VISUAL BASIC 4.0
MULTIMEDIA
HOW-TO

**THE DEFINITIVE PROBLEM-SOLVER
FOR CREATING MULTIMEDIA
APPLICATIONS USING
VISUAL BASIC FOR WINDOWS**

HOW-TO

WAITE GROUP PRESS™
Corte Madera, CA

Noel Jerke

Publisher **Mitchell Waite**
Editor-in-Chief **Charles Drucker**
Acquisitions Editor **Jill Pisoni**
Editorial Director **John Crudo**
Managing Editor **Kurt Stephan**
Content Editor **Harry Henderson**
Technical Reviewer **Steve Peschka**
Copy Editor **Deirdre McDonald Greene**
Production Director **Julianne Ososke**
Production Manager **Cecile Kaufman**
Production Traffic Coordinator **Ingrid Owen**
Designer/Production **Karen Johnston**
Cover Design **Sestina Quarequio**

Printed in the United States of America
95 96 97 98 • 10 9 8 7 6 5 4 3 2 1

Jerke, Noel.
    Visual Basic 4.0 multimedia how-to / Noel Jerke.
        p.   cm.
    Includes index.
    ISBN 1-57169-013-1
    1. Multimedia systems. 2. Microsoft Visual Basic. 3. BASIC
(Computer program language). I. Title.
QA76.575.J47 1995
006.6–dc20   95-11158
                                                                      CIP

DEDICATION

To my wife, Maria, without whose support this book would not be finished.

Message from the
Publisher

WELCOME TO OUR NERVOUS SYSTEM

Some people say that the World Wide Web is a graphical extension of the information superhighway, just a network of humans and machines sending each other long lists of the equivalent of digital junk mail.

I think it is much more than that. To me the Web is nothing less than the nervous system of the entire planet—not just a collection of computer brains connected together, but more like a billion silicon neurons entangled and recirculating electro-chemical signals of information and data, each contributing to the birth of another CPU and another Web site.

Think of each person's hard disk connected at once to every other hard disk on earth, driven by human navigators searching like Columbus for the New World. Seen this way the Web is more of a super entity, a growing, living thing, controlled by the universal human will to expand, to be more. Yet unlike a purposeful business plan with rigid rules, the Web expands in a nonlinear, unpredictable, creative way that echoes natural evolution.

We created our Web site not just to extend the reach of our computer book products but to be part of this synaptic neural network, to experience, like a nerve in the body, the flow of ideas and then to pass those ideas up the food chain of the mind. Your mind. Even more, we wanted to pump some of our own creative juices into this rich wine of technology.

TASTE OUR DIGITAL WINE

And so we ask you to taste our wine by visiting the body of our business. Begin by understanding the metaphor we have created for our Web site—a universal learning center, situated in outer space in the form of a space station. A place where you can journey to study any topic from the convenience of your own screen. Right now we are focusing on computer topics, but the stars are the limit on the Web.

If you are interested in discussing this Web site, or finding out more about the Waite Group, please send me email with your comments and I will be happy to respond. Being a programmer myself, I love to talk about technology and find out what our readers are looking for.

Sincerely,

Mitchell Waite

Mitchell Waite, C.E.O. and Publisher

200 Tamal Plaza
Corte Madera CA 94925
415 924 2575
415 924 2576 fax

Internet email:
mwaite@waite.com

CompuServe email:

75146,3515

Website:
http://www.waite.com/waite

CREATING THE HIGHEST QUALITY COMPUTER BOOKS IN THE INDUSTRY

Waite Group Press
Waite Group New Media

Come Visit
WAITE.COM
Waite Group Press
World Wide Web Site

Now find all the latest information on Waite Group books at our new Web site, **http://www.waite.com/waite**. You'll find an online catalog where you can examine and order any title, review upcoming books, and send email to our authors and editors. Our ftp site has all you need to update your book: the latest program listings, errata sheets, most recent versions of Fractint, POV Ray, Polyray, DMorph, and all the programs featured in our books. So download, talk to us, ask questions, on **http://www.waite.com/waite**.

The New Arrivals Room has all our new books listed by month. Just click for a description, Index, Table of Contents, and links to authors.

The Backlist Room has all our books listed alphabetically.

The People Room is where you'll interact with Waite Group employees

Links to Cyberspace get you in touch with other computer book publishers and other interesting Web sites.

The FTP site contains all program listings, errata sheets, etc.

The Order Room is where you can order any of our books online.

The Subject Room contains typical book pages which show description, Index, Table of Contents, and links to authors.

World Wide Web:

COME SURF OUR TURF—THE WAITE GROUP WEB

http://www.waite.com/waite
Gopher: gopher.waite.com
FTP: ftp.waite.com

ABOUT THE AUTHOR

Noel Jerke is a multimedia enthusiast who currently works in the printing industry at Judd's, Inc., in Strasburg, VA. His background includes receiving a B.S. degree in Computer Science and Economics from Trinity University, San Antonio, TX, developing banking applications, and serving as manager of research and development for a graphics company. Noel is an experienced programmer familiar with C, Basic, and Visual Basic. Currently, his interests include writing about multimedia, project development, and electronic publishing. Noel is a newlywed with no children yet, but keeps busy with his energetic dog and by playing tennis. His other interests include basketball, politics, church activities, and movies.

Noel can be reached on CompuServe at 75554,3514.

TABLE OF CONTENTS

CONTENTS

CONTENTS

ACKNOWLEDGMENTS

I would like to thank Waite Group Press for providing me with the opportunity to write this book. The company's support, vision, and guidance have been immeasurable assets in completing this project. First, for the mechanics, logistics, and details of putting an entire book together I have to thank my managing editor Kurt Stephan. He continually answered my questions and guided me each step of the way.

Additionally, I'd like to thank Mitch Waite and Jill Pisoni for supporting me though the process of authoring for Waite Group Press. Finally, thanks to Harry Henderson and Steve Peschka for doing an excellent job of developmental and technical editing, respectively. Harry did a top-notch job working through the initial draft code and making invaluable comments and suggestions. Steve was a great help in ferreting out the final bugs of the CD.

I have to give a big thanks to my mother-in-law and father-in-law, Rody and Lina Bautista. They were kind enough to welcome us into their home for a short stay while I was writing this book. All of the wonderful Filipino cooking, company, and general support helped to make this a positive and fruitful experience.

I also want to thank my mother, Melody Johnson, and my stepfather, Dr. David Johnson, for providing the wonderful bitmaps and animations used in this book.

Last but certainly not least, I'd like to thank God for providing me with the skills and capabilities to write this book, and for a wife whose support was immeasurable.

Noel Jerke
June 1995

INTRODUCTION

About This Book

Visual Basic 4.0 Multimedia How-To covers a blend of many different state-of-the-art elements found in today's application programming. These include the new version of Visual Basic, the Windows API, and the exciting world of multimedia. This book is about combining all three (and more) to add a new dimension to your programming. It is about user interfaces that go beyond the two-dimensional past. It will show you how to add animation, video, sound, and text to your applications to effectively reach and communicate with your end user.

This book is *not* about great graphic design, creating spectacular 3D animation, or rotoscoped video. But it will show you the techniques to effectively add each of these (and more) elements to your Visual Basic applications.

Organization

Chapter 1, *Windows Multimedia*, introduces you to the terminology of multimedia and how it relates to the Windows environment and Visual Basic programming. In addition, it refers you to specific chapters and How-Tos that incorporate the various multimedia techniques described.

The How-Tos start in Chapters 2 through 7, which explore in detail every facet of Visual Basic multimedia programming, including text, sound, graphics, animation and video, bitmaps and palettes, and low-level Windows multimedia.

Finally, Chapter 8, *Putting It All Together*, shows you how to combine the different techniques developed in the previous chapters into full-featured programs. For example, the hypertext and hot-spot How-Tos developed in Chapters 2 and 4 are combined in this chapter to build a simple hypertext system. You will find seven other sophisticated and exciting projects in Chapter 8, including a How-To on creating a multimedia game.

Question and Answer Format

The How-To format is especially useful for the topic of this book. Each How-To seeks to clearly define the question or task that will be tackled in the section. Each How-To includes an overview of how the task will be accomplished, follows with an explanation of the project code, and finishes with a thorough explanation of the techniques used. At the end of each How-To, comments are provided about how to accomplish variations on the task performed. All of the code, media files, drivers, and other miscellaneous files are provided on the accompanying CD-ROM.

Expected Level of the Reader

Visual Basic 4.0 Multimedia How-To is designed to be used by all levels of readers. However, basic knowledge of Visual Basic programming is assumed. Each How-To is given a complexity rating at the beginning of the discussion. The three levels are Easy, Intermediate, and Advanced. The How-Tos with an Easy rating will be straightforward for any entry-level programmer and do not use any Windows API calls. The Intermediate How-Tos do use the Windows API, but not extensively. Finally, the Advanced How-Tos use the API almost exclusively to solve the proposed question.

Using Visual Basic 4.0

Visual Basic 4.0 takes an already dynamic programming language and offers many new capabilities to the programmer, two of which are used extensively in *Visual Basic 4.0 Multimedia How-To*. The first is the automatic 3D feature, which makes it easy to add that stylish three-dimensional look and feel to your applications. The second is the new class feature, which adds an element of object-oriented programming to your design toolbox. The class feature will be used extensively to encapsulate many of the techniques developed in this book. Through this encapsulation, much of the code developed will be easy to integrate into your own projects.

Using the Windows API

The Windows API is an important and invaluable tool for extensive multimedia programming. The Multimedia Extensions, Multimedia Command Interface (MCI), WinG, and GDI APIs allow for many of the tasks put forth in this book to be accomplished. For example, many of the extensive graphic effects in Chapters 4, 5, and 6 rely extensively on the GDI API. An explanation of how each API is utilized from Visual Basic will be provided to help move you along the path of API programming.

System Requirements

In order to use this book, you will need a PC capable of running Windows 3.1 and Visual Basic 4.0. It is recommended that you run Windows 95. You will need a minimum of a VGA display, with a SVGA display recommended. Most of the How-Tos have been designed to appear correctly at a resolution of 800x600. Also, a CD-ROM drive is required to use the accompanying CD. And, to utilize any of the sound-related How-Tos, a minimum of an 8-bit sound card is required, with a 16-bit card recommended. For further information on the requirements for multimedia development, see Chapter 1.

Program Listing Note

When lines of code must be continued to the next line because of length in the book listings, the ↵ character is used. When you see this character, continue to type the next line in the printed listing on the same line in your Visual Basic code. Do not type a carriage return or the ↵ character.

Visual Basic 3.0 and Visual Basic 4.0 32-Bit Compatibility

All of the How-To code is provided in Visual Basic 4.0 16-bit format and compatibility. Many of the projects utilize the new class feature in version 4.0. The How-Tos that do not have class modules are also provided in Visual Basic 3.0 format. These projects can be found on the CD in the VB30 directory. The following is a listing of the Visual Basic 3.0 How-Tos.

Visual Basic 4.0 also has a 32-bit compatible version for developing applications in 32-bit format for Windows 95. Several of the 16-bit How-Tos that utilize the 16-bit Windows API have been converted to run with the 32-bit version of Visual Basic and access the 32-bit API. These will demonstrate how the 32-bit API is implemented versus the 16-bit API. These projects can be found in the 32Bit directory on the CD. The following is a listing of the 32-bit How-Tos on the CD.

Installation

Installing the How-To Projects

A batch file is provided for each chapter of the CD-ROM to facilitate copying the How-Tos for that chapter to your hard drive. Note that files stored on the CD have a "Read Only" attribute. The batch file takes care of resetting the attribute so the files can be rewritten. If you do not use the batch files, make sure you use the Attribute command to reset the Read Only attribute. To use the batch file, two command line arguments must be provided. The first is the drive you are copying the files from and the second is the drive to copy the files to. The following example demonstrates copying the Chapter 2 How-Tos from the CD-ROM on drive D to the Hard Disk drive designated by C:

```
2COPY D: C:
```

(If your CD drive is not D: or your destination drive is not C:, substitute the appropriate drive letters. This applies to all subsequent instructions).

Note that similiar batch files are provided for the Visual Basic 3.0 and 32-bit-compatible projects in their respective directories.

Installing the Tools

There are four sets of tools provided on the CD that need to be installed. These include the drivers and custom control for playing Autodesk FLC format files. The second is the Apple QuickTime for Windows MCI drivers and development kit. Third, a DLL is provided to facilitate using WinG with Visual Basic. The last is the GoldDisk MCI animation driver for playing AWM animation files.

Installing the WinGHelp DLL and Autodesk Driver

To install both the WinG DLL and the Autodesk DLL and VBX, use the DRIVERS.BAT batch file found on the root directory of the CD. This batch file will copy the files to your Windows system directory. To use the batch file you must provide both the drive to copy from (CD-ROM) and the drive to copy to (hard disk). The following examples copies the drivers from the CD-ROM on drive D to the Windows system directory on drive C:

```
Drivers D: C:
```

Installing QuickTime

To install the QuickTime for Windows package, select the CD from the File Manager for Windows 3.1 or My Computer for Windows 95. From there open the Windows folder and then open the QTW_201 folder. From there open the Setup folder and double-click on the Setup executable. The package will then guide you through the installation. Note that the VBX files needed for How-To 5.10 are installed during this process.

Installing the GoldDisk AWM MCI driver

To install the GoldDisk MCI animation driver with Windows 3.1, open the control panel and select the drivers applet. Choose the option to install a new (unknown) driver. Direct the installation to the Drivers directory (i.e., D:\DRIVERS) on the CD. Once the driver is installed, you can then play AWM animation files through the MCI interface.

To install the GoldDisk drivers from Windows 95, select the Add New Hardware applet from the control panel. Select the Sound, Video, and Game Controllers listing and continue. From there choose to install a 'Microsoft MCI' device and then select the Have Disk button. Point the program to the Drivers directory (i.e., D:\DRIVERS) on the CD. The system will then install the drivers. Once the driver is installed, you can then play AWM animation files through the MCI interface.

Installing WinG

To install WinG select the CD from the File Manager for Windows 3.1 or My Computer for Windows 95. From there open the WinG folder and double-click on the Setup executable. The package will then guide you through the installation.

Media Location Differences Between Windows 3.1 and Windows 95

In Windows 3.1, the standard WAV and MIDI files are stored in the Windows directory. In Windows 95, they are stored in the Media directory under the Windows directory. The How-Tos that reference these files will look for them in the Media directory. If you are using Windows 3.1, be sure to change the directory reference for the media files to the Windows directory.

Visual Basic 4.0 Note: The projects in this book and on the CD-ROM were compiled using a late beta version of Visual Basic 4.0. It is possible that you could encounter problems opening the executable (.EXE) files on the CD using the release version of Visual Basic 4.0. If you experience such problems, please try recompiling the projects with the provided source code on the CD.

1

WINDOWS MULTIMEDIA

1

WINDOWS MULTIMEDIA

This chapter is an introduction to the How-To sections that start in Chapter 2, and gives an overview of the different elements of multimedia that will be introduced in the subsequent chapters. As you can guess, multimedia covers a wide range of topics and interests. For example, the videographer might be interested in digitizing video and presenting it, and the musician may be interested in building a clip library of MIDI music. However, it's *you*, the programmer, who will have the task of bringing it all together into a cohesive and functional format. This chapter introduces you to the terminology of multimedia, gives an overview of the technical topics to be covered, and provides an understanding of how Visual Basic and Windows can combine to create a powerful multimedia development platform. Reviewing this chapter will start you on your way to understanding the different facets of multimedia development. With this foundation, you'll be ready (and eager) to dive into the rest of the chapters to start building your own multimedia applications.

1.1 Introducing Windows Multimedia

In the programming world, Visual Basic has become one of Microsoft's hottest programming tools. In the computer industry, multimedia has become one of the hottest new development markets. To develop multimedia products for the market, it is important to have the right product development tool. Visual Basic is a natural for authoring truly interactive multimedia titles.

Multimedia is the combination of video, sound, text, images, and animation. Your TV set is a multimedia machine. But for the computer world, the key element to add to the list is interaction. It is one thing to witness video and sound passively; it is

3

quite another to interact with each element. With multimedia, information can be portrayed in new and unique ways. Instead of the simple book containing text and a few pictures, the book can now contain sound, hypertext, animation, video, interactive games, and tutorials. Because of all these elements, the book is more enjoyable and useful to the reader.

In a sense, there is almost no limit to what can be done with multimedia. At its essence it is the portrayal of information using many different media. In the real world multimedia meets many specific needs. Table 1-1-1 overviews several areas where multimedia has become a popular tool.

Table 1-1-1 Multimedia development environments

CATEGORY	DESCRIPTION
Business presentations	Communication is an important tool and often a large obstacle for businesses. Multimedia can make business presentations, marketing presentations, and information distribution come to life.
Computer-based training	Requiring workers to have greater technical skills and more specialized knowledge, corporations today are struggling with having a skilled and knowledgeable work force. To train the work force takes time and money. With multimedia, workers can sit down to computer-based training systems that contain video, audio, and logic to assess workers' skills. This saves time and capital in the long run.
Entertainment	Some of the most dazzling multimedia software on the market today can be found in games. Some of the games coming out contain full-length video clips, eye-popping 3D animation, and high levels of interaction.
Education	Children and adults' education can be greatly enhanced through the use of interactive and informative programs. When a child is trying to learn math tables or to read, a computer is tireless and can provide exciting visual and audio effects to make the task interesting and informative.
Information presentation	With the highly interactive and content-filled encyclopedias on the market today, huge amounts of information can be stored on a single CD. Instead of flat text describing a topic, the user can view video and animation and listen to sounds related to the topic.
Interactive kiosks	Kiosks are information booths that are usually found in public places, including malls, universities, and office buildings. Computers today serve as kiosks in that the user can interact with the screen to retrieve specified information.

Each of these multimedia environments benefits from the use of video, 2D and 3D animation, animated text, hypertext, visual graphic effects, and all of the methods developed in this book. And of course, a full programming language such as Visual Basic 4.0 is a key element for developing in these environments. Certainly these are not all of the development environments possible. You can just imagine the uses in vertical markets such as real estate and catalog sales.

Through Visual Basic 4.0, the Windows API and the multimedia extensions are easily accessible. Combining these elements with Visual Basic 4.0 allows you to create nearly any type of interactive multimedia title. All of the popular multimedia file formats are also easily accessible from within Visual Basic 4.0. Table 1-1-2 lists some of the more popular formats.

Table 1-1-2 Standard multimedia file formats

FILE EXTENSION	DESCRIPTION
AVI	Microsoft's Video for Windows Audio Video Interleaved format
WAV	Wave Digital Audio format
AWM	Gold Disk's Animation Works Interactive animation format
MOV	Apple's QuickTime movie format
MID	Musical Instrument Digital Interface (Sequencer)
FLC	Autodesk's Flic animation format
BMP	Bitmap graphics

Standard graphic images have long been a popular method for delivering information. Photos, clip art, and other types of images can be used to communicate ideas and messages. The standard Windows graphic formats include .BMP and .DIB. Bitmap files have a color table or palette associated with the image where each image pixel references a color in the palette. Typically, these images can have 16, 256, thousands, or even millions of colors. The Windows API provides a large set of functions and structures for manipulating existing graphics and creating new images. Throughout this book, various types of manipulations will be done to bitmaps to build interesting animated and visual effects. These include crossfades between two pictures, fade ins and fade outs, and modification of an image's color palette. A Microsoft tool, WinG,

will be introduced for performing high-speed graphics manipulations, including high-speed sprites.

To process digital audio, the electrical signals of the audio data from your source (tape, microphone, etc.) are sampled/recorded into numerical representations called *wave audio*. Today, there are several different formats of wave audio supported by various sound cards on the market. The key characteristics that make up a different format include the number of bits used to represent each sample, the use of stereo or mono recordings, and the number of samples stored for each second of sound.

The amount of data recorded can be stored in 8 or 16 bits per sample. Some cards support 32-bit, but 16-bit has become the standard. If the data is in stereo, there are two channels of recorded data for each sample and only one for mono. Each channel can either be 8-bit or 16-bit, but the two channels must be the same.

The number of samples recorded per second, or *amplitude*, can range from 11,025 to 44,100. This measurement is recorded in hertz and usually represented in kilohertz (kHz). For example, 11,025 hertz would be 11.025 kilohertz (kHz). Almost all sound cards support the minimum standard of 8-bit mono data recorded at 11.025 kHz. The larger the number of bits per sample, number of channels, and amplitude, the larger the file size and the higher the quality of the recording. Several How-Tos in Chapters 3 and 7 give examples of how to use wave data. Table 1-1-3 summarizes the wave format options for bits, channels, and sampling:

Table 1-1-3 Wave format options

BITS	CHANNELS	AMPLITUDE (SAMPLING)
8	1 (Mono)	11 kHz
16	2 (Stereo)	22 kHz
		44 khz

A number of options are available for the type of data to be recorded for the AVI format. The audio component follows the different options laid out above. For video, the compression technique is important. There are several popular compression algorithms for compacting digital data. These include Microsoft Video, Intel's Indeo, and Cinepak. If the user has Video for Windows Runtime installed on his or her system, this will not be a great concern.

Musical Digital Instrument Interface (MIDI) did not originate on the desktop. It was originally used as a way to communicate between instruments for sound mixing. MIDI devices communicate by sending messages to each other. The primary difference between MIDI music and Wave music is that with MIDI the sounds are generated from synthesizers. This does not allow for the development of "custom" sounds. Only the instruments built into the synthesizer can be used to generate sound. On the computer, MIDI has become the standard for long composition playback. To record one of Mozart's symphonies in digital Wave format would require a huge amount of disk space, whereas in the MIDI format, the file size would be comparatively insignificant. Fortunately, the playing of MIDI files (.MID) can be easily accomplished in a number of ways from Visual Basic 4.0. In Chapter 7, an example is given of how to generate MIDI music notes directly from a MIDI-compatible sound board.

A major breakthrough in the delivery of multimedia has been the development of Compact Disc Read-Only Memory (CD-ROM) technology. As you can imagine, video, animation, sound, and full-color graphics take up a lot of room on a hard drive, making delivery of multimedia to the user difficult. With CD-ROM technology, you can deliver hundreds of megabytes of files with ease to your user. A good example is the delivery of the programming content of this book on CD. Today, most major computer manufacturers are building CD-ROMs into their systems as a standard feature.

CD-ROM technology has developed over the years; subsequently, there are various drive technologies on the market today. The two primary characteristics to be concerned with are data transfer rate and access speed. The data transfer rate is measured in kilobytes per second (K/sec), which indicates how much data can be transferred from the drive each second. The standard transfer rate a few years ago was 150K/sec and is typically known as a single spin drive. Today, there are double spin, triple spin, and quadruple spin drives. Double spin drives have a data transfer of 300K/sec. The second measure, access time, indicates how long it takes to find data on the drive. The access time is measured in milliseconds (ms) and usually ranges from 200 ms to 500 ms. By comparison, hard drives usually access from 20 ms or better.

To develop multimedia programs, there are certain hardware and software requirements for supporting and playing the various multimedia elements. Fortunately an organization, the Multimedia PC Marketing Council (MPC), has set up standards for minimal set up for a multimedia computer. Two levels of standards have been developed. MPC Level 1 was set up in 1991 and was considered underpowered almost upon release; MPC Level 2 was released in 1993. Table 1-1-4 details the two standards.

Table 1-1-4 MPC specifications

MPC LEVEL 1 SPECIFICATION	MPC LEVEL 2 SPECIFICATION
16mhz 386sx	25mhz 486sx Processor
2MB RAM	4MB RAM
30MB hard drive	160MB hard drive
640x480 VGA—16 colors	640x480 VGA—65,536 colors
8-bit sound card	16-bit stereo sound card
CD-ROM drive—150K/sec transfer rate	CD-ROM drive—double speed, XA compatible

The MPC Level 2 specification is the standard today. At the publication of this book, the Pentium processor was quickly becoming the standard desktop processor. Also,

high-resolution monitors and triple and quadruple speed CD-ROM drives were becoming standard. For the developer, the system and software requirements for full-fledged multimedia development are considerably greater than the MPC Level 2 specification. Further information on the MPC specifications can be received by contacting:

> Multimedia PC Marketing Council
> 1730 M Street NW, Suite 707
> Washington D.C. 20036

Table 1-1-5 is an overview and a few recommendations of the various system requirements to consider in multimedia production.

Table 1-1-5 MPC specifications

ITEM	DESCRIPTION
Processor	Consider a Pentium processor for development. The target platform is important for performance concerns of video, animation, and sound, and typical systems should be tested.
RAM memory	A minimum of 8MB is recommended, with 16 to 32 (or higher) optimal.
Hard drive	A quick browsing of the files on the CD-ROM with this book will give you an idea of the file sizes of various multimedia elements. At least 500MB is necessary, with higher sizes as necessary.
Monitor	It is important to develop for 640x480 monitors unless you are sure your audience uses higher resolutions. Designing for a higher resolution makes for easier development.
Sound card	A lot of 8-bit mono sound cards are in use today. But the 16-bit stereo standard set forth in the MPC Level 2 specification provides the best quality and use for today's multimedia standards. Most systems have installed a 16-bit sound card as standard.
CD-ROM drive	It is important to consider the type of CD-ROM drive you will be developing for. Because each has different data transfer rates, this can affect the quality of play for video and animation. For development, the CD-ROM drive is not critical other than for potential testing purposes.

A developer should always get as much power as you can get. But it is important to keep in mind the performance issues of playing your multimedia data on target systems.

The multimedia development world pulls together many different elements for a successful full-featured production. These include video, animation, sound, and graphics. But you can easily add simple visual effects that will spice up your everyday applications. This book will show you how to accomplish many of the popular multimedia design elements from Visual Basic 4.0, including animated text, sprite animation, hypertext, image fades and dissolves, and sound manipulation. You can turn to specific How-Tos to begin implementation immediately in your programming, and at the same time work through the book to get a solid feeling for all the possibilities available to you as a Visual Basic 4.0 programmer. Chapter 8 provides more complete and full-featured exercises that show how to pull together various elements in your productions.

Visual Basic 4.0 Classes

One of the new features in Visual Basic 4.0 is the use of class modules for object-oriented programming. Classes act similarly to custom controls or forms. A class object contains properties that govern the behavior of a class, as well as the code that defines properties and methods of the class. When a class is included in your project, you can declare multiple instances of the class. This will be done with Sprite classes so that multiple sprites can be in motion at once.

This new class feature of Visual Basic 4.0 will be used to build reusable modules so you can begin implementing techniques developed in this book into your applications. The beauty of the class feature is the ease with which you can customize and add to the class for your purposes. The primary drawback is that the code is not written in C for greater speed and access to the Windows APIs. Fortunately, with the classes in this book, you can modify them as you wish to suit your needs. Table 1-1-6 summarizes the classes developed and the How-To section they are associated with. Many of the classes are also used in Chapter 8.

Table 1-1-6 Classes developed in this book

CLASS	HOW-TO	DESCRIPTION
WipeClass	4.6	Creates wipes between two images
CrossHatch	4.7	Performs a cross hatch and vertical blind fade in and out on a graphic
ScreenBuild	4.7, 6.6	Builds the cross hatch and vertical blind fade screens

continued on next page

continued from previous page

CLASS	HOW-TO	DESCRIPTION
TransCopy	4.8	Transparently copies one image with a black background onto another using a black and white mask
CompTrns	4.9	Transparently copies one image with a complex background onto another image using two masks
Sprite1	5.4	Develops a user-controlled sprite
Sprite2	5.5, 5.6	Develops a self-running sprite
SimpleSprite	5.6	Controls a simple sprite such as a picture box
PalMod	6.1	Modifies a bitmap's palette with several different tints
Animate	6.2	Animates a picture's color palette
Fade	6.4	Performs a smooth black fade in and out on a graphic
FadeFrames	6.5	Builds a series of fade-in and fade-out bitmap frames for an image
CrossFade	6.6	Crossfades two bitmap images
WinG	6.7 - 6.10	Creates a WinG bitmap
WinGSprite	6.9, 6.10	Creates self-running sprites using WinG bitmaps
WaveTools	7.2	Opens a Wave file using low-level tools and plays the data
WaveTools2	7.3	Opens a Wave file and builds an echo using low-level tools, and also plays the Wave file.
WaveTools3	7.4	Opens a Wave file and reverses the wave data using low-level tools, and plays the Wave file

As you will see throughout the book, the Windows API is an important tool for accomplishing many of the tasks in the How-Tos. Distributed with Visual Basic 4.0

are two important tools that will assist you in learning about and drawing from the API. The first is the Windows SDK Help file, which gives descriptions and syntax about using the various API functions. Most of the functions used in this book can be referenced in this Help file. The second tool is the API Text Viewer program and two API text files, WIN31API.TXT and WINMMSYS.TXT. By using the API Text Viewer, you can open either one of the text files. Then you can search for the function, type, or constant that you need. Once the file is retrieved, the appropriate syntax for accessing the item from Visual Basic 4.0 is copied to the clipboard and can then be copied to your application. The API is used to perform all types of tasks, including memory allocation, bitmap manipulation, and painting.

As a quick browse of the table of contents will show, you can accomplish a wide range of multimedia tasks from Visual Basic 4.0. By using the tools built into Visual Basic 4.0, the Windows API, and the multimedia extensions, and content such as sound, animation, and video, you will be able to develop interactive full-featured multimedia programs.

1.2 The Microsoft Mutimedia Extensions

The ability to develop and use multimedia sound from Microsoft Windows became a reality with the release of the Microsoft Multimedia Extensions. The package was originally marketed as an add-on for Windows 3.0, and then as a part of Windows 3.1. The extensions bring full-featured sound support to the Windows environment and support recording and playing digital sound (WAV), MIDI, and CD-ROM drives.

To use the extensions, you need a CD-ROM drive and a sound board that supports MIDI. Most sound boards today, including the popular Sound Blaster boards, support MIDI.

The extensions consist of more than 30 Multimedia Control Interface (MCI) commands and 100 low-level functions. To perform the tasks laid out in this book, you need only a small subset of these. To manipulate some of the larger amounts of data, you will have to rely on some of the Windows API memory functions because of the data size limits in Visual Basic 4.0. As the different How-Tos will demonstrate, there are varying levels of control for utilizing multimedia: the high-level, simple-to-use sndPlaySound and MessageBeep functions; the mid-level MCI command strings; and the low-level functions.

Throughout the book, you will be using the functions provided in the multimedia extensions. Several of the chapters, especially Chapter 3, focus on using the MCI interface for control of playing multimedia elements. Chapter 7 gives several examples of how the low-level functions can be used to gain greater control and manipulation over your multimedia elements.

1.3 Bitmap Graphics

The use of bitmap graphic images is an important tool for the multimedia developer. An interesting photo, clip art, or other image can provide the desired message.

Fortunately, the Windows API provides a rich set of tools for performing manipulations on bitmap images to help bring them to life. Tables 1-3-1 and 1-3-2 give an overview of the functions and structures that Windows provides for manipulating bitmaps.

Table 1-3-1 Windows API bitmap functions

FUNCTION	DESCRIPTION
BitBlt	Copies a bitmap between device contexts
CreateBitmap	Creates a device-dependent memory bitmap
CreateBitmapIndirect	Creates a bitmap using a BITMAP structure
CreateCompatibleBitmap	Creates a bitmap compatible with a device context
CreateDIBitmap	Creates a bitmap handle from a DIB
CreateDiscardableBitmap	Creates a discardable bitmap
GetBitmapBits	Copies bitmap bits into a buffer
GetBitmapDimension	Retrieves the width and height of a bitmap
GetDIBits	Copies DIB bits into a buffer
GetPixel	Retrieves the RGB color of a specified pixel
LoadBitmap	Loads a bitmap resource
PatBlt	Creates a bit pattern on a device
SetBitmapBits	Sets bitmap bits from an array of bytes
SetBitmapDimension	Sets the width and height of a bitmap
SetDIBits	Sets the bits of a bitmap

FUNCTION	DESCRIPTION
SetDIBitsToDevice	Copies a DIB's bits directly to a rectangle on a device
SetPixel	Sets a pixel to a specified color
StretchBlt	Copies bitmap bits and stretches them as needed to fit the device
StretchDIBits	Moves a DIB from the source to a destination rectangle

Table 1-3-2 Windows API bitmap structures

STRUCTURE	DESCRIPTION
BITMAPFILEHEADER	Describes the header format of a .BMP or .DIB file
BITMAPINFOHEADER	Describes the header data for a bitmap
RGBQUAD	Describes a color consisting of relative intensities of red, green, and blue
BITMAPINFO	Includes the BITMAPINFOHEADER and an array RGBQUAD structure for defining the bitmap's color table

By using these functions and structures, you will be able to read in, write out, and manipulate bitmaps. But to work effectively with bitmaps, you will need to be able to manipulate palettes. Fortunately, Windows provides a set of palette functions and structures for this purpose. These can be used to manipulate a bitmap's palette to perform different visual effects. Tables 1-3-3 and 1-3-4 overview the palette functions and structures.

Table 1-3-3 Windows API palette functions

FUNCTION	DESCRIPTION
AnimatePalette	Replaces entries in a logical palette
CreatePalette	Creates a logical color palette
GetNearestColor	Retrieves the closest available color
GetNearestPaletteIndex	Retrieves the nearest match for a color

continued on next page

continued from previous page

FUNCTION	DESCRIPTION
GetPaletteEntries	Retrieves a range of palette entries
GetSystemPaletteEntries	Retrieves entries from the system palette
GetSystemPaletteUse	Determines access to the entire system palette
RealizePalette	Maps entries from logical to system palette
SelectPalette	Selects a palette into a device context
SetPaletteEntries	Sets colors and flags for a logical palette
SetSystemPaletteUse	Sets the use of static colors in the system palette

Table 1-3-4 Windows API palette structures

STRUCTURE	DESCRIPTION
LOGPALETTE	Defines a logical color palette
PALETTEENTRY	Specifies the color and usage of an entry in a logical color palette

As you can see, a wide range of palette functions is provided for manipulating palettes in Windows. There are many different palette structures, but Table 1-3-4 reflects the two most commonly used in this book.

As you can imagine, managing colors in Windows is an important task. Windows must manage the various colors visible at any one time. It accomplishes this by having one system palette that matches as closely as possible all of the colors that need to be displayed. The system palette is updated each time a window changes or a new window is created; it also creates an optimal set of colors for all of the images currently visible. As you will see in Chapter 6, managing bitmap manipulations with the system palette is an important task.

The combination of the bitmap functions and structures with the palette functions and structures provides a powerful set of tools for performing a wide variety of popular multimedia manipulations on graphics. Chapter 6 leads you through a series of How-Tos that demonstrate effective manipulation of graphics and palettes.

1.4 Overview of WinG

Chapter 6 also introduces Microsoft's WinG. WinG is an optimized set of tools for high-speed bitmap manipulation from Windows. The WinG API provides a set of functions for creating WinG bitmaps and WinG device contexts. You will be able to create WinG bitmaps by using the Windows API bitmap functions and structures in conjunction with WinG. Once you have WinG bitmaps, you can perform a wide variety of manipulation. Table 1-4-1 overviews the WinG functions.

Table 1-4-1 Overview of WinG functions

WinG FUNCTION	DESCRIPTION
WinGCreateDC	Creates a new WinG device context
WinGRecommendDIBFormat	Recommends an optimal DIB format for the WinG bitmap
WinGCreateBitmap	Creates a WinG bitmap from a BITMAPINFO structure
WinGGetDIBPointer	Gets a pointer to the WinG DIB surface (bits)
WinGGetDIBColorTable	Gets the color table of the WinG bitmap
WinGSetDIBColorTable	Sets the WinG color table from the BITMAPINFO structure
WinGCreateHalftonePalette	Creates a halftone palette for converting true color images
WinGCreateHalftoneBrush	Creates a halftone brush
WinGBitBlt	Copies WinG bits from one device to another
WinGStretchBlt	Copies and stretches WinG bits from one device to another
TransparentDIBits	Places the bits into the WinG device; this is not an actual WinG function, but is provided for making WinG easier to use

You may notice that several of the WinG function names are very similar to the Windows API functions. In fact, many of the functions perform the same tasks as the Windows API functions, but are optimized to work in the WinG environment.

The key to understanding WinG is understanding the WinG bitmap and using the WinG device context. The WinG bitmap is built from the data in a bitmap file (.BMP) using several standard Windows API functions. Once the WinG bitmap is created, the bits from the bitmap can be copied onto the WinG device and the color table for the WinG device set. Graphics manipulations on the WinG device can then

be performed. In fact, the WinG device acts in many ways like a bitmap. The standard Windows API drawing functions can be used to draw rectangles, ellipses, and the like directly on to the WinG device and the TransparentDIBits, WinGBitBlt, and WinGStretchBit functions can be used to draw bitmaps directly on to the WinG device.

In Chapter 6, a set of high-speed sprites will be developed using WinG. In Chapter 8, a complete animated scene with animations, sprites, a complex background, and sound will be developed to show the power of WinG. You can compare the sprites developed in Chapter 5 using the Windows API with the sprites developed in Chapter 6 using WinG.

1.5 Overview of MCI

The Multimedia Control Interface (MCI) is based on the concept of sending commands to the system to perform specified tasks. Generally these involve reading multimedia data files, preparing multimedia devices, and performing other tasks needed to record and play multimedia data. The system also provides messages back to the calling application regarding the status of the specified commands.

MCI consists of two levels, the command string interface and MCI commands. The command string interface consists of simple English-like phrases to control the playing of video, animation, wave audio, and MIDI. The following is a typical example:

```
Ex:      open waveaudio
```

The command strings are parsed into direct MCI commands and then sent to the system. MCI commands are more complex and include data structures. The interpretation of the command strings slows down the process of accessing multimedia elements. If you want more direct control of your multimedia elements, MCI commands can be sent directly to the system. Chapter 3 gives examples of interfacing with both the MCI command string interface and the MCI command interface. If you need minute control, the low-level functions can be used.

For most common uses, the command string interface is more than sufficient for accessing the various multimedia elements. Two primary commands are used in the command string interface; mciSendString and mciGetErrorString. The mciSendString function sends the message to the system; if there is an error in carrying out the command, the error can be interpreted by mciGetErrorString. The error messages are also provided in easy-to-understand English phrases.

The MCI command strings work by controlling various devices. Appendix A provides a comprehensive description of the devices that can be controlled and the command strings that can be used with each device. The most common devices include waveaudio for Wave files, digitalvideo for AVI files, sequencer for MIDI, and animation for animation clips. You can also control devices such as a CD-ROM drive.

If you have a standard music CD, you can control the positioning and play of the CD music.

The MCI command set functions require that a set of data structures be filled out and sent to the system with the mciSendCommand function. Developing these data structures involves jumping through a few hoops to get around some of the limitations inherent in passing data directly to the Windows system from Visual Basic. How-To 3.6 provides an example of how to do this. If you must send commands quickly to the system, but don't need to go through the actual reading and manipulation of multimedia data directly (with low-level functions), then consider using MCI commands instead of MCI command strings.

There is one other alternative to using the MCI functions directly. The Visual Basic 4.0 Professional Edition provides an MCI custom control, an easy and familiar interface for adding multimedia elements to your applications. A primary benefit of using the MCI control is that it supports a call back feature, done, to let you know when the specified task has finished. This makes it relatively easy to find out when your multimedia file has finished playing. The control at runtime is represented by a set of VCR-like buttons that control the multimedia file, including recording multimedia data. The control does not have to be visible, and all tasks can be controlled directly from the program.

Table 1-5-1 gives an overview of the types of commands that can be carried out from the control.

Table 1-5-1 MCI custom control commands overview

COMMAND	DESCRIPTION/PROPERTIES USED
Open	Opens a device using the MCI_OPEN command
Close	Closes a device using the MCI_CLOSE command
Play	Plays a device using the MCI_PLAY command; you can also set the from and to properties for play
Pause	Pauses playing or recording
Stop	Stops playing or recording using the MCI_STOP command
Back	Steps backward using the MCI_STEP command
Step	Steps forward using the MCI_STEP command
Prev	Goes to the beginning of the current track using the Seek command

continued on next page

continued from previous page

COMMAND	DESCRIPTION/PROPERTIES USED
Next	Goes to the beginning of the next track using the Seek command
Seek	Seeks a position using the MCI_SEEK command; the position to seek to is specified by the to property of the control
Record	Records using the MCI_RECORD command.; the from and to properties of the control can be set to indicate where to record
Eject	Ejects media using the MCI_SET command
Sound	Plays a sound using the MCI_SOUND command; the name of the sound file is indicated in the file name property
Save	Saves an open file using the MCI_SAVE command; the name of the file is indicated in the file name property

A whole host of properties can be set and checked to control the playing and recording of your multimedia elements. The control will call the done event when a specified command has been accomplished (such as play) if the notify property is set to True. The MCI control supports all of the standard devices including wave audio, sequencer (MIDI), CD-ROM, and digital video. Detailed descriptions of all of the MCI controls properties, methods, and events are found in the Custom Control Help file that comes with Visual Basic 4.0.

1.6 Overview of Audio Services

MCI provides for straightforward method for accessing audio devices. But for general audio services, there are three levels of audio control: the first level includes two functions, MessageBeep and sndPlaySound; the second level is the MCI interface as discussed in the last section; and the third level is low-level services and functions.

The MessageBeep function provides an easy way to access the system sounds specified in the WIN.INI file and set in the control panel. These include asterisk, exclamation, and question system events. The MessageBeep function is actually a part of the standard Windows API. The sndPlaySound function plays the system's sounds, but can also play any Wave file. The Wave files can be played synchronously or asynchronously. If a file is played synchronously, then no actions can be performed while the Wave file is playing. In addition, the function has a feature to play Wave files repeatedly.

MCI provides a fairly straightforward method of accessing and controlling multimedia devices and elements. Although the command string interface is parsed into

MCI commands, ultimately the MCI commands are converted into low-level function calls.

These low-level functions provide the detailed, minute control needed to gain precise control over playing Wave and MIDI data. Through these low-level controls, manipulations such as playing MIDI notes directly and adding echoes to Wave files can be accomplished.

To manipulate Wave data, you must first understand the Resource Interchange File Format (RIFF). The RIFF format is a general format for storing different types of data. Several common formats include .WAV (digital audio), .PAL (palette files), and .AVI (Video for Windows). RIFF files are composed of "chunks" that hold specific data. You can descend or ascend into each chunk. A whole set of functions can be used to read and manipulate RIFF files. Table 1-6-1 gives a brief overview of the primary multimedia input and output functions.

Table 1-6-1 The multimedia file I/O functions

FUNCTION	DESCRIPTION
mmioAscend	Moves up from the current chunk
mmioDescend	Moves down from the current chunk
mmioOpen	Opens a RIFF file
mmioClose	Closes a RIFF file
mmioRead	Reads data from a RIFF file
mmioWrite	Writes data to a RIFF file
mmioCreateChunk	Creates a new chunk in the file

Chapter 7 discusses the RIFF format in greater detail and demonstrates the techniques required to read Wave data, manipulate the data, and rewrite the data to a new file. An obstacle that will be encountered in manipulating large Wave files is memory limitation. The largest variable that you can allocate in Visual Basic 4.0 is a 64K string. To circumvent this limitation, memory functions from the Windows API will be used to allocate memory blocks for storing the Wave data. To read and write the data to and from memory for manipulation, two functions from the Windows ToolHelp library will be used; MemoryRead and MemoryWrite. Table 1-6-2 summarizes the memory allocation and manipulation functions that will be used.

Table 1-6-2 Memory functions

FUNCTION	DESCRIPTION
GlobalAlloc	Allocates the specified block of memory
GlobalFree	Frees up the specified memory block
GlobalLock	Locks the memory block from being moved by the system
GlobalUnlock	Unlocks the memory block from being moved by the system
GlobalHandleToSel	Provides a Windows selector to the memory block that is used in the MemoryRead and MemoryWrite functions
MemoryRead	Reads data from the allocated memory block
MemoryWrite	Writes data to the allocated memory block

The combination of the multimedia I/O functions and the global memory functions gives the greatest control over manipulation of Wave data. Precise timing for starting the playing of a Wave file can be controlled. For example, you can load all of the Wave data into memory and prepare the wave audio device for play. Then, at the exact moment when the Wave data should be played, the appropriate command can be issued to play the data. Compare this to the MCI command string interface, which must parse the commands down to the low-level before Wave data is played.

A set of functions is used to play Wave data on a low level. There are over 30 low-level functions available. Table 1-6-3 highlights several of the functions typically used for playing and manipulating Wave data.

Table 1-6-3 Low-level Wave functions

FUNCTION	DESCRIPTION
waveInGetNumDevs	Retrieves the number of wave devices installed in the system
waveInOpen	Opens the wave device for input
waveInPrepareHeader	Prepares a memory block for recording data
waveInReset	Resets the waveaudio device

FUNCTION	DESCRIPTION
waveInStart	Starts recording Wave data
waveInStop	Stops recording the Wave data
waveInUnprepareHeader	Releases the memory block for recording
waveOutOpen	Opens the wave device for output
waveOutPrepareHeader	Passes the Wave data to the wave audio device
waveOutUnprepareHeader	Releases the Wave data for further use
waveOutClose	Closes the wave device when opened for output
waveOutGetDevCaps	Retrieves the capabilities of the wave audio device; this includes the bits, channels, and sampling supported
waveOutWrite	Outputs the Wave data to the device

Note the difference between supporting recording Wave data and playing Wave data. To record data, the function prefixes start with waveIn for playing, they start with waveOut. There are several excellent complete references to the low-level functions, including Waite Group Press' *Windows API New Testament*. Many of the above functions are also discussed in great detail in Chapter 7. The steps to play Wave data using low-level methods are as follows:

1. Retrieve information about the Wave data from the RIFF file using the multimedia I/O functions

2. Allocate global memory to read the Wave data into memory using the memory functions

3. Read in the data using the multimedia I/O functions

4. Open and prepare the wave audio device for playing the data

5. Ouput (play) the wave data

6. Close the device when finished

Contrast these six steps with the single call of the sndPlaySound function or the few simple functions of the MCI command string interface. But with these steps, you

as the developer have greater control over playing the Wave data. And once the data is read into memory, you can perform digital effects on the Wave data. This includes building echoes and reversing Wave data, as demonstrated in Chapter 7.

For MIDI, a similar set of low-level service functions can be used to perform similar tasks. MIDI devices send messages indicating the commands to be carried out. Two types of messages can be sent to the device, short and long messages. Short messages typically are used to send simple commands such as playing a note. Long messages typically are used to send large sequences of commands to the synthesizer. Table 1-6-4 gives an overview of some of the common low-level MIDI functions.

Table 1-6-4 Low-level MIDI functions

FUNCTION	DESCRIPTION
midiInClose	Closes a MIDI device
midiInGetDevCaps	Determines the capabilities of a MIDI input device
midiInOpen	Opens a MIDI device for input
midiInPrepareHeader	Prepares a memory block for receiving MIDI data
midiInStop	Stops the input of a MIDI device
midiInUnPrepareHeader	Releases the memory block used for receiving messages.
midiOutClose	Closes a MIDI output device
midiOutGetDevCaps	Retrieves the device capabilities of a MIDI device
midiOutGetNumDevs	Retrieves the number of installed MIDI output devices
midiOutLongMsg	Sends a long message to a MIDI device
midiOutOpen	Opens a MIDI device for output
midiOutPrepareHeader	Prepares the memory block for transmission of MIDI data
midiOutShortMsg	Sends a short message to a MIDI device
midiOutUnPrepareHeader	Releases the MIDI data for further use

Note the difference between supporting recording MIDI data and playing MIDI data. As with the Wave functions, to record data, the function prefixes start with midiIn and for playing they start with midiOut. In fact, the functions overall are very similar.

In Chapter 7, an example is given to send notes directly to the system. In Chapter 3 the midiOutGetDevCaps function is used to check the capabilities of the synthesizers installed in the system. A set of standards has been developed for transmitting and receiving MIDI messages. For further information on the MIDI standard, contact the following organization:

The International MIDI Association
5316 W. 57th St.
Los Angeles, CA 90056
213-649-6364

The multimedia extensions provide for several levels of control over playing and accessing audio capabilities. For basic playing of wave audio, the sndPlaySound function can be used. For greater control over playing wave audio and MIDI data, the MCI methods can be used. And for ultimate control, the low-level functions provide for low-level power.

1.7 Overview of Video for Windows

The multimedia extensions are important for adding sound capabilities to Windows. But they do not solve the problems of playing video from Windows. Microsoft's answer is the Video for Windows package. The Video for Windows runtime package allows for playing of AVI video. The Video for Windows development package includes the runtime modules and utilities for capturing and editing video. As you can guess, many considerations must be made because of video's data-intensive format. Single 24-bit images can get very large, even when compressed. You can imagine the difficulties when there are hundreds or thousands of frames with image data in a single clip.

Video can be stored in 8-bit, 16-bit, or 24-bit formats. 24-bit is the closest representation of the original coloring and quality of video. Of course the trade-off is in file size. 8-bit is the most compact, with 16-bit being the middle ground. Video is also stored at a certain frame size. Theoretically, there is no limitation to the size of the frames, but the standards include 320x240 and 160x120. The larger the frame size, the greater the amount of data that must be stored.

We are used to viewing film and TV at 30 frames per second (fps). So normal full motion video, requires 30 frames just to represent one second of video data. On top of all this, it is likely there will be accompanying audio data. Most 486 systems and Pentium systems can support playing 8-bit, 160x120, video at 30 fps from a

double-speed CD-ROM drive. As system performance increases, the higher the bit depth, frame size, and play rate that can be supported.

Fortunately, to control data size, a primary purpose of Video for Windows is to implement compression–decompression schemes (codecs). Four primary codecs are used today: Cinepak, Indeo 3.1 from Intel, Microsoft Video 1, and RLE. The benefit of codecs is the decrease in file size. In fact, digitized video on the desktop would not be realistic even with large storage mediums such as CD-ROMs without codecs. But the drawback is that image quality is sacrificed with the compression. The greater the compression, the greater the image degradation. Even with codecs, file sizes for video data can quickly get very large depending on the size, format, and length of the video. It is not uncommon for simple video clips to reach 10 megabytes or larger.

For video capture, you will need a video capture board and plenty of hard disk space and RAM. The Video for Windows package contains two programs, VidCap and VidEdit, to capture and edit video. The editing program allows for basic frame-by-frame editing of captured clips. You might want to consider using a package such as Adobe Premiere for greater editing control. Appendix C provides a listing of multimedia software companies and their products.

Accessing video from Visual Basic 4.0 is a very straightforward process. The MCI command string interface and MCI command set can be used. Appendix A details the MCI command strings available for working with digital video. The same simple English-like commands make for easy playing of video.

The MCI custom control also makes playing video simple. A benefit of the custom control is that it makes playing video in a specified window simple. Normally when video is played, a window is automatically created for the play of the video. The custom control allows you to specify the handle to the device context you want the video to play in. The custom control interface also provides for natural play and browsing of the video clip. How-To 5.11 provides a comprehensive overview of playing video using the custom control.

You do not have to be concerned with the codec used to compress the video when accessing the clips. The Video for Windows runtime system handles retrieving the data based on the codec scheme. You do need to be concerned with compression and quality when creating your video, but that issue is subjective.

1.8 The Windows API

The Windows Application Programming Interface (API) provides a programming framework for building applications that share a common graphical user interface (GUI) and many other features. Windows provides a set of functions that make this common interface the same for all programs. There are several hundred APIs in the programming set, plus data types and constants. Fortunately, most of these are masked by Visual Basic 4.0 in a design and controls that are familiar to the programmer. Visual Basic 4.0 handles all of the messaging and interaction with the operating system necessary to build forms, set colors, and place controls.

This book uses the Windows API to perform several different multimedia techniques. Appendix B gives a brief overview of the different APIs utilized in the book. Many have already been discussed in this chapter. Others will be used for manipulating fonts, bitmaps, and palettes and for a wide variety of other uses.

The use of graphical data is an important part of multimedia. Nearly everyone is familiar with the digital dissolve that fades one picture out and fades another in. The Windows API will be drawn upon to perform various types of bitmap manipulation. Demonstrating how these types of techniques can be developed directly in Visual Basic 4.0 is an excellent example of the power of Visual Basic 4.0 and the Windows API. Some of the examples will use bitmap functions to read in bitmap data from a file and perform bit and palette manipulations on the data. These type of manipulations can be used to perform the digital image techniques common to multimedia programs.

The API Text Viewer can be used to declare the necessary API functions directly in your application. The Windows Software Development Kit (SDK) help file provided with Visual Basic 4.0 is an excellent reference for the use of the functions. In addition, several very good books are on the market that provide detailed information on how to use the API. One example is Waite Group Press' *Windows API New Testament*.

1.9 Multimedia Authoring in Visual Basic 4.0

There are a variety of tools at your disposal to add multimedia effects to existing or new programs or to develop complete multimedia packages. These tools include Visual Basic 4.0 itself, the multimedia extensions, Video for Windows, the Windows API, WinG, and the MCI custom control. By using these tools and appropriate media (AVI, WAV, FLC), you can add hypertext, digital dissolves and fades, animated sprites and text, and many other multimedia techniques to your applications.

A large number of authoring tools are on the market today. These include the popular Macromedia Director, Authorware, and Multimedia toolbook packages. These packages provide their own language and methods for building multimedia applications. But they tend to lack the all-encompassing control that a full-fledged programming language provides. Most multimedia development is not done in C or C++ because of the higher level of complexity of programming in conjunction with the Windows interface. Visual Basic has become popular because of the ease with which a Windows application can be developed, including forms, text boxes, labels, list boxes, and picture boxes, as well the familiarity of the basic programming language. At the same time, it is easy to add custom controls, access the Windows API, and use object-oriented techniques to extend your applications. It is this flexibility and level of customization of Visual Basic 4.0 that make it an ideal programming environment.

Visual Basic 4.0 provides a wide range of tools for playing media elements. The multimedia extensions and Video for Windows packages provide the necessary functions to play various multimedia format files. And they provide various levels of

control over the playing and control of multimedia elements and devices. Several of the How-Tos demonstrate the various methods for accessing and utilizing the multimedia extensions and Video for Windows, as well as the MCI control.

You may want to consider browsing the How-Tos in Chapter 8 to get an overview of what can be done with Visual Basic 4.0. The exercises range from a computer-based training system to a multimedia tutor. The techniques and methods developed throughout the chapters can be put together in a multitude of combinations to build applications with wide-ranging purposes.

Summary

Now that you've reviewed the basics of multimedia development in Visual Basic and Windows, you're ready to get started with some real programming. The following chapters will lead you through the topics discussed in this chapter and demonstrate programming techniques for using each of the multimedia methods described. So get ready, load up Visual Basic, and let the exciting world of interactive multimedia development begin!

2
TEXT

2

TEXT

How do I...

In multimedia, text is a fundamental avenue for providing information to the target user. We are all familiar with several popular methods of displaying text in multimedia productions. These include hypertext, text shadows, and scrolling marquees, to name a few. By using several of Visual Basic 4.0's standard features you can perform many text manipulations. And for truly powerful text manipulation, you can use the Windows API to gain greater control over the ability to manipulate and display text.

Windows APIs Covered			
DeleteObject	CreateFontIndirect	SelectObject	TextOut

2.1 Pop up an information window when a keyword is selected

You will learn how to implement basic hypertext capabilities using the label control. By clicking on label controls placed appropriately in text, you can access the click and double-click features of the label control to make certain events take place. As an example, a message box will be displayed when a keyword is clicked on.

2.2 Build hypertext jumps to other sections of text

Hypertext features can be implemented using a picture control and the font property capabilities of the picture box. When a keyword is selected out of the text, new text will appear in the picture box. As an example, clicking on a keyword will bring up its definition.

2.3 Display centered and formatted text over a picture

Text can be displayed over a picture box, linking visual and textual information. This How-To will expand on the picture box text printing explained in How-To 2.2 to include a wide range of format options, and the text will also be centered in the picture box. How-Tos 2.2 and 2.3 show the power Visual Basic 4.0 provides for text manipulation in a picture control.

2.4 Scroll text

One popular text manipulation that you see every time you go to the movies is the marquee text scroll as the credits go up the screen. By using the timer control and the picture box text capabilities discussed in How-Tos 2.2 and 2.3, you can easily implement scrolling text.

2.5 Add shadows to text

Shadowed text is an eye grabber for titles and important statements within a project. By using the transparent capabilities of the label control, you can simply and effectively build shadowed text. This project demonstrates how to build shadow text that can be formatted with different text attributes.

2.6 Create simple text animation

This project expands on the use of the picture and timer controls to demonstrate how to develop simple text animation such as a left-justified text slider. The techniques demonstrated will allow for development of a variety of text intro and exit animations.

2.7 Rotate and expand text

The Windows API provides the ultimate in fancy text manipulation. You can create fonts of different specifications using the Logfont structure and building a new font with the CreateFontIndirect API function. The text can then be displayed using the API TextOut function. This How-To demonstrates the power of the Windows API to manipulate and display a great variety of text formats.

2.1 How do I...
Pop up an information window when a keyword is selected?

COMPLEXITY: EASY

Problem

I would like to be able to select a highlighted keyword out of a block of text and have an information window pop up. For example, I might want to provide a definition for difficult words within text.

Technique

By using the label control and the TextWidth function, you can build text with highlighted keywords that can be clicked on for hypertext interaction.

Steps

Open and run 2-1.VBP. The running program appears as shown in Figure 2-1-1.
     The "insipid" and "palatable" keywords can be clicked on to bring up definition message boxes.

1. Create a new project called 2-1.VBP. Add the objects and properties listed in Table 2-1-1 to Form1 and save the form as 2-1.FRM.

Table 2-1-1 Project form's objects and properties

OBJECT	PROPERTY	SETTING
Form	Name	Form1
	Caption	"How - To 2.1"
	Font name	"Arial"
Label	Name	PrimaryText3
	AutoSize	-1 'True
	Caption	"But, he does have a"

continued on next page

continued from previous page

OBJECT	PROPERTY	SETTING
Label	Name	KeyWord2
	AutoSize	-1 'True
	Caption	"palatable"
	ForeColor	&H000000FF&
Label	Name	PrimaryText4
	AutoSize	-1 'True
	Caption	"personality."
Label	Name	PrimaryText2
	AutoSize	-1 'True
	Caption	"and needs extra assistance."
Label	Name	KeyWord1
	AutoSize	-1 'True
	Caption	"insipid"
	ForeColor	&H000000FF&
.Label	Name	PrimaryText1
	AutoSize	-1 'True
	Caption	"Often his style is very"

2. Add the following code to the general declarations section of the form. The BuildText function handles aligning three labels up on one line. The labels are passed as parameters to the subroutine.

```
Private Sub BuildText(Primary1 As Control, Primary2 As Control, KeyWordLabel ↵
As Control)

'   Move the KeyWord label to the same height
'   as the Primary1 label
KeyWordLabel.Top = Primary1.Top

'   Move the KeyWord label to the right of the first
'   primary label.
KeyWordLabel.Left = Primary1.Left + TextWidth(Primary1.Caption + " ")

'   Move the second Primary label to the same
'   height as the first.
Primary2.Top = Primary1.Top

'   Move the second Primary label to the right
```

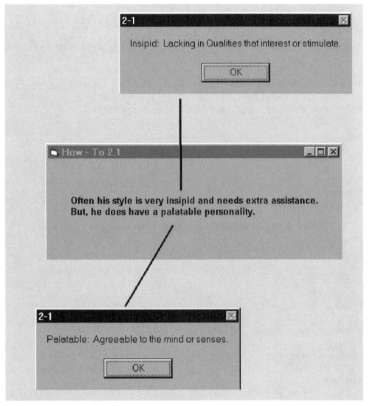

Figure 2-1-1 The form at runtime

```
'  of the KeyWord label
Primary2.Left = KeyWordLabel.Left + TextWidth(KeyWordLabel.Caption + " ")

End Sub
```

3. In the Form_Load routine, the beginning labels for each line are positioned and then the BuildText routine is called to build the sentences.

```
Private Sub Form_Load()

'  Locate the Primary Label on the form.
PrimaryText1.Left = 400
PrimaryText1.Top = 600

'  Lodate the Second Primary label on the form
PrimaryText3.Left = 400
```

continued on next page

continued from previous page

```
'   Note:  We will place the second set of labels
'   directly below the first set of labels.
PrimaryText3.Top = PrimaryText1.Top + TextHeight(PrimaryText1.Caption)

'   Call BuildText which will align the labels.  We pass
'   the two Primary controls and the Keyword Label
BuildText PrimaryText1, PrimaryText2, KeyWord1
BuildText PrimaryText3, PrimaryText4, KeyWord2

End Sub
```

4. When either of the keyword labels is clicked on, an appropriate definition is shown in a MsgBox.

```
Private Sub KeyWord1_Click()

'   When the KeyWord is selected, we will show the
'   definition of Insipid.
MsgBox "Insipid:  Lacking in Qualities that interest or stimulate."

End Sub

Private Sub KeyWord2_Click()

'   When the KeyWord is selected, we will show the
'   definition of Palatable.
MsgBox "Palatable:  Agreeable to the mind or senses."

End Sub
```

How It Works

This straightforward project demonstrates an easy way to add hypertext capabilities to your application. Because label controls provide for transparent display of text, they are ideal for this purpose. The key is placing the keyword label controls in the appropriate part of the main text.

The TextWidth function returns the width of the text for the current font in the object. For this project, all objects use the MS Sans Serif font. By calculating the exact width of the text around the keywords, you can calculate the placement positions of the keywords.

The BuildText routine is a general function that will align a keyword label in the middle of two label controls. The generic function can be used to align any three labels as long as the keyword is not at the end or the beginning of the text.

Comments

By placing these keyword labels in the text, the full range of label events is available to use for the keywords. For example, multiple references to a keyword could be brought up depending on whether a single-click or double-click was performed on the label control.

2.2 How do I...
Build hypertext jumps to other sections of text?

Problem

When a keyword in hypertext is selected, how do I display a new item of text such as a definition? I would like the currently displayed text to be replaced with new text and then returned to the original text.

Technique

In How-To 2.1, the label controls are used to implement keywords in text. In this section, the text is built in a picture box, and while doing so, the locations of the keywords are tracked by using the Picture Box CurrentX and CurrentY properties.

Steps

Open and run 2-2.VBP. The running program appears as shown in Figure 2-2-1.

When you click on the "Mid" keyword, the definition of "Mid" appears. See Figure 2-2-2.

When you click on the "Click Here to Return" statement, the original text appears.

1. Create a new project called 2-2.VBP. Add the objects and properties listed in Table 2-2-1 to Form1 and save the form as 2-2.FRM.

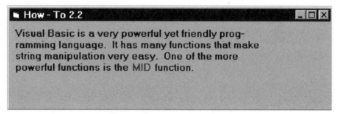

Figure 2-2-1 The form at runtime

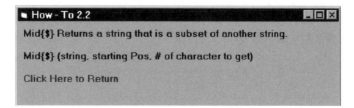

Figure 2-2-2 The "Mid" definition is displayed

Table 2-2-1 Project form's objects and properties

OBJECT	PROPERTY	SETTING
Form	Name	Form1
	Caption	"How - To 2.2"
PictureBox	Name	DispPict
	BorderStyle	0 'None

2. Place the following in the general declarations section. These are global variables that will be used in building and implementing the hypertext.

```
'   TextType serve to let us know whether we
'   are currently displaying the text or
'   the definition
Dim TextType As Integer

'   KeyWords1 and 2 will be used to contain
'   our keywords for the two text paragraphs
Dim KeyWords1 As String
Dim KeyWords2 As String

'   KW-XX and KW-YY will hold the origin coordinate
'   of the hypertext keywords
Dim KW1YY As Integer
Dim KW1XX As Integer
Dim KW2YY As Integer
Dim KW2XX As Integer
```

3. Add the following code to the general declarations section of the form. The PrintText routine handles printing one line of text, with and without keywords. We pass to the function the picture control for the text to be displayed on, the full line of text, and the keyword within the text. XX and YY will be the origin positions of the keyword passed back to the calling routine.

```
Private Sub PrintText(Pict As Control, Text$, KeyWord$, XX, YY)
'   Ensure the starting forecolor is blue
DispPict.ForeColor = RGB(0, 0, 255)

'   Check to see if there are any keywords in this
'   line
If KeyWord$ <> "" Then
    '   Calculate the positon of the keyword in the text
    pos = InStr(Text$, KeyWord$)

    '   In case the keyword is not found in the text,
    '   we will print the full line without a
    '   keyword.
    If pos = 0 Then
        '   Print the line
        Pict.Print Text$
```

```
            'Exit the Sub
            Exit Sub
      End If

      '  We will check to see if the whole line is
      '  to be Hypertext
      If KeyWord$ = Text$ Then
            '  Change the color to red
            DispPict.ForeColor = RGB(255, 0, 0)

            '  Store the x and y coordinates of the hypertext
            XX = DispPict.CurrentX
            YY = DispPict.CurrentY

            '  Print the KeyWord text
            Pict.Print KeyWord$
            Exit Sub
      End If

      '  Print the text left of the keyword
      Pict.Print Left$(Text$, pos - 1);

      '  Store the x and y coord. of the keyword
      XX = DispPict.CurrentX
      YY = DispPict.CurrentY

      '  Print the Keyword in red
      Pict.ForeColor = RGB(255, 0, 0)
      Pict.Print KeyWord$;

      '  Change back to blue
      Pict.ForeColor = RGB(0, 0, 255)

      '  We will get the length of the text to the right
      '  of the keyword
      RightTextlen = Len(Text$) - pos - Len(KeyWord$)

      '  If the value is minus 1, then the keyword is as
      '  the end of the line.  So, we need to set the
      '  value to 0
      If RightTextlen = -1 Then RightTextlen = 0

      '  Print the text to the right of the keyword
      Pict.Print " " + Right$(Text$, RightTextlen)

Else

      '  Print the line and set the XX and YY
      '  values to zero since there are no keywords.
      XX = 0
      YY = 0
      Pict.Print Text$

End If

End Sub
```

4. Add the following code to the general declarations section of the form. The DispDef function handles displaying the definition of the "Mid" keyword. It does this by calling the PrintText function.

```
Private Sub DispDef()
'   We will set TextType to 2 so that the appropriate
'   call will be made when the hypertext click
'   is made
TextType = 2

'   Refresh the picture to remove the current text
DispPict.Refresh

'   Reset the coordinates
DispPict.CurrentX = 0
DispPict.CurrentY = 0

'   Print the text by calling the PrintText function
PrintText DispPict, "Mid{$} Returns a string that is a subset of another ↵
string.", "", Temp, Temp

PrintText DispPict, "", "", Temp, Temp

PrintText DispPict, "Mid{$} (string, starting Pos, # of character to get)", ↵
"", Temp, Temp

PrintText DispPict, "", "", Temp, Temp

'   This time, we have a keyword and will store the keyword
'   orgin values
PrintText DispPict, "Click Here to Return", KeyWords2, KW2XX, KW2YY

End Sub
```

5. The Form_Load procedure handles setting up the keywords and placing the picture.

```
Private Sub Form_Load()
'   Move the picture
DispPict.Move 100, 100

'   Initialize TextType to 1 which indicates that the
'   setup text should be displayed
TextType = 1

'   Set the keywords
KeyWords1 = "MID"
KeyWords2 = "Click Here to Return"
End Sub
```

6. The Form_Paint procedure ensures that the text is still displayed when the form is repainted. The first time the form is painted, the set-up routine is called because the Form_Load procedure TextType is set to 1.

```
Private Sub Form_Paint()

'   Whenever the form is repainted we will redraw the
'   text on the form.  This also serves to show the setup
'   text when the project is started
Select Case TextType
    Case 1  '  Display the standard text
        setup
    Case 2  '  Display the definition
        DispDef
    End Select

End Sub
```

7. The DispPict_MouseDown event performs the necessary checking to see if a keyword(s) has been selected. The check is done according to whether the main text or the definition is displayed. If the keyword(s) has been selected, then the appropriate routine is called to change the text.

```
Private Sub DispPict_MouseDown(Button As Integer, Shift As Integer, x As ↵
Single, y As Single)

'   The following case checks to see whether we are displaying the text
'   or the definition.
Select Case TextType
    Case 1

    '   If the text is displayed and the hypertext word 'MID' is
    '   selected, then we will call the DispDef function.  Note
    '   that XX and YY are global variables that contain the origin
    '   coordinates of the hypertext word.  The If statement checks
    '   to see if the mouse click falls within the bounding box of
    '   the hypertext word.  The TextWidth and TextHeight functions
    '   will serve to provide us with the height and width of the
    '   hypertext word
    If ((x > KW1XX) And (x < KW1XX + TextWidth(KeyWords1))) And ((y > KW1YY) ↵
And (y < KW1YY + TextHeight(KeyWords1))) Then DispDef

    Case 2

    '   This case will redisplay the text instead of the definition
    If ((x > KW2XX) And (x < KW2XX + TextWidth(KeyWords2))) And ((y > KW2YY) ↵
And (y < KW2YY + TextHeight(KeyWords2))) Then setup

    End Select

End Sub
```

8. Add the following code to the general declarations section of the form. The following procedure handles displaying the main body of text. It does this by calling the PrintText function.

```
Private Sub setup()

'  We will set TextType to 1 so that the appropriate
'  call will be made when the hypertext click
'  is made
TextType = 1

'  Clear the current text out of the picture control
DispPict.Refresh

'  Reset the starting position to 0
DispPict.CurrentX = 0
DispPict.CurrentY = 0

'  Print the text
PrintText DispPict, "Visual Basic is a very powerful yet friendly prog-", ↵
"", Throw, Throw

PrintText DispPict, "ramming language.  It has many functions that make", ↵
"", Throw, Throw

PrintText DispPict, "string manipulation very easy.  One of the more ", ↵
"", Throw, Throw

'  This time we have a keyword and will store the
'  keyword origin values
PrintText DispPict, "powerful functions is the MID function.", KeyWords1, ↵
KW1XX, KW1YY

End Sub
```

How It Works

The key to this project is knowing the position of the keyword(s) in the text and the box surrounding the text. When the text is printed into the picture control, the CurrentX and CurrentY of the picture control holds the origin position for the next set of text to be printed. By printing the text in the picture control up to the keywords, an exact fix on the starting location of the keyword text can be calculated. Note that by using a ";" at the end of the print command (e.g., picture1.print A$;), a new line is not started. This allows you to print your keyword in the middle of a line of text. Right before you print the keyword(s), store the CurrentX and CurrentY in a global variable.

The full length and height of the keywords in the picture box can be ascertained by using the TextWidth and TextHeight functions. These will return the height and width of the keyword text. Thus, the box surrounding the keywords is calculated. When the Picture1_MouseDown event is triggered, a check can be performed to see if the click was on a keyword.

Comments

You can use the full set of text attribute features available to the picture control to display different types of keywords. For example, you can use underlines to denote new subjects, red to signify definitions. Hypertext can also be added to graphics to provide a type of hot spot for graphics.

2.3 How do I...
Display centered and formatted text over a picture?

COMPLEXITY: INTERMEDIATE

Problem

I have a picture that I would like to place textual information on. How can I place centered and formatted text over the picture with various font attributes such as underline and italic?

Technique

This How-To expands on the simple printing into a picture box done in How-To 2.2. The picture box control allows you to set font attributes for text displayed in the picture. The TextWidth and TextHeight functions are also used to center the text in the picture.

Steps

Open and run 2-3.VBP. The running program appears as shown in Figure 2-3-1. Select the font attributes you would like to display the text with. Then select Print to show the text. Figure 2-3-2 shows the results of one set of selections.

1. Create a new project called 2-3.VBP. Add the objects and properties listed in Table 2-3-1 to Form1 and save the form as 2-3.FRM.

Table 2-3-1 Project form's objects and properties

OBJECT	PROPERTY	SETTING
Form	Name	Form1
	Caption	"How - To 2.3"
Frame	Name	Frame2
	Caption	"Point Size"

Note: The following two option buttons should be placed on the Frame2 frame.

continued on next page

continued from previous page

OBJECT	PROPERTY	SETTING
OptionButton	Name	Point1
	Caption	"24 Point"
OptionButton	Name	Point2
	Caption	"36 Point"
Frame	Name	Frame1
	Caption	"Color"

Note: The following two option buttons should be placed on the Frame1 frame.

OBJECT	PROPERTY	SETTING
OptionButton	Name	Green
	Caption	"Green"
OptionButton	Name	Red
	Caption	"Red"
CommandButton	Name	Print
	Caption	"Print"
CheckBox	Name	FontUnder
	Caption	"Font Underline"
CheckBox	Name	FontStrike
	Caption	"Font StrikeThru"
CheckBox	Name	FontItal
	Caption	"Font Italic"
CheckBox	Name	FontBld
	Caption	"Font Bold"
PictureBox	Name	DispPict
	Picture	'oranges.bmp'
	AutoSize	-1 'True
	Font	
	name	"Arial"
	size	10.8

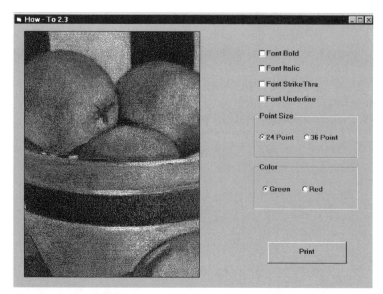

Figure 2-3-1 The form at runtime

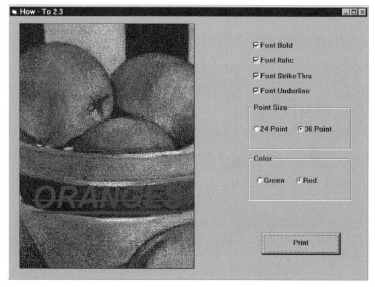

Figure 2-3-2 The picture text shown with various font attributes

2. The following routines handle the check box selections. This includes turning on and off the Font Bold, Font Italic, Font Strikethru, and Font Underline properties, plus the routine also handles changing the font color and point size.

```
Private Sub FontBld_Click()

'  If selected then set the FontBold property
'  to TRUE otherwise set to FALSE
DispPict.FontBold = FontBld.Value
End Sub

Private Sub FontItal_Click()

'  If selected then set the FontItal property
'  to TRUE otherwise set to FALSE
DispPict.FontItalic = FontItal.Value

End Sub

Private Sub FontStrike_Click()

'  If selected then set the FontStrike property
'  to TRUE otherwise set to FALSE
DispPict.FontStrikethru = FontStrike.Value
End Sub

Private Sub FontUnder_Click()

'  If selected then set the FontUnder property
'  to TRUE otherwise set to FALSE
DispPict.FontUnderline = FontUnder.Value
End Sub

Private Sub Green_Click()

'  If green is selected then set the forecolor
If Green.Value = True Then DispPict.ForeColor = RGB(0, 255, 0)

End Sub

Private Sub Point1_Click()

'  Set the fontsize to 24 point
If Point1.Value = True Then DispPict.FontSize = 24

End Sub

Private Sub Point2_Click()

'  Set the fontsize to 36
If Point2.Value = True Then DispPict.FontSize = 36

End Sub
```

```
Private Sub Red_Click()

'  Set the forecolor to red
If Red.Value = True Then DispPict.ForeColor = RGB(255, 0, 0)

End Sub
```

3. The Form_Load procedure sets up the various properties for the picture box and sets the default selections.

```
Private Sub Form_Load()

'  Set the starting font to Arial
DispPict.FontName = "Arial"

'  Set the starting pointsize to 24
DispPict.FontSize = 24

'  Set the forecolor to green
DispPict.ForeColor = RGB(255, 0, 0)

'  Turn off the FontBold property
DispPict.FontBold = False

'  Ensure that 24 Point and Green are selected
'  to start out
Point1.Value = 1
Green.Value = 1
End Sub
```

4. The Print_Click function handles the display of the text on the picture. First, the picture is refreshed to clear out any present text. The ScaleMode property is set to 3 to do the calculations in pixel units. The calculations are then made to center the text (lowered slightly). By dividing the width and height in two, the center of the picture is found. Finally, CurrentX and CurrentY are moved up and left one-half the length and height of the text.

```
Private Sub Print_Click()

'  Refresh the Picture
DispPict.Refresh

DispPict.ScaleMode = 3

'  Set the currentx and currenty
DispPict.CurrentX = DispPict.ScaleWidth / 2 - DispPict.TextWidth("ORANGES") / 2
DispPict.CurrentY = DispPict.ScaleHeight / 2 - DispPict.TextHeight("ORANGES") ↵
/ 2 + 100

'  Print Windows
DispPict.Print "ORANGES"

End Sub
```

How It Works

The key to using the picture box control is placing text at your desired position. By using the TextWidth and TextHeight functions, you can calculate the desired position for your text. The TextWidth and TextHeight functions work by using the current font settings for the picture control; this includes the typeface selected. They also return the size of the current units set by the ScaleMode property. Manipulation of the various font attributes is as simple as setting the font attributes for the picture

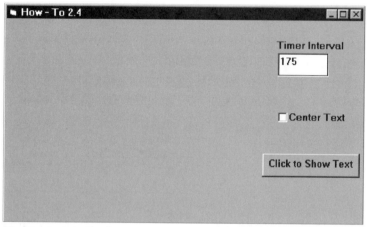

Figure 2-4-1 The form as it appears at runtime

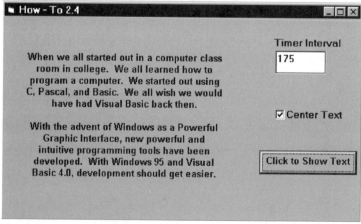

Figure 2-4-2 Centered text scrolling

property appropriately. By setting ForeColor, you can also change the color the text is printed with.

Comments

Using the TextWidth and TextHeight functions and setting the font attributes, you can build text that has various property changes. For example, you could display the following text: **Hello** *Out* There.

2.4 How do I...
Scroll text?

Problem

I would like to scroll text like a film's movie credits. This is an excellent attention grabber and provides for easy reading of text.

Technique

Now that text can be displayed in a picture, the timer control and the placement properties of the picture can be used to perform text scrolling.

Steps

Open and run 2-4.VBP. The running program appears as shown in Figure 2-4-1.

To change the speed of the scrolling, change the timer interval. The higher the interval, the slower the scrolling. The text will scroll left-justified unless you select the Center Text box. Then the text will be centered as shown in Figure 2-4-2. To scroll the text, click on the Click to Show Text button.

1. Create a new project called 2-4.VBP. Add the objects and properties listed in Table 2-4-1 to Form1 and save the form as 2-4.FRM.

Table 2-4-1 Project form's objects and properties

OBJECT	PROPERTY	SETTING
Form	Name	Form1
	BackColor	&H00C0C0C0&
	Caption	"How - To 2.4"
TextBox	Name	intv

continued on next page

continued from previous page

OBJECT	PROPERTY	SETTING
CommandButton	Name	ShowClick
	Caption	"Click to Show Text"
CheckBox	Name	TextCenter
	BackColor	&H00C0C0C0&
	Caption	"Center Text"
PictureBox	Name	ScrollPict
	BackColor	&H00C0C0C0&
	BorderStyle	0 'None
	Font	
	name	"Arial"
	weight	700
Timer	Name	Timer1
	Enabled	0 'False
	Interval	100
Label	Name	TimerLabel
	BackColor	&H00C0C0C0&
	Caption	"Timer Interval"

2. Add the following code to the general declarations section of the form. The ShowClick function handles initializing the scrolling of the text. It calls the PutText function to output the text on the picture. The timer is also started to begin the scrolling.

```
'  This function initiates the display of the text
Private Sub ShowClick_Click()

'  Set the interval to the user entered value
timer1.Interval = Val(intv.Text)

'  Clear the picture
scrollpict.Cls

'  Turn off the timer in case the user
'  clicked during the display of the text
timer1.Enabled = False

'  Turn off the picture
```

```
scrollpict.Visible = False

'  Turn on the automatic redraw
scrollpict.AutoRedraw = -1

'  Set the top of the picture to the bottom of the form
scrollpict.Top = Form1.ScaleHeight

'  Set the current drawing point to the top of the picture
scrollpict.CurrentY = 0

'  The following is the text to be displayed
A$ = "When we all started out in a computer class"
B$ = "room in college.  We all learned how to"
c$ = "program a computer.  We started out using"
D$ = "C, Pascal, and Basic.  We all wish we would"
E$ = "have had Visual Basic back then."
F$ = ""
G$ = "With the advent of Windows as a Powerful"
H$ = "Graphic Interface, new powerful and"
I$ = "intuitive programming tools have been"
J$ = "developed.  With Windows 95 and Visual"
K$ = "Basic 4.0, development should get easier."

'  Print the lines into the picture
PutText A$
PutText B$
PutText c$
PutText D$
PutText E$
PutText F$
PutText G$
PutText H$
PutText I$
PutText J$
PutText K$

'  Turn on the picture
scrollpict.Visible = True

'  Enable Timer1
timer1.Enabled = True

End Sub
```

3. The Form_Load routine moves the picture box to the top left of the form.

```
Private Sub Form_Load()
'  Move the picture to the top left of the form
scrollpict.Move 0, 0
End Sub
```

4. The PutText routine displays the text on the form. Note that for each new line of text, the Print command does an automatic return. If the user wants the text centered, then the center location for the text is calculated.

```
'  T$ is the string to be printed
Private Sub PutText(T$)

'  If the text is to be centered then we calculate
'  the starting position.  TextWidth gives us the width
'  of the string.  We then subtract that from the width
'  of the picture.  We then divide that value by 2. This
'  value is set to CurrentX
If textcenter.Value = 1 Then scrollpict.CurrentX = (scrollpict.ScaleWidth↵
- scrollpict.TextWidth(T$)) / 2

'  Print the Text
scrollpict.Print T$

End Sub
```

5. The timer handles scrolling the picture box up the form. It moves 10 pixels with each timer movement. By changing the timer interval and the size of the move (from 10), you can affect the speed of the scroll.

```
Private Sub Timer1_Timer()

'  Set the scalemode of the form to pixels.
Form1.ScaleMode = 3

'  This check tells us that the top has moved
'  beyond the form such that it is not visible.
'  When the top is above the form higher than
'  the picture height, the picture is no longer
'  visible
If scrollpict.Top + scrollpict.Height > 0 Then
    '  Move the picture up
    scrollpict.Top = scrollpict.Top - 10
Else
    '  Disable the timer
    timer1.Enabled = 0
End If

End Sub
```

How It Works

By using Visual Basic's easy methods of control placement and combining them with the timer control, you can perform text movement over time easily. The timer control is very important to control the movement of the text up the form. It allows you to control the speed with which the picture box is moved. If a simple loop were used, then there would be little control over the speed of the scroll, and the speed would change depending on the system. Once again we see that placing text in the picture box can be handled with a great degree of control by using the TextWidth and TextHeight functions.

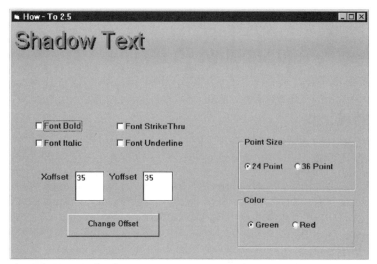

Figure 2-5-1 The form as it appears at runtime

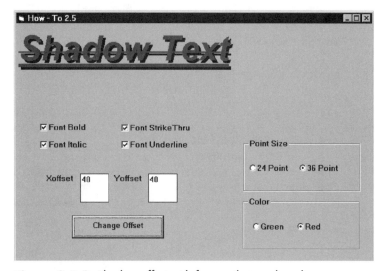

Figure 2-5-2 Shadow offset with font attributes selected

Note that we set the picture's auto-redraw parameter to true when the picture is off the form. This will keep the text constantly displayed in the picture box without being erased.

Comments

Other forms of text transition can be performed by using the timer control, placement methods, and the text, label, and picture box controls.

2.5 How do I...
Add shadows to text?

Problem

I would like to make my text look more solid and striking by adding shadows.

Technique

The label control allows you to set the backstyle property to transparent. This allows objects behind the text in the label to be seen. By using a combination of two label controls, a shadow effect can be built for text.

Steps

Open and run 2-5.VBP. The running program appears as shown in Figure 2-5-1.

You can change the characteristics of the text as well as the front text color and the offset of the shadow. Figure 2-5-2 is an example of the shadow offset changed to 40 with all of the font attributes selected. You can also enter a negative offset(s) to have the shadow appear above, to the left, to the right, or below the text.

1. Create a new project called 2-5.VBP. Add the objects and properties listed in Table 2-5-1 to Form1 and save the form as 2-5.FRM.

Table 2-5-1 Project form's objects and properties

OBJECT	PROPERTY	SETTING
Form	Name	Form1
	Caption	"How - To 2.5"
	Font	
	name	"MS Sans Serif"
	size	19.2
TextBox	Name	Yoff
	Text	"35"
TextBox	Name	xoff
	Text	"35"
Frame	Name	Frame2
	Caption	"Point Size"

OBJECT	PROPERTY	SETTING
Note: The following two option buttons should be added on the Frame2 frame.		
OptionButton	Name	Point1
	Caption	"24 Point"
OptionButton	Name	Point2
	Caption	"36 Point"
Frame	Name	Frame1
	Caption	"Color"
Note: The following two option buttons should be added on the Frame1 frame.		
OptionButton	Name	Green
	Caption	"Green"
OptionButton	Name	Red
	Caption	"Red"
CommandButton	Name	Print
	Caption	"Change Offset"
	Font	
	name	"Arial"
	weight	700
CheckBox	Name	FontUnder
	Caption	"Font Underline"
CheckBox	Name	FontStrike
	Caption	"Font StrikeThru"
CheckBox	Name	FontItal
	Caption	"Font Italic"
CheckBox	Name	FontBld
	Caption	"Font Bold"

continued on next page

continued from previous page

OBJECT	PROPERTY	SETTING
Label	Name	Label2
	Caption	"Yoffset"
Label	Name	Label1
	Caption	"Xoffset"
Label	Name	TopLabel
	AutoSize	-1 'True
	BackStyle	0 'Transparent
	Caption	"Shadow Text"
	Font	
	name	"Arial"
	size	24
Label	Name	BottomLabel
	AutoSize	-1 'True
	BackStyle	0 'Transparent
	Caption	"Shadow Text"
	Font	
	name	"Arial"
	size	24

2. If the bottom or top label has changed, it is important to make sure that the label is sized properly for the text.

```
Private Sub BottomLabel_Change()

'  Autosize the label for any changes
bottomlabel.AutoSize = True

End Sub

Private Sub TopLabel_Change()

'  autosize the label for any new changes
toplabel.AutoSize = True

End Sub
```

3. The following routines handle turning on and off the Font Bold, Font Italic, Font Strikethru, and Font Underline properties. Set the value of each property to that of the check box value.

```
Private Sub FontBld_Click()

'  Turn on or off the fontbold feature for both the
'  top label and the bottom label
toplabel.FontBold = FontBld.Value
bottomlabel.FontBold = FontBld.Value
End Sub

Private Sub FontItal_Click()

'  Turn on or off the fontitalic feature for both the
'  top label and the bottom label
toplabel.FontItalic = FontItal.Value
bottomlabel.FontItalic = FontItal.Value
End Sub

Private Sub FontStrike_Click()

'  Turn on or off the fontstrikethru feature for both the
'  top label and the bottom label
toplabel.FontStrikethru = FontStrike.Value
bottomlabel.FontStrikethru = FontStrike.Value
End Sub

Private Sub FontUnder_Click()

'  Turn on or off the fontunder feature for both the
'  top label and the bottom label
toplabel.FontUnderline = FontUnder.Value
bottomlabel.FontUnderline = FontUnder.Value
End Sub
```

4. The Form_Load routine handles setting up the initial shadow. The initial offsets for the shadow are set and the various font attributes are set.

```
Private Sub Form_Load()
'  Set the starting fontsize to 24
toplabel.FontSize = 24
bottomlabel.FontSize = 24

'  Set the forecolor to green
toplabel.ForeColor = RGB(255, 0, 0)

'  Turn off the fontbold feature
toplabel.FontBold = False
bottomlabel.FontBold = False

'  Start out using Green and 24 point
Point1.Value = 1
Green.Value = 1

'  Set up the initial shadow
toplabel.Left = 50
```

continued on next page

continued from previous page

```
bottomlabel.Left = 85
toplabel.Top = 100
bottomlabel.Top = 135

End Sub
```

5. The following routines handle the changing of the text color and the point size.

```
Private Sub Green_Click()

'  Set the top label to green
If Green.Value = True Then toplabel.ForeColor = RGB(0, 255, 0)

End Sub

Private Sub Red_Click()

'  Set the top label to red
If Red.Value = True Then toplabel.ForeColor = RGB(255, 0, 0)

End Sub

Private Sub Point1_Click()

'  Set the fontsize for both labels to 24 point
If Point1.Value = True Then toplabel.FontSize = 24: bottomlabel.FontSize = 24

End Sub

Private Sub Point2_Click()

'  Set the fontsize for both labels to 36 point
If Point2.Value = True Then toplabel.FontSize = 36: bottomlabel.FontSize = 36

End Sub
```

6. Print_Click handles clicking the Print Command button, which is used to update any offset changes made by the user.

```
Private Sub Print_Click()

'  Refresh form1
Form1.Refresh

'  Move the shadow text to the specified
'  positions
bottomlabel.Left = 50 + Val(xoff.Text)

bottomlabel.Top = 100 + Val(yoff.Text)

End Sub
```

How It Works

Label controls allow you to see objects behind the text if the backstyle property is set to transparent. If two label controls are used with the same text attributes, except that one has a black (or dark) text color and is offset slightly whereas the other is a lighter color or shade, you can build shadowed text. As this project shows, the shadow can work for any type of text formatting and size.

The offset is calculated in this project using the standard visual basic scale mode of twips. We change the offset to the user's desired input. If you enter in two negative values or one negative and one positive value, the shadow will move above and to the left or right of the top text. Note that increasing the offsets too much will cause the shadow effect to disappear.

Comments

A similar technique can be used to build shadow text on pictures. By using the print function and TextWidth and TextHeight, reviewed in How-Tos 2.3 and 2.4, you can also place shadow text over your pictures.

2.6 How do I...
Create simple text animation?

COMPLEXITY: INTERMEDIATE

Problem

I would like to develop simple text animation such as a text slider in my applications.

Technique

By combining the timer control and the picture box, you can perform effective text animation. By using the picture controls left, print, TextWidth, and TextHeight functions you can display and move text. The timer control can be used to adjust the speed of the text movements. In this project, the common effect of having text slide into place from the right of the screen will be implemented.

Steps

Open and run 2-6.VBP. Figure 2-6-1 shows the text while the last line is being animated to the left.

Try changing the movement increment and timer interval values to control the speed and movement of the text. To start the animation, click on the Start Animation button.

1. Create a new project called 2-6.VBP. Add the objects and properties listed in Table 2-6-1 to Form1 and save the form as 2-6.FRM.

Figure 2-6-1 The form at start-up with the text animation in process

Table 2-6-1 Project form's objects and properties

OBJECT	PROPERTY	SETTING
Form	Name	Form1
	Caption	"How - To 2.6"
	Font	
	name	"Arial"
	weight	700
TextBox	Name	Intv
	Text	"5"
TextBox	Name	Movement
	Text	"200"
CommandButton	Name	StartAnim
	Caption	"Start Animation"
PictureBox	Name	AnimPict3
	AutoRedraw	-1 'True
	BorderStyle	0 'None

OBJECT	PROPERTY	SETTING
	Font	
	name	"Arial"
	weight	700
	size	30
	ForeColor	&H0000FF00&
PictureBox	Name	AnimPict2
	AutoRedraw	-1 'True
	BorderStyle	0 'None
	Font	
	name	"Arial"
	weight	700
	size	30
	ForeColor	&H000000FF&
PictureBox	Name	AnimPict1
	AutoRedraw	-1 'True
	BorderStyle	0 'None
	Font	
	name	"Arial"
	weight	700
	size	30
Timer	Name	Timer1
	Enabled	0 'False
	Interval	1
Label	Name	Interval
	Alignment	2 'Center
	AutoSize	-1 'True
	Caption	"Enter a Timer Interval in Milliseconds"
Label	Name	Inc
	Alignment	2 'Center
	AutoSize	-1 'True
	Caption	"Enter a Movement Increment"

2. Add the following code to the general declarations section of the form. The SetText function handles preparing the picture box alignments so that the animated text will be uniform and smooth.

```
Private Sub SetText()

'   We will move the first picture to the top of the form
'   We will then move each successive picture down from
'   the preceding picture by the appropriate text height

'   We will also set the height and width of each
'   picture to that of the text that will be displayed

AnimPict1.Top = 200
AnimPict1.Left = Form1.Width + 10
AnimPict1.Height = AnimPict1.TextHeight(TextArray(1))
AnimPict1.Width = AnimPict1.TextWidth(TextArray(1))

AnimPict2.Top = AnimPict1.Top + AnimPict1.TextHeight(TextArray(1))
AnimPict2.Left = Form1.Width + 10
AnimPict2.Height = AnimPict2.TextHeight(TextArray(2))
AnimPict2.Width = AnimPict2.TextWidth(TextArray(2))

AnimPict3.Top = AnimPict2.Top + AnimPict1.TextHeight(TextArray(2))
AnimPict3.Left = Form1.Width + 10
AnimPict3.Height = AnimPict3.TextHeight(TextArray(3))
AnimPict3.Width = AnimPict3.TextWidth(TextArray(3))

End Sub
```

3. Add the following code to the general declarations section of the form. The MovePict function handles moving the specified picture control to the left by the specified increment. It then reprints the text onto the picture box.

```
Private Sub MovePict(Pict As Control, MoveInc, Text)
'   Move the picture to the left by the
'   specified increment.
Pict.Move Pict.Left - MoveInc

'   Set the CurrentX and CurrentY of the
'   picture to 0
Pict.CurrentX = 0
Pict.CurrentY = 0

'   Print the text on the picture control
Pict.Print Text

End Sub

Private Sub Form_Load()

'   Setup the text to be animated
TextArray(1) = "Presenting"
```

```
TextArray(2) = "A Whole New Concept"
TextArray(3) = "In Computers"

SetText

End Sub
```

4. When the Start Animation button is selected, the pictures are moved off to the right of the form and the timer control is started.

```
Private Sub StartAnim_Click()

'   We will move the pictures to the right of
'   the form so that they are not visible
AnimPict1.Left = Form1.Width + 10
AnimPict2.Left = Form1.Width + 10
AnimPict3.Left = Form1.Width + 10

'   Set the interval to the value of the
'   entered text in the Intv text box
timer1.Interval = Val(Intv.Text)

'   Enable the timer
timer1.Enabled = True

End Sub
```

5. In the timer control, each successive line of text is moved to the left of the form and then the next line of text starts its movement.

```
Private Sub Timer1_Timer()

'   Get the movement increment
Increment = Val(Movement.Text)

'   We don't want to move to the left more
'   than 100 twips to the right of the left
'   edge of the form.  If animpict1 has been
'   moved then we will check animpict2.  The
'   same is true for the following pictures

If AnimPict1.Left > Increment + 100 Then

MovePict AnimPict1, Increment, TextArray(1)

Else

    If AnimPict2.Left > Increment + 100 Then

    MovePict AnimPict2, Increment, TextArray(2)

    Else

        If AnimPict3.Left > Increment + 100 Then
```

continued on next page

continued from previous page

```
        MovePict AnimPict3, Increment, TextArray(3)

        Else

        timer1.Enabled = False

        End If

    End If

  End If

End If

End Sub
```

How It Works

This section is an excellent example of how the picture box capabilities combined with the timer control can affect text animation. We could just as easily have performed animation of right-justified text or had a paragraph built with text dropping from the top of the form. Many of these text transitions/animations are found in the most popular presentation packages.

The heart of this program is the logic in the MovePict function and timer control. With each firing of the timer event, a check is done to see if the picture boxes have been moved to the left edge of the form. If they have not, then the MovePict function is called and passed to the control, text, and increment to perform the move. The MovePict function then changes the left properties of the picture so they are moved by the user-specified increment. The text is then reprinted on the picture control.

Comments

By using the techniques presented in this section, you can implement various text animations. By implementing different text animations, you can provide effective transition for text in your projects. One other idea to keep in mind is having text spelled out over time. You can have characters, not just whole words, transition into the screen.

2.7 How do I...
Rotate and expand text?

COMPLEXITY: ADVANCED

Problem

I would like to rotate and expand text to add special effects to my projects. This will give added visual effectiveness over linear text transitions.

Technique

The Windows API provides for powerful text manipulation. It is possible to create text of different heights, widths, weights, and angles from any of the fonts you have installed in the system.

Steps

Open and run 2-7.VBP. Figure 2-7-1 shows one part of the first phase. Figure 2-7-2 shows the final output of the text manipulation.

1. Create a new project called 2-7.VBP. Add the objects and properties listed in Table 2-7-1 to Form1 and save the form as 2-7.FRM.

Table 2-7-1 Project form's objects and properties

OBJECT	PROPERTY	SETTING
Form	Name	Form1
	Caption	"How - To 2.7"
	Font	
	name	"Arial"
	weight	700
Timer	Name	Timer2
	Enabled	0 'False
	Interval	50
Timer	Name	Timer1
	Enabled	0 'False
	Interval	10
PictureBox	Name	IntroPic
	BorderStyle	0 'None

2. Add the following to a new module called 2-7.BAS. The module defines the Logfont structure for defining a font and the necessary Windows API functions to create and display the font.

```
'   The following type declaration describes the
'   Windows API LOGFONT structure.  THE LOGFONT
'   structure is used by several of the WIN API
'   text functions.

Type LOGFONT
```

continued on next page

continued from previous page

```
        lfHeight As Integer
        lfWidth As Integer
        lfEscapement As Integer
        lfOrientation As Integer
        lfWeight As Integer
        lfItalic As String * 1
        lfUnderline As String * 1
        lfStrikeOut As String * 1
        lfCharSet As String * 1
        lfOutPrecision As String * 1
        lfClipPrecision As String * 1
        lfQuality As String * 1
        lfPitchAndFamily As String * 1
        lfFaceName As String * 24
End Type


'   Declare the Windows API DeleteObject function
Declare Function DeleteObject Lib "GDI" (ByVal hObject As Integer) As Integer

'   Declare the Windows API CreateFontIndirect function
Declare Function CreateFontIndirect Lib "GDI" (lpLogFont As LOGFONT) As Integer

'   Declare the Windows API SelectObject function
```

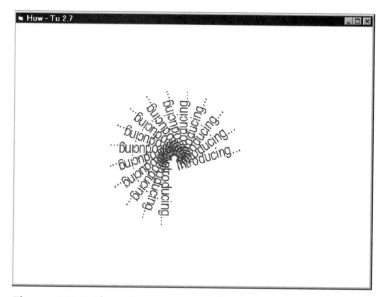

Figure 2-7-1 The project at start-up with the text in mid-rotation

```
Declare Function SelectObject Lib "GDI" (ByVal hDC As Integer, ByVal hObject ↵
As Integer) As Integer

'  Declare the Windows API TextOut function
Declare Function TextOut Lib "GDI" (ByVal hDC As Integer, ByVal X As Integer, ↵
ByVal Y As Integer, ByVal lpString As String, ByVal nCount As Integer) As ↵
Integer
```

3. Add the following code to the general declarations section of Form1. These global variables are used to create the font and calculate appropriate movements.

```
'  CFONT will be our font structure for the text
Dim CFONT As LOGFONT

'  ChangeX and ChangeY will hold the increment to move
'  the text to the upperleft corner.
Dim ChangeX As Integer
Dim ChangeY As Integer
```

4. Add the following code to the general declarations section of the form. The FontOut procedure handles creating the specified font (FontStruct) on the specified control (Pict) at the given coordinates (XX and YY). The Windows API font functions declared in the global module are utilized here.

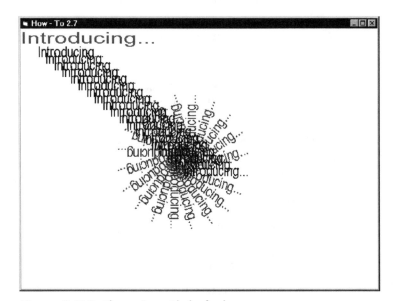

Figure 2-7-2 The project with the final text output

```
Private Sub FontOut(Text$, Pict As Control, xx, yy, FontStruct As LOGFONT)

'   Create the new font
NewFont% = CreateFontIndirect(FontStruct)

'   Select the new font into the picture
'   device context
OldFont% = SelectObject(intropic.hDC, NewFont%)

'   Display the text
Throw% = TextOut(intropic.hDC, xx, yy, Text$, Len(Text$))

'   Select the font back for the original device context
Throw% = SelectObject(Pict.hDC, OldFont%)

'   Delete the newly created font
Throw% = DeleteObject(NewFont%)

End Sub
```

    5. The Form_Load procedure initializes several items, including the Logical Font (Logfont) structure; sets up the picture box; and calculates print coordinates.

```
Private Sub Form_Load()

'   Move the picture to the origin of the form
intropic.Move 0, 0

'   Set the scalemode to 3 (pixels) for the picture
intropic.ScaleMode = 3

'   Set the form to be the same size as the picture.
Form1.Width = intropic.Width
Form1.Height = intropic.Height

'   Set up the initial font structure.  We will
'   use a height of 30 and a width of 10.  The
'   weight will be medium (non-bold), and will
'   use Arial.
CFONT.lfHeight = 30
CFONT.lfWidth = 10
CFONT.lfEscapement = 0
CFONT.lfWeight = 400
CFONT.lfItalic = Chr$(0)
CFONT.lfUnderline = Chr$(0)
CFONT.lfStrikeOut = Chr$(0)
CFONT.lfOutPrecision = Chr$(0)
CFONT.lfClipPrecision = Chr$(0)
CFONT.lfQuality = Chr$(0)
CFONT.lfPitchAndFamily = Chr$(0)
CFONT.lfCharSet = Chr$(0)
CFONT.lfFaceName = "Arial" + Chr$(0)
```

```
'   Locate the currentx and currenty for the first text display
intropic.CurrentX = (intropic.ScaleWidth - intropic.TextWidth(↵
"Introducing...")) / 2

intropic.CurrentY = (intropic.ScaleHeight - intropic.TextHeight( ↵
"Introducing...")) / 2

'   Caclulate the changes for 20 moves of "Introducing..." to the upper corner.
ChangeX = intropic.CurrentX / 20
ChangeY = intropic.CurrentY / 20

'   Start timer1
timer1.Enabled = True

intropic.ForeColor = RGB(255, 0, 0)

End Sub
```

6. The function PLast handles printing the final "Introducing..." at the top of the form.

```
Private Sub PLast()

'   Create a new font with a larger width and height
CFONT.lfWidth = CFONT.lfWidth + 10
CFONT.lfHeight = CFONT.lfHeight + 2

'   Set the color for the font
intropic.ForeColor = RGB(255, 80, 255)

'   Call the FontOut procedure to display the text
FontOut "Introducing...", intropic, X, Y, CFONT

End Sub
```

7. Timer1 handles spinning the text around. The key feature is changing the Escapement for the Logfont structure. Note that the function calls the FontOut routine to handle creating and displaying the text.

```
Private Sub Timer1_Timer()

'   Set the new escapement
CFONT.lfEscapement = CFONT.lfEscapement + 180

'   Calculate the center of the text
X = (intropic.ScaleWidth - intropic.TextWidth("Introducing...")) / 2
Y = (intropic.ScaleHeight - intropic.TextHeight("Introducing...")) / 2

'   For the last print when the font color is white, we will
'   clear the picture and print the text in black
If CFONT.lfEscapement = 3600 Then

    intropic.ForeColor = RGB(0, 0, 0)
```

continued on next page

continued from previous page

```
     '  Turn off timer1
     timer1.Enabled = False
     timer2.Enabled = True

  End If


  '  Call the FontOut procedure to display the text
  FontOut "Introducing...", intropic, X, Y, CFONT

  End Sub
```

8. Timer2 handles moving the text to the upper-left corner of the picture box. Note that the function calls the FontOut routine to handle creating and displaying the text.

```
Private Sub Timer2_Timer()

'  Move up and to the left by the
'  increment stored in ChangeX and ChangeY
X = intropic.CurrentX - ChangeX
Y = intropic.CurrentY - ChangeY

'  Set the new x and y.  Note, we are storing
'  the x and y values here.
intropic.CurrentX = X
intropic.CurrentY = Y

'  Call the FontOut procedure to display the text
FontOut "Introducing...", intropic, X, Y, CFONT

'  If x is greater than 0 but less than the amount
'  of the incremental move (by 1), then we need to stop
'  moving or else the text will not be visible.
If (X > 0) And (X < (ChangeX * 3)) Then

    timer2.Enabled = False

    '  Call the Plast routine to print the final larger
    '  "Introducing..." text
    PLast
End If

End Sub
```

How It Works

In this How-To, the first Windows API functions are introduced. As can be seen in the module, several API functions have been declared. A full description of how to declare Windows API functions is provided in Visual Basic 4.0 Help. Also declared is a Windows structure, Logfont. Visual Basic 4.0 provides text files that contain all of the appropriate API declarations, constants, and structures for Visual Basic. These can easily be imported using the API Text Viewer provided with Visual Basic 4.0. It also provides the Windows SDK help file, which gives complete descriptions of most of the Windows API. For the multimedia extensions as well as the Windows API, Waite Group Press' *Windows API New Testament* is an excellent reference. Throughout *Visual Basic 4.0 Multimedia How-To*, the multimedia extensions and Windows API will be examined to help perform many of the different How-Tos.

The Windows API has several text functions that facilitate creating and displaying text for the screen. This project uses the CreateFontIndirect and TextOut API functions to perform the text effects in this project.

The CreateFontIndirect API function uses the Logfont structure to create a new font. The Logfont structure is fairly straightforward for creating basic text. For this project, the Escapement and Width values of the Logfont are manipulated. The Escapement is measured in tenths of degrees. Thus, a full revolution of the font is 3600 (as opposed to 360). By having the AutoRedraw property set to False for the picture box, the text is not erased.

To create the font from the Logfont structure, the CreateFontIndirect function is utilized. The "Indirect" refers to the fact that the font is created from the Logfont structure. This is opposed to the CreateFont function, which takes the values provided in the Logfont structure directly.

Once the font is created, the SelectObject API function is called to make the font available to the picture control. Note that the SelectObject function returns the handle of the font object to be replaced. You should store this value so it can be reselected when you are done with the new font. Thus, when the TextOut function is called to display the text, the created font will be used.

For the TextOut function, the X and Y coordinates are used to place the text in the picture box at the desired location. For the second-to-last parameter, place the text directly in the function (i.e., "Introducing...") or assign a variable. The last parameter takes the length of the text to be displayed (Len("Introducing...")).

Note: It is important to delete the newly created font by using the DeleteObject function. Before that, the old font needs to be reselected into the picture. This is done by using the handle returned from the first call to SelectObject.

Comments

Using the Windows API to perform text manipulation, you can provide a wide range of text effects for your applications. You can also change the width and height features to provide a text-shrinking or text-enlarging effect.

3
SOUND

3

SOUND

How do I...

The addition of sound to Windows is a significant move forward in bringing interactive information to the user. The multimedia developer has digital audio (Wave) and MIDI capabilities available, as well as CD-audio sound. In this chapter we will explore the powerful utilities the Microsoft Multimedia Extensions provide for manipulating sound from Windows.

The Windows multimedia extensions provide a wide range of audio services. In this chapter, two high-level functions, sndPlaySound and MessageBeep, will be demonstrated. As Chapter 1 discussed, the MCI command string and command message interface are also available for higher levels of control over playing CD-audio, wave, and MIDI data. After you have finished this chapter, you will be able to play various types of multimedia audio data and determine the audio capabilities of the various devices installed in a system.

Windows APIs Covered		
mciSendString	mciGetErrorString	MessageBeep
sndPlaySound	mciSendCommand	waveOutGetDevCaps
waveOutSetVolume	midiOutGetDevCaps	midiOutGetNumDevs

3.1 Play system-alert sounds

You will learn how to use the simple API function, MessageBeep, to play standard system sounds such as Asterisk and Question.

3.2 Add custom sounds to my application

The WIN.INI file allows you to assign sounds to specific keywords. You will learn how to assign sounds in the WIN.INI file and use the sndPlaySound function to access these assignments to play the correct sounds.

3.3 Easily play a wave file

The sndPlaySound function also allows for easy playing of any wave file. The example project implements a simple browser that will allow you to find wave files and play them.

3.4 Play a wave file repeatedly

Under certain circumstances, it is desirable to loop the playing of a wave file. The sndPlaySound function also allows a wave file to be played continuously. The example will develop a simple multiple choice game that will incorporate the repeated playing of the Windows DING.WAV file.

3.5   Play a wave file using MCI command strings

Here is the first look at the mciSendString and mciGetErrorString functions. The wave file browser program developed in How-To 3.3 will be enhanced using the MCI command string interface to expand browsing and wave playing capabilities.

3.6   Play a wave file using MCI command messages

The MCI command string interface provides a straightforward English-like interface for accessing and playing wave files. But the system translates the strings into commands before executing them, which adds slight overhead to the process. The MCI command message interface provides a more direct interface with the system, although the Command message interface is considerably more difficult to implement from Visual Basic. The example uses command messages to play a wave file.

3.7   Adjust the audio level of installed wave audio devices

The ability to change the audio level of a wave audio device is important. The example demonstrates changing the level of audio output via the waveOutSetVolume function.

3.8   Set sample size and sample rate of an audio device and then record a wave file

Wave audio devices can support playing and recording different wave file formats. The example will set the sample size, sample rate, and channels of a wave audio device. You will then record a wave file based on the new settings.

3.9   Get information regarding the capabilities of installed wave audio devices

The type of wave audio device installed in a system is an important determination to make when adding multimedia capabilities to a program. The waveOutGetDevCaps function will be used to determine what capabilities the installed wave audio device supports.

3.10 Easily play MIDI files

MIDI files are an important multimedia sound format that any multimedia developer needs to support. As with wave files, the MCI command string interface allows for straightforward access to and playing of MIDI files. Using the browser developed in How-To 3.3, MIDI files will be accessed and played using the command string interface.

3.11 Determine what MIDI devices are available and their capabilities

It is unusual to find more than one wave audio device installed in a system, but with MIDI devices, more than one driver is often installed. With the midiOutGetNumDevs, the number of MIDI devices installed can be determined. Information about the device(s) can be determined by using the midiOutGetDevCaps function; this includes determining if the synthesizer is internal or external.

3.12 Know when a MIDI (or wave) file has finished playing

Often it is important to know when a wave file has finished playing. The MCI custom control has a Done event that notifies you when a particular command has finished. This feature can be used to notify you when the MIDI file has finished playing. This example implements a simple puzzle that gives the user the duration of the MIDI file as a time limit to solve the puzzle.

3.13 Play CD-audio sound

The MCI command string interface also supports the play of audio CDs. The example will build a simple CD player that will access information about the tracks (songs) on the CD and allow you to browse through and listen to the different tracks.

3.1 How do I...
Play system-alert sounds?

COMPLEXITY: EASY

Problem

I would like to be able to play the standard system-alert sounds assigned in the control panel sound applet.

Technique

The system sounds are the standard feedback given by Windows to users on multimedia systems. These standard events include Asterisk, Critical Stop, Default Beep, Exclamation, Question, Windows Exit, and Windows Start. The MessageBeep function provides a straightforward and simple way to play system-alert sounds. By providing the correct parameter to the function, the appropriate sound will be played.

Steps

To play the system-alert sounds, first ensure that they have been assigned appropriately in the control panel. Open the main folder as shown in Figure 3-1-1.

Figure 3-1-1 The Windows 95 sounds applet

Make sure that you have sounds assigned for the Asterisk, Default Beep, Exclamation, and Question system events.

Open and run 3-1.VBP. The running program is shown in Figure 3-1-2.

Select any one of the option buttons and select the Play Sound button. As you can hear, the sound assigned in the control panel is played.

1. Create a new project called 3-1.VBP. Add the objects and properties listed in Table 3-1-1 to Form1 and save the form as 3-1.FRM.

Table 3-1-1 Project form's objects and properties

OBJECT	PROPERTY	SETTING
Form	Name	Form1
	Caption	"How-To 3.1"
OptionButton	Name	SoundOption
	Caption	"PC Speaker"
OptionButton	Name	SoundOption
	Caption	"System Exclamation"
OptionButton	Name	SoundOption
	Caption	"System Icon"
OptionButton	Name	SoundOption

continued on next page

continued from previous page

OBJECT	PROPERTY	SETTING
	Caption	"System Question"
OptionButton	Name	SoundOption
	Caption	"System Asterisk"
OptionButton	Name	SoundOption
	Caption	"System Default Beep"
CommandButton	Name	PlaySound
	Caption	"Play Sound"
	Font	
	name	"Arial"

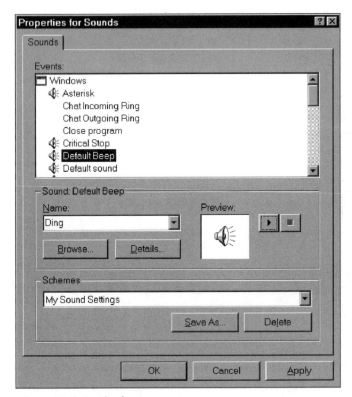

Figure 3-1-2 The form at runtime

2. Add the following code to the general declarations section of the form. The MessageBeep API command is declared along with the appropriate constants for the command.

```
'  The MessgaeBeep command is part of the Windows API.
'  The function takes the value of the system sound
'  to be played.
Private Declare Sub MessageBeep Lib "User" (ByVal vi_Level%)

'  The following Const statements assign the appropriate system
'  sound to be played.  Note, these constants can be found in
'  the VB 4.0 'API Text Viewer' in the WIN31API.TXT file.
Const DEFAULT_SOUND = -1
Const MB_OK = 0
Const MB_ICONHAND = &H10
Const MB_ICONEXCLAMATION = &H20
Const MB_ICONQUESTION = &H30
Const MB_ICONASTERISK = &H40
```

3. Add the following code to the Form_Load procedure. It handles selecting the first option button at start-up.

```
Private Sub Form_Load()
'  Have the first option selected at start up
SoundOption(0).Value = -1
End Sub
```

4. Add the following code to the PlaySound_Click command button function. Each option button in the control array is checked to see if it is selected. For the selected sounds, the MessageBeep function is then given the appropriate parameter and the sound is then played.

```
Private Sub PlaySound_Click()

'  We will check the option button control
'  array to find out which sound to play.

If SoundOption(0) = -1 Then MessageBeep (MB_OK)
If SoundOption(1) = -1 Then MessageBeep (MB_ICONASTERISK)
If SoundOption(2) = -1 Then MessageBeep (MB_ICONQUESTION)
If SoundOption(3) = -1 Then MessageBeep (MB_ICONHAND)
If SoundOption(4) = -1 Then MessageBeep (MB_ICONEXCLAMATION)
If SoundOption(5) = -1 Then MessageBeep (DEFAULT_SOUND)

End Sub
```

How It Works

This straightforward project demonstrates an easy way to access assigned system sounds that are familiar to the user.

The MessageBeep function takes one parameter that is a long integer that indicates which sound to play.

Comments

By using the MessageBeep function, you can play standard system sounds when appropriate events take place in your application. This will help your application conform to the standard multimedia sound interface provided by Windows.

3.2 How do I...

Add custom sounds to my application?

COMPLEXITY: EASY

Problem

I am able to assign sounds to keywords in the WIN.INI file. How can I play these assigned sounds?

Technique

The sndPlaySound function takes the keywords from the sounds section of the WIN.INI file and plays the assigned sound. Unlike the MessageBeep function, sndPlaySound provides several different options for how to play the sound.

Steps

First, it is important to ensure that the appropriate wave keywords are added to the WIN.INI file. Table 3-2-1 shows the LeftMouse, RightMouse, and Click events assigned in the sounds section.

Table 3-2-1 WIN.INI system sound assignments

SOUNDS

SystemAsterisk=chord.wav,Asterisk
SystemHand=chord.wav,Critical Stop
SystemDefault=ding.wav,Default Beep
SystemExclamation=chord.wav,Exclamation
SystemQuestion=chord.wav,Question
SystemExit=chimes.wav,Windows Exit
SystemStart=tada.wav,Windows Start
LeftMouse=chimes.wav,Left Mouse Click
RightMouse=Chord.wav,Right Mouse Click
Exit=tada.wav,Application Exit

Use the notepad application to open the WIN.INI file and add the LeftMouse, RightMouse, and Exit lines to the sound section of your WIN.INI file. The new assigned sounds show up in the control panel as shown in Figure 3-2-1.

Open and run 3-2.VBP. The running program is shown in Figure 3-2-2.

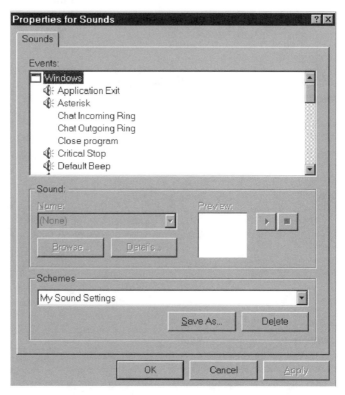

Figure 3-2-1 Windows 95 control panel

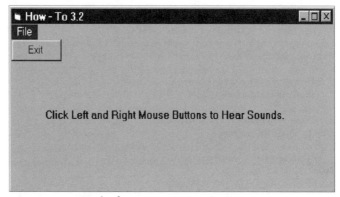

Figure 3-2-2 The form at runtime

Click the left and right mouse buttons anywhere in the form window. As you can hear, the CHIMES and CHORD wave files are played respectively. When you select Exit from the file menu, the TADA wave file is played.

1. Create a new project called 3-2.VBP. Add the objects and properties listed in Table 3-2-2 to Form1 and save the form as 3-2.FRM. Add the menu items as shown in Table 3-2-3.

Table 3-2-2 Project form's objects and properties

OBJECT	PROPERTY	SETTING
Form	Name	Form1
	BackColor	&H00E0E0E0&
	Caption	"How-To 3.2"
Label	Name	LabelCaption
	Alignment	2 'Center
	AutoSize	-1 'True
	Caption	"Click Left and Right Mouse Buttons to Hear Sounds."

Table 3-2-3 Project menu's objects

CAPTION	NAME
"File"	File
"Exit"	Exit

2. Add the following code to the general declarations section of the form.

```
'  Declare the sndPlaySound function.  The function
'  resides in the mmsystem.dll file.
Private Declare Function sndPlaySound Lib "mmsystem" (ByVal SoundName As ↵
String, ByVal wFlags As Integer) As Integer

'  These are the flags for the
'  sndPlaySound function

'  Play synchronously
Const SND_SYNC = &H0

'  Play Asynchronously
Const SND_ASYNC = &H1

'  Don't use the Default Sound
```

```
'  If the specified sound can
'  not be found
Const SND_NODEFAULT = &H2
'  The sound name points to a memory file
Const SND_MEMORY = &H4

'  Loop the Sound
Const SND_LOOP = &H8

'  Don't stop any currently playing sound
Const SND_NOSTOP = &H10
```

3. The sound assigned to the Exit event in the control panel will be played when the Exit menu item is selected.

```
Private Sub Exit_Click()

'  If the menu 'Exit' item is
'  selected then we will play the
'  sound assigned to Exit in the Win.Ini
'  file
Throw% = sndPlaySound("Exit", SND_SYNC)


'  End the program
End

End Sub
```

4. Whenever the MouseUp event is performed on the main form window, a check is performed to see which mouse button was selected. Depending on which was clicked, the appropriate sound is played.

```
Private Sub Form_MouseUp(Button As Integer, Shift As Integer, X As Single, Y ↵
As Single)

'  The If checks to see which mouse button was clicked.

If Button = 1 Then

    '  If it was the left button then play the
    '  sound assigned to LeftMouse in the Win.ini file
    Throw% = sndPlaySound("LeftMouse", SND_SYNC)

Else

    '  If it was the right button then play the
    '  sound assigned to RightMouse in the Win.ini file
    '  The sndPlaySound function returns a value that is
    '  TRUE if the sound was played and FALSE if it was not
    '  played.  In general, throw% will be used when the
    '  return value of an API function is to be
    '  ignored
    Throw% = sndPlaySound("RightMouse", SND_SYNC)
```

continued on next page

continued from previous page
```
End If

End Sub
```

5. Because there is a label on the form, the left and right mouse clicks will also be trapped and the appropriate sound would be played.

```
Private Sub LabelCaption_MouseUp(Button As Integer, Shift As Integer, X ↵
As Single, Y As Single)

'   The If checks to see which mouse button was clicked.
'   We need to make sure that if the label is clicked on
'   that the appropriate sounds are still played.

If Button = 1 Then

    '   If it was the left button then play the
    '   sound assigned to LeftMouse in the Win.ini file
    Throw% = sndPlaySound("LeftMouse", SND_SYNC)

Else

    '   If it was the right button then play the
    '   sound assigned to RightMouse in the Win.ini file
    Throw% = sndPlaySound("RightMouse", SND_SYNC)

End If

End Sub
```

How It Works

The sndPlaySound function provides an easy way to play sounds assigned in the WIN.INI file. In this example, custom assignments have been made in the WIN.INI file (Table 3-2-1). These sounds are then accessed from the program using the sndPlaySound function.

In this example, only the SND_SYNC option is used for the sndPlaySound function. This allows the sounds to be played synchronously. This means that the system does not handle any more events until the sound file has finished playing. As will be seen in later How-Tos in this chapter, the other second parameter options provide for flexible playing of wave files.

Comments

When building your applications, you can develop a set of custom sounds that can be assigned in the WIN.INI file when your application is installed. Then your application can handle playing these sounds in a straightforward fashion using the sndPlaySound function.

3.3 How do I...
Easily play a wave file?

Problem

I would like to play a wave file easily from my application. I want to be able to give useful and simple feedback to my users by playing recorded sounds from my application.

Technique

The sndPlaySound function provides for easy playing of wave files. This section will build a simple browser utility to find and play wave files.

Steps

Open and run 3-3.VBP. The running program appears as shown in Figure 3-3-1.

First find a wave file on the system. Note that the default directory is the Windows directory. Double-click on the wave file you wish to play. The file will stop playing once the end of the wave data is reached.

1. Create a new project called 3-3.VBP. Add the objects and properties listed in Table 3-3-1 to Form1 and save the form as 3-3.FRM.

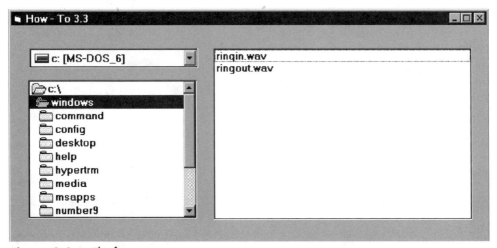

Figure 3-3-1 The form at runtime

85

Table 3-3-1 Project form's objects and properties

OBJECT	PROPERTY	SETTING
Form	Name	Form1
	Caption	"How-To 3.3"
DirListBox	Name	Dir1
DriveListBox	Name	Drive1
FileListBox	Name	File1
	Pattern	"*.wav"

2. Add the following code to the general declarations section of the form. The appropriate declarations for sndPlaySound are made here.

```
'   Declare the sndPlaySound function.  The function
'   resides in the mmsystem.dll file.
Private Declare Function sndPlaySound Lib "mmsystem" (ByVal SoundName As ↵
String, ByVal wFlags As Integer) As Integer

'   These are the flags for the
'   sndPlaySound function

'   Play synchronously
Const SND_SYNC = &H0

'   Play Asynchronously
Const SND_ASYNC = &H1

'   Don't use the Default Sound
'   If the specified sound can
'   not be found
Const SND_NODEFAULT = &H2

'   The sound name points to a memory file
Const SND_MEMORY = &H4

'   Loop the Sound
Const SND_LOOP = &H8

'   Don't stop any currently playing sound
Const SND_NOSTOP = &H10
```

3. When the directory changes, the file list box directory needs to be changed to the new directory.

```
Private Sub Dir1_Change()
```

```
'  When the directory path changes, we need
'  to update the file list path.  Note that
'  we have the pattern property set to *.wav
'  to show only wave files
file1.Path = dir1.Path
End Sub
```

4. When the drive changes, the directory path needs to be updated. When the directory path is updated, it calls the Dir1_Change function, which updates the file list box. Note that error checking is performed to make sure that the selected drive is available.

```
Private Sub Drive1_Change()

'  In case the user selects a drive that
'  is unavailable such as a floppy drive
'  with no disk, then we need to trap that
'  error
On Error GoTo errorcheck

'  Set the new directory listing to the new drive
'  selected
dir1.Path = drive1.Drive


'  Skip around the error handling
GoTo next1


'  The error check section handles notifying
'  the user that the drive is unavailable
'  and resets the drive to the root directory.
errorcheck:

MsgBox "Selected Drive is Unavailable"
drive1.Drive = "c:\"
Resume Next

next1:
End Sub
```

5. When the file is double-clicked, the sound will be played. In this case, the sound will be played asynchronously so that work can continue.

```
Private Sub File1_DblClick()

'  Get the filename of the file to be played
FileName$ = file1.List(file1.ListIndex)

'  Get the path to the file
dirpath$ = dir1.Path

'  If the file is located in the root (C:\), then we
'  don't need to add a trailing "\" to the path
```

continued on next page

continued from previous page

```
'   statement.  Otherwise we do need to add the "\"
'   ex:  directory = c:\windows  filename = tada.wav
'   arg$ = c:\windows\tada.wav
If Right$(dirpath$, 1) <> "\" Then
    arg$ = dirpath$ + "\" + FileName$
Else
    arg$ = dirpath$ + FileName$
End If

'  Play the file found in arg$
Throw% = sndPlaySound(arg$, SND_ASYNC)
End Sub
```

6. When the form is loaded, the default directory is set to C:\windows.

```
Private Sub Form_Load()

'  Set the default path to the windows directory.
dir1.Path = "C:\windows"
End Sub
```

How It Works

This How-To demonstrates the simplicity of playing wave files with the sndPlaySound function. A simple wave file browser program has been built. The SND_ASYNC parameter is used to allow for continued working while the selected sound is played.

The browser part of this section draws on the drive, directory, and file list box custom controls. As you can see, changes have been made in the drive and directories to update changes in the file list box. For the file list box, the default file pattern is set to *.WAV.

Comments

The sndPlaySound function provides one of the simplest ways to play sounds from your applications. You can play the sounds either synchronously or asynchronously. In the next How-To, you will see that you can loop the playing of wave files.

3.4 How do I...
Play a wave file repeatedly?

COMPLEXITY: INTERMEDIATE

Problem

I would like to be able to play a wave file repeatedly for a specific period of time. This can give added emphasis to events in my program or can be used for background effects.

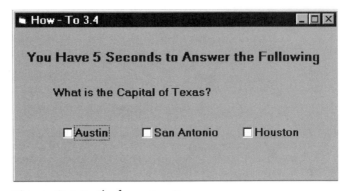

Figure 3-4-1 The form at runtime

Technique

By combining the timer and sndPlaySound functions, you can play a wave file repeatedly for a specified period of time. In this example, a simple multiple choice question game is developed that plays a repeated ding when the user does not answer.

Steps

Open and run 3-4.VBP. The running program appears as shown in Figure 3-4-1.

To hear the repeated playing of the ding sound, don't answer the question. After 5 seconds, the ding sound will play repeatedly for 2 seconds. If you answer correctly or incorrectly, then the program notifies you and plays an appropriate sound.

1. Create a new project called 3-4.VBP. Add the objects and properties listed in Table 3-4-1 to Form1 and save the form as 3-4.FRM.

Table 3-4-1 Project form's objects and properties

OBJECT	PROPERTY	SETTING
Form	Name	Form1
	Caption	"How - To 3.4"
CheckBox	Name	Houston
	Caption	"Houston"
CheckBox	Name	SanAntonio

continued on next page

continued from previous page

OBJECT	PROPERTY	SETTING
	Caption	"San Antonio"
CheckBox	Name	Austin
	Caption	"Austin"
Timer	Name	Timer2
	Enabled	0 'False
	Interval	2000
Timer	Name	Timer1
	Interval	5000
Label	Name	Capital
	Caption	"What is the Capital of Texas?"
Label	Name	Seconds
	Caption	"You Have 5 Seconds to Answer the Following Question."

2. Add the following to the general declarations section of the form. The appropriate declarations for the sndPlaySound function are declared here.

```
'  Declare the sndPlaySound function.  The function
'  resides in the mmsystem.dll file.
Private Declare Function sndPlaySound Lib "mmsystem" (ByVal SoundName As ↵
String, ByVal wFlags As Integer) As Integer

'  These are the flags for the
'  sndPlaySound function

'  Play synchronously
Const SND_SYNC = &H0

'  Play Asynchronously
Const SND_ASYNC = &H1

'  Don't use the Default Sound
'  If the specified sound can
'  not be found
Const SND_NODEFAULT = &H2

'  The sound name points to a memory file
Const SND_MEMORY = &H4
```

```
'  Loop the Sound
Const SND_LOOP = &H8

'  Don't stop any currently playing sound
Const SND_NOSTOP = &H10
```

3. When one of the check boxes is selected, it is important to ensure that the other check boxes are not selected. The best place to do this is in the MouseUp event. If other check box value changes are handled in the click procedure, then the other check box click procedures would fire and none of the boxes would ever be selected. Check boxes were chosen instead of option buttons because with option buttons, one option always has to be selected. In this example, none of the answers (boxes) should be selected at start-up.

```
Private Sub Austin_MouseUp(Button As Integer, Shift As Integer, X As Single, ↵
Y As Single)

'  Once we know that austin has been selected
'  We make sure the other check boxes are
'  not selected
SanAntonio.Value = 0
Houston.Value = 0

End Sub

Private Sub SanAntonio_MouseUp(Button As Integer, Shift As Integer, X As ↵
Single, Y As Single)

'  Once we know that SanAntonio has been selected
'  We make sure the other check boxes are
'  not selected
Austin.Value = 0
Houston.Value = 0

End Sub

Private Sub Houston_MouseUp(Button As Integer, Shift As Integer, X As Single, ↵
Y As Single)

'  Once we know that Houston has been selected
'  We make sure the other check boxes are
'  not selected
Austin.Value = 0
SanAntonio.Value = 0

End Sub
```

4. Timer1 handles timing out the 5 seconds for the user to answer. If none of the boxes are selected, the playing of the ding wave is looped. Timer2 is then started to allow the looping wave to play for 2 seconds. If the user answers, then notification of an incorrect or correct answer is given.

```
Private Sub Timer1_Timer()

'  Turn off timer1
timer1.Enabled = False

'  Once 5000 Milliseconds have passed (5 seconds)
'  We will check the status of the user's response and
'  act accordingly.

If Austin.Value = 0 And SanAntonio.Value = 0 And Houston.Value = 0 Then


'  If none of the boxes were selected then loop the ding
'  sound and start timer2.
timer2.Enabled = True
throw% = sndPlaySound("c:\windows\media\ding.wav", SND_ASYNC Or SND_LOOP)

Else

    '  If a selection was made, we check for the right
    '  answer.
    If Austin.Value = 1 Then

    '  Play tada and congratulate the user.
    throw% = sndPlaySound("c:\windows\tada.wav", SND_ASYNC)
    MsgBox "Congradulations!"

    Else

    '  Play chord wave and tell the user the correct answer.
    throw% = sndPlaySound("c:\windows\media\chord.wav", SND_ASYNC)
    MsgBox "Austin is the Correct Answer."

    End If

End If

End Sub
```

5. Timer2 will allow the wave to loop for 2 seconds. It then notifies the user that no answer was selected. To end the looping of the sound file, the ding wave will be played one more time with the SND_SYNC parameter.

```
Private Sub Timer2_Timer()

'  Play the ding wave one more time and don't loop the
'  sound
throw% = sndPlaySound("c:\windows\media\ding.wav", SND_SYNC)

'  Disable timer2
timer2.Enabled = False

'  Tell the user that a selection was not made
MsgBox "Please Select one of the Cities"
```

```
'  Restart timer1 to check for an answer.
timer1.Enabled = True: n = 0

End Sub
```

How It Works

To time the user's response, a timer is used to count out 5 seconds. When that timer fires, a check is performed to see if a response has been given. If so, the user is notified of a correct or incorrect response and an appropriate wave file is played using the sndPlaySound function.

If the user gives no response a repeated ding sound is played for 2 seconds to get the user's attention. The 2 seconds are counted out by Timer2. The key to looping the playing of the wave file is setting the second parameter of the sndPlaySound function to the following:

SND_ASYNC OR SND_LOOP

The second parameter of the sndPlaySound function is an integer where each bit represents a flag for the function to be performed. Table 3-4-2 presents the binary, decimal, and hex breakdowns for the each flag.

Table 3-4-2 Binary, decimal, and hex properties of flags

FLAG	BINARY	DECIMAL	HEX
SND_ASYNC	... 000000001	1	&H1
SND_LOOP	... 000000100	8	&H8
OR Command	... 000000101	9	&H9

The sndPlaySound function will look to see what bits are set in the (binary) integer value to determine how to play the wave file.

For contrast, Table 3-4-3 would have been the result of an AND operation.

Table 3-4-3 FLag properties as the result of AND operation

FLAG	BINARY	DECIMAL	HEX
SND_ASYNC	... 000000001	1	&H1
SND_LOOP	... 000000100	8	&H8
AND Command	... 000000000	0	&H0

The AND operation will result in a 1 being placed in a bit position only if both bits to be combined are 1. With the OR operation, only one of the bits has to be set to 1 for a 1 to be placed in the result.

As will be seen in later How-Tos, setting bits within numbers is a common occurrence. This is a standard method for passing flags to Windows API functions.

Comments

How-Tos 3.2 through 3.4 have shown ease of use and flexibility of the sndPlaySound function. With this function, system sounds, custom WIN.INI sounds, and any wave file on the system can be played. Sounds can be played synchronously, asynchronously, and looped. The sndPlaySound function hides the steps that must be taken to prepare the wave audio device for playing, ending play, and playing files synchronously or asynchronously.

3.5 How do I...
Play a wave file using MCI command strings?

COMPLEXITY: INTERMEDIATE

Problem

I would like to play a wave file using the MCI command string interface. The interface provides powerful control through a simple interface to the Windows multimedia extensions. Through the MCI interface, sound and video files can be played and manipulated.

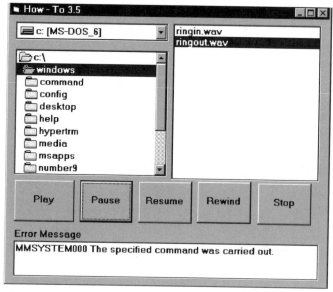

Figure 3-5-1 The form at runtime

Technique

By using the mciSendString and mciGetErrorString functions, wave files can be played and any error messages the system returns regarding the playing of the wave file can be interpreted.

Steps

Open and run 3-5.VBP. The running program appears as shown in Figure 3-5-1.

We have once again implemented the file browsing features to find wave files on the system. When you have selected a wave file, use the Play, Pause, Resume, Rewind, and Stop buttons to control the playing of the file. When each MCI command is carried out, the return message is displayed in the lower text box.

1. Create a new project called 3-5.VBP. Add the objects and properties listed in Table 3-5-1 to Form1 and save the form as 3-5.FRM.

Table 3-5-1 Project form's objects and properties

OBJECT	PROPERTY	SETTING
Form	Name	Form1
	Caption	"How-To 3.5"
TextBox	Name	ErrorText
	MultiLine	-1 'True
CommandButton	Name	Resume
	Caption	"Resume"
CommandButton	Name	Stop
	Caption	"Stop"
CommandButton	Name	Rewind
	Caption	"Rewind"
CommandButton	Name	Pause
	Caption	"Pause"
CommandButton	Name	Play
	Caption	"Play"

continued on next page

continued from previous page

OBJECT	PROPERTY	SETTING
DirListBox	Name	Dir1
DriveListBox	Name	Drive1
FileListBox	Name	File1
	Pattern	"*.wav"
Label	Name	Label1
	AutoSize	-1 'True
	Caption	"Error Message"

2. Add the following to the general declarations section of the form.

```
'   Declare the mciSendString Multimedia API function
Private Declare Function mciSendString Lib "mmsystem" (ByVal MCI_Command ⤶
As String, ByVal returnstring As String, ByVal ReturnLength As Integer, ⤶
ByVal Handle As Integer) As Long

'   Declare the mciGetErrorString Multimedia API function.
'   This will allow us to interpret errors from the
'   mciSendString command
Private Declare Function mciGetErrorString Lib "mmsystem" (ByVal MCI_ERROR ⤶
As Long, ByVal errorstring As String, ByVal ReturnLength As Integer) As Integer

'   filename holds the global value
'   of the currently selected value
Dim filename As String

'   Declare the strings to hold error
'   messages
Dim returnstring As String * 512
Dim errorstring As String * 512
```

3. When the directory changes, the file list box directory needs to be updated.

```
Private Sub Dir1_Change()

'   When the directory path changes, we need
'   to update the file list path.  Note that
'   we have the pattern property set to *.wav
'   to show only wave files
file1.Path = dir1.Path
End Sub
```

4. When the drive is changed, the directory list and file list box need to be updated. Also, any errors regarding the drive not being available are handled.

```
Private Sub Drive1_Change()
```

```
'   In case the user selects a drive that
'   is unavailable such as a floppy drive
'   with no disk, then we need to trap that
'   error
On Error GoTo errorcheck

'   Set the new directory listing to the new drive
'   selected
dir1.Path = drive1.Drive


'   Skip around the error handling
GoTo next1


'   The error check section handles notifying
'   the user that the drive is unavailable
'   and resets the drive to the root directory.
errorcheck:

MsgBox "Selected Drive is Unavailable"
drive1.Drive = "c:\"
Resume Next

next1:
End Sub
```

5. When a file is clicked or double-clicked, filename$ will hold the location and file to be played.

```
Private Sub File1_Click()

'   Get the filename of the file to be played
f$ = file1.List(file1.ListIndex)

'   Get the path to the file
dirpath$ = dir1.Path

'   If the file is located in the root (C:\), then we
'   don't need to add a trailing "\" to the path
'   statement.  Otherwise we do need to add the "\"
'   ex:  directory = c:\windows   filename = tada.wav
'   arg$ = c:\windows\tada.wav
If Right$(dirpath$, 1) <> "\" Then
    filename$ = dirpath$ + "\" + f$
Else
    filename$ = dirpath$ + f$
End If

End Sub

Private Sub File1_DblClick()

'   Get the filename of the file to be played
```

continued on next page

continued from previous page

```
f$ = file1.List(file1.ListIndex)

'   Get the path to the file
dirpath$ = dir1.Path

'   If the file is located in the root (C:\), then we
'   don't need to add a trailing "\" to the path
'   statement.   Otherwise we do need to add the "\"
'   ex:   directory = c:\windows   filename = tada.wav
'   arg$ = c:\windows\tada.wav
If Right$(dirpath$, 1) <> "\" Then
    filename$ = dirpath$ + "\" + f$
Else
    filename$ = dirpath$ + f$
End If

End Sub
```

6. When the form is loaded, the starting directory will be set to C:\windows. The wave audio device is opened.

```
Private Sub Form_Load()

'   Set the default path to the windows directory.
dir1.Path = "C:\windows"

'   Open the Wave Audio Device
MCISTR = "open waveaudio"

'   Send the string to the system.
sendstr MCISTR


End Sub
```

7. When the application is exited, the wave audio device needs to be closed to make sure that the file has stopped playing.

```
Private Sub Form_Unload(Cancel As Integer)

'   When we unload the form, we want
'   to stop the play of the file
MCISTR = "stop " + filename$

'   Call the sendstr function
sendstr MCISTR

'   Close the Wave Audio Device
MCISTR = "close waveaudio"

'   Send the string to the system.
sendstr MCISTR

End Sub
```

8. When the Pause button is selected, the Pause command is sent to the system.

```
Private Sub Pause_Click()

'  Set the string to pause the play of the file
MCISTR = "pause " + filename$

'  Call the sendstr function
sendstr MCISTR


End Sub
```

9. When the Play button is selected, the Play command is sent to the system.

```
Private Sub Play_Click()

'  Set the Play string
MCISTR = "play " + filename$

'  Call the sendstr function
sendstr MCISTR


End Sub
```

10. When the Resume button is selected, the Resume command is sent to the system.

```
Private Sub resume_Click()

'  Resume the playing of the file
MCISTR = "resume " + filename$

'  Call the sendstr function
sendstr MCISTR

End Sub
```

11. When the Rewind button is selected, a seek to the beginning of the file is sent to the system.

```
Private Sub Rewind_Click()
'  Seek to the beginning of the track which
'  in effect does a rewind
MCISTR = "seek " + filename$ + " to 0 "

'  Call the sendstr function
sendstr MCISTR

End Sub
```

12. The sendstr function handles sending the specified string to the system and interpreting the messages returned from the system. The returned message is displayed in the ErrorText text box.

```
Private Sub sendstr(MCISTR)

'  Send the string to the system.
msg& = mciSendString(MCISTR, returnstring, 512, 0)

'  Interpret the error message
throw% = mciGetErrorString(msg&, errorstring, 512)

'  Display the error message
ErrorText.Text = errorstring

End Sub
```

13. When the Stop button is selected, the Stop command is sent to the system.

```
Private Sub Stop_Click()

'  Stop the playing of the file
MCISTR = "stop " + filename$

'  Call the sendstr function
sendstr MCISTR

End Sub
```

How It Works

When using MCI command strings, you have a greater level of control over playing a wave file than you did with the sndPlaySound function. But with greater control comes more responsibility for handling the wave audio device.

Upon loading the form the wave audio device has to be opened. Upon ending the program, the file has to be stopped playing and the device closed. Through this added control, you now have the power to pause, resume, and rewind (among many other options) when playing sounds.

The arguments for the two functions are fairly straightforward. For the mciSendString, they are as follows:

MCI_Command as string	An English-like command phrase
ReturnString as string	Contains any return information
ReturnLength as integer	Specifies the length of the variable provided for ReturnString
Handle as integer	Callback function (rarely used)

The return value is an error code number that can be interpreted by the mciGetErrorString function. Its parameters are as follows:

MCI_ERROR as long	Message number returned from mciSendString
ErrorString as string	Contains the ErrorMessage
ReturnLength as integer	Specifies the length of the variable provided for ErrorString

The return value is also an error code in case an invalid error code was sent to the function.

Appendix A provides a listing of the MCI command strings and several short examples. As will be seen later in this chapter, MCI provides for straightforward and powerful access to multimedia devices.

Comments

This project can also be easily implemented using the MCI custom control. The MCI custom control provides easy and flexible methods for accessing and playing wave files. The MCI command string interface, however, provides direct access to the system through API calls.

3.6 How do I...
Play a wave file using MCI command messages?

Problem

I know that the Windows multimedia extensions also provide for accessing multimedia devices by using MCI command messages. How do I play a wave file using the command message interface?

Technique

The MCI command message interface provides for lower-level access to multimedia devices than the command string interface. Instead of Windows parsing the command strings into command messages, the messages are provided directly. This can speed up the response time needed to carry out the specified actions. But as we will see, in Visual Basic 4.0 the command string interface is much easier to implement than the command message interface. In this How-To, the basic playing of a wave file using command messages will be implemented.

Steps

Open and run 3-6.VBP. The running program appears as shown in Figure 3-6-1.

When you select the Play Sound button, CHORD.WAV is played from the Windows media directory. The return messages from opening the device, playing the file, and closing the device are displayed in the three text boxes.

1. Create a new project called 3-6.VBP. Add the objects and properties listed in Table 3-6-1 to Form1 and save the form as 3-6.FRM.

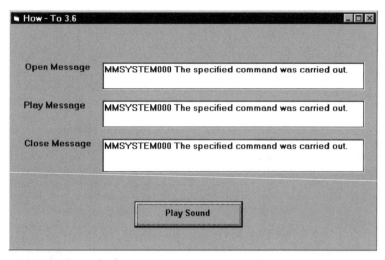

Figure 3-6-1 The form at runtime

Table 3-6-1 Project form's objects and properties

OBJECT	PROPERTY	SETTING
Form	Name	Form1
	Caption	"How-To 3.6"
TextBox	Name	CloseText
TextBox	Name	PlayText
TextBox	Name	OpenText
CommandButton	Name	PlaySound
	Caption	"Play Sound"
	Font	
	name	"Arial"
Label	Name	Close
	Caption	"Close Message"

OBJECT	PROPERTY	SETTING
Label	Name	Play
	Caption	"Play Message"
Label Open	Caption	"Open Message"

2. Add a new file, 3-6.BAS, to your project. Add the following data structures to the file. These data structures will be used for the mciSendCommand function.

```
Type MCI_WAVE_OPEN_PARMS
    dwCallback As Long
    wDeviceID As Integer
    wReserved0 As Integer
    lpstrDeviceType As Long
    lpstrElementName As Long
    lpstrAlias As Long
    dwBufferSeconds As Long
End Type

Type MCI_PLAY_PARMS
    dwCallback As Long
    dwFrom As Long
    dwTo As Long
End Type
```

3. Add the following code to the general declarations section of the form. The appropriate declarations for playing wave files using the MCI command message interface are declared here.

```
'   Declare the mciSendCommand function which will
'   be used to send the MCI commands to the system
Private Declare Function mciSendCommand Lib "MMSystem" (ByVal wDeviceID
As Integer, ByVal wMessage As Integer, ByVal dwParam1 As Long, dwParam2 As
Any) As Long

'   mciGetErrorString will be used to interpret error messages returned
'   from mciSendCommand

Private Declare Function mciGetErrorString Lib "MMSystem" (ByVal dwError
As Long, ByVal lpstrBuffer As String, ByVal wLength As Integer) As Integer

'   We will use AnsiPrev to get the memory
'   address of a string variable
Private Declare Function AnsiPrev Lib "User" (ByVal lpString As String,
ByVal lpString As String) As Long

'   flags for use with the mciSendCommand structure
Const MCI_OPEN = &H803
Const MCI_CLOSE = &H804
Const MCI_PLAY = &H806
Const MCI_OPEN_TYPE = &H2000&
```

continued on next page

continued from previous page

```
Const MCI_OPEN_ELEMENT = &H200&
Const MCI_WAIT = &H2&
```

4. The PlaySound_Click function handles opening and closing the device as well as playing the wave file.

```
Private Sub PlaySound_Click()

'   Declare MCIWaveOpenParms as the
'   MCI_WAVE_OPEN_PARMS structure
Dim MCIWaveOpenParms As MCI_WAVE_OPEN_PARMS

'   Declare the MCIPlayParms as the
'   MCI_Play_Parms structure.
Dim MCIPlayParms As MCI_PLAY_PARMS

'   Declare the ErrorString for the
'   mciGetErrorString function
Dim ErrorString As String * 128

'   Clear out the text boxes
OpenText.Text = ""
PlayText.Text = ""
CloseText.Text = ""


'   We will not support  a call back procedure
MCIWaveOpenParms.dwCallback = 0

'   Set the device ID to 0
MCIWaveOpenParms.wDeviceID = 0

'   Not Used
MCIWaveOpenParms.wReserved0 = 0

'   Set the device type to waveaudio.  The
'   datastructure is setup to have an address of
'   the string in memory.  The AnsiPrev function returns
'   a pointer to the string.  Since we are seeking for the
'   previous character in the beginnng of the string, we will
'   need to add one to the memory address to get the actual
'   address.
MCIWaveOpenParms.lpstrDeviceType = AnsiPrev("waveaudio", "waveaudio") + 1

MCIWaveOpenParms.lpstrElementName = AnsiPrev("c:\windows\media\chord.wav",↵
"c:\windows\media\chord.wav") + 1

'   There will be no alias
MCIWaveOpenParms.lpstrAlias = 0

'   We wont set the buffer seconds
MCIWaveOpenParms.dwBufferSeconds = 0


'   We now call the mciSendCommand function to open the device
```

```
MCIError = mciSendCommand(0, MCI_OPEN, MCI_OPEN_TYPE Or MCI_OPEN_ELEMENT, ↵
MCIWaveOpenParms)

' Get the message returned and display it
Throw% = mciGetErrorString(MCIError, ErrorString, 128)
OpenText.Text = ErrorString


' Set the play back parms.  We will set all the
' values to 0 to support the standard playback.
MCIPlayParms.dwCallback = 0
MCIPlayParms.dwFrom = 0
MCIPlayParms.dwTo = 0

' Play the wave file
MCIError = mciSendCommand(MCIWaveOpenParms.wDeviceID, MCI_PLAY, MCI_WAIT, ↵
MCIPlayParms)

' Get the message returned and display it.
Throw% = mciGetErrorString(MCIError, ErrorString, 128)
PlayText.Text = ErrorString

' Close the device
MCIError = mciSendCommand(MCIWaveOpenParms.wDeviceID, MCI_CLOSE, 0, 0)

' Get the message returned and display it.
Throw% = mciGetErrorString(MCIError, ErrorString, 128)
CloseText.Text = ErrorString

End Sub
```

How It Works

The mciSendCommand function takes four parameters that tell the system what to do. Following is a breakdown of each.

DeviceID as integer	Specifies the device ID to receive the MCI commands
ByVal wMessage as integer	Specifies the command message to be carried out
ByVal dwParam1 as long	Specifies flags on how to carry out the command
dwParam2 as any	This is a structure that contains information for the command and can also receive information back from various commands

Let's look at each command sent to the system in this example. The following is the API call to open the device:

```
MCIError = mciSendCommand(0, MCI_OPEN, MCI_OPEN_TYPE Or
MCI_OPEN_ELEMENT, MCIWaveOpenParms)
```

The default wave audio device is usually 0, so the first parameter is a device ID of 0. The command to be carried out is MCI_OPEN for the second parameter. For the third parameter, the bit flag is set to indicate that the following structure contains the name of the device to open (i.e., wave audio) and the file name to be opened (i.e., CHORD.WAV). See How-To 3.4 for information on how the OR function works with the MCI_OPEN_ELEMENT and MCI_OPEN_TYPE constant values. For the data structure, the variable is declared as follows:

```
Dim MCIWaveOpenParms As MCI_WAVE_OPEN_PARMS
```

The MCI_WAVE_OPEN_PARMS elements are defined as follows:

dwCallback as long	Specifies any call back functions (not used here)
wDeviceID as integer	Specifies the device ID
wReserved0 as integer	Reserved
lpstrDeviceType as long	Specifies a pointer to a string containing the type of device
lpstrElementName as long	Specifies the address of a string containing the file name
lpstrAlias as long	Specifies any alias to be used for the device
dwBufferSeconds as long	Specifies the buffer seconds; most devices are set to a default of 4

The values are set as follows:

```
MCIWaveOpenParms.dwCallback = 0
MCIWaveOpenParms.wDeviceID = 0
MCIWaveOpenParms.wReserved0 = 0
MCIWaveOpenParms.lpstrDeviceType = AnsiPrev("waveaudio","waveaudio")
     + 1
MCIWaveOpenParms.lpstrElementName = AnsiPrev("c:\windows\chord.wav",
     "c:\windows\chord.wav") + 1
MCIWaveOpenParms.lpstrAlias = 0
MCIWaveOpenParms.dwBufferSeconds = 0
```

With Visual Basic 4.0, there is a problem when the address of a string needs to be sent to a function. The lpstrDeviceType and lpstrElementName elements of the data structure are addresses to strings that contain the information the mciSendCommand function needs. To get the addresses of the specified strings, the Windows API function AnsiPrev is used.

The AnsiPrev function moves to the previous character in a string and returns a pointer to that character. By providing the strings as arguments to the function, AnsiPrev tries to get the character preceding the literal string and returns the address. When the address value is incremented by one, the actual address location of the string in memory is returned. A caution flag needs to be raised here. Because Visual Basic 4.0 handles its own memory organization, you should determine the address and then use it immediately. Otherwise, Visual Basic 4.0 may decide to reorganize memory and move your stored string to a new location.

As you can see, the rest of the data structure is set to 0. The only other significant variable is the wDeviceID, which is set to 0.

For playing the wave file, the play command is sent to the system as follows:

```
MCIError = mciSendCommand(MCIWaveOpenParms.wDeviceID, MCI_PLAY, MCI_WAIT,
MCIPlayParms)
```

The first parameter is the Device ID (0), the second parameter is the play command, and the third parameter tells the system to play the sound completely before returning control to the system (MCI_WAIT). The last parameter is the MCI_PLAY_PARMS data structure. The following is a definition for the elements in the structure.

dwCallback as long	- Specifies a call back function (rarely used)
dwFrom as long	- Beginning position to start playing from
dwTo as long	- Ending position to stop playing

For our purposes, all three elements are set to 0. Finally, the device is closed. Note this is done after the wave file is finished playing because the MCI_WAIT argument for the playing of the file was used. The following is the close command:

```
MCIError = mciSendCommand(MCIWaveOpenParms.wDeviceID, MCI_CLOSE, 0, 0)
```

The first parameter is the device ID (0), the second is the close command, and the next two are set to 0 for the close command.

Every operation that can be carried out by mciSendString can also be implemented in message-based form with mciSendCommand. But as this example shows, a significant amount of coding must be done to play a wave file. What would have taken a few short statements in the command string interface took several in the command message interface, and the Windows API had to be dipped into to fill out the data structures for the send commands.

Comments

If speed and timing are critical in accessing and using multimedia devices, then you might want to consider using the MCI command message interface; in most cases, the command string interface is easier to use and implement.

3.7 How do I...
Adjust the audio level of installed wave audio devices?

COMPLEXITY: INTERMEDIATE

Problem

I would like to be able to adjust the audio volume when playing back wave files. This can help control the effect of the sound.

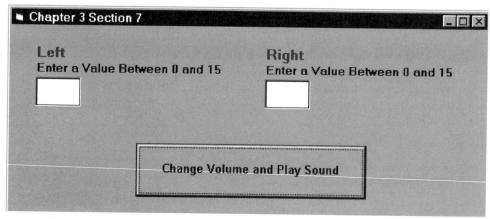

Figure 3-7-1 The form at runtime

Technique

The multimedia extensions include a function called waveOutSetVolume, which allows for adjustment of the left and right audio output of a wave device.

Steps

Open and run 3-10.VBP. The running program appears as shown in Figure 3-7-1.
Change the volume for the left and right channels and click on the Change Volume and Play Sound button. Try setting one value to 0 and the other value to 15 and notice that sound is only played from one speaker.

1. Create a new project called 3-10.VBP. Add the objects and properties listed in Table 3-7-1 to Form1 and save the form as 3-10.FRM.

Table 3-7-1 Project form's objects and properties

OBJECT	PROPERTY	SETTING
Form	Name	Form1
	Caption	"Chapter 3 Section 7"
TextBox	Name	RightText
TextBox	Name	LeftText

OBJECT	PROPERTY	SETTING
CommandButton	Name	Change
	Caption	"Change Volume and Play Sound"
	Font	
	name	"Arial"
Label Right	AutoSize	-1 'True
	Caption	"Right"
	Font	
	name	"MS Sans Serif"
	size	9.6
	ForeColor	&H000000FF&
Label Left	AutoSize	-1 'True
	Caption	"Left"
	Font	
	name	"MS Sans Serif"
	size	9.6
	ForeColor	&H000000FF&
Label	Name	Enter2
	AutoSize	-1 'True
	Caption	"Enter a Value Between 0 and 15"
Label Enter1	AutoSize	-1 'True
	Caption	"Enter a Value Between 0 and 15"

2. Add the following code to the general declarations section of the form. The sndPlaySound and waveOutSetVolume functions are declared.

```
'   Declare the sndPlaySound function to test the
'   volume changes
Private Declare Function sndPlaySound Lib "MMSYSTEM" (ByVal lpszSoundName ↵
As String, ByVal uFlags As Integer) As Integer

'   Use the waveOutSetVolume function to change
'   the audio volume
Private Declare Function waveOutSetVolume Lib "MMSYSTEM" (ByVal udeviceid ↵
As Integer, ByVal dwVolume As Long) As Integer

Const SND_SYNC = &H0     ' play synchronously (default)
```

CHAPTER 3

3. When the Change Volume and Play Sound button is selected, a check is performed to see what entries have been entered. The high- and low-order bits are then set in a long integer according to the value entered. The waveOutSetVolume function is then called to adjust the level.

```
Private Sub Change_Click()

' We need to have three Long Integer variables
' for setting the volume levels
Dim lvol As Long
Dim rvol As Long
Dim vol As Long

' Initialize the variables to -100
lvol& = -100
rvol& = -100

' Check for the volume level entered in the
' left volume text box.  We will set the lvol&
' variable so that the left most bit is set
' to the new value.
If Val(LeftText.Text) = 0 Then lvol& = &H0&
If Val(LeftText.Text) = 1 Then lvol& = &H1000&
If Val(LeftText.Text) = 2 Then lvol& = &H2000&
If Val(LeftText.Text) = 3 Then lvol& = &H3000&
If Val(LeftText.Text) = 4 Then lvol& = &H4000&
If Val(LeftText.Text) = 5 Then lvol& = &H5000&
If Val(LeftText.Text) = 6 Then lvol& = &H6000&
If Val(LeftText.Text) = 7 Then lvol& = &H7000&
If Val(LeftText.Text) = 8 Then lvol& = &H8000&
If Val(LeftText.Text) = 9 Then lvol& = &H9000&
If Val(LeftText.Text) = 10 Then lvol& = &HA000&
If Val(LeftText.Text) = 11 Then lvol& = &HB000&
If Val(LeftText.Text) = 12 Then lvol& = &HC000&
If Val(LeftText.Text) = 13 Then lvol& = &HD000&
If Val(LeftText.Text) = 14 Then lvol& = &HE000&
If Val(LeftText.Text) = 15 Then lvol& = &HF000&

' Check for the volume level entered in the
' right volume text box.  We will set the rvol&
' variable so that the left most bit of the
' right two bytes is set.  Note that we need to
' have the & at the end of the hex value to indicate
' it is a long integer.
If Val(RightText.Text) = 0 Then rvol& = &H0&
If Val(RightText.Text) = 1 Then rvol& = &H10000000
If Val(RightText.Text) = 2 Then rvol& = &H20000000
If Val(RightText.Text) = 3 Then rvol& = &H30000000
If Val(RightText.Text) = 4 Then rvol& = &H40000000
If Val(RightText.Text) = 5 Then rvol& = &H50000000
If Val(RightText.Text) = 6 Then rvol& = &H60000000
If Val(RightText.Text) = 7 Then rvol& = &H70000000
If Val(RightText.Text) = 8 Then rvol& = &H80000000
If Val(RightText.Text) = 9 Then rvol& = &H90000000
If Val(RightText.Text) = 10 Then rvol& = &HA0000000
```

```
If Val(RightText.Text) = 11 Then rvol& = &HB0000000
If Val(RightText.Text) = 12 Then rvol& = &HC0000000
If Val(RightText.Text) = 13 Then rvol& = &HD0000000
If Val(RightText.Text) = 14 Then rvol& = &HE0000000
If Val(RightText.Text) = 15 Then rvol& = &HF0000000

'  If either of the values was not reset to a
'  valid value, then notify the user.
If lvol& = -100 Then
    MsgBox "You need to enter in a value between 0 and 15 for the left value."
    Exit Sub
End If

If rvol& = -100 Then
    MsgBox "You need to enter in a value between 0 and 15 for the right value."
    Exit Sub
End If

'  Add the two values together
vol& = lvol& + rvol&

'  Set the volume.
throw% = waveOutSetVolume(0, vol&)

'  Play a test sound to try out the new volume
throw% = sndPlaySound("c:\windows\media\chord.wav", SND_SYNC)

End Sub
```

How It Works

The key to understanding the waveOutSetVolume function is understanding how to set the second parameter. The LOWORD of the long integer contains the setting for the left volume control, and the HIWORD contains the setting for the right volume control. Remember that a long integer contains 4 bytes, 2 for the LOWORD and 2 for the HIWORD.

This example implements 16 different incremental changes in volume. This makes setting the high and low word bits straightforward. For each incremental value, two variables are set, lvol and rvol. lvol is set to a long integer hex code, where the fourth digit is incremented by one. rvol is set to a long integer hex code, where the eighth digit is incremented by one. As testing will demonstrate, this gives a full range of speaker volumes.

It is important to use the format of &H####& when only using four digits to set the value. The last & indicates that the value should be evaluated as a long integer.

To test the new volume, the simple sndPlaySound function is called on to play a wave file.

Comments

The volume settings of a device can be retrieved by using the waveOutGetVolume function. Interesting effects such as modulating volume between the left and right speaker can be produced.

3.8 How do I...
Set sample size and sample rate of an audio device and then record a wave file?

COMPLEXITY: INTERMEDIATE

Problem

I would like to be able to change the sample size and rate for recording a wave file and then record a new file. I would like to be able to experiment with different combinations of sample size and sample rate so that I can make informed decisions regarding quality and disk space required for different types of audio data.

Technique

The MCI command string interface provides the ability to change the sample size and rate for an audio device. It also supports recording wave files from your sound board. You can record from any standard device your sound board supports, such as a microphone or VCR.

Steps

Open and run 3-8.VBP. The running program appears as shown in Figure 3-8-1.

Set the option buttons to the type of recording you would like to perform. When you are ready to record, select the Record button. When you are done, select the Stop button. Save the file by selecting the Save button and then play the file with the Play button. Note that the wave file is stored in the root directory as TEST.WAV.

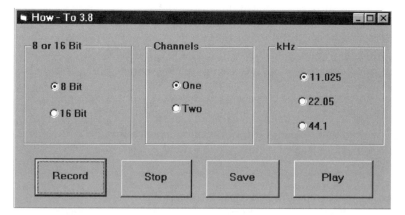

Figure 3-8-1 The form at runtime

1. Create a new project called 3-8.VBP. Add the objects and properties listed in Table 3-8-1 to Form1 and save the form as 3-8.FRM.

Table 3-8-1 Project form's objects and properties

OBJECT	PROPERTY	SETTING
Form	Name	Form1
	Caption	"How - To 3.8"
Frame	Name	channels
	Caption	"Channels"
Note: The following option buttons should be placed on the channels frame.		
OptionButton	Name	two
	Caption	"Two"
OptionButton	Name	one
	Caption	"One"
Frame	Name	khz
	Caption	"kHz"
Note: The following option buttons should be placed on the channels frame.		
OptionButton	Name	khz44
	Caption	"44.1"
OptionButton	Name	khz22
	Caption	"22.05"
OptionButton	Name	khz11
	Caption	"11.025"
	Value	-1 'True
Frame	Name	bit
	Caption	"8 or 16 Bit"

continued on next page

continued from previous page

OBJECT	PROPERTY	SETTING
Note: The following option buttons should be placed on the channels frame.		
OptionButton	Name	bit16
	Caption	"16 Bit"
OptionButton	Name	bit8
	Caption	"8 Bit"
	Value	-1 'True
CommandButton	Name	Save
	Caption	"Save"
CommandButton	Name	Stop
	Caption	"Stop"
CommandButton	Name	Play
	Caption	"Play"
CommandButton	Name	Record
	Caption	"Record"

2. Add the following code to the general declarations section of the form.

```
'   Declare the mciSendString and mciGetErrorString
'   functions.  We will use these to control the
'   recording of the wav file.
Private Declare Function mciSendString Lib "MMSystem" (ByVal lpstrCommand ↵
As String, ByVal lpstrReturnString As String, ByVal wReturnLength As Integer,↵
ByVal hCallback As Integer) As Long

Private Declare Function mciGetErrorString Lib "MMSystem" (ByVal dwError As ↵
Long, ByVal lpstrBuffer As String, ByVal wLength As Integer) As Integer

'   Declare the return and error strings
'   for mciSendString and mciGetErrorString
'   functions
Dim errorstrng As String * 256
Dim returnstrng As String * 256
```

3. When the Play button is selected, the play command is issued. If there is an error, the error-handling routine showerror is called.

```
Private Sub play_Click()

'  Play the wav file
msgval = mciSendString("play c:\test.wav", returnstrng, 256, 0)

'  If there is an error, then call the error
'  handling routine
If msgval <> 0 Then showerror msgval, "play"

End Sub
```

4. When the Record button is selected, the first command is to open the wave audio device. The option buttons are then checked to determine which have been selected by the user and to set the wave audio device accordingly. If there is an error, the error-handling routine showerror is called.

```
Private Sub Record_Click()

'  Open the waveaudio device and give it an alias
msgval = mciSendString("open new type waveaudio alias recwave", ↵
returnstrng, 256, 0)

'  Check for an error
If msgval <> 0 Then showerror msgval, "open"

'  Check to see what the bitspersample will be and
'  set mcistr accordingly
If bit8.Value = True Then mcistr = "set recwave bitspersample 8"
If bit16.Value = True Then mcistr = "set recwave bitspersample 16"

'  Send thhe bitspersample change to the system
msgval = mciSendString(mcistr, returnstrng, 256, 0)

'  Check for an error
If msgval <> 0 Then showerror msgval, "bitspersample"

'  Check for the new samplespersec and set the
'  mcistr variable to hold the command string
If khz11.Value = True Then mcistr = "set recwave samplespersec 11025"
If khz22.Value = True Then mcistr = "set recwave samplespersec 22050"
If khz44.Value = True Then mcistr = "set recwave samplespersec 44100"

'  Send the samplespersec change
msgval = mciSendString(mcistr, returnstrng, 256, 0)

'  Check for an error
If msgval <> 0 Then showerror msgval, "samplespersec"

'  Check if one or two channels should be used and
'  set mcistr accordingly
If one.Value = True Then mcistr = "set recwave channels 1"
If two.Value = True Then mcistr = "set recwave channels 2"
```

continued on next page

continued from previous page

```
'  Send the channels change to the system
msgval = mciSendString(mcistr, returnstrng, 256, 0)

'  Check for any errors
If msgval <> 0 Then showerror msgval, "channels"

'  Begin recording.
msgval = mciSendString("record recwave", returnstrng, 256, 0)

'  check for any errors
If msgval <> 0 Then showerror msgval, "record"

End Sub
```

5. When the Save button is selected, the recorded data is saved to the TEST.WAV file. The device is then closed.

```
Private Sub Save_Click()

'  Save the recorded sound to the test file
msgval = mciSendString("save recwave c:\test.wav", returnstrng, 256, 0)

'  Check for any errors
If msgval <> 0 Then showerror msgval, "save"

'  Close the wave audio device.
msgval = mciSendString("close recwave", returnstrng, 256, 0)

'  Check for any errors
If msgval <> 0 Then showerror msgval, "close"

End Sub
```

6. Add the following routine to the general declarations section of the form. If an error is returned by the mciSendString function; the showerror routine is called. The message code returned is passed from the mciSendString function; c$ holds the name of the command string sent to the system.

```
'  msgval is the value returned from the
'  mciSendString function.  C$ tells us which mci
'  command failed
Private Sub showerror(msgval, c$)

'  This function handles getting any error messages
throw% = mciGetErrorString(msgval, errorstrng, 256)

'  Show the error to the user
MsgBox c$ + " ERROR:   " + errorstrng

End Sub
```

7. When the Stop button is selected, the device stops recording.

```
Private Sub Stop_Click()
```

```
'   Stop the recording
msgval = mciSendString("stop recwave", returnstrng, 256, 0)

'   Check for any errors
If msgval <> 0 Then showerror msgval, "stop"

End Sub
```

How It Works

The MCI command string interface supports setting the sample size, rate, and channels for a wave audio device. Most of the latest wave audio devices support 8- and 16-bits per second sampling. When recording with one channel, you are recording in mono, and with two channels you are recording in stereo. The samples per second are measured in kilohertz; most newer devices typically support 11.025, 22.05, and 44.1 sample rates. Note that when setting the samples per second, the value is provided in hertz (e.g., 11025).

The basic procedure to follow for recording is to open the device; set the channels, bits per second, and samples per second; and then begin recording. When finished recording, save the recorded file and close the device. You can then play the file using the standard MCI play command.

Because not all devices support changing the channels, bits per second, and samples per second, the error message codes need to be sent back from the mciSendString. If the code is not 0, then the showerror routine is called to present the error to the user. The error code (msgval) is passed and a string with the name of the command is sent to the system.

Comments

Later in this chapter, we will see how to determine the capabilities of a wave audio device. This is useful for presenting options for the type of recording to make. Consider experimenting with different settings to see the effects on the file size and the quality of the audio.

3.9 How do I...
Get information regarding the capabilities of installed wave audio devices?

COMPLEXITY: INTERMEDIATE

Problem

I would like to know if the system my software is running on is capable of playing the wave files I have provided. How can I do this?

Technique

The multimedia extensions provide a low-level function, waveOutGetDevCaps, that will return the capabilities of a wave audio device installed in the system.

Steps

Open and run 3-9.VBP. The running program appears as shown in Figure 3-9-1. Select the Get Info button to receive information about the installed wave audio device. The list box will then display all of the supported features of the device.

1. Create a new project called 3-9.VBP. Add the objects and properties listed in Table 3-9-1 to Form1 and save the form as 3-9.FRM.

Table 3-9-1 Project form's objects and properties

OBJECT	PROPERTY	SETTING
Form	Name	Form1
	Caption	"How-To 3.9"
ListBox	Name	InfoList
CommandButton	Name	GetInfo
	Caption	"Get Info"
	Font	
	name	"Arial"

2. Open a new module called 3-9.BAS and add the following structure declaration. This structure will be used to store the device information.

```
'   Declare the WaveOutCaps Structure
Type WaveOutCaps
    wMid As Integer
    wPid As Integer
    vDriverVersion As Integer
    szPName As String * 32
    dwFormats As Long
    wChannels As Integer
    dwSupport As Long
End Type
```

3. Place the following code in the general declarations section of the form. The constants for the waveOutGetDevCaps function and the function itself are declared here.

```
'   This function will retrieve the information on the
'   waveaudio device and store it in the WaveOutCaps
```

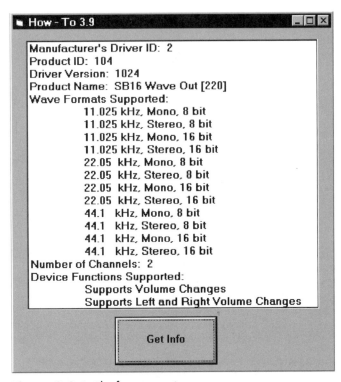

Figure 3-9-1 The form at runtime

```
' data structure
Private Declare Function waveOutGetDevCaps Lib "MMSystem" (ByVal wDeviceID ↵
As Integer, lpCaps As WaveOutCaps, ByVal wSize As Integer) As Integer

' Invalid Format
 Const WAVE_INVALIDFORMAT = &H0
  ' 11.025 kHz, Mono,   8 bit
 Const WAVE_FORMAT_1M08 = &H1
   ' 11.025 kHz, Stereo, 8 bit
 Const WAVE_FORMAT_1S08 = &H2
   ' 11.025 kHz, Mono,   16 bit
 Const WAVE_FORMAT_1M16 = &H4
  ' 11.025 kHz, Stereo, 16 bit
 Const WAVE_FORMAT_1S16 = &H8
   ' 22.05  kHz, Mono,   8 bit
 Const WAVE_FORMAT_2M08 = &H10
  ' 22.05  kHz, Stereo, 8 bit
 Const WAVE_FORMAT_2S08 = &H20
 ' 22.05  kHz, Mono,   16 bit
 Const WAVE_FORMAT_2M16 = &H40
  ' 22.05  kHz, Stereo, 16 bit
 Const WAVE_FORMAT_2S16 = &H80
```

continued on next page

continued from previous page

```
' 44.1   kHz, Mono,   8 bit
Const WAVE_FORMAT_4M08 = &H100
' 44.1   kHz, Stereo, 8 bit
Const WAVE_FORMAT_4S08 = &H200
' 44.1   kHz, Mono,   16 bit
Const WAVE_FORMAT_4M16 = &H400
' 44.1   kHz, Stereo, 16 bit
Const WAVE_FORMAT_4S16 = &H800

' Supports pitch control
Const WAVECAPS_PITCH = &H1

' Supports playback rate control
Const WAVECAPS_PLAYBACKRATE = &H2

' Supports volume control
Const WAVECAPS_VOLUME = &H4

' Supports separate left-right volume control
Const WAVECAPS_LRVOLUME = &H8

'  Support Synchronization
Const WAVECAPS_SYNC = &H10
```

4. The formats routine checks the dwFormats flag to see if the appropriate bits are set to indicate that a specific wave format is supported.

```
Private Sub formats(InfoRecord As WaveOutCaps)

'  This subroutine dissects the dwFormats flags
'  to find out what type of wav formats the device
'  supports.  For each bit that is set in dwFormats
'  we will display the type of device supported.

If InfoRecord.dwFormats And WAVE_FORMAT_1M08 Then
    InfoList.AddItem Chr$(9) + "11.025 kHz, Mono, 8 bit"
End If

If InfoRecord.dwFormats And WAVE_FORMAT_1S08 Then
    InfoList.AddItem Chr$(9) + "11.025 kHz, Stereo, 8 bit"
End If

If InfoRecord.dwFormats And WAVE_FORMAT_1M16 Then
    InfoList.AddItem Chr$(9) + "11.025 kHz, Mono, 16 bit"
End If

If InfoRecord.dwFormats And WAVE_FORMAT_1S16 Then
    InfoList.AddItem Chr$(9) + "11.025 kHz, Stereo, 16 bit"
End If

If InfoRecord.dwFormats And WAVE_FORMAT_2M08 Then
    InfoList.AddItem Chr$(9) + "22.05  kHz, Mono, 8 bit"
End If

If InfoRecord.dwFormats And WAVE_FORMAT_2S08 Then
```

```
        InfoList.AddItem Chr$(9) + "22.05  kHz, Stereo, 8 bit"
End If

If InfoRecord.dwFormats And WAVE_FORMAT_2M16 Then
        InfoList.AddItem Chr$(9) + "22.05  kHz, Mono, 16 bit"
End If

If InfoRecord.dwFormats And WAVE_FORMAT_2S16 Then
        InfoList.AddItem Chr$(9) + "22.05  kHz, Stereo, 16 bit"
End If

If InfoRecord.dwFormats And WAVE_FORMAT_4M08 Then
        InfoList.AddItem Chr$(9) + "44.1   kHz, Mono, 8 bit"
End If

If InfoRecord.dwFormats And WAVE_FORMAT_4S08 Then
        InfoList.AddItem Chr$(9) + "44.1   kHz, Stereo, 8 bit"
End If

If InfoRecord.dwFormats And WAVE_FORMAT_4M16 Then
        InfoList.AddItem Chr$(9) + "44.1   kHz, Mono, 16 bit"
End If

If InfoRecord.dwFormats And WAVE_FORMAT_4S16 Then
        InfoList.AddItem Chr$(9) + "44.1   kHz, Stereo, 16 bit"
End If

End Sub
```

5. When the Get Info button is clicked, the waveOutGetDevCaps function is called. The information returned from the function is stored in the InfoRecord structure. The information stored in the data structure elements is displayed in the InfoList list box.

```
Private Sub GetInfo_Click()

'  Declare InfoRecord as the WaveOutCaps
'  structure
Dim InfoRecord As WaveOutCaps

'  Get info on the wave device installed.  Note that
'  the primary wave audio device will be set to 0.  Most
'  systems only have one driver installed.
valback = waveOutGetDevCaps(0, InfoRecord, Len(InfoRecord))

'  If getting the information failed, then we will notify
'  the user and end the program.
If valback <> 0 Then
    MsgBox "Unable to get information for the specified device"
    End
End If

'  Display the Manufacturer's Driver ID, Product ID,
'  Driver Version and Product name
```

continued on next page

continued from previous page

```
InfoList.AddItem "Manufacturer's Driver ID: " + Str$(InfoRecord.wMid)
InfoList.AddItem "Product ID: " + Str$(InfoRecord.wPid)

InfoList.AddItem "Driver Version: " + Str$(InfoRecord.vDriverVersion)

InfoList.AddItem "Product Name:  " + InfoRecord.szPName

'  Display a title for the wave formats to come
InfoList.AddItem "Wave Formats Supported:"

'  call the formats subroutine and send the InfoRecord structure
'  to the subroutine
formats InfoRecord

'  Display the number of channels supported.
InfoList.AddItem "Number of Channels: " + Str$(InfoRecord.wChannels)

'  Display a header for the device function supported.
InfoList.AddItem "Device Functions Supported:"


'  We will check the dwSupport flag to see what bits have
'  been set to indicate capabilities of the device.
If InfoRecord.dwSupport And WAVECAPS_PITCH Then
    InfoList.AddItem Chr$(9) + "Supports Pitch Control"
End If

If InfoRecord.dwSupport And WAVECAPS_PLAYBACKRATE Then
    InfoList.AddItem Chr$(9) + "Supports Playback Rate Changes"
End If

If InfoRecord.dwSupport And WAVECAPS_VOLUME Then
    InfoList.AddItem Chr$(9) + "Supports Volume Changes"
End If

If InfoRecord.dwSupport And WAVECAPS_LRVOLUME Then
    InfoList.AddItem Chr$(9) + "Supports Left and Right Volume Changes"
End If

If InfoRecord.dwSupport And WAVECAPS_SYNC Then
    InfoList.AddItem Chr$(9) + "Supports Synchronization"
End If

End Sub
```

How It Works

The WaveOutCaps data structure is the key to understanding how this project works. The waveOutGetDevCaps function fills the WaveOutCaps data structure with the information on the wave audio device. The following is a breakdown of the data structure.

wMid as integer	Manufacturer ID
wPid as integer	Product ID
vDriverVersion as integer	Version of driver
szPName as string * 32	Product name
dwFormats as long	Formats supported (bit flags)
wChannels as integer	Number of channels
dwSupport as long	Functionality (bit flags)

The dwFormats and dwSupport flags are long integers that contain bit flags indicating which features are supported. For example, if only the mono, 8 bit, 22.05 kHz format is supported, then the dwSupport integer breaks down as shown in Table 3-9-2 and below.

```
Const WAVE_FORMAT_2M08 = &H10
' 22.05  kHz, Stereo, 8 bit
```

Table 3-9-2 dwSupport flag

FLAG	BINARY	DECIMAL	HEX
dwSupport	... 0000001000	16	&H10

When you AND the various format values with the dwSupport fields, a check is done to see if that particular bit is set to 1. (Remember AND only returns a 1 if both bits are set to 1.) If the format is not supported, then a 0 is returned. The format's subroutine handles checking all of the bits for support.

The same holds true for checking the dwFormats flag. dwFormats indicates whether the device supports pitch control, play back rate control, volume control, left-right volume control, and synchronization.

Comments

Determining the capabilities of a wave audio device is important when distributing applications that support wave audio devices. How-To 3.12 shows how to determine what MIDI devices are available and their capabilities.

3.10 How do I...
Easily play MIDI files?

COMPLEXITY: INTERMEDIATE

Problem

I would like to be able to play MIDI files easily from my applications. This can provide nice background music for my applications and other added effects.

Technique

As with wave files, the MCI command string interface can be used to play MIDI files easily. In this How-To, we explore the MCI interface to retrieve the capabilities of installed MCI devices.

Steps

Open and run 3-11.VBP.   The running program appears as shown in Figure 3-10-1.
Once again, the simple browser will be used to locate and play MIDI files. When you have found a MIDI file to be played, click on the Play button. To stop the playing, click on the Stop button. The error code returned from the mciSendString function is displayed in the text box. Also notice that the capabilities of the sequencer device are displayed in the list box on the right.

1. Create a new project called 3-11.VBP. Add the objects and properties listed in Table 3-10-1 to Form1 and save the form as 3-11.FRM.

Table 3-10-1 Project form's objects and properties

OBJECT	PROPERTY	SETTING
Form	Name	Form1
	Caption	"How-To 3.10"
ListBox	Name	CapList
TextBox	Name	ErrorText
	MultiLine	-1 'True
CommandButton	Name	Stop
	Caption	"Stop"
CommandButton	Name	Play
	Caption	"Play"
DirListBox	Name	Dir1
DriveListBox	Name	Drive1
FileListBox	Name	File1
	Pattern	"*.mid"

OBJECT	PROPERTY	SETTING
Label	Name	Label2
	AutoSize	-1 'True
	Caption	"Capabilities"
Label	Name	Label1
	Caption	"Error Message"

2. Add the following code to the general declarations section of the form.

```
'  Declare the mciSendString Multimedia API function
Private Declare Function mciSendString Lib "mmsystem" (ByVal MCI_Command ↵
As String, ByVal returnstrng As String, ByVal ReturnLength As Integer, ↵
ByVal Handle As Integer) As Long


'  Declare the mciGeterrorstrng Multimedia API function.
'  This will allow us to interpret errors from the
'  mciSendString command
Private Declare Function mciGeterrorstring Lib "mmsystem" (ByVal MCI_ERROR ↵
As Long, ByVal errorstrng As String, ByVal ReturnLength As Integer) As Integer


'  filename holds the global value
'  of the currently selected value
Dim filename As String


'  Declare the strings to hold error
'  and return messages
Dim returnstrng As String * 512
Dim errorstrng As String * 512
```

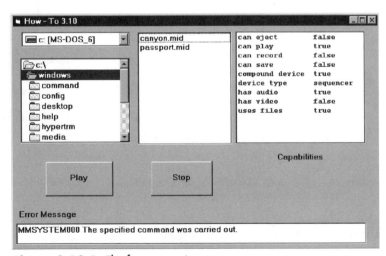

Figure 3-10-1 The form at runtime

3. This function handles updating the file list box when the directory is changed.

```
Private Sub Dir1_Change()

'   When the directory path changes, we need
'   to update the file list path.  Note that
'   we have the pattern property set to *.wav
'   to show only wave files
file1.Path = dir1.Path
End Sub
```

4. When the drive is changed, a check is done to ensure that the new drive is valid. If it is valid, then the directory list box and the file list box are updated.

```
Private Sub Drive1_Change()

'   In case the user selects a drive that
'   is unavailable such as a floppy drive
'   with no disk, then we need to trap that
'   error
On Error GoTo errorcheck

'   Set the new directory listing to the new drive
'   selected
dir1.Path = drive1.Drive


'   Skip around the error handling
GoTo next1


'   The error check section handles notifying
'   the user that the drive is unavailable
'   and resets the drive to the root directory.
errorcheck:

MsgBox "Selected Drive is Unavailable"
drive1.Drive = "c:\"
Resume Next

next1:
End Sub
```

5. When the file name is clicked or double-clicked, the global filename$ variable is set to be the location and name of the MIDI file.

```
Private Sub File1_Click()

'   Get the filename of the file to be played
f$ = file1.List(file1.ListIndex)

'   Get the path to the file
dirpath$ = dir1.Path

'   If the file is located in the root (C:\), then we
```

```
'    don't need to add a trailing "\" to the path
'    statement.  Otherwise we do need to add the "\"
'    ex:  directory = c:\windows  filename = tada.wav
'    arg$ = c:\windows\tada.wav
If Right$(dirpath$, 1) <> "\" Then
     filename$ = dirpath$ + "\" + f$
Else
     filename$ = dirpath$ + f$
End If

End Sub


Private Sub File1_DblClick()

'  Get the filename of the file to be played
f$ = file1.List(file1.ListIndex)

'  Get the path to the file
dirpath$ = dir1.Path

'   If the file is located in the root (C:\), then we
'   don't need to add a trailing "\" to the path
'   statement.  Otherwise we do need to add the "\"
'   ex:  directory = c:\windows  filename = tada.wav
'   arg$ = c:\windows\tada.wav
If Right$(dirpath$, 1) <> "\" Then
     filename$ = dirpath$ + "\" + f$
Else
     filename$ = dirpath$ + f$
End If

End Sub
```

6. When the project is started, the default directory for the directory list box is set to C:\windows. The sequencer device is opened to play the MIDI files. The GetCapabilities function is then called to get information about the device.

```
Private Sub Form_Load()

'  Set the default path to the windows directory.
dir1.Path = "C:\windows"

mcistr = "open sequencer"
'  Send the string to the system.

'  Call the sendstr function to send
'  the string to the system
sendstr mcistr

'  Get the Capabilities of the
'  MIDI Device
GetCapabilities

End Sub
```

7. When you quit the application, it is important to stop playing any MIDI files and close the sequencer device.

```
Private Sub Form_Unload(Cancel As Integer)

'   When we unload the form, we want
'   to stop the play of the file
mcistr = "stop " + filename$

'   Call the sendstr function
sendstr mcistr

mcistr = "close sequencer"

'   Send the string to the system.
sendstr mcistr

End Sub
```

8. GetCapabilities goes through each capability command and gets the information for the sequencer device. The information is then displayed in the list box.

```
Private Sub GetCapabilities()

'   The following set of functions query the
'   sequencer device to see if it can perform
'   the following functions.  With the first system
'   request, we will display an error message if
'   appropriate

'   Note the Chr$(9) is a tab character.
msg& = mciSendString("capability sequencer can eject", returnstrng, 512, 0)

caplist.AddItem "can eject" + Chr$(9) + Chr$(9) + returnstrng

throw% = mciGeterrorstring(msg&, errorstrng, 512)
ErrorText.Text = errorstrng

msg& = mciSendString("capability sequencer can play", returnstrng, 512, 0)
caplist.AddItem "can play" + Chr$(9) + Chr$(9) + returnstrng

msg& = mciSendString("capability sequencer can record", returnstrng, 512, 0)
caplist.AddItem "can record" + Chr$(9) + returnstrng

msg& = mciSendString("capability sequencer can save", returnstrng, 512, 0)
caplist.AddItem "can save" + Chr$(9) + Chr$(9) + returnstrng

msg& = mciSendString("capability sequencer compound device", returnstrng, ↵
512, 0)

caplist.AddItem "compound device" + Chr$(9) + returnstrng

msg& = mciSendString("capability sequencer device type", returnstrng, 512, 0)
caplist.AddItem "device type" + Chr$(9) + returnstrng
```

```
msg& = mciSendString("capability sequencer has audio", returnstrng, 512, 0)
caplist.AddItem "has audio" + Chr$(9) + Chr$(9) + returnstrng

msg& = mciSendString("capability sequencer has video", returnstrng, 512, 0)
caplist.AddItem "has video" + Chr$(9) + Chr$(9) + returnstrng

msg& = mciSendString("capability sequencer uses files", returnstrng, 512, 0)
caplist.AddItem "uses files" + Chr$(9) + Chr$(9) + returnstrng

End Sub
```

9. Play the MIDI file when the Play button is clicked.

```
Private Sub Play_Click()

'  Set the Play string
mcistr = "play " + filename$

'  Call the sendstr function
sendstr mcistr

End Sub
```

10. Add the following to the general declarations section of the form. sendstr is a general function that takes the command to be sent to the system and displays any error messages in the text box.

```
Private Sub sendstr(mcistr)

'  Send the string to the system.
msg& = mciSendString(mcistr, returnstrng, 512, 0)

'  Interpret the error message
throw% = mciGeterrorstring(msg&, errorstrng, 512)

'  Display the error message
ErrorText.Text = errorstrng

End Sub
```

11. Stop playing the MIDI file when the Stop button is clicked.

```
Private Sub Stop_Click()

'  Stop the playing of the file
mcistr = "stop " + filename$

'  Call the sendstr function
sendstr mcistr

End Sub
```

How It Works

As shown in earlier How-Tos, the MCI command string interface provides for simple playing of multimedia files, including MIDI files. Instead of working with wave audio devices, we are now working with sequencer devices. As you can see, the play, open, stop, and close commands are the same as for wave files.

Regarding the capabilities, straightforward English-like commands are used to query whether the sequencer has various capabilities. In this case, the return string from the mciSendString command is used to receive the response. It is important to differentiate this from the errorstring returned from the mciGetErrorString function. These same capabilities can be checked for any device available to the MCI driver.

Comments

Appendix A provides additional information on the different commands available for the sequencer device.

3.11 How do I...
Determine what MIDI devices are available and their capabilities?

COMPLEXITY: INTERMEDIATE

Problem

I would like to determine the number of MIDI devices that are installed in a system and their capabilities. It is important to determine if my MIDI application will run on the system.

Technique

As with wave audio devices, you should determine the specific capabilities of MIDI devices installed in a system. Unlike wave audio devices, often more than one MIDI device is installed.

The midiOutGetDevCaps function will be used to determine what capabilities are available through each MIDI device. The number of devices installed can be determined by using the midiOutGetNumDevs function.

Steps

Open and run 3-11.VBP. The running program appears as shown in Figure 3-11-1.

The number of devices installed in the system is shown in the lower-left label. To get information on a specific device, enter the device number in the upper-left text box. Remember that the first device is signified by 0. To get information on the device, click on the Get Info button. The program determines whether the MIDI device is an external or internal device and displays the determination.

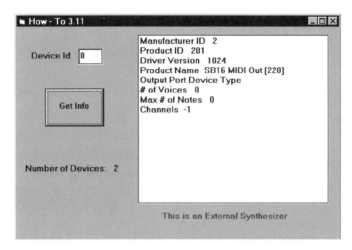

Figure 3-11-1 The form at runtime

1. Create a new project called 3-12.VBP. Add the objects and properties listed in Table 3-11-1 to Form1 and save the form as 3-12.FRM.

Table 3-11-1 Project form's objects and properties

OBJECT	PROPERTY	SETTING
Form	Name	Form1
	Caption	"How-To 3.11"
TextBox	Name	DeviceId
	Text	"0"
CommandButton	Name	GetInfo
	Caption	"Get Info"
	Font	
	name	"Arial"
ListBox	Name	ListInfo
Label	Name	IntExt
	ForeColor	&H000000FF&

continued on next page

continued from previous page

OBJECT	PROPERTY	SETTING
Label	Name	NumDevsLabel
	Caption	"NumDevs"
Label DevId	Caption	"Device Id"

2. Add a new module to the project called 3-12.BAS and add the following data structure. This data structure will hold the information on the MIDI device.

```
' MIDI output device capabilities structure
Type MIDIOUTCAPS
    wMid As Integer            ' manufacturer ID
    wPid As Integer            ' product ID
    vDriverVersion As Integer  ' version of the driver
    szPname As String * 32     ' product name (NULL terminated string)
    wTechnology As Integer     ' type of device
    wVoices As Integer         ' # of voices (internal synth only)
    wNotes As Integer          ' max # of notes (internal synth only)
    wChannelMask As Integer    ' channels used (internal synth only)
    dwSupport As Long          ' functionality supported by driver
End Type
```

3. Add the following code to the general declarations section of Form1. The various constants and functions are declared for accessing the MIDI devices.

```
' The midiOutGetDevCaps function will get information on
' the midi devices installed.  The information is stored
' in the MidiOutCaps structure
Private Declare Function midiOutGetDevCaps Lib "MMSYSTEM" (ByVal udeviceid ⏎
As Integer, lpCaps As MIDIOUTCAPS, ByVal uSize As Integer) As Integer

' midiOutGetNumDevs will return the number of MIDI
' devices installed.
Private Declare Function midiOutGetNumDevs Lib "MMSYSTEM" () As Integer

' flags for wTechnology field of MIDIOUTCAPS structure
Const MOD_MIDIPORT = 1       ' output port
Const MOD_SYNTH = 2          ' generic internal synth
Const MOD_SQSYNTH = 3        ' square wave internal synth
Const MOD_FMSYNTH = 4        ' FM internal synth
Const MOD_MAPPER = 5         ' MIDI mapper

' flags for dwSupport field of MIDIOUTCAPS structure
Const MIDICAPS_VOLUME = &H1  ' supports volume control
Const MIDICAPS_LRVOLUME = &H2 ' separate left-right volume control


' NumDevs stores the number of MIDI devices
' installed in the system.
Dim NumDevs As Integer
```

4. The Form_Load procedure gets the number of devices installed and displays the information in NewDevsLabel.

```
Private Sub Form_Load()

'  We will start out by getting the number
'  of MIDI devices installed
NumDevs = midiOutGetNumDevs()

'  Change1 label2 to show the number of
'  devices
NumDevsLabel.Caption = "Number of Devices:  " + Str$(NumDevs)

'  Autosize the control to the text
NumDevsLabel.AutoSize = True
End Sub
```

5. The midiOutGetDevCaps function returns information on the specified MIDI device and places it in the MidiInfo data structure variable. The information is then displayed in the list box. Finally, a check is performed to see if the synthesizer is internal or external.

```
Private Sub GetInfo_Click()

'  Declare MidiInfo as the MIDIOUTCAPS
'  structure that will hold the information
'  on the MIDI device
Dim MidiInfo As MIDIOUTCAPS

'  Clear out the list box
ListInfo.Clear

'  Get the DeviceID the user wants
'  information on
DeviceID = Val(DeviceID.Text)

'  Call the GetDevCaps function.  The information
'  is stored in the MidiInfo data structure
throw% = midiOutGetDevCaps(DeviceID, MidiInfo, Len(MidiInfo))

'  Display the information for the Manufacturer ID,
'  Product ID, Driver Version, and Product Name
ListInfo.AddItem "Manufacturer ID  " + Str$(MidiInfo.wMid)
ListInfo.AddItem "Product ID  " + Str$(MidiInfo.wPid)
ListInfo.AddItem "Driver Version  " + Str$(MidiInfo.vDriverVersion)
ListInfo.AddItem "Product Name  " + MidiInfo.szPname

'  The wTechnology flag holds the type of device.  We
'  will check for the appropriate value and display
'  the appropriate text
If MidiInfo.wTechnology = 1 Then ListInfo.AddItem "Output Port Device Type"
If MidiInfo.wTechnology = 2 Then ListInfo.AddItem "Generic Internal Synthesizer
Device Type"
```

continued on next page

continued from previous page

```
If MidiInfo.wTechnology = 3 Then ListInfo.AddItem "Square Wave Internal
Synthesizer Device Type"
If MidiInfo.wTechnology = 4 Then ListInfo.AddItem "FM Internal Synthesizer Device
Type"
If MidiInfo.wTechnology = 5 Then ListInfo.AddItem "MIDI Mapper Device Type"

'  Display the # of Voices, Max # of Notes, and Channels
'  in the list box
ListInfo.AddItem "# of Voices  " + Str$(MidiInfo.wVoices)
ListInfo.AddItem "Max # of Notes  " + Str$(MidiInfo.wNotes)
ListInfo.AddItem "Channels  " + Str$(MidiInfo.wChannelMask)

'  If the MIDICAPS_VOLUME flag is set, then the
'  device supports Volume Control
If MidiInfo.dwSupport And MIDICAPS_VOLUME Then
    ListInfo.AddItem "Supports Volume Control"
End If

'  If the MIDICAPS_LRVOLUME flag is set, then the
'  device supports Left and Right Volume Control
If MidiInfo.dwSupport And MIDICAPS_LRVOLUME Then
    ListInfo.AddItem "Supports Separate Left-Right Volume Control"
End If


'  If the device supports notes then we know it
'  is an Internal Synthesizer.
If MidiInfo.wNotes  0 Then
    IntExt.Caption = "This is an Internal Synthesizer"
Else
    IntExt.Caption = "This is an External Synthesizer"
End If

'  size the label to the new text.
IntExt.AutoSize = True

End Sub
```

How It Works

This project is very similar to How-To 3.9. The midiOutGetDevCaps function returns the device information into the MidiOutCaps data structure. The following is a breakdown of the data structure.

wMid as integer	Manufacturer ID
wPid as integer	Product ID
vDriverVersion as integer	Driver version
szPname as string * 32	Product name
wTechnology as integer	Type of device
wVoices as integer	-# of voices (only for internal synthesizers)

wNotes as integer	Max # of notes (only for internal synthesizers)
wChannelMask as integer	Channels used (only for internal synthesizers)
dwSupport As Long	Functionality supported by driver

The dwSupport integer contains bit flags indicating the type of support the MIDI device provides. The device can support volume control and separate left and right volume changes.

As the data structure explanation indicates, it is relatively simple to determine whether a MIDI device is an internal or external synthesizer. If the wVoices, wNotes, and wChannelMask are not set to 0, then the synthesizer is an internal device.

Comments

Using the midiOutGetDevCaps helps you determine what type of MIDI devices are installed in a target system (if any). This combined with the waveOutGetDevCaps function allows you to determine the sound capabilities of a system.

3.12 How do I...
Know when a MIDI (or wave) file has finished playing?

Problem

I would like to be able to know when a MIDI (or wave) file has finished playing so that I can trigger certain events in my application. These would include determining whether or not the user has finished certain tasks within the length of the MIDI music.

Technique

The MCI control provides for easy playing of MIDI and wave files and also supports a notify event that is triggered when the media file (i.e., WAV, AVI) has finished playing. In this example, a simple puzzle game is built that gives the user until the end of the music to solve the puzzle.

Steps

Open and run 3-7.VBP. The running program appears as shown in Figure 3-12-1.

Upon the start of the program, the MIDI music begins playing. You need to move the numbers so they are in order from left to right before the music stops playing. If you finish before the music, click the Done button. The program then

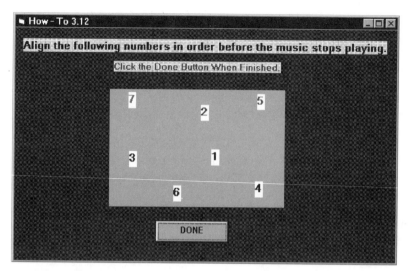

Figure 3-12-1 The form at runtime

Figure 3-12-2 The puzzle correctly solved

checks to see if you solved the puzzle correctly. Try waiting until the music finishes to see how the program responds when the music finishes before you do.

An example of a correctly solved puzzle appears in Figure 3-12-2.

1. Create a new project called 3-7.VBP. Add the MCI control to the project (found in the \Windows \System directory). Add the objects and properties listed in Table 3-12-1 to Form1 and save the form as 3-7.FRM.

Table 3-12-1 Project form's objects and properties

OBJECT	PROPERTY	SETTING
Form	Name	Form1
	BackColor	&H00404000&
	Caption	"How-To 3.12"
.PictureBox	Name	Picture1
	BackColor	&H00C0C0C0&
	BorderStyle	0 'None

Note: The following labels should be placed on the picture control and placed in a control array.

OBJECT	PROPERTY	SETTING
Label	Name	Number
	AutoSize	-1 'True
	Caption	"7"
	DragMode	1 'Automatic
	Font	
	name	"MS Sans Serif"
	size	9.6
	ForeColor	&H00808080&
	Index	6
Label	Name	Number
	AutoSize	-1 'True
	Caption	"6"
	DragMode	1 'Automatic
	Font	
	name	"MS Sans Serif"
	size	9.6
	ForeColor	&H00800000&
	Index	5
Label	Name	Number
	AutoSize	-1 'True
	Caption	"5"
	DragMode	1 'Automatic
	Font	

continued on next page

continued from previous page

OBJECT	PROPERTY	SETTING
	name	"MS Sans Serif"
	size	9.6
	ForeColor	&H00C000C0&
	Index	4
Label	Name	Number
	AutoSize	-1 'True
	Caption	"4"
	DragMode	1 'Automatic
	Font	
	name	"MS Sans Serif"
	size	9.6
	ForeColor	&H00004000&
	Index	3
Label	Name	Number
	AutoSize	-1 'True
	Caption	"3"
	DragMode	1 'Automatic
	Font	
	name	"MS Sans Serif"
	size	9.6
	ForeColor	&H00FF0000&
	Index	2
Label	Name	Number
	AutoSize	-1 'True
	BackColor	&H00FFFFFF&
	Caption	"2"
	DragMode	1 'Automatic
	Font	
	name	"MS Sans Serif"
	size	9.6
	ForeColor	&H000000FF&
	Index	1

OBJECT	PROPERTY	SETTING
Label	Name	Number
	AutoSize	-1 'True
	Caption	"1"
	DragMode	1 'Automatic
	Font	
	name	"MS Sans Serif"
	size	9.6
	Index	0
CommandButton	Name	Done
	Caption	"DONE"
MMControl	Name	MMControl1
	autoenable	0 'False
Label	Name	Click
	AutoSize	-1 'True
	BackColor	&H00E0E0E0&
	Caption	"Click the Done Button When Finished."
	ForeColor	&H000000FF&
Label	Name	Align
	AutoSize	-1 'True
	BackColor	&H00E0E0E0&
	Caption	"Align the following numbers in order before the music stops playing."
	Font	
	name	"MS Sans Serif"
	size	9.6
	ForeColor	&H00000000&

2. Add the following subroutine to the general declarations section of the form. Checkalign will check to see if the numbers have been placed in order from left to right and will notify the user appropriately.

```
Dim flag As Integer
Private Sub checkalign()
```

continued on next page

continued from previous page

```
'   Check to see if the numbers are in order.   We
'   will do this by checking to see if the left
'   values are incrementally larger
For n = 0 To 5

        '   If any one of the labels is further to the
        '   left than its predeccesor, then tell the
        '   user that there is an error
        If Number(n).Left > Number(n + 1).Left Then
            MsgBox "Sorry, Try Again"
            End
        End If

Next n

'   Congratulate the user
MsgBox "Congratulations"

next1:

'   End the program
End

End Sub
```

3. When the Done button is clicked, it will stop playing the MIDI file and call the Checkalign function.

```
Private Sub Done_Click()

'   Close the open device
mmcontrol1.Command = "close"

'   Check the alignment of the numbers
checkalign

End Sub
```

4. When the form is loaded, the system is set up to play the MIDI file and then play it for one-fourth the length of the file. For this example, the CANYON.MID file supplied with Windows is used. Before playing begins, the Notify element of the control is set to True so that notification will be given when play has finished.

```
Private Sub Form_Load()

'   Set the filename to the canyon MIDI file
'   found in the Windows directory
mmcontrol1.FileName = "c:\windows\media\canyon.mid"

'   Set the device type to the sequencer for MIDI
mmcontrol1.DeviceType = "sequencer"

'   Open the device
mmcontrol1.Command = "open"
```

```
'  Start from the beginning of the piece
mmcontrol1.From = 0

'  Play only for a quarter of the length of
'  the selection
mmcontrol1.To = mmcontrol1.Length / 4

'  Turn on the notify feature
mmcontrol1.Notify = True

'  Play the selection
mmcontrol1.Command = "play"

End Sub
```

5. When the program ends, it is important to make sure that the multimedia device is closed.

```
Private Sub Form_Unload(Cancel As Integer)

'  Close the sequencer
mmcontrol1.Command = "close"

End Sub
```

6. The MMControl1_Done event notifies you when the file has finished playing. If normal notification has taken place (value of 1), then the Checkalign subroutine is called.

```
Private Sub MMControl1_Done(NotifyCode As Integer)

'  If it was a normal ending of the playing
'  of our MIDI file then we will check the
'  alignment of numbers.
If NotifyCode = 1 Then checkalign

End Sub
```

7. The DragDrop features of Visual Basic are used to handle moving the number on the picture control. When the DragDrop event is fired for the picture, the dragged control (a number) is moved to the spot where the drop took place. Note that the object is moved to one-half the number's width and height up and left of the mouse. This helps the movement appear more precise. Try not doing that to see the effect.

```
Private Sub Picture1_DragDrop(source As Control, x As Single, y As Single)

'  We are dragging and dropping the labels on
'  the picture control.  When the drop has taken place,
'  we will move the label to the new position.  Note that
'  source contains the control that is being dragged and
'  dropped
```

continued on next page

continued from previous page

```
source.Left = x - (source.Width / 2)
source.Top = y - (source.Height / 2)

End Sub
```

How It Works

This section pulls together many standard Visual Basic 4.0 features to provide effective use of a MIDI file. The MCI custom control provides for easy access to the MCI driver. This example could have just as easily played a wave file.

The MCI control uses English-like phrases to carry out commands to the system. The sequence to play the MIDI file is to set the device type (sequencer), open the Device, set the file name, if necessary set the from/to properties, and then play the file. Playing of the file can be stopped by using the Stop command. Finally, the device is closed with the Close command.

The key to the notification is to ensure that the Notify property is set to true before the file is played. When the file is done playing, the Done event is fired for the control. The Done event is sent a NotifyCode, which can be one of four values:

1	Command completed successfully
2	Command superseded by another command
4	Command aborted by the user
8	Command failed

In our example, a check is done to ensure that a 1 was returned to the Done event.

The other key feature implemented here is the DragDrop feature provided by Visual Basic 4.0. By setting the Drag Mode property of the number label controls to automatic, we have an effective method of moving the numbers around in the picture control. When the number is dropped (you let up on the mouse button), the DragDrop event of the picture control is fired. The DragDrop event is passed to the control that was dropped and the X and Y coordinates of the drop. The label control can then be moved to the dropped position.

The Checkalign function simply loops through the label control array to see if each successive label is to the left of the next label.

Comments

MIDI music provides for an entertaining backdrop to solving the puzzle which is similar to many popular game shows. The MCI control can be used to play most of the popular multimedia file formats, including WAV, MID, and AVI.

3.13 How do I...
Play CD-audio sound?

COMPLEXITY: INTERMEDIATE

Problem

I would like to be able to play musical selections on a CD audio disc.

Technique

The MCI command string interface provides for easy playing of CD-audio sound. As with playing wave and MIDI sound, English-like commands can be used to control the playing of CD-audio sound.

Steps

Open and run 3-13.VBP. The running program appears as shown in Figure 3-13-1.

Each CD is of a certain overall length with each track (or song) a specific length. The program displays the overall playing length of the CD and the length of the selected track. The list box contains a number representing each track on the CD. The program allows you to forward or reverse through the tracks, play the tracks, and stop playing.

1. Create a new project called 3-13.VBP. Add the objects and properties listed in Table 3-13-1 to Form1 and save the form as 3-1.FRM.

Table 3-13-1 Project form's objects and properties

OBJECT	PROPERTY	SETTING
Form	Name	Form1
	Caption	"How-To 3.13"
TextBox	Name	CDLength
CommandButton	Name	Stop
	Caption	"Stop"
TextBox	Name	TrackLength
ListBox	Name	TrackList

continued on next page

continued from previous page

OBJECT	PROPERTY	SETTING
CommandButton	Name	Reverse
	Caption	"Reverse"
CommandButton	Name	Forward
	Caption	"Forward"
CommandButton	Name	Play
	Caption	"Play"
Label	Name	CDLabel
	AutoSize	-1 'True
	Caption	"CD Length"
Label	Name	TrackLabel
	AutoSize	-1 'True
	Caption	"Track Length"
Label	Name	SelectTrack
	Caption	"Select Track"

2. Add the following code to the general declarations section of Form1. The appropriate declarations are made to use the MCI command string interface.

```
' Declare the mciSendString function
Private Declare Function mciSendString Lib "mmsystem" (ByVal lpstrCommand ↵
As String, ByVal lpstrReturnStrng As String, ByVal uReturnLength As Integer, ↵
ByVal hWndCallback As Integer) As Long

' Declare the GetErrorString Message
Private Declare Function mciGetErrorString Lib "mmsystem" (ByVal wError As ↵
Long, ByVal lpstrBuffer As String, ByVal uLength As Integer) As Integer

' ReturnStrng holds the messages sent back from
' the mciSendString function.  ErrorStrng holds
' the message from mciGetErrorString
Dim ErrorStrng As String * 256
Dim ReturnStrng As String * 256

' This variable will hold the number of
' tracks on the CD
Dim NumTracks As Integer
```

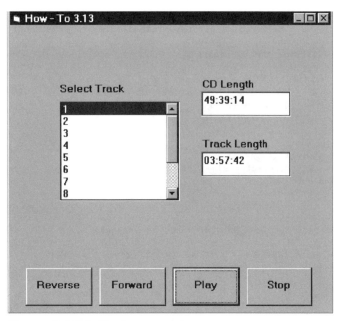

Figure 3-13-1 The form at runtime

3. When the project is started up, the overall length of the CD is determined, the number of tracks on the CD is determined, and the length of the first track is determined. The list box is filled with sequential numbers representing the tracks on the CD.

```
Private Sub Form_Load()

'  Open the cdaudio device and get the
'  total number of tracks
msgval = mciSendString("open cdaudio", ReturnStrng, 256, 0)

'  If there is an error in loading the CD then we will display
'  the message and end the program.
If msgval <> 0 Then
    msgval = mciGetErrorString(msgval, ErrorStrng, 256)
    MsgBox ErrorStrng
    End
End If

msgval = mciSendString("status cdaudio number of tracks", ReturnStrng, 256, 0)

'  Store the number of tracks
NumTracks = Val(ReturnStrng)
```

continued on next page

continued from previous page

```
'  Get the length of the whole CD
msgval = mciSendString("status cdaudio length", ReturnStrng, 256, 0)

'  Display the CD length
cdlength.Text = ReturnStrng

'  Build a list with the number of tracks
For n = 1 To NumTracks
    TrackList.AddItem n
Next n

'  Select the first number in the list.
TrackList.Selected(0) = True
End Sub
```

4. When the application is unloaded, the CD-audio device is closed.

```
Private Sub Form_Unload(Cancel As Integer)

'  Upon ending the program we will close the device
msgval = mciSendString("stop cdaudio", ReturnStrng, 256, 0)

'  Upon ending the program we will close the device
msgval = mciSendString("close cdaudio", ReturnStrng, 256, 0)

End Sub
```

5. When the Forward button is selected, a move is made forward one track in the list box. The new track length is displayed. Then the Stop_Click and Play_Click buttons are called to play the new selection. A check is also done to ensure that a seek has not been done past the end of the CD.

```
Private Sub Forward_Click()

'  Get the current selected track.
track = TrackList.List(TrackList.ListIndex)

'  We need to make sure that we are not trying to
'  seek beyond the last track.
If track <> NumTracks Then

    '  sav will temporarily hold the current selected
    '  device
    sav = TrackList.ListIndex

    '  Select the next track in the list.  Note
    '  that this fires the click event for the list
    '  box and will automatically update the track
    '  length text box.
    TrackList.Selected(sav + 1) = True

    '  Unselect the current track in the list
    TrackList.Selected(sav) = False
```

```
'  Stop the current playing and then play the new track
Stop_Click
Play_Click
```

```
End If
```

```
End Sub
```

6. When the user is ready to play a track, a check is done to find out which track is selected. The track position on the CD is found and a seek is performed to that position, and then the selection is played.

```
Private Sub Play_Click()

'  Get the current selected track
track = TrackList.List(TrackList.ListIndex)

'  Get the position of the current track.
msgval = mciSendString("status cdaudio position track " + Str$(track), ⏎
ReturnStrng, 256, 0)

'  pos will store the position
pos = ReturnStrng

'  seek to the track position
msgval = mciSendString("seek cdaudio to " + pos, ReturnStrng, 256, 0)

'  Play the track
msgval = mciSendString("play cdaudio", ReturnStrng, 256, 0)

End Sub
```

7. When the Reverse button is selected, a move is made back one track. A request is done for the track length and then a call is made to the Stop_Click and Play_Click events to play the new selection. A check is also done to ensure that the user has not tried to move past the beginning of the CD.

```
Private Sub Reverse_Click()

'  Get the currently selected track
track = TrackList.List(TrackList.ListIndex)

'  We need to make sure that we are not trying to
'  go beyond track 1
If track <> 1 Then

    '  sav temporarily stores the currently selected track
    sav = TrackList.ListIndex

    '  Select the new track
    TrackList.Selected(sav - 1) = True

    '  Unselect the currently selected track
```

continued on next page

continued from previous page

```
    TrackList.Selected(sav) = False

    ' Stop the current playing and then play the new track
    Stop_Click
    Play_Click

End If

End Sub
```

8. When the Stop button is selected, play is stopped.

```
Private Sub Stop_Click()

' Stop the device
msgval = mciSendString("stop cdaudio", ReturnStrng, 256, 0)

End Sub
```

9. When a new selection is made in the list box, the track length on the display is updated. To play the new selection, select the Play button.

```
Private Sub TrackList_Click()

' Get the current track
track = TrackList.List(TrackList.ListIndex)

' Get the length of the track
msgval = mciSendString("status cdaudio length track" + Str$(track), ↵
ReturnStrng, 256, 0)

' Display the length in the tracklength text box
tracklength.Text = ReturnStrng

End Sub
```

How It Works

When playing CD-audio tracks, it is important to get information regarding the track's starting positions and lengths. Fortunately, the MCI interface provides for easy access to this information.

The key to playing a specific track is to find the position of the track on the CD. By using the Status cdaudio position track # command, mciSendString fills the ReturnString variable with the position of the specified track. That position is then used in the play command, Play cdaudio from #. The to # could be added to end the track playing at the specified position (which could be the end of the track). In this case, the play continues through the tracks on the CD until the CD ends or another command is issued.

Comments

This simple program, complete with skip forward and reverse functions, repeat, and random play options could easily be built into a full-featured CD player. Playing audio CDs is fairly straightforward with the MCI command string interface. Note that the MCI custom control can also be used to access the cdaudio device.

4

GRAPHICS

4
GRAPHICS

How do I...

A key element in producing multimedia titles is the use and manipulation of graphics. Features such as hot spots, fades, wipes, and bit manipulation can provide visually interesting and powerful effects to your applications.

In this chapter, you will perform various manipulations of graphic effects. Demonstrations of the built-in graphics features of Visual Basic 4.0 will be analyzed, as well as Windows API techniques. This chapter also introduces the new class feature available in Visual Basic 4.0. Several classes will be developed that can easily be integrated with existing applications. A wide range of Windows-based programming topics will be covered, including building bitmaps in memory, bit manipulation with BitBlt, and color palettes.

Windows APIs Covered			
BitBlt	PatBlt	Rectangle	SelectObject
CreatePen	DeleteObject	CreateHatchBrush	CreateSolidBrush
CreateDIBitmap	CreatePatternBrush	StretchBlt	CreatePolygonRgn
PtInRegion			

4.1 Display still pictures

You will learn how to use the image and picture controls to manipulate and display graphics. For example, you can combine the timer control and a picture or image control's height and width properties to change the appearance of an image while your program is running.

4.2 Rotate a picture in a picture box

The picture box control has two properties, Pset and Point, which can be used to rotate a picture from one picture box to another. By using the Pset and Point properties, you can perform interesting effects on picture controls.

4.3 Create simple hot spots using the image control

Hot spots let the user click on objects within an image. The example demonstrates how to create simple hot spots with the image control.

4.4 Create irregularly shaped hot spots on a picture

Often developers have the need to define irregularly shaped hot spots on an image. This project demonstrates a simple puzzle game that uses a hot spot editor and several Windows APIs to develop irregularly shaped hot spots.

4.5 Dissolve a picture with random rectangles

The Windows API provides for powerful graphical manipulation methods. In this How-To, you will couple Visual Basic 4.0's timer control and Rnd function with the Windows BitBlt, Rectangle, and PatBlt functions to dissolve an image with a wide range of rectangular styles.

4.6 Create wipes

Wipe transitions from one image to another are popular multimedia effects. The timer control can be combined with several Windows APIs to build several different types of wipes.

4.7 Perform a cross hatch and vertical blind fade in and out on a picture

The Windows API will be used to learn how to build 8x8 monochrome bitmaps. From these bitmaps, screens will be built that fade the picture in and out using either a cross hatch or a vertical blind fade.

4.8 Display transparent pictures

Often parts of graphics are incomplete and should be transparent when displayed. By creating a special mask of the graphic and using the BitBlt function, you can display only the parts of a graphic you wish to be visible.

4.9 Overlay a complex shape on a picture

Sometimes areas of graphics that should be transparent are not as simple as demonstrated in How-To 4.8. By building on the technique demonstrated in How-To 4.8, you will learn how to filter out any part of a bitmap that you do not want displayed.

4.1 How do I...
Display still pictures?

COMPLEXITY: EASY

Problem

I would like to be able to display basic graphics in my application, for example, with a logo or title screen.

Technique

By using the picture and image controls, you can display images in your applications and accomplish simple graphic effects such as transitions.

Steps

Open and run 4-1.VBP. The running program appears as shown in Figure 4-1-1.

The first phase exits (removes) the first picture from bottom to top. The bottom picture is revealed, and then begins to exit from right to left. Finally, the text "Hello World" is shown. (See Figure 4-1-2.)

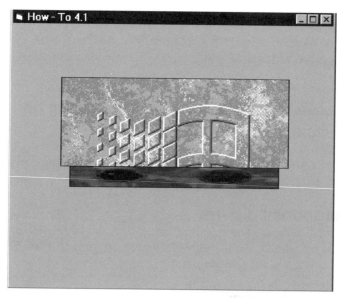

Figure 4-1-1 The program at runtime with the first image in motion

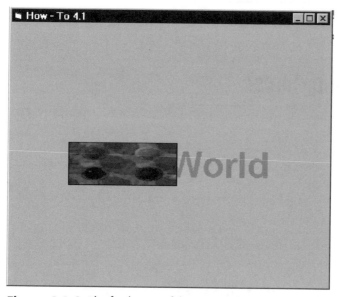

Figure 4-1-2 The final stage of the picture changes

1. Create a new project named 4-1.VBP. Add the objects and properties listed in Table 4-1-1 to Form1 and save the form as 4-1.FRM.

Table 4-1-1 The project form's objects and properties

OBJECT	PROPERTY	SETTING
Form	Name	Form1
	BackColor	&H00800000&
	Caption	"How-To 4.1"
Timer	Name	Timer2
	Enabled	0 'False
	Interval	5
Timer	Name	Timer1
	Interval	1
PictureBox	Name	Picture1
	AutoSize	-1 'True
	Picture	(c:\windows\windows1.bmp)
Image	Name	Image1
	BorderStyle	1 'Fixed Single
	Picture	(c:\windows\manycolo.bmp)
	Stretch	-1 'True
Label	Name	Label1
	AutoSize	-1 'True
	BackStyle	0 'Transparent
	Caption	"Hello World"
	Font	
	name	"Arial"
	ForeColor	&H0000FF00&

2. When the program loads, the images are centered on the form. The image control can stretch the image contained in it. In this case, it is stretched over the "Hello World" text on the label.

```
Private Sub Form_Load()

'   Center the Hello World label on the form
label1.Move Form1.Width / 2 - label1.Width / 2, Form1.Height / 2 - ↵
label1.Height / 2

'   Center the picture on the form
picture1.Move Form1.Width / 2 - picture1.Width / 2, Form1.Height / ↵
2 - picture1.Height / 2


'   Cover the label with the 256Color
'   bitmap
image1.Width = label1.Width + 200
image1.Height = label1.Height
image1.Left = label1.Left - 100
image1.Top = label1.Top

End Sub
```

3. Timer1 handles changing the picture's height to implement the exit from bottom to top.

```
Private Sub Timer1_Timer()

'   We are rolling the picture up in
'   60 unit increments.  We will keep
'   doing that until the height of the
'   picture is less than 60
If picture1.Height > 60 Then

    '   Shorten the height of the picture by 60
    picture1.Height = picture1.Height - 60

Else

    '   Once the height is less than 60, we will
    '   then make the picture invisible, stop this
    '   timer and start timer2
    picture1.Visible = False
    timer1.Enabled = False
    timer2.Enabled = True

End If


End Sub
```

4. Timer2 handles changing the width of the image control.

```
Private Sub Timer2_Timer()

'   We will shrink the image label by
```

```
'  120.
If image1.Width > 120 Then

    ' Decrement the width of the image by 120
    image1.Width = image1.Width - 120

Else

    ' Once the width is less than 120
    ' we make the image invisible and
    ' turn off the timer
    image1.Visible = False
    timer2.Enabled = False

End If


End Sub
```

How It Works

This simple project demonstrates use of the image and picture controls. Both controls have properties that when combined with the timer control, allow for basic transitions to be performed on images. The image control has a unique property, Stretch, that allows the image to be stretched to the size of the control.

Comments

Consider using the image control instead of the picture control. Because it has fewer properties and supports fewer events, the image control takes up less system resources.

4.2 How do I...
Rotate a picture in a picture box?

COMPLEXITY: EASY

Problem

There are two functions, Pset and Point, that allow me to transfer points between two pictures. I would like to be able to rotate a picture, which will help demonstrate the use of these two functions.

Technique

The picture control has two functions, Point and Pset, that allow you to get information about points in one picture and to set points in another picture. This information can be used to "map" one picture point onto another version.

Steps

Open and run 4-2.VBP. The running program appears as shown in Figure 4-2-1.
Click on the Rotate button to create the rotated picture in the right picture box.
Figure 4-2-2 shows the results.

1. Create a new project named 4-2.VBP. Add the objects and properties listed in
Table 4-2-1 to Form1 and save the form as 4-2.FRM.

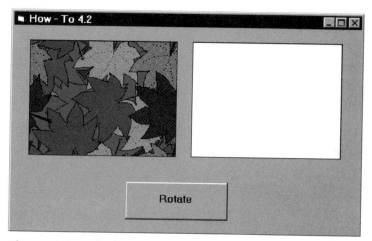

Figure 4-2-1 The form at runtime

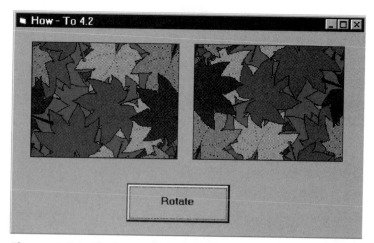

Figure 4-2-2 The form with the rotated picture

Table 4-2-1 The project form's objects and properties

OBJECT	PROPERTY	SETTING
Form	Name	Form1
	BackColor	&H00FFFFFF&
	Caption	"How-To 4.2"
CommandButton	Name	Rotate
	Caption	"Rotate"
PictureBox	Name	Picture2
	AutoRedraw	-1 'True
	ScaleMode	3 'Pixel
PictureBox	Name	Picture1
	AutoSize	-1 'True
	Picture	(C:\windows\leaves.bmp)
	ScaleMode	3 'Pixel

2. Add the following code to the Form_Load and Form_Unload procedures. In the Form_Load procedure, the pictures are set up.

```
Private Sub Form_Load()

'  Set picture2's height and width to picture1
picture2.Width = picture1.Width
picture2.Height = picture1.Height

'  Make sure the pictures are aligned at the top
'  of the form
picture2.Top = picture1.Top
End Sub

Private Sub Form_Unload(Cancel As Integer)

'  End the program when the form is uloaded
End

End Sub
```

3. The For loop in the Rotate_Click function goes through each point in the picture, gets the point's color, and sets the opposite corner point to that color in the

second picture. It is important to make sure that a valid color is received from the Picture1.point() function before the point is set in the second picture.

```
Private Sub rotate_Click()

'  Clear picture2 for the rotation
picture2.Cls

'  The two For loops go through each point in the
'  original picture and get the color values.
For x = 0 To picture1.ScaleWidth

    For y = 0 To picture1.ScaleHeight

        '  Get the color value of the point
        color = picture1.Point(x, y)

        '  Set the opposite point in picture2 to the
        '  color from picture1.  Note that  we need to make
        '  sure that the specified point has a color otherwise
        '  the PSet will return an error.
        If color <> -1 Then picture2.PSet (picture1.ScaleWidth - x - 1, ↵
                        picture1.ScaleHeight - y - 1), color

    Next y

'  Call the DoEvents function so that Windows will
'  continue working on the pixel transfers but you
'  can enter in mouse clicks etc. without being held
'  up by the pixel transfers.
throw% = DoEvents()

Next x

End Sub
```

How It Works

The basic technique is to retrieve the color setting of a pixel in the original picture using the Point function, and then to set the opposite pixel in the new picture using the Pset function. Rotations of 90, 180, and 270 degrees can be done simply by setting the appropriate destination pixel.

Comments

You may wish to consider using the API functions GetPixel and SetPixel to do similar rotations to help speed up the process. Using pixel transfers between images can be useful to provide different types of effects.

4.3 How do I...
Create simple hot spots using the image control?

Problem

I would like to be able to add simple hot spots to my graphic images so that users can select pictures to access program features or to get more information. For example, I would like to be able to have my user click on specific parts of an overall image to get feedback.

Technique

The image control can be used to create simple hot spots on an image. The transparent feature of the image control makes for a perfect invisible hot spot and allows for the Click and Double-Click events to be accessed easily.

Steps

Open and run 4-3.VBP. The running program appears as shown in Figure 4-3-1.

Figure 4-3-1 The form at runtime

Image controls are placed over each of the buttons on the calculator. Click on a button and the text box will give you the appropriate feedback about which button was selected. Because the calculator buttons are rectangular, a single object works effectively to define the hot spots.

1. Create a new project called 4-3.VBP. Add the objects and properties listed in Table 4-3-1 to Form1 and save the form as 4-3.FRM.

Table 4-3-1 The project form's objects and properties

OBJECT	PROPERTY	SETTING
Form	Name	Form1
	Auto3D	-1 'True
	BackColor	&H00404040&
	Caption	"How-To4.3"
TextBox	Name	Feedback
Label	Name	ClickLabel
	AutoSize	-1 'True
	BackColor	&H008080FF&
	Caption	"Click a Button"
	Font	
	name	"Arial"
	size	12

Note: Image2 is a control array of 23 images.

OBJECT	PROPERTY	SETTING
Image	Name	Image2
	Index	0 - 23
Image	Name	Image1
	Picture	(c:\vb40\metafile\business\calcultr.wmf)
	Stretch	-1 'True

2. When the main calculator image is selected, feedback is given to the user.

```
Private Sub Image1_Click()

' Notify the user that the main image was selected
Feedback.Text = "The calculator has been selected."
```

```
End Sub
```

3. Because all of the hot spots are defined with an image control array, Visual Basic 4.0's Case feature is used to check the index and give the appropriate feedback to the user.

```
Private Sub Image2_Click(index As Integer)

'  When one of the hot spots is selected,
'  we check the index and give the appropriate
'  feedback.

Select Case index

Case 0 To 9
    Feedback.Text = "You selected number " + Str$(index) + "."

Case 10
    Feedback.Text = "You Selected Period (.)."

Case 11
    Feedback.Text = "You selected equal (=)."

Case 12 To 15
    Feedback.Text = "You selected a basic math function."

Case 16 To 19
    Feedback.Text = "You selected a memory function."

Case 20

    Feedback.Text = "You selected percent."

Case 21

    Feedback.Text = "You selected square root."

Case 22

    Feedback.Text = "You selected clear."

Case 23

    Feedback.Text = "You selected all clear."

End Select

End Sub
```

How It Works

By building an array of image controls, only one set of code has to be developed to handle indicating which calculator button is selected. The index parameter is used to indicate which hot spot is selected in the feedback text box.

Comments

Using a single image control to cover a rectangular hot spot works fine. But this will not work well when the hot spot to be defined is not rectangular in shape. In the next How-To, this problem is solved.

4.4 How do I...
Create irregularly shaped hot spots on a picture?

COMPLEXITY: INTERMEDIATE

Problem

I would like to be able to define irregularly shaped hot spots that will let users select parts of a complex image.

Technique

By developing a simple hot spot editor and using several of the Windows APIs, you can develp hot spots of any shape and size.

Steps

Open and run OUTLINER.VBP. The running program appears as shown in Figure 4-4-1.

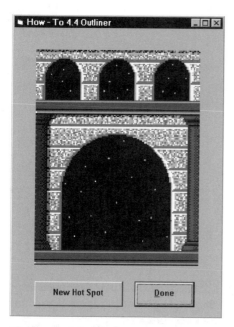

Figure 4-4-1 The form at runtime

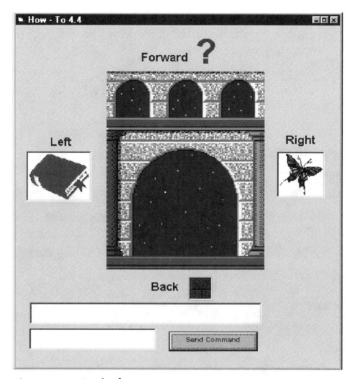

Figure 4-4-2 The form at runtime

To define the hot spots on the arches image, click on the New Hot Spot button. Then begin outlining the hot spot by clicking around it. For the game that will be developed, create hot spots for the four arches, the two columns, and the higher and lower scaffolding. Each hot spot will be saved in succession in a hot# file, where # indicates the hot spot number. The data in the files is the code necessary to outline the hot spot. To see the irregular hot spots in action, open and run 4-4.VBP. The program appears as shown in Figure 4-4-2.

All of the major objects on ARCHES.BMP have been outlined and defined with an irregular polygon. The hot# files are provided with the example. By default, the only area not covered is the stone of the arches. Try clicking on the various objects on the image to see what message is provided in the text box.

This example implements the familiar adventure puzzle/game. By clicking on the various objects on the arches bitmap, feedback will be given about the particular object. Or you can type in "Look <object>" in the command text box to get a description of that object. Your goal is to pick what direction to move in. You can get clues to what lies in a direction by clicking on the icons, such as the ?, next to the direction keywords (e.g., Left). To choose which direction you want to move in, click on a direction label or type in "Go <direction>" (or just "direction") in the command text box. Depending on the direction you have chosen, the program takes the appropriate actions.

1. Create a new project called OUTLINE.VBP. Add the objects and properties listed in Table 4-4-1 to Form1 and save the form as OUTLINE.FRM.

Table 4-4-1 The project form's objects and properties

OBJECT	PROPERTY	SETTING
Form	Name	Form1
	Auto3D	-1 'True
	Caption	"How-To4.4 Outliner"
	FillColor	&H000000FF&
	FillStyle	0 'Solid
	ForeColor	&H00FF0000&
CommandButton	Name	NewHot
	Caption	"New Hot Spot"
	Font	
	name	"Arial"
CommandButton	Name	Done
	Caption	"&Done"
	Font	
	name	"Arial"
Image	Name	backimage
	Picture	"c:\windows\arches.bmp"
	Stretch	-1 'True

2. Add the following code to the general declarations section of the form. The counters for counting the hot spots and points of the outline are declared.

```
'  HotCounter will be used to count through
'  the number of hot spots created
Dim hotcounter As Integer

'  CounterVal tracks the points index
Dim CounterVal As Integer
```

3. When the image is clicked on, the coordinates of the pixel are stored in the file. Note that CounterVal tracks the index into the points array.

```
Private Sub backimage_MouseDown(Button As Integer, Shift As Integer, X ↵
As Single, Y As Single)

Print #1, "pts(" & CounterVal & ").x = " & X
Print #1, "pts(" & CounterVal & ").y = " & Y

CounterVal = CounterVal + 1

End Sub
```

4. When the NewHot button is selected, the hot counter is incremented and the next hot spot file is opened for storage of the points.

```
Private Sub NewHot_Click()

Close #1

hotcounter = hotcounter + 1
CounterVal = 0

file$ = Str$(hotcounter)
file$ = Right$(file$, Len(file$) - 1)
file$ = App.Path + "\hot" + file$

Open file$ For Output As #1

End Sub
```

5. When the Done button is selected, the program is ended.

```
Private Sub Done_Click()
End
End Sub
```

6. Create a new project called 4-4.VBP. Add the objects and properties listed in Table 4-4-2 to Form1 and save the form as 4-4.FRM.

Table 4-4-2 The project form's objects and properties

OBJECT	PROPERTY	SETTING
Form	Name	Form1
	Auto3D	-1 'True
	BackColor	&H00E0E0E0&
	Caption	"How-To 4.4"
PictureBox	Name	BookPict
	AutoSize	-1 'True

continued on next page

continued from previous page

OBJECT	PROPERTY	SETTING
	BorderStyle	0 'None
	Picture	"Book.bmp"
PictureBox	Name	ButterflyPict
	AutoSize	-1 'True
	BorderStyle	0 'None
	Picture	"Outdoor.bmp"
PictureBox	Name	BrickPict
	AutoSize	-1 'True
	Picture	"c:\windows\redbrick.bmp"
TextBox	Name	Comm
CommandButton	Name	Send
	Caption	"Send Command"
	Font	
	name	"Arial"
TextBox	Name	FeedBack
	Enabled	0 'False
	MultiLine	-1 'True
Label	Name	direct
	Alignment	2 'Center
	AutoSize	-1 'True
	BackStyle	0 'Transparent
	Caption	"Left"
	Font	
	name	"Arial"
	size	12.6
Label	Name	direct
	Alignment	2 'Center
	AutoSize	-1 'True
	BackStyle	0 'Transparent
	Caption	"Right"

OBJECT	PROPERTY	SETTING
	Font	
	name	"Arial"
	size	12.6
	Index	2
Label	Name	direct
	Alignment	2 'Center
	AutoSize	-1 'True
	BackStyle	0 'Transparent
	Caption	"Back"
	Font	
	name	"Arial"
	size	12.6
	Index	1
Label	Name	direct
	Alignment	2 'Center
	AutoSize	-1 'True
	BackStyle	0 'Transparent
	Caption	"Forward"
	Font	
	name	"Arial"
	size	12.6
	Index	0
Image	Name	backimage
	Picture	"c:\windows\arches.bmp"
	Stretch	-1 'True
Label	Name	Question
	AutoSize	-1 'True
	BackColor	&H00E0E0E0&
	Caption	"?"
	Font	
	name	"Arial"
	size	36
	ForeColor	&H00C00000&

7. When the image is clicked on, a check is done to see if any of the defined hot spots have been selected. If none of them has been, then by default the stone is selected. Regardless of the case, the appropriate feedback is given.

```
Private Sub backimage_MouseDown(Button As Integer, Shift As Integer, x ↵
As Single, y As Single)

'  Check to see which hot spot was selected
HotSelect = ImageClick(x, y)

'  Depending on the hot spot, the appropriate
'  feed back will be given.
Select Case HotSelect

    Case 1, 5
        '  When any of the scaffolding is selected, we
        '  display the appropriate message.  Note that
        '  to display the " symbol we use the chr$
        '  function
        feedback.Text = "You think to yourself, " + Chr$(34) + "Interesting ↵
                Scaffolding" + Chr$(34)

    Case 2
        '  When any one of the image hot spots of the main
        '  arch has been selected, we will display the
        '  appropriate message.
        feedback.Text = "A steep drop is seen beyond the arch."

    Case 3, 4
        '  When any of the columns are selected we will display
        '  the appropriate message.
        feedback.Text = "The columns are encrypted with weird pictographs. ↵
                If only you had a translation book."

    Case 6, 7, 8
        '  If the first window is selected we then
        '  display the appropriate message.
        feedback.Text = "You see in the sky a small sliver of moon."

    Case Else
        '  If none of the hot spots was selected,
        '  then stone must have been selected
        feedback.Text = "The walls are stony silent"

End Select

End Sub
```

8. The following routines handle giving feedback when the icons are selected.

```
Private Sub BookPict_Click()

'  The following message is given when
'  the book is selected
```

```
feedback.Text = "Maybe a library?"

End Sub

Private Sub BrickPict_Click()

'  The following message is given when
'  the red brick is selected.
feedback.Text = "It looks like brick to me!"

End Sub

Private Sub ButterflyPict_Click()

'  Display the butterfly feedback
feedback.Text = "Butterflies are usually found in the great outdoors."

End Sub

Private Sub Question_Click()

'  When the question mark is selected
'  we give the follwing message
feedback.Text = "Who knows??? Try it!"

End Sub
```

9. The direction array handles clicking on the direction labels. The index of the control array is checked to give appropriate feedback.

```
Private Sub direct_click(Index As Integer)

'  When one of the direction indicators is
'  selected, we will give the appropriate message
'  and take the appropriate action.
If Index = 0 Then MsgBox "You have expired due to multiple injuries from ↵
your steep jump."
If Index = 1 Then feedback.Text = "You run into a brick wall and it ↵
really hurts.": Exit Sub
If Index = 2 Then MsgBox "You have gone right to the great outdoors."
If Index = 3 Then MsgBox "You have gone left into a big library."

End

End Sub
```

10. When the form is loaded, the hot spot regions are defined.

```
Private Sub Form_Load()
'  Make the hot spot regions
MakeRegion
End Sub
```

11. When the form is unloaded, the hot spot regions are deleted.

```
Private Sub Form_Unload(Cancel As Integer)

'   Delete the created regions
DeleteRegions

End Sub
```

12. When the Send button is selected, the text in the comm text box is interpreted. If a valid command is entered, the appropriate action is taken.

```
Private Sub Send_Click()

'   To make interpretation easy, we will make
'   sure that the entered message is all in
'   upper case.
comm.Text = UCase$(comm.Text)

'   For this example, we only allow 5 messages to be
'   entered.  We will check to see which if any of the
'   messages has been entered.  We then call the direct
'   click function to handle presenting the appropriate messages.
If comm.Text = "GO RIGHT" Or comm.Text = "RIGHT" Then direct_click (2)

If comm.Text = "GO FORWARD" Or comm.Text = "FORWARD" Then MsgBox "You ↵
have expired due to multiple injuries from your steep jump.": End

If comm.Text = "GO BACK" Or comm.Text = "BACK" Then direct_click (1): Exit Sub
If comm.Text = "GO LEFT" Or comm.Text = "LEFT" Then direct_click (3)
If comm.Text = "JUMP" Then direct_click (4)

'   In an unknown command has been entered, we notify the user
feedback.Text = "That command is not recognized"

End Sub
```

13. Insert a new module and save it as 4-5.BAS. Add the following code to the general declarations section of the form. The point data structure and the API functions for creating the hot spot regions are declared. Also, the handles to the hot spot regions are declared globally.

```
'   Declare the point structure
Private Type POINTAPI
    x As Integer
    y As Integer
End Type

'   CreatePolygonRgn will create a region that
'   has the specified shape in the points array

Private Declare Function CreatePolygonRgn Lib "GDI" (lpPoints As POINTAPI, ↵
ByVal nCount As Integer, ByVal nPolyFillMode As Integer) As Integer

'   PtInRegion will check to see if a given point
'   is in the specified region
```

```
Private Declare Function PtInRegion Lib "GDI" (ByVal hRgn As Integer, ByVal x ↵
As Integer, ByVal y As Integer) As Integer

' Deletes the object
Private Declare Function DeleteObject Lib "GDI" (ByVal hObject As Integer) ↵
As Integer

' Global handles to the regions
Dim Region1  As Integer
Dim Region2  As Integer
Dim Region3  As Integer
Dim Region4  As Integer
Dim Region5  As Integer
Dim Region6  As Integer
Dim Region7  As Integer
Dim Region8  As Integer
```

14. The MakeRegion function uses the points from the hot# files created in the Outline program. The points are used in the CreatePolygonRgn function to define the hot spots.

```
Public Sub MakeRegion()

' Declare an array of POINTAPI
'   points
Static pts(20) As POINTAPI

' Region 1 coordinates
pts(0).x = 12
pts(0).y = 3912
pts(1).x = 3300
pts(1).y = 3936
pts(2).x = 3312
pts(2).y = 4152
pts(3).x = 12
pts(3).y = 4152
pts(4).x = 0
pts(4).y = 3912

' Create the region
Region1 = CreatePolygonRgn(pts(0), 5, ALTERNATE)

' Region 2 coordinates
pts(0).x = 528
pts(0).y = 3852
pts(1).x = 552
pts(1).y = 2532
pts(2).x = 612
pts(2).y = 2352
pts(3).x = 708
pts(3).y = 2136
pts(4).x = 792
pts(4).y = 2016
pts(5).x = 1068
```

continued on next page

continued from previous page

```
pts(5).y = 1836
pts(6).x = 1248
pts(6).y = 1728
pts(7).x = 1512
pts(7).y = 1668
pts(8).x = 1692
pts(8).y = 1632
pts(9).x = 2052
pts(9).y = 1680
pts(10).x = 2148
pts(10).y = 1752
pts(11).x = 2448
pts(11).y = 1944
pts(12).x = 2616
pts(12).y = 2184
pts(13).x = 2724
pts(13).y = 2484
pts(14).x = 2748
pts(14).y = 2640
pts(15).x = 2748
pts(15).y = 3072
pts(16).x = 2760
pts(16).y = 3852
pts(17).x = 528
pts(17).y = 3840

'   Create the region
Region2 = CreatePolygonRgn(pts(0), 18, ALTERNATE)


'   Region 3 coordinates
pts(0).x = 12
pts(0).y = 3852
pts(1).x = 324
pts(1).y = 3864
pts(2).x = 252
pts(2).y = 3708
pts(3).x = 252
pts(3).y = 1452
pts(4).x = 396
pts(4).y = 1248
pts(5).x = 12
pts(5).y = 1236
pts(6).x = 12
pts(6).y = 3888

'   Create the region
Region3 = CreatePolygonRgn(pts(0), 7, ALTERNATE)

'   Region 4 coordinates
pts(0).x = 2976
pts(0).y = 3864
pts(1).x = 3324
pts(1).y = 3864
pts(2).x = 3312
```

```
pts(2).y = 1248
pts(3).x = 3000
pts(3).y = 1260
pts(4).x = 3084
pts(4).y = 1440
pts(5).x = 3096
pts(5).y = 3660
pts(6).x = 2988
pts(6).y = 3852

'   Create the region
Region4 = CreatePolygonRgn(pts(0), 7, ALTERNATE)

'   Region 5 coordinates
pts(0).x = 0
pts(0).y = 1212
pts(1).x = 3312
pts(1).y = 1224
pts(2).x = 3312
pts(2).y = 972
pts(3).x = 12
pts(3).y = 996
pts(4).x = 12
pts(4).y = 1200

'   Create the region
Region5 = CreatePolygonRgn(pts(0), 5, ALTERNATE)

'   Region 6 coordinates
pts(0).x = 192
pts(0).y = 912
pts(1).x = 192
pts(1).y = 480
pts(2).x = 252
pts(2).y = 360
pts(3).x = 312
pts(3).y = 276
pts(4).x = 420
pts(4).y = 192
pts(5).x = 516
pts(5).y = 168
pts(6).x = 648
pts(6).y = 192
pts(7).x = 780
pts(7).y = 252
pts(8).x = 876
pts(8).y = 348
pts(9).x = 876
pts(9).y = 480
pts(10).x = 864
pts(10).y = 696
pts(11).x = 888
pts(11).y = 876
pts(12).x = 180
pts(12).y = 912
```

continued on next page

continued from previous page

```
'  Create the region
Region6 = CreatePolygonRgn(pts(0), 13, ALTERNATE)

'  Region 7 coordinates
pts(0).x = 1308
pts(0).y = 924
pts(1).x = 1272
pts(1).y = 444
pts(2).x = 1356
pts(2).y = 264
pts(3).x = 1572
pts(3).y = 156
pts(4).x = 1728
pts(4).y = 168
pts(5).x = 1920
pts(5).y = 300
pts(6).x = 1992
pts(6).y = 432
pts(7).x = 2016
pts(7).y = 624
pts(8).x = 2004
pts(8).y = 912
pts(9).x = 1296
pts(9).y = 900

'  Create the region
Region7 = CreatePolygonRgn(pts(0), 10, ALTERNATE)


'  Region 8 coordinates
pts(0).x = 2400
pts(0).y = 924
pts(1).x = 3096
pts(1).y = 924
pts(2).x = 3096
pts(2).y = 408
pts(3).x = 2988
pts(3).y = 288
pts(4).x = 2952
pts(4).y = 192
pts(5).x = 2772
pts(5).y = 144
pts(6).x = 2628
pts(6).y = 216
pts(7).x = 2508
pts(7).y = 264
pts(8).x = 2436
pts(8).y = 360
pts(9).x = 2412
pts(9).y = 456
pts(10).x = 2412
pts(10).y = 924

'  Create the region
```

```
Region8 = CreatePolygonRgn(pts(0), 11, ALTERNATE)

End Sub
```

15. The ImageClick function checks to see if the specified coordinates fall within any of the hot spot regions. The PtInRegion function is used to check the specified region.

```
Public Function ImageClick(x As Single, y As Single) As Integer

    '   Check to see if the point selected
    '   is in any of the hot spot regions.  If
    '   so then return the hot spot selected
    If PtInRegion(Region1, x, y) Then
        ImageClick = 1
        Exit Function
    End If

    If PtInRegion(Region2, x, y) Then
        ImageClick = 2
        Exit Function
    End If

    If PtInRegion(Region3, x, y) Then
        ImageClick = 3
        Exit Function
    End If

    If PtInRegion(Region4, x, y) Then
        ImageClick = 4
        Exit Function
    End If

    If PtInRegion(Region5, x, y) Then
        ImageClick = 5
        Exit Function
    End If

    If PtInRegion(Region6, x, y) Then
        ImageClick = 6
        Exit Function
    End If

    If PtInRegion(Region7, x, y) Then
        ImageClick = 7
        Exit Function
    End If

    If PtInRegion(Region8, x, y) Then
        ImageClick = 8
        Exit Function
    End If

End Function
```

16. The DeleteRegions function deletes the regions created. This function is called when the program ends.

```
Public Sub DeleteRegions()

'  Delete the created regions
throw = DeleteObject(Region1)
throw = DeleteObject(Region2)
throw = DeleteObject(Region3)
throw = DeleteObject(Region4)
throw = DeleteObject(Region5)
throw = DeleteObject(Region6)
throw = DeleteObject(Region7)
throw = DeleteObject(Region8)

End Sub
```

How It Works

The two-step process for defining and using irregular shaped hot spots provides for an effective and straightforward implementation method. The Outline program simply stores pixel locations of the mouse clicks entered by the user. Curves can easily be outlined by many close mouse clicks, and of course angular shapes are easily outlined.

The Outline program stores the mouse clicks in code-ready format in files named hot#, where the # sign indicates the hot spot number. As the game code demonstrates, the point definitions from the hot# files are easily imported and used.

To define the hot spots, several region functions and types are used to create and check for mouse clicks in the hot spots. Table 4-4-3 overviews each.

Table 4-4-3 Memory functions

FUNCTION	DESCRIPTION
POINTAPI	The data structure that describes a Windows point
CreatePolygonRgn	Creates the polygon region based on the set of points passed in
PtInRegion	Checks to see if the specified point falls within the specified region

When the user selects a spot on the image, a check is done to see what hot spot the mouse click falls into, and appropriate action is taken. By default, if the mouse click does not fall in a hot spot, then the stone background of the image is selected.

Comments

The Outline function could easily be expanded to create a complete module that could be added to a project to define hot spots for the specified graphic. This would bypass importing the text from the hot# files.

4.5 How do I...
Dissolve a picture with random rectangles?

COMPLEXITY: ADVANCED

Problem

Many multimedia programs include pictures dissolving with random rectangles of different patterns, colors, and the program background. I would like to add these effects to my graphics.

Technique

The Windows API provides powerful graphics tools that allow you to draw rectangles with various patterns, borders, and even other graphics. This How-To will introduce the Windows BitBlt, PatBlt, and Rectangle functions to demonstrate different drawing methods. It also uses the CreateHatchBrush, CreatePen, and CreateSolidBrush functions to develop different color fills, patterns, and pens.

To dissolve the picture randomly, Visual Basic 4.0's random function will be used to generate a number to indicate which rectangle should be filled. The timer control will be used to change the rate at which the picture is dissolved with the rectangles.

This example sets up an interface for changing the various inputs into the Windows API functions. This will allow you to test the various combinations conveniently and to see how the bitmap is filled in.

Steps

Open and run 4-5.VBP. The running program appears as shown in Figure 4-5-1.

There are literally thousands of color and pattern combinations you can choose to try out. The three main options provided here are copy the background onto the picture (thus dissolving the bitmap with the background), dissolve the picture with colored patterns and solids, and dissolve the picture with API rectangles. The difference between the latter two will become apparent while testing the program.

To change the rate of the rectangle fill, set the time interval to a new millisecond value. To change the number of rectangles, set the number of rows and columns to divide the picture into. The Fill Loops function sets the number of rectangles that will be filled for each timer interval. Increasing this value will speed up the fill.

To reset the picture, click on the Reset button. When this happens, the program takes a snapshot of the background of the picture. If you turn off the marble background, the gray screen will be extracted when the Reset button is selected.

Note that the background copy and the BitBlt copy functions are in a frame together. This signifies that only the background copy uses the BitBlt function and its raster copy options.

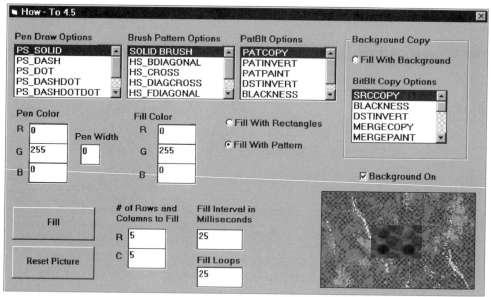

Figure 4-5-1 The form at runtime

1. Create a new project called 4-5.VBP. Add the objects and properties listed in Table 4-5-1 to Form1 and save the form as 4-5.FRM.

Table 4-5-1 The project form's objects and properties

OBJECT	PROPERTY	SETTING
Form	Name	Form1
	BackColor	&H00C0C0C0&
	BorderStyle	3 'Fixed Double
	Caption	"How-To 4.5"
TextBox	Name	FillText
	BackColor	&H00FFFFFF&
	Text	"25"
OptionButton	Name	PatOpt
	BackColor	&H00C0C0C0&
	Caption	"Fill With Pattern"
	Value	-1 'True

OBJECT	PROPERTY	SETTING
CheckBox	Name	BackOn
	BackColor	&H00C0C0C0&
	Caption	"Background On"
	Value	1 'Checked
TextBox	Name	PenWidth
	BackColor	&H00FFFFFF&
	Text	"0"
TextBox	Name	PenR
	BackColor	&H00FFFFFF&
	Text	"0"
TextBox	Name	PenG
	BackColor	&H00FFFFFF&
	Text	"255"
TextBox	Name	PenB
	BackColor	&H00FFFFFF&
	Text	"0"
TextBox	Name	FillR
	BackColor	&H00FFFFFF&
	Text	"0"
TextBox	Name	FillG
	BackColor	&H00FFFFFF&
	Text	"255"
TextBox	Name	FillB
	BackColor	&H00FFFFFF&
	Text	"0"
OptionButton	Name	BackOpt
	BackColor	&H00C0C0C0&

continued on next page

continued from previous page

OBJECT	PROPERTY	SETTING
	Caption	"Fill With Background"
ListBox	Name	BitBltCopy
	BackColor	&H00FFFFFF&
Frame	Name	BackGroundFrame
	BackColor	&H00C0C0C0&
	Caption	"Background Copy"
Label	Name	BitBltOptions
	BackColor	&H00C0C0C0&
	Caption	"BitBlt Copy Options"
ListBox	Name	Patbt
	BackColor	&H00FFFFFF&
CommandButton	Name	PictReset
	Caption	"Reset Picture"
	Font	
	name	"Arial"
TextBox	Name	INTV
	BackColor	&H00FFFFFF&
	Text	"25"
CommandButton	Name	FillButton
	BackColor	&H00C0C0C0&
	Caption	"Fill"
	Font	
	name	"Arial"
ListBox	Name	PenType
	BackColor	&H00FFFFFF&
ListBox	Name	HatchBrush
	BackColor	&H00FFFFFF&

OBJECT	PROPERTY	SETTING
TextBox	Name	COLDIVIDE
	BackColor	&H00FFFFFF&
	Text	"5"
TextBox	Name	ROWDIVIDE
	BackColor	&H00FFFFFF&
	Text	"5"
OptionButton	Name	RectOpt
	BackColor	&H00C0C0C0&
	Caption	"Fill With Rectangles"
PictureBox	Name	HoldBack
	BorderStyle	0 'None
	Visible	0 'False
PictureBox	Name	RectFill
	AutoSize	-1 'True
	BorderStyle	0 'None
	Picture	(c:\windows\manycolo.bmp)
	Visible	0 'False
PictureBox	Name	BackGround
	Picture	(c:\windows\marble.bmp)
Timer	Name	Timer1
	Enabled	0 'False
	Interval	1
Label	Name	LoopsLabel
	AutoSize	-1 'True
	BackColor	&H00C0C0C0&
	Caption	"Fill Loops"
Label	Name	PatBltLabel
	BackColor	&H00C0C0C0&

continued on next page

continued from previous page

OBJECT	PROPERTY	SETTING
	Caption	"PatBlt Options"
Label	Name	BrushPatternLabel
	BackColor	&H00C0C0C0&
	Caption	"Brush Pattern Options"
Label	Name	PenDrawLabel
	BackColor	&H00C0C0C0&
	Caption	"Pen Draw Options"
Label	Name	PenColorLabel
	BackColor	&H00C0C0C0&
	Caption	"Pen Color"
Label	Name	PenWidthLabel
	AutoSize	-1 'True
	BackColor	&H00C0C0C0&
	Caption	"Pen Width"
Label	Name	FillColorLabel
	BackColor	&H00C0C0C0&
	Caption	"Fill Color"
Label	Name	PenRLabel
	AutoSize	-1 'True
	BackColor	&H00C0C0C0&
	Caption	"R"
Label	Name	PenGLabel
	AutoSize	-1 'True
	BackColor	&H00C0C0C0&
	Caption	"G"
Label	Name	PenBLabel
	AutoSize	-1 'True

OBJECT	PROPERTY	SETTING
	BackColor	&H00C0C0C0&
	Caption	"B"
Label	Name	FillRLabel
	AutoSize	-1 'True
	BackColor	&H00C0C0C0&
	Caption	"R"
Label	Name	FillGLabel
	AutoSize	-1 'True
	BackColor	&H00C0C0C0&
	Caption	"G"
Label	Name	FillBLabel
	AutoSize	-1 'True
	BackColor	&H00C0C0C0&
	Caption	"B"
Label	Name	IntvLabel
	BackColor	&H00C0C0C0&
	Caption	"Fill Interval in Milliseconds"
Label	Name	NumRowsLabel
	BackColor	&H00C0C0C0&
	Caption	"# of Rows and Columns to Fill"
Label	Name	ColsLabel
	AutoSize	-1 'True
	BackColor	&H00C0C0C0&
	Caption	"C"
Label	Name	RowsLabel
	AutoSize	-1 'True
	BackColor	&H00C0C0C0&
	Caption	"R"

2. Create a new module and save it as 4-5.BAS. Add the following code to the general declarations section of 4-5.BAS to provide the necessary constants and function declarations for the API.

```
'  The following are the constant values for the type of paint option for BitBlt

Global Const SRCCOPY = &HCC0020
Global Const BLACKNESS = &H42&
Global Const DSTINVERT = &H550009
Global Const MERGECOPY = &HC000CA
Global Const MERGEPAINT = &HBB0226
Global Const NOTSRCCOPY = &H330008
Global Const NOTSRCERASE = &H1100A6
Global Const PATCOPY = &HF00021
Global Const PATINVERT = &H5A0049
Global Const PATPAINT = &HFB0A09
Global Const SRCAND = &H8800C6
Global Const SRCERASE = &H440328
Global Const SRCINVERT = &H660046
Global Const SRCPAINT = &HEE0086
Global Const WHITENESS = &HFF0062


'  The following are the constant values for the type of Hatch Pattern for the
'          188      188'  CreateHatchBrush function
Global Const HS_BDIAGONAL = 3
Global Const HS_CROSS = 4
Global Const HS_DIAGCROSS = 5
Global Const HS_FDIAGONAL = 2
Global Const HS_HORIZONTAL = 0
Global Const HS_VERTICAL = 1


'  The following are the constant values for the type of Pen
Global Const PS_SOLID = 0
Global Const PS_DASH = 1
Global Const PS_DOT = 2
Global Const PS_DASHDOT = 3
Global Const PS_DASHDOTDOT = 4
Global Const PS_NULL = 5
Global Const PS_INSIDEFRAME = 6


'  These are the bitmap manipulation functions
'  that will be used for the image manipulation.

Declare Function BitBlt Lib "GDI" (ByVal hDestDC As Integer, ByVal X As ↵
Integer, ByVal Y As Integer, ByVal nWidth As Integer, ByVal nHeight As ↵
Integer, ByVal hSrcDC As Integer, ByVal XSrc As Integer, ByVal YSrc As ↵
Integer, ByVal dwRop As Long) As Integer

Declare Function PatBlt Lib "GDI" (ByVal hDC As Integer, ByVal X As Integer, ↵
ByVal Y As Integer, ByVal nWidth As Integer, ByVal nHeight As Integer, ByVal ↵
dwRop As Long) As Integer

Declare Function Rectangle Lib "GDI" (ByVal hDC As Integer, ByVal X1 As ↵
Integer, ByVal Y1 As Integer, ByVal X2 As Integer, ByVal Y2 As Integer) ↵
As Integer
```

```
Declare Function SelectObject Lib "GDI" (ByVal hDC As Integer, ByVal hObject ↵
As Integer) As Integer

Declare Function CreatePen Lib "GDI" (ByVal nPenStyle As Integer, ByVal ↵
nWidth  As Integer, ByVal crColor As Long) As Integer

Declare Function DeleteObject Lib "GDI" (ByVal hObject As Integer) As Integer

Declare Function CreateHatchBrush Lib "GDI" (ByVal nIndex As Integer, ByVal ↵
crColor As Long) As Integer

Declare Function CreateSolidBrush Lib "GDI" (ByVal crColor As Long) As Integer
```

3. Add the following code to the general declarations section of Form1 to provide values to track the selected graphics parameters.

```
' This global value stores whether the form paint function has captured the
' background behind the rect fill picture
Dim FIRST As Integer

' These two values store the number of rows and columns to fill the picture
' in with
Dim DIVIDEr As Integer
Dim DIVIDEc As Integer

' Array to store the x and y coordinates of the rectangles to be filled
Dim Pts() As Double

' When we are random filling the picture, we need to store if a rectangle
' has all ready been filled
Dim Hit() As Integer

' The bltcopy variable stores the copy option - used in the BitBlt function
Dim BltCopy As Double

' The penp variable stores the type of pen copy to be performed - used in the '
' CreatePen function
Dim PenP As Integer

' Stores the hatch pattern selected - used in the CreateHatchBrush function
Dim Hatch  As Integer

' Stores the type of Pattern Copy to be performed - used in the
' PatCopy function
Dim PatC As Double

' Stores the handle to the pen we will create
Dim hpen As Integer

' stores the handle to the old pen that was selected
Dim HpenOld As Integer

' stores the handle to the brush we will create
Dim Hbr As Integer
```

continued on next page

continued from previous page

```
' stores the handle to the previous brush selected
Dim HbrOld As Integer
```

4. Add this code to the BackOn function. This code turns on and off the background picture.

```
Private Sub BackOn_Click()
' The following two statements check to see if the back on
' box is x'd  or not.  If it is then the background is visible
' otherwise its visible property is set to false
If BackOn.Value = 0 Then BackGround.Visible = False
If BackOn.Value = 1 Then BackGround.Visible = True
End Sub
```

5. Add the following code to the general declarations section of the form. In general, this code allows a specific number of digits to be typed into the text boxes. It also allows the backspace key to be used.

```
Private Sub checkkey(key As Integer, Txt As Control)

' The following code will only allow three numerical digits
' to be entered in the text field.  We also check to see
' if the BackSpace character was selected and allow it to
' be used to delete values

If key <> 8 Then
    If Len(Txt.Text) > 2 Then key = 0
End If

If key = 8 Then
    If Len(Txt.Text) > 3 Then key = 0
End If

If key <> 8 Then
    If key < 48 Or KeyAscii > 57 Then key = 0
End If

End Sub
```

6. Add the following code to the specified functions. The Checkkey function is called to make sure the key entered is a digit.

```
Private Sub COLDIVIDE_KeyPress(KeyAscii As Integer)

' Check the character entered
checkkey KeyAscii, coldivide

End Sub

Private Sub FillB_KeyPress(KeyAscii As Integer)

' Check the character entered
checkkey KeyAscii, fillb
```

```
End Sub

Private Sub FillG_KeyPress(KeyAscii As Integer)

'  Check the character entered
checkkey KeyAscii, fillg

End Sub

Private Sub FillR_KeyPress(KeyAscii As Integer)

'  Check the character entered
checkkey KeyAscii, fillr

End Sub

Private Sub filltext_KeyPress(KeyAscii As Integer)

'  Check the character entered
checkkey KeyAscii, filltext

End Sub

Private Sub INTV_KeyPress(KeyAscii As Integer)

'  Check the character entered
checkkey KeyAscii, intv

End Sub

Private Sub PenB_KeyPress(KeyAscii As Integer)

'  Check the character entered
checkkey KeyAscii, penb

End Sub

Private Sub ROWDIVIDE_KeyPress(KeyAscii As Integer)

'  Check the character entered
checkkey KeyAscii, rowdivide

End Sub

Private Sub PenG_KeyPress(KeyAscii As Integer)

'  Check the character entered
checkkey KeyAscii, peng

End Sub

Private Sub PenR_KeyPress(KeyAscii As Integer)

'  Check the character entered
```

continued on next page

continued from previous page

```
checkkey KeyAscii, penr

End Sub

Private Sub PenWidth_KeyPress(KeyAscii As Integer)

'   Check the character entered
checkkey KeyAscii, penwidth

End Sub
```

7. Add the following code to the general declarations section of Form1. This code interprets the list box selections.

```
'   This function will take the selected values in the list boxes and set
'   the variables for each API function that may be called
Private Sub ConVal()

'   The following if statements find out which BitBlt copy
'   option is selected.  It then sets the global BltCopy
'   variable to have the value stored in the appropriate constant
If BitBltCopy.Selected(0) = True Then BltCopy = SRCCOPY
If BitBltCopy.Selected(1) = True Then BltCopy = BLACKNESS
If BitBltCopy.Selected(2) = True Then BltCopy = DSTINVERT
If BitBltCopy.Selected(3) = True Then BltCopy = MERGECOPY
If BitBltCopy.Selected(4) = True Then BltCopy = MERGEPAINT
If BitBltCopy.Selected(5) = True Then BltCopy = NOTSRCCOPY
If BitBltCopy.Selected(6) = True Then BltCopy = NOTSRCERASE
If BitBltCopy.Selected(7) = True Then BltCopy = PATCOPY
If BitBltCopy.Selected(8) = True Then BltCopy = PATINVERT
If BitBltCopy.Selected(9) = True Then BltCopy = PATPAINT
If BitBltCopy.Selected(10) = True Then BltCopy = SRCAND
If BitBltCopy.Selected(11) = True Then BltCopy = SRCERASE
If BitBltCopy.Selected(12) = True Then BltCopy = SRCINVERT
If BitBltCopy.Selected(13) = True Then BltCopy = SRCPAINT
If BitBltCopy.Selected(14) = True Then BltCopy = WHITENESS

'   The following if statements find out which hatch brush
'   option is selected.  It then sets the global Hatch
'   variable to have the value stored in the appropriate constant
If HatchBrush.Selected(1) = True Then Hatch = HS_BDIAGONAL
If HatchBrush.Selected(2) = True Then Hatch = HS_CROSS
If HatchBrush.Selected(3) = True Then Hatch = HS_DIAGCROSS
If HatchBrush.Selected(4) = True Then Hatch = HS_FDIAGONAL
If HatchBrush.Selected(5) = True Then Hatch = HS_HORIZONTAL
If HatchBrush.Selected(6) = True Then Hatch = HS_VERTICAL

'   The following if statements find out which pen copy
'   option is selected.  It then sets the global PenP
'   variable to have the value stored in the appropriate constant
If PenType.Selected(0) = True Then PenP = PS_SOLID
If PenType.Selected(1) = True Then PenP = PS_DASH
If PenType.Selected(2) = True Then PenP = PS_DOT
If PenType.Selected(3) = True Then PenP = PS_DASHDOT
If PenType.Selected(4) = True Then PenP = PS_DASHDOTDOT
```

```
If PenType.Selected(5) = True Then PenP = PS_NULL
If PenType.Selected(6) = True Then PenP = PS_INSIDEFRAME


'   The following if statements find out which PatCopy copy
'   option is selected.  It then sets the global PatC
'   variable to have the value stored in the appropriate constant
If PatBt.Selected(0) = True Then PatC = PATCOPY
If PatBt.Selected(1) = True Then PatC = PATINVERT
If PatBt.Selected(2) = True Then PatC = PATPAINT
If PatBt.Selected(3) = True Then PatC = DSTINVERT
If PatBt.Selected(4) = True Then PatC = BLACKNESS
If PatBt.Selected(5) = True Then PatC = WHITENESS

End Sub
```

8. Add the following code to the FillButton_Click event. This code sets up dissolving the picture.

```
Private Sub FillButton_Click()

'   Call the ConVal function to set the neccessary variables for
'   the Win API functions
ConVal

'   This will seed the random number generator
Randomize

'   Set the row and column divide values
DIVIDEr = rowdivide.Text
DIVIDEc = coldivide.Text


'   Get the time interval entered by the user and set the timer
timer1.Interval = intv.Text

'   Make sure the user has not entered in a timer, row or column of 0.
'   If they have then we will default to 1
If DIVIDEr = 0 Then DIVIDEr = 1
If DIVIDEc = 0 Then DIVIDEc = 1
If timer1.Interval = 0 Then timer1.Interval = 1

'   Dimension the Pts array to store the indices of the rectangles to be filled
ReDim Pts(DIVIDEr * DIVIDEc, 2)

'   Dimension the Hit array to store whether or not a certain rectangle has
'   been filled
ReDim Hit(DIVIDEr * DIVIDEc)

'   The following for loop calculates the upper left corner coordinate of
'   each point to be filled.  C counts through the array to store the values
c = 1

For n = 1 To DIVIDEr
    For M = 1 To DIVIDEc
```

continued on next page

continued from previous page

```
      Pts(c, 0) = (RectFill.ScaleWidth / DIVIDEc) * (M - 1)
      Pts(c, 1) = (RectFill.ScaleHeight / DIVIDEr) * (n - 1)
      c = c + 1
      Next M
Next n


'  Get the integer value of the pen width
p = penwidth.Text

'  Get the integer values of the RGB values for the pen
r = penr.Text
g = peng.Text
b = penb.Text

'  Make sure that the RGB values entered are not over 255.  If
'  they are, then reset the r,g,b values and the text
If r > 255 Then penr.Text = "255": r = 255
If g > 255 Then peng.Text = "255": g = 255
If b > 255 Then penb.Text = "255": b = 255

'  Create the type of pen selected by the user.  CreatePen takes in the
'  type of pen to paint (PenP), the width (P), and the color (r,g,b)
hpen = CreatePen(PenP, p, RGB(r, g, b))

'  We need to select the created pen into the device (our fill rectangle)
'  SelectObject returns the handle of the object being replaced
HpenOld = SelectObject(RectFill.hDC, hpen)

'  Get the integer values of the RGB values for the fill
r = fillr.Text
g = fillg.Text
b = fillb.Text

'  Make sure that the RGB values entered are not over 255.  If
'  they are, then reset the r,g,b values and the text
If r > 255 Then penr.Text = "255": r = 255
If g > 255 Then peng.Text = "255": g = 255
If b > 255 Then penb.Text = "255": b = 255


'  We first need to see if a solid brush was selected, which
'  is the first item in the list.  If so, we will use the
'  create solid brush API function to make the brush with the
'  appropriate color.  We will store the handle in Hbr.  Otherwise
'  we will create the hatch brush selected with the
'  fill colors selected.
If HatchBrush.Selected(0) = True Then
    Hbr = CreateSolidBrush(RGB(r, g, b))
Else
    Hbr = CreateHatchBrush(Hatch, RGB(r, g, b))
End If


'  Select the new brush to be used in the picture to be
```

```
'  filled (RectFill)
HbrOld = SelectObject(RectFill.hDC, Hbr)


'  Enable timer1 to begin randomly filling the picture
timer1.Enabled = True

End Sub
```

9. Add the following code to the Form_Load procedure. It ensures that the picture boxes are set up appropriately. Also, it calls the ListFill function to set up the list boxes.

```
Private Sub Form_Load()
'  Set First to 1 so that the code in the Form_Paint
'  is triggered.
FIRST = 1

'  Set the scale mode for the three pictures on the form to pixels
'  The Windows GDI API functions (i.e. BitBlt, PatBlt, Rectangle)
'  work in pixel coordinates.
RectFill.ScaleMode = 3
BackGround.ScaleMode = 3
HoldBack.ScaleMode = 3

'  Set the picture that will hold the background (HoldBack) to
'  have the same dimensions as the RectFill picture
HoldBack.Width = RectFill.Width
HoldBack.Height = RectFill.Height

'  Set up the lists
ListFill

End Sub
```

10. Add the following code to the Form_Paint procedure. This takes a snapshot of the background of the picture.

```
Private Sub Form_Paint()
'  Check to see if this is the first time we have been in the form paint
'  procedure.  Note that FIRST is set back to 0 when the Reset Picture button is
'  clicked.  That way if the background is off, then the form section will be
'  grabbed instead of the BackGround Picture

If FIRST = 1 Then

    '  Reset FIRST so that when the form is repainted, this code will not
    '  be executed
    FIRST = 0

    '  Turn on the HoldBack AutoRedraw picture to true.
    HoldBack.AutoRedraw = True

    '  Note that currently the RectFill picture is not visible so that the
    '  following BitBlt function will copy the current image from the RectFill
```

continued on next page

continued from previous page

```
'   picture, which when RectFill is not visible, is the image behind the
'   RectFill picture.  In this case it will either be the gray of the form
'   or the BackGround picture
throwaway = BitBlt(HoldBack.hDC, 0, 0, RectFill.ScaleWidth, ↵
RectFill.ScaleHeight, RectFill.hDC, 0, 0, SRCCOPY)

'   Refresh the HoldBack picture so that it now 'shows' and stores the image
HoldBack.Refresh

'   Make the RectFill picture visible
RectFill.Visible = True

End If

End Sub
```

11. Add the following code to the general declarations section of Form1. This code sets up the list boxes.

```
Private Sub ListFill()

'   The following code adds the appropriate items
'   to each list box.
BitBltCopy.AddItem "SRCCOPY"
BitBltCopy.AddItem "BLACKNESS"
BitBltCopy.AddItem "DSTINVERT"
BitBltCopy.AddItem "MERGECOPY"
BitBltCopy.AddItem "MERGEPAINT"
BitBltCopy.AddItem "NOTSRCCOPY"
BitBltCopy.AddItem "NOTSRCERASE"
BitBltCopy.AddItem "PATCOPY"
BitBltCopy.AddItem "PATINVERT"
BitBltCopy.AddItem "PATPAINT"
BitBltCopy.AddItem "SRCAND"
BitBltCopy.AddItem "SRCERASE"
BitBltCopy.AddItem "SRCINVERT"
BitBltCopy.AddItem "SRCPAINT"
BitBltCopy.AddItem "WHITENESS"
BitBltCopy.Selected(0) = True

HatchBrush.AddItem "SOLID BRUSH"
HatchBrush.AddItem "HS_BDIAGONAL"
HatchBrush.AddItem "HS_CROSS"
HatchBrush.AddItem "HS_DIAGCROSS"
HatchBrush.AddItem "HS_FDIAGONAL"
HatchBrush.AddItem "HS_HORIZONTAL"
HatchBrush.AddItem "HS_VERTICAL"
HatchBrush.Selected(0) = True

PenType.AddItem "PS_SOLID"
PenType.AddItem "PS_DASH"
PenType.AddItem "PS_DOT"
PenType.AddItem "PS_DASHDOT"
PenType.AddItem "PS_DASHDOTDOT"
PenType.AddItem "PS_NULL"
```

```
PenType.AddItem "PS_INSIDEFRAME"
PenType.Selected(0) = True


PatBt.AddItem "PATCOPY"
PatBt.AddItem "PATINVERT"
PatBt.AddItem "PATPAINT"
PatBt.AddItem "DSTINVERT"
PatBt.AddItem "BLACKNESS"
PatBt.AddItem "WHITENESS"
PatBt.Selected(0) = True

End Sub
```

12. Add the following code to the Picture Reset button click event. It executes Form_Paint to restore the picture.

```
Private Sub PictReset_Click()
'  Make sure the timer is disabled if the user
'  clicks the button while a fill is taking place
timer1.Enabled = False

'  Turn off the RectFill Picture so that the Form_Paint Procedure will grab
'  the image behind it
RectFill.Visible = False

'  Set First so that the code in Form_Paint is executed
FIRST = 1

'  Call the Form_Paint procedure
Form_Paint
End Sub
```

13. Add the following code to the Timer1_Timer event. This is the main code that handles the dissolving of the picture.

```
Private Sub Timer1_Timer()

'  Dim the CWidth and RHeight variable to be double
'  to calculate each rectangle's height and width
'  accordingly
Dim CWidth As Double
Dim RHeight As Double

'  We will use this for loop to speed up the fill
'  beyond that of the timer.
For z = 1 To Val(filltext.Text)

'  The following do loop will generate a random
'  number in the specified range (# of rectangles)
'  Then we will signify that that rectangle has been
'  filled by setting the Hit array
Do
```

continued on next page

continued from previous page

```
    c = Int((DIVIDEc * DIVIDEr) * Rnd + 1)
Loop Until Hit(c) <> 1

Hit(c) = 1


'  Check to see if all of the rectangles have been filled.
'  If there is an unfilled rectangle, then set the FLAG
'  to 1.
Flag = 0
For n = 1 To DIVIDEr * DIVIDEc
    If Hit(n) <> 1 Then Flag = 1
Next n


'  Get the X and Y coordinates from PTS array which stores
'  the upper left points of each rectangle to be filled
XC = Pts(c, 0)
YC = Pts(c, 1)

'  Calculate the width and height of each rectangle.  It is important
'  to add a little 'padding' to the width and height to account
'  for rounding that may make the width or height          too short
CWidth = (RectFill.ScaleWidth / DIVIDEc) + 0.5
RHeight = (RectFill.ScaleHeight / DIVIDEr) + 0.5


'  The following checks to see if the fill with rectangle option is selected.
'  (RectOpt)  If so, we create a rectangle at the XC and YC coordinates with the
'  lower right points being at XC and YC coord plus the rectangle's width and
'  height.  The rectangle function uses the pen and brush selected.

If RectOpt.Value = True Then throwaway = Rectangle(RectFill.hDC, XC, YC, XC ↵
+ CWidth, YC + RHeight)

'  The following checks to see if the fill with pattern option is selected.
'  (PatOpt)  If so, we use the PatBlt option to draw in the specified pattern
'  into the RectFill picture.  The pattern will start at the XC and YC
'  coordinates with the Cwidth and RHeight width and height.  The PatC variable
'  represents the pattern chosen by the user.

If PatOpt.Value = True Then throwaway = patblt(RectFill.hDC, XC, YC, CWidth, ↵
RHeight, PatC)

'  The following checks to see if the fill with background option is selected.
'  (BacKOpt)  If so, we use the BitBlt option to take the specified rectangle
'  rectangle from the HoldBack picture and draw them into the RectFill Picture.

If backopt.Value = True Then throwaway = BitBlt(RectFill.hDC, XC, YC, CWidth, ↵
RHeight, HoldBack.hDC, XC, YC, BltCopy)

'  If flag was not set to 1 above (indicating unpainted rectangles), then the
'  random fill is done
If Flag = 0 Then
    '  Turn off the timer
```

```
            timer1.Enabled = False

            '  Delete the Pen and Brush objects created
            throwaway = deleteobject(hpen)
            throwaway = deleteobject(Hbr)

            '  Reset the form Pen and Brush objects for the RectFill picture
            throwaway = SelectObject(RectFill.hDC, HpenOld)
            throwaway = SelectObject(RectFill.hDC, HbrOld)

            '  Make sure the for loop ends.
            z = Val(filltext.Text)
End If

Next z

End Sub
```

How It Works

This How-To demonstrates several of the Windows API functions. Three primary keys to this How-To are important to analyze.

Windows API Functions

The three main "paint" functions are the BitBlt, PatBlt, and Rectangle functions. The BitBlt function allows you to copy from one device context (picture, form) to another. The raster option allows you to combine the source image with the destination image in different ways to perform different effects.

The PatBlt function is similar to the BitBlt function, but uses the current brush to paint on the device context. BitBlt copies from another device context (picture).

The Rectangle function draws rectangles with the current pen and brush for the device context being painted to (in this case a picture).

By using the brush, pen, and various paint functions, you can achieve interesting and effective image manipulation.

Random Fill

The FillButton_Click function handles setting up the random fill routine. It calculates the upper-left points (using the scale mode values of the picture) of the rectangles. The number and size of the rectangles are determined by the row and column values provided by you.

The Timer1_Timer function performs the dissolve. The hit() array is dimensioned to the number of rectangles the picture is to be dissolved with. When a new random rectangle is filled, the appropriate position in the hit() array is to set to 1. Once all the elements of the hit() array are set to 1, all the rectangles are filled. You can set the rate of the dissolve by setting the timer interval. You can speed up the fill by changing the number of fills per timer interval.

Background Copy

To dissolve a bitmap with the background showing through, a copy of the background of the picture must be made before the picture is displayed. This can be accomplished at the start of the form. Make sure that the picture visible property is set to false. When the form starts up, the Form_Paint procedure is called. This is where you can use BitBlt to copy the image in the picture to a storage area (another picture). Because the picture is not visible, its background is visible. In fact, the picture now contains a copy of the background. The BitBlt function makes a copy of the background stored in the picture. Then at the end of the Form_Paint event, you can make the picture visible. Make sure that the code in the Form_Paint event is not executed every time it is called. Otherwise you will not keep your copy of the picture intact when the Form_Paint event is called for other than these purposes.

The Pen Draw, Brush Pattern, and PatBlt options define the type of fill that takes place. The Rectangle API function can be changed by setting the various pen variables. As you will see later, the border on the filled rectangles changes.

The Windows API defines several standard brushes. These are listed in the Brush Pattern Options list box. The Pattern Fill and the Rectangle Fill options are affected by the type of brush selected. The CreateSolidBrush function is used for a solid brush and the CreateHatchBrush function is used to create a pattern brush.

BitBlt and PatBlt allow for different methods of "painting" the image. For example, BLACKNESS or WHITENESS will fill the image with black or white rectangles. Table 4-5-2 is a list of the logical operators used for each option.

Table 4-5-2 Descriptions of the various bitmap function parameters

PARAMETER	DESCRIPTION
SRCCOPY	Copies the source bitmap to the destination bitmap
BLACKNESS	Fills the destination bitmap with black pixels
DSTINVERT	Inverts the destination bitmap
MERGECOPY	Combines the pattern and the source bitmap by using the the Boolean AND operator
MERGEPAINT	Combines the inverted source bitmap with the destination bitmap by using the Boolean OR operator
NOTSRCCOPY	Copies the inverted source bitmap to the destination

PARAMETER	DESCRIPTION
NOTSRCERASE	Inverts the result of combining the destination and source bitmaps by using the Boolean OR operator
PATCOPY	Copies the pattern to the destination bitmap
PATINVERT	Combines the destination bitmap with the pattern by using the Boolean XOR operator
PATPAINT	Combines the inverted source bitmap with the pattern by using the Boolean OR operator. Combines the result of this operation with the destination bitmap by using the Boolean OR operator
SRCAND	Combines pixels of the destination and source bitmaps by using the Boolean AND operator
SRCERASE	Inverts the destination bitmap and combines the result with the source bitmap by using the Boolean AND operator
SRCINVERT	Combines pixels of the destination and source bitmaps by using the Boolean XOR operator
SRCPAINT	Combines pixels of the destination and source bitmaps by using the Boolean OR operator
WHITENESS	Fills the destination bitmap with white pixels

Comments

By using the various methods for dissolving a picture presented here, you can provide fast and effective image dissolves to enhance your programs. One feature not implemented here is to develop a "quilt" effect, with each rectangle filled in with a different color and pattern.

Keep in mind the rounding issues when calculating the rectangle's height and width values. This is not a problem for solid and picture dissolves as long as you always round up. But for the rectangle control, the pen widths may be noticeably off. Experiment with taking the rounding padding off in the Timer1_Timer event. Try using different row and column values to see what happens.

4.6 How do I...
Create wipes?

COMPLEXITY: ADVANCED

Problem

I would like to create popular image wipes such as top-to-bottom, left-to-right, and snake, that allow for smooth transition from one picture to another.

Technique

Once again you will see that by using the BitBlt API function and the timer control, you can build effective transitions between two different pictures. In this section, the new class features of Visual Basic 4.0 will be introduced. A new Wipe class will be developed to perform wipes between two images.

Steps

Open and run 4-6.VBP. The running program appears as shown in Figure 4-6-1. Select the different command buttons to view the different type of transitions. You can change the size of each rectangle fill by changing the number of rows and

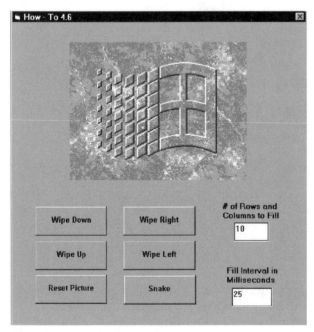

Figure 4-6-1 The form at runtime

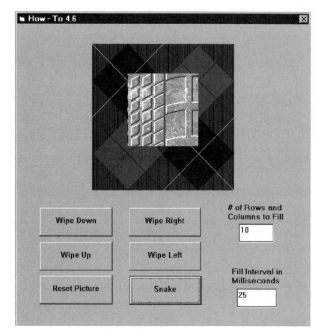

Figure 4-6-2 The snake wipe

columns to divide the transferred image into. Also, the speed of the fill can be changed by changing the timer interval. Figure 4-6-2 shows the snake wipe in mid-wipe.

1. Create a new project called 4-6.VBP. Add the objects and properties listed in Table 4-6-1 to Form1 and save it as 4-6.FRM.

Table 4-6-1 The project form's objects and properties

OBJECT	PROPERTY	SETTING
Form	Name	Form1
	BackColor	&H00C0C0C0&
	BorderStyle	3 'Fixed Double
	Caption	"How-To 4.6"
CommandButton	Name	WipeButton
	BackColor	&H00C0C0C0&
	Caption	"Snake"

continued on next page

CHAPTER 4

continued from previous page

OBJECT	PROPERTY	SETTING
	Font	
	name	"Arial"
CommandButton	Name	WipeButton
	BackColor	&H00C0C0C0&
	Caption	"Reset Picture"
	Font	
	name	"Arial"
CommandButton	Name	WipeButton
	BackColor	&H00C0C0C0&
	Caption	"Wipe Right"
	Font	
	name	"Arial"
CommandButton	Name	WipeButton
	BackColor	&H00C0C0C0&
	Caption	"Wipe Left"
	Font	
	name	"Arial"
CommandButton	Name	WipeButton
	BackColor	&H00C0C0C0&
	Caption	"Wipe Up"
	Font	
	name	"Arial"
TextBox	Name	ROWDIVIDE
	BackColor	&H00FFFFFF&
	Text	"10"
PictureBox	Name	Picture3
	BackColor	&H00C0C0C0&
	BorderStyle	0 'None
TextBox	Name	INTV

OBJECT	PROPERTY	SETTING
	BackColor	&H00FFFFFF&
	Text	"25"
CommandButton	Name	WipeButton
	BackColor	&H00C0C0C0&
	Caption	"Wipe Down"
	Font	
	name	"Arial"
PictureBox	Name	Picture1
	AutoSize	-1 'True
	BackColor	&H00C0C0C0&
	BorderStyle	0 'None
	Picture	(c:\windows\windows1.bmp)
PictureBox	Name	Picture2
	AutoSize	-1 'True
	BackColor	&H00C0C0C0&
	BorderStyle	0 'None
	Picture	(c:\windows\tartan.bmp)
Timer	Name	Timer1
	Enabled	0 'False
	Interval	1
Label	Name	FillIntLabel
	BackColor	&H00C0C0C0&
	Caption	"Fill Interval in Milliseconds"
Label	Name	RowColLabel
	BackColor	&H00C0C0C0&
	Caption	"# of Rows and Columns to Fill"

2. Create a new class module and save it as 4-6.CLS. Add the following code to the general declarations section of the class to set up BitBlt.

```
'  These are the constants for the wipes
Const WDOWN = 1
Const WRIGHT = 2
Const WLEFT = 3
Const WUP = 4
Const WSNAKE = 5

'  The following are the constant values for the type of paint option for BitBlt
Const SRCCOPY = &HCC0020

'  BitBlt will be used to do the bit transfers
Private Declare Function BitBlt Lib "GDI" (ByVal hDestDC As Integer, ByVal X ↵
As Integer, ByVal Y As Integer, ByVal nWidth As Integer, ByVal nHeight As ↵
Integer, ByVal hSrcDC As Integer, ByVal XSrc As Integer, ByVal YSrc As ↵
Integer, ByVal dwRop As Long) As Integer

' Declare the four primary objects used in the wipe process
Private m_Pict1 As Object
Private m_Pict2 As Object
Private m_Pict3 As Object
Private m_timer As Object

'  Declare the m_PTS array, which will be used to handle
'  the filling of the snake wipe
Dim m_PTS() As Integer

'  Done will be used to indicate when the wipe is finished
Dim m_done As Integer

'  counter1 and counter2 will be used to
'  count through the rows and colums of the
'  image
Dim m_counter1 As Integer
Dim m_counter2 As Integer

'  divider and dividec will be used to hold
'  the number of rows and colums to divide
'  the picture into
Dim m_divider As Integer
Dim m_dividec As Integer
```

3. When the Wipe function is called, a parameter is sent to indicate which wipe will be performed. Depending on that, the appropriate function is called.

```
'  Wipe will be used to call the appropriate
'  wipe function
Public Sub Wipe(Wtype)
    If Wtype = WDOWN Then WIPEDOWN
    If Wtype = WUP Then WIPEUP
    If Wtype = WRIGHT Then WIPERIGHT
    If Wtype = WLEFT Then WIPELEFT
    If Wtype = WSNAKE Then snakewipe
End Sub
```

4. In the following functions, the appropriate objects for the wipes are passed into the class.

```
'  Get the timer control and assign
'   to a private variable
Public Property Set Timer(aControl As Object)
    Set m_timer = aControl
End Property


'  Get the picture control and assign
'   to a private variable
Public Property Set Pict3(aControl As Object)
    Set m_Pict3 = aControl
End Property


'  Get the picture control and assign
'   to a private variable
Public Property Set Pict2(aControl As Object)
    Set m_Pict2 = aControl
End Property


'  Get the picture control and assign
'   to a private variable
Public Property Set Pict1(aControl As Object)
    Set m_Pict1 = aControl
End Property
```

5. The Pictreset function handles resetting the wiped picture.

```
'  The initially displayed picture will be
'   reset
Public Sub pictreset()
    m_Pict1.Visible = True
    m_Pict1.Cls
End Sub
```

6. The Setup function handles preparing the two images for the wipe. Note that a special function is called to set up for the snake wipe.

```
Public Sub setup(wipetype, rowcol, interval)

'  A check is performed to see if a snake wipe is to
'   be performed.  If so, we call the snakesetup
'   function to setup for the snake wipe.
If wipetype = WSNAKE Then snakesetup rowcol, interval: Exit Sub

'  Set the number of rows and columns
m_divider = rowcol
m_dividec = rowcol

'  Check to see if a WDOWN or WRIGHT wipe
'   is to be performed.  If so, we set the
'   counter properties appropriately
If wipetype = WDOWN Or wipetype = WRIGHT Then
    '  Set counter1 to 1 and counter2 to 0   Note
```

continued on next page

continued from previous page

```
        '   that counter2 is incremented immediately
        '   to 1 in the timer
        m_counter1 = 1
        m_counter2 = 0
End If

'   Check to see if a WUP or WLEFT wipe is
'   to be performed.  If so, we set the
'   counter properties appropriately.
If wipetype = WUP Or wipetype = WLEFT Then

        '   Set counter1 to the number of rows
        '   and counter2 to the number of columns.
        '   Note that counter2 decreased immediately
        '   in the timer.
        m_counter1 = m_divider
        m_counter2 = m_dividec + 1
End If

'   Reset the done flag
m_done = 0

'   Make sure a 0 row and column has not been
'   entered
If m_divider = 0 Then m_divider = 1
If m_dividec = 0 Then m_dividec = 1

'   Set the timer interval
m_timer.interval = interval

'   Make sure a 0 timer interval has not been
'   entered
If m_timer.interval = 0 Then m_timer.interval = 1

'   Enable the timer
m_timer.Enabled = True

End Sub
```

7. The Snakesetup function handles preparing the two images for the wipe.

```
Private Sub snakesetup(rowcol, interval)

'   Reset the two counters
m_counter1 = 0
m_counter2 = 0

'   We get the number of rows and columns
'   that the image will be filled with.  We
'   will only use the row value to ensure that
'   a perfectly square snake fill is done.
m_divider = rowcol
m_dividec = rowcol
m_done = 0
```

```
'   PTS will hold the origin points of each square
'   to be filled.  The number of squares is equal to
'   the number of rows times the number of columns.
'   To make the snake fill logic straightforward we
'   will actually fill the diagonal blocks twice, so
'   we need to dimension extra points for those diagonal
'   blocks.  In some cases we will need one extra square
ReDim m_PTS((m_divider * m_dividec) + (m_divider * 2) + 1, 2)

'   Set the timer to the interval
m_timer.interval = interval

'   Check to make sure that a 0 interval has not been
'   entered.
If m_timer.interval = 0 Then m_timer.interval = 1

'   Set z to the number of rows (and columns) + 1
'   note z is decremented immediately, which is why
'   we set it to 1 greater
z = m_divider + 1

'   reset c, which is our counter
c = 0

'   diag will calculate the number of
'   squares diagonally to the center
Dim diag As Double

'   y will be used to convert that value to
'   an integer
Dim Y As Integer

'   calculate the number of diagonal squares
diag = (m_divider / 2) + 0.5

'   convert diag to an integer
Y = diag

'   Example 5.5 matrix
'
'   1,1  2,1  3,1  4,1  5,1
'   1,2  2,2  3,2  4,2  5,2
'   1,3  2,3  3,3  4,3, 5,3
'   1,4  2,4  3,4  4,4  5,5
'   1,5  2,5  3,5  4,5  5,5

'   This for loop will calculate the points of
'   each snake square in order to be filled.  We use
'   Y to calculate the number of row/columns from one
'   side into the center
For n = 1 To Y

    '   z will hold the number of squares in each
    '   row/column
    z = z - 1
```

continued on next page

CHAPTER 4

continued from previous page

```
' This for loop calculates the left column points
For a = n To z
c = c + 1

' Example points for a first column 5x5 break up:
' 1,1  1,2  1,3  1,4  1,5
m_PTS(c, 0) = n
m_PTS(c, 1) = a
Next a

' This for loop calculates the bottom row points
For g = n To z
c = c + 1

' Example points for a bottom row 5x5 break up:
' 1,5  2,5  3,5  4,5  5,5
m_PTS(c, 0) = g
m_PTS(c, 1) = z
Next g

' This for loop calculates the right column points
For d = z To n Step -1
c = c + 1

' Example points for a right column 5x5 break up:
' 5,5  5,4  5,3  5,2  5,1
m_PTS(c, 0) = z
m_PTS(c, 1) = d
Next d

' This for loop calculates the top row points
For e = z To n Step -1
c = c + 1

' Example points for a top row 5x5 break up:
' 5,1  4,1  3,1  2,1  1,1
m_PTS(c, 0) = e
m_PTS(c, 1) = n
Next e

Next n

' m is used as a counter if timer5, we need to reset it
m = 0

' enable timer5
m_timer.Enabled = True

End Sub
```

8. The Wipeup function is called from the timer event in the project with each timer tick. It performs the wipe from the bottom to the top of the image.

```
Private Sub WIPEUP()
```

```
'  To speed up the wipe we will fill Dividec number
'  of squares for each timer event
For a = m_dividec To 1 Step -1

'  We decrement counter2 which moves along the columns.
m_counter2 = m_counter2 - 1

'  If the top row has been reached then we stop the wipe
If m_counter1 = 0 Then m_done = 1: Exit Sub

'  if we have reached the first column we then reset counter2
'  to the last column (Dividec) and move up a row
If m_counter2 = 0 Then m_counter2 = m_dividec: m_counter1 = m_counter1 - 1

'  Calculate the actual pixel point of the origin of the
'  square.  Note that the origin is actually counter1 and
'  counter2 - 1
xc = (m_Pict1.ScaleWidth / m_dividec) * (m_counter2 - 1)
yc = (m_Pict1.ScaleHeight / m_divider) * (m_counter1 - 1)

'  Calculate the square width and height to be transferred
cwidth = (m_Pict1.ScaleWidth / m_dividec) + 0.5
rheight = (m_Pict1.ScaleHeight / m_divider) + 0.5

'  BitBlt the square to the image
throwaway = BitBlt(m_Pict1.hDC, xc, yc, cwidth, rheight, m_Pict3.hDC, xc, ↵
yc, SRCCOPY)

Next a

End Sub
```

9. The Wiperight function is called from the timer event in the project with each timer tick. It performs the wipe from the left to the right of the image.

```
Private Sub WIPERIGHT()

'  The code here is essentially the same as wipeup
'  except the xc and yc are reversed as explained
'  and the for loop runs to Divider and not Dividec
For a = 1 To m_divider

m_counter2 = m_counter2 + 1

If m_counter1 = m_divider + 1 Then m_done = 1: Exit Sub

If m_counter2 = m_dividec + 1 Then m_counter2 = 1: m_counter1 = m_counter1 + 1

'  counter1 and counter2 are switched from that of wipeup
'  that in effect switches the wipe from top to bottom to
'  left to right
xc = (m_Pict1.ScaleWidth / m_dividec) * (m_counter1 - 1)
yc = (m_Pict1.ScaleHeight / m_divider) * (m_counter2 - 1)
```

continued on next page

continued from previous page

```
cwidth = (m_Pict1.ScaleWidth / m_dividec) + 0.5
rheight = (m_Pict1.ScaleHeight / m_divider) + 0.5

throwaway = BitBlt(m_Pict1.hDC, xc, yc, cwidth, rheight, m_Pict3.hDC, xc, ↵
yc, SRCCOPY)

Next a

End Sub
```

10. The Wipeleft function is called from the timer event in the project with each timer tick. It performs the wipe from the right to the left of the image.

```
Private Sub WIPELEFT()

'   The code here is essentially the same as wipeup
'   except the xc and yc are reversed as explained
'   and the for loop runs to Divider and not Dividec

For a = m_divider To 1 Step -1

m_counter2 = m_counter2 - 1

If m_counter1 = 0 Then m_done = 1: Exit Sub

If m_counter2 = 0 Then m_counter2 = m_dividec: m_counter1 = m_counter1 - 1

'   counter1 and counter2 are switched from that of wipeup
'   that in effect switches the wipe from top to bottom to
'   right to left
xc = (m_Pict1.ScaleWidth / m_dividec) * (m_counter1 - 1)
yc = (m_Pict1.ScaleHeight / m_divider) * (m_counter2 - 1)

cwidth = (m_Pict1.ScaleWidth / m_dividec) + 0.5
rheight = (m_Pict1.ScaleHeight / m_divider) + 0.5

throwaway = BitBlt(m_Pict1.hDC, xc, yc, cwidth, rheight, m_Pict3.hDC, xc, ↵
yc, SRCCOPY)

Next a

End Sub
```

11. The Snakewipe function is called from the timer event in the project with each timer tick. It performs the spiraling transition.

```
Private Sub snakewipe()

'   To speed up the wipe we will fill Dividec number
'   of squares for each timer event
For a = 1 To m_divider

'   counter2 will increment through the pts array to get
'   the coordinates of the next square to be transferred
m_counter2 = m_counter2 + 1
```

```
'  We check to see if we have reached the last point
If m_counter2 = (m_divider * m_dividec) + (m_divider * 2) Then m_done = 1: ↵
Exit Sub

'  We will get the actual pixel point origins
xc = (m_Pict1.ScaleWidth / m_dividec) * (m_PTS(m_counter2, 0) - 1)
yc = (m_Pict1.ScaleHeight / m_divider) * (m_PTS(m_counter2, 1) - 1)

'  Calculate the width and height of the square to be
'   transferred
cwidth = (m_Pict1.ScaleWidth / m_dividec) + 0.5
rheight = (m_Pict1.ScaleHeight / m_divider) + 0.5

'  Transfer the square
throwaway = BitBlt(m_Pict1.hDC, xc, yc, cwidth, rheight, m_Pict3.hDC, xc, ↵
yc, SRCCOPY)

Next a

End Sub
```

12. The Wipedown function is called from the timer event in the project with each timer tick. It performs the wipe from the top to the bottom of the image.

```
Private Sub WIPEDOWN()

'  To speed up the wipe we will fill Divider number
'   of squares for each timer event
For a = 1 To m_dividec

'  increment m to move along the columns.
m_counter2 = m_counter2 + 1

'  We check to see if n has moved past the last row.  If so
'  we end the wipe
If m_counter1 = m_divider + 1 Then m_done = 1: Exit Sub

'  If m has been incremented past the last column, we then
'  reset m and move down a row
If m_counter2 = m_dividec + 1 Then m_counter2 = 1: m_counter1 = m_counter1 + 1

'  We calculate the actual pixel point in the picture to
'  move from.  Note that the origin of the square is actually
'  m and n minus 1.
xc = (m_Pict1.ScaleWidth / m_dividec) * (m_counter2 - 1)
yc = (m_Pict1.ScaleHeight / m_divider) * (m_counter1 - 1)

'  Calculate width and height of the square to be filled
cwidth = (m_Pict1.ScaleWidth / m_dividec) + 0.5
rheight = (m_Pict1.ScaleHeight / m_divider) + 0.5

throw% = BitBlt(m_Pict1.hDC, xc, yc, cwidth, rheight, m_Pict3.hDC, xc, ↵
yc, SRCCOPY)
```

continued on next page

continued from previous page

```
Next a

End Sub
```

13. Pictset handles setting up the pictures to have the appropriate properties. It also builds the transition picture, which will be large enough to transition over the displayed image.

```
Public Sub pictset()

' Make sure that all 3 pictures are set to
' a scalemode of 3 (pixels)
m_Pict1.ScaleMode = 3
m_Pict2.ScaleMode = 3
m_Pict3.ScaleMode = 3

'  Also ensure that the autoredraw
'  features are true on the two working
'  pictures
m_Pict2.AutoRedraw = True
m_Pict3.AutoRedraw = True

'  Since the two pictures are of different
'  sizes, we need to set our two working
'  pictures to the maximum dimensions of the
'  two combined.
If m_Pict1.Width > m_Pict2.Width Then W = m_Pict1.Width Else W = m_Pict2.Width

If m_Pict1.Height > m_Pict2.Height Then H = m_Pict1.Height Else ↵
H = m_Pict2.Height

'  Set picture1 and picture3 to have the
'  maximum dimensions of the two graphics.
'  Note:  Since the form and the two picture
'  boxes have the same back color, we cannot
'  tell that they are not autosized.
m_Pict1.Width = W
m_Pict1.Height = H
m_Pict3.Width = W
m_Pict3.Height = H

'  We are going to be transferring the picture from
'  picture2 to picture3.  We will center the image
'  in picture3.  When we go to wipe out picture1
'  with the new image in picture3, the gray area round
'  picture3 will effectively wipe out all of picture1
'  with the image centered.
xc = m_Pict3.ScaleWidth / 2 - m_Pict2.ScaleWidth / 2
yc = m_Pict3.ScaleHeight / 2 - m_Pict2.ScaleHeight / 2

throwaway = BitBlt(m_Pict3.hDC, xc, yc, m_Pict2.ScaleWidth, ↵
m_Pict2.ScaleHeight,  m_Pict2.hDC, 0, 0, SRCCOPY)

End Sub
```

14. When the wipe is done, the m_done flag is set to 1. The timer event needs to check this to end the wipe.

```
'  Return the value of m_done
Public Property Get done() As Integer
done = m_done
End Property
```

15. Add the following code to the general declarations section of the form. First, the Wipe class is declared globally. The button variable indicates which wipe the user wants to perform.

```
'  Globally declare our class
Dim WipeClass As WipeClass

'  Button will indicate which wipe was selected
Dim Button As Integer
```

16. Checkkey ensures that only three-digit numbers are entered into the text box.

```
Private Sub checkkey(KeyAscii As Integer, CText As Control)

'  We ensure that only a 3 digit number can be
'  entered.  We also allow the backspace key to
'  be used.
If KeyAscii <> 8 Then
    If Len(CText.Text) > 3 Then KeyAscii = 0
End If

If KeyAscii = 8 Then
    If Len(CText.Text) > 4 Then KeyAscii = 0
End If

If KeyAscii <> 8 Then
    If KeyAscii < 48 Or KeyAscii > 57 Then KeyAscii = 0
End If

End Sub
```

17. Form_Load handles setting up the class. It is important to pass the timer and the three pictures to the class. The Pictset function is then called to set up the pictures for the wipes.

```
Private Sub Form_Load()

'  Declare the new WipeClass object
Set WipeClass = New WipeClass

'  Initialize WipeClass with the appropriate timer
'  and three picture controls.
Set WipeClass.Timer = timer1
Set WipeClass.Pict1 = picture1
Set WipeClass.Pict2 = picture2
Set WipeClass.Pict3 = picture3
```

continued on next page

continued from previous page

```
'  Setup the pictures for the wip
WipeClass.pictset

End Sub
```

18. The following two functions handle checking to make sure the user is entering only digits into the text boxes.

```
Private Sub INTV_KeyPress(KeyAscii As Integer)

'  Ensure only valid keys have been entered
checkkey KeyAscii, intv

End Sub

Private Sub ROWDIVIDE_KeyPress(KeyAscii As Integer)

'  Ensure only valid keys have been entered
checkkey KeyAscii, rowdivide

End Sub
```

19. The timer handles calling the wipe procedures from the class. The done property of the class is checked to see when the wipe is finished.

```
Private Sub Timer1_Timer()

'  Run the Wipe method for the
'  the wipe specified in Button
WipeClass.Wipe Button

'  Check to see if the wipe has
'  been finished.
If WipeClass.done = 1 Then timer1.Enabled = False

End Sub
```

20. The wipe buttons are a control array with the correct index number set for each wipe. If the Picture Reset button is selected, then the Pictreset function is called. Otherwise, the Wipe setup function is called. The button variable is used to store which wipe is selected.

```
Private Sub WipeButton_Click(Index As Integer)

'  Check to see reset was selected, otherwise
'  setup the wipe selected and store the wipe
'  value in Button.  Note that Index will be the
'  appropriate constant for the setup routine.
If Index = 6 Then
    WipeClass.pictreset
Else
    WipeClass.setup Index, Val(rowdivide.Text), Val(intv.Text)
    Button = Index
```

```
End If

End Sub
```

How It Works

In this How-To, the new class features of Visual Basic 4.0 are introduced. An independent class has been developed that you can add to any of your projects to perform fades between two pictures. If you look at the code in the form closely, you will see that very few calls are made. Table 4-6-2 is an overview of the public (accessible) class functions and properties.

Table 4-6-2 The Wipe class properties and functions

PROPERTY/FUNCTION	DESCRIPTION
Done	Indicates whether or not a wipe procedure is in process (1 = true)
PictReset	Resets the originally displayed image
Pictset	Sets up the image for the wipes
Timer	This is the timer used to perform the wipe
Pict1	The displayed image
Pict2	The image to be transitioned in
Pict3	The temporary image built to ensure the transition works appropriately
Wipe	A function that handles calling the right procedures for the specified wipes
Setup	This function sets up for the specified wipe

When the form is loaded, a new instance of the class is created (Set WipeClass = New WipeClass). It is then important to set up the properties of the class. The Pict1, Pict2, Pict3, and Timer properties are set to the pictures on the form. Then the Pictset function is called to set up the images for the wipe. Next, the wipe selected by you needs to be set up. This is done with the Setup function. Finally, in each tick of the timer, the wipe procedure needs to be called with the specified wipe to be performed. When the wipe is finished, the Done property is set to one. Note that the nomenclature used in the class for variables and objects is the m_*Item*. The m_ indicates the item is a member of the class.

To understand how the class works, you must understand how the images are set up for the wipe. The original image is the one that appears at the start of the project. The transition image is the new image that will be "wiped" in. The transferred image is the image that is built in the Setup function of the class.

The set-up program builds a transfer picture that contains the transition image but it has a height and width that will cover both images. Figure 4-6-3 depicts how this new image is built. (Note: A, B, C, and D represent the rectangle's dimensions.)

Figure 4-6-3 Wipe image set up

The new transition image is now large enough in width and height to cover the displayed image and to hold the transition image. It is important to note that the back color of the form and all three pictures are set to the same shade of gray. The newly constructed image has a gray border around it. When the transition takes place, if the displayed image is wider or taller, the area that is not covered by the transition image is covered in gray and blends with the form. The best way to see this effect is to set the back color of Picture3 to white (or any other color). You may want to bypass building the new transition image to see what happens.

When one of the wipes is selected, the specified function moves through each row or column (depending on the wipe) and transfers the appropriate rectangle. The image is broken down into indices that reflect the number of rows and columns to divide the image into. Figure 4-6-4 is a good example. (Note: 30 represents the length of the height and width.)

When a block is transferred from one image to another, the origin of the square and the width and height are calculated from the overall image width and height. Using Figure 4-6-4, Table 4-6-3 represents the blocks transferred in the wipe.

Figure 4-6-4 Sample image divided into rows and columns

Table 4-6-3 Example transfer blocks

POINTS	PIXEL ORIGIN	BLOCK WIDTH AND HEIGHT
1,1	0,0	10x10
1,2	0,10	10x10
1,3	0,20	10x10
2,1	10,0	10x10
2,2	20,10	10x10
2,3	30,20	10x10
3,1	20,0	10x10
3,2	20,10	10x10
3,3	20,20	10x10

The image could be divided into several rows and one column (or vice versa) but several columns (or rows) give a more fluid effect. For slower systems, you may want to set the DivideC or DivideR variables to 1, depending on the wipe, to speed up the process.

In the Wipe functions, you will notice that several sections are transferred at once (e.g., For a = DivideR to 1 Step -1) in each call. This speeds up the wipe by wiping a larger section of the image for each Timer event. This is especially important if you are dividing the image into a large number of sections.

For the snake wipe, a slightly different approach is taken to do the transition. When the snake wipe is selected, an array is set up that will hold the indices in order of the snake fill. The pts() array would have indices in the following order for Figure 4-6-4.

pts() = (1,1) (2,1) (3,1) (3,2) (3,3) (2,3) (1,3) (1,3) (1,2) (1,1) (2,2)

The corners are represented twice in the array, and thus will be filled twice. To keep the programming logic simple and straightforward, this double counting is not accounted for. And it is only noticeable on very large snake fills, which tend to be very slow due to the number of transfers being done. The function then goes through the pts() array and displays each corresponding rectangle.

Comments

By using a few simple techniques, wipes and transitions between two images can be done effectively using the Windows API and Visual Basic 4.0. The new Wipe class can easily be added to your applications using the simple methods demonstrated.

4.7 How do I...
Perform a cross hatch and vertical blind fade in and out on a picture?

COMPLEXITY: ADVANCED

Problem

I would like to be able to fade images in and out using screens such as a cross hatch and vertical blind. This provides a visually effective method for having images transition in and out of my application.

Technique

In this section, we will reach into the Windows API functions to learn how to build monochrome bitmaps that can then be used as brushes for painting and filling images. Two new classes, CrossHatch and ScreenBuild, will be developed to perform the transition fades.

Steps

Open and run 4-7.VBP. The running program appears as shown in Figure 4-7-1. To change between the cross hatch and vertical blind fades, select the appropriate command button. To fade the image in or out, select the appropriate command button. If you would like to see the 8x8 bitmap and see the fade in slow motion, select the Slow Display box. This will allow you to see the various fade bitmaps and for a longer period. Figure 4-7-2 shows the cross hatch fade in progress.

1. Create a new project called 4-7.VBP. Add the objects and properties listed in Table 4-7-1 to Form1 and save the form as 4-7.FRM.

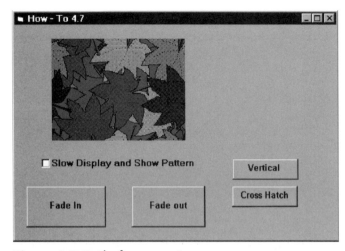

Figure 4-7-1 The form at runtime

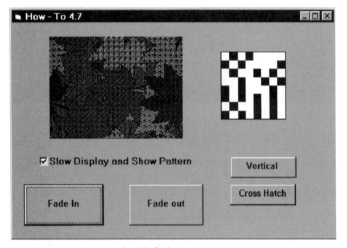

Figure 4-7-2 Cross hatch fade in progress

Table 4-7-1 The project form's objects and properties

OBJECT	PROPERTY	SETTING
Form	Name	Form1
	AutoRedraw	-1 'True
	Caption	"How-To 4.7"
CommandButton	Name	Cross

continued on next page

continued from previous page

OBJECT	PROPERTY	SETTING
	Caption	"Cross Hatch"
	Font	
	name	"Arial"
CommandButton	Name	Vertical
	Caption	"Vertical "
	Font	
	name	"Arial"
CheckBox	Name	SlowDisp
	Caption	"Slow Display and Show Pattern"
PictureBox	Name	BlowUpPict
	ScaleMode	3 'Pixel
	Visible	0 'False
CommandButton	Name	FadeOut
	Caption	"Fade out"
	Font	
	name	"Arial"
CommandButton	Name	FadeIn
	Caption	"Fade In"
	Font	
	name	"Arial"
PictureBox	Name	Picture4
	AutoSize	-1 'True
	BorderStyle	0 'None
PictureBox	Name	Picture2
	AutoSize	-1 'True
	BorderStyle	0 'None
	Picture	(c:\windows\leaves.bmp)
PictureBox	Name	Picture3

OBJECT	PROPERTY	SETTING
	AutoSize	-1 'True
	BorderStyle	0 'None
	ScaleMode	3 'Pixel
Timer	Name	Timer1
	Enabled	0 'False
	Interval	20
PictureBox	Name	Picture1
	AutoSize	-1 'True
	BorderStyle	0 'None
	Picture	(c:\windows\leaves.bmp)

2. Create a new class module and save it as SCREEN.CLS. Add the following code to the general declarations section of the form to hold the screen template bits.

```
'  m_array will hold the string of
'  1's and 0's, which indicates the
'  screen to be built.
Private m_array() As String * 8
```

3. BitArraySet is called to send in the string, which indicates which bits should be set in the 8x8 screen bitmap. The m_array variable stores these bits. Ultimately, this function is called eight times for each screen to send the representation of the 64 bits needed for the monochrome bitmap.

```
'  This routine is called to set
'  the array data
Public Sub BitArraySet(s, index)

m_array(index) = s

End Sub
```

4. When the class is initialized, the m_array is dimensioned to 8.

```
Private Sub Class_Initialize()

'  Dimension m_array
ReDim m_array(8) As String * 8

End Sub
```

5. The BitBuild routine handles taking the string representation of the bitmap in m_array and setting up the data appropriately in the string variable passed to the function.

```
Public Sub BitBuild(s As String)

'  We will loop through each element in the array
For counter = 1 To 8

    '  v will hold the value of the bit pattern, we
    '  need to reset it for each row
    v = 0

    '  We will loop through each row and set the bit values
    For c = 0 To 7

    '  We check for a 1 in the array and if it is 1 we
    '  then calculate the decimal value of the binary postion
    '  for example in 00000100, the 1 is = to 2^2 = 4
    If Mid$(m_array(counter), c + 1, 1) = "1" Then v = v + 2 ^ c
    Next c
    Mid$(s, (counter - 1) * 4 + 1, 1) = Chr$(v)

Next counter

End Sub
```

6. Create a new class module and save it as CROSSHAT.CLS. Add the following code to the general declarations section of the form. The declarations for building the bitmap and doing the image transfers are made here. Also, many of the member variables are declared here for the class.

```
'  The BITMAPINFOHEADER contains basic informtion
'  about the bitmap we will create
Private Type BITMAPINFOHEADER '40 bytes
        biSize As Long
        biWidth As Long
        biHeight As Long
        biPlanes As Integer
        biBitCount As Integer
        biCompression As Long
        biSizeImage As Long
        biXPelsPerMeter As Long
        biYPelsPerMeter As Long
        biClrUsed As Long
        biClrImportant As Long
End Type


'  This data structure holds the header info as
'  well as the color data
Private Type BITMAPINFO
    bmiHeader As BITMAPINFOHEADER
    bmiColors As String * 8 ' Array length is arbitrary; may be changed
End Type


'  Used to transfer m_bits from one picture to another
Private Declare Function BitBlt% Lib "GDI" (ByVal hDestDC%, ByVal X%, ByVal ↵
Y%, ByVal nWidth%, ByVal nHeight%, ByVal hSrcDC%, ByVal XSrc%, ByVal YSrc%, ↵
```

```
ByVal dwRop&)

'   Selects an object into a device context
Private Declare Function SelectObject% Lib "GDI" (ByVal hDC%, ByVal hObject%)

'   Creates a DIB Bitmap
Private Declare Function CreateDIBitmap% Lib "GDI" (ByVal hDC%, lpInfoHeader ↵
As BITMAPINFOHEADER, ByVal dwUsage&, ByVal lpInitBits$, lpInitInfo As ↵
BITMAPINFO, ByVal wUsage%)

'   Deletes a created object
Private Declare Function DeleteObject% Lib "GDI" (ByVal hObject%)

'   Creates a pattern brush
Private Declare Function CreatePatternBrush Lib "GDI" (ByVal HBITMAP As ↵
Integer) As Integer

'   Paints a picture with the specified pattern
Private Declare Function PatBlt Lib "GDI" (ByVal hDC As Integer, ByVal X ↵
As Integer, ByVal Y As Integer, ByVal nWidth As Integer, ByVal nHeight As ↵
Integer, ByVal dwRop As Long) As Integer

'   Transfers data from one picture to another and stretches to the new
'   picture dimensions
Private Declare Function StretchBlt% Lib "GDI" (ByVal hDC%, ByVal X%, ByVal ↵
Y%, ByVal nWidth%, ByVal nHeight%, ByVal hSrcDC%, ByVal XSrc%, ByVal YSrc%, ↵
ByVal nSrcWidth%, ByVal nSrcHeight%, ByVal dwRop&)

'   Specifies that the bitmap color table contains RGB colors
Const DIB_RGB_COLORS = 0

'   Indicates to CreateDIBitmap that the bitmap is initialized with the m_bits
'   specified by the lpvBits and lpbmi parameters.
Const CBM_INIT = &H4&

'   Copy the bitmap as is to the destination picture
Const SRCCOPY = &HCC0020

'   Use logical AND to combine the bitmaps
Const SRCAND = &H8800C6

'   Copy the pattern to the bitmap
Const PATCOPY = &HF00021

'   Specifies that the bitmap is not compressed
Const BI_RGB = 0&

'   Declare m_BitInfoH as type BITMAPINFOHEADER
Dim m_BitInfoH As BITMAPINFOHEADER

'   Declare m_BitInfo as type BITMAPINFO
Dim m_BitInfo As BITMAPINFO

Dim m_bits As ScreenBuild
```

continued on next page

continued from previous page

```
Dim m_scrn(10) As String * 32

'  m_counter will act as a counter for our timer
Dim m_counter As Integer

'  Declare our objects to be passed in
Private m_pict1 As Object
Private m_pict2 As Object
Private m_pict3 As Object
Private m_pict4 As Object
Private m_blowuppict As Object
Private m_timer As Object

'  m_show will indicate whether to show the
'  blown up copy of the pattern
Private m_show As Integer
```

7. The blow-up property is used to indicate whether or not the blown-up pattern should be shown in the independent picture.

```
Public Property Let blowup(n As Integer)
'  Retrieve the setting
Let m_show = n

End Property
```

8. Buildbitmap handles setting up the main settings of the bitmap.

```
Public Sub buildbitmap()

'  Standard 40 Byte Header
m_BitInfoH.biSize = 40

'  This will be an 8 by 8 bitmap
m_BitInfoH.biWidth = 8
m_BitInfoH.biHeight = 8

'  One Plane
m_BitInfoH.biPlanes = 1

'  Specifies the number of bits per pixel
m_BitInfoH.biBitCount = 1

'   No Compression
m_BitInfoH.biCompression = BI_RGB

'  These values are rarely used
m_BitInfoH.biSizeImage = 0
m_BitInfoH.biXPelsPerMeter = 0
m_BitInfoH.biYPelsPerMeter = 0

'  Two colors used
m_BitInfoH.biClrUsed = 2

'  This ensures that all colors are important
```

```
m_BitInfoH.biClrImportant = 0


'  This will be a monochrome bitmap
m_BitInfo.bmiColors = "0000" + Chr$(255) + Chr$(255) + Chr$(255) + "0"

End Sub
```

9. BuildScrns handles building the bitmap screens for the cross hatch and vertical fades. Index indicates which should be performed.

```
Public Sub BuildScrns(index)

If index = 1 Then

'  This function builds the different screens to
'  fill the picture with

'  Dimension m_scrn to hold 10 screens
'ReDim m_scrn(10) As String * 32

'  For each of the successive 10 screens, we
'  will build a binary string of 1s and 0s
'  to represent the 8x8 screen that will be
'  used to fill the picture.  We call the
'  BitArraySet function in the ScreenBuild class

m_bits.BitArraySet "11111111", 1
m_bits.BitArraySet "11111111", 2
m_bits.BitArraySet "11111111", 3
m_bits.BitArraySet "11111111", 4
m_bits.BitArraySet "11111111", 5
m_bits.BitArraySet "11111111", 6
m_bits.BitArraySet "11111111", 7
m_bits.BitArraySet "11111111", 8

'  We now setup the bit data in scrn
m_bits.BitBuild m_scrn(1)


'  The code is the same as above
m_bits.BitArraySet "11101111", 1
m_bits.BitArraySet "10111111", 2
m_bits.BitArraySet "11111011", 3
m_bits.BitArraySet "11111111", 4
m_bits.BitArraySet "11111111", 5
m_bits.BitArraySet "11111111", 6
  m_bits.BitArraySet "11111110", 7
m_bits.BitArraySet "11111111", 8

m_bits.BitBuild m_scrn(2)

m_bits.BitArraySet "11101011", 1
m_bits.BitArraySet "10111111", 2
m_bits.BitArraySet "11111010", 3
```

continued on next page

continued from previous page

```
m_bits.BitArraySet "11111011", 4
m_bits.BitArraySet "11011111", 5
m_bits.BitArraySet "11101111", 6
m_bits.BitArraySet "11111110", 7
m_bits.BitArraySet "11110111", 8

m_bits.BitBuild m_scrn(3)

m_bits.BitArraySet "10101011", 1
m_bits.BitArraySet "10111101", 2
m_bits.BitArraySet "11101010", 3
m_bits.BitArraySet "10111011", 4
m_bits.BitArraySet "11011011", 5
m_bits.BitArraySet "11101101", 6
m_bits.BitArraySet "01111110", 7
m_bits.BitArraySet "11110111", 8

m_bits.BitBuild m_scrn(4)

m_bits.BitArraySet "10101010", 1
m_bits.BitArraySet "10101101", 2
m_bits.BitArraySet "10101010", 3
m_bits.BitArraySet "10111010", 4
m_bits.BitArraySet "01011011", 5
m_bits.BitArraySet "10101101", 6
m_bits.BitArraySet "01111010", 7
m_bits.BitArraySet "11110101", 8

m_bits.BitBuild m_scrn(5)

m_bits.BitArraySet "10101010", 1
m_bits.BitArraySet "10100101", 2
m_bits.BitArraySet "10101010", 3
m_bits.BitArraySet "00111010", 4
m_bits.BitArraySet "01001011", 5
m_bits.BitArraySet "10100101", 6
m_bits.BitArraySet "01011010", 7
m_bits.BitArraySet "10110101", 8

m_bits.BitBuild m_scrn(6)

m_bits.BitArraySet "10001010", 1
m_bits.BitArraySet "00100101", 2
m_bits.BitArraySet "10100010", 3
m_bits.BitArraySet "00101010", 4
m_bits.BitArraySet "01001001", 5
m_bits.BitArraySet "00100101", 6
m_bits.BitArraySet "01001010", 7
m_bits.BitArraySet "10110100", 8

m_bits.BitBuild m_scrn(7)

m_bits.BitArraySet "10001000", 1
m_bits.BitArraySet "00100001", 2
m_bits.BitArraySet "00100010", 3
```

```
m_bits.BitArraySet "00100010", 4
m_bits.BitArraySet "01001000", 5
m_bits.BitArraySet "00100100", 6
m_bits.BitArraySet "00001010", 7
m_bits.BitArraySet "10010100", 8

m_bits.BitBuild m_scrn(8)

m_bits.BitArraySet "10000000", 1
m_bits.BitArraySet "00000001", 2
m_bits.BitArraySet "00100000", 3
m_bits.BitArraySet "00000010", 4
m_bits.BitArraySet "00001000", 5
m_bits.BitArraySet "00000100", 6
m_bits.BitArraySet "00000010", 7
m_bits.BitArraySet "10000000", 8

m_bits.BitBuild m_scrn(9)

m_bits.BitArraySet "00000000", 1
m_bits.BitArraySet "00000000", 2
m_bits.BitArraySet "00000000", 3
m_bits.BitArraySet "00000000", 4
m_bits.BitArraySet "00000000", 5
m_bits.BitArraySet "00000000", 6
m_bits.BitArraySet "00000000", 7
m_bits.BitArraySet "00000000", 8

m_bits.BitBuild m_scrn(10)

Else

'   This function builds the different screens to
'   fill the picture with

'   Dimension m_scrn to hold 10 screens
ReDim m_scrn(10) As String * 32

'   For each of the successive 10 screens, we
'   will build a binary string of 1s and 0s
'   to represent the 8x8 screen that will be
'   used to fill the picture.  We call the
'   BitArraySet function in the ScreenBuild class

m_bits.BitArraySet "11111111", 1
m_bits.BitArraySet "11111111", 2
m_bits.BitArraySet "11111111", 3
m_bits.BitArraySet "11111111", 4
m_bits.BitArraySet "11111111", 5
m_bits.BitArraySet "11111111", 6
m_bits.BitArraySet "11111111", 7
m_bits.BitArraySet "11111111", 8

'   We now setup the bit data in scrn
m_bits.BitBuild m_scrn(1)
```

continued on next page

continued from previous page

```
m_bits.BitArraySet "11111110", 1
m_bits.BitArraySet "11111110", 2
m_bits.BitArraySet "11111110", 3
m_bits.BitArraySet "11111110", 4
m_bits.BitArraySet "11111110", 5
m_bits.BitArraySet "11111110", 6
m_bits.BitArraySet "11111110", 7
m_bits.BitArraySet "11111110", 8

m_bits.BitBuild m_scrn(2)

m_bits.BitArraySet "11111100", 1
m_bits.BitArraySet "11111100", 2
m_bits.BitArraySet "11111100", 3
m_bits.BitArraySet "11111100", 4
m_bits.BitArraySet "11111100", 5
m_bits.BitArraySet "11111100", 6
m_bits.BitArraySet "11111100", 7
m_bits.BitArraySet "11111100", 8

m_bits.BitBuild m_scrn(3)

m_bits.BitArraySet "11111000", 1
m_bits.BitArraySet "11111000", 2
m_bits.BitArraySet "11111000", 3
m_bits.BitArraySet "11111000", 4
m_bits.BitArraySet "11111000", 5
m_bits.BitArraySet "11111000", 6
m_bits.BitArraySet "11111000", 7
m_bits.BitArraySet "11111000", 8

m_bits.BitBuild m_scrn(4)

m_bits.BitArraySet "11110000", 1
m_bits.BitArraySet "11110000", 2
m_bits.BitArraySet "11110000", 3
m_bits.BitArraySet "11110000", 4
m_bits.BitArraySet "11110000", 5
m_bits.BitArraySet "11110000", 6
m_bits.BitArraySet "11110000", 7
m_bits.BitArraySet "11110000", 8

m_bits.BitBuild m_scrn(5)

m_bits.BitArraySet "11100000", 1
m_bits.BitArraySet "11100000", 2
m_bits.BitArraySet "11100000", 3
m_bits.BitArraySet "11100000", 4
m_bits.BitArraySet "11100000", 5
m_bits.BitArraySet "11100000", 6
m_bits.BitArraySet "11100000", 7
m_bits.BitArraySet "11100000", 8

m_bits.BitBuild m_scrn(6)
```

```
m_bits.BitArraySet "11000000", 1
m_bits.BitArraySet "11000000", 2
m_bits.BitArraySet "11000000", 3
m_bits.BitArraySet "11000000", 4
m_bits.BitArraySet "11000000", 5
m_bits.BitArraySet "11000000", 6
m_bits.BitArraySet "11000000", 7
m_bits.BitArraySet "11000000", 8

m_bits.BitBuild m_scrn(7)

m_bits.BitArraySet "10000000", 1
m_bits.BitArraySet "10000000", 2
m_bits.BitArraySet "10000000", 3
m_bits.BitArraySet "10000000", 4
m_bits.BitArraySet "10000000", 5
m_bits.BitArraySet "10000000", 6
m_bits.BitArraySet "10000000", 7
m_bits.BitArraySet "10000000", 8

m_bits.BitBuild m_scrn(8)

m_bits.BitArraySet "00000000", 1
m_bits.BitArraySet "00000000", 2
m_bits.BitArraySet "00000000", 3
m_bits.BitArraySet "00000000", 4
m_bits.BitArraySet "00000000", 5
m_bits.BitArraySet "00000000", 6
m_bits.BitArraySet "00000000", 7
m_bits.BitArraySet "00000000", 8

m_bits.BitBuild m_scrn(9)

m_bits.BitArraySet "00000000", 1
m_bits.BitArraySet "00000000", 2
m_bits.BitArraySet "00000000", 3
m_bits.BitArraySet "00000000", 4
m_bits.BitArraySet "00000000", 5
m_bits.BitArraySet "00000000", 6
m_bits.BitArraySet "00000000", 7
m_bits.BitArraySet "00000000", 8

m_bits.BitBuild m_scrn(10)

End If

End Sub
```

10. The Fadein function handles setting up for the fade-in process.

```
Public Sub fadein()

'   Check to see if the user wants to see the
'   fade in slow motion
```

continued on next page

continued from previous page

```
If m_show = 1 Then m_timer.Interval = 500 Else m_timer.Interval = 1

'   Set m_counter to 11, note that the timer
'   immediately increments it to 10
m_counter = 11

'   start the timer
m_timer.Enabled = True

End Sub
```

11. The Fadeout function handles setting up for the fade-out process.

```
Public Sub fadeout()
'   Check to see if the user wants to
'   display the picture slowly
If m_show = 1 Then m_timer.Interval = 500 Else m_timer.Interval = 1

'   Set m_counter to 0, note that the timer
'   immediately increments it
m_counter = 0

'   Start timer
m_timer.Enabled = True

End Sub
```

12. The Intick procedure is performed with every tick of the timer and performs the fade in.

```
Public Sub intick()
'   Decrement m_counter which will grab the appropriate
'   screen
m_counter = m_counter - 1

'   Stop the process when m_counter reaches 0
If m_counter = 0 Then m_timer.Enabled = False: GoTo next2

'   Set the BitmapInfoHeader field of m_BitInfo
m_BitInfo.bmiHeader = m_BitInfoH

'   Create the 8x8 bitmap specified by m_scrn(m_counter)
compbitmap% = CreateDIBitmap(m_pict3.hDC, m_BitInfoH, CBM_INIT, ↵
m_scrn(m_counter), m_BitInfo, DIB_RGB_COLORS)

'   Create the bitmap pattern from the screen
hbr% = CreatePatternBrush(compbitmap%)

'   Select the brushes into picture3 and picture5
OldBP1% = SelectObject(m_pict3.hDC, hbr%)
If m_show = 1 Then OldBP2% = SelectObject(m_blowuppict.hDC, hbr%)


'   Because we are slowly "brightening" the picture, we need to
'   copy in a whole new copy of the picture.  If we just copy in
```

```
'   the pattern, it will not be seen.  If we use the picture1.refresh
'   capability, we can notice a slight flicker in the process, which
'   does not look good.  So, we will use picture4 to hold the original
'   image from picture1.

'   Picture2 hold an original copy of picture1.  We copy that into picture4
throw% = BitBlt(m_pict4.hDC, 0, 0, m_pict2.ScaleWidth, m_pict2.ScaleHeight, ↵
m_pict2.hDC, 0, 0, SRCCOPY)

'   Build the pattern screen in picture3
throw% = PatBlt(m_pict3.hDC, 0, 0, m_pict3.ScaleWidth, m_pict3.ScaleHeight, ↵
PATCOPY)

'   Show a blown up copy of the screen in picture5
If m_show = 1 Then throw% = StretchBlt%(m_blowuppict.hDC, 0, 0, ↵
m_blowuppict.ScaleWidth, m_blowuppict.ScaleHeight, m_pict3.hDC, 0, 0, 8, 8,
SRCCOPY)

'   Copy the screen into picture4
throw% = BitBlt(m_pict4.hDC, 0, 0, m_pict1.ScaleWidth, m_pict1.ScaleHeight, ↵
m_pict3.hDC, 0, 0, SRCAND)

'   Transfer the new screened image in picture4 to picture1
throw% = BitBlt(m_pict1.hDC, 0, 0, m_pict1.ScaleWidth, m_pict1.ScaleHeight, ↵
m_pict4.hDC, 0, 0, SRCCOPY)


'   Select the original brushes into picture3 and picture5
throw% = SelectObject(m_pict3.hDC, OldBP1%)
If m_show = 1 Then throw% = SelectObject(m_blowuppict.hDC, OldBP2%)

'   Delete the created brush
throw% = DeleteObject(hbr%)

'   Delete the created bitmap
throw% = DeleteObject%(compbitmap%)

next2:

End Sub
```

13. The Outtick procedure is performed with every tick of the timer and performs the fade out.

```
Public Sub outtick()
'   Increment m_counter, which will be used to grab the correct screen.
m_counter = m_counter + 1

'   When m_counter = 11 then we will stop the timer and exit the routine
If m_counter = 11 Then m_timer.Enabled = False: GoTo next1

'   Set the BitmapInfoHeader field of the m_BitInfo structure
m_BitInfo.bmiHeader = m_BitInfoH

'   We call the CreateDIBitmap function to build the 8x8 bitmap
```

continued on next page

continued from previous page

```
'   designated in m_scrn(m_counter)
compbitmap% = CreateDIBitmap(m_pict1.hDC, m_BitInfoH, CBM_INIT, ↵
m_scrn(m_counter), m_BitInfo, DIB_RGB_COLORS)


'   We then create a pattern brush from the bitmap built
hbr% = CreatePatternBrush(compbitmap%)


'   We then select the brush into picture3 and picture5
OldBP1% = SelectObject(m_pict3.hDC, hbr%)
If m_show = 1 Then OldBP2% = SelectObject(m_blowuppict.hDC, hbr%)


'   We fill picture3 with the pattern
throw% = PatBlt(m_pict3.hDC, 0, 0, m_pict3.ScaleWidth, m_pict3.ScaleHeight, ↵
PATCOPY)


'   We show a blown up copy of the 8x8 screen
If m_show = 1 Then throw% = StretchBlt%(m_blowuppict.hDC, 0, 0,
m_blowuppict.ScaleWidth, m_blowuppict.ScaleHeight, m_pict3.hDC, 0, 0, 8, 8, ↵
SRCCOPY)


'   From picture3, we copy the screen into our display picture,
'   picture1
throw% = BitBlt(m_pict1.hDC, 0, 0, m_pict1.ScaleWidth, m_pict1.ScaleHeight, ↵
m_pict3.hDC, 0, 0, SRCAND)


'   We select the original brushes back into picture3
'   and picture5
throw% = SelectObject(m_pict3.hDC, OldBP1%)
If m_show = 1 Then throw% = SelectObject(m_blowuppict.hDC, OldBP2%)


'   Delete the created brush
throw% = DeleteObject(hbr%)


'   Delete the created bitmap
throw% = DeleteObject%(compbitmap%)

next1:

End Sub
```

14. The Setup procedure handles preparing the images for the fade in and out.

```
Public Sub setup()
'   Make sure that the working pictures
'   are all set to autoredraw of true
m_pict2.AutoRedraw = True
m_pict3.AutoRedraw = True
m_pict4.AutoRedraw = True


'   Make sure that all of the pictures are
'   the same height and width as picture1
m_pict3.Width = m_pict1.Width
m_pict3.Height = m_pict1.Height

m_pict2.Width = m_pict1.Width
```

```
m_pict2.Height = m_pict1.Height

m_pict4.Width = m_pict1.Width
m_pict4.Height = m_pict1.Height

'  Make sure that all of the pictures
'  have the same scalemode
m_pict4.ScaleMode = 3
m_pict1.ScaleMode = 3
m_pict2.ScaleMode = 3
m_pict3.ScaleMode = 3

End Sub
```

15. The following properties handle receiving the necessary picture and timer controls.

```
Public Property Set Pict1(aControl As Object)
Set m_pict1 = aControl
End Property

Public Property Set pict2(aControl As Object)
  Set m_pict2 = aControl
End Property

Public Property Set pict3(aControl As Object)
    Set m_pict3 = aControl
End Property

Public Property Set pict4(aControl As Object)
    Set m_pict4 = aControl
End Property

Public Property Set blowuppict(aControl As Object)
    Set m_blowuppict = aControl
End Property

Public Property Set timer(aControl As Object)
    Set m_timer = aControl
End Property
```

16. When the class is initialized, a new instance of the ScreenBuild class is declared.

```
Private Sub Class_Initialize()

Set m_bits = New ScreenBuild

End Sub
```

17. Add the following to the general declarations section of the form. Here the CrossHatch class is globally declared and the button variable is used to indicate which type of fade is to be performed.

```
'  Declare our global class CrossHatch
```

continued on next page

continued from previous page

```
Dim CrossHatch As CrossHatch

'  Button will indicate which button
'  was selected
Dim Button As Integer
```

18. When the Cross_Click button is selected, the screens for the cross hatch fade are built.

```
Private Sub Cross_Click()

'  Build the CrossHatch Screen
CrossHatch.BuildScrns 1

End Sub
```

19. When the FadeIn button is selected, the fade-in routine of the CrossHatch class is called. This sets up for the fade-in process.

```
Private Sub FadeIn_Click()

'  Prepare for the Fade In
CrossHatch.fadein

'  Indicate a FadeIn is to be performed
Button = 1

End Sub
```

20. When the FadeOut button is selected, the fade-out routine of the CrossHatch class is called. This sets up for the fade-out process.

```
Private Sub FadeOut_Click()

'  Prepare for the FadeOut
CrossHatch.fadeout

'  Indicate a FadeOut is to be performed
Button = 2

End Sub
```

21. When the form is loaded, the class is initialized and the appropriate properties are set. The setup routine is also called to prepare for the overall fade-in and fade-out process.

```
Private Sub Form_Load()

'  Declare the new class
Set CrossHatch = New CrossHatch

'  Send the pictures necessary to the class
Set CrossHatch.Pict1 = picture1
Set CrossHatch.pict2 = picture2
```

```
Set CrossHatch.pict3 = picture3
Set CrossHatch.pict4 = picture4

'   Setup the pictures
CrossHatch.setup

'   Indicate no blow up of the pattern will be
'   shown
Let CrossHatch.blowup = 0

'   Send in the picture in case the pattern
'   is to be shown blown up
Set CrossHatch.blowuppict = blowuppict

'   Pass the timer to the class
Set CrossHatch.timer = timer1

'   Call the setup bitmap function
CrossHatch.buildbitmap

'   Build the cross hatch screens
CrossHatch.BuildScrns 1

End Sub
```

22. When the SlowDisp check box is selected, the blown-up 8x8 bitmap screen is turned on or off.

```
Private Sub slowDisp_Click()

'   If the user wants to see the
'   blown up patterns then we will
'   turn on the picture and set the
'   appropriate variables in the class
If slowDisp.Value = 1 Then
    blowuppict.Visible = True
    Let CrossHatch.blowup = 1
    Set CrossHatch.blowuppict = blowuppict
Else
    '   The user no longer wants to see the
    '   blown up pattern
    blowuppict.Visible = False
    Let CrossHatch.blowup = 0
End If

End Sub
```

23. The timer handles performing the fade in or fade out. The Intick and Outtick procedures are called to perform the process. Note that the timer is disabled from within the class when the fade is finished.

```
Private Sub Timer1_Timer()

'   Depending on which button was
'   selected, perform the appropriate
```

continued on next page

continued from previous page

```
'   transition
If Button = 1 Then
     CrossHatch.intick
Else
     CrossHatch.outtick
End If

End Sub
```

24. When you want to do a vertical fade, the appropriate screens are built.

```
Private Sub Vertical_Click()

'   Build the vertical screens
CrossHatch.BuildScrns 2

End Sub
```

How It Works

Two classes are introduced in this How-To. The ScreenBuild class handles setting up the bitmap data for the functions that will build the 8x8 monochrome bitmap. This class could easily be implemented within the CrossHatch class, but the ScreenBuild class shows how multiple classes can be used to modularize code. ScreenBuild handles converting the screen matrices into bit data that can be used by the API functions. The CrossHatch class handles building the bitmaps with the bit data from ScreenBuild. Review the Form_Load procedure to see how the class is initialized. There are two important elements to understand about doing the two fades. The first is how the bitmap is built, and consequently how the brush is built. The second is how the screens and fades are developed.

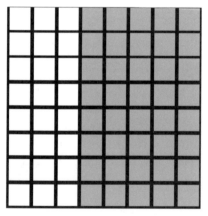

Figure 4-7-3 An image representation of the array

For the cross hatch screens and the vertical blinds, an appropriate 8x8 monochrome bitmap is built for each stage of the fade. To make building the bitmap simple, the patterns are built using string arrays that contain a 0 where the bit will be black and a 1 where the bit will be white. The list below and Figure 4-7-3 show the relationship between the array and the actual 8x8 bitmap.

m_array(1) = "00000111"
m_array(2) = "00000111"
m_array(3) = "00000111"
m_array(4) = "00000111"
m_array(5) = "00000111"
m_array(6) = "00000111"
m_array(7) = "00000111"
m_array(8) = "00000111"

Notice that the image is flipped from the array settings. The bitmap is built from the right-bottom up. As you can see, where there is a 0 in the array, the black pixel is set in the 8x8 bitmap. Each screen is stored in the m_scrn() array. When the image is filled, each screen is looped through and the appropriate bitmap is created.

In the ScreenBuild.BitBuild function, every fourth character is set in the 32 character strings. This is because the CreateDIBitmap function expects the bitmap data to be placed in 4-byte blocks. In other words, each row of data must end on a 4-byte boundary. But for an 8x8 monochrome bitmap, only the first 8 bits are needed to define the data for each row.

To set the bits, you need to calculate the appropriate binary number for each row in the screen. For the first row in the example above, the following list calculates the appropriate value for each position and sums up the values.

2^0	= 1	
2^1	= 1	
2^2	= 4	
Total = 7	Binary Representation = 00000111	

Thus, the first of 4 bytes is set to chr$(7), which is then interpreted by the CreateDIBitmap function. In the bmiColors element of the BITMAPINFO structure, white is defined as 1 and black as 0. Thus, the 1's in the binary image are white and the 0's are black.

The CreateDIBitmap function takes six parameters that build the bitmap. Table 4-7-2 is a breakdown of each.

Table 4-7-2 CreateDIBitmap parameters

PARAMETER	DESCRIPTION
ByVal hDC%	The device context to build the bitmap in
lpInfoHeader as BITMAPINFOHEADER	The bitmap definition
ByVal dwUsage&	Defines whether or not the bitmap is initialized
ByVal lpInitBits$	Defines the actual bitmap data
lpInitInfo as BITMAPINFO	Contains the bitmap and color information
ByVal wUsage%	Specifies whether the colors contain explicit red, green, blue (RGB) values or palette indices

The m_scrn() array is set up to contain the lpInitBits data. As the code comments reflect, the BITMAPINFOHEADER is set up to define an 8x8 monochrome bitmap. The bmiColors element of the BITMAPINFO array holds RGB color values (black and white).

From these 8x8 monochrome bitmaps, the screens can be built. This is where the CreatePatternBrush and PatBlt functions come into play. Once the bitmap is created, a pattern brush can be created from the bitmap. Once the pattern brush is created, PatBlt is used to fill an image with the pattern. For the fade-out process, each screen works with the following process:

1. Fill an empty picture box with the pattern using PatBlt.

2. Copy the pattern to the displayed image using BitBlt.

For the fade-in process, a few more steps must be done, because with each step more of the picture must be shown.

1. Fill an empty picture box with the pattern using PatBlt.

2. Copy a back-up copy of the original image to a temporary image using BitBlt.

3. Fill the temporary image with the pattern from Step 1 using BitBlt.

4. Copy the temporary image to the visible image on the screen using BitBlt.

If you try to transfer the full image and then the pattern to the visible image, you will notice a flicker, especially on slower systems. By building the screened image in a temporary picture, you avoid any flickering.

Comments

Experiment with building different bit pattern screens, such as horizontal blind. You could build the bitmaps using the m_array() string array more efficiently, but we did it this way to illustrate the process.

4.8 How do I...
Display transparent pictures?

COMPLEXITY: ADVANCED

Problem

I would like to be able to display one image over another without the black background surrounding the top image being visible. This allows me to display images with transparent backgrounds in my application.

Technique

The API BitBlt function can be used with special monochrome versions of the image to build the transparent effect.

Steps

Open and run 4-8.VBP. The running program appears as shown in Figure 4-8-1. Click on the background to show ARCHES.BMP. As Figure 4-8-2 shows, the arches show the background image through them.

Figure 4-8-1 The form at runtime

Figure 4-8-2 The transparent bitmap is displayed

1. Create a new project called 4-8.VBP. Add the objects and properties listed in Table 4-8-1 to Form1 and save the form as 4-8.FRM.

Table 4-8-1 The project form's objects and properties

OBJECT	PROPERTY	SETTING
Form	Name	Form1
	BackColor	&H00FFFFFF&
	Caption	"How-To 4.8"
PictureBox	Name	Background
	BorderStyle	0 'None
	ScaleMode	3 'Pixel
PictureBox	Name	TempBack
	AutoRedraw	-1 'True
	AutoSize	-1 'True
	BackColor	&H00FFFFFF&
	BorderStyle	0 'None
	Picture	(c:\windows\flock.bmp)
	ScaleMode	3 'Pixel
	Visible	0 'False
PictureBox	Name	Mask
	AutoSize	-1 'True
	BorderStyle	0 'None
	Picture	(arches2.bmp)
	Visible	0 'False
PictureBox	Name	FullPict
	AutoSize	-1 'True
	BackColor	&H00FFFFFF&
	BorderStyle	0 'None
	Picture	(c:\windows\arches.bmp)
	Visible	0 'False
Label	Name	ClickLabel

continued on next page

continued from previous page

OBJECT	PROPERTY	SETTING
	Alignment	2 'Center
	Caption	"Click on Picture to Show Transparent Image"
	ForeColor	&H000000FF&

2. Create a new class called TRANSCOP.CLS. Add the following code to the general declarations section. The appropriate declarations are made to perform the bitmap transfers. Also, the member declarations for the class are made here.

```
'  BitBlt will be used to make the transparent effect.
Private Declare Function BitBlt Lib "GDI" (ByVal hDestDC As Integer, ByVal x ↵
As Integer, ByVal y As Integer, ByVal nWidth As Integer, ByVal nHeight As ↵
Integer, ByVal hSrcDC As Integer, ByVal XSrc As Integer, ByVal YSrc As ↵
Integer, ByVal dwRop As Long) As Integer


'  Constants for BitBlt and StretchBlt
Const SRCCOPY = &HCC0020
Const SRCAND = &H8800C6
Const SRCINVERT = &H660046


'  Declare our three pictures
Private m_BackPict As Object
Private m_MaskPict As Object
Private m_PrimaryPict As Object


'  x and y coord to display pictures
Private m_X As Integer
Private m_Y As Integer
```

3. The following property settings pass in the picture objects necessary to perform the transparent transfer. The scale-mode and auto-redraw properties are also set for the pictures.

```
Public Property Set BackGroundPict(aControl As Object)
'  Background Picture
Set m_BackPict = aControl
'  Ensure that the picture scalemode is three
m_BackPict.ScaleMode = 3
End Property

Public Property Set MaskPict(aControl As Object)
'  The Mask
Set m_MaskPict = aControl
'  Ensure the autoredraw and scalemode features
'  are set
m_MaskPict.ScaleMode = 3
m_MaskPict.AutoRedraw = True
End Property

Public Property Set PrimaryPict(aControl As Object)
'  This is the original image to be transfered
Set m_PrimaryPict = aControl
```

continued on next page

continued from previous page

```
'   Ensure the autoredraw and scalemode features
'   are set
m_PrimaryPict.ScaleMode = 3
m_PrimaryPict.AutoRedraw = True
End Property
```

4. Showtrans handles building the transparent bitmap on the form. First the black and white mask is copied to the background, then the main image is transferred to the same position.

```
Public Sub showtrans(xx, yy)

'   X coord. to disp. picture
m_X = xx

'   Y coord. to disp. picture
m_Y = yy

'   We will first transfer the black and white mask to the
'   background pict.  We use the SRCAND constant to combine the bits
'   using the AND logic
throw% = BitBlt(m_BackPict.hDC, m_X, m_Y, m_MaskPict.ScaleWidth, ↵
m_MaskPict.ScaleHeight, m_MaskPict.hDC, 0, 0, SRCAND)

'   We now transfer the main image to the background using the
'   SRCINVERT constant.  Wherever there is a black pixel in
'   the mask, the original image will show through.  Wherever
'   there is a white pixel in the mask and a black pixel in the
'   main image, the transparent effect will take place.
throw% = BitBlt(m_BackPict.hDC, m_X, m_Y, m_PrimaryPict.ScaleWidth, ↵
m_PrimaryPict.ScaleHeight, m_PrimaryPict.hDC, 0, 0, SRCINVERT)

End Sub
```

5. Add the following code to the general declarations section of the form. The global class is declared, as well as the StretchBlt function.

```
'   Globally declare our class
Dim Trans As TransCopy

'   We will use StretchBlt to expand the flock.bmp image
'   to fit in the form.
Private Declare Function StretchBlt% Lib "GDI" (ByVal hDC%, ByVal x%, ByVal ↵
y%, ByVal nWidth%, ByVal nHeight%, ByVal hSrcDC%, ByVal XSrc%, ByVal YSrc%, ↵
ByVal nSrcWidth%, ByVal nSrcHeight%, ByVal dwRop&)

'   Used for the StretchBlt copy
Const SRCCOPY = &HCC0020
```

6. When the background is clicked on, the center of the image is calculated and passed to the Class Showtrans function. Showtrans performs the actual transparent transfer.

```
Private Sub background_Click()
'   x and y are calculated such that the arches image
'   will be centered on the background
x = background.ScaleWidth / 2 - mask.ScaleWidth / 2
y = background.ScaleHeight / 2 - mask.ScaleHeight / 2

'   Show the transparent image at x and y
Trans.showtrans x, y

End Sub
```

7. When the form is loaded, the width and height are set and the Trans class is initialized with the necessary picture controls.

```
Private Sub Form_Load()

'   Set the form width and height
Form1.Width = background.Width + 70
Form1.Height = background.Height + 900

'   Create the new class
Set Trans = New TransCopy

'   Send in the three pictures
Set Trans.BackGroundPict = background
Set Trans.MaskPict = mask
Set Trans.PrimaryPict = FullPict

'   Move the background
background.Move 0, 0

End Sub
```

8. In the Form_Paint procedure, the small FLOCKS.BMP image is stretched into the background picture using StretchBlt.

```
Private Sub Form_Paint()

'   In order to use the StretchBlt, we have to have
'   the background picture have a scalemode of 3
background.ScaleMode = 3

'   Stretch the flock.bmp image to fit in
'   the form.
throw% = StretchBlt%(background.hDC, 0, 0, background.ScaleWidth, ↵
background.ScaleHeight, TempBack.hDC, 0, 0, TempBack.ScaleWidth, ↵
TempBack.ScaleHeight, SRCCOPY)

End Sub
```

How It Works

The TransCopy class handles performing the transparent copy. It has three properties that need to be set. The first is the background picture that the transparent image is to be placed on. The second is the mask image. The third is the full image to be placed (transparently) on the background. The ShowTrans routine member of the class takes in the X and Y coordinates of where you would like to have the image placed on the background.

You can make a transparent bitmap simply by using two important steps. The first is to create a monochrome version of the bitmap to be displayed. The second is to use two modes of bitmap transfer using BitBlt.

To create the mask, you want all of the areas visible when the bitmap is displayed to be filled with black. All the areas filled with white should be transparent. You can easily accomplish this using the paint fill feature of any paint program (including PaintBrush). Save that image as a new file. In the primary image to be displayed, make sure that the areas to be transparent are completely filled with black. The two versions of the arches bitmap are shown in Figure 4-8-3.

To show the transparent image, SRCAND and the SRCINVERT are used. When SRCAND is used to copy the mask to the background, the background image shows through wherever there are white pixels. Wherever there are black pixels, the background is turned to black.

The SRCINVERT uses the XOR operation to combine the pixels. Wherever there are black pixels, no change takes place in the background. Wherever there are black pixels in the background, no changes are made to the transferred image.

Figure 4-8-3a and Figure 4-8-3b The arches graphics

Comments

The intermediate step of transferring the mask to the bitmap can be seen by placing a MsgBox function in between the two BitBlt calls.

4.9 How do I...
Overlay a complex shape on a picture?

COMPLEXITY: ADVANCED

Problem

I would like to be able to filter a general background color out of a bitmap and then display the image. This technique is often referred to as "blue screening." This is useful for showing a part of a bitmap graphic over the top of another.

Technique

We will see how to filter out the background color and then use the technique from How-To 4.8 to display the transparent image. A new class will be developed to handle this process.

Steps

Open and run 4-9.VBP. The running program appears as shown in Figure 4-9-1. To demonstrate how the process works, the steps will be shown on the screen. The bottom of the screen shows the original bitmap, the blue screen mask, and the black and white mask. Click on the Combine1 bitmap twice to show the blue screen filter. You need to click twice to make the image appear because the auto-redraw property of the picture box is set to true, which forces an immediate redraw of the previous contents. Then click on the Combine2 bitmap to show the final transparent display. As Figure 4-9-2 shows, the blue background and blue spot on the bird have been filtered out. Note that you can resize the form to cover all of the mask images and the temporary picture. The process will still work correctly.

1. Create a new project called 4-9.VBP. Add the objects and properties listed in Table 4-9-1 to Form1 and save the form as 4-9.FRM.

Table 4-9-1 The project form's objects and properties

OBJECT	PROPERTY	SETTING
Form	Name	Form1
	BackColor	&H00404040&
	Caption	"How-To 4.9"
	ScaleMode	3 'Pixel

continued on next page

continued from previous page

OBJECT	PROPERTY	SETTING
PictureBox	Name	Picture1
	AutoSize	-1 'True
	BackColor	&H00FFFFFF&
	BorderStyle	0 'None
	Picture	(c:\windows\windows1.bmp)
	ScaleMode	3 'Pixel
PictureBox	Name	TmpPict
	AutoSize	-1 'True
	BackColor	&H00FFFFFF&
	BorderStyle	0 'None
CommandButton	Name	Combine2
	Caption	"Combine2"
PictureBox	Name	Mask
	AutoSize	-1 'True
	BorderStyle	0 'None
	Index	1
	Picture	(bird3.bmp)
CommandButton	Name	Combine1
	Caption	"Combine1"
PictureBox	Name	Mask
	AutoSize	-1 'True
	BorderStyle	0 'None
	Index	0
	Picture	(bird2.bmp)
PictureBox	Name	FullPict
	AutoSize	-1 'True
	BackColor	&H00FFFFFF&
	BorderStyle	0 'None
	Picture	(fullpict.bmp)

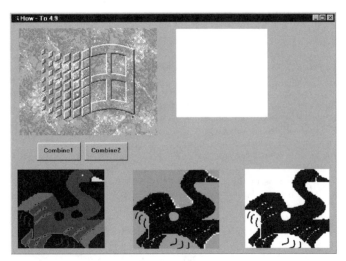

Figure 4-9-1 The form at runtime

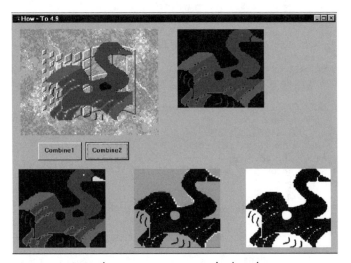

Figure 4-9-2 The transparent image displayed

2. Create a new class module called COMPTRNS.CLS. Add the following code to the general declarations section of the form to handle the BitBlt and declare the global members of the class.

```
'  BitBlt will be our main tool to do the transfer
Private Declare Function BitBlt Lib "GDI" (ByVal hDestDC As Integer, ByVal x ↵
As Integer, ByVal y As Integer, ByVal nWidth As Integer, ByVal nHeight As ↵
Integer, ByVal hSrcDC As Integer, ByVal XSrc As Integer, ByVal YSrc As ↵
Integer, ByVal dwRop As Long) As Integer
```

continued on next page

continued from previous page

```
'  SRCAND and SRCINVERT will be used to do the
'  bit transfers
Const SRCAND = &H8800C6
Const SRCINVERT = &H660046
Const SRCCOPY = &HCC0020 ' (DWORD) dest = source

'  Declare our private picture objects
Private m_primarypict As Object
Private m_mask1 As Object
Private m_mask2 As Object
Private m_backpict As Object
Private m_temppict As Object

'  X and Y will be the coordinates to display
'  the image at
Private m_X As Integer
Private m_Y As Integer
```

3. The following code handles setting the picture properties for the class. The three necessary pictures along with their scale-mode and auto-redraw properties, are set.

```
Public Property Set PrimaryPict(acontrol As Object)
'  Primary Image
Set m_primarypict = acontrol
'  Set autoredraw and scalemode
m_primarypict.ScaleMode = 3
m_primarypict.AutoRedraw = True
End Property


Public Property Set Mask1(acontrol As Object)
'  First Mask
Set m_mask1 = acontrol
'  Set autoredraw and scalemode
m_mask1.ScaleMode = 3
m_mask1.AutoRedraw = True
End Property


Public Property Set mask2(acontrol As Object)
'  Second Mask
Set m_mask2 = acontrol
'  Set autoredraw and scalemode
m_mask2.ScaleMode = 3
m_mask2.AutoRedraw = True
End Property


Public Property Set BackgroundPict(acontrol As Object)
'  Background image to transfer to
Set m_backpict = acontrol
'  Only set scalemode
m_backpict.ScaleMode = 3
End Property


Public Property Set temppict(acontrol As Object)
'  Temporary picture for image transfers
Set m_temppict = acontrol
```

```
'   set autoredraw and scalemode
m_temppict.ScaleMode = 3
m_temppict.AutoRedraw = True
End Property
```

4. This code transfers the blue mask to the temporary picture. It then transfers the primary image to the temporary picture using SRCINVERT. It also ensures that all the images are of the same dimensions.

```
Public Sub combine1()

'   Make sure the temporary picture is sized to
'   the other images
m_temppict.Width = m_primarypict.Width
m_temppict.Height = m_primarypict.Height

'   Clear the form and picture for the transfer
m_backpict.Refresh
m_temppict.Refresh

'   We will first copy the first mask to the
'   temporary picture.
throw% = BitBlt(m_temppict.hDC, 0, 0, m_mask1.ScaleWidth, ↵
m_mask1.ScaleHeight, m_mask1.hDC, 0, 0, SRCCOPY)

'   Combine the full picture and the background
'   in the temporary picture.  We will use arg$
throw% = BitBlt(m_temppict.hDC, 0, 0, m_primarypict.ScaleWidth, ↵
m_primarypict.ScaleHeight, m_primarypict.hDC, 0, 0, SRCINVERT)

End Sub
```

5. In Combine2, the standard transparent bitmap transfer is done.

```
Public Sub combine2(xx, yy)
'   x and y will be the offset into the form for
'   the final bit transfers
m_X = xx
m_Y = yy

'   We now copy the second mask on to the background which
'   will only show the black bits
throw% = BitBlt(m_backpict.hDC, m_X, m_Y, m_mask2.ScaleWidth, ↵
m_mask2.ScaleHeight, m_mask2.hDC, 0, 0, SRCAND)

'   We now copy the new image in TempPict onto the background
'   image.  We use the SRCINVERT flag to only copy bits
'   that are black on the form.
throw% = BitBlt(m_backpict.hDC, m_X, m_Y, m_temppict.ScaleWidth, ↵
m_temppict.ScaleHeight, m_temppict.hDC, 0, 0, SRCINVERT)

End Sub
```

6. Add the following code to the general declarations section of the form. The global CompTrns class is declared here.

```
'   Declare a global copy of our class
Dim CompTrns As CompTrns
```

7. When the first button is selected, the first bitmap transfers are done.

```
Private Sub Combine1_Click()

'   Do the first combining
CompTrns.combine1

End Sub
```

8. When the second button is selected, the Combine2 class routine is called. It is passed to the location where the transparent image will be displayed on the background.

```
Private Sub Combine2_Click()

'   Do the second actual combining
CompTrns.combine2 60, 30

End Sub
```

9. In the Form_Load procedure, the picture properties of the class are set with the appropriate images.

```
Private Sub Form_Load()

'   Create the new class
Set CompTrns = New CompTrns

'   Send in the necessary pictures
Set CompTrns.PrimaryPict = FullPict
Set CompTrns.Mask1 = mask(0)
Set CompTrns.mask2 = mask(1)
Set CompTrns.BackgroundPict = Picture1
Set CompTrns.temppict = TmpPict

End Sub
```

How It Works

The complex transparent class, CompTrns, is set up to build and display the transparent bitmap. The class needs the original picture to be displayed, the two masks for building the transparent bitmap, the background picture to be transferred to, and a temporary picture for doing some of the work. (See the Form_Load procedure for the initialization of the class.) For purposes of showing the transparent process, two routines are built in the class, Combine1 and Combine2. These can easily be combined to make one simple call to the class.

To perform the process, the first step is to create a mask with the pixels of the image that should be shown turned to black. The simplest way to do this is either to use a black tool fill in a paint program or to eliminate the colors in the original palette of the pixels that should be shown. The latter method is the easiest for very complex images and most paint packages support this feature. An example is the first mask (BIRD2.BMP) in the program. The second step is to create the monochrome bitmap with the black pixels where the image should show and the white pixels where the image should be transparent.

When you select the first command button, the BIRD2.BMP mask is transferred to the temporary picture. This is done with a straight copy (SRCCOPY). It then copies the primary image to the temporary picture using the SRCINVERT parameter for BitBlt. As you can see, wherever there are black pixels in the BIRD2.BMP mask, the original pixels stay intact. Wherever there are blue pixels in the BIRD2.BMP mask, they are turned to black in the temporary picture. We now have a version of the picture that has the sections that are to be transparent set to black and the visible pixels intact. Now the monochrome mask (BIRD3.BMP) can be combined with the temporary picture image using the techniques learned in How-To 4.8. As you can see, the blue sections of the original image are now transparent.

Comments

The key to making this function successful is building the mask that will filter out the color pixels that should be transparent. In fact, you can filter out many colors at once. Just make sure that the pixels that should be visible are turned to black. From that mask, you should build the monochrome mask. This will help ensure that all of the image boundaries are aligned.

5

ANIMATION AND VIDEO

5

ANIMATION AND VIDEO

How do I...

The use of animation and video is an important part of multimedia programming. Animation can be implemented in many different ways to enhance your applications. In this chapter, we will explore the use of standard animation files formats, as well as the creation of animation from applications.

Animation can be generated from within Visual Basic 4.0 using a wide variety of techniques. Simple animation can be accomplished using the picture and image controls along with a timer. Shapes can be animated using the timer and the shape control. Using the Windows API, you can develop a wide variety of animation techniques. Sprites, which are animated bitmap graphics, can be manipulated to have their own movement. By using sprites in your application, you have real-time control over animation.

If you want to develop more sophisticated animations, you can use packages such as Animation Works Interactive and Autodesk's Animator or 3D Studio. But do not worry, these can easily be accessed from within your Visual Basic 4.0 applications.

The use of video can also be effective in getting your message across to your audience. Audio Visual Interleaved (AVI) and Apple's QuickTime are two popular formats of video available for use from Windows. We will explore the use of both of these from Windows.

Windows APIs Covered			
BitBlt	PatBlt	Rectangle	SelectObject
DeleteObject	GetDC	ReleaseDC	CreateSolidBrush

5.1 Start my application with an animated look
This How-To will show you how to start your application with a catchy animated look to capture your user's attention as soon as your program starts.

5.2 Easily create animations with graphics controls
It is easy to create simple animations using the shape control and the timer. This How-To shows three different shapes moving across a form.

5.3 Make a picture-box flip book
Another simple approach to animation is to flip through successive images. This How-To demonstrates animation by flipping through a series of image controls.

5.4 Create simple sprite animations
Sprites are graphical objects that either move on their own or can be controlled and interacted with by the user. Sprites allow for real-time control over graphical objects from the user or by your program code. This How-To will develop a technique for displaying sprites on a background and for moving them around using the arrow keys.

5.5   Create simple path-based sprite movements

This section will build on the technique developed in How-To 5.4. But instead of keyboard control, the sprite will move around the form on its own.

5.6   Detect sprite collisions

For games and other tasks, it is important to be able to detect sprite collisions. You will build a simple game that involves detecting when two sprites collide by building on the techniques developed in How-Tos 5.4 and 5.5.

5.7   Add animated highlights to text

One popular multimedia effect is to add animated highlights to text. Animated text highlights can be developed by using the text manipulation techniques from Chapter 2 and the sprite techniques developed earlier in this chapter.

5.8   Display animations created by Animation Works Interactive

You can create more sophisticated animations with Animation Works Interactive (AWI), a popular Windows animation package. AWI animation files can be played easily from your Visual Basic 4.0 applications by using GoldDisk's MCI driver and the MCI control.

5.9   Display animations created by Autodesk Animator

Autodesk's FLC animation format is an industry standard. This How-To demonstrates using Autodesk's custom control to make playing FLC files straightforward.

5.10 Display QuickTime movies

The QuickTime video format can be played from Windows using Apple's QuickTime for Windows. The package also provides a custom control for Visual Basic 4.0 that provides for easy playing of QuickTime files.

5.11 Display audio-visual interleaved animation files

Audio-visual interleaved (AVI) files have become a standard for Windows-based video and animation. AVI files can be easily played and manipulated by using the MCI control and Video for Windows.

5.1 How do I...
Start my application with an animated look?

Problem

When my application starts up, I would like to be able to catch my user's attention with an animated look. My animation can also occupy the user's attention while the program reads files, initializes data, and the like.

Technique

By using a few simple Windows API calls, you can draw animated rectangles where the form ultimately will appear.

Steps

Open and run 5-1.VBP. The running program appears as shown in Figure 5-1-1.

As you noticed when you started the application, a series of expanding red rectangles fills the space where the form will appear. To view the other transitional animated effects, select the appropiate option button.

1. Create a new project named 5-1.VBP. Add the objects and properties listed in Table 5-1-1 to the form and save the form as 5-1.FRM.

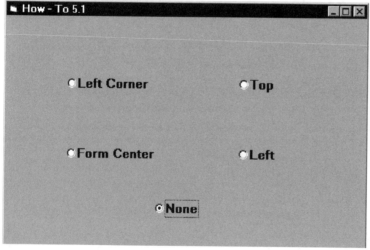

Figure 5-1-1 The form at runtime

Table 5-1-1 The project's objects and properties

OBJECT	PROPERTY	SETTING
Form	Name	form1
	BackColor	&H00C0C0C0&
	BorderStyle	1 'Fixed Single
	Caption	"How-To 5.1"
	ScaleMode	3 'Pixel
OptionButton	Name	None
	BackColor	&H00C0C0C0&
	Caption	"None"
	Value	-1 'True
OptionButton	Name	Left
	BackColor	&H00C0C0C0&
	Caption	"Left"
OptionButton	Name	Top
	BackColor	&H00C0C0C0&
	Caption	"Top"
OptionButton	Name	Center
	BackColor	&H00C0C0C0&
	Caption	"Form Center"
OptionButton	Name	LeftCorner
	BackColor	&H00C0C0C0&
	Caption	"Left Corner"

2. Open a new module called 5-1.BAS and add the following code. The Rect data type is used to define the dimensions of Windows rectangles.

```
'  Rect is used to define a Windows rectangle.
Type RECT
    Left As Integer
    Top As Integer
    Right As Integer
    Bottom As Integer
End Type
```

3. Add the following code to the general declarations section of the form. The appropriate API declarations are made to build the animated rectangles.

```
'  GetWindowRect will be used to get the rectangle
'  information about the form
Private Declare Sub GetWindowRect Lib "User" (ByVal hWnd As Integer, lpRect ↵
As RECT)

'  GetDC will get the Device Context of the screen
Private Declare Function GetDC Lib "User" (ByVal hWnd As Integer) As Integer

'  ReleaseDC will be used to release the DeviceContext
'  of the screen
Private Declare Function ReleaseDC Lib "User" (ByVal hWnd As Integer, ByVal ↵
hDC As Integer) As Integer

'  Rectangle will draw a rectangle on the specified
'  device context with the specified dimensions
Private Declare Sub Rectangle Lib "GDI" (ByVal hDC As Integer, ByVal X1 ↵
As Integer, ByVal Y1 As Integer, ByVal X2 As Integer, ByVal Y2 As Integer)

'  CreateSolidBrush will be used to create a red
'  brush to paint the animated rectangle
Private Declare Function CreateSolidBrush Lib "GDI" (ByVal crColor As Long) ↵
As Integer

'  SelectObject will select the specified object into the
'  specified device context
Private Declare Function SelectObject Lib "GDI" (ByVal hDC As Integer, ByVal ↵
hObject As Integer) As Integer

'  DeleteObject deletes the specified object
Private Declare Sub DeleteObject Lib "GDI" (ByVal hObject As Integer)

'  Trans will hold the specified transition
Dim Trans As Integer
```

4. Add the following code to the general declarations section of the form. Aniform handles performing the transition specified by the Trans parameter.

```
Private Sub AniForm(Trans As Integer)

'  Declare R as type Rectangle
Dim R As RECT

'  Increments will control the speed of the
'  transition
Increments = 0.001

'  GetWindowRect gets the rectangle dimensions
'  of the form
GetWindowRect form1.hWnd, R

'  FormWidth and FormHeight hold the width
```

```
'  and height of the form
FormWidth = R.Right - R.Left
FormHeight = R.Bottom - R.Top

'  Get the Screen Device Context
Scrn% = GetDC(0)

'  We will create a red sold brush
hbr% = CreateSolidBrush(QBColor(4))

'  Select the brush into the screen
'  device context
hbrold% = SelectObject(Scrn%, hbr%)

'  This for loop will increase the dimensions of
'  the rectangle with each iteration
For N = 0 To 1 Step Increments

    '  Since N is a percentage value, we multiply
    '  the percentage times the form width and height
    ChangeX = FormWidth * N
    ChangeY = FormHeight * N

    '  Perform the left corner animation
    If Trans% = 1 Then
        X = R.Left
        Y = R.Top
        Rectangle Scrn%, X, Y, X + ChangeX, Y + ChangeY
    End If

    '  Perform the center animation
    If Trans% = 2 Then
        X = R.Left + (FormWidth - ChangeX) / 2
        Y = R.Top + (FormHeight - ChangeY) / 2
        Rectangle Scrn%, X, Y, X + ChangeX, Y + ChangeY
    End If

    '  Perform the top animation
    If Trans% = 3 Then
        Y = R.Top
        Rectangle Scrn%, R.Left, R.Top, R.Left + FormWidth, Y + ChangeY
    End If

    '  Perform the left side animation
    If Trans% = 4 Then
        X = R.Left
        Rectangle Scrn%, R.Left, R.Top, X + ChangeX, R.Top + FormHeight
    End If

Next N

'  Select the original brush into the screen
'  device context
throw% = SelectObject(Scrn%, hbrold%)
```

continued on next page

continued from previous page

```
'   Release the Screen Device Context
throw% = ReleaseDC(0, Scrn%)

'   Delete the created brush
DeleteObject (hbr%)

'   Show the form
form1.Visible = True

'   Select the None option box
None.Value = -1

End Sub
```

5. The following code handles the selection of the different option buttons. Each initiates an appropriate animated transition.

```
Private Sub Center_Click()

    '   Set the animation and start the process
    Trans% = 2
    Unload form1
    Load form1

End Sub

Private Sub Left_Click()

    '   Set the animation and start the process
    Trans% = 4
    Unload form1
    Load form1

End Sub

Private Sub LeftCorner_Click()

    '   Set the animation and start the process
    Trans% = 1
    Unload form1
    Load form1

End Sub

Private Sub Top_Click()

    '   Set the animation and start the process
    Trans% = 3
    Unload form1
    Load form1

End Sub
```

6. The Form_Load procedure initiates the animation transition.

```
Private Sub Form_Load()

'   The first time the form starts up, Trans
'   will be 0 so we will perform the animation
'   transition
If Trans% = 0 Then Trans% = 2

'   Call the AniForm to do the Animated Start
AniForm Trans%

End Sub
```

How It Works

The animated look is generated by drawing rectangles directly onto the screen device context, which is retrieved from the GetDC function. The parameter used for GetDC is 0, which by default gives the screen context.

The GetWindowRect function is then used to retrieve the dimensions in screen coordinates of the specified rectangle (Form1). The Rectangle function is used to draw rectangles on the screen device. The rectangles are drawn where the form ultimately will appear.

To accomplish the animated effect, successive rectangles are drawn larger. The simplest way to do this is to make the rectangle width and height approach the form width and height. This is done by multiplying the form width and height by a successively larger percentage until they reach 100 percent and the animation is finished.

```
ChangeX = FormWidth * N

ChangeY = FormHeight * N
```

N is counted from 0 to 1 using steps of .001. Thus, ChangeX and ChangeY are an increasing percentage of the actual form width and height.

Comments

Consider reversing the process to give an animated finish to your program.

5.2 How do I...
Easily create animations with graphics controls?

COMPLEXITY: EASY

Problem

I would like to be able to create line, rectangular, and circular animated objects. These objects can provide simple animated effects in my applications.

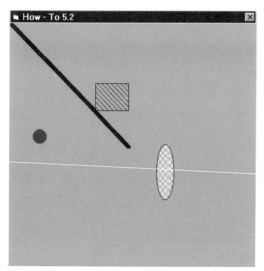

Figure 5-2-1 The form at runtime

Technique

The shape control provided in Visual Basic 4.0, combined with the timer control, provides for effective and simple shape animation. There is also an added benefit in that the shape control takes very few system resources.

Steps

Open and run 5-2.VBP. The running program appears as shown in Figure 5-2-1. To begin the animation, click on the back of the form.

1. Create a new project named 5-2.VBP. Add the objects and properties listed in Table 5-2-1 and save the form as 5-2.FRM.

Table 5-2-1 The project's objects and properties

OBJECT	PROPERTY	SETTING
Form	Name	form1
	BackColor	&H00C0C0C0&
	BorderStyle	3 'Fixed Double
	Caption	"How-To 5.2"
Timer	Name	Timer1

OBJECT	PROPERTY	SETTING
	Enabled	0 'False
	Interval	20
Line	Name	Line1
	BorderStyle	6 'Inside Solid
	BorderWidth	5
Shape	Name	Shape3
	BackColor	&H00FFFF80&
	BackStyle	1 'Opaque
	Shape	2 'Oval
Shape	Name	Shape2
	BackColor	&H0080FF80&
	BackStyle	1 'Opaque
	FillStyle	4 'Upward Diagonal
Shape	Name	Shape1
	BackColor	&H000000FF&
	BorderStyle	0 'Transparent
	FillColor	&H000000FF&
	FillStyle	0 'Solid
	Shape	3 'Circle

2. Add the following code to the Form_Click procedure. This procedure starts the timer to animate the objects.

```
Private Sub Form_Click()

'  Start the timer
timer1.Enabled = True

End Sub
```

3. The Form_Load procedure handles setting up the objects for the animation. This includes moving the objects of the form so they are not visible.

```
Private Sub Form_Load()

'  Set the form width and height
form1.Height = 5000
form1.Width = 5000
```

continued on next page

continued from previous page

```
'  Move the shapes off of the form
shape1.Top = 0 - shape1.Height
shape2.Left = 0 - shape2.Width
shape3.Left = form1.Width + shape3.Width

'  Initialize the line
Line1.X1 = 0
Line1.Y1 = 0
Line1.X2 = 0
Line1.Y2 = 0

End Sub
```

4. Timer1 handles moving the objects each interval and it checks to see if the largest object (the rectangle) has moved off the form. If it has, then the objects are reset and moved off the form so the process can take place again.

```
Private Sub Timer1_Timer()

'  We check to see if shape2 (the largest) has moved
'  off the form
If shape2.Left > form1.Width + shape2.Width Then

    '  Stop the timer and reset the shapes
    timer1.Enabled = False
    shape1.Top = 0 - shape1.Height
    shape2.Left = 0 - shape2.Width
    shape3.Left = form1.Width + shape3.Width

    Line1.X1 = 0
    Line1.Y1 = 0
    Line1.X2 = 0
    Line1.Y2 = 0

Else

    '  Move the shapes and lengthen the line
    shape1.Top = shape1.Top + 100
    shape2.Left = shape2.Left + 100
    shape3.Left = shape3.Left - 100
    Line1.X2 = Line1.X2 + 100
    Line1.Y2 = Line1.Y2 + 100

End If

End Sub
```

How It Works

The various shapes are defined by setting the properties of the shape controls. For the circle, oval, and rectangle, the position properties move left with every timer event to accomplish the animation. For the line control, the X2 and Y2 properties are changed to make the line longer with every timer event. Because the origin is 0,0 in effect the program draws a diagonal line across the form. The animation stops when the largest object, the rectangle, moves beyond the right edge of the form.

Comments

Collisions between the graphic objects can be detected by comparing the bounding coordinates of each object and seeing if there is an intersection.

5.3 How do I...
Make a picture-box flip book?

COMPLEXITY: EASY

Problem

I would like to be able to flip through a series of pictures to perform animation and various graphic effects.

Technique

By using an image control, you can load a series of images in a control array and flip through them at various speeds using a timer control.

Steps

Open and run 5-3.VBP. The running program appears as shown in Figure 5-3-1. Select the Animate button to see the images animated. Change the timer interval to control the speed of the animation.

1. Create a new project called 5-3.VBP. Add the objects and properties listed in Table 5-3-1 to Form1 and save the form as 5-3.FRM.

Table 5-3-1 The project's objects and properties

OBJECT	PROPERTY	SETTING
Form	Name	form1
	BackColor	&H00C0C0C0&
	BorderStyle	3 'Fixed Double
	Caption	"How-To 5.3"
	ScaleMode	3 'Pixel
TextBox	Name	Text1

continued on next page

continued from previous page

OBJECT	PROPERTY	SETTING
	Text	"25"
CommandButton	Name	Animate
	Caption	"Animate"
Timer	Name	Timer1
	Enabled	0 'False
	Interval	25
Label	Name	Label1
	AutoSize	-1 'True
	BackStyle	0 'Transparent
	Caption	"Interval"
Image	Name	flip
	Index	0

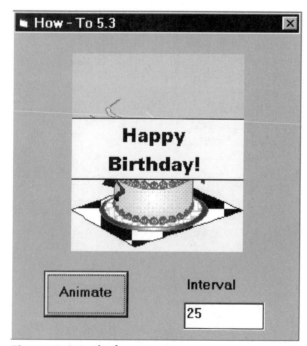

Figure 5-3-1 The form at runtime

2. Add the following code to the general declarations section of the form. N is used to count the images in the timer control.

```
'   n will be used to count through the image
'   controls
Dim n As Integer
```

3. This code handles starting the animation process. N is reset to -1 and the timer is started.

```
Private Sub Animate_Click()

'   Reset n to -1, note it will be
'   incremented immediately
n = -1

'   Set the timer interval
timer1.Interval = Val(text1.Text)

'   Enable the timer
timer1.Enabled = True

'   Make sure the last image is not visible
'   from the last animation.
flip(23).Visible = False

End Sub
```

4. The Form_Load procedure handles adding additional control arrays and then loading the appropriate images.

```
Private Sub Form_Load()

'   Visual Basic allows us to add controls at
'   runtime by using the control array.  We will
'   use Load to create copies of the flip image control
For n = 1 To 23
    Load flip(n)

flip(n - 1).Picture = LoadPicture(App.Path + "\" + Right$(Str$(n), ↵
Len(Str$(n)) - 1) + ".bmp")

Next n

n = 24

flip(n - 1).Picture = LoadPicture(App.Path + "\" + Right$(Str$(n), ↵
Len(Str$(n)) - 1) + ".bmp")

End Sub
```

5. Timer1 handles loading each successive image. It turns off the last image and makes the next one visible.

```
Private Sub Timer1_Timer()

'  Increment n
n = n + 1

'  Check to see if we have reached the next to
'  last picture
If n = 22 Then timer1.Enabled = False

'  For each timer iteration, we will make
'  the currently displayed image invisible
'  and make the image to be displayed visible
flip(n).Visible = False
flip(n + 1).Visible = True

End Sub
```

How It Works

You will notice that Form1 contains only one image control. In the Form_Load procedure, you add additional image controls by adding to the image control array. The following is the code:

```
For n = 1 To 23
        Load flip(n)
Next n
```

There are a total of 24 images to be flipped through. You add 23 images to the control array by using the Load function and you designate the index number of the control to be added (flip(n)). In the next section of the Form_Load procedure, you load the appropriate bitmaps into the image controls.

The timer event makes the next image control visible. But it is important to make the previous image control invisible. By flipping through the image controls, you implement effective animation.

Comments

The flip book developed here can be expanded to provide for user control of flipping through the images.

5.4 How do I...
Create simple sprite animations?

Problem

I would like to be able to create animations from bitmap graphics and control their movement. This will allow me to build animations directly from my program and control their interaction with the user.

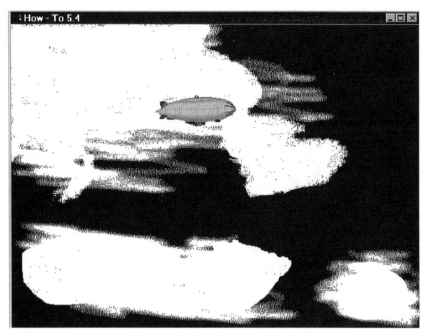

Figure 5-4-1 The form at runtime

Technique

It is nice to create animations in an application such as Autodesk Animator or Animation Works and play them from your applications. But it is difficult to interact with the objects in the animation. As this How-To will demonstrate, you can develop sprite animations from prebuilt bitmaps and have control over their interaction. To do this you will use the techniques developed in How-To 4.8 to display transparent bitmaps and develop additional techniques to control the bitmap sprites. You will animate an "airship" sprite in this example.

In this How-To, the first of three sprite classes will be developed. By using these classes, you will be able to add sprite animations to your applications easily.

Steps

Open and run 5-4.VBP. The running program appears as shown in Figure 5-4-1. Move the airship around using the arrow keys. As you can see, with every press of an arrow key, the airship moves in the selected direction.

1. Create a new project called 5-4.VBP. Add the objects and properties listed in Table 5-4-1 to Form1 and save the form as 5-4.FRM.

Table 5-4-1 The project's objects and properties

OBJECT	PROPERTY	SETTING
Form	Name	Form1
	BackColor	&H00C0C0C0&
	Caption	"How-To 5.4"
	KeyPreview	-1 'True
PictureBox	Name	Picture2
	AutoSize	-1 'True
	BorderStyle	0 'None
PictureBox	Name	Transf1
	AutoSize	-1 'True
	BorderStyle	0 'None
PictureBox	Name	Mask1
	AutoSize	-1 'True
	BorderStyle	0 'None
	Picture	(air3.bmp)
PictureBox	Name	TempPict
	AutoSize	-1 'True
	BackColor	&H00FFFFFF&
	BorderStyle	0 'None
PictureBox	Name	Mask2
	AutoSize	-1 'True
	BorderStyle	0 'None
	Picture	(air2.bmp)
PictureBox	Name	FullPict
	AutoSize	-1 'True
	BackColor	&H00FFFFFF&
	BorderStyle	0 'None
	Picture	(air1.bmp)
PictureBox	Name	Picture1

OBJECT	PROPERTY	SETTING
	AutoSize	-1 'True
	BackColor	&H00FFFFFF&
	BorderStyle	0 'None
	Picture	(clouds.bmp)

2. Add a new module, SPRITE1.CLS. to the application. Add the following code to the general declarations section of the form. The appropriate API declarations and global members are declared for the class.

```
'  BitBlt will be our primary function to handle
'  the sprite animation
Private Declare Function BitBlt Lib "GDI" (ByVal hDestDC As Integer, ByVal x ↵
As Integer, ByVal y As Integer, ByVal nWidth As Integer, ByVal nHeight As ↵
Integer, ByVal hSrcDC As Integer, ByVal XSrc As Integer, ByVal YSrc As ↵
Integer, ByVal dwRop As Long) As Integer

'  We will use the transparent bitmap techniques
'  developed in chapter4
Const SRCAND = &H8800C6
Const SRCINVERT = &H660046
Const SRCCOPY = &HCC0020

'  These are the global members of the class
Dim m_primarypict As Object
Dim m_mask1pict As Object
Dim m_mask2pict As Object
Dim m_background As Object
Dim m_dispback As Object
Dim m_transf1pict As Object
Dim m_temppict As Object
```

3. The following are the declarations for the properties of the class. These are the picture boxes needed to animate the sprite.

```
'  This is the original image of the sprite
Public Property Set PrimaryPict(acontrol As Object)
    Set m_primarypict = acontrol
End Property

'  This is the first mask
Public Property Set mask1pict(acontrol As Object)
    Set m_mask1pict = acontrol
End Property

'  This is the second mask (black and white)
Public Property Set mask2pict(acontrol As Object)
    Set m_mask2pict = acontrol
End Property
```

continued on next page

continued from previous page

```
'  This is the displayed background
Public Property Set background(acontrol As Object)
    Set m_background = acontrol
End Property


'   This is the background to be displayed
Public Property Set dispback(acontrol As Object)
    Set m_dispback = acontrol
End Property


'  This will be the working picture for building
'  the movement of the sprite.
Public Property Set transf1pict(acontrol As Object)
    Set m_transf1pict = acontrol
End Property


'  This will hold the mask that converts the
'  background around the airship to black
Public Property Set temppict(acontrol As Object)
    Set m_temppict = acontrol
End Property
```

4. MoveImage handles moving the sprite to the new location. Mstep indicates the change in movement from the last position. Mstep is used to calculate where the last position of the sprite was. The last position of the sprite needs to be covered up in the transfer so that no artifacts from it can be seen.

```
Public Sub MoveImage(x, y, Mstep)

'  First copy the background from the backup
'  of the background.  The copy is made from where
'  the airship is to be placed minus the move of
'  the airship.
throw% = BitBlt(m_transf1pict.hDC, 0, 0, m_transf1pict.ScaleWidth + (Mstep * ↵
2), m_transf1pict.ScaleHeight + (Mstep * 2), m_dispback.hDC, x - Mstep, y - ↵
Mstep, SRCCOPY)

'  Build the airship on the new section of the background  using
'  the transparent techniques developed in How-To 4.8
throw% = BitBlt(m_transf1pict.hDC, Mstep, Mstep, m_mask1pict.ScaleWidth, ↵
m_mask1pict.ScaleHeight, m_mask1pict.hDC, 0, 0, SRCAND)

throw% = BitBlt(m_transf1pict.hDC, Mstep, Mstep, m_temppict.ScaleWidth, ↵
m_temppict.ScaleHeight, m_temppict.hDC, 0, 0, SRCINVERT)

'  Copy the new image to the displayed background.  Note that
'  the image is placed where the the previous airship was
'  located.  This will cover the old airship with background.
throw% = BitBlt(m_background.hDC, x - Mstep, y - Mstep, ↵
m_transf1pict.ScaleWidth, m_transf1pict.ScaleHeight, m_transf1pict.hDC, 0, ↵
0, SRCCOPY)


End Sub
```

5. CreateMask handles filtering out the color background around the sprite. See How-To 4.9 for further information on this process.

```
Private Sub CreateMask()

'   m_temppict will hold the mask needed for the transparent
'   display.  We first copy the full picture into m_temppict
throw% = BitBlt(m_temppict.hDC, 0, 0, m_mask2pict.ScaleWidth,
m_mask2pict.ScaleHeight, m_mask2pict.hDC, 0, 0, SRCCOPY)

'  We now copy in the Mask, which will clear the background
'  to black
throw% = BitBlt(m_temppict.hDC, 0, 0, m_primarypict.ScaleWidth, ↵
m_primarypict.ScaleHeight, m_primarypict.hDC, 0, 0, SRCINVERT)

End Sub
```

6. The setup routine initializes the pictures passed in as properties and calls the CreateMask function to build the necessary masks. The last action taken is to copy the picture that contains the background (background) to the picture that displays the background and the animation (dispback). The background picture holds a copy of the background image to be displayed.

```
Public Sub setup()

'  Make sure that our picture that will hold
'  the background is the same size as the
'  background.
m_dispback.Width = m_background.Width
m_dispback.Height = m_background.Height

'  It is important to ensure that all of the
'  masks are set to the same size as the original
'  airship image.
m_primarypict.AutoSize = True

m_mask2pict.Width = m_primarypict.Width
m_mask2pict.Height = m_primarypict.Height

m_mask1pict.Width = m_primarypict.Width
m_mask1pict.Height = m_primarypict.Height

m_temppict.Width = m_primarypict.Width
m_temppict.Height = m_primarypict.Height

'  The picture used for building the movements
'  of the sprite needs to be large enough to hold
'  the additional background to cover the previous
'  location of the sprite.
m_transf1pict.Width = m_transf1pict.Width * 1.1
m_transf1pict.Height = m_transf1pict.Height * 1.1

'  The following statements ensure that
'  all of the images are operating with
```

continued on next page

continued from previous page

```
'   a pixel scalemode
m_temppict.ScaleMode = 3
m_primarypict.ScaleMode = 3
m_mask2pict.ScaleMode = 3
m_mask1pict.ScaleMode = 3
m_transf1pict.ScaleMode = 3
m_dispback.ScaleMode = 3
m_background.ScaleMode = 3


'   All but the displayed background needs
'   to be set to autoredraw so the bit manipulations
'   can be done while the images are not visible.
m_temppict.AutoRedraw = True
m_primarypict.AutoRedraw = True
m_mask2pict.AutoRedraw = True
m_mask1pict.AutoRedraw = True
m_transf1pict.AutoRedraw = True
m_dispback.AutoRedraw = True


'   Create the mask from m_primarypict and m_mask2pict
CreateMask


'   Transfer background to the dispback
'   picture, which will hold a copy of it
throw% = BitBlt(m_dispback.hDC, 0, 0, m_background.ScaleWidth, ↵
m_background.ScaleHeight, m_background.hDC, 0, 0, SRCCOPY)

End Sub
```

7. Add the following code to the general declarations section of the form. The sprite object is declared globally, along with the variables necessary to track the sprite's movement.

```
'   Globally declare the sprite object
Dim Sprite As Sprite


'   x and y will be used to hold the current location
'   of the sprite
Dim x As Integer
Dim y As Integer


'   Mstep will be used to calculate the amount of
'   movement for each sprite movement
Dim Mstep As Integer


'   First is used to execute
'   the code in form_paint only once
Dim First As Integer


'   The sprite is moved around using the arrow keys
'   These are the constant values for each key
Const KEY_LEFT = &H25
Const KEY_UP = &H26
Const KEY_RIGHT = &H27
Const Key_Down = &H28
```

8. When the user presses a key, the program checks to see if an arrow key has been selected. If so, the necessary adjustments are made to the sprite's position variables and the MoveImage event of the sprite is called.

```
Private Sub Form_KeyDown(KeyCode As Integer, Shift As Integer)

'   Depending on the key selected, we increment or
'   decrement x or y and call MoveImage function of
'   the sprite.
If KeyCode = KEY_RIGHT Then x = x + Mstep: Sprite.MoveImage x, y, Mstep
If KeyCode = KEY_LEFT Then x = x - Mstep: Sprite.MoveImage x, y, Mstep
If KeyCode = Key_Down Then y = y + Mstep: Sprite.MoveImage x, y, Mstep
If KeyCode = KEY_UP Then y = y - Mstep: Sprite.MoveImage x, y, Mstep

End Sub
```

9. When the form is loaded, a new sprite object is created. The appropriate picture properties and the variables for tracking the sprite's movement are set.

```
Private Sub Form_Load()

'   Create a new instance of the class
Set Sprite = New Sprite

'   Pass in the appropriate images
'   to initialize the class
Set Sprite.PrimaryPict = FullPict
Set Sprite.mask1pict = Mask1
Set Sprite.mask2pict = Mask2
Set Sprite.background = picture1
Set Sprite.dispback = Picture2
Set Sprite.transf1pict = Transf1
Set Sprite.temppict = temppict

'   Move the picture to the upper
'   left corner and size the form
'   to the picture
picture1.Move 0, 0
Form1.Width = picture1.Width
Form1.Height = picture1.Height

'   Mstep holds the amount of each movement
Mstep = 15

'   Start x amd y as 0
y = 0
x = 0

End Sub
```

10. When the form is painted for the first time, the setup event of the sprite is called. It is important to do the setup after the form is painted. In the setup routine, the

background for the animation is displayed in Picture2 on the form. If setup is
called before the form is painted, the background is not displayed.

```
Private Sub Form_Paint()

'   Make sure this code is only
'   executed once.
If First = 0 Then

'   When the form is first painted,
'   the sprites need to be set up
Sprite.setup

'   Make the first move on the airship
'   so it will be visible when the form starts up.
Form_KeyDown Key_Down, 0

First = 1

End If

End Sub
```

How It Works

In How-To 4.9, you learned how to take an image with a colored background and
filter out the background so that only the desired image is visible. You then used the
techniques learned in How-To 4.8 to display the desired image with a transparent
surrounding background.

You now add to those techniques the ability to control the location of the airship
by using the arrow keys. To do that, use the Form_KeyDown event to capture the
KeyCode value of the selected key. You don't use the Form_KeyPress event, because
this returns the ASCII value of the selected key, and the arrow keys do not have an
ASCII value. You could use the Form_KeyUp event, but the Form_KeyDown event
allows you to hold the key down for repeated movement of the airship.

With the added dimension of movement of the airship, you have to account for
clearing the previous airship image on the form. If you just transfer the airship in its
original size to the new location, parts of the original airship will still be visible. To
account for this, we use the following steps to display the new airship and cover the
last airship position with the original background. These steps are implemented in
the sprite class.

1. Keep an original copy of the background in a nonvisible picture (background
   member)

2. Use a second picture the size of the background for building the transfer bitmap
   (Transf1pict)

3. Use Mstep to define the distance of each movement of the airship. Figure 5-4-2 depicts a right arrow move of the airship.

When you build the next airship for transfer, you need to transfer an image that will be large enough to cover the last position of the airship. To do this, copy the background from background to Transf1pict. As the code shows in MoveImage, you actually copy a section of the background that is equal to the airship image with the 2*Mstep added to the height and width. This accounts for movement in any direction. Copy the background into Transf1pict at the new airship position minus Mstep (in both directions). The final result is that, regardless of the original image position and the new position, the first airship is completely covered.

4. Next, copy the black and white mask to the Transf1pict picture at the new position.

5. Then copy the image created from CreateMask (TempPict) to Transf1pict.

6. Finally, copy the newly created image (Transf1pict) to the displayed background (disppict). Note that the image transferred is placed on the form at the new airship position minus Mstep, and the size of the image transferred is the size of the airship plus 2*Mstep added to the height and width.

The final result is the airship in its new position with the previous airship completely covered. This basic process will move the airship in any direction.

The two masks were developed using the techniques developed in How-To 4.9. To increase performance as much as possible, the airships are tightly cropped. Note that all of the bitmaps are identical in size. This is important or the transfer effect will not be correct.

Note that the updated image is developed out of sight from the user on Transf1pict. If you were to do the work directly on the form, the user would notice

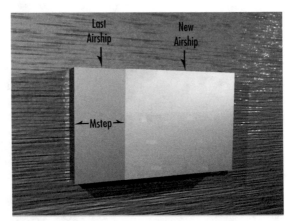

Figure 5-4-2   Depiction of sprite movement

flickers in the process and the animation would seem jerky. By transferring the final new airship position to the form only once, the animation appears fairly smooth and flicker-free.

Comments

The technique developed here can be used with various types of bitmaps. The next two How-Tos will expand on this technique to perform different tasks.

5.5 How do I...
Create simple path-based sprite movements?

Problem

I would like to be able to have my sprite move along its own path. This allows for the user to control the movement of sprites in my application.

Figure 5-5-1 The form at runtime

Technique

You will expand on the class developed in the last How-To. But instead of having the sprite controlled by key movements, you will have the airship travel along its own path using the timer event. You will also add an airship that will point to the left when it is moving to the left.

Steps

Open and run 5-5.VBP. The running program appears as shown in Figure 5-5-1.

The airship is set in motion by the timer. It will bounce around the form along a path that is determined by the amount of movement for each timer event.

1. Create a new project called 5-5.VBP. Add the objects and properties listed in Table 5-5-1 to Form1 and save the form as 5-5.FRM.

Table 5-5-1 The project's objects and properties

OBJECT	PROPERTY	SETTING
Form	Name	Form1
	BackColor	&H00C0C0C0&
	Caption	"How-To 5.5"
	KeyPreview	-1 'True
PictureBox	Name	Picture2
	AutoSize	-1 'True
	BackColor	&H00FFFFFF&
	BorderStyle	0 'None
PictureBox	Name	Transf2
	AutoSize	-1 'True
	BorderStyle	0 'None
PictureBox	Name	TempPict2
	AutoSize	-1 'True
	BackColor	&H00FFFFFF&
	BorderStyle	0 'None
PictureBox	Name	FullPict2
	AutoSize	-1 'True
	BackColor	&H00FFFFFF&

continued on next page

continued from previous page

OBJECT	PROPERTY	SETTING
	BorderStyle	0 'None
	Picture	(air4.bmp)
PictureBox	Name	Mask4
	AutoSize	-1 'True
	BorderStyle	0 'None
	Picture	(air5.bmp)
PictureBox	Name	Mask3
	AutoSize	-1 'True
	BorderStyle	0 'None
	Picture	(air6.bmp)
Timer	Name	Timer1
	Interval	1
PictureBox	Name	Transf1
	AutoSize	-1 'True
	BorderStyle	0 'None
PictureBox	Name	Mask1
	AutoSize	-1 'True
	BorderStyle	0 'None
	Picture	(air3.bmp)
PictureBox	Name	TempPict
	AutoSize	-1 'True
	BackColor	&H00FFFFFF&
	BorderStyle	0 'None
PictureBox	Name	Mask2
	AutoSize	-1 'True
	BorderStyle	0 'None
	Picture	(air2.bmp)
PictureBox	Name	FullPict

OBJECT	PROPERTY	SETTING
	AutoSize	-1 'True
	BackColor	&H00FFFFFF&
	BorderStyle	0 'None
	Picture	(air1.bmp)
PictureBox	Name	Picture1
	AutoSize	-1 'True
	BackColor	&H00FFFFFF&
	BorderStyle	0 'None
	Picture	(clouds.bmp)

2. Add a new module, SPRITE2.CLS, to the application. Add the following code to the general declarations section of the class. The appropriate API declarations and global members are declared for the class. Also, the bounds in which the sprite moves are declared as members of the class.

```
'  BitBlt will be our primary function to handle
'  the sprite animation
Private Declare Function BitBlt Lib "GDI" (ByVal hDestDC As Integer, ByVal x ↵
As Integer, ByVal y As Integer, ByVal nWidth As Integer, ByVal nHeight As ↵
Integer, ByVal hSrcDC As Integer, ByVal XSrc As Integer, ByVal YSrc As ↵
Integer, ByVal dwRop As Long) As Integer

'  We will use the transparent bitmap techniques
'  developed in chapter4
Const SRCAND = &H8800C6
Const SRCINVERT = &H660046
Const SRCCOPY = &HCC0020

'  These are the global members of the class
Dim m_primarypict As Object
Dim m_mask1pict As Object
Dim m_mask2pict As Object
Dim m_background As Object
Dim m_dispback As Object
Dim m_transf1pict As Object
Dim m_temppict As Object

'  Declare the boundaries for detecting collisions
Dim m_rightbound As Integer
Dim m_bottombound As Integer
Dim m_topbound As Integer
Dim m_leftbound As Integer
```

3. The following are the declarations for the properties of the class. These are the picture boxes needed to animate the sprite. Also, the boundaries in which the sprite moves are set up.

```
'  Set the right boundary
Public Property Let RightBound(n As Integer)
    Let m_rightbound = n
End Property
'  Set the bottom boundary
Public Property Let Bottombound(n As Integer)
    Let m_bottombound = n
End Property
'  Set the Top boundary
Public Property Let TopBound(n As Integer)
    Let m_topbound = n
End Property
'  Set the left boundary
Public Property Let Leftbound(n As Integer)
    Let m_leftbound = n
End Property

'  This is the original image of the sprite
Public Property Set PrimaryPict(acontrol As Object)
    Set m_primarypict = acontrol
End Property

'  This is the first mask
Public Property Set mask1pict(acontrol As Object)
    Set m_mask1pict = acontrol
End Property

'  This is the second mask (black and white)
Public Property Set mask2pict(acontrol As Object)
    Set m_mask2pict = acontrol
End Property

'  This is the displayed background
Public Property Set background(acontrol As Object)
    Set m_background = acontrol
End Property

'   This is the background to be displayed
Public Property Set dispback(acontrol As Object)
    Set m_dispback = acontrol
End Property

'  This will be the working picture for building
'  the movement of the sprite.
Public Property Set transf1pict(acontrol As Object)
    Set m_transf1pict = acontrol
End Property

'  This will hold the mask that converts the
'  background around the airship to black
Public Property Set temppict(acontrol As Object)
```

```
      Set m_temppict = acontrol
End Property
```

4. The Collide function handles checking to see if the sprite has crossed its boundaries. If so, the function returns a change of direction.

```
Public Sub collide(x, y, direction)

'   We check to see if the airship has reached the right
'   side of the form.  If so, we change direction
'   appropriately
If x + m_primarypict.ScaleWidth > m_rightbound Then
    If direction = "UR" Then direction = "UL"
    If direction = "DR" Then direction = "DL"
End If

'   We check to see if the airship has reached the left
'   side of the form.  If so, we change direction
'   appropriately
If x < m_leftbound Then
    If direction = "UL" Then direction = "UR"
    If direction = "DL" Then direction = "DR"
End If

'   We check to see if the airship has reached the
'   bottom side of the form.  If so, we change direction
'   appropriately
If y + m_primarypict.ScaleHeight > m_bottombound Then
    If direction = "DL" Then direction = "UL"
    If direction = "DR" Then direction = "UR"
End If

'   We check to see if the airship has reached the top
'   side of the form.  If so, we change direction
'   appropriately
If y < m_topbound Then
    If direction = "UL" Then direction = "DL"
    If direction = "UR" Then direction = "DR"
End If

End Sub
```

5. MoveImage handles moving the sprite to the new location, xstep indicates the change in left-right movement from the last position, and ystep indicates the change in the up-down direction. Xstep and ystep are used to calculate the last position of the sprite. The last position of the sprite needs to be covered up in the transfer so that no artifacts of the sprite in the last position can be seen.

```
Public Sub MoveImage(x, y, xstep, ystep)

'   First copy the background from the backup
'   of the background.  The copy is made from where
'   the airship is to be placed minus the move of
'   the airship.
```

continued on next page

continued from previous page

```
throw% = BitBlt(m_transf1pict.hDC, 0, 0, m_transf1pict.ScaleWidth + (xstep * ↵
2), m_transf1pict.ScaleHeight + (ystep * 2), m_dispback.hDC, x - xstep, y - ↵
ystep, SRCCOPY)

'  Build the airship on the new section of the background  using
'  the transparent techniques developed in How-To 4.8
throw% = BitBlt(m_transf1pict.hDC, xstep, ystep, m_mask1pict.ScaleWidth, ↵
m_mask1pict.ScaleHeight, m_mask1pict.hDC, 0, 0, SRCAND)

throw% = BitBlt(m_transf1pict.hDC, xstep, ystep, m_temppict.ScaleWidth, ↵
m_temppict.ScaleHeight, m_temppict.hDC, 0, 0, SRCINVERT)

'  Copy the new image to the displayed background.  Note that
'  the image is placed where the previous airship was
'  located.  This will cover the old airship with background.
throw% = BitBlt(m_background.hDC, x - xstep, y - ystep, ↵
m_transf1pict.ScaleWidth, m_transf1pict.ScaleHeight, m_transf1pict.hDC, 0, ↵
0, SRCCOPY)

'm_collision = "None"

'collide x, y

End Sub
```

6. CreateMask handles filtering out the color background around the sprite. See How-To 4.9 for further information on this process.

```
Private Sub CreateMask()

'  m_temppict will hold the mask needed for the transparent
'  display.  We first copy the full picture into m_temppict
throw% = BitBlt(m_temppict.hDC, 0, 0, m_mask2pict.ScaleWidth, ↵
m_mask2pict.ScaleHeight, m_mask2pict.hDC, 0, 0, SRCCOPY)

'  We now copy in the mask, which will clear the background
'  to black
throw% = BitBlt(m_temppict.hDC, 0, 0, m_primarypict.ScaleWidth, ↵
m_primarypict.ScaleHeight, m_primarypict.hDC, 0, 0, SRCINVERT)

End Sub
```

7. The setup routine initializes the pictures passed in as properties and calls the CreateMask function to build the necessary masks. The last action taken is to copy the picture that contains the background (background) to the picture that displays the background and the animation (dispback). The background picture holds a copy of the background image to be displayed.

```
Public Sub setup()

'  Make sure that our picture that will hold
'  the background is the same size as the
'  background.
m_dispback.Width = m_background.Width
```

```
m_dispback.Height = m_background.Height

'  It is important to ensure that all of the
'  masks are set to the same size as the original
'  airship image.
m_primarypict.AutoSize = True

m_mask2pict.Width = m_primarypict.Width
m_mask2pict.Height = m_primarypict.Height

m_mask1pict.Width = m_primarypict.Width
m_mask1pict.Height = m_primarypict.Height

m_temppict.Width = m_primarypict.Width
m_temppict.Height = m_primarypict.Height

'  The picture used for building the movements
'  of the sprite needs to be large enough to hold
'  the additional background to cover the previous
'  location of the sprite.
m_transf1pict.Width = m_transf1pict.Width * 1.12
m_transf1pict.Height = m_transf1pict.Height * 1.12

'  The following statements ensure that
'  all of the images are operating with
'  a pixel scalemode
m_temppict.ScaleMode = 3
m_primarypict.ScaleMode = 3
m_mask2pict.ScaleMode = 3
m_mask1pict.ScaleMode = 3
m_transf1pict.ScaleMode = 3
m_dispback.ScaleMode = 3
m_background.ScaleMode = 3

'  All but the displayed background needs
'  to be set to autoredraw so the bit manipulations
'  can be done while the images are not visible.
m_temppict.AutoRedraw = True
m_primarypict.AutoRedraw = True
m_mask2pict.AutoRedraw = True
m_mask1pict.AutoRedraw = True
m_transf1pict.AutoRedraw = True
m_dispback.AutoRedraw = True

'  Create the mask from m_primarypict and m_mask2pict
CreateMask

'  Transfer background to the dispback
'  picture, which will hold a copy of it
throw% = BitBlt(m_dispback.hDC, 0, 0, m_background.ScaleWidth,
m_background.ScaleHeight, m_background.hDC, 0, 0, SRCCOPY)

End Sub
```

8. Add the following code to the general declarations section of the form. Note that two global sprites are declared. The first is the right-pointing airship and the second is the left-pointing airship. The variables needed to track the movements of the sprites are also declared.

```
'  Globally declare out two sprites
Dim Sprite1 As Sprite
Dim Sprite2 As Sprite

'  X and Y will be used to track and move the airship
Dim x As Integer
Dim y As Integer

'  First will be used to execute the code in the
'  form paint event only once
Dim First As Integer

'  XStep and YStep will hold the amount for each movement
'  of the sprites for each timer tick.
Dim xstep As Integer
Dim ystep As Integer

'  Direction will track the direction the airship
'  is moving
Dim direction As String
```

9. In the Form_Load procedure, the two sprite properties are set. The variables for tracking the sprite are also initialized.

```
Private Sub Form_Load()

'  Create two instances of the class
Set Sprite1 = New Sprite
Set Sprite2 = New Sprite

'  Pass in the appropriate images
'  to initialize the class
Set Sprite1.PrimaryPict = fullpict
Set Sprite1.mask1pict = mask1
Set Sprite1.mask2pict = mask2
Set Sprite1.background = picture1
Set Sprite1.dispback = Picture2
Set Sprite1.transf1pict = Transf1
Set Sprite1.temppict = temppict

'  Intialize the second sprite
Set Sprite2.PrimaryPict = FullPict2
Set Sprite2.mask1pict = Mask3
Set Sprite2.mask2pict = Mask4
Set Sprite2.background = picture1
Set Sprite2.dispback = Picture2
Set Sprite2.transf1pict = Transf2
Set Sprite2.temppict = TempPict2

'  The x step will be 3 and the y step will be 1
```

```
' this is the amount the airship is moved each time
xstep = 3
ystep = 1

' Start out at the origin
y = 0
x = 0

' Our direction is down and right
' To begin with
direction = "DR"

' Move the picture to the top right
picture1.Move 0, 0

' Set the form width and height to the
' background picture
Form1.Width = picture1.Width
Form1.Height = picture1.Height + 300

End Sub
```

10. When the form is painted for the first time, the sprites are set up. Also, the bound properties are set up for both sprites to be that of the displayed picture (Picture1).

```
Private Sub Form_Paint()

If First = 0 Then

    ' Setup sprite1 and sprite2
    Sprite1.setup
    Sprite2.setup

    ' Reset first
    First = 1

    ' In order to detect the collisions,
    ' the boundaries of the sprite need to be set
    ' In this case these will be the boundaries of the
    ' background picture

    Let Sprite1.Leftbound = 0
    Let Sprite1.TopBound = 0
    Let Sprite1.RightBound = picture1.ScaleWidth
    Let Sprite1.Bottombound = picture1.ScaleHeight

    Let Sprite2.Leftbound = 0
    Let Sprite2.TopBound = 0
    Let Sprite2.RightBound = picture1.ScaleWidth
    Let Sprite2.Bottombound = picture1.ScaleHeight

End If

End Sub
```

11. The timer event handles moving the sprites. If the direction is Up Left or Down Left then Sprite2 is called (the left-pointing airship). If the direction is Up Right or Down Right, then Sprite1 is called (the right-pointing airship). With each movement, the collide routine is called to check for a collision. If a collision is detected, then the direction is changed.

```
Private Sub Timer1_Timer()

'  With each timer event we will make 15 moves
For n = 1 To 5

    '  Depending on the direction, we will increment or
    '  decrement X and Y appropriately.  Then the image
    '  is moved and we check for a collision with the
    '  collide function.
    Select Case direction

    Case "UL"
        x = x - xstep
        y = y - ystep
        Sprite2.MoveImage x, y, xstep, ystep
        Sprite2.collide x, y, direction

    Case "UR"
        x = x + xstep
        y = y - ystep
        Sprite1.MoveImage x, y, xstep, ystep
        Sprite1.collide x, y, direction

    Case "DL"
        x = x - xstep
        y = y + ystep
        Sprite2.MoveImage x, y, xstep, ystep
        Sprite2.collide x, y, direction

    Case "DR"
        x = x + xstep
        y = y + ystep
        Sprite1.MoveImage x, y, xstep, ystep
        Sprite1.collide x, y, direction

    End Select

Next n

End Sub
```

How It Works

Displaying and moving the airship follow the same logic as that of the Sprite1 class in the previous How-To, with two major additions. The first is the addition of the collide function, which includes the boundary properties. The second is allowing the

MoveImage function to move different degrees in the *x* and *y* direction with xstep and ystep. The collide function checks to see if the appropriate edge of the sprite hits a boundary. To change direction, the program checks to see if the *x* and *y* coordinates have reached an edge of the form. If the direction is Up-Right and the sprite has reached the right edge of the form, the direction is changed to Up-Left. The airship continues to move up, but will now move to the left.

The timer control drives the movement of the airship. In each timer event, the program moves the airship 15 times. Depending on the left or right direction of the airship, the program calls either the Sprite1 or the Sprite2 MoveImage functions. Sprite1 is the right-pointing airship and Sprite2 is the left-pointing airship. After each move of the airship, the collide function is called to see if a boundary has been crossed. If so, the class changes the direction appropriately.

The same techniques developed in How-To 5.4 to ensure the previous airship is completely covered are implemented here. But because the sprite is moving in the x and y direction with each movement, you need to account for covering up the previous airship that is not just to the left, right, top, or bottom of the new ship. The final transferred image is the size of the airship plus 2*xstep and 2*ystep. This ensures that the last airship is completely covered.

Comments

By changing the xstep and ystep values, the speed and direction of the airship can be changed. Other types of sprite movements can be developed and movement along the path can be timed using the timer control.

5.6 How do I...
Detect sprite collisions?

COMPLEXITY: ADVANCED

Problem

I would like to be able to detect when two sprites collide. This will allow me to build in interaction between animated objects.

Technique

By using the techniques developed in the previous How-To and adding a picture control sprite, you can develop a simple game that uses sprite collisions.

Steps

Open and run 5-6.VBP. The running program appears as shown in Figure 5-6-1. The goal of this simple game is to cross the red square you control with the arrow keys with the red square centered on the airship. When that happens, the game ends and displays an appropriate message.

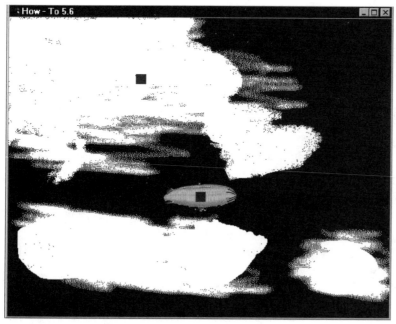

Figure 5-6-1 The form at runtime

1. Create a new project called 5-6.VBP. Add the objects and properties listed in Table 5-6-1 to Form1 and save the form as 5-6.FRM.

Table 5-6-1 The project's objects and properties

OBJECT	PROPERTY	SETTING
Form	Name	Form1
	BackColor	&H00C0C0C0&
	Caption	"How-To 5.6"
	KeyPreview	-1 'True
PictureBox	Name	Picture2
	AutoSize	-1 'True
	BackColor	&H00FFFFFF&
	BorderStyle	0 'None
PictureBox	Name	TempPict2

OBJECT	PROPERTY	SETTING
	AutoSize	-1 'True
	BackColor	&H00FFFFFF&
	BorderStyle	0 'None
PictureBox	Name	FullPict2
	AutoSize	-1 'True
	BackColor	&H00FFFFFF&
	BorderStyle	0 'None
	Picture	(air4.bmp)
PictureBox	Name	Mask4
	AutoSize	-1 'True
	BorderStyle	0 'None
	Picture	(air5.bmp)
PictureBox	Name	Mask3
	AutoSize	-1 'True
	BorderStyle	0 'None
	Picture	(air6.bmp)
Timer	Name	Timer1
	Interval	1
PictureBox	Name	Transf1
	AutoSize	-1 'True
	BorderStyle	0 'None
PictureBox	Name	Mask1
	AutoSize	-1 'True
	BorderStyle	0 'None
	Picture	(air3.bmp)
PictureBox	Name	TempPict
	AutoSize	-1 'True
	BackColor	&H00FFFFFF&
	BorderStyle	0 'None

continued on next page

continued from previous page

OBJECT	PROPERTY	SETTING
PictureBox	Name	Mask2
	AutoSize	-1 'True
	BorderStyle	0 'None
	Picture	(air2.bmp)
PictureBox	Name	FullPict
	AutoSize	-1 'True
	BackColor	&H00FFFFFF&
	BorderStyle	0 'None
	Picture	(air1.bmp)
PictureBox	Name	Picture1
	AutoSize	-1 'True
	BackColor	&H00FFFFFF&
	BorderStyle	0 'None
	Font	
	name	"Arial"
	size	48
	ForeColor	&H00000000&
	Picture	(clouds.bmp)
	Scalemode	3 'Pixel
PictureBox	Name	MisslePict
	BackColor	&H000000FF&
	BorderStyle	0 'None
	Visible	0 'False

2. Add a new class module, SIMSPR.CLS, to your application. Add the following code to the general declarations section of the form. The appropriate API declarations are made, as well as the member variables of the class.

```
'  BitBlt will be our primary function to handle
'  the sprite animation
Private Declare Function BitBlt Lib "GDI" (ByVal hDestDC As Integer, ByVal x ↵
As Integer, ByVal y As Integer, ByVal nWidth As Integer, ByVal nHeight As ↵
Integer, ByVal hSrcDC As Integer, ByVal XSrc As Integer, ByVal YSrc As ↵
Integer, ByVal dwRop As Long) As Integer

'  We will use the transparent bitmap techniques
'  developed in chapter4
```

```
Const SRCAND = &H8800C6
Const SRCINVERT = &H660046
Const SRCCOPY = &HCC0020


'  These will hold the x and y position of the simple
'  sprite.  These can then be checked in the collision
'  routine
Dim m_xx As Integer
Dim m_yy As Integer

'  These are the global properties of the simple sprite.
Public m_RightBound As Integer
Public m_Leftbound As Integer
Public m_TopBound As Integer
Public m_Bottombound As Integer
Public m_missle As Object
Public m_background As Object
Public m_dispback As Object
```

3. This Collide function checks to see if the simple sprite has collided with the coordinates passed into the function. A check is done of each point of the four corners of the sprite to see if it lies within the coordinates.

```
'  Collide checks to see if a collision has been
'  detected between the coordinates passed in and the
'  position of the sprite
Public Sub collide(x, y, Width, Height, coll)

'  Start out as a false collision
coll = "False"

'  Check the upper left point of the square sprite to
'  see if it is within the bounds
If m_xx >= x And m_xx <= x + Width Then If m_yy >= y And m_yy <= y + Height Then
coll = "True":  Exit Sub

'  Check to see if the lower right point of the square sprite
'  is within the bounds
If m_xx + m_missle.ScaleWidth >= x And m_xx + m_missle.ScaleWidth <= x + Width
Then If m_yy + m_missle.ScaleHeight >= y And m_yy + m_missle.ScaleHeight <= y +
Height Then coll = "True": Exit Sub

'  Check the upper right point
If m_xx >= x And m_xx <= x + Width Then If m_yy + m_missle.ScaleHeight >= y And
m_yy + m_missle.ScaleHeight <= y + Height Then coll = "True": Exit Sub

'  Check the lower left point
If m_xx + m_missle.ScaleWidth >= x And m_xx + m_missle.ScaleWidth <= x + Width
Then If m_yy >= y And m_yy <= y + Height Then coll = "True": Exit Sub

End Sub
```

4. The Move function is called each time the sprite is to be moved. Unlike the MoveImage function in the Sprite2 class, this class tracks the position internally.

When the Move function is called, only the direction of the move has to be given. When the move is made, the original position of the sprite is covered with the background. Also, a check is done to see if the boundaries have been met. If so, the sprite is not moved.

```
Public Sub move(Direction As String)

'   Save the last XX and YY postion of the red
'   square
XXLast = m_xx
YYLast = m_yy

'   Depending on the key selected, we move the sprite
'   appropriately.  Note that we only move 9/10 of the
'   actual width and height to ensure all area is covered
If Direction = "LEFT" Then m_xx = m_xx - (m_missle.ScaleWidth * 0.9)
If Direction = "UP" Then m_yy = m_yy - (m_missle.ScaleWidth * 0.9)
If Direction = "RIGHT" Then m_xx = m_xx + (m_missle.ScaleWidth * 0.9)
If Direction = "DOWN" Then m_yy = m_yy + (m_missle.ScaleWidth * 0.9)

'   We check to see if the sprite has reached the
'   specified boundaries.  If so, we don't make
'   the move
If m_xx > m_RightBound Then m_xx = XXLast
If m_yy > m_Bottombound Then m_yy = YYLast
If m_xx < m_Leftbound Then m_xx = XXLast
If m_yy < m_TopBound Then m_yy = YYLast

'   Move the picture
m_missle.Left = m_xx
m_missle.Top = m_yy

'   Copy the original background to the
'   last spot the sprite was placed in.
throw% = BitBlt(m_dispback.hDC, XXLast, YYLast, m_missle.ScaleWidth, ↵
m_missle.ScaleHeight, m_background.hDC, XXLast, YYLast, SRCCOPY)

End Sub
```

5. Setup handles initializing the sprite. The various images sent in are set up. Also, the starting position of the sprite is sent to the function. This determines where the sprite will first appear.

```
Public Sub setup(xx, yy)

'   Ensure that the displayed background and
'   the copy of the background has a scalemode
'   set to pixel
m_dispback.ScaleMode = 3
m_background.ScaleMode = 3

'   It is important to ensure that the
'   autoredraw of the hidden background is
'   set to True
```

```
m_background.AutoRedraw = True

'  Store the origin starting point of the
'  sprite
m_xx = xx
m_yy = yy

'  Make sure the scalemode is pixels
m_missle.ScaleMode = 3

'  Move the sprite to the origin point
m_missle.move m_xx, m_yy

'  Make sure the sprite is visible
m_missle.Visible = True
End Sub
```

6. Following are the properties for the class. These include the sprite picture, the background, the displayed background, and the sprite's boundaries.

```
'  This is the displayed background
Public Property Set dispback(acontrol As Object)
    Set m_dispback = acontrol
End Property

'  This is a copy of the background
Public Property Set background(acontrol As Object)
    Set m_background = acontrol
End Property

'  This is the moving sprite, missle
Public Property Set Missle(acontrol As Object)
    Set m_missle = acontrol
End Property

'  The following properties set boundaries
'  for the sprite to move in.
Public Property Let RightBound(n As Integer)
    Let m_RightBound = n
End Property

Public Property Let Bottombound(n As Integer)
    Let m_Bottombound = n
End Property

Public Property Let TopBound(n As Integer)
    Let m_TopBound = n
End Property

Public Property Let Leftbound(n As Integer)
    Let m_Leftbound = n
End Property
```

7. This following is the code for SPRITE2.CLS. This is the same class as discussed in the last How-To.

```
'  BitBlt will be our primary function to handle
'  the sprite animation
Private Declare Function BitBlt Lib "GDI" (ByVal hDestDC As Integer, ByVal x ↵
As Integer, ByVal y As Integer, ByVal nWidth As Integer, ByVal nHeight As ↵
Integer, ByVal hSrcDC As Integer, ByVal XSrc As Integer, ByVal YSrc As ↵
Integer, ByVal dwRop As Long) As Integer

'  We will use the transparent bitmap techniques
'  developed in chapter4
Const SRCAND = &H8800C6
Const SRCINVERT = &H660046
Const SRCCOPY = &HCC0020

'  These are the global members of the class
Dim m_primarypict As Object
Dim m_mask1pict As Object
Dim m_mask2pict As Object
Dim m_background As Object
Dim m_dispback As Object
Dim m_transf1pict As Object
Dim m_temppict As Object

'  Declare the boundaries for detecting collisions
Dim m_rightbound As Integer
Dim m_bottombound As Integer
Dim m_topbound As Integer
Dim m_leftbound As Integer

'  Set the right boundary
Public Property Let RightBound(n As Integer)
    Let m_rightbound = n
End Property
'  Set the bottom boundary
Public Property Let Bottombound(n As Integer)
    Let m_bottombound = n
End Property
'  Set the Top boundary
Public Property Let TopBound(n As Integer)
    Let m_topbound = n
End Property
'  Set the left boundary
Public Property Let Leftbound(n As Integer)
    Let m_leftbound = n
End Property

'  This is the original image of the sprite
Public Property Set PrimaryPict(acontrol As Object)
    Set m_primarypict = acontrol
End Property

'  This is the first mask
Public Property Set mask1pict(acontrol As Object)
```

```
        Set m_mask1pict = acontrol
End Property


'  This is the second mask (black and white)
Public Property Set mask2pict(acontrol As Object)
        Set m_mask2pict = acontrol
End Property


'  This is the displayed background
Public Property Set background(acontrol As Object)
        Set m_background = acontrol
End Property


'   This is the background to be displayed
Public Property Set dispback(acontrol As Object)
        Set m_dispback = acontrol
End Property


'  This will be the working picture for building
'  the movement of the sprite.
Public Property Set transf1pict(acontrol As Object)
        Set m_transf1pict = acontrol
End Property


'  This will hold the mask, which converts the
'  background around the airship to black
Public Property Set temppict(acontrol As Object)
        Set m_temppict = acontrol
End Property


Public Sub collide(x, y, direction)

'  We check to see if the airship has reached the right
'  side of the form.  If so, we change direction
'  appropriately
If x + m_primarypict.ScaleWidth > m_rightbound Then
        If direction = "UR" Then direction = "UL"
        If direction = "DR" Then direction = "DL"
End If


'  We check to see if the airship has reached the left
'  side of the form.  If so, we change direction
'  appropriately
If x < m_leftbound Then
        If direction = "UL" Then direction = "UR"
        If direction = "DL" Then direction = "DR"
End If


'  We check to see if the airship has reached the
'  bottom side of the form.  If so, we change direction
'  appropriately
If y + m_primarypict.ScaleHeight > m_bottombound Then
        If direction = "DL" Then direction = "UL"
        If direction = "DR" Then direction = "UR"
End If
```

continued on next page

CHAPTER 5

continued from previous page

```
'  We check to see if the airship has reached the top
'  side of the form.  If so, we change direction
'  appropriately
If y < m_topbound Then
    If direction = "UL" Then direction = "DL"
    If direction = "UR" Then direction = "DR"
End If

End Sub

Public Sub MoveImage(x, y, xstep, ystep)

'  First copy the background from from the backup
'  of the background.  The copy is made from where
'  the airship is to be placed minus the move of
'  the airship.
throw% = BitBlt(m_transf1pict.hDC, 0, 0, m_transf1pict.ScaleWidth + (xstep * ↵
2), m_transf1pict.ScaleHeight + (ystep * 2), m_dispback.hDC, x - xstep, y - ↵
ystep, SRCCOPY)

'  Build the airship on the new section of the background  using
'  the transparent techniques developed in How-To 4.8
throw% = BitBlt(m_transf1pict.hDC, xstep, ystep, m_mask1pict.ScaleWidth, ↵
m_mask1pict.ScaleHeight, m_mask1pict.hDC, 0, 0, SRCAND)

throw% = BitBlt(m_transf1pict.hDC, xstep, ystep, m_temppict.ScaleWidth, ↵
m_temppict.ScaleHeight, m_temppict.hDC, 0, 0, SRCINVERT)

'  Copy the new image to the displayed background.  Note that
'  the image is placed where the previous airship was
'  located.  This will cover the old airship with background.
throw% = BitBlt(m_background.hDC, x - xstep, y - ystep, ↵
m_transf1pict.ScaleWidth, m_transf1pict.ScaleHeight, m_transf1pict.hDC, 0, ↵
0, SRCCOPY)

'm_collision = "None"

'collide x, y

End Sub

Private Sub CreateMask()

'  m_temppict will hold the mask needed for the transparent
'  display.  We first copy the full picture into m_temppict
throw% = BitBlt(m_temppict.hDC, 0, 0, m_mask2pict.ScaleWidth, ↵
m_mask2pict.ScaleHeight, m_mask2pict.hDC, 0, 0, SRCCOPY)

'  We now copy in the mask, which will clear the background
'  to black
throw% = BitBlt(m_temppict.hDC, 0, 0, m_primarypict.ScaleWidth, ↵
m_primarypict.ScaleHeight, m_primarypict.hDC, 0, 0, SRCINVERT)

End Sub
```

```
Public Sub setup()

'   Make sure that our picture that will hold
'   the background is the same size as the
'   background.
m_dispback.Width = m_background.Width
m_dispback.Height = m_background.Height


'   It is important to ensure that all of the
'   masks are set to the same size as the original
'   airship image.
m_primarypict.AutoSize = True

m_mask2pict.Width = m_primarypict.Width
m_mask2pict.Height = m_primarypict.Height

m_mask1pict.Width = m_primarypict.Width
m_mask1pict.Height = m_primarypict.Height

m_temppict.Width = m_primarypict.Width
m_temppict.Height = m_primarypict.Height


'   The picture used for building the movements
'   of the sprite needs to be large enough to hold
'   the additional background to cover the previous
'   location of the sprite.
m_transf1pict.Width = m_transf1pict.Width * 1.12
m_transf1pict.Height = m_transf1pict.Height * 1.12


'   The following statements ensure that
'   all of the images are operating with
'   a pixel scalemode
m_temppict.ScaleMode = 3
m_primarypict.ScaleMode = 3
m_mask2pict.ScaleMode = 3
m_mask1pict.ScaleMode = 3
m_transf1pict.ScaleMode = 3
m_dispback.ScaleMode = 3
m_background.ScaleMode = 3


'   All but the displayed background needs
'   to be set to autoredraw so the bit manipulations
'   can be done while the images are not visible.
m_temppict.AutoRedraw = True
m_primarypict.AutoRedraw = True
m_mask2pict.AutoRedraw = True
m_mask1pict.AutoRedraw = True
m_transf1pict.AutoRedraw = True
m_dispback.AutoRedraw = True


'   Create the mask from m_primarypict and m_mask2pict
CreateMask


'   Transfer background to the dispback
```

continued on next page

continued from previous page

```
'  picture, which will hold a copy of it
throw% = BitBlt(m_dispback.hDC, 0, 0, m_background.ScaleWidth, ↵
m_background.ScaleHeight, m_background.hDC, 0, 0, SRCCOPY)

End Sub
```

8. Add the following code to the general declarations section of the form. The BitBlt function is declared to copy the target on to the sprites. Also, the variables for tracking the sprites are declared.

```
'  BitBlt will be our primary function to handle
'  the sprite animation
Private Declare Function BitBlt Lib "GDI" (ByVal hDestDC As Integer, ByVal x ↵
As Integer, ByVal y As Integer, ByVal nWidth As Integer, ByVal nHeight As ↵
Integer, ByVal hSrcDC As Integer, ByVal XSrc As Integer, ByVal YSrc As ↵
Integer, ByVal dwRop As Long) As Integer

'  We will use the transparent bitmap techniques
'  developed in chapter4
Const SRCCOPY = &HCC0020

'  Globally declare our class objects
Dim Sprite1 As Sprite
Dim Sprite2 As Sprite
Dim Missle As SimpleSprite

'  X and Y will be used to track and move the airship
Dim x As Integer
Dim y As Integer

'  xx and yy will be used to track the red square
Dim xx As Integer
Dim yy As Integer

'  This will hold the origin point of the red
'  square to be placed on the airship picture
Dim airx As Integer
Dim airy As Integer

'  First will be used to execute the code in the
'  form paint event only once
Dim First As Integer

'  XStep and YStep will hold the amount for each movement
Dim XSTep As Integer
Dim YStep As Integer

'  Direction will track the direction the airship
'  is moving
Dim Direction As String

'  These constants will be used to check and see if
'  the arrow keys have been selected.
Const KEY_LEFT = &H25
Const KEY_UP = &H26
```

```
Const KEY_RIGHT = &H27
Const KEY_DOWN = &H28
```

9. Add the following code to the general declarations section of the form. The Winner function is called whenever the user successfully hits the target with the sprite.

```
Private Sub winner()

'   Center and print 'You win' on the
'   picture to indicate when the user
'   has succesfully crossed the red
'   squares.
picture1.CurrentX = (picture1.ScaleWidth / 2) - (picture1.TextWidth(⏎
"YOU WIN!!!") / 2)

picture1.CurrentY = (picture1.ScaleHeight / 2) - (picture1.TextWidth(⏎
"YOU WIN!!!") / 2)

picture1.Print "YOU WIN!"

End Sub
```

10. When a key is selected, a check is done to see if it is one of the arrow keys. If so, the missile sprite is moved.

```
Private Sub Form_KeyDown(KeyCode As Integer, Shift As Integer)

'   Depending on the key selected, we move the red square
'   appropriately.  Note that we only move 9/10 of the
'   actual red square width and height.
If KeyCode = KEY_LEFT Then Missle.move "LEFT"
If KeyCode = KEY_UP Then Missle.move "UP"
If KeyCode = KEY_RIGHT Then Missle.move "RIGHT"
If KeyCode = KEY_DOWN Then Missle.move "DOWN"

End Sub
```

11. The Form_Load procedure handles setting up the sprites and initializes the tracking variables for the sprites. Also, the target is placed on the airship sprites.

```
Private Sub Form_Load()

'  Create instances of the class objects
Set Sprite1 = New Sprite
Set Sprite2 = New Sprite
Set Missle = New SimpleSprite

'  Setup the Missile sprite
Set Missle.Missle = MisslePict
Set Missle.background = picture2
Set Missle.dispback = picture1
Let Missle.RightBound = picture1.ScaleWidth-10
Let Missle.TopBound = 0
```

continued on next page

continued from previous page

```
Let Missle.Bottombound = picture1.ScaleHeight-10
Let Missle.Leftbound = 0

'  Pass in the appropriate images
'  to initialize the class
Set Sprite1.PrimaryPict = fullpict
Set Sprite1.mask1pict = mask1
Set Sprite1.mask2pict = mask2
Set Sprite1.background = picture1
Set Sprite1.dispback = picture2
Set Sprite1.transf1pict = transf1
Set Sprite1.temppict = temppict

'  Intialize the second sprite
Set Sprite2.PrimaryPict = fullpict2
Set Sprite2.mask1pict = mask3
Set Sprite2.mask2pict = mask4
Set Sprite2.background = picture1
Set Sprite2.dispback = picture2
Set Sprite2.transf1pict = transf1
Set Sprite2.temppict = TempPict2


'  We are going to copy the misslepict image
'  onto the FullPict images to make that our moving
'  target to be hit.  In order to do this, we need
'  to ensure that the scalemode of the images is
'  pixel and that the MisslePict autoredraw property is
'  true so that BitBlt  will have access to its image.
picture1.ScaleMode = 3
MisslePict.ScaleMode = 3
MisslePict.AutoRedraw = True
fullpict.ScaleMode = 3
fullpict2.ScaleMode = 3
fullpict.AutoRedraw = True
fullpict2.AutoRedraw = True

'  Calculate the center of airship images.
airx = fullpict.ScaleWidth / 2 - MisslePict.ScaleWidth / 2
airy = fullpict.ScaleHeight / 2 - MisslePict.ScaleHeight / 2

'  We now copy the square to the center of the images.  Note that
'  this is successful because the two images are tightly cropped
'  around the airship, so the center will be the same.
throw% = BitBlt(fullpict.hDC, airx, airy, MisslePict.ScaleWidth, ↵
MisslePict.ScaleHeight, MisslePict.hDC, 0, 0, SRCCOPY)

throw% = BitBlt(fullpict2.hDC, airx, airy, MisslePict.ScaleWidth, ↵
MisslePict.ScaleHeight, MisslePict.hDC, 0, 0, SRCCOPY)


'  Set the moving boundaries for the sprites
Let Sprite1.Leftbound = 0
Let Sprite1.TopBound = 0
Let Sprite1.RightBound = picture1.ScaleWidth
```

```
Let Sprite1.Bottombound = picture1.ScaleHeight

Let Sprite2.Leftbound = 0
Let Sprite2.TopBound = 0
Let Sprite2.RightBound = picture1.ScaleWidth
Let Sprite2.Bottombound = picture1.ScaleHeight

'  The x step will be 3 and the y step will be 1
'  This is the amount the airship is moved each time
XSTep = 3
YStep = 1

'  Start at the origin
y = 0
x = 0

'  Our direction is down and right
Direction = "DR"

'  Move the picture to the top right
picture1.move 0, 0

'  Set the form width and height to the
'  background picture
Form1.Width = picture1.Width
Form1.Height = picture1.Height + 300

End Sub
```

12. When the form is painted, the airship sprites are set up, as well as the missile sprite.

```
Private Sub Form_Paint()

If First = 0 Then

    '  Set up sprite1 and sprite2
    Sprite1.setup
    Sprite2.setup

    '  Reset first
    First = 1

    '  Set up the simple sprite
    Missle.setup 0, 0

End If

End Sub
```

13. The first part of the timer works the same way as in the last How-To. The appropriate airship is moved and a check is done to see if it has collided with the boundaries. Also, a check is done to see if the missile sprite has hit the target.

```
Private Sub Timer1_Timer()
```

continued on next page

continued from previous page

```
'  With each timer event we will make 15 moves
For n = 1 To 5

        '   Depending on the direction, we will increment or
        '   decrement X and Y appropriately and move the sprite.
        '   We will also check to see if the boundaries have been
        '   hit for the airship sprites.
        Select Case Direction

        Case "UL"
             x = x - XSTep
             y = y - YStep
             Sprite2.MoveImage x, y, XSTep, YStep
             Sprite2.collide x, y, Direction

        Case "UR"
             x = x + XSTep
             y = y - YStep
             Sprite1.MoveImage x, y, XSTep, YStep
             Sprite1.collide x, y, Direction

        Case "DL"
             x = x - XSTep
             y = y + YStep
             Sprite2.MoveImage x, y, XSTep, YStep
             Sprite2.collide x, y, Direction

        Case "DR"
             x = x + XSTep
             y = y + YStep
             Sprite1.MoveImage x, y, XSTep, YStep
             Sprite1.collide x, y, Direction

        End Select


        '   Check to see if the red square has
        '   collided with the airship red square
             Missle.collide x + airx, y + airy, MisslePict.ScaleWidth, ⏎
MisslePict.ScaleHeight, coll

        '   If there was a collision, then turn off
        '   the timer and run the winner routine
        If coll = "True" Then Timer1.Enabled = False: winner

Next n

End Sub
```

How It Works

You have combined the sprite class from the last section with a simple sprite class. When you move the airship, you have to ensure that the last location of the airship is completely covered, and you have to do the same for the picture box sprite. In the Move function of the class, copy from background (the background copy) the appropriate image to where the picture box was last located. This is done by storing the last position of the red square in the XXLast and YYLast variables. Also check to see if the box has moved to any of the set boundaries. If so, ignore any attempt to move outside the form.

In the Form_Load procedure, you actually copy the red square image into the full image airship pictures (fullpict and fullpict2). This allows you to add a simple target to the airship. Because the images are closely cropped and the target is centered, regardless of the left- or right-pointing airship, the target is in the same centered spot.

The SimpleSprite collide function checks to see if the target red square and the moving red square have crossed. It does this by passing the coordinates of the target red square. AirX and AirY hold the location on the airship sprites. By adding these values to the current X and Y location of the airship, the origin of the target is ascertained. When the Collide function is called, the width and height of the target are also passed in. The Collide function then checks to see if the two boxes have crossed.

Comments

The picture control you are using to create the moving red square could also contain a bitmap image. It also could be expanded to support control of a transparent bitmap.

5.7 How do I...
Add animated highlights to text?

COMPLEXITY: ADVANCED

Problem

I would like to add animated highlights to my displayed text.

Technique

You will use the transparent bitmap techniques developed in How-To 4.8 with the picture-box flip book from earlier in this chapter to create a highlight effect for text.

Steps

Open and run 5-7.VBP. The running program appears as shown in Figure 5-7-1. Click on the back of the form to make the highlight sparkle effect appear.

1. Create a new project called 5-7.VBP. Add the objects and properties listed in Table 5-7-1 to Form1 and save the form as 5-7.FRM.

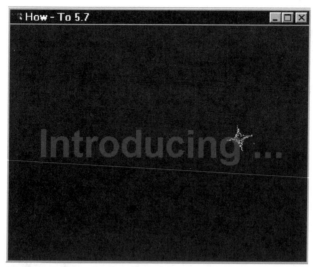

Figure 5-7-1 The form at runtime

Table 5-7-1 The project's objects and properties

OBJECT	PROPERTY	SETTING
Form	Name	Form1
	BackColor	&H00FFFFFF&
	Caption	"How-To 5.7"
	Font	
	name	"Arial"
	size	30
	ForeColor	&H000000FF&
	KeyPreview	-1 'True
PictureBox	Name	smask5
	AutoRedraw	-1 'True
	AutoSize	-1 'True
	BackColor	&H00FFFFFF&
	BorderStyle	0 'None
	Picture	(Smask5.bmp)
	ScaleMode	3 'Pixel
	Visible	0 'False

OBJECT	PROPERTY	SETTING
PictureBox	Name	smask4
	AutoRedraw	-1 'True
	AutoSize	-1 'True
	BackColor	&H00FFFFFF&
	BorderStyle	0 'None
	Picture	(Smask4.bmp)
	ScaleMode	3 'Pixel
	Visible	0 'False
PictureBox	Name	spark5
	AutoRedraw	-1 'True
	AutoSize	-1 'True
	BackColor	&H00FFFFFF&
	BorderStyle	0 'None
	Picture	(Spark5.bmp)
	ScaleMode	3 'Pixel
	Visible	0 'False
PictureBox	Name	spark4
	AutoRedraw	-1 'True
	AutoSize	-1 'True
	BackColor	&H00FFFFFF&
	BorderStyle	0 'None
	Picture	(Spark4.bmp)
	ScaleMode	3 'Pixel
	Visible	0 'False
PictureBox	Name	Picture1
	BackColor	&H00FF0000&
	BorderStyle	0 'None
	ForeColor	&H000000FF&
PictureBox	Name	smask3
	AutoRedraw	-1 'True
	AutoSize	-1 'True
	BackColor	&H00FFFFFF&

continued on next page

311

continued from previous page

OBJECT	PROPERTY	SETTING
	BorderStyle	0 'None
	Picture	(Smask3.bmp)
	ScaleMode	3 'Pixel
	Visible	0 'False
PictureBox	Name	smask2
	AutoRedraw	-1 'True
	AutoSize	-1 'True
	BorderStyle	0 'None
	Picture	(Smask2.bmp)
	ScaleMode	3 'Pixel
	Visible	0 'False
PictureBox	Name	smask1
	AutoRedraw	-1 'True
	AutoSize	-1 'True
	BorderStyle	0 'None
	Picture	(Smask1.bmp)
	ScaleMode	3 'Pixel
	Visible	0 'False
Timer	Name	Timer1
	Enabled	0 'False
	Interval	75
PictureBox	Name	spark1
	AutoRedraw	-1 'True
	AutoSize	-1 'True
	BorderStyle	0 'None
	Picture	(Spark1.bmp)
	Visible	0 'False
PictureBox	Name	spark2
	AutoRedraw	-1 'True
	AutoSize	-1 'True
	BorderStyle	0 'None

OBJECT	PROPERTY	SETTING
	Picture	(Spark2.bmp)
	ScaleMode	3 'Pixel
	Visible	0 'False
PictureBox	Name	spark3
	AutoRedraw	-1 'True
	AutoSize	-1 'True
	BackColor	&H00FFFFFF&
	BorderStyle	0 'None
	Picture	(Spark3.bmp)
	ScaleMode	3 'Pixel
	Visible	0 'False

2. Add the following code to the general declarations section of the form.

```
'  BitBlt will be used to copy the picture and sparkles
'  to the form.
Private Declare Function BitBlt Lib "GDI" (ByVal hDestDC As Integer, ByVal X ↵
As Integer, ByVal Y As Integer, ByVal nWidth As Integer, ByVal nHeight As ↵
Integer, ByVal hSrcDC As Integer, ByVal XSrc As Integer, ByVal YSrc As ↵
Integer, ByVal dwRop As Long) As Integer

'  These will be used for transferring the images
Const SRCAND = &H8800C6
Const SRCINVERT = &H660046
Const SRCCOPY = &HCC0020

'  N will be used to count through the sparkles
Dim N As Integer

'  X and Y will be used to calculate the position
'  of the sparkles0
Dim X As Integer
Dim Y As Integer

'  Flag will be used to count how many times
'  the sparkle spins
Dim Flag As Integer

'  First will be used to perform the Form_Paint
'  code only once
Dim First As Integer
```

3. Add the following code to the general declarations section of the form. This function handles displaying the text on the picture control. It also calculates where the sparkle will take place.

```
Private Sub Distext()

'  We will clear picture1
picture1.Cls

'  Dis$ holds the string to be displayed
Dis$ = "Introducing ..."

'  X and Y hold the center for printing the
'  text on the picture.
X = (picture1.ScaleWidth / 2) - (picture1.TextWidth(Dis$) / 2)
Y = (picture1.ScaleHeight / 2) - (picture1.TextHeight(Dis$) / 2)

'  Set the currentx and currenty to the X and Y
'  location.
picture1.CurrentX = X
picture1.CurrentY = Y

'  Print the text on the picture
picture1.Print Dis$

'  We now calculate the location of the sparkle, which will
'  be at the end of the lower case g.  For Y we move down to the
'  top of the g by dividing the g height by 2.8.
X = (picture1.ScaleWidth / 2) - (picture1.TextWidth(Dis$) / 2) + ↵
picture1.TextWidth("Introducing") - (picture1.TextWidth("g") / 11)

Y = (picture1.ScaleHeight / 2) - (picture1.TextHeight(Dis$) / 2) + ↵
(picture1.TextHeight("g") / 2.8)

End Sub
```

4. When the form is clicked on, the sparkle will start.

```
Private Sub Form_Click()

'  Set Flag to 0
Flag = 0

'  Set N to 0
N = 0

'  Set the picture scalemode to 3
picture1.ScaleMode = 3

'  Start the timer.
timer1.Enabled = True

End Sub
```

5. Add the following code to the Form_Load procedure.

```
Private Sub Form_Load()

'  Set First to 1 so that the code
```

```
'  in Form_Paint will be executed.
First = 1

End Sub
```

6. The Form_Paint procedure handles displaying the picture at start up.

```
Private Sub Form_Paint()

'  Only execute this code the first time
'  the event is fired.
If First = 1 Then

    '  Set the form width and height to that
    '  of the picture.  Note that we add 400 to
    '  the height so that all of the picture is
    '  exposed.
    Form1.Width = picture1.Width
    Form1.Height = picture1.Height + 300

    '  Turn on the autoredraw feature of the picture
    '  Set the picture1 and form1 scalemode to pixel
    picture1.AutoRedraw = True
    picture1.ScaleMode = 3
    Form1.ScaleMode = 3

    '  Set First to 0 so that this code is not
    '  executed again.
    First = 0

    '  Display the text
    Distext

    '  Copy the picture to the form.
    throw% = BitBlt(Form1.hDC, 0, 0, picture1.ScaleWidth, ↵
        picture1.ScaleHeight, picture1.hDC, 0, 0, SRCCOPY)

End If

End Sub
```

7. The timer handles "flipping" through the different steps of the sparkle and displays the transparent image.

```
Private Sub Timer1_Timer()

'  Increment N
N = N + 1

'  Display the text
Distext

'  If we have displayed sparkle three times, we
'  then display the picture without the sparkle.
If Flag = 3 Then
```

continued on next page

continued from previous page

```
      timer1.Enabled = False
      N = 6
      throw% = BitBlt(Form1.hDC, 0, 0, picture1.ScaleWidth, ↵
          picture1.ScaleHeight, picture1.hDC, 0, 0, SRCCOPY)
End If



'  Each If checks to see which sparkle should be displayed
If N = 1 Then
    '  Calculate the center of the sparkle
    a = smask1.ScaleWidth / 2
    b = smask1.ScaleHeight / 2

    '  Display the sparkle at the X and Y location minus the
    '  width and height of the sparkle.  This ensures that the
    '  sparkles will all be displayed at the same spot.
    throw% = BitBlt(picture1.hDC, X - a, Y - b, smask1.ScaleWidth, ↵
        smask1.ScaleHeight, smask1.hDC, 0, 0, SRCAND)

        throw% = BitBlt(picture1.hDC, X - a, Y - b, spark1.ScaleWidth, ↵
        spark1.ScaleHeight, spark1.hDC, 0, 0, SRCINVERT)
End If

'  For the rest of the sparkles, see the code above.
If N = 2 Then
    a = smask2.ScaleWidth / 2
    b = smask2.ScaleHeight / 2

    throw% = BitBlt(picture1.hDC, X - a, Y - b, smask2.ScaleWidth, ↵
        smask2.ScaleHeight, smask2.hDC, 0, 0, SRCAND)

    throw% = BitBlt(picture1.hDC, X - a, Y - b, spark2.ScaleWidth, ↵
        spark2.ScaleHeight, spark2.hDC, 0, 0, SRCINVERT)
End If


If N = 3 Then
    a = smask3.ScaleWidth / 2
    b = smask3.ScaleHeight / 2

    throw% = BitBlt(picture1.hDC, X - a, Y - b, smask3.ScaleWidth,↵
        smask3.ScaleHeight, smask3.hDC, 0, 0, SRCAND)

    throw% = BitBlt(picture1.hDC, X - a, Y - b, spark3.ScaleWidth, ↵
        spark3.ScaleHeight, spark3.hDC, 0, 0, SRCINVERT)
End If


If N = 4 Then
    a = smask4.ScaleWidth / 2
    b = smask4.ScaleHeight / 2

    throw% = BitBlt(picture1.hDC, X - a, Y - b, smask4.ScaleWidth, ↵
        smask4.ScaleHeight, smask4.hDC, 0, 0, SRCAND)
```

```
      throw% = BitBlt(picture1.hDC, X - a, Y - b, spark4.ScaleWidth, ↵
         spark4.ScaleHeight, spark4.hDC, 0, 0, SRCINVERT)
End If

If N = 5 Then
    a = smask5.ScaleWidth / 2
    b = smask5.ScaleHeight / 2

    throw% = BitBlt(picture1.hDC, X - a, Y - b, smask5.ScaleWidth, ↵
        smask5.ScaleHeight, smask5.hDC, 0, 0, SRCAND)

    throw% = BitBlt(picture1.hDC, X - a, Y - b, spark5.ScaleWidth, ↵
        spark5.ScaleHeight, spark5.hDC, 0, 0, SRCINVERT)
End If

'  Last we copy the picture to the form so that the
'  image is updated.  Note:  To speed up the display
'  only the section with the sparkle could be transferred.
throw% = BitBlt(Form1.hDC, 0, 0, picture1.ScaleWidth, picture1.ScaleHeight, ↵
picture1.hDC, 0, 0, SRCCOPY)

'  When we reach the last sparkle, we set n to 0 to
'  start over and increment Flag.
If N = 5 Then N = 0: Flag = Flag + 1

End Sub
```

How It Works

The sparkle animation was developed in a paint program. Different frames rotate the growing and shrinking sparkle. Black and white masks are then developed from the original images.

You use the techniques developed in Chapter 2 to display text in the picture control. You also use these techniques to calculate the position of the sparkle on the text. Once you have the text displayed, copy the contents of the picture control to the form. The reason you do not display the text on the form and animate the sparkle directly on the form is because for each new cell of the sparkle, you need to clear out the last sparkle. If you use the FORM.CLS event, a flicker will be noticeable between the display of each sparkle cell. Instead, you do the animation on the picture box and then copy the contents to the form.

The timer control handles updating the picture with the next appropriate sparkle cell. To make the sparkle highlight effective, you need to perform the sparkle animation at least twice. This is counted in the timer control using the flag variable.

Comments

You might also want to consider moving the sparkle along the text. A simple character-to-character path could be developed using the TextWidth function. Smaller and larger sparkles can be developed using the StretchBlt API function.

5.8 How do I...
Display animations created by Animation Works Interactive?

Problem

I would like to be able to play animations developed by GoldDisk's Animations Works Interactive (AWI).

Technique

GoldDisk provides a MCI driver that allows you to access the animations using the MCI control provided with Visual Basic 4.0.

Steps

Open and run 5-8.VBP. The running program appears as shown in Figure 5-8-1.

1. Create a new project called 5-8.VBP. Add the objects and properties listed in Table 5-8-1 to Form1 and save the form as 5-8.FRM.

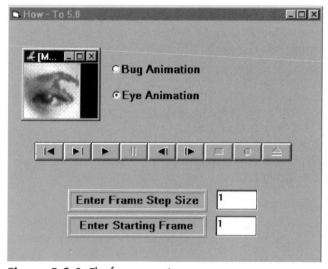

Figure 5-8-1 The form at runtime

Table 5-8-1 The project's objects and properties

OBJECT	PROPERTY	SETTING
Form	Name	Form1
	BackColor	&H00808080&
	Caption	"How-To 5.8"
OptionButton	Name	Option2
	BackColor	&H00C0C0C0&
	Caption	"Eye Animation"
OptionButton	Name	Option1
	BackColor	&H00C0C0C0&
	Caption	"Bug Animation"
	Value	-1 'True
TextBox	Name	FrameStart
	Text	"1"
TextBox	Name	FrameStep
	Text	"1"
SSPanel	Name	Panel3D4
	Caption	"Enter Starting Frame"
	Bevelinner	1
SSPanel	Name	Panel3D1
	Caption	"Enter Frame Step Size"
	Bevelinner	1
MMControl	Name	MMControl1
	Playenabled	-1 'True

2. Add the following code to the Form_Load procedure to set up the MCI control.

```
Private Sub Form_Load()

' CENTER SCREEN
Move (Screen.Width - Form1.Width) / 2, (Screen.Height - Form1.Height) / 2

' We are going to initialize the MCI Control by making sure it is closed
```

continued on next page

CHAPTER 5

continued from previous page

```
mmcontrol1.Command = "Close"

' Load the file name to the directory where we are running the project from.
mmcontrol1.FileName = App.Path + "\bug.awm"

' Open the file for play
mmcontrol1.Command = "Open"

End Sub
```

3. Add the following code to the appropriate procedures. It checks to ensure that only numbers are entered into the text boxes.

```
Private Sub FrameStart_KeyPress(KeyAscii As Integer)

' We will not allow anything but numbers to be typed into the text box
If KeyAscii > 58 Or KeyAscii < 47 Then KeyAscii = 0

End Sub

Private Sub FrameStep_KeyPress(KeyAscii As Integer)

' We will not allow anything but numbers to be typed into the text box
If KeyAscii > 58 Or KeyAscii < 47 Then KeyAscii = 0

End Sub
```

4. Whenever the user selects to go back in the animation, the animation moves the number of frames entered in the Frame Step text box.

```
Private Sub MMControl1_BackClick(Cancel As Integer)

' If the back button is clicked we want to go back the current
' number of frames set in the Framestep text box
mmcontrol1.Frames = Framestep.Text
End Sub
```

5. When the animation is played, it starts at the frame selected by the user.

```
Private Sub MMControl1_PlayClick(Cancel As Integer)

' Check to make sure that the starting frame is not invalid
If Val(FrameStart.Text) > mmcontrol1.Length Then MsgBox "The starting frame ↵
is larger than the number of frames in the clip": GoTo SETO

If Val(FrameStart.Text) < 0 Then MsgBox "The starting frame is smaller than ↵
0": GoTo SETO

' set the starting frame to the one entered
mmcontrol1.From = FrameStart.Text: GoTo ENDPLAY

' Reset starting frame to 0
SETO:
FrameStart.Text = 0
```

ENDPLAY:

End Sub

6. If the user wants to step through the animation, it steps the number of frames set in the Frame Step text box.

```
Private Sub MMControl1_StepClick(Cancel As Integer)

' If the step button is clicked, we want to go back the current
' number of frames set in the Framestep text box
mmcontrol1.Frames = Framestep.Text
End Sub
```

7. The following two option click procedures handle changing between the two animations.

```
Private Sub Option2_Click()

' We are going to initialize the MCI Control by making sure it is closed
mmcontrol1.Command = "Close"

' Load the file name to the directory where we are running the project from.
mmcontrol1.FileName = App.Path + "\eye.awm"

' Open the file for play
mmcontrol1.Command = "Open"

End Sub

Private Sub Option1_Click()

' We are going to initialize the MCI Control by making sure it is closed
mmcontrol1.Command = "Close"

' We are going to set the play window to the picture on form1
'mmcontrol1.hWndDisplay = picture1.hWnd

' Load the file name to the directory where we running the project from.
mmcontrol1.FileName = App.Path & "\bug.awm"

' Open the file for play
mmcontrol1.Command = "Open"

End Sub
```

How It Works

Using the MCI control with the GoldDisk MCI driver makes accessing and playing GoldDisk animations straightforward. The uniform MCI interface provides for simple changes to play WAV, AVI, and AWM files. You will find that this section is similar to How-To 5.11.

Comments

If you have an MCI device installed in your system, the same basic principles as found here can be implemented to access the device.

5.9 How do I...
Display animations created by Autodesk Animator?

Problem

I would like to be able to play the popular FLC animations created by Autodesk Animator.

Technique

Autodesk provides a custom control and DLL, which allow easy and flexible playing of FLC/FLI animation files.

Steps

Open and run 5-9.VBP. The running program appears as shown in Figure 5-9-1.

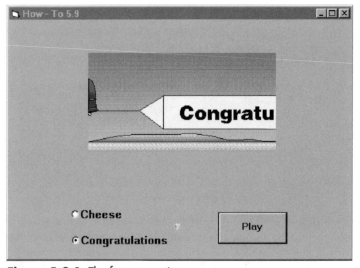

Figure 5-9-1 The form at runtime

Select the animation you wish to play and click on the Play button to play it.

1. Create a new project called 5-9.VBP. Add the objects and properties listed in Table 5-9-1 to Form1 and save as 5-9.FRM.

Table 5-9-1 The project's objects and properties

OBJECT	PROPERTY	SETTING
Form	Name	Form1
	BackColor	&H00808080&
	Caption	"How-To 5.9"
	FillStyle	0 'Solid
PictureBox	Name	Picture2
	AutoSize	-1 'True
	BorderStyle	0 'None
	Picture	(r001.bmp)
	Visible	0 'False
PictureBox	Name	Picture1
	AutoSize	-1 'True
	BorderStyle	0 'None
	Picture	(p001.bmp)
	Visible	0 'False

Note: This is a custom control.

VBAnimation	Name	Animation1
	AutoPlay	-1 'True
	BeginFade	0 'Cut
	BeginFadeTime	500
	ColorCycling	-1 'True
	EndFade	0 'Cut
	EndFadeTime	500
	EndLoop	0
	LoopFrame	-1 'True

continued on next page

continued from previous page

OBJECT	PROPERTY	SETTING
CommandButton	Name	Play
	Caption	"Play"
OptionButton	Name	Option2
	BackColor	&H00C0C0C0&
	Caption	"Congratulations"
OptionButton	Name	Option1
	BackColor	&H00C0C0C0&
	Caption	"Cheese"
	Value	-1 'True

2. Add the following code in the general declarations section of the form. First is used in the Form_Paint procedure.

```
' First will be used to indicate the first time
' we have loaded the form
Dim First As Integer
```

3. In the Form_Load procedure, center the form on the screen.

```
Private Sub Form_Load()

' CENTER SCREEN
Move (Screen.Width - Form1.Width) / 2, (Screen.Height - Form1.Height) / 2

End Sub
```

4. In the Form_Paint procedure, play the animation by calling the Play_Click procedure.

```
Private Sub Form_Paint()

' Play the animation the first time
' we load the form
If First = 0 Then Play_Click: First = 1

End Sub
```

5. In the Play_Click procedure, load and play the appropriate animation.

```
Private Sub Play_Click()

' Check to see if the Cheese option button has been
' selected
If option1.Value = -1 Then
    ' Disable the animation
```

```
        animation1.Enabled = False

        '   Turn off the autoplay
        animation1.AutoPlay = False

        '   Set the animation file
        animation1.Animation = App.Path + "\photochs.flc"

        '   Set the animation width and height to that
        '   of the template in picture1
        animation1.Width = picture1.Width
        animation1.Height = picture1.Height

        '   Center the animation
        animation1.Move (Form1.Width / 2) - (animation1.Height / 2), ↵
            ((Form1.Height / 2) - (animation1.Height / 2)) - 800

Else

        '   Disable the animation
        animation1.Enabled = False

        '   Turn off the autoplay
        animation1.AutoPlay = False

        '   Set the animation file
        animation1.Animation = App.Path + "\raccong.flc"

        '   Set the animation width and height to that
        '   of the template in picture2
        animation1.Width = picture2.Width
        animation1.Height = picture2.Height

        '   Center the animation
        animation1.Move (Form1.Width / 2) - (animation1.Width / 2), ↵
            ((Form1.Height / 2) - (animation1.Height / 2)) - 800
End If

'   Make the animation visible
animation1.Visible = True

'   Have the animation pause at the end
animation1.PauseAtEnd = 700

'   Only play the animation once
animation1.EndLoop = 1

'   Set the autoplay to true to play the animation
animation1.AutoPlay = True

End Sub
```

How It Works

In the Play_Click procedure, you set up the playing of the animation. Once you load the animation by setting the file name, set the AutoPlay procedure to true. That will start the playing of the animation. It is also important to set the EndLoop member to 1. This will play the animation once. If you want to play the animation more than once in sequence, change EndLoop to the number of iterations you desire.

Because the custom control does not provide a feature to automatically size the control to the animation, you have to use a roundabout method to make sure the control is sized to the animation. You will notice that two picture files are loaded onto the form. One picture contains a single frame from the first animation and the second contains a single frame from the second. When the animation is loaded into the control, the program sets the width and height to that of the appropriate picture. The animation package can get the single frame from the animations, or you can create one by pushing Print Screen while the animation is in progress and using a paint tool to cut out the animation image.

Comments

The Autodesk custom control provides for many additional features. These can be accessed and tested by clicking on the AnimSettings in the Properties windows. You can add a timed fade in and fade out of the animation and other effects.

5.10 How do I...
Display QuickTime movies?

Problem

Apple's QuickTime is a popular video format. How can I play Macintosh QuickTime files from my Visual Basic 4.0 application?

Technique

Apple provides a flexible custom control with its QuickTime for Windows package. You will use this control to play QuickTime files.

Steps

Open and run 5-10.VBP. The running program appears as shown in Figure 5-10-1.

Select the QuickTime movie you would like to play and then click on the play button on the video window. You can adjust the size of the window by selecting the lower right of the video window. The rooster movie has sound with it; the volume of the sound can be adjusted by selecting the speaker icon to the right of the video window.

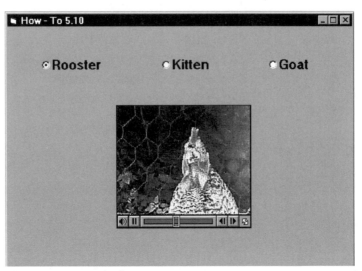

Figure 5-10-1 The form at runtime

1. Create a new project called 5-10.VBP. Add the objects and properties listed in Table 5-10-1 to Form1 and save the form as 5-10.FRM.

Table 5-10-1 The project's objects and properties

OBJECT	PROPERTY	SETTING
Form	Name	Form1
	BackColor	&H00808080&
	Caption	"How-To 5.10"
	FillStyle	0 'Solid
OptionButton	Name	Kitten
	BackColor	&H00808080&
	Caption	"Kitten"
	ForeColor	&H0000FFFF&
OptionButton	Name	Goat
	BackColor	&H00808080&
	Caption	"Goat"
	ForeColor	&H0000FFFF&

continued on next page

continued from previous page

OBJECT	PROPERTY	SETTING
OptionButton	Name	Rooster
	BackColor	&H00808080&
	Caption	"Rooster"
	ForeColor	&H0000FFFF&
	Value	-1 'True
Note: This is a custom control.		
QTMovie	Name	QTMovie1
	AutoSize	-1 'True
	GrowBox	-1 'True
	Visible	-1 'True

2. The Form_Load procedure centers the form on the screen.

```
Private Sub Form_Load()

' CENTER SCREEN
Move (Screen.Width - Form1.Width) / 2, (Screen.Height - Form1.Height) / 2

'   Load the Rooster Movie
Rooster_Click

End Sub
```

3. When any one of the three option buttons is selected, it loads the movie and centers the video box on the form.

```
Private Sub Goat_Click()

'   Load the Goat Movie and place it on the form
qtmovie1.MovieName = App.Path + "\goat.mov"

qtmovie1.Move Form1.Width / 2 - qtmovie1.Width / 2, Form1.Height / 2 ↵
- qtmovie1.Height / 2 + 200

End Sub

Private Sub Kitten_Click()

'   Load the Kitten Movie and place it on the form
qtmovie1.MovieName = App.Path + "\kitten.mov"

qtmovie1.Move Form1.Width / 2 - qtmovie1.Width / 2, Form1.Height / 2 ↵
- qtmovie1.Height / 2 + 200

End Sub
```

```
Private Sub Rooster_Click()

'  Load the Rooster Movie and place it on the form
qtmovie1.MovieName = App.Path + "\rooster.mov"

qtmovie1.Move Form1.Width / 2 - qtmovie1.Width / 2, Form1.Height / 2 ↵
- qtmovie1.Height / 2 + 200

End Sub
```

How It Works

Although the QuickTime custom control does not provide as many options to play the video files as the Autodesk control, it does provide for flexible and easy playing of QuickTime video. The only real programming to be concerned with is setting the file name.

```
qtmovie1.MovieName = app.Path + "\rooster.mov"
```

The ability to size the video can be turned off by setting the Grow Box property to false.

Comments

The QuickTime for Windows package also installs an MCI driver. By using the MCI control demonstrated earlier in the chapter, QuickTime movies can be played. The custom control has the benefit of giving the user direct control of playing the video, as well as control of the sound, without additional programming.

5.11 How do I...
Display audio-visual interleaved animation files?

COMPLEXITY: INTERMEDIATE

Problem

I would like to be able to play an audio-visual interleaved (AVI) file and use some of the MCI techniques to control the playback of the file.

Technique

With the MCI control in the Professional Edition of Visual Basic 4.0, you have a powerful tool that allows you to have complete control of playing your AVI files. This How-To will show you how to load and manipulate your AVI files using several different methods.

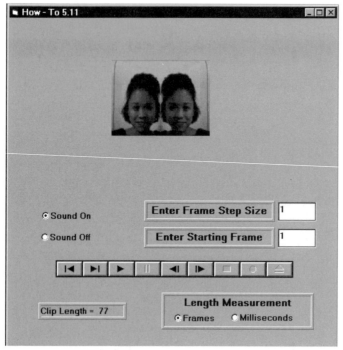

Figure 5-11-1 The form at runtime

Steps

Open and run 5-11.VBP. The running program appears as shown in Figure 5-11-1.

If the AVI file you are playing has sound, you can turn it off and on by using the two option buttons. The Clip Length window tells you the number of frames in the AVI clip. You can also view the length in milliseconds by selecting the Milliseconds button. For the backward and forward (step) buttons (buttons 5 and 6), you can specify how many frames to move each click by setting the value in the Enter Frame Step Size text box. When you go to play the clip (button 3), you can specify the starting frame by entering the frame number in the Enter Starting Frame text box.

1. Create a new project called 5-11.VBP. Add the objects and properties listed in Table 5-11-1 to Form1 and save the form as 5-11.FRM.

Table 5-11-1 The project's objects and properties

OBJECT	PROPERTY	SETTING
Form	Name	Form1
	BackColor	&H00808080&

OBJECT	PROPERTY	SETTING
	Caption	"How-To 5.11"
TextBox	Name	FrameStart
	Text	"1"
SSPanel	Name	Panel3D4
	BevelInner	1 'Inset
	Caption	"Enter Starting Frame"
SSPanel	Name	Panel3D3
	AutoSize	1 'AutoSize Panel Width To Caption
	BevelInner	1 'Inset
Label	Name	Label1
	BackColor	&H00C0C0C0&
	Caption	"Label1"
SSPanel	Name	Panel3D2
	Alignment	6 'Center - TOP
	BevelInner	1 'Inset
	Caption	"Length Measurement"
OptionButton	Name	Milli
	BackColor	&H00C0C0C0&
	Caption	"Milliseconds"
OptionButton	Name	Frames
	BackColor	&H00C0C0C0&
	Caption	"Frames"
SSPanel	Name	Panel3D1
	BevelInner	1 'Inset
	Caption	"Enter Frame Step Size"
TextBox	Name	FrameStep
	Text	"1"

continued on next page

continued from previous page

OBJECT	PROPERTY	SETTING
MMControl	Name	MMControl1
	PlayEnabled	-1 'True
PictureBox	Name	Picture1
	BackColor	&H00808080&
	BorderStyle	0 'None
OptionButton	Name	SoundOff
	BackColor	&H0080FFFF&
	Caption	"Sound Off"
OptionButton	Name	SoundOn
	BackColor	&H0080FFFF&
	Caption	"Sound On"

2. Most of the code in this section is used to set up the placement of the objects on the form. The code also initializes the MCI control and sets the file to play. The clip length label is initialized to the number of frames in the clip.

```
Private Sub Form_Load()

' The following placement commands will set the placement of the objects in the
' appropriate places on the screen.  This will help to ensure that the form looks
'  correct in all resolutions


' CENTER SCREEN
Move (Screen.Width - Form1.Width) / 2, (Screen.Height - Form1.Height) / 2

' Place Movie Window
picture1.Move (Form1.Width / 2) - (picture1.Width / 2), (Form1.Height / 2) ↵
- (picture1.Height / 2) - 1300

' Place Length Window and Autosize Panel
' Also set the caption to the number of frames for the label
' contained in the panel3d3 window

panel3d3.Move (Form1.Width / 2) - (panel3d3.Width / 2) - 1800, (Form1.Height ↵
/ 2) - (panel3d3.Height / 2) + 2300

panel3d3.AutoSize = 1
label1.Caption = "Clip Length = " + Str$(mmcontrol1.Length)
label1.AutoSize = True

' Place Frames/Milliseconds Window
panel3d2.Move (Form1.Width / 2) - (panel3d2.Width / 2) + 1250, (Form1.Height ↵
/ 2) - (panel3d2.Height / 2) + 2300
```

```
' Place MCI Control
mmcontrol1.Move (Form1.Width / 2) - (mmcontrol1.Width / 2), (Form1.Height / 2) ↵
(mmcontrol1.Height / 2) + 1500

' Place FrameStep Window
Framestep.Move (Form1.Width / 2) - (Framestep.Width / 2) + 2400, ↵
(Form1.Height   / 2) - (Framestep.Height / 2) + 400

' Place Frames Label
panel3d1.Move (Form1.Width / 2) - (panel3d1.Width / 2) + 700, (Form1.Height ↵
/ 2) - (panel3d1.Height / 2) + 400


' Place FrameStart Window
FrameStart.Move (Form1.Width / 2) - (FrameStart.Width / 2) + 2400, ↵
(Form1.Height / 2) - (FrameStart.Height / 2) + 900

' Place panel3d4 Label
panel3d4.Move (Form1.Width / 2) - (panel3d4.Width / 2) + 700, (Form1.Height ↵
/ 2) - (panel3d4.Height / 2) + 900

' Place Sound On Option
Soundon.Move (Form1.Width / 2) - (Soundon.Width / 2) - 2000, (Form1.Height / ↵
2) - (Soundon.Height / 2) + 500

' Place Sound Off Option
soundoff.Move (Form1.Width / 2) - (soundoff.Width / 2) - 2000, (Form1.Height ↵
/ 2) - (soundoff.Height / 2) + 900

' Turn on the Frames Measurement Option
Frames.Value = 1

' We are going to initialize the MCI Control by making sure it is closed
mmcontrol1.Command = "Close"

' We are going to set the play window to the picture on form1
mmcontrol1.hWndDisplay = picture1.hWnd

' Load the file name to the directory where we are running the project from.
mmcontrol1.FileName = App.Path & "\EIM.AVI"

' Open the file for play
mmcontrol1.Command = "Open"

' set the time format measurement to Milliseconds (0)
mmcontrol1.TimeFormat = 3

' update the length caption to reflect the milliseconds length
label1.Caption = "Clip Length = " + Str$(mmcontrol1.Length)
label1.AutoSize = True
panel3d3.AutoSize = 1

End Sub
```

3. If the user wants to view the number of frames in the clip, then the MCI control TimeFormat setting should be updated to 3, which sets the length property to a measurement in frames. To display the new measurement, update the Label1 caption to the new length. The MCI control allows you to measure the length of the clips in various time formats.

```
Private Sub Frames_Click()

' Set the time format measurement value to Frames (3)
mmcontrol1.TimeFormat = 3

' Update the caption to contain the new timer format measurement
label1.Caption = "Clip Length = " + Str$(mmcontrol1.Length)
label1.AutoSize = True
panel3d3.AutoSize = 1

End Sub
```

4. Because the starting frame is measured numerically, ensure that the user enters in only numeric values.

```
Private Sub FrameStart_KeyPress(KeyAscii As Integer)

' We will not allow anything but numbers to be typed into the text box
If KeyAscii > 58 Or KeyAscii < 47 Then KeyAscii = 0

End Sub
```

5. Because the frame step is measured numerically, ensure that the user enters in only numeric values.

```
Private Sub FrameStep_KeyPress(KeyAscii As Integer)

' We will not allow anything but numbers to be typed into the text box
If KeyAscii > 58 Or KeyAscii < 47 Then KeyAscii = 0

End Sub
```

6. Set the clip length measurement to milliseconds (TimeFormat = 0). Label1 must be updated to reflect the new measurement.

```
Private Sub Milli_Click()

' set the time format measurement to Milliseconds (0)
mmcontrol1.TimeFormat = 0

' update the length caption to reflect the milliseconds length
label1.Caption = "Clip Length = " + Str$(mmcontrol1.Length)
label1.AutoSize = True
panel3d3.AutoSize = 1

End Sub
```

7. If the user clicks the back button, then the program needs to move back the appropriate number of frames. The user can specify the number of frames by entering the value in the Frame Step box. The Frames property specifies the number of frames to skip for each BackClick and StepClick event.

```
Private Sub MMControl1_BackClick(Cancel As Integer)

' If the back button is clicked, we want to go back the current
' number of frames set in the Framestep text box
mmcontrol1.Frames = Framestep.Text
End Sub
```

8. Because you are allowing the user to specify the starting frame, make sure that the starting frame is valid. The first check ensures that the starting frame is not past the length of the clip. The second check ensures that a negative frame number has not been entered. If an invalid entry is entered, then reset the value to 0 and play the clip. Otherwise, set the from setting to the specified starting frame. The clip will then play.

```
Private Sub MMControl1_PlayClick(Cancel As Integer)

' Check to make sure that the starting frame is not invalid
If Val(FrameStart.Text) > mmcontrol1.Length Then MsgBox "The starting frame ↵
is larger than the number of frames in the clip": GoTo SET0

If Val(FrameStart.Text) < 0 Then MsgBox "The starting frame is smaller than ↵
0": GoTo SET0

' set the starting frame to the one entered
mmcontrol1.From = FrameStart.Text: GoTo ENDPLAY

' Reset starting frame to 0
SET0:
FrameStart.Text = 0

ENDPLAY:

End Sub
```

9. If the user clicks the forward button, then advance the appropriate number of frames. The user can specify the number of frames by entering the value in the Frame Step box. Set the Frames property to the FrameStep value.

```
Private Sub MMControl1_StepClick(Cancel As Integer)

' If the step button is clicked we want to go back the current
' number of frames set in the Framestep text box
mmcontrol1.Frames = Framestep.Text
End Sub
```

10. The silent property of the MCI control allows the sound to be enabled or disabled for the clip. If the user selects the Sound Off box, then set the silent property to true.

```
Private Sub SoundOff_Click()

' turn the silent setting to true so that the avi sound will not play
mmcontrol1.Silent = True
End Sub


Private Sub SoundOn_Click()

' turn the silent setting to false so that the avi sound will play
mmcontrol1.Silent = False
End Sub
```

How It Works

This project demonstrates how easy it is to play and manipulate an AVI file using the MCI control. The user-defined values of the starting frame and step value allow the user to manipulate the viewing of the clip. By placing the picture control on the form, the clip appears to be playing on the same plane as the overall application. You might want to try commenting out the following statement from the Form_Load event subroutine to see how the application differs.

```
mmcontrol1.hWndDisplay = picture1.hWnd
```

As you can see, the AVI plays in its own window. The MCI control has many other events and properties that can be utilized to enhance the viewing of and interaction with your video clips. The events and properties demonstrated here give you a good sampling of what can be done with the MCI control.

Comments

The MCI control can be just as effective when used with other mediums such as MIDI, WAV, and Gold Disk animations. With the Video for Windows tool kit from Microsoft, you can convert your FLC clips to AVI format if you want to use the MCI control with your animations.

6

BITMAPS AND PALETTES

6

BITMAPS AND PALETTES

How do I...

Chapters 4 and 5 covered techniques using video, animation, and graphics. In this chapter, low-level bitmap and palette manipulation will be used to perform a variety of effective and useful techniques common to multimedia programming. WinG, a Microsoft programming tool for Windows, will be used to perform advanced bitmap manipulation techniques.

In How-To 4.7, bitmap brushes were built to develop crosshatch and vertical blind fade-in and fade-out effects. In this chapter, actual data from bitmap files will be manipulated to perform several different types of effects on bitmap graphics. These techniques include learning how to read in and write out bitmap files, how to perform manipulation on the bitmap's color table, and how to create WinG bitmaps.

Central to working with bitmaps is the use and manipulation of the bitmap's color palette as well as the system palette. This chapter will work exclusively with 256-color bitmap images. By manipulating a bitmap's palette, effects such as a cross-fade, palette cycling, and color tinting can be performed. Also, the system palette can be manipulated to build blinking lights and other types of simple animation.

WinG is a set of tools developed by Microsoft to help developers overcome many of the difficulties with high-speed graphics programming in Windows. These include limitations in the current Windows graphics tools and inability to have lower level control over VGA devices. WinG allows the programmer to create GDI-compatible bitmaps with a DIB bitmap file as the basis. You can use the standard GDI routines such as BitBlt and PatBlt to draw on a WinG device and use WinG to copy the contents to the screen rapidly. You can also use WinG to send image data between different WinG bitmaps. Along with WinG, TransparentDIBits is provided, which uses WinG to perform transparent bitmap copying (similar to How-To 4.8) easily and rapidly.

Windows APIs Covered

AnimatePalette	BitBlt	CreateCompatibleDC	CreateDIBitmap
CreatePalette	CreateSolidBrush	CreatePatternBrush	DeleteDC
DeleteObject	GlobalAlloc	GlobalFree	GlobalHandleToSel
GlobalLock	GlobalUnlock	_lopen	_lread
_lclose	_hread	lstrcpy	MemoryWrite
MemoryRead	PatBlt	RealizePalette	Rectangle
SelectObject	SelectPalette	StretchBlt	StretchDIBits
TransparentDIBits	WinGCreateDC	WinGBitBlt	WinGStretchBlt
WinGGetDIBPointer	WinGCreateBitmap	WinGRecommendDIBFormat	
WinGGetDIBColorTable	WinGSetDIBColorTable		
WinGCreateHalftonePalette	WinGCreateHalftoneBrush		
CreateCompatibleBitmap			

6.1 Modify a picture's color palette

One of the easiest ways to manipulate the appearance of an image is to modify its palette. Each pixel in a bitmap references a color table palette position stored within the file. If you change values for any of the entries in the color table, every pixel in the bitmap that references that entry will be changed. This How-To will demonstrate methods for reading a bitmap file and modifying its color table.

6.2 Perform rapid color cycling

A unique and interesting effect can be performed on graphics when the color entries for the bitmap are rapidly cycled from their original position through the 256-color logical palette array back to their original position. When the system palette is updated with the new entries, the bitmap is dramatically affected. This How-To will build on the techniques for reading a bitmap file's palette and will introduce new techniques to quickly modify its palette and update the system.

6.3 Perform palette animation

Using several API palette functions, standard API palette structures, and the Windows GDI, you can implement animations such as blinking and rotating lights. By manipulating the system palette, you do not need files such as bitmap graphics and animation to perform simple animation. This project will implement a series of rotating lights to develop a simple pump-monitoring simulation.

6.4 Fade pictures in to and out from black

In Chapter 4, a cross hatch and a vertical blind fade were implemented by developing a series of bitmap pattern brushes and filling in a displayed image with the brushes. In this How-To, a graphics palette will be manipulated to fade the picture uniformly to and from black.

6.5 Add fade-in and fade-out transitions to video clips

Adding digital image manipulations to video can help enhance the overall effectiveness of the video clip. Using Microsoft's Video for Windows VidEdit program and a little bitmap manipulation, you can add fade-in and fade-out effects to a video clip. This How-To will demonstrate how to build a series of fade-in and fade-out bitmap graphics files consisting of the first and last frame of a video clip, and then how to import them into VidEdit to build the final clip.

6.6 Perform a crossfade between two images

Perhaps one of the most popular graphic effects is the crossfade between two images. Unfortunately this is one of the most challenging to implement. Using the pattern bitmaps built in How-To 4.7 and techniques developed earlier in this chapter, you will develop crossfades between images.

6.7 Display and manipulate graphics with WinG

This How-To will introduce the WinG API and how to use it to read in and manipulate bitmap graphics. A simple graphics browser will be implemented that allows for the display and size manipulation of the graphic images.

6.8 Perform flip book animations with WinG

In How-To 5.3, a simple image flip book was developed for implementing animation. In this How-To, the same concept will be used to develop animation in WinG. A series of bitmaps will be rapidly rotated to perform animation. Also, a complex background will be used as a backdrop to show the versatility of WinG.

6.9 Build sprites with WinG

In How-Tos 5.4 through 5.6, sprite animation was developed using the Windows GDI functions. In this How-To, the sprite classes from Chapter 5 will be reworked to use WinG for faster graphics performance and greater flexibility.

6.10 Build scenes with multiple sprites, animations, and sounds with WinG

This How-To will use WinG and the sound API to perform several actions at once. This project will demonstrate the power and flexibility of the WinG API. Also, different techniques for controlling the timing of sprites will be implemented.

6.1 How do I...
Modify a picture's color palette?

COMPLEXITY: INTERMEDIATE

Problem

I would like to be able to modify a bitmap picture's color palette to perform such effects as adding colored tints, switching colors, and adding graininess to the image. This can help add interesting visual effects to my applications.

Technique

Several new techniques will be introduced in this How-To. These include using several Windows API memory functions to read in a bitmap and its data and then write out to a new file the corresponding changes. To do this, you will use various bitmap header structures to interpret the bitmap file and create a new file. The modifications to the picture's palette will create such effects as color tinting and pixel diffusion.

Steps

Open and run 6-1.VBP. The running program appears as shown in Figure 6-1-1.

Select the Read button to read in the bitmap file. Then select the Write button to view the picture without modifications. Figure 6-1-2 shows the original image.

Select the Diffuse/Smudge option and then select the Tint button. The palette of the file has now been modified. To store the data in the NEW.BMP file and view the new bitmap, select the Write button. Figure 6-1-3 shows the diffused image.

To try different tints, select the Read button to read the original data. Note that you can perform multiple tints on the same image.

1. Create a new project called 6-1.VBP. Add the objects and properties listed in Table 6-1-1 to Form1 and save the form as 6-1.FRM.

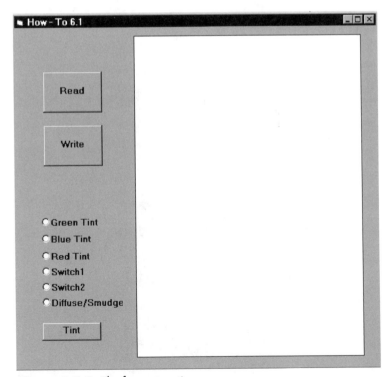

Figure 6-1-1 The form at runtime

Figure 6-1-2 The unaltered image

Figure 6-1-3 The Diffuse/Smudge alteration

Table 6-1-1 Project form's objects and properties

OBJECT	PROPERTY	SETTING
Form	Name	Form1
	Auto3D	-1 'True
	Caption	"How-To 6.1"
OptionButton	Name	Diffuse
	Caption	"Diffuse/Smudge"
OptionButton	Name	Switch2
	Caption	"Switch2"
OptionButton	Name	Switch1
	Caption	"Switch1"
CommandButton	Name	TintSel
	Caption	"Tint"
OptionButton	Name	Red
	Caption	"Red Tint"
OptionButton	Name	Blue
	Caption	"Blue Tint"
OptionButton	Name	Green
	Caption	"Green Tint"
CommandButton	Name	Write
	Caption	"Write"
CommandButton	Name	Read
	Caption	"Read"
PictureBox	Name	DispPict
	AutoSize	-1 'True
	ScaleMode	3 'Pixel

2. Add the following code to the general declarations section of the form. The palette modification class is globally declared.

```
'  Globally declare the class
Dim PalMod As PalMod
```

3. When the form is loaded, the new class is created and set up. This includes setting the picture property and the file name.

```
Private Sub Form_Load()

'  Create the new class
Set PalMod = New PalMod

'  Set the Display Picture Property
Set PalMod.DispPict = DispPict

'  Set the filename
Let PalMod.filename = App.Path + "\oranges.bmp"

End Sub
```

4. When the Tint button is selected, the option buttons are checked to see which tint should be performed. Then the Tint function of the class is called.

```
Private Sub TintSel_Click()

'  Depending on the option button selected, the appropriate
'  tint will be performed
If Red.Value = True Then PalMod.Tint 1
If Green.Value = True Then PalMod.Tint 2
If Blue.Value = True Then PalMod.Tint 3
If Switch1.Value = True Then PalMod.Tint 4
If Switch2.Value = True Then PalMod.Tint 5
If Diffuse.Value = True Then PalMod.Tint 6

End Sub
```

5. When the Read button is selected, the ReadBitmapFile function of the class is called.

```
Private Sub Read_Click()

'  Read the bitmap file
PalMod.ReadBitmapFile

End Sub
```

6. When the Write button is selected, the WriteBitmapFile function of the class is called.

```
Private Sub Write_Click()
```

```
'  Write the bitmap file to a new file
PalMod.WriteBitmapFile

End Sub
```

7. Create a new class module for the project and save it as PALMOD.CLS. Add the following code to the general declarations section of the form. The API functions for allocating memory to read the bitmap, the data structures for the bitmap format, and the appropriate global variables for the class are declared.

```
'  Declare the memory functions needed to
'  read in the bitmap data
Private Declare Function GlobalAlloc Lib "Kernel" (ByVal wFlags As Integer, ↵
ByVal dwBytes As Long) As Integer

Private Declare Function GlobalHandleToSel Lib "ToolHelp.DLL" (ByVal hMem As ↵
Integer) As Integer

Private Declare Function MemoryWrite Lib "ToolHelp.DLL" (ByVal wSel As ↵
Integer,ByVal dwOffSet As Long, lpvBuf As Any, ByVal dwcb As Long) As Long

Private Declare Function MemoryRead Lib "ToolHelp.DLL" (ByVal wSel As ↵
Integer, ByVal dwOffSet As Long, lpvBuf As Any, ByVal dwcb As Long) As Long

Private Declare Function GlobalFree Lib "Kernel" (ByVal hMem As Integer) ↵
As Integer

Private Declare Function GlobalLock Lib "Kernel" (ByVal hMem As Integer) As Long

Private Declare Function GlobalUnlock Lib "Kernel" (ByVal hMem As Integer) ↵
As Integer

'  These are the constants necessary for indicating
'  how the memory block should be allocated
Const GMEM_MOVEABLE = &H2
Const GMEM_ZEROINIT = &H40

'  This is the bitmap header information
'  structure
Private Type BITMAPINFOHEADER
    biSize              As Long
    biWidth             As Long
    biHeight            As Long
    biPlanes            As Integer
    biBitCount          As Integer
    biCompression       As Long
    biSizeImage         As Long
    biXPelsPerMeter     As Long
    biYPelsPerMeter     As Long
    biClrUsed           As Long
    biClrImportant      As Long
End Type

'  These structures define the palette
```

continued on next page

continued from previous page

```
'   entries in the bitmap file
Private Type RGBQUAD
      rgbBlue              As String * 1
      rgbGreen             As String * 1
      rgbRed               As String * 1
      rgbReserved          As String * 1
End Type


'   Overall bitmap structure for the
'   bitmap data.
Private Type BITMAPINFO
      bmiHeader As BITMAPINFOHEADER
      bmiColors(0 To 255)  As RGBQUAD
End Type


'   Header data for the bitmap file
Private Type BITMAPFILEHEADER
      bfType               As Integer
      bfSize               As Long
      bfReserved1          As Integer
      bfReserved2          As Integer
      bfOffBits            As Long
End Type


'   The selector to the global memory block
Private m_BitDataSelector As Integer


'   The pointer to the global memory block
Private m_BitData As Long


'   The following two structures will be used to
'   read in the bitmap file.
Private m_bmFileHeader As BITMAPFILEHEADER
Private m_bmInfo As BITMAPINFO


'   The filename to be read in
Private m_FileName As String


'   The picture for the image to be displayed in
Private m_DispPict As Object
```

8. The following two functions set the file name and picture properties.

```
'   The filename indicates the bitmap to be opened
Public Property Let filename(s As String)
    Let m_FileName = s
End Property


'   The picture to display the image in
Public Property Set DispPict(acontrol As Control)
    Set m_DispPict = acontrol
End Property
```

9. The Tint function will perform the specified manipulation on the bitmap palette. The TintType parameter indicates the type of manipulation to be performed. The function loops through the palette entries and performs the necessary manipulation.

```
Public Sub Tint(TintType As Integer)

'  Loop through the palette to perform
'  the desired modification
For n = 0 To 254

    '  Get the ascii values of the  current
    '  palette position
    r = Asc(m_bmInfo.bmiColors(n).rgbRed)
    g = Asc(m_bmInfo.bmiColors(n).rgbGreen)
    B = Asc(m_bmInfo.bmiColors(n).rgbBlue)

    '  Peform the Red Tint
    If TintType = 1 Then
        '  Every palette position will be brightened,
        '  with the red being brightened more.  This
        '  helps to add more of a 'glare' to the
        '  tint
        r = r + 95: If r > 255 Then r = 255
        g = g + 10: If g > 255 Then g = 255
        B = B + 10: If B > 255 Then B = 255

        '  Set the original palette positions
        m_bmInfo.bmiColors(n).rgbRed = Chr$(r)
        m_bmInfo.bmiColors(n).rgbGreen = Chr$(g)
        m_bmInfo.bmiColors(n).rgbBlue = Chr$(B)
    End If

    '  Perform the Green Tint
    If TintType = 2 Then
        '  Every palette position will be brightened,
        '  with the green being brightened more.  This
        '  helps to add more of a 'glare' to the
        '  tint
        r = r + 10: If r > 255 Then r = 255
        g = g + 95: If g > 255 Then g = 255
        B = B + 10: If B > 255 Then B = 255

        '  Set the original palette positions
        m_bmInfo.bmiColors(n).rgbRed = Chr$(r)
        m_bmInfo.bmiColors(n).rgbGreen = Chr$(g)
        m_bmInfo.bmiColors(n).rgbBlue = Chr$(B)
    End If

    '  Perform the blue tint
    If TintType = 3 Then
        '  Every palette position will be brightened,
        '  with the blue being brightened more.  This
        '  helps to add more of a 'glare' to the
        '  tint
```

continued on next page

continued from previous page

```
              r = r + 10: If r > 255 Then r = 255
              g = g + 10: If g > 255 Then g = 255
              B = B + 95: If B > 255 Then B = 255


              '  Set the original palette positions
              m_bmInfo.bmiColors(n).rgbRed = Chr$(r)
              m_bmInfo.bmiColors(n).rgbGreen = Chr$(g)
              m_bmInfo.bmiColors(n).rgbBlue = Chr$(B)
          End If


      '  This switch provides for a simple
      '  cycling of the colors, which turns
      '  the image to an overall blue hue
      If TintType = 4 Then
          '  Rotate the colors
          m_bmInfo.bmiColors(n).rgbRed = Chr$(g)
          m_bmInfo.bmiColors(n).rgbGreen = Chr$(B)
          m_bmInfo.bmiColors(n).rgbBlue = Chr$(r)
      End If


      '  This switch provides for a simple
      '  cycling of the colors, which turns
      '  the image to an overall green hue
      If TintType = 5 Then
          '  Rotate the colors
          m_bmInfo.bmiColors(n).rgbRed = Chr$(B)
          m_bmInfo.bmiColors(n).rgbGreen = Chr$(r)
          m_bmInfo.bmiColors(n).rgbBlue = Chr$(g)
      End If


      '  To make a diffused effect, every other palette
      '  entry will be darkened.  This provides for a dark
      '  grainy effect for the image
      If TintType = 6 And n Mod 2 = 0 Then
          '  Set the new palette position to be half
          '  the original value
          m_bmInfo.bmiColors(n).rgbRed = Chr$(r / 2)
          m_bmInfo.bmiColors(n).rgbGreen = Chr$(g / 2)
          m_bmInfo.bmiColors(n).rgbBlue = Chr$(B / 2)
      End If

Next n

End Sub
```

10. The ReadBitmapFile function opens the bitmap file and retrieves the bitmap file
    header, the bitmap data header, and the bitmap pixel data. The bitmap pixel data
    is read into memory using several API memory functions.

```
Public Sub ReadBitmapFile()

'  NumBitPixels holds the number of pixels
'  in the image
Dim NumBitPixels As Long
```

```
'  MemPos will store the current position
'  in memory while reading in the data
Dim MemPos As Long

'  BitBuffer will be used to read in the
'  pixels from the file and then written
'  to memory.  Note the buffer size is
'  2024
Dim BitBuffer As String * 2024

'  Open the image file
Open m_FileName For Binary As 1

'  Read in the header
Get 1, 1, m_bmFileHeader

'  Read in the bitmap info
Get 1, Len(m_bmFileHeader) + 1, m_bmInfo

'  Retrieve the size of the image
NumBitPixels = m_bmInfo.bmiHeader.biSizeImage

'  Set the starting memory position
MemPos = 0

'  Allocate memory for reading in the
'  data
m_BitData = GlobalAlloc(GMEM_MOVEABLE Or GMEM_ZEROINIT, NumBitPixels)

'  Get a selector to the data
m_BitDataSelector = GlobalHandleToSel(m_BitData)

'  Read in the memory
Do While NumBitPixels > 0

    '  Read the first set of data
    Get 1, , BitBuffer

    '  Check to see if the amount of data left
    '  to be read is less than our 2024 buffer
    '  size.  If so, then only read in the amount
    '  of data left
    If 2024 < NumBitPixels Then
        Size = 2024
    Else
        Size = NumBitPixels
    End If

    '  Write the new data to memory
    Throw = MemoryWrite(m_BitDataSelector, MemPos, ByVal BitBuffer, Size)

    '  Increment the memory position
    MemPos = MemPos + 2024

    '  Count down the number of bits read
```

continued on next page

CHAPTER 6

continued from previous page

```
    NumBitPixels = NumBitPixels - 2024
Loop

'   Close the file
Close 1

End Sub
```

11. The WriteBitmapFile function writes the new bitmap out to the NEW.BMP file. Note that if any changes are made by the Tint function to the bitmap palette, these changes are written out into the new file.

```
Public Sub WriteBitmapFile()

'   NumBitPixels holds the number of pixels
'   in the image
Dim NumBitPixels As Long

'   MemPos will store the current position
'   in memory while reading in the data
Dim MemPos As Long

'   BitBuffer will be used to read in the
'   pixels from the file and then written
'   to memory.  Note the buffer size is
'   2024
Dim BitBuffer As String * 2024

'   Open the new.bmp file for output
'   of the new manipulated image
Open App.Path + "\new.bmp" For Binary As 1

'   Place the original file header
Put 1, 1, m_bmFileHeader

'   Place the bitmap info
Put 1, Len(m_bmFileHeader) + 1, m_bmInfo

'   Set the image size
NumBitPixels = m_bmInfo.bmiHeader.biSizeImage

'   Set the starting memory position
MemPos = 0

'   Read the bits from memory and write
'   them out to the file
Do While NumBitPixels > 0


'   Check to see if the amount of data left
'   to be read is less than our 2024 buffer
'   size.  If so then only read in the amount
'   of data left
If 2024 < NumBitPixels Then
    Size = 2024
```

```
        Else
            Size = NumBitPixels
        End If

        '   Read the data from memory
        Throw = MemoryRead(m_BitDataSelector, MemPos, ByVal BitBuffer, Size)

        '   Set the new memory position
        MemPos = MemPos + 2024

        '   Decrease the pixel counter
        NumBitPixels = NumBitPixels - 2024

        '   Store the read memory
        Put 1, , BitBuffer
Loop

'   Close the file
Close 1

'   Display the picture
m_DispPict.Picture = LoadPicture(App.Path + "\new.bmp")

End Sub
```

How It Works

In this How-To, a new class is developed to perform various manipulations on an image. The class handles reading the bitmap data, modifying the palette, and writing and displaying the new image. A quick review of Form1 shows that the implementation of the class from within the main project is straightforward. The class is declared globally in the general declarations section of Form1. It is then created in the Form_Load procedure. Also, the two properties of the class are set up. These include the file name and the display picture.

Throughout many of the file-intensive How-Tos in this chapter, the global memory functions will be used to read in and manipulate large amounts of data. The largest variable in Visual Basic 4.0 is a 64K string. This is not enough for reading large bitmap image files. Fortunately, there are API methods to handle storing and manipulating large blocks of data. Table 6-1-2 overviews the functions used.

Table 6-1-2 Memory functions

FUNCTION	DESCRIPTION
GlobalAlloc	Allocates the specified block of memory
GlobalFree	Frees up the specified memory block
GlobalLock	Locks the memory block from being moved by the system
GlobalUnlock	Unlocks the memory block so it can be moved by the system

continued on next page

continued from previous page

FUNCTION	DESCRIPTION
GlobalHandleToSel	Provides a Windows selector to the allocated memory block
MemoryRead	Reads data from the allocated memory block
MemoryWrite	Writes data to the allocated memory block

When the bitmap pixel data is read from the file, it is stored into the memory allocated by GlobalAlloc. The size of memory allocated is determined from the bitmap structure biSizeImage field. To read and write from memory, a Windows selector to the memory block is needed. Because Windows does not store memory in contiguous chunks, the selector provides the necessary information to read and write data from the allocated memory. The MemoryRead and MemoryWrite functions must have a selector to know how to read and write from noncontiguous memory. The GlobalHandleToSel function takes in the pointer to the memory block returned from GlobalAlloc and returns the needed selector.

The bitmap file is read in using standard bitmap data structures. Each bitmap file has a header, BITMAPFILEHEADER, which is a standard Windows API data structure. Once the file header is read, the bitmap data can be read. This includes a standard header structure, BITMAPINFO. This structure contains two fields, BITMAPINFOHEADER and bmiColors. The BITMAPINFOHEADER structure contains the header information for the bitmap data and describes the type of bitmap and the size of the bitmap data among other things. The second field, bmiColors, defines the color palette for the bitmap file. The array of 256 entries (for a 256-color bitmap) contains the RGBQUAD data structure. Each entry defines the red, green, and blue colors for the palette entry. For further discussion on bitmap data structures, see How-To 4.7.

The palette is easily modified by manipulating the RGBQUAD palette entries in the bitmap structure. Each of the 256 entries is modified to change the whole image. For example, the blue, green, and red tints are developed by increasing the appropriate color components values. To help give the effect of the entire image emanating a color, the other two color components are brightened by increasing their values, which brightens the image.

Finally, when the Write button is selected, the new file is created with the same file header, bitmap header, and pixel data (from memory). The only change has been made on the bmiColors structure entries.

Comments

Many different types of palette manipulations can be performed to provide interesting effects. For example, a completely red image can be developed by setting the blue and green components to 0. This will create a picture that has only shades of red.

6.2 How do I...
Perform rapid color cycling?

COMPLEXITY: INTERMEDIATE

Problem

Rapid color cycling can provide for eye-catching effects such as explosions and lightning. How can I perform rapid color cycling on a bitmap graphic from Visual Basic 4.0?

Technique

The Windows API provides a function, AnimatePalette, that allows you to perform rapid palette manipulation. The AnimatePalette function replaces entries in a device context's logical palette. But you do not have to update the device context with the new palette because AnimatePalette instructs Windows to map new entries into the system palette immediately. To perform this technique, a new class will be developed so that you can easily implement rapid color cycling in your applications.

Steps

Open and run 6-2.VBP. The running program appears as shown in Figure 6-2-1.

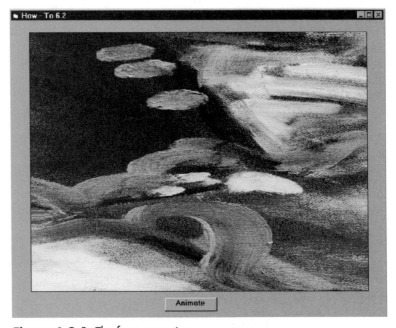

Figure 6-2-1 The form at runtime

Select the Animate button to see the rapid palette cycling. Each entry in the bitmaps color palette is rotated through every position in the array and ends up at its original position.

1. Create a new project called 6-2.VBP. Add the objects and properties listed in Table 6-2-1 to Form1 and save the form as 6-2.FRM.

Table 6-2-1 Project form's objects and properties

OBJECT	PROPERTY	SETTING
Form	Name	Form1
	Auto3D	-1 'True
	Caption	"How-To 6.2"
CommandButton	Name	ShowAnimate
	Caption	"Animate"
PictureBox	Name	DispPict
	AutoSize	-1 'True
	Picture	"Colormix.bmp"
	ScaleMode	3 'Pixel

2. Add the following code to the general declarations section of the form. The palette animation class is globally declared.

```
' Declare the animate class
Dim Animate As Animate
```

3. When the Command button is selected, the palette animation is shown.

```
Private Sub ShowAnimate_Click()

' Perform the animation cycling
Animate.Show

End Sub
```

4. When the form is loaded, the class is set up with the bitmap file name and the picture in which to display the palette cycling.

```
Private Sub Form_Load()

' Create the animate class
Set Animate = New Animate
```

```
'  Set the picture for the animation
Set Animate.pict = DispPict

'  Set the file to be animated
Let Animate.File = App.Path + "\colormix.bmp"

End Sub
```

5. Insert a new class into the project titled ANIMATE.CLS. Add the following code to the general declarations section of the form. The appropriate data structures and functions for reading the bitmap file are declared here, as are the necessary palette functions and structures.

```
'  Declare the bitmap file header
'   structure
Private Type BITMAPINFOHEADER
     biSize             As Long
     biWidth            As Long
     biHeight           As Long
     biPlanes           As Integer
     biBitCount         As Integer
     biCompression      As Long
     biSizeImage        As Long
     biXPelsPerMeter    As Long
     biYPelsPerMeter    As Long
     biClrUsed          As Long
     biClrImportant     As Long
End Type

'  Declare the RGBQUAD structure for the
'   bitmap palette entries
Private Type RGBQUAD
     rgbBlue            As String * 1
     rgbGreen           As String * 1
     rgbRed             As String * 1
     rgbReserved        As String * 1
End Type

' Declare the overall bitmap structure
Private Type BITMAPINFO
     bmiHeader As BITMAPINFOHEADER
     bmiColors(0 To 255)  As RGBQUAD
End Type

'  Declare the bitmap file header structure
Private Type BITMAPFILEHEADER
     bfType             As Integer
     bfSize             As Long
     bfReserved1        As Integer
     bfReserved2        As Integer
     bfOffBits          As Long
End Type
```

continued on next page

continued from previous page

```
'   Declare the palette entry structure
'   for the palette entries in a logical
'   palette
Private Type PALETTEENTRY
    peRed As String * 1
    peGreen As String * 1
    peBlue As String * 1
    peFlags As String * 1
End Type

'   Declare the logical palette structure
Private Type LOGPALETTE
    palVersion As Integer
    palNumEntries As Integer
    palPalEntry(255) As PALETTEENTRY
End Type

'   palette index used for animation
Const PC_RESERVED = &H1

'   SelectPalette will be used to select the created palette
'   into the specified device context
Private Declare Function SelectPalette Lib "User" (ByVal hDC As Integer, ↵
ByVal hPalette As Integer, ByVal bForceBackground As Integer) As Integer

'   RealizePalette realizes the current palette in the device
'   context into the system palette
Private Declare Function RealizePalette Lib "User" (ByVal hDC As Integer) ↵
As Integer

'   DeleteObject deletes the selected object
Private Declare Function DeleteObject Lib "GDI" (ByVal hObject As Integer) ↵
As Integer

'   CreatePalette creates a palette from the
'   logical palette structure
Private Declare Function CreatePalette Lib "GDI" (lpLogPalette As LOGPALETTE) ↵
As Integer

'   AnimatePalette maps the new palette directly
'   to the system
Private Declare Sub AnimatePalette Lib "GDI" (ByVal hPalette As Integer, ↵
ByVal wStartIndex As Integer, ByVal wNumEntries As Integer, lpPaletteColors ↵
As PALETTEENTRY)

'   The displayed picture
Dim m_pict As Object

'   The bitmap image file to be selected
Dim m_filename As String
```

6. Pass in the picture to display the bitmap.

```
'   The public pict property
```

```
Public Property Set pict(acontrol As Control)
    Set m_pict = acontrol
End Property
```

7. Pass in the bitmap file name of the displayed picture.

```
'  The public filename property
Public Property Let File(filename As String)
    Let m_filename = filename
End Property
```

8. The Show function opens the bitmap file and reads in the color table. It then builds a logical palette and cycles the colors in the palette. To show the palette being animated, the AnimatePalette function is used. Note that the first time the palette is changed, a palette is created with CreatePalette. It is then selected into the picture device context. This is done so that the system will track the new logical palette color set for the picture.

```
Sub Show()
'Load the picture
m_pict. Picture = LoadPicture (m_filename)
'  Declare the bitmap file header and
'  bitmap header structures
Dim bmFileHeader As BITMAPFILEHEADER
Dim bmInfo As BITMAPINFO

'  Declare the LOGPALETTE structure
'  for building the animated palettes
Dim LogicalPalette As LOGPALETTE

Dim Flag As Integer

'  Open the bitmap file
Open m_filename For Binary As 1

'  Read in the file header
Get 1, 1, bmFileHeader

'  Read in the bitmap header
Get 1, Len(bmFileHeader) + 1, bmInfo

'  Close the file
Close

'  Set the initial values from the bitmap palette
For n = 0 To 255
    LogicalPalette.palPalEntry(n).peRed = bmInfo.bmiColors(n).rgbRed
    LogicalPalette.palPalEntry(n).peGreen = bmInfo.bmiColors(n).rgbGreen
    LogicalPalette.palPalEntry(n).peBlue = bmInfo.bmiColors(n).rgbBlue
    LogicalPalette.palPalEntry(n).peFlags = Chr$(PC_RESERVED)
Next n

'  Loop through the palette rotation
For Counter = 0 To 255
```

continued on next page

continued from previous page

```
        '  Switch the positions, i.e. palette entry 1 will be in 2.
        '  2 in 3 and so on.
        For n = 0 To 254
            LogicalPalette.palPalEntry(n).peRed = LogicalPalette.palPalEntry(n ↵
                + 1).peRed

            LogicalPalette.palPalEntry(n).peGreen = LogicalPalette.palPalEntry(n ↵
                + 1).peGreen

            LogicalPalette.palPalEntry(n).peBlue = LogicalPalette.palPalEntry(n ↵
                + 1).peBlue

            LogicalPalette.palPalEntry(n).peFlags = Chr$(PC_RESERVED)
        Next n

            '  Place the first palette entry in 255 to
            '  complete the rotation
            LogicalPalette.palPalEntry(255).peRed = LogicalPalette.↵
              palPalEntry(0).peRed

            LogicalPalette.palPalEntry(255).peGreen = LogicalPalette.↵
              palPalEntry(0).peGreen

            LogicalPalette.palPalEntry(255).peBlue = LogicalPalette.↵
              palPalEntry(0).peBlue

            LogicalPalette.palPalEntry(255).peFlags = Chr$(PC_RESERVED)
            LogicalPalette.palVersion = &H300
            LogicalPalette.palNumEntries = 256

    '  The first time this loop is called
    '  the palette will be created, selected
    '  into the device context and realized.
    If Flag = 0 Then
        Pal = CreatePalette(LogicalPalette)
        throw = SelectPalette(m_pict.hDC, Pal, 0)
        throw = RealizePalette(m_pict.hDC)
        Flag = 1
    End If

    '  Animate the palette.
    AnimatePalette Pal, 0, 255, LogicalPalette.palPalEntry(0)

Next Counter

' Refresh the Picture
m_pict.refresh

End Sub
```

How It Works

The techniques for opening and reading in a bitmap covered in the last How-To are used here to open the file and read in the color table. Note that the image's bitmap pixel data does not have to be read. You are only interested in building a color palette based on the bitmap color table.

To build a logical palette, use two primary API structures along with several API functions. The logical palette structure, LOGPALETTE, is used by the CreatePalette function to create a palette. The LOGPALETTE structure uses a sub structure, PAL ETTEENTRY, to hold the RGB values as well as flags for the palette entries. Tables 6-2-2 and 6-2-3 overview the two structures.

Table 6-2-2 LOGPALETTE structure

DATA MEMBER	DESCRIPTION
palVersion as integer	Version of the palette set to &H300
palNumEntries as integer	The number of entries up to 256
palPalEntry(255) as PALETTEENTRY	The number of entries as PALETTEENTRY

Table 6-2-3 PALETTEENTRY structure

DATA MEMBER	DESCRIPTION
peRed As String * 1	The red value for the palette entry
peGreen As String * 1	The green value for the palette entry
peBlue As String * 1	The blue value for the palette entry
peFlags As String * 1	The flags for the palette entry

There are several options with which to set the peFlags structure member. These flags determine how the specific palette entries are interpreted and used by the system. Table 6-2-4 gives a brief description of each.

Table 6-2-4 peFlags options

FLAG	DESCRIPTION
PC_EXPLICIT	Indicates that the palette entry actually represents an index into the currently displayed palette
PC_NOCOLLAPSE	Indicates that the palette entry should be placed in an unused position in the current system palette; if there are no unused entries, then it is matched to the closest entry
PC_RESERVED	Specifies that the logical palette entry will be used for palette animation

To create a new palette, the CreatePalette function is used. The palette must then be selected with SelectPalette into the device context where it will be used. Finally, RealizePalette is used to have the colors mapped to the system palette. Table 6-2-5 overviews the palette functions used.

Table 6-2-5 Palette functions and parameters

PARAMETER	DESCRIPTION
SelectPalette	
ByVal hDC as integer	The device context to select the palette into
ByVal hPalette as integer	The handle to the palette
ByVal bForceBackground as integer	
RealizePalette	
ByVal hDC as integer	The device context where the palette is selected
CreatePalette	
lpLogPalette as LOGPALETTE	The logical palette structure to create from
AnimatePalette	
ByVal hPalette as integer	The handle of the palette
ByVal wStartIndex as integer	The beginning entry to animate from
ByVal wNumEntries as integer	The number of entries to animate
lpPaletteColors As PALETTEENTRY)	The palette entries structure

The palette cycling is done by rotating the bitmap palette entries in the LOGPALETTE array. For instance, if a blue color is in position 0, then throughout the cycling it will go through positions 2–255 and then end up in position 0. With each rotation of the colors, the AnimatePalette function is called to map the new palette to the system palette. When this happens, the colors in the displayed image are immediately updated to reference the new color positions. As the program shows, this can provide for a dramatic effect on the image.

Comments

This How-To runs through the complete rotation of the palette entries. But shorter palette cycling can be done by developing different algorithms to switch the palette entries. For the image to appear correctly, though, it is important that the final palette used by AnimatePalette be the original.

6.3 How do I...
Perform palette animation?

COMPLEXITY: INTERMEDIATE

Problem

I know that through manipulation of palettes and the use of the GDI API functions, I can develop a type of simple animation. This type of animation is useful because large files do not need to be utilized nor does extensive bitmap manipulation need to be done. How can I accomplish this type of animation with Visual Basic 4.0?

Technique

A variation on the technique used in the last How-To can be used to develop palette animation such as blinking and rotating lights. The same palette structures and functions used in the last How-To will be utilized here. To create the colored and animated images, the Rectangle and CreateSolidBrush API functions will be used.

Steps

Open and run 6-3.VBP. The running program appears as shown in Figure 6-3-1.

The program develops a simple operations control panel for a pump. The flashing lights indicate its pumping action. The gauges meter the flow of the pump.

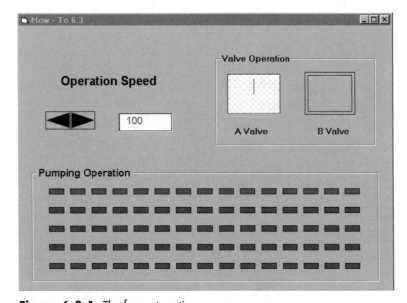

Figure 6-3-1 The form at runtime

The speed of the operation can be increased or decreased using the Spin button. The rate of the pump (timer interval) is shown in the text box. The higher the value, the longer the interval between pumping actions. The lower the value, the shorter the interval between pumping actions.

1. Create a new project called 6-3.VBP. Add the objects and properties listed in Table 6-3-1 to Form1 and save the form as 6-3.FRM.

Table 6-3-1 Project form's objects and properties

OBJECT	PROPERTY	SETTING
Form	Name	Form1
	Auto3D	-1 'True
	BackColor	&H00FFFFFF&
	Caption	"How-To 6.3"
	FillColor	&H8000000A&
	ForeColor	&H00000000&
	ScaleMode	3 'Pixel
TextBox	Name	OpSpeed
	Enabled	0 'False
	Font	
	name	"Arial"
	weight	700
	size	10.2
	ForeColor	&H00000000&
	Text	"100"
Frame	Name	Frame2
	Caption	"Valve Operation"

Note: The following two labels and gauges are placed on the frame.

OBJECT	PROPERTY	SETTING
Label	Name	Label2
	AutoSize	-1 'True
	Caption	"B Valve"
Label	Name	Label1

OBJECT	PROPERTY	SETTING
	AutoSize	-1 'True
	Caption	"A Valve"
Gauge	Name	Gauge2
	Value	50
	Autosize	0 'False
	Needlewidth	1
Gauge	Name	Gauge1
	Style	3
	Needlewidth	1

Note: The picture box should be placed on the frame.

.

OBJECT	PROPERTY	SETTING
Frame	Name	Frame1
	Caption	"Pumping Operation"
	Font	
	name	"Arial"
	size	10.2
PictureBox	Name	AniPict
	BackColor	&H00C0C0C0&
	BorderStyle	0 'None
	ScaleMode	3 'Pixel
Timer	Name	Timer1
	Interval	100
Label	Name	Label3
	AutoSize	-1 'True
	Caption	"Operation Speed"
	Font	
	name	"Arial"
	size	12
SpinButton	Name	SpinButton1
	spinorientation	1

2. Add the following code to the general declarations section of the form. The appropriate API functions and data structures are declared for creating logical palettes and drawing rectangles. Also, global variables for tracking the animated rectangles are declared.

```
'  Used to create the palette from the
'  logical palette
'  ColorRotate is used to count through the words missing at end of comment
Private Declare Function CreatePalette Lib "GDI" (LPStoreLogPalette ↵
As LOGPALETTE) As Integer

'  Used to select the created palette
'  into the device context
Private Declare Function SelectPalette Lib "User" (ByVal hdc As Integer, ↵
ByVal hPalette As Integer, ByVal bForceBackground As Integer) As Integer

'  Used to realize the newly selected palette
Private Declare Function RealizePalette Lib "User" (ByVal hdc As Integer) ↵
As Integer

'  Creates a brush of the specified ColorRotate
Private Declare Function CreateSolidBrush Lib "GDI" (ByVal crColor As Long) ↵
As Integer

'  Selects an object into a device context
Private Declare Function SelectObject Lib "GDI" (ByVal hdc As Integer, ↵
ByVal hObject As Integer) As Integer

'  Deletes an object
Private Declare Function DeleteObject Lib "GDI" (ByVal hObject As Integer) ↵
As Integer

'  Maps the palette entries directly to the
'  system palette
Private Declare Sub AnimatePalette Lib "GDI" (ByVal hPalette As Integer, ↵
ByVal wStartIndex As Integer, ByVal wNumEntries As Integer, ↵
LPStorePaletteColors As PALETTEENTRY)

'  Creates a rectangle in the specified device context
Private Declare Function Rectangle Lib "GDI" (ByVal hdc As Integer, ByVal X1 ↵
As Integer, ByVal Y1 As Integer, ByVal X2 As Integer, ByVal Y2 As Integer) ↵
As Integer

'  The handle to the created palette
Dim PAL As Integer

'  The primary logical palette
Dim LP As LOGPALETTE

'  LPStore will be used to store the
'  two primary colors in the palette.
'  This will be used to easily rotate
'  through the palette indices and change
'  the colors
```

```
Dim LPStore As LOGPALETTE


'  palette entries in the timer
Dim ColorRotate As Integer
```

3. When the form is loaded, two logical palettes are developed. The first contains the nonanimated color of the rectangles. The second holds a copy of the nonanimated color and the animated color. Also, a palette is created from the first logical palette using the CreatePalette function.

```
Private Sub Form_Load()

'  Set up the palette with the correct number
'  of entries and as a Win 3.0 (or higher) version
LP.palVersion = &H300
LP.palNumEntries = 5

'  Set up the palette with the correct number
'  of entries and as a Win 3.0 (or higher) version
LPStore.palVersion = &H300
LPStore.palNumEntries = 2

'  Build the initial palette with five color entries
'  One for each vertical square that will be drawn
For N = 0 To 4
    LP.palPalEntry(N).peRed = Chr$(80)
    LP.palPalEntry(N).peGreen = Chr$(80)
    LP.palPalEntry(N).peBlue = Chr$(80)
    LP.palPalEntry(N).peFlags = Chr$(PC_RESERVED)
Next N

'  Set the first color in the Store palette
'  to that of the colors in the LP Palette
LPStore.palPalEntry(0) = LP.palPalEntry(0)

'  Set up the second entry in the Store palette
'  to have the color that will show the animation.
LPStore.palPalEntry(1).peRed = Chr$(255)
LPStore.palPalEntry(1).peGreen = Chr$(15)
LPStore.palPalEntry(1).peBlue = Chr$(100)
LPStore.palPalEntry(1).peFlags = Chr$(PC_RESERVED)

'  Create our primary palette
PAL = CreatePalette(LP)

End Sub
```

4. When the form is painted, a series of rectangles is drawn onto the picture. Each row of rectangles is drawn using its own brush. Instead of each brush using an explicit color, an index in the currently selected palette is referenced, which in this case is the logical palette created when the form was loaded.

```
Private Sub Form_Paint()

'   Brush will hold the
Dim Brush(4) As Integer

'   Select the palette into the picture
Throw = SelectPalette(AniPict.hdc, PAL, False)

'   Realize the palette
Throw = RealizePalette(AniPict.hdc)

'   Create the five brushes.  Note that the index
'   into the current palette method is used for
'   indicating the color.  Instead of an explicit
'   RGB value, the &H1000000 indicates that a palette
'   index entry is to be used.  N will be the palette
'   entry.   So each successive brush points to a
'   palette entry in our new palette
For N = 0 To 4
    Brush(N) = CreateSolidBrush(&H1000000 Or N)
Next N

'   Set the box width and height
BWidth = 25
BHeight = 10

'   x the starting x origin
x = 15

'   Y is the starting y height
y = AniPict.ScaleHeight - 20

'   Fifteen rows of boxes will be drawn.  Each
'   row will be five high
For z = 0 To 14

    '   Increment the x value
    x = 15 + (z * 10) + (z * BWidth)

    '   Reset the y position
    y = AniPict.ScaleHeight - 20

    '   Loop through and create the stacked five
    '   boxes
    For N = 0 To 4
        '   Select the brush into the picture
        Throw = SelectObject(AniPict.hdc, Brush(N))

        '   Draw the rectangle
        Throw = Rectangle(AniPict.hdc, x, y, x + BWidth, y + BHeight)

        '   Decrement (move up the picture) the
        '   y value
        y = y - BHeight * 3
    Next N
```

```
Next z


'   Delete the created brushes
For N = 0 To 4
    Throw = DeleteObject(Brush(N))
Next N

End Sub
```

5. The palette created for the rectangles must be deleted when the program is exited.

```
Private Sub Form_Unload(Cancel As Integer)
'   Delete the palette
Throw = DeleteObject(PAL)
End Sub
```

6. On the spin-down click, the value of the timer is decreased and the displayed text is updated. The smaller the timer interval, the smaller the time between pumping actions.

```
Private Sub SpinButton1_SpinDown()

'   Make sure the timer interval is not 0
If Timer1.Interval <> 0 Then
    '   Decrement the timer value and show
    '    the value in the text box
    Timer1.Interval = Timer1.Interval - 20
    OpSpeed.Text = Timer1.Interval
End If

End Sub
```

7. On the spin-up click, the value of the timer is increased and the displayed text is updated. The longer the timer interval, the longer the time between pumping actions.

```
Private Sub SpinButton1_SpinUp()

    '   Increment the timer value
    Timer1.Interval = Timer1.Interval + 20
    '   Show the timer value
    OpSpeed.Text = Timer1.Interval
End Sub
```

8. With each timer interval, the actual palette animation takes place. The logical palette that is currently selected into the device context is reset to its original color values. The animation is performed by setting one of the entries in the logical palette to be that of the animation color. With each timer tick, the position of the animated color is rotated through the logical palette and the simulation

gauge values are updated. When their values reach 100, they are reset to 0. This gives the appearance of continuous monitoring of the pump.

```
Private Sub Timer1_Timer()

'   Increment the two guage values
Gauge1.Value = Gauge1.Value + 1
Gauge2.Value = Gauge2.Value + 2

'   Rotate the values back if the maximum
'   value of 100 has been reached
If Gauge1.Value = 100 Then Gauge1.Value = 0
If Gauge2.Value = 100 Then Gauge2.Value = 0

'   To rotate the colors in the palette, the
'   ColorRotate variable is used.  There are five
'   positions in the palette, so when five is reached
'   the variable is set back to 0.
If ColorRotate = 5 Then ColorRotate = 0

'   Reset the original palette entries to
'   the original color
For N = 0 To 4
    LP.palPalEntry(N) = LPStore.palPalEntry(0)
Next N

'   Set the ColorRotate position to be the animated
'   color
LP.palPalEntry(ColorRotate) = LPStore.palPalEntry(1)

'   Animate the palette
AnimatePalette PAL, 0, 5, LP.palPalEntry(0)

'   Increment ColorRotate
ColorRotate = ColorRotate + 1

End Sub
```

9. Insert a new module into the class and save it as 6-3.BAS. The palette data structures and flags are declared.

```
'   Palette entries for the logical palette
Type PALETTEENTRY
    peRed As String * 1
    peGreen As String * 1
    peBlue As String * 1
    peFlags As String * 1
    End Type

' Logical Palette
Type LOGPALETTE
        palVersion As Integer
        palNumEntries As Integer
        palPalEntry(255) As PALETTEENTRY ' Array length is arbitrary; may be changed
End Type
```

```
'  palette index used for animation
Global Const PC_RESERVED = &H1
```

How It Works

This How-To demonstrates a technique for developing simple animation without the use of bitmap graphics. The LOGPALETTE structures introduced in the last How-To are used to develop a simple palette with five entries. Note that this corresponds to the number of rows of squares, one palette entry for each row.

When the brush for the rectangles is created, it references a position in the system palette rather than a specific color. The following code accomplishes this:

```
For N = 0 To 4
    Brush(N) = CreateSolidBrush(&H1000000 Or N)
Next N
```

The &H1000000 indicates that the color is an index into the palette. The For loop builds the references for 0 through 4. The brushes are stored in an array for use when each row of rectangles is created. When a new row of rectangles is drawn, the next brush is selected into the picture device context; consequently, the row uses the color in the palette index used to create the brush. The next set of rectangles drawn then references the specified position in the palette.

The timer function handles setting each row in succession to the animated color and resetting the last row. This is done by changing the color of the appropriate position in the LOGPALETTE and resetting the last animated position to the original color. AnimatePalette is then used to update those positions in the system palette rapidly, which then directly updates the rectangles. The final result is rotating lights on the pump control panel.

Comments

Many different types of palette animation can be developed. For example, blinking lights or rotating lights can be easily developed.

6.4 How do I...
Smoothly fade pictures in to and out from black?

COMPLEXITY: ADVANCED

Problem

In How-To 4.7, I learned how to build a cross hatch and vertical blind fade in and out on a displayed image. I would also like to be able to perform the popular smooth fade in and out from black on my images. This provides for effective and smooth graphics transition in my applications. How can I do this using Visual Basic 4.0?

Figure 6-4-1 The form at runtime

Technique

In How-To 4.7, fade-in and fade-out effects were developed by creating bitmap patterns to fill in an image. In this How-To, the color table from the image file will be manipulated to build successive palettes to fade out the bitmap. From the original bitmap header and pixel data, a new DIB bitmap is created in memory for the new color table. Then the StretchDIBits API function will be used to copy the new DIB image to the display. Each successive DIB will have a darker palette, with a final palette of all black.

A new class will be developed for performing the fade in and fade out. This class can easily be added to your existing applications to build this effect for your graphics.

Steps

Open and run 6-4.VBP. The running program appears as shown in Figure 6-4-1.

Select the Fade In and Fade Out buttons to perform the two effects. As you can see, the image smoothly transitions in and out from black.

1. Create a new project called 6-4.VBP. Add the objects and properties listed in Table 6-4-1 to Form1 and save the form as 6-4.FRM.

Table 6-4-1 Project form's objects and properties

OBJECT	PROPERTY	SETTING
Form	Name	Form1
	Auto3D	-1 'True
	Caption	"How-To 6.4"
CommandButton	Name	OutFade
	Caption	"Fade Out"
	Font	
	name	"Arial"
	size	10.2
CommandButton	Name	InFade
	Caption	"Fade In"
	Font	
	name	"Arial"
	size	10.2
PictureBox	Name	DispPict
	AutoSize	-1 'True
	ScaleMode	3 'Pixel
	Visible	0 'False

2. Add the following code to the general declarations section of the form. The Fade class is globally declared.

```
'  Globally declare the fade class
Dim Fade As fade
```

3. When the form is loaded, the Fade class is declared and set up.

```
Private Sub Form_Load()

'  Create the fade class
Set fade = New fade

'  Set the display picture
Set fade.Pict = DispPict
```

continued on next page

continued from previous page

```
'   Set the filename
Let fade.File = App.Path + "\flower.bmp"

' Setup for the fade
fade.Setup

End Sub
```

4. When the form is painted, the Display method of the class is called. This ensures that the image is visible.

```
Private Sub Form_Paint()

'   Display the picture
fade.display

End Sub
```

5. When the form is unloaded, it is important to free up the memory allocated by the class.

```
Private Sub Form_Unload(Cancel As Integer)

'   Free the memory allocated
fade.MemFree

End Sub
```

6. When the Fade In button is selected, the FadeIn method of the class is called. This performs the fade-in effect on the image.

```
Private Sub InFade_Click()

'   Peform the fade in
fade.FadeIn

End Sub
```

7. When the Fade Out button is selected, the FadeOut method of the class is called to perform the fade-out effect on the image.

```
Private Sub OutFade_Click()

'   Perform the fade out
fade.FadeOut

End Sub
```

8. Create a new class and save it as FADE.CLS. Add the following code to the general declarations section. The functions for reading the image into memory are declared, as are the data structures for reading the bitmap data. The functions for creating the DIB bitmaps and displaying the fade images are also declared, as are all global members of the class.

```
'   Declare the bitmap information
'   header data structure
Private Type BITMAPINFOHEADER
     biSize                As Long
     biWidth               As Long
     biHeight              As Long
     biPlanes              As Integer
     biBitCount            As Integer
     biCompression         As Long
     biSizeImage           As Long
     biXPelsPerMeter       As Long
     biYPelsPerMeter       As Long
     biClrUsed             As Long
     biClrImportant        As Long
End Type


'   Declare the data structure the
'   pallete entries
Private Type RGBQUAD
     rgbBlue               As String * 1
     rgbGreen              As String * 1
     rgbRed                As String * 1
     rgbReserved           As String * 1
End Type


'   Declare the overall structure for
'   the bitmap data
Private Type BITMAPINFO
     bmiHeader As BITMAPINFOHEADER
     bmiColors(0 To 255)  As RGBQUAD
End Type


'   Declare the bitmap file header
'   structure
Private Type BITMAPFILEHEADER
     bfType                As Integer
     bfSize                As Long
     bfReserved1           As Integer
     bfReserved2           As Integer
     bfOffBits             As Long
End Type



'   Declare the memory functions for reading in the
'   bitmap data
Private Declare Function GlobalAlloc Lib "Kernel" (ByVal wFlags As Integer, ↵
ByVal dwBytes As Long) As Integer

Private Declare Function GlobalHandleToSel Lib "ToolHelp.DLL" (ByVal hMem As ↵
Integer) As Integer

Private Declare Function MemoryWrite Lib "ToolHelp.DLL" (ByVal wSel As ↵
Integer,ByVal dwOffSet As Long, lpvBuf As Any, ByVal dwcb As Long) As Long
```

continued on next page

continued from previous page

```
Private Declare Function MemoryRead Lib "ToolHelp.DLL" (ByVal wSel As ↵
Integer, ByVal dwOffSet As Long, lpvBuf As Any, ByVal dwcb As Long) As Long

Private Declare Function GlobalFree Lib "Kernel" (ByVal hMem As Integer) ↵
As Integer

Private Declare Function GlobalLock Lib "Kernel" (ByVal hMem As Integer) As Long

Private Declare Function GlobalUnlock Lib "Kernel" (ByVal hMem As Integer) ↵
As Integer


' Two constants for allocating
' memory
Const GMEM_MOVEABLE = &H2
Const GMEM_ZEROINIT = &H40


' PatBlt will be used to paint a picture black
Private Declare Function PatBlt Lib "GDI" (ByVal hDC As Integer, ByVal x ↵
As Integer, ByVal y As Integer, ByVal nWidth As Integer, ByVal nHeight ↵
As Integer, ByVal dwRop As Long) As Integer


' CreateDIBitmap creates a new DIB from the
' specified structures
Private Declare Function CreateDIBitmap Lib "GDI" (ByVal hDC As Integer, ↵
lpInfoHeader As BITMAPINFOHEADER, ByVal dwUsage As Long, ByVal lpInitBits&,↵
 lpInitInfo As BITMAPINFO, ByVal wUsage As Integer) As Integer


' StretchDIBits will copy the specified bits to
' the screen
Private Declare Function StretchDIBits Lib "GDI" (ByVal hDC As Integer, ByVal ↵
DestX As Integer, ByVal DestY As Integer, ByVal nDestWidth As Integer, ByVal ↵
nDestHeight As Integer, ByVal SrcX As Integer, ByVal SrcY As Integer, ByVal ↵
nSrcWidth As Integer, ByVal nSrcHeight As Integer, ByVal lpBits As Long, ↵
lpBitsInfo As BITMAPINFO, ByVal wUsage As Integer, ByVal dwRop As Long) ↵
As Integer


' SelectObject and DeleteObject select and delete the
' specified objects
Private Declare Function SelectObject Lib "GDI" (ByVal hDC As Integer, ByVal ↵
hObject As Integer) As Integer

Private Declare Function DeleteObject Lib "GDI" (ByVal hObject As Integer) ↵
As Integer


' Declare two constants for bitmap
' copies
Const BLACKNESS = &H42&
Const SRCCOPY = &HCC0020


' CBM_INIT is used to initialize the bitmap in
' CreateDIBitmap
Const CBM_INIT = &H4&


' Indicates that the colors are
' in the RGB Quad format
```

```
Const DIB_RGB_COLORS = 0

'  This array will store the palette
'  increments to perform the fades
Dim m_bmInfoStore(20) As BITMAPINFO

'  A pointer to the locked memory
Dim m_lpDIBits As Long

'  Pointer to the allocated memory block
Dim m_BitData As Long

'  Stores the bitmap filename
Dim m_FileName As String

'  The picture to be displayed
Dim m_Pict As Object
```

9. The following properties set the file name of the bitmap image and the display picture for performing the fade.

```
'  Set the filename
Public Property Let File(acontrol As String)
    Let m_FileName = acontrol
End Property

'  Set the picture for display
Public Property Set Pict(acontrol As Object)
    Set m_Pict = acontrol
End Property
```

10. When the display method is called, the picture is loaded into the display. Also, the picture is made visible. To help keep the load clean visually, the picture box is not made visible until the image is loaded.

```
Public Sub Display()

    '  Display the picture
    m_Pict.Picture = LoadPicture(m_FileName)

    '  Make the picture visible
    m_Pict.Visible = True

End Sub
```

11. The Setup function opens the bitmap file and reads in the bitmap header and pixel data. It then develops 20 transition bitmap headers that fade each color to black. Finally, the bitmaps are stored in a global array for quick access when the fade takes place.

```
Public Sub Setup()

'  Declare the file header structure
Dim bmFileHeader As BITMAPFILEHEADER
```

continued on next page

continued from previous page

```
'  Declare the bitmap header info
Dim bmInfo As BITMAPINFO

'   This is the selector to the memory
Dim m_BitDataSelector As Integer

'  NumBits will be the number of pixel
'  bits to read
Dim NumBits As Long

'  BitBuffer will be used to read in
'  the bit data
Dim BitBuffer As String * 2048

'  MemOffset will hold the position in
'  memory for the data
Dim MemOffset As Long

'  Open the bitmap file
Open m_FileName For Binary As 1

'  Read in the file header
Get 1, 1, bmFileHeader

'  Read in the bitmap data
Get 1, Len(bmFileHeader) + 1, bmInfo

'  Set NumBits to the size of the pixel
'  data
NumBits = bmInfo.bmiHeader.biSizeImage

'  set the Memory offset
MemOffset = 0

'  Allocate the memory
m_BitData = GlobalAlloc(GMEM_MOVEABLE Or GMEM_ZEROINIT, NumBits)

'  Get a selector to the memory
m_BitDataSelector = GlobalHandleToSel(m_BitData)

'  Read the data until all of the pixel
'  bits have been read.
Do While NumBits > 0

    '  Read in the pixel data into the buffer
    Get 1, , BitBuffer

    '  Write the data to memory
    Throw = MemoryWrite(m_BitDataSelector, MemOffset, ByVal BitBuffer, 2048)

    '  Increment the memory offset to the new
    '  position
    MemOffset = MemOffset + 2048
```

```
      '  Count down the number of bits
      '  read
      NumBits = NumBits - 2048
Loop

'  Close the file
Close #1

'  Lock the memory.  m_lpDIBits will
'  hold a pointer to the locked
'  memory
m_lpDIBits& = GlobalLock(m_BitData)

'  Build the 20 steps to the fade
For Counter = 0 To 20

      '  Loop through the palette
      For n = 0 To 255

            '  Get the ASCII value of the red
            '  component
            T = Asc(bmInfo.bmiColors(n).rgbRed)

            '  Decrease the value and ensure that
            '  it does not go below 0
            If T > 19 Then T = T - 20 Else T = 0

            '  Set the new color
            bmInfo.bmiColors(n).rgbRed = Chr$(T)

            '  Get the ASCII value of the Green
            '  component
            T = Asc(bmInfo.bmiColors(n).rgbGreen)

            '  Decrease the value and ensure that
            '  it does not go below 0
            If T > 19 Then T = T - 20 Else T = 0

            '  Set the new color
            bmInfo.bmiColors(n).rgbGreen = Chr$(T)

            '  Get the ASCII value of the Blue
            '  component
            T = Asc(bmInfo.bmiColors(n).rgbBlue)

            '  Decrease the value and ensure that
            '  it does not go below 0
            If T > 19 Then T = T - 20 Else T = 0

            '  Set the new color
            bmInfo.bmiColors(n).rgbBlue = Chr$(T)

            '  Set the reserved value
            bmInfo.bmiColors(n).rgbReserved = Chr$(0)
```

continued on next page

continued from previous page

```
              '   Set the colors for the appropriate
              '   position in the array
              m_bmInfoStore(Counter).bmiColors(n).rgbBlue = bmInfo.↵
                bmiColors(n).rgbBlue
              m_bmInfoStore(Counter).bmiColors(n).rgbGreen = bmInfo.↵
                bmiColors(n).rgbGreen

              m_bmInfoStore(Counter).bmiColors(n).rgbRed = bmInfo.bmiColors(n).rgbRed

              m_bmInfoStore(Counter).bmiColors(n).rgbReserved = bmInfo.↵
                bmiColors(n).rgbReserved

        Next n

        '   Store the header
        m_bmInfoStore(Counter).bmiHeader = bmInfo.bmiHeader

Next Counter

End Sub
```

12. The FadeOut function loops through the fade bitmaps created in the Setup function and copies the bits to the display. When the final image is displayed, the picture display is filled with black to ensure a complete fade.

```
Public Sub FadeOut()

'   See the FadeIn procedure for comments
'   the two functions work in reverse
For Counter = 0 To 20

              Throw% = StretchDIBits(m_Pict.hDC, 0, 0, m_Pict.ScaleWidth, ↵
                m_Pict.ScaleHeight, 0, 0, m_Pict.ScaleWidth, m_Pict.ScaleHeight, ↵
                m_lpDIBits&, m_bmInfoStore(Counter), DIB_RGB_COLORS, SRCCOPY)

Next Counter

'   Fill the picture black to
'   ensure a complete fade
Throw% = PatBlt(m_Pict.hDC, 0, 0, m_Pict.ScaleWidth, m_Pict.ScaleHeight, ↵
BLACKNESS)

End Sub
```

13. The FadeIn function loops through the fade bitmaps created in the Setup function and copies the bits to the display.

```
Public Sub FadeIn()

'   Loop through the created bitmaps and
'   copy the bits to the display.
For Counter = 20 To 0 Step -1
              '   Copy the bits into the picture
              Throw% = StretchDIBits(m_Pict.hDC, 0, 0, m_Pict.ScaleWidth, ↵
```

```
                m_Pict.ScaleHeight, 0, 0, m_Pict.ScaleWidth, m_Pict.ScaleHeight, ↵
                m_lpDIBits&, m_bmInfoStore(Counter), DIB_RGB_COLORS, SRCCOPY)
Next Counter

End Sub
```

14. The MemFree function frees up the memory created by GlobalAlloc.

```
Public Sub MemFree()
    ' Free the globally allocated memory
    Throw% = GlobalFree(m_BitData)
End Sub
```

How It Works

The basic concept behind building the fade is a series of bitmaps with palettes that fade to or from black. In this project, each palette progresses over a series of 20 steps. To do this, the red, green, and blue values of each palette entry must be incremented or decremented accordingly.

It is important to have the fade progress as smoothly as possible. A quick review of the FadeIn and FadeOut functions shows that only the StretchDIBits function has to be called to perform the fade. Thus, each step of the fade consists of only one API call. The array of fade bitmaps is already developed in the Setup function and has the same header information as the original image. Each successive bitmap has its palette RGB entry values deducted by 15, which reaches 0 over 20 steps. The final bitmap is a completely black image because each RGB value in the palette array is set to black. Thus, each pixel, regardless of what palette position it references, is represented by black.

To display the successive images, the StretchDIBits function is used to copy the bitmap bits to the display. Table 6-4-2 overviews the StretchDIBits function and its parameters.

Table 6-4-2 The StretchDIBits function and its parameters

PARAMETER	DESCRIPTION
ByVal hDC As Integer	Device context to copy the bitmaps into
ByVal DestX as integer	X origin destination coordinate
ByVal DestY as integer	Y origin destination coordinate
ByVal nDestWidth as integer	Width to copy the bits into
ByVal nDestHeight as integer	Height to copy the bits into
ByVal SrcX as integer	X origin of the source to copy from
ByVal SrcY as integer	Y origin of the source to copy from
ByVal nSrcWidth as integer	Width of the source to copy from
ByVal nSrcHeight as Integer	Height of the source to copy from

continued on next page

continued from previous page

PARAMETER	DESCRIPTION
ByVal lpBits as long	Pointer to the bit data in memory
lpBitsInfo as Bitmapinfor	Bitmap header
ByVal wUsage as integer	RGB or palette indices for color table
ByVal dwRop as long	Type of ROP copy (i.e., SRCCOPY)

The FadeIn and FadeOut functions loop through the bitmap array with faded color tables. The lpBitsInfo parameter is set to the different bitmap headers. In each case, the lpBits parameter points to the locked memory block containing the pixel data read from the bitmap file. Note that the wUsage parameter should indicate that the color table references standard RGB values and not indices into the system palette by using the DIB_RGB_COLORS API constant.

Comments

Different variations of the fade can be performed. You might want to consider building a parameter that indicates the total number of fade steps to be performed so that the fade can be faster or slower. Also, the StretchDIBits function can copy the bits to different sized images. The class could also be expanded to fade the image to different sizes so that a new image of a different size could be faded in.

6.5 How do I...
Add fade-in and fade-out transitions to video clips?

COMPLEXITY: ADVANCED

Problem

Now that I can perform fade-in and fade-out transitions on my static bitmap graphics, is there a way I can add these same transitions to the beginning and end of my video clips? This would provide effective entry and exit effects for the video.

Technique

In the last How-To a series of bitmaps was built and displayed to build fade transitions. In this How-To, Microsoft's VidEdit, provided with the Video for Windows package, will be used to help build a fade-in and fade-out effect for a video clip. VidEdit can be used to extract the first and last frame of a clip easily. Transitions of each bitmap image can be built using bitmap and palette techniques developed in the last How-To. Finally, VidEdit can be used to import the transitions images into the beginning and end of the clip.

Steps

To get started, the provided sample MAZE.AVI video clip will be used to build a fade-in and fade-out effect. First extract the first and last frames from the video clip to which you want to add the effects. This can easily be done with Microsoft's VidEdit program. Open the VidEdit program and load in the MAZE.AVI video file. Then extract the first and last frames as Microsoft DIB files and save them in the project directory as MAZE1.DIB and MAZE2.DIB respectively. Figure 6-5-1 shows the first frame being extracted.

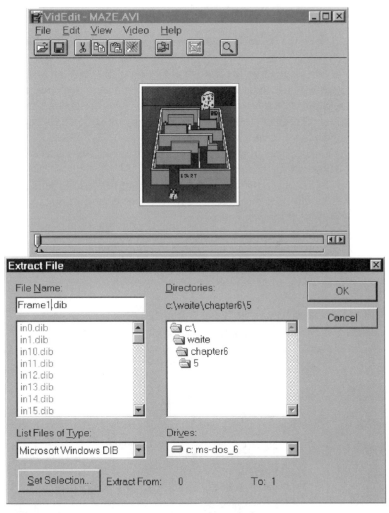

Figure 6-5-1 Extracting a DIB using the VidEdit program

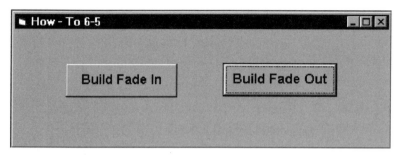

Figure 6-5-2 The form as it appears at runtime

Open the 6.5 project and run the program. Figure 6-5-2 shows the running program.

The program builds a series of DIB bitmaps. For the fade-in bitmaps, each file begins with the In designation and a corresponding sequence number. For the fade-out bitmaps each file name begins with the Out designation and a corresponding sequence number. These series of DIB bitmaps can then be imported into the beginning and end of your video clip using VidEdit. To do this, return to VidEdit and move to the beginning of the clip. Import the In DIB sequence into the clip. Figure 6-5-3 shows the process.

To import the fade-out sequences, move to the last frame in the clip and import the Out DIB sequence. Finally, save the new video clip. Figure 6-5-4 shows a fade-in step of the maze video clip.

1. Create a new project called 6-5.VBP. Add the objects and properties listed in Table 6-5-1 to Form1 and save the form as 6-5.FRM.

Table 6-5-1 Project form's objects and properties

OBJECT	PROPERTY	SETTING
Form	Name	Form1
	Auto3D	-1 'True
	Caption	"How-To 6-5"
CommandButton	Name	FadeIn
	Caption	"Build Fade In"
	Font	
	name	"Arial"
	size	10.2

OBJECT	PROPERTY	SETTING
CommandButton	Name	FadeOut
	Caption	"Build Fade Out"
	Font	
	name	"Arial"
	size	10.2

2. Add the following code to the general declarations section of the form. The FadeFrames class is globally declared.

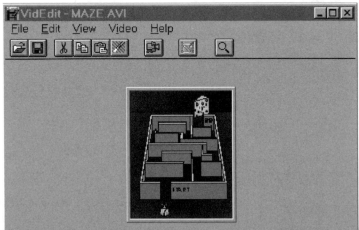

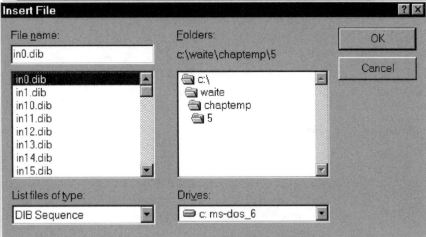

Figure 6-5-3 Importing DIB sequences into VidEdit

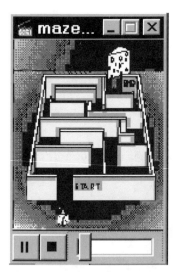

Figure 6-5-4 Fade-in step on
the maze video clip

```
'  Globally declare the fade class
Dim FadeFrames As FadeFrames
```

3. When the Fade Out button is selected, the file name from which to build the fade-out series is set. Then the BuildFrames method of the class is called. The FadeOut parameter is sent to the BuildFrames function to indicate that the fade-out frames should be built.

```
Private Sub FadeOut_Click()

'  Set the filename for the class
Let FadeFrames.File = App.Path + "\maze2.dib"

'  Build the Fade Out frames
FadeFrames.BuildFrames "FadeOut"

End Sub
```

4. When the Fade In button is selected, the file name from which to build the fade-in series is set. Then the BuildFrames method of the class is called. The FadeIn parameter is sent to the BuildFrames function to indicate that the fade-in frames should be built.

```
Private Sub FadeIn_Click()
```

```
'  Set the filename
Let FadeFrames.File = App.Path + "\maze1.dib"

'  Build the Fade In Frames
FadeFrames.BuildFrames "FadeIn"

End Sub
```

5. When the form is loaded, the FadeFrames class is created.

```
Private Sub Form_Load()

'  Create the new class
Set FadeFrames = New FadeFrames

End Sub
```

6. Create a new class and save it as FADEFRMS.CLS. Add the following code to the general declarations section of the form. The memory functions for reading and writing the bitmap data are declared, as are the appropriate bitmap data structures and global member variables.

```
'  Declare the bitamp header info
'   structure
Private Type BITMAPINFOHEADER
    biSize              As Long
    biWidth             As Long
    biHeight            As Long
    biPlanes            As Integer
    biBitCount          As Integer
    biCompression       As Long
    biSizeImage         As Long
    biXPelsPerMeter     As Long
    biYPelsPerMeter     As Long
    biClrUsed           As Long
    biClrImportant      As Long
End Type


'  Declare the RGBQUAD structure for
'   storing the palette entries
Private Type RGBQUAD
    rgbBlue             As String * 1
    rgbGreen            As String * 1
    rgbRed              As String * 1
    rgbReserved         As String * 1
End Type


'  Declare the overall structure
'   for the bitmap
Private Type BITMAPINFO
    bmiHeader As BITMAPINFOHEADER
    bmiColors(0 To 255)  As RGBQUAD
End Type
```

continued on next page

CHAPTER 6

continued from previous page

```
'  Declare the file header structure
Private Type BITMAPFILEHEADER
    bfType              As Integer
    bfSize              As Long
    bfReserved1         As Integer
    bfReserved2         As Integer
    bfOffBits           As Long
End Type

'  Declare the global memory functions
Private Declare Function GlobalAlloc Lib "Kernel" (ByVal wFlags As Integer, ↵
ByVal dwBytes As Long) As Integer

Private Declare Function GlobalHandleToSel Lib "ToolHelp.DLL" (ByVal hMem As ↵
Integer) As Integer

Private Declare Function MemoryWrite Lib "ToolHelp.DLL" (ByVal wSel As ↵
Integer, ByVal dwOffSet As Long, lpvBuf As Any, ByVal dwcb As Long) As Long

Private Declare Function MemoryRead Lib "ToolHelp.DLL" (ByVal wSel As ↵
Integer, ByVal dwOffSet As Long, lpvBuf As Any, ByVal dwcb As Long) As Long

Private Declare Function GlobalFree Lib "Kernel" (ByVal hMem As Integer) ↵
As Integer

Private Declare Function GlobalLock Lib "Kernel" (ByVal hMem As Integer) As Long

Private Declare Function GlobalUnlock Lib "Kernel" (ByVal hMem As Integer) ↵
As Integer

'  Declare the constants for allocating
'  memory
Const GMEM_MOVEABLE = &H2
Const GMEM_ZEROINIT = &H40

'  Pointer to the globally allocated memory
Dim m_BitData As Long

'  The filename of the image
Dim m_FileName As String
```

7. The file name property sets the file name for the fade frames to be built.

```
'  Filename property
Public Property Let File(acontrol As String)
    Let m_FileName = acontrol
End Property
```

8. The BuildFrames function handles reading in the DIB bitmap and builds the 25 fade frames. Depending on the FadeType, the DIB sequence file names are built with the appropriate In or Out leading extension followed by the number

388

sequence. The technique used in the last How-To to build fade palettes is also used here. The fade-out files are then written out to the successive bitmap files.

```
Public Sub BuildFrames(FadeType)

'   Declare the bitmap file header structure
Dim bmFileHeader As BITMAPFILEHEADER

'   Declare the bitmap header structure
Dim bmInfo As BITMAPINFO

'   This is the selector to the pixel data
Dim BitDataSelector As Integer

'   The number of bits in the pixel data
Dim NumBits As Long

'   The buffer to read in the data
Dim BitBuffer As String * 2048

'   Tracks the offset into memory for
'   reading and writing
Dim MemOffset As Long

'   The number of fade bitmaps to build
Dim num As Integer

'   Build 26 fades
num = 26

'   Open the filename
Open m_FileName For Binary As 1

'   Read in the file header
Get 1, 1, bmFileHeader

'   Read in the bitmap header
Get 1, Len(bmFileHeader) + 1, bmInfo

'   Get the number of pixel bits
NumBits = bmInfo.bmiHeader.biSizeImage

'   Set the offset to 0
MemOffset = 0

'   Allocate a memory block to hold the pixels
m_BitData = GlobalAlloc(GMEM_MOVEABLE Or GMEM_ZEROINIT, NumBits)

'   Get a selector to the memory block
BitDataSelector = GlobalHandleToSel(m_BitData)

'   Read in the pixel data
Do While NumBits > 0

    '   Read in the pixel data
```

continued on next page

continued from previous page

```
    Get 1, , BitBuffer

    ' Write it to memory
    Throw = MemoryWrite(BitDataSelector, MemOffset, ByVal BitBuffer, 2048)

    ' Increment the offset
    MemOffset = MemOffset + 2048

    ' Decrement the number of bits to be read
    NumBits = NumBits - 2048

Loop

' Close the file
Close #1


' Build the frames
For counter = 0 To 25

    ' Loop through the palette
    For n = 0 To 255

        ' Get the ASCII value of Red
        T = Asc(bmInfo.bmiColors(n).rgbRed)

        ' Decrement the value ensuring that the
        ' increment does not go below 0
        If T > 9 Then T = T - 10 Else T = 0

        ' Set the palette entry
        bmInfo.bmiColors(n).rgbRed = Chr$(T)

        ' Get the ASCII value of Green
        T = Asc(bmInfo.bmiColors(n).rgbGreen)

        ' Decrement the value ensuring that the
        ' increment does not go below 0
        If T > 9 Then T = T - 10 Else T = 0

        ' Set the palette entry
        bmInfo.bmiColors(n).rgbGreen = Chr$(T)

        ' Get the ASCII value of Blue
        T = Asc(bmInfo.bmiColors(n).rgbBlue)

        ' Decrement the value ensuring that the
        ' increment does not go below 0
        If T > 9 Then T = T - 10 Else T = 0

        ' Set the palette entry
        bmInfo.bmiColors(n).rgbBlue = Chr$(T)

        ' Set the reserved value
        bmInfo.bmiColors(n).rgbReserved = Chr$(0)
```

```
    Next n

'   Build the filename depending on
'   whether it is a fade out or fade in
If FadeType = "FadeOut" Then

    Open App.Path + "\out" + Right$(Str$(counter), Len(Str$(counter)) - 1) ↵
      + ".dib" For Binary As 1

Else

    '   Num will be decreased to build the file names
    num = num - 1
    Open App.Path + "\in" + Right$(Str$(num), Len(Str$(num)) - 1) + ".dib" ↵
      For Binary As 1

End If

'   Put the file header and and bitmap header
'   in the file
Put 1, 1, bmFileHeader
Put 1, Len(bmFileHeader) + 1, bmInfo

'   Get the bitmap size
NumBits = bmInfo.bmiHeader.biSizeImage

'   Reset the memory offset
MemOffset = 0

'   Write the data to the file
Do While NumBits > 0

    '   Read the data from memory
    Throw = MemoryRead(BitDataSelector, MemOffset, ByVal BitBuffer, 2048)

    '   Increment the offset
    MemOffset = MemOffset + 2048

    '   Decrement the number of bits written
    NumBits = NumBits - 2048

    '   Store the data in the file
    Put 1, , BitBuffer

Loop

'   Close the file
Close 1

Next counter

End Sub
```

9. The MemFree function frees up the global memory allocated to read in the image file's pixel data.

```
Public Sub MemFree()

'  Free the global memory
Throw% = GlobalFree(m_BitData)

End Sub
```

How It Works

In many ways, the techniques developed in this How-To closely match those of the last How-To. The bitmap file is read in and several versions of the color table are developed to perform the fade effect. In this case, the technique for writing bitmap data to file from How-To 6.1 is used to write the new bitmap and color table out to successive files. The only real difference between each file is the color table. The header and pixel data are identical.

The program builds 25 successive frames, in which each successive frame's color table RGB values are brightened or darkened to reach either black or its original color. The speed of the fade can easily be manipulated by reducing the number of frames developed. But it is important to ensure that the RGB values reach their final values within the specified number of frames.

The VidEdit program provides for flexible frame-by-frame manipulation of video files, in this case, the easy extraction of the first and last frames of a video clip and the easy insertion of the DIB sequence into the beginning and end of the video clip. A DIB sequence is simply a series of bitmap files that have the same beginning extension, in this case either In or Out, and a series of numbers after the beginning of the extension. Review the sample files provided with this How-To to see the numbering sequence of the fade frames. When the DIB files are imported, each DIB is added to the video clip in sequence.

If you should encounter unusual palette cycling because of the many new colors added to the video clip, VidEdit provides a utility to build an optimal palette for the video clip. Use this utility to optimize the entire clip to include the new frames. It is important to point out that the fade-in and fade-out sequences (and other manipulations) can only be performed on video clips that use 8-bit color (256 colors). If your clip uses more colors, VidEdit can convert the clip to 8-bit. You can then use these tools to manipulate various frames in the clip and import them.

Comments

This example shows only one of many different effects that can be performed on bitmap video frames. For example, if you have several sections of a video clip between which you would like to have transition frames, you can extract the beginning and ending clip of each section and develop and insert fades. The tint techniques from How-To 6.1 can be used to color a single frame or many successive frames. The basic elements demonstrated in this How-To combined with bitmap manipulation and VidEdit can allow you to develop effective custom effects for your video clips.

6.6 How do I...
Perform a crossfade between two images?

Problem

One of the most popular multimedia effects is the crossfade between two images. How can I perform this popular graphic effect using my Visual Basic 4.0 applications?

Technique

Although the crossfade may be one of the most popular graphic visual effects, it is also one of the most challenging to implement. First, there is the obstacle of how to combine the pixels of the two images into a visually effective pattern. Second, the palettes of the two images may be vastly different and the transition frames need to accurately reflect all of the colors between the two images that have to be built.

To solve the first problem, How-To 4.7 is used to help build successful transition patterns between the images. In this case, the pattern will not be black but will be a pattern of the image to transition to. To solve the palette transition problem, techniques used for building the fade transition palettes in the last two How-Tos will be used. But instead of fading the palette to black, the palette will transition to the palette of the final image.

Steps

Open and run 6-6.VBP. The running program appears as shown in Figure 6-6-1.

To perform the crossfade, click on the CrossFade button. To reset the picture to perform the crossfade again, click on the Reset button. Figure 6-6-2 shows the transition in progress.

The final image is shown in the Figure 6-6-3.

1. Create a new project called 6-6.VBP. Add the objects and properties listed in Table 6-6-1 to Form1 and save the form as 6-6.FRM.

Table 6-6-1 Project form's objects and properties.

OBJECT	PROPERTY	SETTING
Form	Name	Form1
	Auto3D	-1 'True
	Caption	"How-To 6.6"

continued on next page

continued from previous page

OBJECT	PROPERTY	SETTING
CommandButton	Name	Cfade
	Caption	"CrossFade"
CommandButton	Name	Reset
	Caption	"Reset"
Timer	Name	Timer1
	Enabled	0 'False
	Interval	1
PictureBox	Name	DispPict
	AutoSize	-1 'True
	BackColor	&H00C0C0C0&
	BorderStyle	0 'None
	ScaleMode	3 'Pixel

2. Add the following code to the general declarations section of the form. The CrossFade class is globally declared, along with global variables for the form.

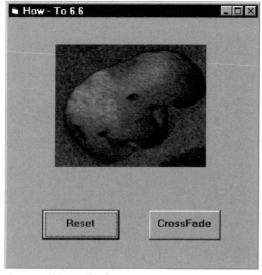

Figure 6-6-1 The form as it appears at runtime

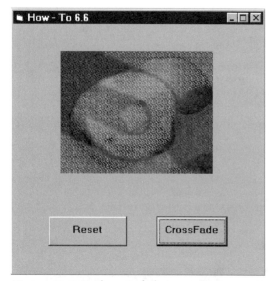

Figure 6-6-2 The crossfade in progress

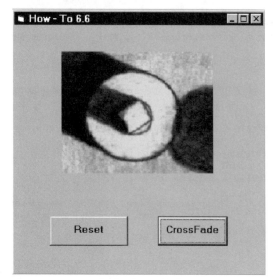

Figure 6-6-3 The final crossfade image

```
'   Globally declare the crossfade class
Dim crossfade As New crossfade

'   Flag is used in the Form
'   Paint procedure
Dim flag As Integer
```

3. When the CrossFade button is selected, the Fade method of the CrossFade class is called.

```
Private Sub Cfade_Click()
'   Setup for the fade
crossfade.Fade
End Sub
```

4. When the form is loaded, the CrossFade class is created and the display picture, timer, and fade file name properties are set.

```
Private Sub Form_Load()

'   Create the new class
Set crossfade = New crossfade

'   Set the fade picture
Set crossfade.picture = DispPict

'   Set the fade timer
Set crossfade.timer = Timer1

'   Set the two files to fade to and from
Let crossfade.FromFile = App.Path + "\rock.bmp"
Let crossfade.ToFile = App.Path + "\boiler.bmp"

End Sub
```

5. The first time the form is painted, the pattern bitmaps are created and the cross-fade is initialized by calling the Setup function of the CrossFade class.

```
Private Sub Form_Paint()

'   Setup the first time the form is
'   loaded
If flag = 0 Then

    '   Setup for the fade.  Set the parameter
    '   to 2 if you want a vertical blind fade
    crossfade.setup 1
    flag = 1
End If

End Sub
```

6. When the form is unloaded, the MemFree method is called to free up the memory allocated by the GlobalAlloc function.

```
Private Sub Form_Unload(Cancel As Integer)
'   Free the memory up
crossfade.MemFree
End Sub
```

7. When the Reset button is selected, the original bitmap is displayed by calling the DisplayBitmap method of the CrossFade class.

```
Private Sub Reset_Click()
'  Display the original bitmap
crossfade.DisplayBitmap
End Sub
```

8. With every tick of the timer, the TimerTick method of the class is called to perform the next step of the crossfade.

```
Private Sub Timer1_Timer()
'  Perform a step of the fade
crossfade.TimerTick
End Sub
```

9. Insert a new class into the project and save it as CROSSFAD.CLS. Add the following code to the general declarations section of the form. The necessary GDI and memory functions are declared for performing the crossfade, as are the appropriate bitmap structures and global members of the class.

```
'  Used to transfer m_bits from one picture to another
Private Declare Function BitBlt% Lib "GDI" (ByVal hDestDC%, ByVal x%, ByVal ↵
y%, ByVal nWidth%, ByVal nHeight%, ByVal hSrcDC%, ByVal XSrc%, ByVal YSrc%, ↵
ByVal dwRop&)

'  Selects an object into a device context
Private Declare Function SelectObject% Lib "GDI" (ByVal hDC%, ByVal hObject%)

'  Creates a DIB Bitmap
Private Declare Function CreateDIBitmap% Lib "GDI" (ByVal hDC%, lpInfoHeader ↵
As BITMAPINFOHEADER, ByVal dwUsage&, ByVal lpInitBits$, lpInitInfo As ↵
BITMAPINFO2, ByVal wUsage%)

'  Deletes a created object
Private Declare Function DeleteObject% Lib "GDI" (ByVal hObject%)

'  Creates a pattern brush
Private Declare Function CreatePatternBrush Lib "GDI" (ByVal hBitmap As ↵
Integer) As Integer

'  Paints a picture with the specified pattern
Private Declare Function PatBlt Lib "GDI" (ByVal hDC As Integer, ByVal x As ↵
Integer, ByVal y As Integer, ByVal nWidth As Integer, ByVal nHeight As ↵
Integer, ByVal dwRop As Long) As Integer

'  Transfers data from one picture to another and stretches to the new
'  picture dimensions
Private Declare Function StretchBlt% Lib "GDI" (ByVal hDC%, ByVal x%, ByVal ↵
y%, ByVal nWidth%, ByVal nHeight%, ByVal hSrcDC%, ByVal XSrc%, ByVal YSrc%, ↵
ByVal nSrcWidth%, ByVal nSrcHeight%, ByVal dwRop&)

' Declare solid brush function
Private Declare Function CreateSolidBrush Lib "GDI" (ByVal crColor As Long) ↵
```

continued on next page

CHAPTER 6

continued from previous page

```
As Integer

'   Deletes a created device context
Private Declare Function DeleteDC Lib "GDI" (ByVal hDC As Integer) As Integer

'   Copies the DIB bits to the device context
Private Declare Function StretchDIBits Lib "GDI" (ByVal hDC As Integer, ByVal ↵
DestX As Integer, ByVal DestY As Integer, ByVal nDestWidth As Integer, ByVal ↵
nDestHeight As Integer, ByVal SrcX As Integer, ByVal SrcY As Integer, ByVal ↵
nSrcWidth As Integer, ByVal nSrcHeight As Integer, ByVal lpBits As Long, ↵
lpBitsInfo As BITMAPINFO, ByVal wUsage As Integer, ByVal dwRop As Long) ↵
As Integer

'   Deletes an object
Private Declare Function DeleteObject Lib "GDI" (ByVal hObject As Integer) ↵
As Integer

'   Creates a palette from a logical palette
Private Declare Function CreatePalette Lib "GDI" (lpLogPalette As LOGPALETTE) ↵
As Integer

'   Creates a compatible bitmap to the device context
Private Declare Function CreateCompatibleBitmap Lib "GDI" (ByVal hDC As ↵
Integer, ByVal nWidth As Integer, ByVal nHeight As Integer) As Integer

'   Creates a compatible device context
Private Declare Function CreateCompatibleDC Lib "GDI" (ByVal hDC As Integer) ↵
As Integer

'   SelectPalette will be used to select the created palette
'   into the specified device context
Private Declare Function SelectPalette Lib "User" (ByVal hDC As Integer, ↵
ByVal Pal As Integer, ByVal bForceBackground As Integer) As Integer

'   RealizePalette realizes the current palette in the device
'   context into the system palette
Private Declare Function RealizePalette Lib "User" (ByVal hDC As Integer) ↵
As Integer

'   Declare the paletteentry structure
'   for the palette entries in a logical
'   palette
Private Type PALETTEENTRY
    peRed       As String * 1
    peGreen     As String * 1
    peBlue      As String * 1
    peFlags     As String * 1
End Type

'   Declare the logical palette structure
Private Type LOGPALETTE
    palVersion          As Integer
    palNumEntries       As Integer
    PalEntry(255)       As PALETTEENTRY
End Type
```

```
'  palette index used for animation
Const PC_RESERVED = &H1

'  Defines the bitmap header structure
Private Type BITMAPINFOHEADER
        biSize                As Long
        biWidth               As Long
        biHeight              As Long
        biPlanes              As Integer
        biBitCount            As Integer
        biCompression         As Long
        biSizeImage           As Long
        biXPelsPerMeter       As Long
        biYPelsPerMeter       As Long
        biClrUsed             As Long
        biClrImportant        As Long
End Type


'  This data structure holds the header info as
'  well as the color data.  Special monochrome
'  version for the pattern bitmaps.  bmiColors
'  is a simple string that will hold two colors
Private Type BITMAPINFO2
     bmiHeader As BITMAPINFOHEADER
     bmiColors As String * 8 ' Array length is arbitrary; may be changed
End Type

'  Stores the palette colors for the bitmap
Private Type RGBQUAD
     rgbBlue      As String * 1
     rgbGreen     As String * 1
     rgbRed       As String * 1
     rgbReserved  As String * 1
End Type

'  Overall Bitmap Header Structure
Private Type BITMAPINFO
     bmiHeader As BITMAPINFOHEADER
     bmiColors(0 To 255)  As RGBQUAD
End Type

'  Bitmap file header structure
Private Type BITMAPFILEHEADER
     bfType       As Integer
     bfSize       As Long
     bfReserved1  As Integer
     bfReserved2  As Integer
     bfOffBits    As Long
End Type


'  The global memory functions
Private Declare Function GlobalAlloc Lib "Kernel" (ByVal wFlags As Integer, ↵
```

continued on next page

continued from previous page

```
ByVal dwBytes As Long) As Integer

Private Declare Function GlobalHandleToSel Lib "ToolHelp.DLL" (ByVal hMem As ↵
Integer) As Integer

Private Declare Function MemoryWrite Lib "ToolHelp.DLL" (ByVal wSel As ↵
Integer, ByVal dwOffset As Long, lpvBuf As Any, ByVal dwcb As Long) As Long

Private Declare Function MemoryRead Lib "ToolHelp.DLL" (ByVal wSel As ↵
Integer, ByVal dwOffset As Long, lpvBuf As Any, ByVal dwcb As Long) As Long

Private Declare Function GlobalFree Lib "Kernel" (ByVal hMem As Integer) ↵
As Integer

Private Declare Function GlobalLock Lib "Kernel" (ByVal hMem As Integer) As Long

Private Declare Function GlobalUnlock Lib "Kernel" (ByVal hMem As Integer) ↵
As Integer

'   Constants for allocating memory
Const GMEM_MOVEABLE = &H2
Const GMEM_ZEROINIT = &H40

'   Specifies that the bitmap color table contains RGB colors
Const DIB_RGB_COLORS = 0

'   Indicates to CreateDiBitmap that the bitmap is initialized with the m_bits
'   specified by the lpvBits and lpbmi parameters.
Const CBM_INIT = &H4&

'   Copy the bitmap as is to the destination picture
Const SRCCOPY = &HCC0020

'   Use logical AND to combine the bitmaps
Const SRCAND = &H8800C6

'   Copy the pattern to the bitmap
Const PATCOPY = &HF00021

' (DWORD) dest = (source AND pattern)
Const MERGECOPY = &HC000CA

'   Specifies that the bitmap is not compressed
Const BI_RGB = 0&

'   Raster Operations used for
'   building the cross fade bitmaps
Const SPDSxax = &HAC0744

'   DissolveCnt counts through
'   the dissolve steps
Dim DissolveCnt As Integer

'   The two pointers to the global memory
Dim m_BitData1 As Integer
```

```
Dim m_BitData2 As Integer

'   Palette handle
Dim Pal As Integer

'   Handle to the bitmap of the memory
'   device context used for building
'   the fade
Dim NewBitmap As Integer

'   The memory device context used
'   for the fade
Dim NewDc As Integer

'   Array to store header information
'   for the two bitmaps
Dim bmInfoStore(2) As BITMAPINFO

'   Array to hold the pointer information for
'   the two bitmap bits
Dim lpDIBits(2) As Long

'   Holds the palette steps for
'   the fade
Dim LogicalPalette(10) As LOGPALETTE

'   The file to fade from
Dim m_FromFIle As String

'   The file to fade to
Dim m_ToFIle As String

'   The timer
Dim m_timer As Object

'   The display picture
Private m_DispPict As Object

'   Declare m_BitInfoH as type BITMAPINFOHEADER
'   This is used to create the patterns
Dim m_BitInfoH As BITMAPINFOHEADER

'   Declare m_BitInfo as type BITMAPINFO
'   This is used to create the simple monochrome
'   bitmaps.
Dim m_BitInfo As BITMAPINFO2

'   Declare the screen class
Dim m_bits As ScreenBuild

'   Stores the pattern screens
Dim m_scrn(10) As String * 32

'   Dim the global variable to store the
'   transition palette handles
```

continued on next page

continued from previous page

```
Dim Pal() as integer

'   Stores the handle to the
'   pattern bitmaps
Private m_hbr() As Integer
```

10. The following properties set the display picture for the crossfade, the timer, the file to fade from, and the file to fade to.

```
'   Get the display picture
Public Property Set picture(acontrol As Control)
    Set m_DispPict = acontrol
End Property

'   Get the timer control
Public Property Set timer(acontrol As Control)
    Set m_timer = acontrol
End Property

'   Get the bitmap to fade from
Public Property Let FromFile(S As String)
    Let m_FromFIle = S
End Property

'   Get the bitmap to fade to
Public Property Let ToFile(S As String)
    Let m_ToFIle = S
End Property
```

11. The ReadFiles function reads in the two images and sets the first and last logical palettes of the transition palette array. The first palette should be that of the fade-from image and the last should be that of the fade-to image. The intermediate logical palettes are developed by calling the CreatePalettes function.

```
Public Sub ReadFiles()

'   Declare the file header structure
Dim bmFileHeader As BITMAPFILEHEADER

'   NumBits will hold the number of bits
'   in the bitmap
Dim NumBits As Long

'   BitBuffer will be used to read in the
'   bitmap data
Dim BitBuffer As String * 2048

'   Open the file
Open m_FromFIle For Binary As 1

'   Read in the file and bitmap header
Get 1, 1, bmFileHeader
Get 1, Len(bmFileHeader) + 1, bmInfoStore(1)
```

```
'  Get the number of bits in the file
NumBits = bmInfoStore(1).bmiHeader.biSizeImage

'  Allocate the memory
m_BitData1 = GlobalAlloc(GMEM_MOVEABLE Or GMEM_ZEROINIT, NumBits)

'  Get a selector to the memory
m_Bitdataselector = GlobalHandleToSel(m_BitData1)

'  Read in the bitmap bits
Do While NumBits > 0
    Get 1, , BitBuffer
    throw = MemoryWrite(m_Bitdataselector, memoffset, ByVal BitBuffer, 2048)
    memoffset = memoffset + 2048
    NumBits = NumBits - 2048
Loop

'  Close the file
Close #1

'  Get the pointer to the memory block
LpDIBits&(1) = GlobalLock(m_BitData1)


'  Build the logical palette for the beginning fade
'  palette.  Note that we do not want the system
'  palette positions to be reserved so that they
'  will be mapped as they should be
For n = 10 To 245
    LogicalPalette(1).PalEntry(n).peRed = bmInfoStore(1).bmiColors(n).rgbRed
    LogicalPalette(1).PalEntry(n).peGreen = bmInfoStore(1).bmiColors(n).rgbGreen
    LogicalPalette(1).PalEntry(n).peBlue = bmInfoStore(1).bmiColors(n).rgbBlue
    LogicalPalette(1).PalEntry(n).peFlags = Chr$(PC_RESERVED)

Next n


'  Open the second file for reading
Open m_ToFIle For Binary As 1

'  Read in the header of the file and the bitmap
Get 1, 1, bmFileHeader
Get 1, Len(bmFileHeader) + 1, bmInfoStore(2)

'  Get the number of bits
NumBits = bmInfoStore(2).bmiHeader.biSizeImage

'  Reset the memory offset
memoffset = 0

'  Allocate the memory and get a selector
m_BitData2 = GlobalAlloc(GMEM_MOVEABLE Or GMEM_ZEROINIT, NumBits)
m_Bitdataselector = GlobalHandleToSel(m_BitData2)

'  Read in the data
```

continued on next page

continued from previous page

```
Do While NumBits > 0
    Get 1, , BitBuffer
    throw = MemoryWrite(m_Bitdataselector, memoffset, ByVal BitBuffer, 2048)
    memoffset = memoffset + 2048
    NumBits = NumBits - 2048
Loop

'  Close the file
Close #1

'  Get a pointer to the memory block
lpDIBits&(2) = GlobalLock(m_BitData2)

'  Setup the ending logical palette
For n = 10 To 245
    LogicalPalette(10).PalEntry(n).peRed = bmInfoStore(2).bmiColors(n).rgbRed
    LogicalPalette(10).PalEntry(n).peGreen = bmInfoStore(2).↵
    bmiColors(n).rgbGreen

    LogicalPalette(10).PalEntry(n).peBlue = bmInfoStore(2).bmiColors(n).rgbBlue
    LogicalPalette(10).PalEntry(n).peFlags = Chr$(PC_RESERVED)
Next n

'  Call the CreatePalettes function to create
'  the series of palettes for the fade
CreatePalettes

End Sub
```

12. The CreatePalettes function handles building the transition palettes between the original image and the fade-to image. The individual RGB entries of each palette entry are transitioned to the values of the final palette. Keep in mind that the value can go either up or down. At the end of the function, the Pal() array is filled with handles to the 10 transition palettes.

```
Private Sub CreatePalettes()

'  Loop through all of the palette positions.  For
'  each postion ten steps will be built to fade the
'  red, green, and blue components to the ending palette
For n = 10 To 245

'  Check to see if the beginning Red component is larger
'  than the ending component.
If Asc(LogicalPalette(1).PalEntry(n).peRed) > ↵
Asc(LogicalPalette(10).PalEntry(n).peRed) Then

    '  Calculate the difference between the two positions
    palincs = Asc(LogicalPalette(1).PalEntry(n).peRed) - ↵
      Asc(LogicalPalette(10).PalEntry(n).peRed)

    '  Calculate the step increment EX:
    '  Origial Value of 255
    '  Final Value of 205
```

```
'  The increment will be 5
palincs = palincs / 8

'  For the 8 intermediate palette positions,
'  calculate the new value
For b = 2 To 9

'  Set the Red value to subtract the appropriate
'  multiple of the increment.
LogicalPalette(b).PalEntry(n).peRed = Chr$(Asc(LogicalPalette(1).↵
  PalEntry(n).peRed) - (palincs * (b - 1)))
LogicalPalette(b).PalEntry(n).peFlags = Chr$(PC_RESERVED)
Next b

'  Otherwise the beginning Red value is smaller
'  than the ending value
Else

'  Calculate the beginning value from the ending value
palincs = Asc(LogicalPalette(10).PalEntry(n).peRed) - ↵
  Asc(LogicalPalette(1).PalEntry(n).peRed)

'  Calculate the 8 step increment
palincs = palincs / 8

'  For the 8 intermediate palettes, the
'  values will be calculated
For b = 2 To 9

'  Set the Red value for the specified position
LogicalPalette(b).PalEntry(n).peRed = Chr$(Asc(LogicalPalette(1).↵
  PalEntry(n).peRed) + (palincs * (b - 1)))
LogicalPalette(b).PalEntry(n).peFlags = Chr$(PC_RESERVED)
Next b

End If


'  The Green and Blue palette components
'  are calculated the same as the red.
If Asc(LogicalPalette(1).PalEntry(n).peGreen) > ↵
Asc(LogicalPalette(10).PalEntry(n).peGreen) Then

palincs = Asc(LogicalPalette(1).PalEntry(n).peGreen) - ↵
  Asc(LogicalPalette(10).PalEntry(n).peGreen)
palincs = palincs / 8

For b = 2 To 9
LogicalPalette(b).PalEntry(n).peGreen = Chr$(Asc(LogicalPalette(1).↵
  PalEntry(n).peGreen) - (palincs * (b - 1)))
  LogicalPalette(b).PalEntry(n).peFlags = Chr$(PC_RESERVED)
Next b

Else
palincs = Asc(LogicalPalette(10).PalEntry(n).peGreen) - ↵
```

continued on next page

continued from previous page

```
            Asc(LogicalPalette(1).PalEntry(n).peGreen)

     palincs = palincs / 8

     For b = 2 To 9
     LogicalPalette(b).PalEntry(n).peGreen = Chr$(Asc(LogicalPalette(1).↵
       PalEntry(n).peGreen) + (palincs * (b - 1)))
        LogicalPalette(b).PalEntry(n).peFlags = Chr$(PC_RESERVED)
             End If
     Next b

End If


If Asc(LogicalPalette(1).PalEntry(n).peBlue) > ↵
Asc(LogicalPalette(10).PalEntry(n).peBlue) Then

     palincs = Asc(LogicalPalette(1).PalEntry(n).peBlue) - ↵
       Asc(LogicalPalette(10).PalEntry(n).peBlue)

     palincs = palincs / 8

     For b = 2 To 9

     LogicalPalette(b).PalEntry(n).peBlue = Chr$(Asc(LogicalPalette(1).↵
       PalEntry(n).peBlue) - (palincs * (b - 1)))
          LogicalPalette(b).PalEntry(n).peFlags = Chr$(PC_RESERVED)
     Next b

Else
     palincs = Asc(LogicalPalette(10).PalEntry(n).peBlue) - ↵
       Asc(LogicalPalette(1).PalEntry(n).peBlue)

     palincs = palincs / 8

     For b = 2 To 9

     LogicalPalette(b).PalEntry(n).peBlue = Chr$(Asc(LogicalPalette(1).↵
       PalEntry(n).peBlue) + (palincs * (b - 1)))
        LogicalPalette(b).PalEntry(n).peFlags = Chr$(PC_RESERVED)
     Next b

End If


Next n

'  Set the version and number of entries
'  up for each palette
For n = 1 To 10

    LogicalPalette(n).palVersion = &H300
    LogicalPalette(n).palNumEntries = 256

    '  Create the palettes and store them
```

```
    '  in the Pal array
    Pal(n) = CreatePalette(LogicalPalette(n))

Next n

End Sub
```

13. The MemFree function frees up the memory allocated by the GlobalAlloc function for reading in the bitmap pixel data.

```
Public Sub MemFree()

'  Free the allocated memory
throw% = GlobalFree(m_BitData1)
throw% = GlobalFree(m_BitData2)

End Sub
```

14. With each timer tick, the next transition palette is selected into the device context. Using StretchDIBits and a special ROP function, the pattern and the two bitmaps are combined to perform the fade.

```
Public Sub TimerTick()

'  Select the bitmap brush into the device context
Bselect NewDc, DissolveCnt

'  Select the palette into the new device context
'  as well as the display picture
throw = SelectPalette(NewDc, Pal(DissolveCnt), 0)
LastPal = SelectPalette(m_DispPict.hDC, Pal(DissolveCnt), 0)

'  Realize the palette
throw = RealizePalette(m_DispPict.hDC)

'  Copy the new image into the device context.  The result
'  is the opposite of the pattern is copied to the Device
'  context.
'  SPDSxax  is:
'  Source Bitmap is XORed with the Destination
'  The result is ANDed with the Pattern
'  The result is XORed with the Source
throw = StretchDIBits(NewDc, 0, 0, m_DispPict.ScaleWidth, ↵
m_DispPict.ScaleHeight, 0, 0, bmInfoStore(2).bmiHeader.biWidth, ↵
bmInfoStore(2).bmiHeader.biHeight, lpDIBits(2), bmInfoStore(2), ↵
DIB_RGB_COLORS, SPDSxax)

'  Copy the image to the display picture
throw = BitBlt(m_DispPict.hDC, 0, 0, m_DispPict.ScaleWidth, ↵
m_DispPict.ScaleHeight, NewDc, 0, 0, SRCCOPY)

'  Increment the dissolve counter
DissolveCnt = DissolveCnt + 1

'  If the last step has been
```

continued on next page

continued from previous page

```
'  reached then disable the timer
If DissolveCnt = 11 Then m_timer.Enabled = False

End Sub
```

15. The Setup function handles building the pattern bitmaps that combine the two images. Note that several of these functions came from the CrossHatch class developed in How-To 4.7 and they access the ScreenBuild class also developed in How-To 4.7. The parameter of the Setup function indicates whether cross hatch or vertical blind screens should be built. The function calls the ReadFiles function to read in the two images, and then displays the initial image.

```
Public Sub Setup(ScrnType As Integer)

'  Build the bitmaps
buildbitmap

'  Build the screens
BuildScrns ScrnType

'  Build the bitmaps
BuildHandles

'  Read in the bitmap files
ReadFiles

'  Create a compatible memory
'  device context to that of the
'  picture
NewDc = CreateCompatibleDC(m_DispPict.hDC)

'  Create a compatible bitmap to that of
'  the picture
NewBitmap = CreateCompatibleBitmap(m_DispPict.hDC, m_DispPict.ScaleWidth, ↵
m_DispPict.ScaleHeight)

'  Select the NewBitmap into the New Device context
throw = SelectObject(NewDc, NewBitmap)

'  Select the palette into the new device context
'  as well as the display picture
throw = SelectPalette(NewDc, Pal, 0)
LastPal = SelectPalette(m_DispPict.hDC, Pal, 0)

'  Realize the palette
LastPal = RealizePalette(m_DispPict.hDC)

'  Display the initial bitmap
DisplayBitmap

End Sub
```

16. The Fade function enables the timer and resets the DissolveCnt parameter.

```
Public Sub Fade()

'   Set the DissolveCnt counter
DissolveCnt = 1

' Start the timer
m_timer.Enabled = True

End Sub
```

17. The ReStart function handles deleting the created device context, bitmaps, and transition palettes. This function is called when the class is terminated.

```
Public Sub ReStart()

'   Delete the brushes
BDelete

'   Delete the new device context and
'   the new bitmap
throw = DeleteDC(NewDc)
throw = DeleteObject(NewBitmap)

'   Delete the transition palettes
For N = 1 to 10
        throw = DeleteObject(Pal(N))
Next N

End Sub
```

18. When the class is initialized, the ScreenBuild class is created. This is called by the functions that create the pattern bitmaps.

```
Private Sub Class_Initialize()
        Set m_bits = New ScreenBuild
End Sub
```

19. When the class is terminated, the ReStart function is called to delete all the objects created for the crossfade.

```
Private Sub Class_Terminate()
        ReStart
End Sub
```

20. The DisplayBitmap function displays the initial bitmap image. The StretchDIBits function is used to copy the bits to the display. Also, the palette for the initial image is selected into the display device context to ensure that the system palette accurately reflects the colors in the image.

```
Public Sub DisplayBitmap()

'   Create the appropriate palette for the step
'   we are on.
```

continued on next page

continued from previous page

```
Pal(1) = CreatePalette(LogicalPalette(1))

'  Select the palette into the new device context
'  as well as the display picture
throw = SelectPalette(NewDc, Pal(1), 0)
LastPal = SelectPalette(m_DispPict.hDC, Pal(1), 0)

'  Realize the palette
throw = RealizePalette(m_DispPict.hDC)

'  Copy the bitmap bits to the memory context
ErrCode = StretchDIBits(NewDc, 0, 0, m_DispPict.ScaleWidth, ↵
m_DispPict.ScaleHeight, 0, 0, bmInfoStore(1).bmiHeader.biWidth, ↵
bmInfoStore(1).bmiHeader.biHeight, lpDIBits(1), bmInfoStore(1), ↵
DIB_RGB_COLORS, SRCCOPY)

'  Copy the image to the display picture
ErrCode = BitBlt(m_DispPict.hDC, 0, 0, m_DispPict.ScaleWidth, ↵
m_DispPict.ScaleHeight, NewDc, 0, 0, SRCCOPY)

End Sub
```

21. The BuildScrns routine builds cross hatch pattern brushes or vertical blind pattern brushes. For further information on this process, see How-To 4.7.

```
Public Sub BuildScrns(index)

If index = 1 Then

'  This function builds the different screens to
'  fill the picture with

'  a will hold a string representation of
'  the screen
ReDim A(8) As String * 8

'  For each of the successive 10 screens, we
'  will build a binary string of 1s and 0s
'  to represent the 8x8 screen that will be
'  used to fill the picture.  We call the
'  BitArraySet fun
ction in the ScreenBuild class

m_bits.BitArraySet "11111111", 1
m_bits.BitArraySet "11111111", 2
m_bits.BitArraySet "11111111", 3
m_bits.BitArraySet "11111111", 4
m_bits.BitArraySet "11111111", 5
m_bits.BitArraySet "11111111", 6
m_bits.BitArraySet "11111111", 7
m_bits.BitArraySet "11111111", 8

'  We now setup the bit data in scrn
m_bits.BitBuild m_scrn(1)
```

```
'   The code is the same as above
m_bits.BitArraySet "11101111", 1
m_bits.BitArraySet "10111111", 2
m_bits.BitArraySet "11111011", 3
m_bits.BitArraySet "11111111", 4
m_bits.BitArraySet "11111111", 5
m_bits.BitArraySet "11111111", 6
m_bits.BitArraySet "11111110", 7
m_bits.BitArraySet "11111111", 8

m_bits.BitBuild m_scrn(2)

m_bits.BitArraySet "11101011", 1
m_bits.BitArraySet "10111111", 2
m_bits.BitArraySet "11111010", 3
m_bits.BitArraySet "11111011", 4
m_bits.BitArraySet "11011111", 5
m_bits.BitArraySet "11101111", 6
m_bits.BitArraySet "11111110", 7
m_bits.BitArraySet "11110111", 8

m_bits.BitBuild m_scrn(3)

m_bits.BitArraySet "10101011", 1
m_bits.BitArraySet "10111101", 2
m_bits.BitArraySet "11101010", 3
m_bits.BitArraySet "10111011", 4
m_bits.BitArraySet "11011011", 5
m_bits.BitArraySet "11101101", 6
m_bits.BitArraySet "01111110", 7
m_bits.BitArraySet "11110111", 8

m_bits.BitBuild m_scrn(4)

m_bits.BitArraySet "10101010", 1
m_bits.BitArraySet "10101101", 2
m_bits.BitArraySet "10101010", 3
m_bits.BitArraySet "10111010", 4
m_bits.BitArraySet "01011011", 5
m_bits.BitArraySet "10101101", 6
m_bits.BitArraySet "01111010", 7
m_bits.BitArraySet "11110101", 8

m_bits.BitBuild m_scrn(5)

m_bits.BitArraySet "10101010", 1
m_bits.BitArraySet "10100101", 2
m_bits.BitArraySet "10101010", 3
m_bits.BitArraySet "00111010", 4
m_bits.BitArraySet "01001011", 5
m_bits.BitArraySet "10100101", 6
m_bits.BitArraySet "01011010", 7
m_bits.BitArraySet "10110101", 8
```

continued on next page

continued from previous page

```
m_bits.BitBuild m_scrn(6)

m_bits.BitArraySet "10001010", 1
m_bits.BitArraySet "00100101", 2
m_bits.BitArraySet "10100010", 3
m_bits.BitArraySet "00101010", 4
m_bits.BitArraySet "01001001", 5
m_bits.BitArraySet "00100101", 6
m_bits.BitArraySet "01001010", 7
m_bits.BitArraySet "10110100", 8

m_bits.BitBuild m_scrn(7)

m_bits.BitArraySet "10001000", 1
m_bits.BitArraySet "00100001", 2
m_bits.BitArraySet "00100010", 3
m_bits.BitArraySet "00100010", 4
m_bits.BitArraySet "01001000", 5
m_bits.BitArraySet "00100100", 6
m_bits.BitArraySet "00001010", 7
m_bits.BitArraySet "10010100", 8

m_bits.BitBuild m_scrn(8)

m_bits.BitArraySet "10000000", 1
m_bits.BitArraySet "00000001", 2
m_bits.BitArraySet "00100000", 3
m_bits.BitArraySet "00000010", 4
m_bits.BitArraySet "00001000", 5
m_bits.BitArraySet "00000100", 6
m_bits.BitArraySet "00000010", 7
m_bits.BitArraySet "10000000", 8

m_bits.BitBuild m_scrn(9)

m_bits.BitArraySet "00000000", 1
m_bits.BitArraySet "00000000", 2
m_bits.BitArraySet "00000000", 3
m_bits.BitArraySet "00000000", 4
m_bits.BitArraySet "00000000", 5
m_bits.BitArraySet "00000000", 6
m_bits.BitArraySet "00000000", 7
m_bits.BitArraySet "00000000", 8

m_bits.BitBuild m_scrn(10)

Else

'   This function builds the different screens to
'   fill the picture with


'   a will hold a string representation of
'   the screen
ReDim A(8) As String * 8
```

```
'   For each of the successive 10 screens, we
'   will build a binary string of 1s and 0s
'   to represent the 8x8 screen that will be
'   used to fill the picture.  We call the
'   BitArraySet function in the ScreenBuild class

m_bits.BitArraySet "11111111", 1
m_bits.BitArraySet "11111111", 2
m_bits.BitArraySet "11111111", 3
m_bits.BitArraySet "11111111", 4
m_bits.BitArraySet "11111111", 5
m_bits.BitArraySet "11111111", 6
m_bits.BitArraySet "11111111", 7
m_bits.BitArraySet "11111111", 8


'   We now setup the bit data in scrn
m_bits.BitBuild m_scrn(1)

m_bits.BitArraySet "11111110", 1
m_bits.BitArraySet "11111110", 2
m_bits.BitArraySet "11111110", 3
m_bits.BitArraySet "11111110", 4
m_bits.BitArraySet "11111110", 5
m_bits.BitArraySet "11111110", 6
m_bits.BitArraySet "11111110", 7
m_bits.BitArraySet "11111110", 8

m_bits.BitBuild m_scrn(2)

m_bits.BitArraySet "11111100", 1
m_bits.BitArraySet "11111100", 2
m_bits.BitArraySet "11111100", 3
m_bits.BitArraySet "11111100", 4
m_bits.BitArraySet "11111100", 5
m_bits.BitArraySet "11111100", 6
m_bits.BitArraySet "11111100", 7
m_bits.BitArraySet "11111100", 8

m_bits.BitBuild m_scrn(3)

m_bits.BitArraySet "11111000", 1
m_bits.BitArraySet "11111000", 2
m_bits.BitArraySet "11111000", 3
m_bits.BitArraySet "11111000", 4
m_bits.BitArraySet "11111000", 5
m_bits.BitArraySet "11111000", 6
m_bits.BitArraySet "11111000", 7
m_bits.BitArraySet "11111000", 8

m_bits.BitBuild m_scrn(4)

m_bits.BitArraySet "11110000", 1
m_bits.BitArraySet "11110000", 2
m_bits.BitArraySet "11110000", 3
```

continued on next page

continued from previous page

```
m_bits.BitArraySet "11110000", 4
m_bits.BitArraySet "11110000", 5
m_bits.BitArraySet "11110000", 6
m_bits.BitArraySet "11110000", 7
m_bits.BitArraySet "11110000", 8

m_bits.BitBuild m_scrn(5)

m_bits.BitArraySet "11100000", 1
m_bits.BitArraySet "11100000", 2
m_bits.BitArraySet "11100000", 3
m_bits.BitArraySet "11100000", 4
m_bits.BitArraySet "11100000", 5
m_bits.BitArraySet "11100000", 6
m_bits.BitArraySet "11100000", 7
m_bits.BitArraySet "11100000", 8

m_bits.BitBuild m_scrn(6)

m_bits.BitArraySet "11000000", 1
m_bits.BitArraySet "11000000", 2
m_bits.BitArraySet "11000000", 3
m_bits.BitArraySet "11000000", 4
m_bits.BitArraySet "11000000", 5
m_bits.BitArraySet "11000000", 6
m_bits.BitArraySet "11000000", 7
m_bits.BitArraySet "11000000", 8

m_bits.BitBuild m_scrn(7)

m_bits.BitArraySet "10000000", 1
m_bits.BitArraySet "10000000", 2
m_bits.BitArraySet "10000000", 3
m_bits.BitArraySet "10000000", 4
m_bits.BitArraySet "10000000", 5
m_bits.BitArraySet "10000000", 6
m_bits.BitArraySet "10000000", 7
m_bits.BitArraySet "10000000", 8

m_bits.BitBuild m_scrn(8)

m_bits.BitArraySet "00000000", 1
m_bits.BitArraySet "00000000", 2
m_bits.BitArraySet "00000000", 3
m_bits.BitArraySet "00000000", 4
m_bits.BitArraySet "00000000", 5
m_bits.BitArraySet "00000000", 6
m_bits.BitArraySet "00000000", 7
m_bits.BitArraySet "00000000", 8

m_bits.BitBuild m_scrn(9)

m_bits.BitArraySet "00000000", 1
m_bits.BitArraySet "00000000", 2
m_bits.BitArraySet "00000000", 3
```

```
m_bits.BitArraySet "00000000", 4
m_bits.BitArraySet "00000000", 5
m_bits.BitArraySet "00000000", 6
m_bits.BitArraySet "00000000", 7
m_bits.BitArraySet "00000000", 8

m_bits.BitBuild m_scrn(10)

End If

End Sub
```

22. The BuildHandles function creates the bitmaps for each pattern brush and stores the handles in the m_hbr() array. These pattern brushes are used to blend the two images together.

```
Public Sub BuildHandles()

'   m_counter will count down the bitmaps
'   to be built
m_counter = 11

'   Dimension the bitmap array to hold
'   the brush handles
ReDim m_hbr(10)

'   Loop to create the 10 bitmaps
For b = 11 To 1 Step -1

'    Decrement m_counter
m_counter = m_counter - 1

'   Stop the process when m_counter reaches 0
If m_counter = 0 Then Exit Sub

'   Set the BitmapInfoHeader field of m_BitInfo
m_BitInfo.bmiHeader = m_BitInfoH

'   Create the 8x8 bitmap specified by m_scrn(m_counter)
compbitmap% = CreateDIBitmap(m_DispPict.hDC, m_BitInfoH, CBM_INIT, ↵
m_scrn(m_counter), m_BitInfo, DIB_RGB_COLORS)

'   Create the bitmap pattern from the screen
m_hbr(m_counter) = CreatePatternBrush(compbitmap%)

Next b

End Sub
```

23. The Bselect function selects the specified brush into the specified device context. This makes the pattern available for combining the two images.

```
Public Sub Bselect(hMemDC, n)
      '   Select the pattern brush into the specified
      '   memory device context
      throw = SelectObject(hMemDC, m_hbr(n))
End Sub
```

24. The BDelete function deletes the pattern brushes created in the BuildHandles function.

```
Public Sub BDelete()
'  Delete the Bitmaps
For n = 1 To 10
    throw = DeleteObject(m_hbr(n))
Next n

End Sub
```

25. The BuildBitmap function sets up a bitmap header for creating the pattern bitmaps used to create the pattern brushes.

```
Public Sub BuildBitmap()

'  Standard 40 Byte Header
m_BitInfoH.biSize = 40

'  This will be an 8 by 8 bitmap
m_BitInfoH.biWidth = 8
m_BitInfoH.biHeight = 8

'  One Plane
m_BitInfoH.biPlanes = 1

'  Specifies the number of bits per pixel
m_BitInfoH.biBitCount = 1

'   No Compression
m_BitInfoH.biCompression = BI_RGB

'  These values are rarely used
m_BitInfoH.biSizeImage = 0
m_BitInfoH.biXPelsPerMeter = 0
m_BitInfoH.biYPelsPerMeter = 0

'  Two colors used
m_BitInfoH.biClrUsed = 255

'  This ensures that all colors are important
m_BitInfoH.biClrImportant = 0

'  This will be a monochrome bitmap
m_BitInfo.bmiColors = "0000" + Chr$(255) + Chr$(255) + Chr$(255) + "0"

End Sub
```

26. Add the SCREEN.CLS class from How-To 4.7 to the project. To review how this class works, see How-To 4.7.

```
'  m_array will hold the string of
'  1's and 0's, which indicates the
'  screen to be built.
```

```
Private m_array() As String * 8

'  This routine is called to set
'  the array data
Public Sub BitArraySet(s, index)

m_array(index) = s

End Sub

Private Sub Class_Initialize()

'  Dimension m_array
ReDim m_array(8) As String * 8

End Sub


Public Sub BitBuild(s As String)

'  We will loop through each element in the a array
For counter = 1 To 8

    '  v will hold the value of the bit pattern, we
    '  need to reset it for each row
    v = 0

    '  We will loop through each row and set the bit values
    For c = 0 To 7

    '  We check for a 1 in the array and if it is one we
    '  then calculate the decimal value of the binary position,
    '  for example in 00000100, the 1 is = to 2^2 = 4
    If Mid$(m_array(counter), c + 1, 1) = "1" Then v = v + 2 ^ c
    Next c
    Mid$(s, (counter - 1) * 4 + 1, 1) = Chr$(v)

Next counter

End Sub
```

How It Works

This project encompasses many different topics. The first challenge is to find an effective way to combine the two bitmaps during the crossfade. One of the most obvious obstacles to overcome is two differently sized images. This is easily overcome with the StretchDIBits function. The bitmaps can be crossed with the same display dimensions. StretchDIBits can stretch the bitmap bits to meet the dimensions provided to the function. Another challenge is to develop a method for determining what bits of the first image will be replaced with bits from the second image for each step. Fortunately, the pattern bitmaps developed in How-To 4.7 provide an effective pattern for blending the bits.

The next issue is how to get the pattern copied onto the original image to have the bits from the new image. To do this, you can turn to the Windows GDI Raster Operations (ROP). So far, you have used simple raster operations such as SRCCOPY and SRCINVERT. But a wide variety of raster operations is available to combine source, destination, and patterns bitmaps—255 to be exact. A simple equation can be built to represent different types of raster operations. Table 6-6-2 is an overview of the different components that can make up an equation.

Table 6-6-2 Raster operation components

LETTER CODE	NAME	DESCRIPTION
D	Destination	The value of the destination pixel
S	Source	The value of the source pixel
P	Pattern	The value of the pixel in the pattern
a	AND	AND Operation
n	NOT	NOT Operation
o	OR	OR Operation
X	XOR	XOR Operation

Equations using these ROP components are written in Reverse Polish Notation (RPN). This means that the equation is interpreted from left to right, with each action affecting the operation to its left. For example, the SRCAND ROP is written as follows:

DSa   SRCAND ROP

In this case, the source and the destination pixels are combined using the AND operator. For the purposes of this How-To, the following ROP equation is used to build a pattern containing the fade-to image pixels:

SPDSxax   ROP used for Crossfade

The source and destination pixels are XORed together. Thus, anywhere the pixels are not the same, the bits are retained. The result of that is ANDed with the pattern to keep only the pattern bits pixels. That final result is XORed with the source to copy the original image bits. The new image is then copied to the specified device context. The final result is an image that has the fade-to bitmap's pixels in the pattern bitmap positions and the original bitmap's pixels in the nonpattern positions.

For each step in the crossfade, the corresponding brush must be selected into the working memory device context. The bitmap brushes are developed from the functions used in the CrossHatch class from How-To 4.7. The functions implemented include the BuildScrns function, which sets up the pattern screens; the BuildBitmap function, which sets up the bitmap header for the pattern bitmap; and the BuildHandles function, which creates the pattern brushes and stores the handles to each. Before the StretchDIBits function is called with the SPDSxax ROP, the appropriate pattern brush must be selected into the working memory device context.

The above manipulation only solves half the problem of performing the crossfade. The other problem is to make sure that the intervening palettes in the crossfade keep an appropriate representation of the two bitmap colors. Also, it is important to ensure that the final palette is that of the fade-to image.

To solve this problem, you need to build incremental palettes for each step of the crossfade. For each of the 245 non–system reserved palette entries in the color table of the original bitmap, the separate RGB values must approach the final RGB values of the fade-to palette. The CreatePalettes function for the class handles building this transition. In this function, each of the original palette entry's separate red, green, and blue color value is incremented eight steps to the corresponding fade-to palette's red, green, and blue. The increment is calculated by dividing the difference between the two corresponding values by eight. Each step is stored in a logical palette structure. Once the 10 logical structures (including the first and last) are developed, a palette is created for each. When the crossfade is in progress, each successive palette is selected into the display device context and the working memory device context. The new palette is also realized into the system palette using the RealizePalette function. As each color begins its transition, so does the overall set of pixels for the bitmap image that references the specific palette colors.

The combination of the pattern-blended set of pixels between the two images and the transitioning palettes provides for an effective crossfade between the two images. Note that you can also use the vertical blind screens to perform the crossfade. In the Form_Paint event, change the class set-up call to a 2 parameter value instead of a 1. That indicates to the class that the vertical blind patterns are to be used.

A benefit of using the StretchDIBits function for the crossfade is that either of the two image dimensions (or neither) can be used for performing the crossfade. But note that if the two images are not the same size, one or both may be severely distorted to fit the crossfade into the display context. Keep this in mind when choosing graphics for performing the operation. Ideally, the two images will have identical dimensions or be very similar.

One final procedure should be performed for implementing crossfades between any two images. It is important that the two bitmaps use the standard Windows identity palette. In the Windows system palette, the first and last 10 entries contain 20 reserved colors. A bitmap has an identity palette if the first and last 10 positions are the same as the system palette. This ensures that all colors referenced in these positions are correctly mapped from one palette to the next. Converting the bitmap's palette entries to an identity palette can easily be done with Microsoft's Video for Windows BitEdit program. To do this, open the bitmap file with the BitEdit program. Next, press F7 to start the PalEdit program and show the bitmap's palette. Next, under the palette menu, select the Make Identity Palette option. Figure 6-6-4 shows the process.

By doing this, you will ensure that the images are smoothly transitioned without any unusual image effects occurring because of unusual entries in the reserved system palette locations.

Comments

By using the pattern brushes to combine the two bitmaps, a wide variety of 8x8 patterns can be used to combine the pixels. The ones used here provide for a fluid transition between the two images, but others are possible, as the vertical blinds option demonstrates.

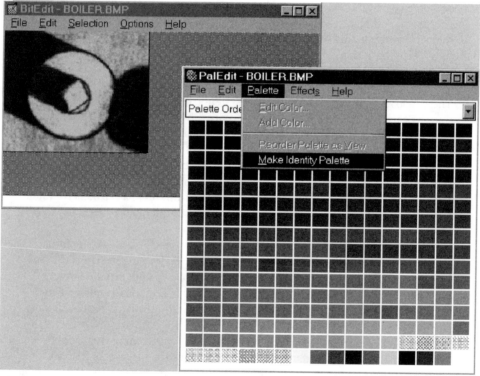

Figure 6-6-4 Converting a bitmap's palette to an identity palette

6.7 How do I...
Display and manipulate graphics with WinG?

COMPLEXITY: INTERMEDIATE

Problem

I know that Microsoft has developed a set of tools, WinG, for developing high-speed graphics in Windows. I also know that the WinG library was developed primarily for C and C++ programmers. How can I use WinG from my Visual Basic 4.0 applications?

Technique

When WinG is installed on your system, a new WinG bitmap device context becomes available. WinG creates a device context that is compatible with the WinG functions, as well as with most of the existing GDI functions. Functions such as BitBlt and PatBlt can be used to copy to and from the WinG device context.

There are two primary advantages to using WinG over a standard memory device context. WinG is actually more of a bitmap than a standard device context. With WinG, you always have direct access to the pixel data of the bitmap. Thus, you can draw directly to and from the device context's bitmap image. In addition, WinG is optimized for bitmap image performance. The routines for moving bit data from WinG devices to the display are very fast and optimized for bitmap use.

In this How-To, a WinG class will be developed for creating a WinG bitmap and filling in the bitmap with data from a bitmap file. Once a WinG bitmap is created from the image file, various types of manipulations can be performed on the image data.

This How-To also introduces a new set of API functions for reading in the bitmap data. These will make it easier to pass the necessary data about the bitmap to the WinG API.

Steps

Open and run 6-7.VBP. The running program appears as shown in Figure 6-7-1.

The initial trees image is shown. Various manipulations on the different bitmaps can be performed, including blowing up the image to twice and five times its size as well as half its size. Figure 6-7-2 shows the fish image at half its size. Figure 6-7-3 shows the fish image at five times its size.

1. Create a new project called 6-7.VBP. Add the objects and properties listed in Table 6-7-1 to Form1 and save the form as 6-7.FRM.

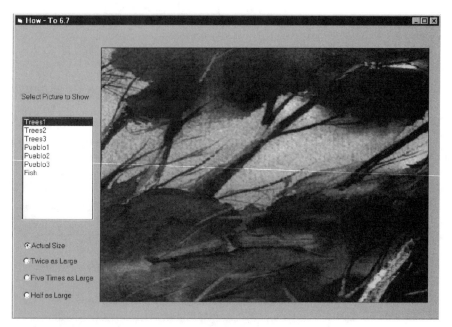

Figure 6-7-1 The form as it appears at runtime

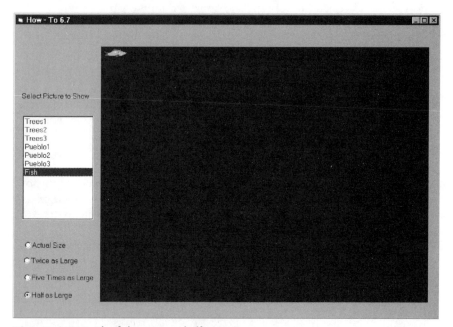

Figure 6-7-2 The fish image at half its size

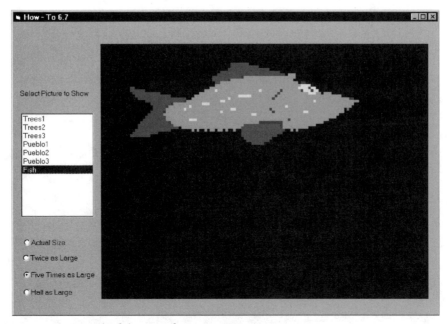

Figure 6-7-3 The fish image five times its size

Table 6-7-1 Project form's objects and properties

OBJECT	PROPERTY	SETTING
Form	Name	Form1
	Auto3D	-1 'True
	Caption	"How-To 6.7"
	KeyPreview	-1 'True
	ScaleMode	3 'Pixel
OptionButton	Name	IncFive
	Caption	"Five Times as Large"
OptionButton	Name	Reduce
	Caption	"Half as Large"
OptionButton	Name	Increase
	Caption	"Twice as Large"

continued on next page

continued from previous page

OBJECT	PROPERTY	SETTING
OptionButton	Name	Actual
	Caption	"Actual Size"
	Value	-1 'True
ListBox	Name	PicList
PictureBox	Name	Picture1
	AutoSize	-1 'True
	ScaleMode	3 'Pixel
PictureBox	Name	Picture2
	AutoSize	-1 'True
	ScaleMode	3 'Pixel
Label	Name	Label1
	AutoSize	-1 'True
	Caption	"Select Picture to Show"

2. Add the following code to the general declarations section of the form. Several WinG functions are declared, as well as GDI functions for displaying the bitmap images. Also, the new WinG class is globally declared.

```
'  PatBlt will be used to fill the background
'  of the picture box with black
Private Declare Function PatBlt Lib "GDI" (ByVal hDC As Integer, ByVal X As _
Integer, ByVal Y As Integer, ByVal nWidth As Integer, ByVal nHeight As _
Integer, ByVal dwRop As Long) As Integer

'  Used to copy different sizes of the bitmap
Private Declare Function WinGStretchBlt Lib "wing.dll" (ByVal hdcDest As _
Integer, ByVal nXOriginDest As Integer, ByVal nYOriginDest As Integer, ByVal _
nWidthDest As Integer, ByVal nHeightDest As Integer, ByVal hdcSrc As Integer, _
ByVal nXOriginSrc As Integer, ByVal nYOriginSrc As Integer, ByVal nWidthSrc _
As Integer, ByVal nHeightSrc As Integer) As Boolean

'  Standard bit copy
Private Declare Function WinGBitBlt Lib "wing.dll" (ByVal hdcDest As Integer, _
ByVal nXOriginDest As Integer, ByVal nYOriginDest As Integer, ByVal _
nWidthDest As Integer, ByVal nHeightDest As Integer, ByVal hdcSrc As _
Integer, ByVal nXOriginSrc As Integer, ByVal nYOriginSrc As Integer) As Boolean

'  Create a new WinG Device Context
Private Declare Function WinGCreateDC Lib "wing.dll" () As Integer
```

```
'   Delete the specified device context
Private Declare Function DeleteDC Lib "GDI" (ByVal hDC As Integer) As Integer

'   Used with PatBlt
Const BLACKNESS = &H42&   ' (DWORD) dest = BLACK

'   Globally declare the WinG Class
Dim WinG As WinG

'   WingDc will store the handle
'   to the device context
Dim WingDc As Integer
```

3. When the Actual size button is selected, the PicList_Click function is called to process the image and display it at its actual size.

```
Private Sub Actual_Click()
'   Trigger the picture list click event
PicList_Click
End Sub
```

4. When the form is loaded, the list box is filled with the image names. The WinG class is created and set up and the first image in the list box is selected.

```
Private Sub Form_Load()
'   Make sure the picture is properly sized
Picture2.Autosize = True
'   Load the list box with the picture names
PicList.AddItem "Trees1"
PicList.AddItem "Trees2"
PicList.AddItem "Trees3"
PicList.AddItem "Pueblo1"
PicList.AddItem "Pueblo2"
PicList.AddItem "Pueblo3"
PicList.AddItem "Fish"

'   Create a new instance of WinG
Set wing = New wing

'   Create a WinG device context
WingDc = WinGCreateDC()

'   Set the class device context
Let wing.wdc = WingDc

'   Set the class picture
Set wing.picture = Picture1

PicList.Selected(0) = True
End Sub
```

5. When the form is painted, the PicList_Click function is called to display the image.

```
Private Sub Form_Paint()

'  Trigger the picture list click event
PicList_Click

End Sub
```

6. When the form is unloaded the WinG device context must be deleted and the WinG class must be terminated. When the class is terminated, the terminate function of the class is called.

```
Private Sub Form_Unload(Cancel As Integer)

'  Delete the device context when we exit
throw = DeleteDC(WingDc)
Set wing = Nothing

End Sub
```

7. Call the PicList_Click function to blow up the image by five times its size.

```
Private Sub IncFive_Click()

'  Trigger the picture list click event
PicList_Click

End Sub
```

8. Call the PicList_Click function to blow up the image by twice its size.

```
Private Sub Increase_Click()

'  Trigger the picture list click event
PicList_Click

End Sub
```

9. When this function is called, the file name of the image selected is set for the WinG class. Then the MakeWinGBit function is called to read in the file and build the WinG bitmap. To copy the bit data from the file to the WinG bitmap, the Transbits function is called. Finally, the SetPal function is called to set up the palette of the WinG device. Once the WinG bitmap is completely set up, it is copied to the display by using the WinGBitBlt and WinGStretchBlt functions. WinGStretchBlt is used to display the image at various sizes. WinGBitBlt is used to copy the image at its original size.

```
Sub PicList_Click()

'  Find out which image was selected
For n = 0 To 6
    If PicList.Selected(n) = True Then Pict = n
Next n
```

```
'   Depending on the image selected, set
'   the filename
Select Case Pict

    Case 0
        Let wing.Filename = App.Path + "\trees1.bmp"

    Case 1
        Let wing.Filename = App.Path + "\trees2.bmp"

    Case 2
        Let wing.Filename = App.Path + "\trees3.bmp"

    Case 3
        Let wing.Filename = App.Path + "\pueblo1.bmp"

    Case 4
        Let wing.Filename = App.Path + "\pueblo2.bmp"

    Case 5
        Let wing.Filename = App.Path + "\pueblo3.bmp"

    Case 6
        Let wing.Filename = App.Path + "\fish.bmp"

End Select

'   Build the Bitmap for the
'   new image
wing.MakeWinGBit

'   Set the bits in the bitmap
wing.transbits

'   Set the screen palette
wing.setpal


'   Depending on the type of transfer
'   to be performed the image in the
'   WinG device context is transferred
'   to the screen
'   Copy in a black background
throw = PatBlt(Picture1.hDC, 0, 0, Picture1.ScaleWidth, ↵
        Picture1.ScaleHeight,BLACKNESS)

'   Actual size
If Actual.Value = -1 Then
    Call WinGBitBlt(Picture1.hDC, 0, 0, Picture2.ScaleWidth, ↵
        Picture2.ScaleHeight, WingDc, 0, 0)
    Exit Sub

End If

'   Twice the size
```

continued on next page

continued from previous page

```
If Increase.Value = -1 Then
    Call WinGStretchBlt(Picture1 * 2.hDC, 0, 0, Picture2.ScaleWidth * 2, ↵
        Picture2.ScaleHeight * 2, WingDc, 0, 0, Picture2.ScaleWidth ↵
        Picture2.ScaleHeight)
    Exit Sub

End If

'  Half the size
If Reduce.Value = -1 Then
    Call WinGStretchBlt(Picture1.hDC, 0, 0, Picture2.ScaleWidth / 2, ↵
        Picture2.ScaleHeight / 2, WingDc, 0, 0, Picture2.ScaleWidth, ↵
        Picture2.ScaleHeight)
    Exit Sub
End If

'  Five times the size
If IncFive.Value = -1 Then

    Call WinGStretchBlt(Picture1.hDC, 0, 0, Picture2.ScaleWidth * 5, ↵
        Picture2.ScaleHeight * 5, WingDc, 0, 0, Picture2.ScaleWidth, ↵
        Picture2.ScaleHeight)

End If

End Sub
```

10. Call the PicList_Click function to shrink the image to half its size.

```
Private Sub Reduce_Click()

'  Trigger the picture list click event
PicList_Click

End Sub
```

11. Insert a new class into the project and save it as WING.CLS. Add the following code to the general declarations section of the form. The WinG functions are declared, along with the necessary API functions and structures to read in the bitmap file. Also, the palette functions and structures for building a logical palette and the global members of the class are declared.

```
'  TransparentDIBits is used to place the bits
'  into the WinG device
Private Declare Function TransparentDIBits Lib "winghelp.dll" (dstInfo As ↵
Any, dstBuffer As Any, ByVal destx As Integer, ByVal desty As Integer, ↵
srcBuffer As Any, srcInfo As Any, ByVal srcx As Integer, ByVal srcy As ↵
Integer, ByVal iUsage As Integer, ByVal TransparentColor As Byte) As Boolean

'  Creates the WinG device context
Private Declare Function WinGCreateDC Lib "wing.dll" () As Integer

'  Recomends an optimal DIB format
Private Declare Function WinGRecommendDIBFormat Lib "wing.dll" (pBitmapInfo ↵
```

```
As Any) As Boolean

'  Creates a WinG bitmap
Private Declare Function WinGCreateBitmap Lib "wing.dll" (ByVal WingDc ↵
As Integer, pBitmapInfo As Any, ppBits As Any) As Integer

'  Gets a pointer to the WinG DIB
Private Declare Function WinGGetDIBPointer Lib "wing.dll" (ByVal WinGBitmap ↵
As Integer, pBitmapInfo As Any) As Long

'  Gets the color table of the WinG bitmap
Private Declare Function WinGGetDIBColorTable Lib "wing.dll" (ByVal WingDc ↵
As Integer, ByVal StartIndex As Integer, ByVal NumberOfEntries As Integer, ↵
pRgbQuadColors As Any) As Integer

'  Sets the WinG color table
Private Declare Function WinGSetDIBColorTable Lib "wing.dll" (ByVal WingDc ↵
As Integer, ByVal StartIndex As Integer, ByVal NumberOfEntries As Integer, ↵
pRgbQuadColors As Any) As Integer

'  Will create a halftone palette for converting
'  24 bit images to 8 bit
Private Declare Function WinGCreateHalftonePalette Lib "wing.dll" () As Integer

'  Creates a halftone brush
Private Declare Function WinGCreateHalftoneBrush Lib "wing.dll" (ByVal ↵
Context As Integer, ByVal crColor As Long, ByVal DitherType As Integer) ↵
As Integer

'  Transfers from a WinG device context to
'  either another device context or a display
'  device context
Private Declare Function WinGBitBlt Lib "wing.dll" (ByVal hdcDest As Integer, ↵
ByVal nXOriginDest As Integer, ByVal nYOriginDest As Integer, ByVal ↵
nWidthDest As Integer, ByVal nHeightDest As Integer, ByVal hdcSrc As ↵
Integer, ByVal nXOriginSrc As Integer, ByVal nYOriginSrc As Integer) As Boolean

'  Transfers from a WinG device context to
'  either another device context or a display
'  device context.  Will stretch the bits to
'  fit the dimensions
Private Declare Function WinGStretchBlt Lib "wing.dll" (ByVal hdcDest As ↵
Integer, ByVal nXOriginDest As Integer, ByVal nYOriginDest As Integer, ByVal ↵
nWidthDest As Integer, ByVal nHeightDest As Integer, ByVal hdcSrc As Integer, ↵
ByVal nXOriginSrc As Integer, ByVal nYOriginSrc As Integer, ByVal nWidthSrc ↵
As Integer, ByVal nHeightSrc As Integer) As Boolean

'  Deletes an object
Private Declare Function DeleteObject Lib "GDI" (ByVal hObject As Integer) ↵
As Integer

'  Creates a palette from a logical palette
Private Declare Function CreatePalette Lib "GDI" (lpLogPalette As LOGPALETTE) ↵
As Integer
```

continued on next page

continued from previous page

```
'   Selects a palette into the specified
'   device context
Private Declare Function SelectPalette Lib "User" (ByVal hDC As Integer, ↵
ByVal hPalette As Integer, ByVal bForceBackground As Integer) As Integer

'   Realizes the specified palette into the
'   screen palette
Private Declare Function RealizePalette Lib "User" (ByVal hDC As Integer) ↵
As Integer

'   Selects an object into a device context
Private Declare Function SelectObject Lib "GDI" (ByVal hDC As Integer, ↵
ByVal hObject As Integer) As Integer

'   Opens a file
Private Declare Function lopen Lib "Kernel" Alias "_lopen" (ByVal lpPathName ↵
As String, ByVal iReadWrite As Integer) As Integer

'   Reads from the file
Private Declare Function lread Lib "Kernel" Alias "_lread" (ByVal hfile ↵
As Integer, lpBuffer As Any, ByVal wBytes As Integer) As Integer

'   Closes the file
Private Declare Function lclose Lib "Kernel" Alias "_lclose" (ByVal hfile ↵
As Integer) As Integer

'   Reads large blocks of data
'   from a file
Private Declare Function hread Lib "Kernel" Alias "_hread" (ByVal hfile ↵
As Integer, buffer As Any, ByVal n As Long) As Long

'   Used to get a pointer to the dib bits
'   Needed for transblt
Private Declare Function lstrcpy Lib "Kernel" (dest As Any, src As Any) As Long

'   Used for lopen
Const OPEN_READ = 0

'   Standard Logical Palette structures
Private Type RGBQUAD
    rgbBlue      As String * 1
    rgbGreen     As String * 1
    rgbRed       As String * 1
    rgbReserved  As String * 1
End Type

Private Type PALETTEENTRY
    peRed        As String * 1
    peGreen      As String * 1
    peBlue       As String * 1
    peFlags      As String * 1
End Type

Private Type LOGPALETTE
    version      As Integer
```

```
        nEntries              As Integer
        palpalentry(256)      As PALETTEENTRY
End Type


'   Standard palette constants
Const PC_RESERVED = &H1        '   palette index used for animation
Const PC_NOCOLLAPSE = &H4      '   do not match color to system palette
Const DIB_RGB_COLORS = 0       '   color table in RGBTriples


'   Standard bitmap headers
Private Type BITMAPFILEHEADER
    bfType        As Integer
    bfSize        As Long
    bfReserved1   As Integer
    bfReserved2   As Integer
    bfOffBits     As Long
End Type

Private Type BITMAPINFOHEADER
    biSize          As Long
    biWidth         As Long
    biHeight        As Long
    biPlanes        As Integer
    biBitCount      As Integer
    biCompression   As Long
    biSizeImage     As Long
    biXPelsPerMeter As Long
    biYPelsPerMeter As Long
    biClrUsed       As Long
    biClrImportant  As Long
End Type


Private Type BITMAPINFO
    bmiHeader       As BITMAPINFOHEADER
    bmiColors(256)  As RGBQUAD
End Type


'   hbitmap is the handle to the WinG bitmap
Private hbitmap As Integer

'   m_pict is the display picture
Private m_pict As Object

'   The handle to the WinG device context
Private m_WinGDc As Integer

'   The WinG bitmap header
Private WGBminfo As BITMAPINFO

'   The bitmap file header
Private bminfo As BITMAPINFO

'   The handle to the surface to copy
```

continued on next page

continued from previous page

```
'   the bitmap data to
Private psurface As Long

'   The handle to the palette of the
'   bitmap
Private Pal As Integer

' The handle to the dib bit data
Private bitdata() As Byte

'   The file name to read
Private m_filename As String

'   The surface of this WinG bitmap
Private m_psurface As Long
```

12. The ReadBitmap function uses several API tools to read in the bitmap data from the image file. Also, the bit data of the image is read into memory for later use.

```
Private Sub ReadBitmap()

'   Declare the logical palette
Dim LogicalPal     As LOGPALETTE

'   Declare the bitmap file header
Dim FileHeader      As BITMAPFILEHEADER

'   Open the file
FileP = lopen(m_filename, OPEN_READ)

'   Read the file header
throw = lread(FileP, FileHeader, Len(FileHeader)) = Len(FileHeader)

'   Read the bitmap header
throw = lread(FileP, bminfo.bmiHeader.biSize, Len(bminfo.bmiHeader))

'   Read the color table
throw = lread(FileP, bminfo.bmiColors(0), Len(bminfo.bmiColors(0)) * 256)

'   Build the logical palette
For n = 0 To 255
    LogicalPal.palpalentry(n).peRed = bminfo.bmiColors(n).rgbRed
    LogicalPal.palpalentry(n).peGreen = bminfo.bmiColors(n).rgbGreen
    LogicalPal.palpalentry(n).peBlue = bminfo.bmiColors(n).rgbBlue

    If (n > 9) And (n < 246) Then
            LogicalPal.palpalentry(n).peFlags = Chr$(PC_RESERVED)
        Else
            LogicalPal.palpalentry(n).peFlags = Chr$(0)
    End If
Next n

'   Set up the logical palette
LogicalPal.version = &H300
LogicalPal.nEntries = 256
```

```
'  Create the logical palette
Pal = CreatePalette(LogicalPal)

'  Set the bitdata array to
'  store the bitmap data
ReDim bitdata(bminfo.bmiHeader.biSizeImage)

'  Read in the bit data
throw = hread(FileP, bitdata(0), bminfo.bmiHeader.biSizeImage)

'  Close the file
Call lclose(FileP)

End Sub
```

13. The MakeWinGBit function creates a WinG bitmap in the specified WinG device context. The bitmap is set up to have the standard 8-bit (256-color) header. The WinGCreateBitmap function is used to create the bitmap, and it is selected into the WinG device context. The color table is selected into the device context using the WinGSetDIBColorTable function.

```
Public Sub MakeWinGBit()

'  Read the bitmap
ReadBitmap

'  Setup the WinG bitmap header
WGBminfo.bmiHeader.biSize = 40
WGBminfo.bmiHeader.biWidth = m_pict.ScaleWidth
WGBminfo.bmiHeader.biHeight = m_pict.ScaleHeight
WGBminfo.bmiHeader.biPlanes = 1
WGBminfo.bmiHeader.biBitCount = 8
WGBminfo.bmiHeader.biCompression = 0
WGBminfo.bmiHeader.biSizeImage = 0
WGBminfo.bmiHeader.biXPelsPerMeter = 0
WGBminfo.bmiHeader.biYPelsPerMeter = 0
WGBminfo.bmiHeader.biClrUsed = 256
WGBminfo.bmiHeader.biClrImportant = 0

'  Create the WinG bitmap
hbitmap = WinGCreateBitmap(m_WinGDc, WGBminfo, psurface)

'  Select the bitmap into the WinG device
'  context
throw = SelectObject(m_WinGDc, hbitmap)

'  Set the WinG color table to that
'  of the bitmap
Call WinGSetDIBColorTable(m_WinGDc, 0, 256, bminfo.bmiColors(0))

End Sub
```

14. The SetPal function selects the bitmap's palette into the display device context. This ensures that the system palette can accurately represent the bitmap images.

```
Public Sub SetPal()

'  Select the palette into the
'  display device
holdPal = SelectPalette(m_pict.hDC, Pal, False)

'  Delete the old palette
throw = DeleteObject(holdPal)

'  Realize the palette into
'  the display context
Call RealizePalette(m_pict.hDC)

End Sub
```

15. The Transbits function copies the pixel data from memory to the WinG surface. The function requires pointers to the location of the information for the pixel data and bitmap header. This can be done by performing a simple string copy of the bitdata(0) and bminfo variables. The value returned from the Lstrcpy function is the necessary pointer needed by the TransparentDIBits function for both sets of data.

```
Public Sub Transbits()

'  Get pointers to the specified
'  objects
BytesAsLong& = lstrcpy(bitdata(0), bitdata(0))
InfoAsLong& = lstrcpy(bminfo, bminfo)

'  Copy the bit data onto the
'  this WinG bitmap's surface
Call TransparentDIBits(WGBminfo, ByVal psurface, 0, 0, ByVal BytesAsLong&, ↵
ByVal InfoAsLong&, 0, 0, 0, 1)

End Sub
```

16. The Transbits2 function handles copying the pixel data for this WinG bitmap onto another WinG bitmap set by the m_psurface property. Because TransparentDIBits makes a transparent copy, the black background around the image is not visible.

```
Public Sub Transbits2(X, Y)

'  Get pointers to the specified
'  objects
BytesAsLong& = lstrcpy(bitdata(0), bitdata(0))
InfoAsLong& = lstrcpy(bminfo, bminfo)

'  Copy the bit data onto the
'  specified WinG bitmap surface
Call TransparentDIBits(WGBminfo, ByVal m_psurface, X, Y, ByVal ↵
```

```
BytesAsLong&, ByVal InfoAsLong&, 0, 0, 0, 0)

End Sub
```

17. The following sets the properties for the class. These include the picture that displays the bitmap, the WinG device context to be used, the file name to be read in, and another WinG bitmap surface to copy the bitmap data onto. Also, the surface of this WinG bitmap can be retrieved.

```
'  Set the display picture
Public Property Set picture(acontrol As Control)
        Set m_pict = acontrol
End Property

'  Set the WinG device context
Public Property Let wdc(n As Integer)
        Let m_WinGDc = n
End Property

'  Set the filename
Public Property Let filename(s As String)
        Let m_filename = s
End Property

'  Set the surface to copy
'  bits onto in Transbits2
Public Property Let surface(n As Long)
    m_psurface = n
End Property

'  Return the surface to this
'  bitmap
Public Property Get surface() As Long
    surface = psurface
End Property
```

18. When the class is terminated, it is important to delete the created WinG bitmap.

```
'  When the class is terminated,
'  then the WinG bitmap is deleted
Private Sub Class_Terminate()

    throw = DeleteObject(hbitmap)

End Sub
```

How It Works

Several new API calls are introduced in this How-To both to create the WinG bitmap and to read in the bitmap data from the file. Table 6-7-2 overviews all the WinG functions. Although not all of these are used in the class, they are declared for your future reference and use.

Table 6-7-2 WinG functions

WinG FUNCTION	DESCRIPTION
WinGCreateDC	Creates a new WinG device context
WinGRecommendDIBFormat	Recommends an optimal DIB format for the WinG bitmap
WinGCreateBitmap	Creates a WinG bitmap from a BITMAPINFO structure
WinGGetDIBPointer	Gets a pointer to the WinG DIB surface (bits)
WinGGetDIBColor	Gets the colortable of the WinG bitmap
WinGSetDIBColorTable	Sets the WinG color table from the bmicolors field of the BITMAPINFO structure
WinGCreateHalftonePalette	Creates a halftone palette for converting true color images
WinGCreateHalftoneBrush	Creates a half-tone brush
WinGBitBlt	Transfers from a WinG device context to either another device context or a display device context
WinGStretchBlt	Transfers from a WinG device context either another device context or to a display device context; it will stretch the bits to fit the specified dimensions
TransparentDIBits	Places the bits into the WinG device; this is not an actual WinG function, but is provided for easy creation of the WinG bitmap and for Transparent image building

To read in the bitmap file information, a new set of functions is used instead of the standard Visual Basic 4.0 file I/O functions. Table 6-7-3 overviews each. Note that the actual API functions begin with the underscore (_) character. An alias name is used when the functions are declared to make the functions easier to read and use in the code.

Table 6-7-3 API file reading functions

WinG FUNCTION	DESCRIPTION
lopen	Opens a file
lread	Reads from the file
lclose	Closes the file
hread	Reads large blocks of data from a file
lstrcpy	Gets a pointer to the DIB bits needed for TransparentDIBits

The process for opening and reading in the data is the same as before. The BITMAPFILEHEADER and BITMAPINFO structures are filled in with the appropriate data. Then the pixel data is read into memory using the Hread function, which is used specifically to read in large blocks of data.

To make a WinG bitmap, several steps must take place. First, a WinG device must be created using the WinGCreateDC function. Once a device is created, a bitmap can be selected into the device. The bitmap must be created by the WinGCreateBitmap function. A standard 8-bit BITMAPINFOHEADER bitmap is set up to create the WinG bitmap. The bitmap is selected into the WinG device using SelectObject.

Once the bitmap is created, it must have a color table for the pixel data. This is easily set by using the WinGSetDIBColorTable function. The bmicolors member of the BITMAPINFOHEADER structure is used to set the color table for the WinG bitmap. Once the color table is set up, the final step is to copy the bitmap pixel bits into the WinG bitmap surface. When the WinGCreateBitmap function is called, it returns a variable that points to where the pixel data should be copied.

The TransparentDIBits function copies pixel data stored in memory to the surface of the WinG bitmap. The TransparentDIBits function is provided as a high-speed tool for copying bitmap data from memory to a WinG bitmap surface and for performing transparent copies of one image onto another. Table 6-7-4 overviews the parameters of the function.

Table 6-7-4 TransparentDIBits parameters

PARAMETER	DESCRIPTION
dstInfo as any	WinG bitmap structure
dstBuffer as any	The surface of the WinG bitmap to copy the bitmap bits into;
	this variable is set by the WinGCreateBitmap function
ByVal destx as integer	X orgin to begin the copy

continued on next page

continued from previous page

PARAMETER	DESCRIPTION
ByVal desty as integer	Y origin to begin the copy
srcBuffer as any	Pointer to the memory block where the pixel data is stored
srcInfo as any	Pointer to the memory location of the bitmap header of the file
ByVal srcx as integer	X origin to begin the copy from
ByVal srcy as integer	Y origin to begin the copy from
ByVal iUsage as integer	Usage of the function, usually set to 0
ByVal TransparentColor as byte	Indicates the transparent color

To pass the correct reference for the srcBuffer and the srcInfo parameters, the API lstrcpy function must be used. The function copies one string into another and returns a pointer to the address of the new string. By simply copying the two variables back onto themselves, a pointer is retrieved to their location in memory. This pointer can then be used for the srcBuffer and srcInfo parameters. Once this function is called, the image data is copied onto the WinG bitmap surface.

From this point, WinGBitBlt and WinGStretchBlt functions can be used to copy the data from the WinG bitmap onto the display device context. These functions work in a manner similar to that of the standard BitBlt and StretchBlt functions of the Windows GDI API. But the device to be copied from must be a WinG device. The device to copy to can be a memory device context, a display device context, or another WinG device.

As the project demonstrates, the WinG interface provides a powerful set of optimized utilities for bitmap manipulation. Many of the functions are very similar to the Windows GDI, and in fact share similar naming. Through a few simple manipulations to get around Visual Basic 4.0 limitations, the bitmap file's pixel data and bitmap header can be used by the TransparentDIBits function to copy image data onto a WinG bitmap.

Comments

The next several How-Tos will expand on using the WinG class developed here. With these basic utilities, you can perform many different types of image manipulation. For example, most of the GDI drawing functions can be used to manipulate the image data in a WinG bitmap directly. Once these manipulations have taken place, WinGBitBlt and WinGStretchBlt can be used to copy the new image to the screen rapidly.

6.8 How do I...
Perform flip book animations with WinG?

COMPLEXITY: INTERMEDIATE

Problem

I would like to be able to perform faster flip book animations than can be accomplished using Visual Basic 4.0 or the standard GDI. How can I do this using WinG?

Technique

In How-To 5.3, a simple picture box flip book was created by loading a series of bitmaps into an image control array. In this How-To, a series of WinG bitmaps will be created from bitmap images representing a chest opening and closing. Also, a WinG bitmap will be created for the background of the scene. The TransparentDIBits function will be used to copy the chest images transparently onto the background. This How-To will use the WinG class developed in the last How-To to create and use the WinG bitmaps.

Steps

Open and run 6-8.VBP. The running program appears as shown in Figure 6-8-1. The box top is opening and closing in the animation. Figure 6-8-2 shows the box top completely opened.

Figure 6-8-1 The form as it appears at runtime

Figure 6-8-2 The animation with box top open

1. Create a new project called 6-8.VBP. Add the objects and properties listed in Table 6-8-1 to Form1 and save the form as 6-8.FRM.

Table 6-8-1 Project form's objects and properties

OBJECT	PROPERTY	SETTING
Form	Name	Form1
	Auto3D	-1 'True
	Caption	"How-To 6.8"
	ScaleMode	3 'Pixel
PictureBox	Name	Picture2
	AutoSize	-1 'True
	BorderStyle	0 'None
	ScaleMode	3 'Pixel
Timer	Name	Timer1
	Interval	50

OBJECT	PROPERTY	SETTING
PictureBox	Name	Picture1
	BorderStyle	0 'None
	ScaleMode	3 'Pixel

2. Add the following code to the general declarations section of the form. The necessary WinG and Windows API functions are declared for displaying the WinG bitmaps and performing the animation. Also, the WinG class is globally declared.

```
' WinG functions
Private Declare Function WinGCreateDC Lib "wing.dll" () As Integer

Private Declare Function WinGBitBlt Lib "wing.dll" (ByVal hdcDest As Integer, ↵
ByVal nXOriginDest As Integer, ByVal nYOriginDest As Integer, ByVal ↵
nWidthDest As Integer, ByVal nHeightDest As Integer, ByVal hdcSrc As ↵
Integer, ByVal nXOriginSrc As Integer, ByVal nYOriginSrc As Integer) As Boolean

' Deletes specified Device Context
Private Declare Function DeleteDC Lib "GDI" (ByVal hDC As Integer) As Integer

' PatBlt for copying blackness bits
' to the WinG device
Private Declare Function PatBlt Lib "GDI" (ByVal hDC As Integer, ByVal x ↵
As Integer, ByVal y As Integer, ByVal nWidth As Integer, ByVal nHeight As ↵
Integer, ByVal dwRop As Long) As Integer

Const BLACKNESS = &H42&   ' (DWORD) dest = BLACK

' Globally declare the WinG backgound
' and chest
Dim Back As WinG
Dim Back2 As WinG
Dim Chest(9) As WinG

' The Handles to the WinG
' device contexts
Dim wingDC1 As Integer
Dim wingDC2 As Integer
Dim wingDC3 As Integer

' N will be used to count through the boxes
Dim N As Integer

' Flag will be used in form_paint
Dim flag As Integer
```

3. When the form is loaded, three WinG device contexts are created. One is for the series of WinG bitmaps that will hold the chest animation; one is for the working device context; and one is for the copy of the background for the scene. The bitmaps for the background of the scene and the overall scene are set up. The

WinG bitmaps for the individual chest cells are also set up. Note that only one device context is needed for the chest bitmaps because the actual contents of the device will not be displayed. The contents of the chest WinG bitmaps are copied onto the scene background in the first device context. When the chest class instances are set up, the surface of the primary scene background is passed into the class. This is the primary working surface for the displayed scene.

```
Private Sub Form_Load()

'   Create the WinG device Contexts
wingDC1 = WinGCreateDC()
wingDC2 = WinGCreateDC()
wingDC3 = WinGCreateDC()

'   Set N to 1
N = 1

'   Create the Background
Set Back = New WinG

'   Create second background
Set Back2 = New WinG

'   Set the filename for the background
Let Back.filename = App.Path + "\sea.bmp"
Let Back2.filename = App.Path + "\sea.bmp"

'   Set the device context for the background
Let Back.wdc = wingDC1
Let Back2.wdc = wingDC3

'   Set the display picture for the background
Set Back.picture = Picture1
Set Back2.picture = Picture1

'   Make the background WinG bitmap
Back.MakeWinGBit
Back2.MakeWinGBit

'   Set the palette for the background
'   display
Back.setpal

'   Setup the WinG bitmaps
'   for the chest animation
For a = 1 To 9
    '   Create the new Chest
    Set Chest(a) = New WinG

    '   Get the String representation
    '   of A
    num$ = Str$(a)
    num$ = Right$(num$, Len(num$) - 1)
```

```
'  Set the filename
Let Chest(a).filename = App.Path + "\c00" + num$ + ".bmp"

'  Set the device context
Let Chest(a).wdc = wingDC2

'  Set the display picture
Set Chest(a).picture = Picture1

'  Make the new bitmap
Chest(a).MakeWinGBit

'  Get the background surface
psurface = Back.surface

'  Set the surface to copy to
Chest(a).surface = psurface

Next a

End Sub
```

4. When the form is painted, the background bits for the scene are copied to the WinG bitmaps by calling the Transbits function of each class. After that, the background is copied to the display context by using WinGBitBlt.

```
Private Sub Form_Paint()

'  Only perform once
If flag = 0 Then

    '  setup the initial background
    Back.Transbits
    Back2.Transbits

    '  Copy the full background to the display
    Call WinGBitBlt(Picture1.hDC, 0, 0, Picture1.ScaleWidth, ↵
            Picture1.ScaleHeight, wingDC3, 0, 0)

    flag = 1
End If

End Sub
```

5. When the form is unloaded, it is important to delete the WinG devices created when the form was loaded. It is also important to terminate the various WinG classes by setting them to nothing. This will call the Terminate method of the class, which deletes all objects created by the class.

```
Private Sub Form_Unload(Cancel As Integer)

'  Delete the WinG device contexts
throw = DeleteDC(wingDC1)
throw = DeleteDC(wingDC2)
```

continued on next page

CHAPTER 6

continued from previous page

```
throw = DeleteDC(wingDC3)

'  Terminate the Chest instances
For a = 1 To 9
    Set Chest(a) = Nothing
Next a

'  Terminate the background
Set Back = Nothing
Set Back2 = Nothing

End Sub
```

6. The Timer function handles the actual animation of the chest. With each tick of the timer, the background is restored by copying from the back-up copy of the background to the working device context. The next image in the chest animation is copied onto the working device context by using the Transbit2 method of the WinG bitmap class. This transparently copies the chest bits onto the newly restored background. After that, the newly updated area is copied onto the display. Note that only the section of the background where the chest is being animated is updated and copied to the display. The entire background could be updated and copied, but the implemented method increases the speed of the operation by requiring fewer bits to be updated and copied.

```
Private Sub Timer1_Timer()

'  Check to see if the last
'  chest has been reached
If N = 10 Then N = 1

'  Restore the background in WingDC1 from
'  backup background in WingDC3
Call WinGBitBlt(wingDC1, 65, 280, Picture2.ScaleWidth, Picture2.ScaleHeight, ↵
wingDC3, 65, 280)

'  Copy the chest onto the background
'  surface
Chest(N).transbits2 65, 280

'  Copy the square of the chest
'  to the screen
Call WinGBitBlt(Picture1.hDC, 65, 280, Picture2.ScaleWidth, ↵
Picture2.ScaleHeight, wingDC1, 65, 280)

'  Increment N
N = N + 1

End Sub
```

7. The following is the class code from the last How-To. For a detailed discussion of each function in the class, see that How-To. Various comments regarding the code and the animation of the chest are made for the necessary functions.

444

```
'   TransparentDIBits is used to place the bits
'   into the WinG device
Private Declare Function TransparentDIBits Lib "winghelp.dll" (dstInfo As ⏎
Any, dstBuffer As Any, ByVal destx As Integer, ByVal desty As Integer, ⏎
srcBuffer As Any, srcInfo As Any, ByVal srcx As Integer, ByVal srcy As ⏎
Integer, ByVal iUsage As Integer, ByVal TransparentColor As Byte) As Boolean

Private Declare Sub CopyDIBits Lib "winghelp.dll" (pBuffer As Any, ByVal ⏎
destOffset As Long, pSource As Any, ByVal sourceOffset As Long, ByVal ⏎
dstWidth As Integer, ByVal dstHeight As Integer, ByVal dstScanWidth As ⏎
Long, ByVal srcScanWidth As Long)


'   Creates the WinG device context
Private Declare Function WinGCreateDC Lib "wing.dll" () As Integer


'   Reccomends an optimal DIB format
Private Declare Function WinGRecommendDIBFormat Lib "wing.dll" (pBitmapInfo ⏎
As Any) As Boolean


'   Creates a WinG bitmap
Private Declare Function WinGCreateBitmap Lib "wing.dll" (ByVal wingDC As ⏎
Integer, pBitmapInfo As Any, ppBits As Any) As Integer


'   Gets a pointer to the WinG DIB
Private Declare Function WinGGetDIBPointer Lib "wing.dll" (ByVal WinGBitmap ⏎
As Integer, pBitmapInfo As Any) As Long


'   Gets the color table of the WinG bitmap
Private Declare Function WinGGetDIBColorTable Lib "wing.dll" (ByVal wingDC ⏎
As Integer, ByVal StartIndex As Integer, ByVal NumberOfEntries As Integer, ⏎
pRgbQuadColors As Any) As Integer


'   Sets the WinG color table
Private Declare Function WinGSetDIBColorTable Lib "wing.dll" (ByVal wingDC ⏎
As Integer, ByVal StartIndex As Integer, ByVal NumberOfEntries As Integer, ⏎
pRgbQuadColors As Any) As Integer


'   Will create a halftone palette for converting
'   24 bit images to 8 bit
Private Declare Function WinGCreateHalftonePalette Lib "wing.dll" () As Integer


'   Creates a halftone brush
Private Declare Function WinGCreateHalftoneBrush Lib "wing.dll" (ByVal ⏎
Context As Integer, ByVal crColor As Long, ByVal DitherType As Integer) ⏎
As Integer


'   Transfers from a WinG device context to
'   either another device context or a display
'   device context
Private Declare Function WinGBitBlt Lib "wing.dll" (ByVal hdcDest As Integer, ⏎
ByVal nXOriginDest As Integer, ByVal nYOriginDest As Integer, ByVal ⏎
nWidthDest As Integer, ByVal nHeightDest As Integer, ByVal hdcSrc As Integer, ⏎
ByVal nXOriginSrc As Integer, ByVal nYOriginSrc As Integer) As Boolean
```

continued on next page

CHAPTER 6

continued from previous page

```
'  Transfers from a WinG device context to
'  either another device context or a display
'  device context.  Will stretch the bits to
'  fit the dimensions
Private Declare Function WinGStretchBlt Lib "wing.dll" (ByVal hdcDest As ⏎
Integer, ByVal nXOriginDest As Integer, ByVal nYOriginDest As Integer, ByVal ⏎
nWidthDest As Integer, ByVal nHeightDest As Integer, ByVal hdcSrc As Integer,⏎
ByVal nXOriginSrc As Integer, ByVal nYOriginSrc As Integer, ByVal nWidthSrc ⏎
As Integer, ByVal nHeightSrc As Integer) As Boolean

'  Deletes an object
Private Declare Function DeleteObject Lib "GDI" (ByVal hObject As Integer) ⏎
As Integer

'  Creates a palette from a logical palette
Private Declare Function CreatePalette Lib "GDI" (lpLogPalette As LOGPALETTE) ⏎
As Integer

'  Selects a palette into the specified
'  device context
Private Declare Function SelectPalette Lib "User" (ByVal hDC As Integer, ⏎
ByVal hPalette As Integer, ByVal bForceBackground As Integer) As Integer

'  Realizes the specified palette into the
'  screen palette
Private Declare Function RealizePalette Lib "User" (ByVal hDC As Integer) ⏎
As Integer

'  Selects an object into a device context
Private Declare Function SelectObject Lib "GDI" (ByVal hDC As Integer, ⏎
ByVal hObject As Integer) As Integer

'  Opens a file
Private Declare Function lopen Lib "Kernel" Alias "_lopen" (ByVal lpPathName ⏎
As String, ByVal iReadWrite As Integer) As Integer

'  Reads from the file
Private Declare Function lread Lib "Kernel" Alias "_lread" (ByVal hfile As ⏎
Integer, lpBuffer As Any, ByVal wBytes As Integer) As Integer

'  Closes the file
Private Declare Function lclose Lib "Kernel" Alias "_lclose" (ByVal hfile As ⏎
Integer)          As Integer

'  Reads large blocks of data
'  from a file
Private Declare Function hread Lib "Kernel" Alias "_hread" (ByVal hfile As ⏎
Integer, buffer As Any, ByVal N As Long) As Long

'  Used to get a pointer to the dib bits
'  Needed for transblt
Private Declare Function lstrcpy Lib "Kernel" (dest As Any, src As Any) As Long

'  Used for lopen
Const OPEN_READ = 0
```

```
'  Standard Logical Palette structures
Private Type RGBQUAD
    rgbBlue      As String * 1
    rgbGreen     As String * 1
    rgbRed       As String * 1
    rgbReserved  As String * 1
End Type

Private Type PALETTEENTRY
    peRed        As String * 1
    peGreen      As String * 1
    peBlue       As String * 1
    peFlags      As String * 1
End Type

Private Type LOGPALETTE
    version           As Integer
    nEntries          As Integer
    palpalentry(256)  As PALETTEENTRY
End Type

'  Standard palette constants
Const PC_RESERVED = &H1     '  palette index used for animation
Const PC_NOCOLLAPSE = &H4   '  do not match color to system palette
Const DIB_RGB_COLORS = 0    '  color table in RGBTriples


'  Standard bitmap headers
Private Type BITMAPFILEHEADER
    bfType       As Integer
    bfSize       As Long
    bfReserved1  As Integer
    bfReserved2  As Integer
    bfOffBits    As Long
End Type

Private Type BITMAPINFOHEADER
    biSize           As Long
    biWidth          As Long
    biHeight         As Long
    biPlanes         As Integer
    biBitCount       As Integer
    biCompression    As Long
    biSizeImage      As Long
    biXPelsPerMeter  As Long
    biYPelsPerMeter  As Long
    biClrUsed        As Long
    biClrImportant   As Long
End Type

Private Type BITMAPINFO
    bmiHeader        As BITMAPINFOHEADER
    bmiColors(256) As RGBQUAD
End Type
```

continued on next page

continued from previous page

```
'  hbitmap is the handle to the WinG bitmap
Private hbitmap As Integer

'  m_pict is the display picture
Private m_pict As Object

'  The handle to the WinG device context
Private m_WinGDc As Integer

'  The WinG bitmap header
Private WGBminfo As BITMAPINFO

'  The bitmap file header
Private bminfo As BITMAPINFO

'  The handle to the surface to copy
'  the bitmap data to
Private psurface As Long

'  The handle to the palette of the
'  bitmap
Private Pal As Integer

' The handle to the dib bit data
Private bitdata() As Byte

'  The filenname to read
Private m_filename As String

'  The surface of this WinG bitmap
Private m_psurface As Long


Private Sub ReadBitmap()

'  Declare the logical palette
Dim LogicalPal     As LOGPALETTE

'  Declare the bitmap file header
Dim FileHeader     As BITMAPFILEHEADER

'  Open the file
FileP = lopen(m_filename, OPEN_READ)

'  Read the file header
throw = lread(FileP, FileHeader, Len(FileHeader)) = Len(FileHeader)

'  Read the bitmap header
throw = lread(FileP, bminfo.bmiHeader.biSize, Len(bminfo.bmiHeader))

'  Read the color table
throw = lread(FileP, bminfo.bmiColors(0), Len(bminfo.bmiColors(0)) * 256)

'  Build the logical palette
```

```
For N = 0 To 255
    LogicalPal.palpalentry(N).peRed = bminfo.bmiColors(N).rgbRed
    LogicalPal.palpalentry(N).peGreen = bminfo.bmiColors(N).rgbGreen
    LogicalPal.palpalentry(N).peBlue = bminfo.bmiColors(N).rgbBlue
    If (N > 9) And (N < 246) Then
            LogicalPal.palpalentry(N).peFlags = Chr$(PC_RESERVED)
        Else
            LogicalPal.palpalentry(N).peFlags = Chr$(0)
    End If
Next N

'  Set up the logical palette
LogicalPal.version = &H300
LogicalPal.nEntries = 256

'  Create the logical palette
Pal = CreatePalette(LogicalPal)

'  Set the bitdata array to
'  store the bitmap data
ReDim bitdata(bminfo.bmiHeader.biSizeImage)

'  Read in the bit data
throw = hread(FileP, bitdata(0), bminfo.bmiHeader.biSizeImage)

'  Close the file
Call lclose(FileP)

End Sub
```

8. Note that the m_WinGDc variable is the same for all the chest WinG bitmaps. When the chest image is copied onto the background, the TransparentDIBits function does not need to reference the specified device context, only the bit and header data. So a WinG device context is necessary only for using the WinGCreateBitmap function and for setting the color table.

```
Public Sub MakeWinGBit()

'  Read the bitmap
ReadBitmap

'  Setup the WinG bitmap header
WGBminfo.bmiHeader.biSize = 40
WGBminfo.bmiHeader.biWidth = m_pict.ScaleWidth
WGBminfo.bmiHeader.biHeight = m_pict.ScaleHeight
WGBminfo.bmiHeader.biPlanes = 1
WGBminfo.bmiHeader.biBitCount = 8
WGBminfo.bmiHeader.biCompression = 0
WGBminfo.bmiHeader.biSizeImage = 0
WGBminfo.bmiHeader.biXPelsPerMeter = 0
WGBminfo.bmiHeader.biYPelsPerMeter = 0
WGBminfo.bmiHeader.biClrUsed = 256
WGBminfo.bmiHeader.biClrImportant = 0
```

continued on next page

continued from previous page

```
'   Create the WinG bitmap
hbitmap = WinGCreateBitmap(m_WinGDc, WGBminfo, psurface)

'   Select the bitmap into the WinG device
'   context
throw = SelectObject(m_WinGDc, hbitmap)

'   Set the WinG color table to that
'   of the bitmap
Call WinGSetDIBColorTable(m_WinGDc, 0, 256, bminfo.bmiColors(0))

End Sub

Public Sub setpal()

'   Select the palette into the
'   display device
holdPal = SelectPalette(m_pict.hDC, Pal, False)

'   Delete the old palette
throw = DeleteObject(holdPal)

'   Realize the palette into
'   the display context
Call RealizePalette(m_pict.hDC)

End Sub
```

9. Transbits is used to copy the bit data for the file specified in the class into the WinG bitmap created in the class.

```
Public Sub Transbits()

'   Get pointers to the specified
'   objects
BytesAsLong& = lstrcpy(bitdata(0), bitdata(0))
InfoAsLong& = lstrcpy(bminfo, bminfo)

'   Copy the bit data onto
'   this WinG bitmaps surface
Call TransparentDIBits(WGBminfo, ByVal psurface, x, y, ByVal BytesAsLong&, ↵
ByVal InfoAsLong&, 0, 0, 0, 1)

End Sub
```

10. Transbits2 is used to copy this WinG bitmaps data onto the surface of another WinG bitmap. The x and y variables indicate where to copy the image data. Note that the m_psurface parameter of the TransparentDIBits call is set as one of the properties of the class.

```
Public Sub Transbits2(x, y)

'   Get pointers to the specified
'   objects
```

```
BytesAsLong& = lstrcpy(bitdata(0), bitdata(0))
InfoAsLong& = lstrcpy(bminfo, bminfo)

'  Copy the bit data onto the
'  specified WinG bitmap surface
Call TransparentDIBits(WGBminfo, ByVal m_psurface, x, y, ByVal BytesAsLong&, ↵
ByVal InfoAsLong&, x, y, 0, 0)

End Sub

'  Set the display picture
Public Property Set picture(acontrol As Control)
  Set m_pict = acontrol
End Property

'  Set the WinG device context
Public Property Let wdc(N As Integer)
  Let m_WinGDc = N
End Property

'  Set the filename
Public Property Let filename(s As String)
  Let m_filename = s
End Property
```

11. This property is set to indicate what surface these WinG bitmaps bits should be transferred to when the Transbits2 function is called.

```
'  Set the surface to copy
'  bits onto in Transbits2
Public Property Let surface(N As Long)
    m_psurface = N
End Property
```

12. If another WinG class needs to draw on this WinG bitmaps surface, the pointer to the surface is returned by calling this property.

```
'  Return the surface to this
'  bitmap
Public Property Get surface() As Long
    surface = psurface
End Property

'  When the class is terminated,
'  the WinG bitmap is deleted
Private Sub Class_Terminate()
    throw = DeleteObject(hbitmap)
End Sub
```

How It Works

After reading through the discussion of the code for this project, you may have realized that there seems to be one crucial topic not dealt with in manipulating the bitmaps for the animation, namely palettes. You would assume that each of the 256 images used in the scene would have its own palette, and that these differences would need to be reconciled. The assumption would be partly correct. The differences do have to be reconciled, but the images themselves have already been updated to have the same palettes for each image.

The directory where the project is located contains a file called PAL.PAL. This is a Windows palette file created to optimize the palettes for the background and chest images. This file was created by using the Microsoft Video for Windows BitEdit and PalEdit tools. The background was loaded into the BitEdit program. From the BitEdit program, the PalEdit program was loaded and the palette of the image was saved to a file. Figure 6-8-3 depicts the setup.

Once the palette for the background image is saved, the palette can be imported into the series of chest bitmaps. The Apply From File option can be used to import the background palette file into the chest bitmaps. The program will match the original palette colors as close as possible to the new palette colors.

If you find that drastic changes have taken place in the image from the new palette, you might consider using the VidEdit program to build an optimal palette for all of your WinG images. Each individual image can be imported into the VidEdit program and an optimal palette for all frames can be made. When VidEdit does this, the palette is pasted to the clipboard. You can then use PalEdit to copy the palette

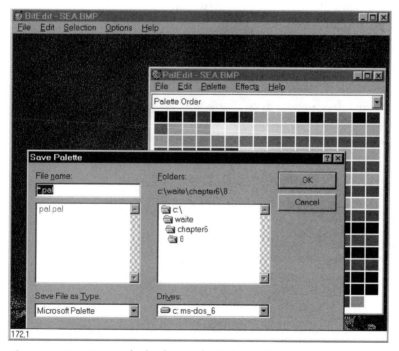

Figure 6-8-3 Saving the background palette to a file

from the clipboard and save it to a file. That palette can then be imported into each bitmap image. This should produce a set of images that has an optimized palette for each.

Once the palette hurdles have been overcome, the WinG class provides an effective method of building animated graphic scenes. Conceptually, the full scene is built frame by frame in a WinG device context. The primary bitmap in the working device context is the sea background image. For the sea background to be placed in the working device context, it must first be converted into a WinG bitmap using the class tools. A clean copy of the background is kept in a separate WinG bitmap. This copy is used to update any background areas of the working WinG device context. For example, the area behind the animated chest needs to be updated with every move of the animation. The area behind the chest is copied from the back-up image to the working device context.

The chest bitmaps also need to be converted into WinG bitmaps with the class tools. In the project, a WinG class array is created to hold the various chest images. The Transbits2 function of each chest is called to copy the chest bits onto the working device context, which holds a copy of the background. Note that the WinGBitBlt function is not used to transfer bits from the chest bitmaps to the working device context. The TransparentDIBits function copies the actual pixel data onto the surface of the working device bitmap and filters out the black background.

The overall process followed for each timer tick is to update the working WinG bitmap where the chest is located with a clean copy of the background, then to copy the chest image transparently to the working WinG bitmap. Lastly, the final image from the working WinG device context is copied to the display. Note that only the area updated by the chest needs to be copied to the display.

Comments

This How-To shows the versatility and ease of use of the WinG API. The animated chest performs smoothly on a complex background. Note that, unlike the GDI functions, only one bitmap image is needed to perform the transparent copy. In the next two How-Tos, the sprite methods developed in Chapter 5 will be converted to use WinG.

6.9 How do I...
Build sprites with WinG?

Problem

In Chapter 5, several techniques were developed for building sprites in Visual Basic 4.0. How can I use those methods in conjunction with WinG to build high-performance sprites?

Technique

The methods for updating and tracking sprites developed in How-Tos 5.4, 5.5, and 5.6 can be converted to use the WinG device context and bitmaps. The flip book animation developed in the last How-To is a simple stationary sprite; the technique for showing its different frames can be used in developing WinG sprites. In this How-To, a fish sprite will be added to the animated scene developed in the last How-To.

Steps

Open and run 6-9.VBP. The running program appears as shown in Figure 6-9-1. The figure shows the chest animation as well as the self-running fish sprite.

1. Create a new project called 6-9.VBP. Add the objects and properties listed in Table 6-9-1 to Form1 and save the form as 6-9.FRM.

Table 6-9-1 Project form's objects and properties

OBJECT	PROPERTY	SETTING
Form	Name	Form1
	Auto3D	-1 'True
	Caption	"How-To 6.9"
	ScaleMode	3 'Pixel
PictureBox	Name	Picture3
	AutoRedraw	-1 'True
	AutoSize	-1 'True
	BorderStyle	0 'None
	ScaleMode	3 'Pixel
PictureBox	Name	Picture2
	AutoRedraw	-1 'True
	AutoSize	-1 'True
	BorderStyle	0 'None
	ScaleMode	3 'Pixel
Timer	Name	Timer1
	Interval	10
PictureBox	Name	Picture1
	BorderStyle	0 'None
	ScaleMode	3 'Pixel

Figure 6-9-1 The form as it appears at runtime

2. Add the following code to the general declarations section of the form. The appropriate functions and variables are declared for creating the WinG device contexts and tracking the sprite's movement. The WinG bitmaps for the chest, the working WinG device context, the background WinG device context, and the fish sprite classes are globally declared.

```
'  WinG functions
Private Declare Function WinGCreateDC Lib "wing.dll" () As Integer

Private Declare Function WinGBitBlt Lib "wing.dll" (ByVal hdcDest As Integer, ↵
ByVal nXOriginDest As Integer, ByVal nYOriginDest As Integer, ByVal ↵
nWidthDest As Integer, ByVal nHeightDest As Integer, ByVal hdcSrc As ↵
Integer, ByVal nXOriginSrc As Integer, ByVal nYOriginSrc As Integer) As Boolean

'  DeleteDC to delete the WinG device
'  contexts
Private Declare Function DeleteDC Lib "GDI" (ByVal hDC As Integer) As Integer

'  X and Y will be used to track and move the fish
Dim x As Integer
Dim y As Integer
```

continued on next page

continued from previous page

```
'  First will be used only to execute the code in the
'  form paint event  once
Dim First As Integer

'  XStep an YStep will hold the amount for each movement
'  of the sprites for each timer tick.
Dim xstep As Integer
Dim ystep As Integer

'  Direction will track the direction the fish
'  is moving
Dim direction As String

'  Declare two copies of the background
Dim Back As WinG
Dim Back2 As WinG

'  Fish1 is the right pointing fish
'  and Fish2 the left
Dim Fish1 As WinGSprite
Dim Fish2 As WinGSprite

'  Declare the WinG bitmaps for
'  the chest
Dim chest(9) As WinG

'  The three WinG device contexts
Dim wingDC1 As Integer
Dim wingDC2 As Integer
Dim wingdc3 As Integer

'  N will be used to count through
'  the chest frames
Dim N As Integer
```

3. When the form is loaded, several actions take place. First, the background and working WinG device context are created and set up. The sprites for handling the left- and right-pointing fish are created and set up, with their tracking variables initialized. Also, the chest WinG bitmaps are created and set up for performing the opening and closing chest animation.

```
Private Sub Form_Load()

'  Set N to 1 for counting through
'  the chest boxes
N = 1

'  Create the background instances
Set Back = New WinG
Set Back2 = New WinG

'  Create the Fish sprites
Set Fish1 = New WinGSprite
Set Fish2 = New WinGSprite
```

```
'  Set the filenames for the fish
Fish1.filename = App.Path + "\fish1.bmp"
Fish2.filename = App.Path + "\fish2.bmp"

'  Set the picture where the background
'  is to be displayed
Set Fish1.dispback = picture1
Set Fish2.dispback = picture1

'  Create the WinG bitmaps for the fish
Fish1.create
Fish2.create

'  Create our WinG Device contexts
wingDC1 = WinGCreateDC()
wingDC2 = WinGCreateDC()
wingdc3 = WinGCreateDC()


'  Set up the two backgrounds.  One
'  is for working on and the other
'  is a clean copy.
Let Back.filename = App.Path + "\sea.bmp"
Let Back.wdc = wingDC1
Set Back.picture = picture1

Let Back2.filename = App.Path + "\sea.bmp"
Let Back2.wdc = wingdc3
Set Back2.picture = picture1

'  Make the background WinG bitmaps
Back.MakeWinGBit
Back2.MakeWinGBit

'  Set the palette
Back.setpal

'  Create the WinG bitmaps for
'  the chest

For a = 1 To 9

    '  Create the instance
    Set chest(a) = New WinG

    '  Get a string representation of A
    num$ = Str$(a)
    num$ = Right$(num$, Len(num$) - 1)

    '  Setup the filenames, DC, and
    '  picture
    Let chest(a).filename = App.Path + "\c00" + num$ + ".bmp"
    Let chest(a).wdc = wingDC2
    Set chest(a).picture = picture1
```

continued on next page

continued from previous page

```
        '  Make the bitmap
        chest(a).MakeWinGBit

        '  Get the surface to copy bits to
        psurface = Back.surface

        '  Set the surface to copy bits to
        chest(a).surface = psurface

Next a

'  Set the surfaces to copy bits to
Fish1.surface = psurface
Fish2.surface = psurface

'  Set the horizontal and vertical
'  increments of moving the fish
xstep = 7
ystep = 4

'  Start out at the origin
y = 0
x = 0

'  Our direction is Down and Right
'  To begin with
direction = "DR"

'  Set the collision boundaries for
'  the fish
Let Fish1.Leftbound = 0
Let Fish1.TopBound = 0
Let Fish1.RightBound = picture1.ScaleWidth
Let Fish1.Bottombound = picture1.ScaleHeight

Let Fish2.Leftbound = 0
Let Fish2.TopBound = 0
Let Fish2.RightBound = picture1.ScaleWidth
Let Fish2.Bottombound = picture1.ScaleHeight

End Sub
```

4. When the form is painted, the background bits for the working device context and the holding copy of the background are copied into their respective WinG bitmap surfaces using Transbits. Then the background is copied to the display picture using WinGBitBlt.

```
Private Sub Form_Paint()

'  The first time the form is painted
'  copy the bits of the background
'  and show the background
If First = 0 Then
```

```
      Back.Transbits
      Back2.Transbits
      Call WinGBitBlt(picture1.hDC, 0, 0, picture1.ScaleWidth, ⏎
                picture1.ScaleHeight, wingDC1, 0, 0)
      First = 1
End If

End Sub
```

5. When the form is unloaded, it is important to delete the WinG devices created when the form was loaded. It is also important to terminate the WinG classes as well as the sprite classes so that any objects created in the classes will be deleted.

```
Private Sub Form_Unload(Cancel As Integer)

'   Delete our 3 WinG device contexts
throw = DeleteDC(wingDC1)
throw = DeleteDC(wingDC2)
throw = DeleteDC(wingdc3)

'   Terminate the Chest WinG bitmaps
For a = 1 To 9
    Set chest(a) = Nothing
Next a

'   Terminate the Fish and backgrounds
Set Back = Nothing
Set Back2 = Nothing
Set Fish1 = Nothing
Set Fish2 = Nothing

End Sub
```

6. The timer controls the actual movement of the sprites and the animation of the chest. With each tick of the timer, the original positions of the fish and the chest are updated on the working device context from the back-up copy of the background. At that point, the next cell in the chest animation is copied to the working device context. The fish is then updated to be at its new position with the MoveImage function of the Sprite class. Note that the update is done on the working device context. Then a check is done to see if the sprite has collided with any of the boundaries of the picture box. If so, the Sprite class changes the direction of the sprite. Finally, the current position of the sprite and the current position of the chest are copied to the display. Note that enough of the background is copied to cover up the last position of the fish sprite.

```
Private Sub Timer1_Timer()

'   If N reaches 10 then reset N to 1
If N = 10 Then N = 1

'   Copy the original background into
'   our working background.  This covers up
```

continued on next page

continued from previous page

```
'   the original positions of the Fish and
'   Chest objects
Call WinGBitBlt(wingDC1, 65, 280, Picture3.ScaleWidth, Picture3.ScaleHeight, ↵
wingdc3, 65, 280)

Call WinGBitBlt(wingDC1, x, y, Picture2.ScaleWidth + xstep * 2, ↵
Picture2.ScaleHeight + ystep * 2, wingdc3, x, y)

'  Copy the next chest into our working background
chest(N).transbits2 65, 280

        '  Depending on the direction, we will increment or
        '  decrement X and Y appropriately.  Then the image
        '  is moved and we check for a collision with the
        '  collide function.
        Select Case direction

        Case "UL"
             x = x - xstep
             y = y - ystep
             Fish2.MoveImage x, y
             Fish2.collide x, y, direction, Picture2.ScaleWidth, Picture2.ScaleHeight

        Case "UR"
             x = x + xstep
             y = y - ystep
             Fish1.MoveImage x, y
             Fish1.collide x, y, direction, Picture2.ScaleWidth, Picture2.ScaleHeight

        Case "DL"
             x = x - xstep
             y = y + ystep
             Fish2.MoveImage x, y
             Fish2.collide x, y, direction, Picture2.ScaleWidth, Picture2.ScaleHeight

        Case "DR"
             x = x + xstep
             y = y + ystep
             Fish1.MoveImage x, y
             Fish1.collide x, y, direction, Picture2.ScaleWidth, Picture2.ScaleHeight

        End Select

'  Copy to the display the new fish and chest
Call WinGBitBlt(picture1.hDC, 65, 280, Picture3.ScaleWidth, ↵
Picture3.ScaleHeight, wingDC1, 65, 280)

Call WinGBitBlt(picture1.hDC, x - xstep, y - ystep, Picture2.ScaleWidth + ↵
xstep * 2, Picture2.ScaleHeight + ystep * 2, wingDC1, x - xstep, y - ystep)

'   Increment N
N = N + 1

End Sub
```

7. Insert a new class into the project and save it as WSPRITE.CLS. Add the following code to the general declarations section of the form. The WinG functions for creating the WinG bitmap and device context are created. Also, the WinG class is globally declared, along with the necessary member variables for the sprite. For detailed information on the overall sprite function, see How-Tos 5.4, 5.5, and 5.6. The following comments discuss the changes made to support WinG.

```
'   Standard WinG functions
Private Declare Function DeleteDC Lib "GDI" (ByVal hDC As Integer) As Integer
Private Declare Function WinGCreateDC Lib "wing.dll" () As Integer

'   Globally declare the WinG bitmap
'   for the sprite
Dim WinGBitmap As WinG

Dim m_dispback As Object

'   Declare the boundaries for detecting collisions
Dim m_rightbound  As Integer
Dim m_bottombound As Integer
Dim m_topbound    As Integer
Dim m_leftbound   As Integer

'   The surface to copy the bitmap onto
Dim m_psurface As Long

'   The filename to open
Dim m_filename As String

'   The device WinG context for the sprite
Dim WInGDC As Integer
```

8. The following properties set the boundaries for the sprite's movement, the background picture for the sprite to be displayed on, and the file name for the bitmap. The WinG bitmap surface for the sprite to be copied onto is passed into the sprite.

```
'   Set the surface for bits to be
'   copied to
Public Property Let surface(N As Long)
    m_psurface = N
End Property

'   Set the right boundary
Public Property Let RightBound(N As Integer)
    Let m_rightbound = N
End Property

'   Set the bottom boundary
Public Property Let Bottombound(N As Integer)
    Let m_bottombound = N
End Property
```

continued on next page

continued from previous page

```
'   Set the Top boundary
Public Property Let TopBound(N As Integer)
    Let m_topbound = N
End Property

'   Set the left boundary
Public Property Let Leftbound(N As Integer)
    Let m_leftbound = N
End Property

'    This is the background to be displayed
Public Property Set dispback(acontrol As Object)
    Set m_dispback = acontrol
End Property

'   The file to be opened
Public Property Let filename(s As String)
    Let m_filename = s
End Property
```

9. The Collide function checks to see if the sprite has crossed any of the boundaries set by the property values. If so, the direction is appropriately updated.

```
Public Sub collide(x, y, direction, width, height)

'   We check to see if the sprite has reached the right
'   side of the form.  If so, we change direction
'   appropriately
If x + width > m_rightbound Then
    If direction = "UR" Then direction = "UL"
    If direction = "DR" Then direction = "DL"
End If

'   We check to see if the sprite has reached the left
'   side of the form.  If so, we change direction
'   appropriately
If x < m_leftbound Then
    If direction = "UL" Then direction = "UR"
    If direction = "DL" Then direction = "DR"
End If

'   We check to see if the sprite has reached the
'   bottom side of the form.  If so, we change direction
'   appropriately
If y + height > m_bottombound Then
    If direction = "DL" Then direction = "UL"
    If direction = "DR" Then direction = "UR"
End If

'   We check to see if the sprite has reached the top
'   side of the form.  If so, we change direction
'   appropriately
If y < m_topbound Then
    If direction = "UL" Then direction = "DL"
    If direction = "UR" Then direction = "DR"
```

End If

End Sub

10. In the original Sprite class, the MoveImage function went through a series of bitmap manipulations to copy the sprite to the new position and to cover up the previous position. Here the Transbits2 function of the WinG class is used to copy the sprite onto the surface passed into the sprite and represented by m_psurface.

```
Public Sub MoveImage(x, y)

'  Set the surface to copy the bits to
WinGBitmap.surface = m_psurface

'  Copy the bits
WinGBitmap.transbits2 x, y

End Sub
```

11. The Create function of the sprite creates the WinG bitmap necessary to represent the bitmap file data. The function uses the MakeWinGBit function of the WinG class to build the WinG bitmap.

```
'  Create the WinG bitmap for the sprite
Public Sub create()
    Let WinGBitmap.filename = m_filename
    Set WinGBitmap.picture = m_dispback
    WinGBitmap.MakeWinGBit

    '  Delete the device context because
    '  we are finished with it
    throw = DeleteDC(WInGDC)
End Sub
```

12. When the class is created, a WinG device context is created, as well as the new WinG class.

```
'  When the class is intialized, the
'  new WinG device context is set
'  and the WinGBitmap created
Private Sub Class_Initialize()
    WInGDC = WinGCreateDC()
    Set WinGBitmap = New WinG
    Let WinGBitmap.wdc = WInGDC
End Sub
```

13. When the sprite is terminated, it is important also to terminate the WinG class.

```
'  Be sure to terminate the
'  WinG bitmap and delete the
'  device context.
Private Sub Class_Terminate()
    Set WinGBitmap = Nothing
End Sub
```

14. Add the WinG class developed in the last two How-Tos to the project. Refer to the last two How-Tos for detailed information on how the WinG class works. Various comments are made about the class regarding building the WinG sprites.

```
Private Declare Function TransparentDIBits Lib "winghelp.dll" (dstInfo As ↵
Any, dstBuffer As Any, ByVal destx As Integer, ByVal desty As Integer, ↵
srcBuffer As Any, srcInfo As Any, ByVal srcx As Integer, ByVal srcy As ↵
Integer, ByVal iUsage As Integer, ByVal TransparentColor As Byte) As Boolean

Private Declare Sub CopyDIBits Lib "winghelp.dll" (pBuffer As Any, ByVal ↵
destOffset As Long, pSource As Any, ByVal sourceOffset As Long, ByVal ↵
dstWidth As Integer, ByVal dstHeight As Integer, ByVal dstScanWidth As ↵
Long, ByVal srcScanWidth As Long)

Private Declare Function WinGCreateDC Lib "wing.dll" () As Integer

Private Declare Function WinGRecommendDIBFormat Lib "wing.dll" (pBitmapInfo ↵
As Any) As Boolean

Private Declare Function WinGCreateBitmap Lib "wing.dll" (ByVal wingDC ↵
As Integer, pBitmapInfo As Any, ppBits As Any) As Integer

Private Declare Function WinGGetDIBPointer Lib "wing.dll" (ByVal WinGBitmap ↵
As Integer, pBitmapInfo As Any) As Long

Private Declare Function WinGGetDIBColorTable Lib "wing.dll" (ByVal wingDC ↵
As Integer, ByVal StartIndex As Integer, ByVal NumberOfEntries As Integer,
pRgbQuadColors As Any) As Integer

Private Declare Function WinGSetDIBColorTable Lib "wing.dll" (ByVal wingDC ↵
As Integer, ByVal StartIndex As Integer, ByVal NumberOfEntries As Integer, ↵
pRgbQuadColors As Any) As Integer

Private Declare Function WinGCreateHalftonePalette Lib "wing.dll" () As Integer

Private Declare Function WinGCreateHalftoneBrush Lib "wing.dll" (ByVal ↵
Context As Integer, ByVal crColor As Long, ByVal DitherType As Integer) ↵
As Integer

Private Declare Function WinGBitBlt Lib "wing.dll" (ByVal hdcDest As ↵
Integer, ByVal nXOriginDest As Integer, ByVal nYOriginDest As Integer, ByVal ↵
nWidthDest As Integer, ByVal nHeightDest As Integer, ByVal hdcSrc As Integer, ↵
ByVal nXOriginSrc As Integer, ByVal nYOriginSrc As Integer) As Boolean

Private Declare Function WinGStretchBlt Lib "wing.dll" (ByVal hdcDest ↵
As Integer, ByVal nXOriginDest As Integer, ByVal nYOriginDest As Integer, ↵
ByVal nWidthDest As Integer, ByVal nHeightDest As Integer, ByVal hdcSrc As ↵
Integer, ByVal nXOriginSrc As Integer, ByVal nYOriginSrc As Integer, ByVal ↵
nWidthSrc As Integer, ByVal nHeightSrc As Integer) As Boolean

Private Declare Function DeleteObject Lib "GDI" (ByVal hObject As Integer) ↵
As Integer

Private Declare Function CreatePalette Lib "GDI" (lpLogPalette As LOGPALETTE) ↵
As Integer
```

```
Private Declare Function SelectPalette Lib "User" (ByVal hDC As Integer, ↵
ByVal hPalette As Integer, ByVal bForceBackground As Integer) As Integer

Private Declare Function RealizePalette Lib "User" (ByVal hDC As Integer) ↵
As Integer

Private Declare Function SelectObject Lib "GDI" (ByVal hDC As Integer, ByVal ↵
hObject As Integer) As Integer

Private Declare Function lopen Lib "Kernel" Alias "_lopen" (ByVal lpPathName ↵
As String, ByVal iReadWrite As Integer) As Integer

Private Declare Function lread Lib "Kernel" Alias "_lread" (ByVal hfile ↵
As Integer, lpBuffer As Any, ByVal wBytes As Integer) As Integer

Private Declare Function lclose Lib "Kernel" Alias "_lclose" (ByVal hfile ↵
As Integer) As Integer

Private Declare Function hread Lib "Kernel" Alias "_hread" (ByVal hfile As ↵
Integer, buffer As Any, ByVal n As Long) As Long

Private Declare Function hwrite Lib "Kernel" Alias "_hwrite" (ByVal hfile As ↵
Integer, buffer As Any, ByVal n As Long) As Long

Private Declare Function lstrcpy Lib "Kernel" (dest As Any, src As Any) As Long

Const OPEN_READ = 0

Const SRCCOPY = &HCC0020
Const WHITENESS = &HFF0062
Const BLACKNESS = &H42&

Private Type RGBQUAD
    rgbBlue        As String * 1
    rgbGreen       As String * 1
    rgbRed         As String * 1
    rgbReserved    As String * 1
End Type

Private Type PALETTEENTRY
    peRed          As String * 1
    peGreen        As String * 1
    peBlue         As String * 1
    peFlags        As String * 1
End Type

Private Type LOGPALETTE
    version            As Integer
    nEntries           As Integer
    palpalentry(256)   As PALETTEENTRY
End Type

Const PC_RESERVED = &H1      ' palette index used for animation
Const PC_NOCOLLAPSE = &H4    ' do not match color to system palette
```

continued on next page

465

CHAPTER 6

continued from previous page

```
Const DIB_RGB_COLORS = 0      '  color table in RGBTriples

Private Type BITMAPFILEHEADER
    bfType       As Integer
    bfSize       As Long
    bfReserved1  As Integer
    bfReserved2  As Integer
    bfOffBits    As Long
End Type

Private Type BITMAPINFOHEADER
    biSize          As Long
    biWidth         As Long
    biHeight        As Long
    biPlanes        As Integer
    biBitCount      As Integer
    biCompression   As Long
    biSizeImage     As Long
    biXPelsPerMeter As Long
    biYPelsPerMeter As Long
    biClrUsed       As Long
    biClrImportant  As Long
End Type

Private Type BITMAPINFO
    bmiHeader        As BITMAPINFOHEADER
    bmiColors(256)   As RGBQUAD
End Type


Private hbitmap    As Integer
Private m_pict     As Object
Private m_WinGDc   As Integer
Private WGBminfo   As BITMAPINFO
Private bminfo     As BITMAPINFO
Private psurface   As Long
Private pal        As Integer
Private bitdata()  As Byte
Private m_filename As String
Private m_psurface As Long


Private Sub ReadBitmap()

Dim LogicalPal As LOGPALETTE
Dim FileHeader As BITMAPFILEHEADER

FileP = lopen(m_filename, OPEN_READ)

throw = lread(FileP, FileHeader, Len(FileHeader)) = Len(FileHeader)
throw = lread(FileP, bminfo.bmiHeader.biSize, Len(bminfo.bmiHeader))
throw = lread(FileP, bminfo.bmiColors(0), Len(bminfo.bmiColors(0)) * 256)

For n = 0 To 255
    LogicalPal.palpalentry(n).peRed = bminfo.bmiColors(n).rgbRed
```

```
      LogicalPal.palpalentry(n).peGreen = bminfo.bmiColors(n).rgbGreen
      LogicalPal.palpalentry(n).peBlue = bminfo.bmiColors(n).rgbBlue
      If (n > 9) And (n < 246) Then
              LogicalPal.palpalentry(n).peFlags = Chr$(PC_RESERVED)
          Else
              LogicalPal.palpalentry(n).peFlags = Chr$(0)
      End If
Next n

LogicalPal.version = &H300
LogicalPal.nEntries = 256
pal = CreatePalette(LogicalPal)

ReDim bitdata(bminfo.bmiHeader.biSizeImage)
throw = hread(FileP, bitdata(0), bminfo.bmiHeader.biSizeImage)

Call lclose(FileP)

End Sub


Public Sub MakeWinGBit()

ReadBitmap

WGBminfo.bmiHeader.biSize = 40
WGBminfo.bmiHeader.biWidth = m_pict.ScaleWidth
WGBminfo.bmiHeader.biHeight = m_pict.ScaleHeight
WGBminfo.bmiHeader.biPlanes = 1
WGBminfo.bmiHeader.biBitCount = 8
WGBminfo.bmiHeader.biCompression = 0
WGBminfo.bmiHeader.biSizeImage = 0
WGBminfo.bmiHeader.biXPelsPerMeter = 0
WGBminfo.bmiHeader.biYPelsPerMeter = 0
WGBminfo.bmiHeader.biClrUsed = 256
WGBminfo.bmiHeader.biClrImportant = 0

hbitmap = WinGCreateBitmap(m_WinGDc, WGBminfo, psurface)
throw = SelectObject(m_WinGDc, hbitmap)

Call WinGSetDIBColorTable(m_WinGDc, 0, 256, bminfo.bmiColors(0))

End Sub

Public Sub SetPal()
holdPal = SelectPalette(m_pict.hDC, pal, False)

throw = DeleteObject(holdPal)

Call RealizePalette(m_pict.hDC)

End Sub
```

15. Note that, for sprites, this function is never called. The sprite bits must always be copied onto another WinG surface and not their own.

```
Public Sub Transbits()
BytesAsLong& = lstrcpy(bitdata(0), bitdata(0))
InfoAsLong& = lstrcpy(bminfo, bminfo)

Call TransparentDIBits(WGBminfo, ByVal psurface, 0, 0, ByVal BytesAsLong&, ByVal
InfoAsLong&, 0, 0, 0, 0)

End Sub
```

16. Transbits2 is the primary function used for moving the sprite.

```
Public Sub Transbits2(x, y)

BytesAsLong& = lstrcpy(bitdata(0), bitdata(0))
InfoAsLong& = lstrcpy(bminfo, bminfo)

Call TransparentDIBits(WGBminfo, ByVal m_psurface, x, y, ByVal BytesAsLong&, ↵
ByVal InfoAsLong&, 0, 0, 0, 1)

End Sub
```

17. All of the properties for the WinG class are set by the sprite class. Several,
    including the WinG surface for copying the sprite onto, the file name, and
    picture, passed into the Sprite class from the overall project.

```
Public Property Set picture(acontrol As Control)
        Set m_pict = acontrol
End Property

Public Property Let wdc(n As Integer)
        Let m_WinGDc = n
End Property

Public Property Let filename(s As String)
        Let m_filename = s
End Property

Public Property Let surface(n As Long)
    m_psurface = n
End Property

Public Property Get surface() As Long
    surface = psurface
End Property

Private Sub Class_Terminate()
throw = DeleteObject(hbitmap)
End Sub
```

How It Works

The chest animation from the last How-To is used as the foundation for adding the
sprite to the animated scene. All the code for showing the background and the chest
was used from the last How-To. The addition made here is a new Sprite class.

The Sprite class developed originally in How-To 5.5 is used as the basis for building the WinG Sprite class. In the original class, a complex set of bitmap transfers was done on various masks of the bitmap to build the transparent sprite. In this class, only one bitmap image is needed with a black background, and its palette is set to that of the other images to be displayed. This is because the TransparentDIBits function handles copying the bits transparently onto the surface of another WinG bitmap. The PAL.PAL palette file from the last How-To is used for the fish. In this case, the form code handles setting up the background WinG bitmap that the sprites are copied onto. The surface of this working bitmap is passed into the WinG sprite, which is in turn passed into the WinG bitmap for the sprite. To move the sprite, the MoveImage method calls the Transbits2 function of the WinG bitmap to copy the sprite onto the working background WinG bitmap.

In the Timer function, each new image is created in the working WinG device context and bitmap. The original positions of the sprite (and chest) are covered from the WinG bitmap copy of the background. Then the fish is copied to its new position. At the same time, the chest is updated appropriately. Once the new scene is set up, the sections of the scene where the background and fish are updated are copied to the display using WinGBitBlt. Note that when the new fish is copied to the display, enough of the background is copied to cover up the last position of the fish.

As with the How-Tos in Chapter 5, collisions boundaries for the sprite are set up. With each move of the fish, a check is done to see if the fish has collided with any of the boundaries. If so, then the direction of the fish is updated. If the fish is moving to the right, then the right-pointing fish is moved. If the fish is moving to the left, then the left-pointing fish is used.

Comments

As this How-To demonstrates, WinG simplifies and enhances the building and use of sprites in Windows. The next How-To will demonstrate how the sprite and animation techniques of WinG can be expanded to include sound and additional sprites.

6.10 How do I...
Build scenes with multiple sprites, animations, and sounds with WinG?

COMPLEXITY: ADVANCED

Problem

It is nice to have one or two sprites being manipulated at once using WinG or the Windows GDI functions. But how can I add additional sprites and sound to make the animation scenes more effective and at the same time have greater control over the timing of the different actions?

Technique

By building on the foundation developed in the last How-To for animating sprites, you can add an additional sprite to the animated scene. At the same time you can add background music and make the ding wave file play when the chest is to be shut. Also, you can slow down the speed at which the chest opens and closes. This How-To demonstrates the power and speed of WinG by easily animating three objects in the scene using additional resources to play sounds. It also shows various techniques for using a single timer for controlling sprites that need to be updated at different intervals.

Steps

Open and run 6-10.VBP. The running program appears as shown in Figure 6-10-1.
The red fish will continue to rotate from the left to the right of the animated scene. The ding wave is played each time the chest closes.

1. Create a new project called 6-10.VBP. Add the objects and properties listed in Table 6-10-1 to Form1 and save the form as 6-10.FRM.

Figure 6-10-1 The form as it appears at runtime

Table 6-10-1 Project form's objects and properties

OBJECT	PROPERTY	SETTING
Form	Name	Form1
	Auto3D	-1 'True
	Caption	"How-To 6.10"
	ScaleMode	3 'Pixel
PictureBox	Name	Picture3
	AutoRedraw	-1 'True
	AutoSize	-1 'True
	BorderStyle	0 'None
	ScaleMode	3 'Pixel
PictureBox	Name	Picture2
	AutoRedraw	-1 'True
	AutoSize	-1 'True
	BorderStyle	0 'None
	ScaleMode	3 'Pixel
Timer	Name	Timer1
	Interval	1
PictureBox	Name	Picture1
	BorderStyle	0 'None
	ScaleMode	3 'Pixel
MMControl	Name	MMControl1
	Visible	0 'False
	BorderStyle	1

2. Add the following code to the general declarations section of the form. The WinG functions and the necessary functions for playing the ding wave are declared. Variables for creating and tracking the WinG bitmaps and sprites are also declared.

```
' WinG Functions
Private Declare Function WinGBitBlt Lib "wing.dll" (ByVal hdcDest As Integer, _
ByVal nXOriginDest As Integer, ByVal nYOriginDest As Integer, ByVal _
nWidthDest As Integer, ByVal nHeightDest As Integer, ByVal hdcSrc As Integer, _
ByVal nXOriginSrc As Integer, ByVal nYOriginSrc As Integer) As Boolean
```

continued on next page

continued from previous page

```
Private Declare Function WinGCreateDC Lib "wing.dll" () As Integer

' Delete Device Context
Private Declare Function DeleteDC Lib "GDI" (ByVal hDC As Integer) As Integer

' Used to play the Ding.Wav sound
' when the chest shuts
Private Declare Function sndPlaySound Lib "mmsystem" (ByVal lpszSoundName ↵
As String, ByVal uFlags As Integer) As Integer

Const SND_ASYNC = &H1                    ' play asynchronously

' X and Y will be used to track and move
' the first Fish
Dim X As Integer
Dim Y As Integer

' XX and YY will be used for the second
Dim XX As Integer
Dim YY As Integer

' First will be used only to execute the code in the
' form paint event once
Dim first As Integer

' XStep an YStep will hold the amount for each movement
' of the sprites for each timer tick.
Dim xstep       As Integer
Dim ystep       As Integer
Dim xxstep      As Integer
Dim yystep      As Integer

' Direction will track the direction the sprites
' are moving
Dim direction   As String
Dim direction2  As String

' Declare the working and backup
' backgrounds
Dim Back  As WinG
Dim Back2 As WinG

' Globally declare the Fish sprites
Dim Fish1 As WinGSprite
Dim Fish2 As WinGSprite
Dim Fish3 As WinGSprite

' Declare the Chest Bitmaps
Dim Chest(9) As WinG

' The WinG device contexts
Dim wingDC1 As Integer
Dim wingDC2 As Integer
Dim wingDC3 As Integer
```

```
'   N will be used to count times
'   for the chest animations
Dim N As Integer

'   BoxCount is used to count
'   through the chest bitmaps
Dim BoxCount As Integer
```

3. When the form is loaded, the three fish sprites, the chest WinG images, and the background and working background WinG bitmaps are set up. Also, the variables for tracking the sprites are initialized and the background music is started.

```
Private Sub Form_Load()

'   Start the play of the music
MMControl1.DeviceType = "Sequencer"
MMControl1.filename = "c:\windows\media\canyon.mid"
MMControl1.Command = "close"
MMControl1.Command = "open"
MMControl1.Command = "play"

'   Set the starting positions and direction
'   for the Red Fish sprite
XX = -150
YY = 50
direction2 = "UR"

'   Initialize BoxCount and N to 1
BoxCount = 1
N = 1

'   Create the background instances
Set Back = New WinG
Set Back2 = New WinG

'   Create the Fish Sprites
Set Fish1 = New WinGSprite
Set Fish2 = New WinGSprite
Set Fish3 = New WinGSprite

'   Set the Fish file names
Fish1.filename = App.Path + "\fish1.bmp"
Fish2.filename = App.Path + "\fish2.bmp"
Fish3.filename = App.Path + "\fish3.bmp"

'   Set the Fish display backgrounds
Set Fish1.dispback = picture1
Set Fish2.dispback = picture1
Set Fish3.dispback = picture1

'   Create the Fish WinG bitmaps
Fish1.create
Fish2.create
Fish3.create
```

continued on next page

CHAPTER 6

continued from previous page

```
'  Create the WinG Device Contexts
wingDC1 = WinGCreateDC()
wingDC2 = WinGCreateDC()
wingDC3 = WinGCreateDC()

'  Setup the backgrounds
Let Back.filename = App.Path + "\sea.bmp"
Let Back.wdc = wingDC1
Set Back.picture = picture1

Let Back2.filename = App.Path + "\sea.bmp"
Let Back2.wdc = wingDC3
Set Back2.picture = picture1

'  Make the background WinG bitmaps
Back.MakeWinGBit
Back2.MakeWinGBit

'  Set the palette for the animation
Back.setpal


'  Create the chest WinG bitmaps
For A = 1 To 9

    '  Create the WinG instance
    Set Chest(A) = New WinG

    '  Get the string representation of A
    num$ = Str$(A)
    num$ = Right$(num$, Len(num$) - 1)

    '  Set the chest file name, WinG device context
    '  and picture
    Let Chest(A).filename = App.Path + "\c00" + num$ + ".bmp"
    Let Chest(A).wdc = wingDC2
    Set Chest(A).picture = picture1

    '  Make the WinG bitmap
    Chest(A).MakeWinGBit

    '  Get the surface to copy to
    psurface = Back.surface

    '  Set the surface to copy to
    Chest(A).surface = psurface

Next A

'  Set the Fish surfaces to copy to
Fish1.surface = psurface
Fish2.surface = psurface
Fish3.surface = psurface

'  The x step will be 4 and the y step will be 2
```

```
'  this is the amount the sprite is moved each time
xstep = 4
ystep = 2

'  Start out at the origin
Y = 0
X = 0

'  Our direction is Down and Right
'  To begin with
direction = "DR"

'  Set the boundaries for the fish movements
Let Fish1.Leftbound = 0
Let Fish1.TopBound = 0
Let Fish1.RightBound = picture1.ScaleWidth
Let Fish1.Bottombound = picture1.ScaleHeight

Let Fish2.Leftbound = 0
Let Fish2.TopBound = 0
Let Fish2.RightBound = picture1.ScaleWidth
Let Fish2.Bottombound = picture1.ScaleHeight

Let Fish3.Leftbound = 0
Let Fish3.TopBound = 0
Let Fish3.RightBound = picture1.ScaleWidth + Picture3.ScaleWidth * 2
Let Fish3.Bottombound = picture1.ScaleHeight

'  Set the Red Fish xstep to 8
xxstep = 8
End Sub
```

4. When the form is painted, the background WinG bitmaps have their corresponding pixel data copied. Then the background is shown on the display context using WinGBitBlt.

```
Private Sub Form_Paint()

'  The first time the form is painted
'  execute the following actions
If first = 0 Then
    '  Copy the bitmap bits into
    '  the background WinG bitmap
    Back.transbits
    Back2.transbits

    '  Display the background
    Call WinGBitBlt(picture1.hDC, 0, 0, picture1.ScaleWidth, ↵
              picture1.ScaleHeight, wingDC1, 0, 0)

    first = 1
End If

End Sub
```

5. When the form is unloaded, it is important to delete the WinG device context created when the form is loaded. It is also important to terminate the chest, background, and fish classes so that any objects created in the classes can be deleted.

```
Private Sub Form_Unload(Cancel As Integer)

'  Delete the WinG instances
throw = DeleteDC(wingDC1)
throw = DeleteDC(wingDC2)
throw = DeleteDC(wingDC3)

'  Terminate the Chest bitmaps
For A = 1 To 9
    Set Chest(A) = Nothing
Next A

'  Terminate the backgrounds
Set Back = Nothing
Set Back2 = Nothing

'  Terminate the Fish instances
Set Fish1 = Nothing
Set Fish2 = Nothing
Set Fish3 = Nothing

End Sub
```

6. The timer control handles updating the scene with every timer tick. The opening and closing of the chest is performed on every fourth timer tick. When the next-to-the-last-frame of the chest closing is shown, the ding wave file is played. By the time the wave file is finished playing, the last frame of the chest animation is shown. Also, the fish sprites are updated and moved and a check is done to see if any of the boundaries have been reached.

```
Private Sub Timer1_Timer()

'  When N reaches 40 set N to 1
If N = 40 Then N = 1

'  When BoxCount reaches 10 then set to 1
If BoxCount = 10 Then BoxCount = 1

'  When the box is about to shut,
'  play the ding wave
If N = 28 Then throw = sndPlaySound("c:\windows\media\ding.wav", SND_ASYNC)

'  Copy the original background over the current
'  fish and chest positions
Call WinGBitBlt(wingDC1, XX - xxstep * 2, YY - yystep * 2, ↵
Picture3.ScaleWidth  + 5, Picture3.ScaleHeight, wingDC3, XX - xxstep * 2, ↵
YY - yystep * 2)

Call WinGBitBlt(wingDC1, 65, 280, Picture2.ScaleWidth * 3, ↵
Picture2.ScaleHeight * 4, wingDC3, 65, 280)
```

```
Call WinGBitBlt(wingDC1, X - xstep, Y - ystep, Picture2.ScaleWidth + xstep ↵
* 2, Picture2.ScaleHeight + ystep * 2, wingDC3, X - xstep, Y - ystep)

'  Copy the chest
Chest(BoxCount).transbits2 65, 280

'  Check to see if the Red fish has changed direction
'  If so reset to the left of the picture and set
'  the direction back
If direction2 = "UL" Then direction2 = "UR": XX = -150

'  Increase the Red fish position
XX = XX + xxstep

    '  Depending on the direction, we will increment or
    '  decrement X and Y appropriately.  Then the image
    '  is moved and we check for a collision with the
    '  collide function.
    Select Case direction

    Case "UL"
        X = X - xstep
        Y = Y - ystep
        Fish2.MoveImage X, Y
        Fish2.collide X, Y, direction, Picture2.ScaleWidth, Picture2.ScaleHeight

    Case "UR"
        X = X + xstep
        Y = Y - ystep
        Fish1.MoveImage X, Y
        Fish1.collide X, Y, direction, Picture2.ScaleWidth, Picture2.ScaleHeight

    Case "DL"
        X = X - xstep
        Y = Y + ystep
        Fish2.MoveImage X, Y
        Fish2.collide X, Y, direction, Picture2.ScaleWidth, Picture2.ScaleHeight

    Case "DR"
        X = X + xstep
        Y = Y + ystep
        Fish1.MoveImage X, Y
        Fish1.collide X, Y, direction, Picture2.ScaleWidth, Picture2.ScaleHeight

    End Select

'  Move the Red Fish and check for a collision
Fish3.MoveImage XX, YY
Fish3.collide XX, YY, direction2, Picture3.ScaleWidth, Picture3.ScaleHeight

'  Copy the three objects to the screen
Call WinGBitBlt(picture1.hDC, XX - xxstep * 2, YY - yystep * 2, ↵
Picture3.ScaleWidth + 5, Picture3.ScaleHeight, wingDC1, XX - xxstep * 2, ↵
YY - yystep * 2)
```

continued on next page

continued from previous page

```
Call WinGBitBlt(picture1.hDC, X - xstep, Y - ystep, Picture2.ScaleWidth + ↵
xstep * 2, Picture2.ScaleHeight + ystep * 2, wingDC1, X - xstep, Y - ystep)

Call WinGBitBlt(picture1.hDC, 65, 280, Picture2.ScaleWidth * 3, ↵
Picture2.ScaleHeight * 4, wingDC1, 65, 280)

'   Check to see if four ticks on the clock
'   have counted off.  If so, then increment
'   BoxCount
If N Mod 4 = 0 Then BoxCount = BoxCount + 1

'   Increment N
N = N + 1

End Sub
```

7. Add the Sprite class from the How-To 6-9 to the project. Note that there are actually three sprites declared in the project. Two define the green fish when moving in different directions from left to right. The third defines the red fish. Various comments are made regarding the use of class in this How-To.

```
'   Standard WinG functions
Private Declare Function DeleteDC Lib "GDI" (ByVal hDC As Integer) As Integer
Private Declare Function WinGCreateDC Lib "wing.dll" () As Integer

'   Globally declare the WinG bitmap
'   for the sprite
Dim WinGBitmap As WinG

Dim m_dispback As Object

'   Declare the boundaries for detecting collisions
Dim m_rightbound    As Integer
Dim m_bottombound   As Integer
Dim m_topbound      As Integer
Dim m_leftbound     As Integer

'   The surface to copy the bitmap onto
Dim m_psurface As Long

'   The filename to open
Dim m_filename As String

'   The device WinG context for the sprite
Dim WInGDC As Integer

'   Set the right boundary
Public Property Let RightBound(N As Integer)
    Let m_rightbound = N
End Property

'   Set the bottom boundary
Public Property Let Bottombound(N As Integer)
```

```
      Let m_bottombound = N
End Property

'   Set the Top boundary
Public Property Let TopBound(N As Integer)
      Let m_topbound = N
End Property

'   Set the left boundary
Public Property Let Leftbound(N As Integer)
      Let m_leftbound = N
End Property

'   This is the background to be displayed
Public Property Set dispback(acontrol As Object)
      Set m_dispback = acontrol
End Property

'   The file to be opened
Public Property Let filename(s As String)
      Let m_filename = s
End Property
```

8. Note that the Collide method of the class is used for the red fish even though the
fish moves in only one direction. The class does not actually control the direction
of the sprite, it indicates that a boundary has been hit and a direction change
should be made. In the Timer function, when the red fish direction changes, the
appropriate actions take place to set the fish back to the left of the scene.

```
Public Sub Collide(X, Y, direction, width, height)

'   We check to see if the sprite has reached the right
'   side of the form.  If so, we change direction
'   appropriately
If X + width > m_rightbound Then
      If direction = "UR" Then direction = "UL"
      If direction = "DR" Then direction = "DL"
End If

'   We check to see if the sprite has reached the left
'   side of the form.  If so, we change direction
'   appropriately
If X < m_leftbound Then
      If direction = "UL" Then direction = "UR"
      If direction = "DL" Then direction = "DR"
End If

'   We check to see if the sprite has reached the
'   bottom side of the form.  If so, we change direction
'   appropriately
If Y + height > m_bottombound Then
      If direction = "DL" Then direction = "UL"
      If direction = "DR" Then direction = "UR"
End If
```

continued on next page

continued from previous page

```
'   We check to see if the sprite has reached the top
'   side of the form.  If so, we change direction
'   appropriately
If Y < m_topbound Then
     If direction = "UL" Then direction = "DL"
     If direction = "UR" Then direction = "DR"
End If

End Sub

Public Sub MoveImage(X, Y)

'   Set the surface to copy the bits to
WinGBitmap.surface = m_psurface

'   Copy the bits
WinGBitmap.transbits2 X, Y

End Sub

'   Set the surface for bits to be
'   copied to
Public Property Let surface(N As Long)
    m_psurface = N
End Property

'   Create the WinG bitmap for the sprite
Public Sub create()
    Let WinGBitmap.filename = m_filename
    Set WinGBitmap.picture = m_dispback
    WinGBitmap.MakeWinGBit

    '   Delete the device context because
    '   we are finished with it
    throw = DeleteDC(WInGDC)
End Sub

'   When the class is intialized, the
'   new WinG device context is set
'   and the WinGBitmap created
Private Sub Class_Initialize()
    WInGDC = WinGCreateDC()
    Set WinGBitmap = New WinG
    Let WinGBitmap.wdc = WInGDC
End Sub

'   Be sure to terminate the
'   WinG bitmap and delete the
'   device context.
Private Sub Class_Terminate()
    Set WinGBitmap = Nothing
End Sub
```

9. Add the WinG sprite class developed in the last three How-Tos. Each sprite uses the class to read in the bitmap file and create a WinG bitmap. Plus, the chest and background images are created through the WinG class. Various comments about the WinG class are made pertaining to this How-To.

```
Private Declare Function TransparentDIBits Lib "winghelp.dll" (dstInfo As ↵
Any, dstBuffer As Any, ByVal destx As Integer, ByVal desty As Integer, ↵
srcBuffer As Any, srcInfo As Any, ByVal srcx As Integer, ByVal srcy As ↵
Integer, ByVal iUsage As Integer, ByVal TransparentColor As Byte) As Boolean

Private Declare Sub CopyDIBits Lib "winghelp.dll" (pBuffer As Any, ByVal ↵
destOffset As Long, pSource As Any, ByVal sourceOffset As Long, ByVal ↵
dstWidth As Integer, ByVal dstHeight As Integer, ByVal dstScanWidth As ↵
Long, ByVal srcScanWidth As Long)

Private Declare Function WinGCreateDC Lib "wing.dll" () As Integer

Private Declare Function WinGRecommendDIBFormat Lib "wing.dll" (pBitmapInfo ↵
As Any) As Boolean

Private Declare Function WinGCreateBitmap Lib "wing.dll" (ByVal wingDC As ↵
Integer, pBitmapInfo As Any, ppBits As Any) As Integer

Private Declare Function WinGGetDIBPointer Lib "wing.dll" (ByVal WinGBitmap ↵
As Integer, pBitmapInfo As Any) As Long

Private Declare Function WinGGetDIBColorTable Lib "wing.dll" (ByVal wingDC ↵
As Integer, ByVal StartIndex As Integer, ByVal NumberOfEntries As Integer, ↵
pRgbQuadColors As Any) As Integer

Private Declare Function WinGSetDIBColorTable Lib "wing.dll" (ByVal wingDC ↵
As Integer, ByVal StartIndex As Integer, ByVal NumberOfEntries As Integer, ↵
pRgbQuadColors As Any) As Integer

Private Declare Function WinGCreateHalftonePalette Lib "wing.dll" () As Integer

Private Declare Function WinGCreateHalftoneBrush Lib "wing.dll" (ByVal ↵
Context As Integer, ByVal crColor As Long, ByVal DitherType As Integer) ↵
As Integer

Private Declare Function WinGBitBlt Lib "wing.dll" (ByVal hdcDest As Integer, ↵
ByVal nXOriginDest As Integer, ByVal nYOriginDest As Integer, ByVal ↵
nWidthDest As Integer, ByVal nHeightDest As Integer, ByVal hdcSrc As Integer, ↵
ByVal nXOriginSrc As Integer, ByVal nYOriginSrc As Integer) As Boolean

Private Declare Function WinGStretchBlt Lib "wing.dll" (ByVal hdcDest As ↵
Integer, ByVal nXOriginDest As Integer, ByVal nYOriginDest As Integer, ByVal ↵
nWidthDest As Integer, ByVal nHeightDest As Integer, ByVal hdcSrc As Integer, ↵
ByVal nXOriginSrc As Integer, ByVal nYOriginSrc As Integer, ByVal nWidthSrc ↵
As Integer, ByVal nHeightSrc As Integer) As Boolean

Private Declare Function DeleteObject Lib "GDI" (ByVal hObject As Integer) ↵
As Integer
```

continued on next page

CHAPTER 6

continued from previous page

```
Private Declare Function CreatePalette Lib "GDI" (lpLogPalette As LOGPALETTE) ↵
As Integer

Private Declare Function SelectPalette Lib "User" (ByVal hDC As Integer, ↵
ByVal hPalette As Integer, ByVal bForceBackground As Integer) As Integer

Private Declare Function RealizePalette Lib "User" (ByVal hDC As Integer) ↵
As Integer

Private Declare Function SelectObject Lib "GDI" (ByVal hDC As Integer, ↵
ByVal hObject As Integer) As Integer

Private Declare Function lopen Lib "Kernel" Alias "_lopen" (ByVal lpPathName ↵
As String, ByVal iReadWrite As Integer) As Integer

Private Declare Function lread Lib "Kernel" Alias "_lread" (ByVal hfile ↵
As Integer, lpBuffer As Any, ByVal wBytes As Integer) As Integer

Private Declare Function lclose Lib "Kernel" Alias "_lclose" (ByVal hfile ↵
As Integer) As Integer

Private Declare Function hread Lib "Kernel" Alias "_hread" (ByVal hfile ↵
As Integer, buffer As Any, ByVal n As Long) As Long

Private Declare Function hwrite Lib "Kernel" Alias "_hwrite" (ByVal hfile ↵
As Integer, buffer As Any, ByVal n As Long) As Long

Private Declare Function lstrcpy Lib "Kernel" (dest As Any, src As Any) As Long

Const OPEN_READ = 0

Const SRCCOPY = &HCC0020
Const WHITENESS = &HFF0062
Const BLACKNESS = &H42&

Private Type RGBQUAD
    rgbBlue      As String * 1
    rgbGreen     As String * 1
    rgbRed       As String * 1
    rgbReserved  As String * 1
End Type

Private Type PALETTEENTRY
    peRed        As String * 1
    peGreen      As String * 1
    peBlue       As String * 1
    peFlags      As String * 1
End Type

Private Type LOGPALETTE
    version         As Integer
    nEntries        As Integer
    palpalentry(256) As PALETTEENTRY
End Type
```

```
Const PC_RESERVED = &H1     '  palette index used for animation
Const PC_NOCOLLAPSE = &H4 '  do not match color to system palette
Const DIB_RGB_COLORS = 0    '  color table in RGBTriples

Private Type BITMAPFILEHEADER
    bfType        As Integer
    bfSize        As Long
    bfReserved1   As Integer
    bfReserved2   As Integer
    bfOffBits     As Long
End Type

Private Type BITMAPINFOHEADER
    biSize          As Long
    biWidth         As Long
    biHeight        As Long
    biPlanes        As Integer
    biBitCount      As Integer
    biCompression   As Long
    biSizeImage     As Long
    biXPelsPerMeter As Long
    biYPelsPerMeter As Long
    biClrUsed       As Long
    biClrImportant  As Long
End Type

Private Type BITMAPINFO
    bmiHeader       As BITMAPINFOHEADER
    bmiColors(256)  As RGBQUAD
End Type


Private hbitmap      As Integer
Private m_pict       As Object
Private m_WinGDc     As Integer
Private WGBminfo     As BITMAPINFO
Private bminfo       As BITMAPINFO
Private psurface     As Long
Private pal          As Integer
Private bitdata()    As Byte
Private m_filename   As String
Private m_psurface   As Long


Private Sub ReadBitmap()

Dim LogicalPal  As LOGPALETTE
Dim FileHeader  As BITMAPFILEHEADER

FileP = lopen(m_filename, OPEN_READ)

throw = lread(FileP, FileHeader, Len(FileHeader)) = Len(FileHeader)
throw = lread(FileP, bminfo.bmiHeader.biSize, Len(bminfo.bmiHeader))
throw = lread(FileP, bminfo.bmiColors(0), Len(bminfo.bmiColors(0)) * 256)
```

continued on next page

continued from previous page

```
For n = 0 To 255
    LogicalPal.palpalentry(n).peRed = bminfo.bmiColors(n).rgbRed
    LogicalPal.palpalentry(n).peGreen = bminfo.bmiColors(n).rgbGreen
    LogicalPal.palpalentry(n).peBlue = bminfo.bmiColors(n).rgbBlue
    If (n > 9) And (n < 246) Then
            LogicalPal.palpalentry(n).peFlags = Chr$(PC_RESERVED)
        Else
            LogicalPal.palpalentry(n).peFlags = Chr$(0)
    End If
Next n

LogicalPal.version = &H300
LogicalPal.nEntries = 256
pal = CreatePalette(LogicalPal)

ReDim bitdata(bminfo.bmiHeader.biSizeImage)
throw = hread(FileP, bitdata(0), bminfo.bmiHeader.biSizeImage)

Call lclose(FileP)

End Sub


Public Sub MakeWinGBit()

ReadBitmap

WGBminfo.bmiHeader.biSize = 40
WGBminfo.bmiHeader.biWidth = m_pict.ScaleWidth
WGBminfo.bmiHeader.biHeight = m_pict.ScaleHeight
WGBminfo.bmiHeader.biPlanes = 1
WGBminfo.bmiHeader.biBitCount = 8
WGBminfo.bmiHeader.biCompression = 0
WGBminfo.bmiHeader.biSizeImage = 0
WGBminfo.bmiHeader.biXPelsPerMeter = 0
WGBminfo.bmiHeader.biYPelsPerMeter = 0
WGBminfo.bmiHeader.biClrUsed = 256
WGBminfo.bmiHeader.biClrImportant = 0

hbitmap = WinGCreateBitmap(m_WinGDc, WGBminfo, psurface)
throw = SelectObject(m_WinGDc, hbitmap)

Call WinGSetDIBColorTable(m_WinGDc, 0, 256, bminfo.bmiColors(0))

End Sub

Public Sub setpal()
holdPal = SelectPalette(m_pict.hDC, pal, False)

throw = DeleteObject(holdPal)

Call RealizePalette(m_pict.hDC)

End Sub
```

10. The Transbits method copies the pixel data on to this WinG's bitmap surface and not on to the working device context for the scene. This is used to set up the background for the working device context and the copy of the background.

```
Public Sub Transbits()
BytesAsLong& = lstrcpy(bitdata(0), bitdata(0))
InfoAsLong& = lstrcpy(bminfo, bminfo)

Call TransparentDIBits(WGBminfo, ByVal psurface, 0, 0, ByVal BytesAsLong&, ↵
ByVal InfoAsLong&, 0, 0, 0, 1)

End Sub
```

11. Transbits2 copies this WinG bitmap's pixel data onto another WinG bitmap, represented by m_psurface.

```
Public Sub Transbits2(x, y)

BytesAsLong& = lstrcpy(bitdata(0), bitdata(0))
InfoAsLong& = lstrcpy(bminfo, bminfo)

Call TransparentDIBits(WGBminfo, ByVal m_psurface, x, y, ByVal BytesAsLong&, ↵
ByVal InfoAsLong&, 0, 0, 0, 0)

End Sub


Public Property Set picture(acontrol As Control)
Set m_pict = acontrol
End Property

Public Property Let wdc(n As Integer)
Let m_WinGDc = n
End Property

Public Property Let filename(s As String)
Let m_filename = s
End Property

Public Property Let surface(n As Long)
    m_psurface = n
End Property

Public Property Get surface() As Long
    surface = psurface
End Property

Private Sub Class_Terminate()
throw = DeleteObject(hbitmap)
End Sub
```

How It Works

In this How-To, several actions are taking place in the animated scene that are pulling on system resources. These include an animation, three sprites, background music, and a wave file. This demonstrates the benefits of WinG over standard GDI functions. Animated scenes developed using WinG tend to run more smoothly and more quickly because of the optimization for using bitmaps.

In the Timer function, several checks are done to see what actions should take place during the current timer tick. To slow down the chest opening and closing, on every fourth tick of the timer the next frame is shown. To accomplish this, a variable is used to count from 1 to 40. The mod 4 of the variable counter is used to indicate when the chest should be updated. To time the playing of the ding wave with the closing of the chest, the wave file is played on the frame before the chest is to be closed. By the time the ding wave has finished playing, the trunk is closed.

With each tick of the timer, both the green and the red fish are moved. Each has a different step distance to move with each tick. This gives the appearance of one fish moving more quickly than the other. The red fish moves in only one direction, from left to right. A check is done each time the fish is moved to see if it has crossed the right side of the picture box. If so, it is reset to begin moving from the left again.

Although there is only one timer in the project, it appears that each event is moving along its own time scale. The chest is animated on every fourth timer tick, with the ding wave played on the appropriate frame. The fish sprites each move at their own rate. By using one timer instead of several, less system overhead is used.

Comments

Because WinG provides speed and flexibility over the Windows GDI interface, multiple effects can be implemented in a scene. In Chapter 8, a full-featured animated scene will be developed.

7

LOW-LEVEL WINDOWS
MULTIMEDIA

7

LOW-LEVEL WINDOWS MULTIMEDIA

How do I...

In the previous chapters, the high-level multimedia extensions were used to play various multimedia file formats such as AVI, Wave, and MIDI. As one would expect, these high-level functions make accessing these files easy by hiding much of the technical underpinnings.

This chapter will explore the low-level Windows multimedia formats and tools. The basic foundation for the multimedia formats is the RIFF file format. How-To 7.1 will look specifically at the Wave RIFF file format. In the next three How-Tos, the low-level wave APIs will be used to play and manipulate Wave files. How-To 7.5 will demonstrate use of several of the low-level MIDI APIs.

Low-level control over playing Wave and MIDI data provides the type of detailed control over playing sounds that is needed for performing time-sensitive and precise tasks. Timing sounds to specific events such as mouse movements requires that the sound be started and stopped at a precise moment. With the sndPlaySound function and the MCI interface, the system must process the commands into the low-level calls. These low-level calls and techniques will be used in this chapter.

Several of the How-Tos will be implemented using Visual Basic 4.0's class feature. This will allow you to integrate many of the low-level features implemented in the chapter directly into your applications. As the examples in this chapter are laid out, you will notice that, to implement many of these tasks in Visual Basic 4.0, the Windows API functions relating to memory must be heavily relied on to solve some of the problems that will be encountered.

Windows APIs Covered			
midiOutOpen	midiOutShortMsg	midiOutClose	GlobalHandleToSel
MemoryRead	MemoryWrite	GlobalAlloc	GlobalFree
GlobalLock	GlobalUnlock	mmioOpen	mmioRead
mmioClose	mmioWrite	mmioDescend	mmioAscend
mmioSeek	mmioCreateChunk	waveOutOpen	waveOutClose
waveOutUnprepareHeader	waveOutPrepareHeader		

7.1 Build a Wave RIFF browser

RIFF files are a standard file format for storing a wide range of data. This example will explore the use of the RIFF file format for storing Wave data.

7.2 Play Wave files using low-level APIs

Often there is a need to have strong low-level control over the playing of Wave files. Precise control over when the wave file begins and ends playing can be important in applications such as games with actions that have corresponding sounds. To gain this greater degree of control, you must exhibit a greater degree of work and responsibility. This example will show how to allocate large memory blocks for the Wave data and how to use the low-level API functions to read the Wave file and play the data. The implementation will be built into a class that can be reused in your applications.

7.3 Add echoes to a Wave file

One popular audio-digital effect is to add echoes to a Wave file. By building on the methods developed in the last How-To, you can develop additional manipulations of the Wave data to add echoes to the Wave.

7.4 Play a Wave file backwards

Another popular and interesting digital effect is to play a Wave file backwards. This How-To will add several functions to the class developed in How-To 7.3 that will show how to reverse the data in a Wave file.

7.5 Play MIDI notes using low-level APIs

As with Wave files, there are a similar set of low-level APIs for accessing MIDI devices. This How-To demonstrates opening a MIDI device and playing notes directly from your application.

7.1 How do I...
Build a Wave RIFF browser?

Problem

I would like to be able to browse the contents of Wave files that are in the RIFF file format. This will allow me to make determinations about the contents and format of a Wave file. This will be important so that low-level manipulations of the Wave data can be done properly.

Technique

The Windows Multimedia Extensions provide a set of functions that allow you to browse through RIFF format files.

Steps

Open and run 7-1.VBP. The running program appears as shown in Figure 7-1-1.

To understand the basics of the program, you must understand the basic format of RIFF files. RIFF is an acronym for Resource Interchange File Format. RIFF provides a general format for storing different types of data. Several common formats that can be included in a RIFF file are .WAV (digital audio), .PAL (palette files), and .AVI (video for Windows). RIFF files are composed of "Chunks" that hold specific data. Each RIFF file begins with a standard RIFF chunk that has the 4-byte string designation of RIFF. Figure 7-1-2 depicts a general RIFF file structure.

The primary chunk for the file is the RIFF chunk. Each chunk can contain subchunks. Figure 7-1-2 depicts two subchunks within the primary RIFF chunk. Each chunk contains a header of the following format:

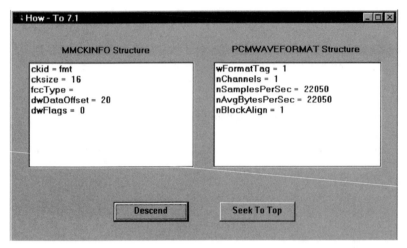

Figure 7-1-1 The FMT and PCMWave structures

```
Type MMCKINFO
    ckid As String * 4              '  chunk ID
    cksize As Long          '  chunk size
    fccType As String * 4   '  form type or list type
    dwDataOffset As Long    '  offset of data portion of chunk
    dwFlags As Long         '  flags used by MMIO functions
End Type
```

For the primary RIFF chunk, the ckid field will be set to RIFF and the fccType will be Wave. Figure 7-1-3 depicts a typical Wave format file.

A primary RIFF chunk indicates that the file is in RIFF format and the data contained in the RIFF file is Wave data. The first subchunk is the FMT chunk, which contains the Wave format data. The second subchunk is the Wave data itself. By using the Windows Multimedia I/O extensions, the different subchunks of the Wave format can be walked through and analyzed.

The program allows you to descend into the various chunks of the Wave file using the Descend button. The left-hand list box shows the chunk MMCKINFO data; the second list box shows Wave format data when the FMT chunk is accessed. To go back to the top of the RIFF file, use the Seek button.

1. Create a new project named 7-1-1.VBP. Add the objects and properties listed in Table 7-1-1 to the form and save the form as 7-1.FRM.

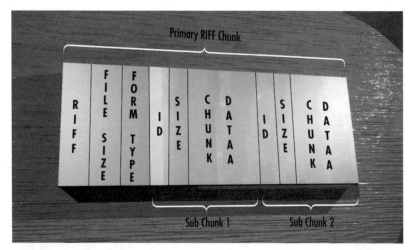

Figure 7-1-2 Basic RIFF file structure

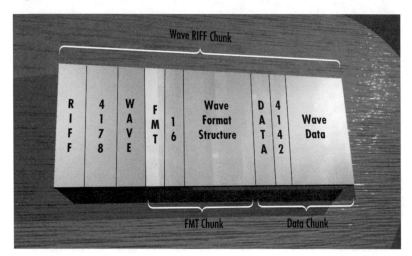

Figure 7-1-3 The wave RIFF structure

Table 7-1-1 The form's objects and properties

OBJECT	PROPERTY	SETTING
Form	Name	Form1
	Auto3D	-1 'True
	Caption	"How-To 7.1"
ListBox	Name	PCMList

continued on next page

continued from previous page

OBJECT	PROPERTY	SETTING
ListBox	Name	ChunkList
CommandButton	Name	Seek
	Caption	"Seek To Top"
	Font	
	name	"Arial"
CommandButton	Name	Descend
	Caption	"Descend"
	Font	
	name	"Arial"
Label	Name	MMCKINFOLabel
	AutoSize	-1 'True
	Caption	"MMCKINFO Structure"
Label	Name	PCMLabel
	AutoSize	-1 'True
	Caption	"PCMWAVEFORMAT Structure"

2. Open a new module called 7-1.BAS and add the following code.

```
'  Chunk Info
Type MMCKINFO
    ckid As String * 4      '  chunk ID
    cksize As Long          '  chunk size
    fccType As String * 4   '  form type or list type
    dwDataOffset As Long    '  offset of data portion of chunk
    dwFlags As Long         '  flags used by MMIO functions
End Type

'  general waveform format structure (information common to all formats)
Type WAVEFORMAT
    wFormatTag As Integer   '  format type
    nChannels As Integer    '  number of channels (i.e. mono, stereo, etc.)
    nSamplesPerSec As Long  '  sample rate
    nAvgBytesPerSec As Long '  for buffer estimation
    nBlockAlign As Integer  '  block size of data
End Type

'  specific waveform format structure for PCM data
Type PCMWAVEFORMAT
    wf As WAVEFORMAT
    wBitsPerSample As Integer
```

```
End Type
```

3. Add the following code to the general declarations section of Form1. The proper declarations are made for the multimedia I/O functions.

```
'  These are the standard RIFF functions
Private Declare Function mmioOpen Lib "MMSystem" (ByVal szFilename As ↵
String, ByVal lpMMIOINFO As Any, ByVal dwOpenFlags As Long) As Integer

Private Declare Function mmioDescend Lib "MMSystem" (ByVal hmmio As Integer, ↵
lpck As MMCKINFO, ByVal lpckParent As Any, ByVal uFlags As Integer) As Integer

Private Declare Function mmioRead Lib "MMSystem" (ByVal hmmio As Integer, pch ↵
As Any, ByVal cch As Long) As Long

Private Declare Function mmioSeek Lib "MMSystem" (ByVal hmmio As Integer, ↵
ByVal lOffset As Long, ByVal iOrigin As Integer) As Long

Private Declare Function mmioClose Lib "MMSystem" (ByVal hmmio As Integer, ↵
ByVal uFlags As Integer) As Integer

'  Handle to the file
Dim hmmio As Integer

'  FMTInfo will hold the Chunk Info
Dim FMTInfo As MMCKINFO

'  PCMWaveData will hold the wave data information
Dim PCMWaveData As PCMWAVEFORMAT
```

4. Add the following code to the general declarations section of Form1. This routine handles descending into the different RIFF file chunks.

```
Private Sub Descend_Click()

'  Descent into the first chunk
er% = mmioDescend(hmmio, FMTInfo, 0&, 0)

'  Clear the list
ChunkList.Clear

'  We check to see if there was an error in reading
'  the files.
If er% = 0 Then

    '  We will report the information in the FMTInfo Structure
    ChunkList.AddItem "ckid = " + FMTInfo.ckid
    ChunkList.AddItem "cksize = " + Str$(FMTInfo.cksize)
    ChunkList.AddItem "fccType = " + FMTInfo.fccType
    ChunkList.AddItem "dwDataOffset = " + Str$(FMTInfo.dwDataOffset)
    ChunkList.AddItem "dwFlags = " + Str$(FMTInfo.dwFlags)

    '  We will clear PCMList
    PCMList.Clear
```

continued on next page

continued from previous page

```
     ' If we are in the Format chunk, we will read the
     ' wave data format into the PCMWaveData structure
    If FMTInfo.ckid = "fmt " Then

         ' Read the data
        Throw = mmioRead(hmmio, PCMWaveData, FMTInfo.cksize)

         ' We will report the wave data in the second list box
        PCMList.AddItem "wFormatTag = " + Str$(PCMWaveData.wf.wFormatTag)
        PCMList.AddItem "nChannels = " + Str$(PCMWaveData.wf.nChannels)

        PCMList.AddItem "nSamplesPerSec = " + ↵
            Str$(PCMWaveData.wf.nSamplesPerSec)

        PCMList.AddItem "nAvgBytesPerSec = " + ↵
            Str$(PCMWaveData.wf.nAvgBytesPerSec)

        PCMList.AddItem "nBlockAlign = " + Str$(PCMWaveData.wf.nBlockAlign)

    End If


Else

     ' If there was an error and it was 265, then we have
     ' reached the end of the file
    If er% = 265 Then
        ChunkList.AddItem "End of file."
    End If

End If

End Sub
```

5. The Form_Load procedure handles setting up the program to read the RIFF file.

```
Private Sub Form_Load()

'  Set the wave file
FileName = "C:\windows\media\chord.wav"

'  Open the wave file
hmmio = mmioOpen(FileName, 0&, 0&)

'  If the file was not opened, we will
'  report it to the user.
If hmmio = 0 Then
    MsgBox "Unable to open " + FileName
    Throw% = mmioClose(hmmio, 0)
    End
End If

End Sub
```

6. The Form_Unload procedure handles closing the open Wave file.

```
Private Sub form_unload(Cancel As Integer)

'  Close the file.
Throw% = mmioClose(hmmio, 0)

End Sub
```

7. The Seek button will seek to the top of the file.

```
Private Sub Seek_Click()

'  Clear out the lists
ChunkList.Clear
PCMList.Clear

'  Seek to the beginning of the file
Throw% = mmioSeek(hmmio, 0, 0)

End Sub
```

How It Works

The key to understanding this How-To is the Multimedia I/O extensions. Table 7-1-2 is a list of the various key functions used to manipulate RIFF files.

Table 7-1-2 The multimedia file I/O functions

FUNCTION	DESCRIPTION
mmioAscend	Moves from a child (or sub) chunk to a parent chunk
mmioDescend	Descends to a child (or sub) chunk from a parent chunk
mmioOpen	Opens a file and returns a file pointer
mmioClose	Closes a file
mmioSeek	Moves to a new location in a RIFF file
mmioRead	Reads data from a RIFF file
mmioWrite	Writes data to a RIFF file
mmioCreateChunk	Creates a chunk in the RIFF file

The parameters of the functions are important to understand to learn how to pass information into and out of the RIFF structure. Table 7-1-3 lists the functions used in this How-To and a description of their parameters.

Table 7-1-3 The multimedia file I/O function parameters

FUNCTION	PARAMETER	DESCRIPTION
mmioOpen	ByVal szFilename as string	The file name
	ByVal lpMMIOINFO as any	Set to 0
	ByVal dwOpenFlags as long	Specifies how the file will be opened. These include
		MMIO_READ, MMIO_WRITE, MMIO_CREATE,
		MMIO_READWRITE
mmioDescend	ByVal hmmio as integer	The RIFF file pointer from mmioOpen
	lpck as MMCKINFO	The data structure to read the chunk header into
	ByVal lpckParent as any	Normally set to 0.
	ByVal uFlags as integer	Normally set to 0
mmioAscend	ByVal hmmio as integer	The RIFF file pointer from mmioOpen
	lpck As MMCKINFO	The chunk descended from
	ByVal uFlags as integer	Not used
mmioRead	ByVal hmmio as integer	The RIFF file pointer from mmioOpen
	pch as any	A pointer to a data structure to read the information
		into; in this example it is the PCMwave data structure
	ByVal cch as long	The number of bytes to read
mmioWrite	ByVal hmmio as integer	The RIFF file pointer from mmioOpen
	pch as any	A pointer to a data structure to write from
	ByVal cch as long	The number of bytes to write
mmioSeek	ByVal hmmio as integer	The RIFF file pointer from mmioOpen
	ByVal lOffset as long	The number of positive or negative bytes to move
	ByVal iOrigin as integer	Specifies where to seek from; SEEK_SET for the
		beginning, SEEK_CUR for the current position, and
		SEEK_END for the end
mmioClose	ByVal hmmio as integer	The RIFF file pointer from mmioOpen
	ByVal uFlags as integer	Normally set to 0
mmioCreateChunk	ByVal hmmio as integer	The RIFF file pointer from mmioOpen
	lpck as MMCKINFO	The filled in chunk header structure
	ByVal uFlags as integer	Normally set to 0

In this How-To, the mmioDescend, mmioOpen, mmioClose, and mmioSeek functions are used to browse the Wave RIFF file. The other functions will be used in the next three How-Tos. When the Descend command button is selected, the mmioDescend function is called. The header information of the chunk is read into the MMCKINFO data structure. From this data structure, the type of chunk you are reading can be identified and information about the chunk can be retrieved. For example, if the ckid field is set to format (FMT), the chunk contains information on the Wave data. This information can then be read into the PCMWAVEFORMAT data structure. This information includes the number of channels and the sample rate. To restart the browsing of the data, the top of the file is moved using the mmioSeek function when the Seek to Top button is clicked.

Comments

In the next three How-Tos, the ability to browse through Wave RIFF files will be built on to perform various manipulations of the Wave data.

7.2 How do I...
Play Wave files using low-level APIs?

COMPLEXITY: ADVANCED

Problem

The MCI command string interface provides a simple method for playing Wave files, but there are times when I need greater control over accessing and playing Wave files. For example, I need to time sounds closely to a user's action. It is important to have the sound play when the action is finished. The MCI interface takes time to be parsed and the timing is off. How can I do this using the low-level wave APIs?

Technique

Using the techniques for browsing through Wave RIFF files elucidated in the last How-To, you will add several memory functions along with low-level wave APIs to play Wave data from a Wave file.

Steps

Open and run 7-2.VBP. The running program appears as shown in Figure 7-2-1.
   To open the Wave file, click on the appropriate command button. To play the Wave file, select the play button.

1. Create a new project named 7-2.VBP. Add the objects and properties listed in Table 7-2-1 and save the form as 7-2.FRM.

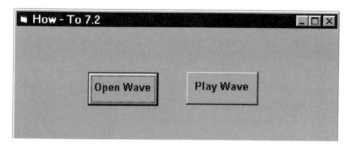

Figure 7-2-1 The form at runtime

Table 7-2-1 The form's objects and properties

OBJECT	PROPERTY	SETTING
Form	Name	Form1
	Caption	"How-To 7.2"
CommandButton	Name	Play
	Caption	"Play Wave"
	Font	
	name	"Arial"
CommandButton	Name	Open
	Caption	"Open Wave"
	Font	
	name	"Arial"

2. Create a new class module called WAVETOOL.CLS and add the following code to the general declarations section. The data structures, multimedia I/O functions, and data members of the class are declared here.

```
' general waveform format structure (information common to all formats)
Private Type WAVEFORMAT
    wFormatTag As Integer      '  format type
    nChannels As Integer       '  number of channels (i.e. mono, stereo, etc.)
    nSamplesPerSec As Long     '  sample rate
    nAvgBytesPerSec As Long    '  for buffer estimation
    nBlockAlign As Integer     '  block size of data
End Type

' specific waveform format structure for PCM data
Private Type PCMWAVEFORMAT
```

```
        wf As WAVEFORMAT
        wBitsPerSample As Integer
End Type


'  wave data block header
Private Type WAVEHDR
        lpData As Long                    '  pointer to locked data buffer
        dwBufferLength As Long            '  length of data buffer
        dwBytesRecorded As Long           '  used for input only
        dwUser As Long                    '  for client's use
        dwFlags As Long                   '  assorted flags (see defines)
        dwLoops As Long                   '  loop control counter
        wavehdr_tag As Long               '  reserved for driver
        reserved As Long                  '  reserved for driver
End Type


' RIFF chunk information data structure
Private Type MMCKINFO
        ckid As String * 4
        cksize As Long
        fccType As String * 4
        dwDataOffset As Long
        dwFlags As Long
End Type


'  Multimedia File I/O functions for reading the
'  WAVE RIFF file
Private Declare Function mmioRead Lib "MMSystem" (ByVal m_hmmio As Integer, ↵
pch As Any, ByVal cch As Long) As Long

Private Declare Function mmioReadPtrVal Lib "MMSystem" Alias "mmioRead" ↵
(ByVal m_hmmio As Integer, ByVal HugePtr As Long, ByVal cch As Long) As Long

Private Declare Function mmioOpen Lib "MMSystem" (ByVal szFilename As String, ↵
ByVal lpMMIOINFO As Any, ByVal dwOpenFlags As Long) As Integer

Private Declare Function mmioClose Lib "MMSystem" (ByVal m_hmmio As Integer, ↵
ByVal wFlags As Integer) As Integer

Private Declare Function mmioDescend Lib "MMSystem" (ByVal m_hmmio As ↵
Integer, lpck As MMCKINFO, ByVal lpckParent As Any, ByVal uFlags As Integer) ↵
As Integer


'  Low Level WAVE API functions to play the wave file
Private Declare Function waveOutOpen Lib "MMSystem" (lpWaveout As Integer, ↵
ByVal UINT As Integer, lpformat As Any, ByVal dwCallback As Long, ByVal ↵
dwInstance As Long, ByVal flags As Long) As Integer

Private Declare Function waveOutClose Lib "MMSystem" (ByVal hWaveOut As ↵
Integer) As Integer

Private Declare Function waveOutPrepareHeader Lib "MMSystem" (ByVal hWaveOut ↵
As Integer, WH As WAVEHDR, ByVal uSize As Integer) As Integer

Private Declare Function waveOutUnprepareHeader Lib "MMSystem" (ByVal ↵
```

continued on next page

continued from previous page

```
hWaveOut As Integer, WH As WAVEHDR, ByVal uSize As Integer) As Integer

Private Declare Function waveOutWrite Lib "MMSystem" (ByVal hWaveOut As ↵
Integer, WH1 As WAVEHDR, ByVal uSize As Integer) As Integer

'   Constants for the various functions
Const MMIO_READ = &H0                        '   open file for reading only
Const WHDR_DONE = &H1                        '   done bit

'   Functions used for reading the Wave data
'   into memory.
Private Declare Function GlobalAlloc Lib "Kernel" (ByVal wFlags As Integer,↵
ByVal dwBytes As Long) As Integer

Private Declare Function GlobalFree Lib "Kernel" (ByVal hMem As Integer) ↵
As Integer

Private Declare Function GlobalLock Lib "Kernel" (ByVal hMem As Integer) As Long

Private Declare Function GlobalUnlock Lib "Kernel" (ByVal hMem As Integer) ↵
As Integer

'   Constants for the memory functions
Const GMEM_MOVEABLE = &H2
Const GMEM_ZEROINIT = &H40

'   m_WaveHeader will be used to hold the wave data
Dim m_WaveHeader As WAVEHDR

'   m_PCMWave will hold the information on the
'   format of the wave data.
Dim m_PCMWave As PCMWAVEFORMAT

'   m_WaveData will hold the pointer to the
'   allocated memory block
Dim m_WaveData As Integer

'   m_filename holds the name of the wave file
Dim m_filename As String

'   m_hmmio is the handle to the wave file
Dim m_hmmio As Integer
```

3. The file name property will take in the name and location of the Wave file to be opened and played.

```
Public Property Let filename(file As String)

'   Set the filename for the wave file
Let m_filename = file

End Property
```

4. Add the following function to the general declarations section of the form. ReadWave handles getting information on the Wave data and reads the Wave data into memory.

```
Public Sub readwave()

'  Declare Chunk for holding the Chunk Information
Dim Chunk As MMCKINFO

'  Open the file for reading.
m_hmmio = mmioOpen(m_filename, 0&, 0&)

'  Read the RIFF Chunk
Throw = mmioDescend(m_hmmio, Chunk, 0&, 0)

' Read the FMT Chunk
Throw = mmioDescend(m_hmmio, Chunk, 0&, 0)

' Read the m_m_PCMWave Data
Throw = mmioRead(m_hmmio, m_PCMWave, Chunk.cksize)

' Descend to the Data Chunk
Throw = mmioDescend(m_hmmio, Chunk, 0&, 0)

'  Allocate the memory to read the data
m_WaveData = GlobalAlloc(GMEM_MOVEABLE Or GMEM_ZEROINIT, Chunk.cksize)

'  Get a Ptr to the data.  GlobalLock will notify the
'  system to keep the memory from being moved.
WaveDataPtr = GlobalLock(m_WaveData)

'  We will now read the data into the memory block.  Note that we have
'  a pointer to the memory.  We have a special version of mmioRead that
'  will accept a pointer to the memory block instead of the actual data
Throw = mmioReadPtrVal(m_hmmio, WaveDataPtr, Chunk.cksize)

'  We will now unlock the data
Throw = GlobalUnlock(m_WaveData)

'  We will set the size of the data in the
'  m_WaveHeader data structure
m_WaveHeader.dwBufferLength = Chunk.cksize

End Sub
```

5. The data from the ReadWave function is used in conjunction with the low-level API functions to play the Wave data.

```
Public Sub PlayWave()

'  HWav will hold the handle to the wave device
Dim HWav As Integer

'  Set the m_WaveHeader data to the locked memory
'  block
```

continued on next page

continued from previous page

```
m_WaveHeader.lpData = GlobalLock(m_WaveData)

' Open the wave device
Throw = waveOutOpen(HWav, 0, m_PCMWave, 0, 0, 0)

' Prepare the Header of the Wave Data
Throw = waveOutPrepareHeader(HWav, m_WaveHeader, Len(m_WaveHeader))

' Send the Wave data to the Wave Device
Throw = waveOutWrite(HWav, m_WaveHeader, Len(m_WaveHeader))

'  When the wave file is finished playing, the WHDR_DONE
'  bit of the m_WaveHeader.dwFlags field will be set.  This
'  is done to ensure that the wave file has finished playing
'  before we move on.
Do Until (m_WaveHeader.dwFlags And WHDR_DONE)
Loop

' Unprepare the Header of the Wave Data
Throw = waveOutUnprepareHeader(HWav, m_WaveHeader, Len(m_WaveHeader))

' Close the Wave Device
Throw = waveOutClose(HWav)

'  Unlock the Memory
Throw = GlobalUnlock(m_WaveData)

End Sub
```

6. When the user is done playing the file, it is important to free up the allocated memory.

```
Public Sub CloseWave()

'  Before we free up the memory, we need
'  to ensure that it was calculated
If m_WaveData <> 0 Then

    '  Free up the memory
    Throw = GlobalFree(m_WaveData)

End If

End Sub
```

7. Add the following to the general declarations section of the form. The WaveTools class is declared globally.

```
Dim wave As WaveTools
```

8. When the form is loaded, a new class object is created.

```
Private Sub Form_Load()
```

```
Set wave = New WaveTools

End Sub
```

9. When the application is exited, it is important to call the CloseWave function of the class. This will free up the memory allocated for the Wave data.

```
Private Sub Form_Unload(Cancel As Integer)

wave.closewave

End Sub
```

10. When the open button is selected, the file name property of the class is set.

```
Private Sub Open_Click()

'  Set the name of the wave file
filename = App.Path + "\roostM8.wav"

Let wave.filename = filename

'  Read the wave file
wave.readwave filename

End Sub
```

11. When the play button is selected, the PlayWave function of the class is called.

```
Private Sub Play_Click()

wave.playwave

End Sub
```

How It Works

The functions developed to perform the low-level Wave manipulations have been placed into the WaveTools class to allow easy access from your applications. A brief scan of the project's form code will give you the basics of how the class is to be implemented.

The basics for browsing RIFF files developed in the last How-To are found in the beginning of the ReadWave function. Once the data chunk is reached, the Wave data must be read into memory. A Visual Basic 4.0 string can hold up to 64K of memory, but Wave data will often exceed this limit. As demonstrated in Chapter 5, the Windows API memory functions will be used to read in the Wave data. Table 7-2-2 is a brief overview of the memory functions used.

Table 7-2-2 Memory functions

FUNCTION	DESCRIPTION
GlobalAlloc	Allocates the specified block of memory
GlobalFree	Frees up the specified memory block
GlobalLock	Locks the memory block from being moved by the system
GlobalUnlock	Unlocks the memory block from being moved by the system

When you make the final mmioDescend call in ReadWave, you are positioned at the data chunk in the RIFF file. The chunk header information contains the size of the data in the Chunk.cksize field. You need to allocate a memory block that is large enough to hold the data. The following is the command used to allocate the memory:

```
WaveData = GlobalAlloc(GMEM_MOVEABLE Or GMEM_ZEROINIT, Chunk.cksize)
```

The WaveData variable contains a handle to the memory block. The GMEM_MOVEABLE flag tells the system that the memory block is moveable for memory management. The GMEM_ZEROINIT flag initializes the memory to zero. You now have a memory block available into which to read the Wave data. Before the data is read into the memory, it needs to be locked with the GlobalLock function, so that the memory management system does not move it during access. The GlobalLock function returns a pointer to the data in memory, rather than to the memory location itself. Once the data is read into memory, the GlobalUnlock function is used to allow the memory to be moved by the system.

At the end of the ReadWave function, the data is read into memory and the appropriate information on the Wave data is stored in a MMCKINFO data structure. Note that at the end of the ReadWave function, the WaveHeader.dwBufferLength field is set to the Chunk.cksize field. This contains the size of the data and is used in low-level Wave functions.

To play the Wave data read from the RIFF file, several low-level Wave functions are necessary to prepare the Wave device and send the data. Tables 7-2-3 and 7-2-4 are overviews of the functions and their parameters.

Table 7-2-3 Low-level Wave functions

FUNCTION	DESCRIPTION
waveOutOpen	Opens a Wave audio device
waveOutClose	Closes a Wave audio device
waveOutPrepareHeader	Prepares data to play on a Wave audio device
waveOutUnprepareHeader	Releases data containing Wave audio data
waveOutWrite	Sends Wave data to the Wave audio device

Table 7-2-4 Low-level Wave functions and their parameters

FUNCTION	PARAMETER	DESCRIPTION
waveOutOpen	lpWaveout as integer	This variable contains the handle to the device
	ByVal UINT as integer	The Device ID of the device (usually 0)
	lpformat as any	PCMWave data structure
	ByVal dwCallback as long	Call back functions - usually not used from VB4.0
	ByVal dwInstance as long	Set to 0
	ByVal flags as long	Set to 0
waveOutClose	ByVal hWaveOut as integer	The waveOutOpen handle of the Wave device
waveOutPrepareHeader	ByVal hWaveOut as integer	The waveOutOpen handle of the Wave device
	WH as WAVEHDR	Header of the Wave data (WaveHdr Structure)
	ByVal uSize as integer	The size of the structure
waveOutUnprepareHeader	ByVal hWaveOut as integer	The waveOutOpen handle of the Wave device
	WH as WAVEHDR	Header of the Wave data (WaveHdr Structure)
	ByVal uSize as integer	The size of the structure
waveOutWrite	ByVal hWaveOut as integer	The waveOutOpen handle of the Wave device
	WH1 as WAVEHDR	Header of the Wave data (WaveHdr Structure)
	ByVal uSize as integer	The size of the structure

These are the primary functions used to play Wave data. It is important to note that the waveOutPrepareHeader and waveOutUnprepareHeader functions need to have the Wave data passed in a memory block allocated by GlobalAlloc and locked by GlobalLock. The WAVEHDR structure contains the lpData field, which contains the locked value returned from GlobalLock.

When the play button is selected, the following steps are used to play the Wave data from the ReadWave function.

1. Set up the WaveHeader that will be sent to the Wave API functions. To do this, the memory needs to be locked using the GlobalLock function. The WaveHeader.lpData member is set to the pointer returned from the GlobalLock function.

2. Open the Wave device. Note that in the waveOutOpen call, the PCMWaveFormat data structure that was filled in the ReadWave function is sent to the function. This structure contains information on the format of the Wave data.

3. Copy the Wave data to the output device. This is done with the waveOutPrepareHeader function, which prepares the device for playing of the data.

4. Use the waveOutWrite function to play the data.

5. Wait until the data is finished playing. This is done by checking the WaveHeader.dwFlags field to see if the WHDR_DONE bit has been set. When the flag is set, the data has finished playing.

6. Call the waveOutUnprepareHeader function to free up the memory from the device.

7. Close the device using the waveOutClose function.

8. Use the GlobalUnlock function to release the memory.

When the program is unloaded, it is important to free up the allocated memory for further use. It is also important to note that the Wave API functions expect the data sent to them to have been allocated by GlobalAlloc and locked by the GlobalLock function.

Comments

The next two How-Tos will further explore manipulations of the actual Wave data.

7.3 How do I...
Add echoes to a Wave file?

COMPLEXITY: ADVANCED

Problem

I would like to be able to add echoes to my Wave files. This can provide unique and interesting effects to my existing Wave files.

Technique

This example will expand on the techniques developed in the last two How-Tos, and add several functions to handle building the Wave echoes and writing out the data to a new file.

Steps

Open and run 7-3.VBP. The running program appears as shown in Figure 7-3-1.

Depending on the format of the Wave file, the method for building the echo will vary. The sound of a rooster crowing is provided in the four most common formats, mono 8 bit, mono 16 bit, stereo 8 bit, and stereo 16 bit. Select the Add Echo button to build the echoes for the specified file format. To play the new file (stored in

Figure 7-3-1 The form at runtime

ECHO.WAV), select the Play button. Note that the program gives you feedback on where in the process the program is.

1. Create a new project called 7-3.VBP. Add the objects and properties listed in Table 7-3-1 to Form1 and save the form as 7-3.FRM.

Table 7-3-1 The form's objects and properties

OBJECT	PROPERTY	SETTING
Form	Name	Form1
	Caption	"How-To 7.3"
TextBox	Name	Text1
OptionButton	Name	Option4
	Caption	"16 Bit Stereo Rooster"
OptionButton	Name	Option3
	Caption	"8 Bit Stereo Rooster"
OptionButton	Name	Option2
	Caption	"16 Bit Mono Rooster"

continued on next page

continued from previous page

OBJECT	PROPERTY	SETTING
OptionButton	Name	Option1
	Caption	"8 Bit Mono Rooster"
CommandButton	Name	Command2
	Caption	"Play"
	Font	
	name	"Arial"
CommandButton	Name	Command1
	Caption	"Add Echo"
	Font	
	name	"Arial"
Label	Name	Label1
	AutoSize	-1 'True
	Caption	"Status"

2. Create a new class module called WAVETLS.CLS and add the following code to the general declarations section. The data structures, multimedia I/O functions, and data members of the class are declared here.

```
' general waveform format structure (information common to all formats)
Private Type WAVEFORMAT
    wFormatTag As Integer        ' format type
    nChannels As Integer         ' number of channels (i.e. mono, stereo, etc.)
    nSamplesPerSec As Long       ' sample rate
    nAvgBytesPerSec As Long      ' for buffer estimation
    nBlockAlign As Integer       ' block size of data
End Type

' specific waveform format structure for PCM data
Private Type PCMWaveFORMAT
    wf As WAVEFORMAT
    wBitsPerSample As Integer
End Type

' wave data block header
Private Type WAVEHDR
    lpData As Long               ' pointer to locked data buffer
    dwbufferlength As Long       ' length of data buffer
    dwBytesRecorded As Long      ' used for input only
    dwUser As Long               ' for client's use
    dwFlags As Long              ' assorted flags (see defines)
    dwLoops As Long              ' loop control counter
    wavehdr_tag As Long          ' reserved for driver
```

```
        reserved As Long                '  reserved for driver
End Type


' RIFF chunk information data structure
Private Type MMCKINFO
    ckid As String * 4
    cksize As Long
    fccType As String * 4
    dwDataOffset As Long
    dwFlags As Long
End Type


'  These are the datatypes to represent the wave
'  data of the various formats
Private Type Mono8Data
    Channel1 As String * 1
End Type


Private Type Stereo8Data
    Channel1 As String * 1
    Channel2 As String * 1
End Type


Private Type Mono16Data
    Channel1 As Integer
End Type


Private Type Stereo16Data
    Channel1 As Integer
    Channel2 As Integer
End Type


'  These are the functions used to read and write
'  the wave RIFF files
Private Declare Function mmioRead Lib "MMSYSTEM" (ByVal m_hmmio As Integer, ↵
pch As Any, ByVal cch As Long) As Long

Private Declare Function mmioReadPtrVal Lib "MMSYSTEM" Alias "mmioRead" ↵
(ByVal m_hmmio As Integer, ByVal HugePtr As Long, ByVal cch As Long) As Long

Private Declare Function mmioOpen Lib "MMSYSTEM" (ByVal szm_filename As ↵
String, ByVal lpMMIOINFO As Any, ByVal dwOpenFlags As Long) As Integer

Private Declare Function mmioClose Lib "MMSYSTEM" (ByVal m_hmmio As ↵
Integer, ByVal wFlags As Integer) As Integer

Private Declare Function mmioDescend Lib "MMSYSTEM" (ByVal m_hmmio As ↵
Integer, lpck As MMCKINFO, ByVal lpckParent As Any, ByVal uFlags As Integer) ↵
As Integer

Private Declare Function mmioAscend Lib "MMSYSTEM" (ByVal m_hmmio As Integer, ↵
lpck As MMCKINFO, ByVal uFlags As Integer) As Integer

Private Declare Function mmioWrite Lib "MMSYSTEM" (ByVal m_hmmio As Integer, ↵
pch As Any, ByVal cch As Long) As Long
```

continued on next page

continued from previous page

```
Private Declare Function mmioWritePtr Lib "MMSYSTEM" Alias "mmioWrite" (ByVal ↵
m_hmmio As Integer, ByVal HugePtr As Long, ByVal cch As Long) As Long

Private Declare Function mmioCreateChunk Lib "MMSYSTEM" (ByVal m_hmmio As ↵
Integer, lpck As MMCKINFO, ByVal uFlags As Integer) As Integer

' These functions are used to play the wave file
Private Declare Function waveOutOpen Lib "MMSYSTEM" (lpWaveout As Integer, ↵
ByVal UINT As Integer, lpformat As Any, ByVal dwCallback As Long, ByVal ↵
dwInstance As Long, ByVal flags As Long) As Integer

Private Declare Function waveOutClose Lib "MMSYSTEM" (ByVal hWaveOut As ↵
Integer) As Integer

Private Declare Function waveOutPrepareHeader Lib "MMSYSTEM" (ByVal hWaveOut ↵
As Integer, wh As WAVEHDR, ByVal uSize As Integer) As Integer

Private Declare Function waveOutUnprepareHeader Lib "MMSYSTEM" (ByVal ↵
hWaveOut As Integer, wh As WAVEHDR, ByVal uSize As Integer) As Integer

Private Declare Function waveOutWrite Lib "MMSYSTEM" (ByVal hWaveOut As ↵
Integer, WH1 As WAVEHDR, ByVal uSize As Integer) As Integer

' This flag is used to open the wave file
' for reading and writing
Const MMIO_CREATE = &H1000                    ' create new file (or truncate file)
Const MMIO_CREATERIFF = &H20                  ' mmioCreateChunk: make a LIST chunk

' read/write mode numbers (bit field MMIO_RWMODE)
Const MMIO_READ = &H0                         ' open file for reading only
Const MMIO_WRITE = &H1                        ' open file for writing only

' This lets us know that the wave file
' is finished playing
Const WHDR_DONE = &H1

' These functions are used to allocate
' memory for the wave data
Private Declare Function GlobalAlloc Lib "Kernel" (ByVal wFlags As Integer,↵
ByVal dwBytes As Long) As Integer

Private Declare Function GlobalHandleToSel Lib "ToolHelp.DLL" (ByVal hMem ↵
As Integer) As Integer

Private Declare Function MemoryWrite Lib "ToolHelp.DLL" (ByVal wSel As ↵
Integer,  ByVal dwOffset As Long, lpvBuf As Any, ByVal dwcb As Long) As Long

Private Declare Function MemoryRead Lib "ToolHelp.DLL" (ByVal wSel As ↵
Integer, ByVal dwOffset As Long, lpvBuf As Any, ByVal dwcb As Long) As Long

Private Declare Function GlobalFree Lib "Kernel" (ByVal hMem As Integer) ↵
As Integer

Private Declare Function GlobalLock Lib "Kernel" (ByVal hMem As Integer) As Long
```

```
Private Declare Function GlobalUnlock Lib "Kernel" (ByVal hMem As Integer) ↵
As Integer

'  Flags for the GlobalAlloc function.  This
'  will allow the memory to be moveable for
'  memory management.
Const GMEM_MOVEABLE = &H2

'  m_WaveHeader will be used to hold the
'  wave data and is accessed in the wave
'  playing functions.
Dim m_WaveHeader As WAVEHDR

'  m_PCMWave will hold the wave information
Dim m_PCMWave As PCMWaveFORMAT

'  m_WaveData will hold the pointer to
'  the global memory block
Dim m_WaveData As Integer

'  m_WTYPE will hold the type of wave file
Dim m_WTYPE As String

'  Holds the wave filename
Dim m_filename As String

'  m_hmmio will be the handle to the wave file
Dim m_hmmio As Integer

'  These will hold the information on
'  the chunks orignally read.  This will
'  be updated and rewritten in the writewave
'  function
Dim m_RIFFchunk As MMCKINFO
Dim m_FMTchunk As MMCKINFO
Dim m_DATAchunk As MMCKINFO
```

3. Each of the following four routines handles adding echoes to the specified Wave file format. Note that these are private routines that are only accessible from within the class.

```
Private Sub BuildM16Echo(selector)

'  Mono16 and OrgMono16 will be used to read and
'  access the wave data.  Note the data structure consists
'  of one integer for reading the 16 bit data.
Dim Mono16 As Mono16Data
Dim OrgMono16 As Mono16Data

'  Set the data to 0
OrgMono16.Channel1 = 0

'  Set the EchoLength to two times the samples per second
'  this will set the starting point of the echo
```

continued on next page

continued from previous page

```
EchoLength = m_PCMWave.wf.nSamplesPerSec * 2


'  We are going to end the echo
EndData = m_WaveHeader.dwbufferlength + EchoLength * 2


' Initialize the memory block to the mid value of
'  an integer (0)
For N = m_WaveHeader.dwbufferlength To EndData Step 2
     throw = MemoryWrite(selector, N, OrgMono16, 2)
Next N


'  We now average the move through the memory data
For N = EchoLength To EndData Step 2

     '  Read the data starting at echo length
     throw = MemoryRead(selector, N, Mono16, 2)

     '  We read the original wave data
     throw = MemoryRead(selector, N - EchoLength, OrgMono16, 2)

     '  We average the data together
     Mono16.Channel1 = Mono16.Channel1 / 2 + OrgMono16.Channel1 / 2

     '  We write the new data to memory
     throw = MemoryWrite(selector, N, Mono16, 2)
Next N


'  We set the new length of the data
m_WaveHeader.dwbufferlength = m_WaveHeader.dwbufferlength + EchoLength * 2


'  Write the wave data to a file
writewave


End Sub


Private Sub BuildM8Echo(selector)


'  Declare the type declarations for the mono 8 bit
'  data.  Note that one byte represents each sample
'  of data
Dim mono8 As Mono8Data
Dim Orgmono8 As Mono8Data


'  Set the length of the echo
EchoLength = m_PCMWave.wf.nSamplesPerSec


'  Set the end of the data to the
EndData = m_WaveHeader.dwbufferlength + EchoLength * 2


'  We will initialize the memory to the mid value
'  of a byte (0 - 256)
Orgmono8.Channel1 = Chr$(128)


'  Initialize the data
For N = m_WaveHeader.dwbufferlength To EndData
```

```
      throw = MemoryWrite(selector, N, Orgmono8, 1)
Next N

'  Perform the building of the echo
For N = EchoLength To EndData
    '  Read the data starting at echolength
    throw = MemoryRead(selector, N, mono8, 1)

    '  Read the original mono 8 bit data
    throw = MemoryRead(selector, N - EchoLength, Orgmono8, 1)

    '  Average the data together
    mono8.Channel1 = Chr$((Asc(mono8.Channel1) / 2 + Asc(Orgmono8.Channel1) ↵
        / 2))

    '  Write the new data
    throw = MemoryWrite(selector, N, mono8, 1)
Next N

'  Set the new length of the data
m_WaveHeader.dwbufferlength = m_WaveHeader.dwbufferlength + EchoLength * 2

'  Write the data to a file
writewave

End Sub

Private Sub BuildS16Echo(selector)
'  Declare Stereo16 and OrgStereo16 for reading
'  the two channel 16 bit data.  Note that the
'  structure contains two fields of integer data.
Dim Stereo16 As Stereo16Data
Dim OrgStereo16 As Stereo16Data

'  Set the echo length.
EchoLength = m_PCMWave.wf.nSamplesPerSec * 4

'  Set the end of the data in memory
EndData = m_WaveHeader.dwbufferlength + EchoLength * 2

'  Set the initialized value for the memory
OrgStereo16.Channel1 = 0
OrgStereo16.Channel2 = 0

'  Initialize the new memory
For N = m_WaveHeader.dwbufferlength To EndData Step 4
    throw = MemoryWrite(selector, N, OrgStereo16, 4)
Next N


'  Build the Echo
For N = EchoLength To EndData Step 4
    '  Read from the start of the echo
    throw = MemoryRead(selector, N, Stereo16, 4)
```

continued on next page

continued from previous page

```
        '  Read the original data
        throw = MemoryRead(selector, N - EchoLength, OrgStereo16, 4)

        '  Average each channel
        Stereo16.Channel1 = Stereo16.Channel1 / 2 + OrgStereo16.Channel1 / 2
        Stereo16.Channel2 = Stereo16.Channel2 / 2 + OrgStereo16.Channel2 / 2

        '  Write the data to memory
        throw = MemoryWrite(selector, N, Stereo16, 4)
Next N

'  Set the new length of the data
m_WaveHeader.dwbufferlength = m_WaveHeader.dwbufferlength + EchoLength * 2

'  Write the echo to a file
writewave

End Sub

Private Sub BuildS8Echo(selector)

'  Declare two variables for reading the
'  wave data
Dim Stereo8 As Stereo8Data
Dim OrgStereo8 As Stereo8Data

'  Set the EchoLength
EchoLength = m_PCMWave.wf.nSamplesPerSec * 2

'  Set the end of the new memory data
EndData = m_WaveHeader.dwbufferlength + EchoLength * 2

'  Initialize the memory to the mid value
OrgStereo8.Channel1 = Chr$(128)
OrgStereo8.Channel2 = Chr$(128)

'  Initialze the memory
For N = m_WaveHeader.dwbufferlength To EndData Step 2
    throw = MemoryWrite(selector, N, OrgStereo8, 2)
Next N


'  Build the echo
For N = EchoLength To EndData Step 2
    '  Read from the start of EchoLength
    throw = MemoryRead(selector, N, Stereo8, 2)

    '  Read the original wave data
    throw = MemoryRead(selector, N - EchoLength, OrgStereo8, 2)

    '  Average the data
    Stereo8.Channel1 = Chr$((Asc(Stereo8.Channel1) / 2 + ↵
      Asc(OrgStereo8.Channel1) / 2))

    Stereo8.Channel2 = Chr$((Asc(Stereo8.Channel2) / 2 ↵
```

```
        + Asc(OrgStereo8.Channel2) / 2))

    '  Write the data to memory
    throw = MemoryWrite(selector, N, Stereo8, 2)
Next N

'  Set the length of the new data
m_WaveHeader.dwbufferlength = m_WaveHeader.dwbufferlength + EchoLength * 2

'  Write the wave data to file
writewave

End Sub
```

4. The ReadWave function is similar to the function documented in the last How-To. The primary difference is the calculation to allocate memory for the echo Wave data. Because there will be additional Wave data, extra memory needs to be allocated to hold the echoes.

```
Public Sub ReadWave()
'  Open the File
m_hmmio = mmioOpen(m_filename, 0&, 0&)

'  Decend to the RIFF chunk
throw = mmioDescend(m_hmmio, m_RIFFchunk, 0&, 0)

'  Descend to the FMT chunk
throw = mmioDescend(m_hmmio, m_FMTchunk, 0&, 0)

'  Read the wave data format information
throw = mmioRead(m_hmmio, m_PCMWave, m_FMTchunk.cksize)

'  Descend to the data chunk
throw = mmioDescend(m_hmmio, m_DATAchunk, 0&, 0)

'  Determine the type of wave file
If m_PCMWave.wf.nChannels = 1 Then m_WTYPE$ = "M" Else m_WTYPE$ = "S"

m_WTYPE$ = m_WTYPE$ + Right$(Str$(m_PCMWave.wBitsPerSample), ↵
Len(Str$(m_PCMWave.wBitsPerSample)) - 1)

'  Depending on the type of wave file we will use N to allocate
'  the appropriate amount of memory.  Note that N is equal to the
'  number of bytes needed to hold each sample of wave data.
If m_WTYPE$ = "M8" Then N = 1
If m_WTYPE$ = "S8" Or m_WTYPE$ = "M16" Then N = 2
If m_WTYPE$ = "S16" Then N = 4

'  Allocate the appropriate amount of memory.  Note that 2
'  is the number of echos.
m_WaveData = GlobalAlloc(GMEM_MOVEABLE, m_DATAchunk.cksize + ↵
m_PCMWave.wf.nSamplesPerSec * N * 2)

'  We lock the memory so that the system will not
```

continued on next page

continued from previous page

```
'  move it and we also get a pointer to the data.
m_WaveDataPtr = GlobalLock(m_WaveData)

'  We use our special version of mmdioRead that will accept
'  a pointer to the allocated memory block.
throw = mmioReadPtrVal(m_hmmio, m_WaveDataPtr, m_DATAchunk.cksize + ↵
m_PCMWave.wf.nSamplesPerSec * N * 2)

'  Unlock the memory so the system can perform memory
'  management
throw = GlobalUnlock(m_WaveData)

'  Set the current length of the wave data to the original
'  data size
m_WaveHeader.dwbufferlength = m_DATAchunk.cksize

End Sub
```

5. WriteWave handles writing the echoes out to the Wave file. The function uses the saved chunks from the ReadWave function.

```
Private Sub WriteWave()
'  Set N to calculate the amount of allocated memory.  Note
'  that N is the number of bytes needed to define each sample
'  of data.
If m_WTYPE$ = "M8" Then N = 1
If m_WTYPE$ = "S8" Or m_WTYPE$ = "M16" Then N = 2
If m_WTYPE$ = "S16" Then N = 4

'  We will close the currently opened RIFF file
throw = mmioClose(m_hmmio, 0)

'  Set the new file name
m_filename = App.Path + "\echo.wav"

'  Open the Echo.wav file for creation and writing
m_hmmio = mmioOpen(m_filename, 0&, MMIO_CREATE Or MMIO_WRITE)

'  Add the additional data onto the chunk size
m_RIFFchunk.cksize = m_RIFFchunk.cksize + m_PCMWave.wf.nSamplesPerSec * N * 2

'  Create the RIFF chunk
throw = mmioCreateChunk(m_hmmio, m_RIFFchunk, MMIO_CREATERIFF)

'  Create the FMT chunk
throw = mmioCreateChunk(m_hmmio, m_FMTchunk, 0)

'  Write the wave data
throw = mmioWrite(m_hmmio, m_PCMWave, m_FMTchunk.cksize)

'  Ascend back to the FMT chunk so that the
'  DATA chunk will be a sub chunk of the
'  RIFF chunk
throw = mmioAscend(m_hmmio, m_FMTchunk, 0)
```

```
'  Set the new data chunk size
m_DATAchunk.cksize = m_DATAchunk.cksize + m_PCMWave.wf.nSamplesPerSec * N * 2

'  Create the data chunk
throw = mmioCreateChunk(m_hmmio, m_DATAchunk, 0)

'  Lock the memory and get a Pointer to the data
m_WaveDataPtr = GlobalLock(m_WaveData)

'  Write the memory data to file.  This version of
'  mmioWrite takes a pointer to the global memory as does
'  our mmioReadPtr function.
throw = mmioWritePtr(m_hmmio, m_WaveDataPtr, m_DATAchunk.cksize)

'  Unlock the memory.
throw = GlobalUnlock(m_WaveData)
n1:
'  Close the file
throw = mmioClose(m_hmmio, 0)
End Sub
```

6. The filename property handles setting the file name of the Wave file on which to perform the echo.

```
Public Property Let Filename(file As String)

Let m_filename = file

End Property
```

7. The AddEcho function handles calling the appropriate function for the Wave file format on which you are working.

```
Public Sub AddEcho()

'  The MemoryWrite and MemoryRead functions take a selector
'  to the allocated memory block.  The Windows API
'  GlobalHandleToSel function will return a selector to the
'  memory block
selector = GlobalHandleToSel(m_WaveData)

'  Depending on the type of wave file we
'  are working on, we will call the appropriate
'  function to build the echo.
If m_WTYPE$ = "M8" Then BuildM8Echo selector
If m_WTYPE$ = "M16" Then BuildS8Echo selector
If m_WTYPE$ = "S8" Then BuildS8Echo selector
If m_WTYPE$ = "S16" Then BuildS16Echo selector

End Sub
```

8. The PlayWave function handles playing the new Wave file with the added echoes.

```
Public Sub PlayWave()
'  HWav will be a handle to the opened
```

continued on next page

continued from previous page

```
' wave device
Dim HWav As Integer

' Set the lpData field of the m_WaveHeader function
' to the ptr to the allocated memory
m_WaveHeader.lpData = GlobalLock(m_WaveData)

' Open the wave output device
throw = waveOutOpen(HWav, 0, m_PCMWave, 0, 0, 0)

' Prepare the device header
throw = waveOutPrepareHeader(HWav, m_WaveHeader, Len(m_WaveHeader))

' Send the wave data to the opened device
throw = waveOutWrite(HWav, m_WaveHeader, Len(m_WaveHeader))

' We will continue to loop until the WHDR_DONE bit
' of the dwFlags parameter has been set.  This lets
' us know that the wave file has finished playing.
Do Until (m_WaveHeader.dwFlags And WHDR_DONE)
Loop

' Clear the Header
throw = waveOutUnprepareHeader(HWav, m_WaveHeader, Len(m_WaveHeader))

' close the opened device
throw = waveOutClose(HWav)

' Unlock the global data
throw = GlobalUnlock(m_WaveData)

End Sub
```

9. The CloseWave function releases the allocated memory and ensures that the Wave file is closed.

```
Public Sub CloseWave()

' Check to see if global memory
' has been allocated
If m_WaveData <> 0 Then

    ' Free up the allocated memory
    throw = GlobalFree(m_WaveData)

    ' Ensure that the last file opened
    ' has been closed
    throw = mmioClose(m_hmmio, 0)

End If

End Sub
```

10. Add the following code to the general declarations section of the form. The WaveTools2 class is declared globally.

```
'  Dimension the global wave tools class
Dim wave As WaveTools2
```

11. Depending on the type of Wave file selected, the appropriate file name is set. The DoEvents function ensures that the text is displayed on the screen before the Wave file manipulations are started. The Wave file is read and the echoes are built.

```
Private Sub Command1_Click()
'  Depending on the option button selected, we will set
'  the m_filename appropriately
If option1.Value = -1 Then filename = App.Path + "\roostM8.wav"
If option2.Value = -1 Then filename = App.Path + "\roostM16.wav"
If option3.Value = -1 Then filename = App.Path + "\roostS8.wav"
If option4.Value = -1 Then filename = App.Path + "\roostS16.wav"

'  Set the wave filename
Let wave.filename = filename

'  Show the status to the user
text1.Text = "Reading Wave File"

'  Ensure that the text is displayed before the wave is read
throw = DoEvents()

'  Read the wave file
wave.readwave

'  Update the status to the user
text1.Text = "Building Echo"

'  Ensure that the text is displayed before the echo is called
throw = DoEvents()

'  Add an echo to the wave file
wave.addecho

'  Update the status to the user
text1.Text = "Done Building Echo"

End Sub
```

12. When the user selects the Play button, the new ECHO.WAV file is played.

```
Private Sub Command2_Click()

'  Update the status to the user
text1.Text = "Playing New ECHO.WAV file"

'  Ensure that the text is displayed before the echo is played
throw = DoEvents()
```

continued on next page

continued from previous page

```
'  Play the wave file
wave.playwave

'  Notify the user that the file has finished playing
text1.Text = "Done Playing New ECHO.WAV file"

End Sub
```

13. When the form is loaded, the new class is created and the first option is selected.

```
Private Sub Form_Load()

'  Create a new instance of the class
Set wave = New WaveTools2

'  Select the first option
option1.Value = -1

End Sub
```

14. When the form is unloaded, the Wave file is closed by calling the CloseWave function.

```
Private Sub Form_Unload(Cancel As Integer)

'  Close the wave file
wave.closewave

End Sub
```

How It Works

The basics of opening the Wave RIFF file, reading the data into memory, and playing the Wave file with the low-level APIs are the same as the last How-To. What has been added are functions to read and write from the global memory and the steps necessary to manipulate the Wave data to add echoes.

To add the echoes, you need to be able to read and write from the global memory block you have allocated. To do this, three of the API functions provided in the Microsoft ToolHelp library provided with Windows are used. Two of the functions, MemoryRead and MemoryWrite, are provided to help read and write from Windows memory. Windows has an elaborate memory management system that does not store allocated memory for programs in contiguous memory blocks. Reading and writing from such a memory block scheme can be problematic at best from Visual Basic 4.0.

Fortunately, the MemoryRead and MemoryWrite functions make doing this easy. The two functions require a selector to the memory. A selector provides a Windows-protected mode address value to the memory. The ToolHelp library includes a function, GlobalHandleToSel, that will provide a selector to a global memory block. In the AddEcho class routine, this function is called and the selector is passed to the appropriate echo-building function. The MemoryRead and MemoryWrite functions can read or write any specified amount of bytes to and from memory.

To build the echo, copy data from the beginning of the Wave and overlay it in later parts of the Wave. Where the echo will start is set by the SamplesPerSec member in the PCMWaveFormat record. Depending on the format of the Wave file, multiply SamplesPerSec by the number of bytes to define each sample. This will move you one second into the playing of the Wave file. Because you are adding trailing echoes to the Wave file, you will need the appropriate amount of memory allocated to handle the additional Wave data. In this example, you multiply SamplesPerSec by the number of bytes for each sample and then by 2. This How-To allows you to add several echoes to the Wave file. The ReadWave function from the last section has been modified to allocate additional memory for the echo data.

Each Wave format sample size is dependent on the type of the Wave data. For mono 8-bit data, 1 byte defines each sample. For mono 16-bit data, 2 bytes define each sample. For stereo data, there are two channels to be defined. Stereo 8-bit data takes 1 byte for each channel and stereo 16-bit data takes 2 bytes for each channel. Depending on the format of data being manipulated, use the MemoryRead function to read the original data into the data structures that define the samples for each Wave format. The echo is built by adding the data in front of the echo to the current echo position. Then divide the value by two to decrease the volume of the sound. The new Wave data is then written to memory with the MemoryWrite function. This process is repeated until the end of the memory has been reached.

Once the echo has been added to the Wave data, the WriteWave function is called to write the new Wave data to a new file. In the WriteWave function, a new function is introduced called mmioCreateChunk. The Wave file must be reconstructed due to the changes in the data chunk sizes and overall file sizes. Note that the mmioOpen function now contains two flags, mmio_CREATE and mmio_WRITE. These will open the file for creation and for writing. Note that the original chunks are stored in global variables. First, the primary RIFF chunk is written and the RIFFChunk.cksize parameter is updated to include the additional echo data. The mmio_CREATERIFF parameter is used to indicate that a RIFF chunk should be written. Then the FMT chunk and the corresponding Wave header data are written. The next chunk to be written is the data chunk. DATAChunk.cksize must be updated to reflect the additional Wave data. Then the data chunk is written to the file. Finally, the Wave data is written to the file. Note that a special version of the mmioWrite function is used to accept a pointer to the global memory.

The Wave data is then played the same as it was in the previous How-To. Note that the new echo version of the Wave is found in ECHO.WAV in the application directory.

Comments

Various effects can be performed on Wave data. The next How-To demonstrates how to reverse the Wave data so that the Wave file can be played backwards.

7.4 How do I...
Play a Wave file backwards?

Problem

I would like to be able to play a Wave file backwards. This provides unusual and catchy effects to my Wave files.

Technique

The methods used for building the wave echo can easily be modified to reverse the data in a Wave file and then play it backwards. The class developed in the last How-To will be updated to implement the new reverse procedures.

Steps

Open and run 7-4.VBP. The running program appears as shown in Figure 7-4-1. To reverse the Wave data, select the Reverse button. To play the reversed Wave, select the Play button.

1. Create a new project called 7-4.VBP. Add the objects and properties listed in Table 7-4-1 to Form1 and save the form as 7-4.FRM.

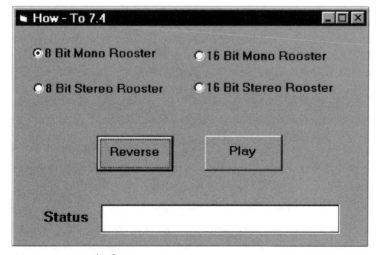

Figure 7-4-1 The form at runtime

Table 7-4-1 The form's objects and properties

OBJECT	PROPERTY	SETTING
Form	Name	Form1
	Caption	"How-To 7.4"
TextBox	Name	Text1
OptionButton	Name	Option4
	Caption	"16 Bit Stereo Rooster"
OptionButton	Name	Option3
	Caption	"8 Bit Stereo Rooster"
OptionButton	Name	Option2
	Caption	"16 Bit Mono Rooster"
OptionButton	Name	Option1
	Caption	"8 Bit Mono Rooster"
CommandButton	Name	Command2
	Caption	"Play"
CommandButton	Name	Command1
	Caption	"Reverse"
Label	Name	Label1
	AutoSize	-1 'True
	Caption	"Status"

2. Create a new module called WAVETLS3.BAS and add the following code to the general declarations section. This code is the same as that developed in the Wavetls2 class.

```
' general waveform format structure (information common to all formats)
Private Type WAVEFORMAT
    wFormatTag As Integer        ' format type
    nChannels As Integer         ' number of channels (i.e. mono, stereo, etc.)
    nSamplesPerSec As Long       ' sample rate
    nAvgBytesPerSec As Long      ' for buffer estimation
    nBlockAlign As Integer       ' block size of data
```

continued on next page

continued from previous page

```
End Type


'   specific waveform format structure for PCM data
Private Type PCMWaveFORMAT
    wf As WAVEFORMAT
    wBitsPerSample As Integer
End Type

'   wave data block header
Private Type WAVEHDR
    lpData As Long                  ' pointer to locked data buffer
    dwbufferlength As Long          ' length of data buffer
    dwBytesRecorded As Long         ' used for input only
    dwUser As Long                  ' for client's use
    dwFlags As Long                 ' assorted flags (see defines)
    dwLoops As Long                 ' loop control counter
    wavehdr_tag As Long             ' reserved for driver
    reserved As Long                ' reserved for driver
End Type

' RIFF chunk information data structure
Private Type MMCKINFO
    ckid As String * 4
    cksize As Long
    fccType As String * 4
    dwDataOffset As Long
    dwFlags As Long
End Type


'   These are the datatypes to represent the wave
'   data of the various formats
Private Type Mono8Data
    Channel1 As String * 1
End Type


Private Type Stereo8Data
    Channel1 As String * 1
    Channel2 As String * 1
End Type


Private Type Mono16Data
    Channel1 As Integer
End Type


Private Type Stereo16Data
    Channel1 As Integer
    Channel2 As Integer
End Type


'   These are the functions used to read and write
'   the wave RIFF files
Private Declare Function mmioRead Lib "MMSYSTEM" (ByVal m_hmmio As Integer, ↵
pch As Any, ByVal cch As Long) As Long

Private Declare Function mmioReadPtrVal Lib "MMSYSTEM" Alias "mmioRead" ↵
```

```
(ByVal m_hmmio As Integer, ByVal HugePtr As Long, ByVal cch As Long) As Long

Private Declare Function mmioOpen Lib "MMSYSTEM" (ByVal szm_filename As ↵
String, ByVal lpMMIOINFO As Any, ByVal dwOpenFlags As Long) As Integer

Private Declare Function mmioClose Lib "MMSYSTEM" (ByVal m_hmmio As Integer,↵
ByVal wFlags As Integer) As Integer

Private Declare Function mmioDescend Lib "MMSYSTEM" (ByVal m_hmmio As ↵
Integer, lpck As MMCKINFO, ByVal lpckParent As Any, ByVal uFlags As Integer) ↵
As Integer

Private Declare Function mmioAscend Lib "MMSYSTEM" (ByVal m_hmmio As Integer, ↵
lpck As MMCKINFO, ByVal uFlags As Integer) As Integer

Private Declare Function mmioWrite Lib "MMSYSTEM" (ByVal m_hmmio As Integer, ↵
pch As Any, ByVal cch As Long) As Long

Private Declare Function mmioWritePtr Lib "MMSYSTEM" Alias "mmioWrite" (ByVal ↵
m_hmmio As Integer, ByVal HugePtr As Long, ByVal cch As Long) As Long

Private Declare Function mmioCreateChunk Lib "MMSYSTEM" (ByVal m_hmmio As ↵
Integer, lpck As MMCKINFO, ByVal uFlags As Integer) As Integer


' These functions are used to play the wave file
Private Declare Function waveOutOpen Lib "MMSYSTEM" (lpWaveout As Integer, ↵
ByVal UINT As Integer, lpformat As Any, ByVal dwCallback As Long, ByVal ↵
dwInstance As Long, ByVal flags As Long) As Integer

Private Declare Function waveOutClose Lib "MMSYSTEM" (ByVal hWaveOut As ↵
Integer) As Integer

Private Declare Function waveOutPrepareHeader Lib "MMSYSTEM" (ByVal hWaveOut ↵
As Integer, wh As WAVEHDR, ByVal uSize As Integer) As Integer

Private Declare Function waveOutUnprepareHeader Lib "MMSYSTEM" (ByVal ↵
hWaveOut As Integer, wh As WAVEHDR, ByVal uSize As Integer) As Integer

Private Declare Function waveOutWrite Lib "MMSYSTEM" (ByVal hWaveOut As ↵
Integer, WH1 As WAVEHDR, ByVal uSize As Integer) As Integer

' This flag is used to open the wave file
' for reading and writing
Const MMIO_CREATE = &H1000          ' create new file (or truncate file)
Const MMIO_CREATERIFF = &H20        ' mmioCreateChunk: make a LIST chunk

' read/write mode numbers (bit field MMIO_RWMODE)
 Const MMIO_READ = &H0              ' open file for reading only
 Const MMIO_WRITE = &H1            ' open file for writing only

' This lets us know that the wave file
' is finished playing
Const WHDR_DONE = &H1
```

continued on next page

continued from previous page

```
'   These functions are used to allocate
'   memory for the wave data
Private Declare Function GlobalAlloc Lib "Kernel" (ByVal wFlags As Integer, ↵
ByVal dwBytes As Long) As Integer

Private Declare Function GlobalHandleToSel Lib "ToolHelp.DLL" (ByVal hMem ↵
As Integer) As Integer

Private Declare Function MemoryWrite Lib "ToolHelp.DLL" (ByVal wSel As ↵
Integer, ByVal dwOffset As Long, lpvBuf As Any, ByVal dwcb As Long) As Long

Private Declare Function MemoryRead Lib "ToolHelp.DLL" (ByVal wSel As ↵
Integer, ByVal dwOffset As Long, lpvBuf As Any, ByVal dwcb As Long) As Long

Private Declare Function GlobalFree Lib "Kernel" (ByVal hMem As Integer) ↵
As Integer

Private Declare Function GlobalLock Lib "Kernel" (ByVal hMem As Integer) As Long

Private Declare Function GlobalUnlock Lib "Kernel" (ByVal hMem As Integer) ↵
As Integer

'   Flags for the GlobalAlloc function.  This
'   will allow the memory to be moveable for
'   memory management.
Const GMEM_MOVEABLE = &H2

'   m_WaveHeader will be used to hold the
'   wave data and is accessed in the wave
'   playing functions.
Dim m_WaveHeader As WAVEHDR

'   m_PCMWave will hold the wave information
Dim m_PCMWave As PCMWaveFORMAT

'   m_WaveData will hold the pointer to
'   the global memory block
Dim m_WaveData As Integer

'   m_WTYPE will hold the type of wave file
Dim m_WTYPE As String

'   Holds the wave filename
Dim m_filename As String

'   m_hmmio will be the handle to the wave file
Dim m_hmmio As Integer

'   These will hold the information on
'   the chunks orignally read.  This will
'   be updated and rewritten in the writewave
'   function
Dim m_RIFFchunk As MMCKINFO
Dim m_FMTchunk As MMCKINFO
Dim m_DATAchunk As MMCKINFO
```

3. The following code is the same as in WAVETLS2.CLS. The only change is that in the BuildEcho functions, the ECHO.WAV file name is sent at the end of each routine.

```
Private Sub BuildM16Echo(selector)

'   Mono16 and OrgMono16 will be used to read and
'   access the wave data.  Note the data structure consists
'   of one integer for reading the 16 bit data.
Dim Mono16 As Mono16Data
Dim OrgMono16 As Mono16Data

'   Set the data to 0
OrgMono16.Channel1 = 0

'   Set the EchoLength to two times the samples per second
'   this will set the starting point of the echo
EchoLength = m_PCMWave.wf.nSamplesPerSec * 2

'   We are going to end the echo
EndData = m_WaveHeader.dwbufferlength + EchoLength * 2

' Initialize the memory block to the mid value of
'   an integer (0)
For N = m_WaveHeader.dwbufferlength To EndData Step 2
    throw = MemoryWrite(selector, N, OrgMono16, 2)
Next N

'   We now average the move through the memory data
For N = EchoLength To EndData Step 2

    '   Read the data starting at echo length
    throw = MemoryRead(selector, N, Mono16, 2)

    '   We read the original wave data
    throw = MemoryRead(selector, N - EchoLength, OrgMono16, 2)

    '   We average the data together
    Mono16.Channel1 = Mono16.Channel1 / 2 + OrgMono16.Channel1 / 2

    '   We write the new data to memory
    throw = MemoryWrite(selector, N, Mono16, 2)
Next N

'   We set the new length of the data
m_WaveHeader.dwbufferlength = m_WaveHeader.dwbufferlength + EchoLength * 2

'   Set the new file name
m_filename = App.Path + "\echo.wav"

'   Write the wave data to a file
writewave 1

End Sub
```

continued on next page

continued from previous page

```
Private Sub BuildM8Echo(selector)

'  Declare the type declarations for the mono 8 bit
'  data.  Note that one byte represents each sample
'  of data
Dim mono8 As Mono8Data
Dim Orgmono8 As Mono8Data

'  Set the length of the echo
EchoLength = m_PCMWave.wf.nSamplesPerSec

'  Set the end of the data to the
EndData = m_WaveHeader.dwbufferlength + EchoLength * 2

'  We will initialize the memory to the mid value
'  of a byte (0 - 256)
Orgmono8.Channel1 = Chr$(128)

'  Initialize the data
For N = m_WaveHeader.dwbufferlength To EndData
     throw = MemoryWrite(selector, N, Orgmono8, 1)
Next N

'  Perform the building of the echo
For N = EchoLength To EndData
    '  Read the data starting at echolength
    throw = MemoryRead(selector, N, mono8, 1)

    '  Read the original mono 8 bit data
    throw = MemoryRead(selector, N - EchoLength, Orgmono8, 1)

    '  Average the data together
    mono8.Channel1 = Chr$((Asc(mono8.Channel1) / 2 + Asc(Orgmono8.Channel1)↵
        / 2))

    '  Write the new data
    throw = MemoryWrite(selector, N, mono8, 1)
Next N

'  Set the new length of the data
m_WaveHeader.dwbufferlength = m_WaveHeader.dwbufferlength + EchoLength * 2

'  Set the new file name
m_filename = App.Path + "\echo.wav"

'  Write the data to a file
writewave 1

End Sub

Private Sub BuildS16Echo(selector)
'  Declare Stereo16 and OrgStereo16 for reading
'  the two channel 16 bit data.  Note that the
'  structure contains two fields of integer data.
```

```
Dim Stereo16 As Stereo16Data
Dim OrgStereo16 As Stereo16Data

'  Set the echo length.
EchoLength = m_PCMWave.wf.nSamplesPerSec * 4

'  Set the end of the data in memory
EndData = m_WaveHeader.dwbufferlength + EchoLength * 2

'  Set the initialized value for the memory
OrgStereo16.Channel1 = 0
OrgStereo16.Channel2 = 0

'  Initialize the new memory
For N = m_WaveHeader.dwbufferlength To EndData Step 4
    throw = MemoryWrite(selector, N, OrgStereo16, 4)
Next N


'  Build the Echo
For N = EchoLength To EndData Step 4
    '  Read from the start of the echo
    throw = MemoryRead(selector, N, Stereo16, 4)

    '  Read the original data
    throw = MemoryRead(selector, N - EchoLength, OrgStereo16, 4)

    '  Average each channel
    Stereo16.Channel1 = Stereo16.Channel1 / 2 + OrgStereo16.Channel1 / 2
    Stereo16.Channel2 = Stereo16.Channel2 / 2 + OrgStereo16.Channel2 / 2

    '  Write the data to memory
    throw = MemoryWrite(selector, N, Stereo16, 4)
Next N

'  Set the new length of the data
m_WaveHeader.dwbufferlength = m_WaveHeader.dwbufferlength + EchoLength * 2

'  Set the new file name
m_filename = App.Path + "\echo.wav"

'  Write the echo to a file
writewave 1

End Sub

Private Sub BuildS8Echo(selector)

'  Declare two variables for reading the
'  wave data
Dim Stereo8 As Stereo8Data
Dim OrgStereo8 As Stereo8Data

'  Set the EchoLength
EchoLength = m_PCMWave.wf.nSamplesPerSec * 2
```

continued on next page

continued from previous page

```
'  Set the end of the new memory data
EndData = m_WaveHeader.dwbufferlength + EchoLength * 2

'  Initialize the memory to the mid value
OrgStereo8.Channel1 = Chr$(128)
OrgStereo8.Channel2 = Chr$(128)

'  Initialze the memory
For N = m_WaveHeader.dwbufferlength To EndData Step 2
    throw = MemoryWrite(selector, N, OrgStereo8, 2)
Next N


'  Build the echo
For N = EchoLength To EndData Step 2
    '  Read from the start of EchoLength
    throw = MemoryRead(selector, N, Stereo8, 2)

    '  Read the original wave data
    throw = MemoryRead(selector, N - EchoLength, OrgStereo8, 2)

    '  Average the data
    Stereo8.Channel1 = Chr$((Asc(Stereo8.Channel1) / 2 ↵
    '  + Asc(OrgStereo8.Channel1) / 2))
    Stereo8.Channel2 = Chr$((Asc(Stereo8.Channel2) / 2 ↵
    '  + Asc(OrgStereo8.Channel2) / 2))

    '  Write the data to memory
    throw = MemoryWrite(selector, N, Stereo8, 2)
Next N

'  Set the length of the new data
m_WaveHeader.dwbufferlength = m_WaveHeader.dwbufferlength + EchoLength * 2

'  Set the new file name
m_filename = App.Path + "\echo.wav"

'  Write the wave data to file
writewave 1

End Sub

Public Sub ReadWave()
'  Open the File
m_hmmio = mmioOpen(m_filename, 0&, 0&)

'  Decend to the RIFF chunk
throw = mmioDescend(m_hmmio, m_RIFFchunk, 0&, 0)

'  Descend to the FMT chunk
throw = mmioDescend(m_hmmio, m_FMTchunk, 0&, 0)

'  Read the wave data format information
throw = mmioRead(m_hmmio, m_PCMWave, m_FMTchunk.cksize)
```

```
'  Descend to the data chunk
throw = mmioDescend(m_hmmio, m_DATAchunk, O&, 0)

'  Determine the type of wave file
If m_PCMWave.wf.nChannels = 1 Then m_WTYPE$ = "M" Else m_WTYPE$ = "S"
m_WTYPE$ = m_WTYPE$ + Right$(Str$(m_PCMWave.wBitsPerSample), ↵
Len(Str$(m_PCMWave.wBitsPerSample)) - 1)

'  Depending on the type of wave file we will use N to allocate
'  the appropriate amount of memory.  Note that N is equal to the
'  number of bytes needed to hold each sample of wave data.
If m_WTYPE$ = "M8" Then N = 1
If m_WTYPE$ = "S8" Or m_WTYPE$ = "M16" Then N = 2
If m_WTYPE$ = "S16" Then N = 4

'  Allocate the appropriate amount of memory.  Note that 2
'  is the number of echos.
m_WaveData = GlobalAlloc(GMEM_MOVEABLE, m_DATAchunk.cksize ↵
+ m_PCMWave.wf.nSamplesPerSec * N * 2)

'  We lock the memory so that the system will not
'  move it and we also get a pointer to the data.
m_WaveDataPtr = GlobalLock(m_WaveData)

'  We use our special version of mmdioRead that will accept
'  a pointer to the allocated memory block.
throw = mmioReadPtrVal(m_hmmio, m_WaveDataPtr, m_DATAchunk.cksize ↵
+ m_PCMWave.wf.nSamplesPerSec * N * 2)

'  Unlock the memory so the system can perform memory
'  management
throw = GlobalUnlock(m_WaveData)

'  Set the current length of the wave data to the original
'  data size
m_WaveHeader.dwbufferlength = m_DATAchunk.cksize

End Sub

Private Sub WriteWave(REVECHO)
'  Set N to calculate the amount of allocated memory.  Note
'  that N is the number of bytes needed to define each sample
'  of data.
If m_WTYPE$ = "M8" Then N = 1
If m_WTYPE$ = "S8" Or m_WTYPE$ = "M16" Then N = 2
If m_WTYPE$ = "S16" Then N = 4

'  We will close the currently opened RIFF file
throw = mmioClose(m_hmmio, 0)

'  Open the Echo.wav file for creation and writing
m_hmmio = mmioOpen(m_filename, O&, MMIO_CREATE Or MMIO_WRITE)

'  Add the additional data onto the chunk size if an
```

continued on next page

continued from previous page

```
'  echo is to be updated
If REVECHO = 1 Then m_RIFFchunk.cksize = m_RIFFchunk.cksize +
m_PCMWave.wf.nSamplesPerSec * N * 2


'  Create the RIFF chunk
throw = mmioCreateChunk(m_hmmio, m_RIFFchunk, MMIO_CREATERIFF)


'  Create the FMT chunk
throw = mmioCreateChunk(m_hmmio, m_FMTchunk, 0)


'  Write the wave data
throw = mmioWrite(m_hmmio, m_PCMWave, m_FMTchunk.cksize)


'  Ascend back to the FMT chunk so that the
'  DATA chunk will be a sub chunk of the
'  RIFF chunk
throw = mmioAscend(m_hmmio, m_FMTchunk, 0)


'  Set the new data chunk size if an echo
'  update is to be done
If REVECHO = 1 Then m_DATAchunk.cksize = m_DATAchunk.cksize +
m_PCMWave.wf.nSamplesPerSec * N * 2


'  Create the data chunk
throw = mmioCreateChunk(m_hmmio, m_DATAchunk, 0)


'  Lock the memory and get a Pointer to the data
m_WaveDataPtr = GlobalLock(m_WaveData)


'  Write the memory data to file.  This version of
'  mmioWrite takes a pointer to the global memory as does
'  our mmioReadPtr function.
throw = mmioWritePtr(m_hmmio, m_WaveDataPtr, m_DATAchunk.cksize)


'  Unlock the memory.
throw = GlobalUnlock(m_WaveData)


'  Close the file
throw = mmioClose(m_hmmio, 0)
End Sub


Public Property Let Filename(file As String)

Let m_filename = file

End Property


Public Sub AddEcho()

'  The MemoryWrite and MemoryRead functions take a selector
'  to the allocated memory block.  The Windows API
'  GlobalHandleToSel function will return a selector to the
'  memory block
selector = GlobalHandleToSel(m_WaveData)
```

```
'   Depending on the type of wave file we
'   are working on, we will call the appropriate
'   function to build the echo.
If m_WTYPE$ = "M8" Then BuildM8Echo selector
If m_WTYPE$ = "M16" Then buildm16echo selector
If m_WTYPE$ = "S8" Then builds8echo selector
If m_WTYPE$ = "S16" Then BuildS16Echo selector

End Sub


Public Sub PlayWave()
'   HWav will be a handle to the opened
'   wave device
Dim HWav As Integer

'   Set the lpData field of the m_WaveHeader function
'   to the ptr to the allocated memory
m_WaveHeader.lpData = GlobalLock(m_WaveData)

' Open the wave output device
throw = waveOutOpen(HWav, 0, m_PCMWave, 0, 0, 0)

' Prepare the device header
throw = waveOutPrepareHeader(HWav, m_WaveHeader, Len(m_WaveHeader))

' Send the wave data to the opened device
throw = waveOutWrite(HWav, m_WaveHeader, Len(m_WaveHeader))

'   We will continue to loop until the WHDR_DONE bit
'   of the dwFlags parameter has been set.  This lets
'   us know that the wave file has finished playing.
Do Until (m_WaveHeader.dwFlags And WHDR_DONE)
Loop

' Clear the Header
throw = waveOutUnprepareHeader(HWav, m_WaveHeader, Len(m_WaveHeader))

' close the opened device
throw = waveOutClose(HWav)

'   Unlock the global data
throw = GlobalUnlock(m_WaveData)

End Sub

Public Sub CloseWave()

'   Check to see if global memory
'   has been allocated
If m_WaveData <> 0 Then

    '   Free up the allocated memory
    throw = GlobalFree(m_WaveData)
```

continued on next page

continued from previous page

```
    '   Ensure that the last file opened
    '   has been closed
    throw = mmioClose(m_hmmio, 0)

End If

End Sub
```

4. The Reverse function handles calling the appropriate build reverse function for the type of Wave file being accessed.

```
Public Sub Reverse()

    '   The MemoryWrite and MemoryRead functions take a selector
    '   to the allocated memory block.  The Windows API
    '   GlobalHandleToSel function will return a selector to the
    '   memory block
    selector = GlobalHandleToSel(m_WaveData)

    '   Depending on the type of wave file we
    '   are working on, we will call the appropriate
    '   function to build the Reverse.
    If m_WTYPE$ = "M8" Then BuildM8Rev selector
    If m_WTYPE$ = "M16" Then BuildM16Rev selector
    If m_WTYPE$ = "S8" Then BuildS8Rev selector
    If m_WTYPE$ = "S16" Then BuildS16Rev selector

End Sub
```

5. The following four functions handle reversing the Wave data in memory.

```
Private Sub BuildM16Rev(selector)

    '   Mono16 and EndMono16 will be used to read and
    '   access the wave data.  Note the data structure consists
    '   of one integer for reading the 16 bit data.
    Dim Mono16 As Mono16Data
    Dim EndMono16 As Mono16Data

    '   We will go half way through the data and
    '   swap the data in the beginning of the file with
    '   the end
    For N = 0 To m_WaveHeader.dwbufferlength / 2

        '   Read from the beginning of the file
        throw = MemoryRead(selector, N, Mono16, 1)

        '   Read from the End of the file
        throw = MemoryRead(selector, m_WaveHeader.dwbufferlength - N, EndMono16, 1)

        '   Write the data from the begining to the end
        throw = MemoryWrite(selector, m_WaveHeader.dwbufferlength - N, Mono16, 1)

        '   Write the data from the end of the file to
        '   the beginning
```

```
        throw = MemoryWrite(selector, N, EndMono16, 1)

Next N

'  Set the new file name
m_filename = App.Path + "\reverse.wav"

'  Write the wave data to a file
writewave 2

End Sub

Private Sub BuildM8Rev(selector)

'  Declare the type declarations for the mono 8 bit
'  data.  Note that one byte represents each sample
'  of data
Dim mono8 As Mono8Data
Dim EndMono8 As Mono8Data

'  We will go half way through the data and
'  swap the data in the beginning of the file with
'  the end
For N = 0 To m_WaveHeader.dwbufferlength / 2

    '  Read from the beginning of the file
    throw = MemoryRead(selector, N, mono8, 1)

    '  Read from the End of the file
    throw = MemoryRead(selector, m_WaveHeader.dwbufferlength - N, EndMono8, 1)

    '  Write the data from the begining to the end
    throw = MemoryWrite(selector, m_WaveHeader.dwbufferlength - N, mono8, 1)

    '  Write the data from the end of the file to
    '  the beginning
    throw = MemoryWrite(selector, N, EndMono8, 1)

Next N

'  Set the new file name
m_filename = App.Path + "\reverse.wav"

'  Write the wave data to a file
writewave 2

End Sub

Private Sub BuildS16Rev(selector)

'  Declare Stereo16 and EndStereo16 for reading
'  the two channel 16 bit data.  Note that the
'  structure contains two fields of integer data.
Dim Stereo16 As Stereo16Data
Dim EndStereo16 As Stereo16Data
```

continued on next page

continued from previous page

```
'  We will go half way through the data and
'  swap the data in the beginning of the file with
'  the end
For N = 0 To m_WaveHeader.dwbufferlength / 2

     '  Read from the beginning of the file
     throw = MemoryRead(selector, N, Stereo16, 1)

     '  Read from the End of the file
     throw = MemoryRead(selector, m_WaveHeader.dwbufferlength - N, ↵
             EndStereo16, 1)

     '  Write the data from the begining to the end
     throw = MemoryWrite(selector, m_WaveHeader.dwbufferlength - N, Stereo16, 1)

     '  Write the data from the end of the file to
     '  the beginning
     throw = MemoryWrite(selector, N, EndStereo16, 1)

Next N

'  Set the new file name
m_filename = App.Path + "\reverse.wav"

'  Write the wave data to a file
writewave 2

End Sub

Private Sub BuildS8Rev(selector)

'  Declare two variables for reading the
'  wave data
Dim Stereo8 As Stereo8Data
Dim EndStereo8 As Stereo8Data


'  We will go half way through the data and
'  swap the data in the beginning of the file with
'  the end
For N = 0 To m_WaveHeader.dwbufferlength / 2

     '  Read from the beginning of the file
     throw = MemoryRead(selector, N, Stereo8, 1)

     '  Read from the End of the file
     throw = MemoryRead(selector, m_WaveHeader.dwbufferlength - N, EndStereo8, 1)

     '  Write the data from the begining to the end
     throw = MemoryWrite(selector, m_WaveHeader.dwbufferlength - N, Stereo8, 1)

     '  Write the data from the end of the file to
     '  the beginning
     throw = MemoryWrite(selector, N, EndStereo8, 1)
```

```
Next N

'  Set the new file name
m_filename = App.Path + "\reverse.wav"

'  Write the wave data to file
writewave 2

End Sub
```

6. Add the following code to the general declarations section of the form. The WaveTools3 class is globally declared here.

```
Dim wave As WaveTools3
```

7. When the user is ready to build the reverse Wave, the file name is set for the class, the ReadWave function is called, and then the Reverse function is called to reverse the data.

```
Private Sub Command1_Click()

'  Depending on the option button selected, we will set
'  the filename appropriately
If option1.Value = -1 Then filename = App.Path + "\roostM8.wav"
If option2.Value = -1 Then filename = App.Path + "\roostM16.wav"
If option3.Value = -1 Then filename = App.Path + "\roostS8.wav"
If option4.Value = -1 Then filename = App.Path + "\roostS16.wav"

Let wave.filename = filename

'  Show the status to the user
text1.Text = "Reading Wave File"

'  Ensure the text is displayed
throw% = DoEvents

'  Read the wave file
wave.readwave

'  Update the status to the user
text1.Text = "Reversing Data"

'  Ensure the text is displayed
throw% = DoEvents

wave.Reverse

'  Update the status to the user
text1.Text = "Done Building Reverse"
End Sub
```

8. When the Play button is selected, the PlayWave class function is called.

```
Private Sub Command2_Click()
```

continued on next page

continued from previous page

```
'   Update the status to the user
text1.Text = "Playing New reverse.wav file"

'   Ensure the text is displayed
throw% = DoEvents

wave.playwave

'   Notify the user that the file has finished playing
text1.Text = "Done Playing New reverse.wav file"

End Sub
```

9. When the form is loaded, a new instance of the class is created and the first Wave option is selected.

```
Private Sub Form_Load()
Set wave = New WaveTools3

'   Select the first option
option1.Value = -1

End Sub
```

10. It is important to make sure that the Wave file is closed by calling the CloseWave function.

```
Private Sub Form_Unload(Cancel As Integer)

wave.closewave

End Sub
```

How It Works

This How-To is closely aligned with the previous one. All of the functions and declarations are the same with the exception of the four new functions that build the reverse data and the Reverse function. Reverse handles calling the appropriate reverse building procedure for the type of Wave data being worked on.

To reverse the Wave data, the corresponding bytes in the first half of the file are swapped with the bytes in the second half of the file. In the For loops where the swapping of the data takes place, bytes are read from the beginning of the Wave data and then the corresponding bytes from the end of the data are read. Their positions are then swapped when the data is written back out to memory. When the Reverse is finished, the final result is a rooster crowing backwards. A truly interesting effect!

Comments

Many other digital effects can be added to the Wave data now that a set of programming procedures to read, play, and write Wave data have been developed.

7.5 How do I...
Play MIDI notes using low-level APIs?

COMPLEXITY: INTERMEDIATE

Problem

I would like to be able to use low-level MIDI APIs to play MIDI notes. There are times when I would like to be able to play single notes from my application. This would be easier than having to access prerecorded MIDI files.

Technique

As with the low-level Wave APIs, a set of low-level MIDI APIs provides for greater control over installed MIDI devices.

Steps

Open and run 7-5.VBP. The running program appears as shown in Figure 7-5-1. The notes range from 0 to 127. To play a note, select the number either by using the spinner control or by entering the number in the text box.

1. Create a new project called 7-5.VBP. Add the objects and properties listed in Table 7-5-1 to Form1 and save the form as 7-5.FRM.

Table 7-5-1 The project's objects and properties

OBJECT	PROPERTY	SETTING
Form	Name	Form1
	BackColor	&H00C0C0C0&
	Caption	"How-To 7.5"
TextBox	Name	Text1
CommandButton	Name	PlayNote
	Caption	"Play Note"
	Font	
	name	"Arial"
SpinButton	Name	Spin1
	borderthickness	0
	delay	30

continued on next page

continued from previous page

OBJECT	PROPERTY	SETTING
LabelLabel1		
	Alignment	2 'Center
	AutoSize	-1 'True
	BackColor	&H00C0C0C0&
	Caption	"Note Value"

2. Add the following code to the general declarations section of the form.

```
' These are the MIDI API functions
Private Declare Function midiOutOpen Lib "mmsystem.dll" (hMidiOut As Long, ↵
ByVal DeviceId As Integer, ByVal C As Long, ByVal I As Long, ByVal F As Long) ↵
As Integer

Private Declare Function midiOutShortMsg Lib "mmsystem.dll" (ByVal hMidiOut ↵
As Integer, ByVal MidiMessage As Long) As Integer

Private Declare Function midiOutClose Lib "mmsystem.dll" (ByVal hMidiOut ↵
As Integer) As Integer

'   HMidi is the handle to the
'   open MIDI Device
Dim HMidi As Long

'   MIDI Mapper
Const MIDI_MAPPER = -1
```

3. The Form_Load procedure handles setting up the playing of the MIDI notes.

```
Private Sub Form_Load()

'  Set the text display value
text1.Text = Int(127 / 2)

'  Open the MIDI Mapper Device 0
Er = midiOutOpen(HMidi, MIDI_MAPPER, 0, 0, 0)

'  We will ensure that the device was opened properly
If Er <> 0 Then
    MsgBox "There is an Error Opening the MIDI Device."
'    End
End If

End Sub
```

4. When the application is finished, ensure that the MIDI device is closed.

```
Private Sub Form_Unload(Cancel As Integer)

'  Close the MIDI Device
Throw = midiOutClose(HMidi)

End Sub
```

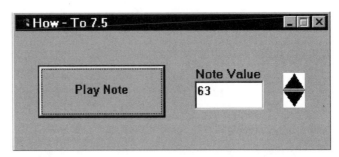

Figure 7-5-1 The form at runtime

5. When the user selects to play a note, build the message for the midiOutShortMsg function and then send the message to the system.

```
Private Sub PlayNote_Click()

'  Ensure that Note and Message are
'  Long Integers
Dim Note As Long
Dim Message As Long

'  Get the Note Value
Note = Val(text1.Text)

'  Make sure we have a valid note
If Note < 128 And Note > -1 Then

'  &H90 Is the Note On Command.  The 0 in
'  &H90 can be changed to change the channel
'  NOTE is the value of the note to be played.
'  We multiply the value times 256 to set the
'  second set of bits
'  &H7F0000 is setting the volume to 127 (&H7F)
'  but we are setting the high order bits
'  The final Hex value for a Hex Note of 40
'  would be &H7F4090.
Message = &H90 + (Note * 256) + &H7F0000

'  Send the message to the device
Throw = midiOutShortMsg(HMidi, Message)

End If

End Sub
```

6. The SpinDown and SpinUp events handle checking to ensure that the data in the text box is within the specified range. Note that if the user enters alpha text, it will be converted to a number.

```
Private Sub Spin1_SpinDown()

' Get the value of the text
A = Val(text1.Text)

' Make sure it is in the bounds
If A > 0 And A < 128 Then A = A - 1

' Set the text to the new value
text1.Text = A

End Sub

Private Sub Spin1_SpinUp()

' Get the value of the text
A = Val(text1.Text)

' Make sure it is in the bounds
If A < 127 And A > -1 Then A = A + 1

' Set the text to the new value
text1.Text = A

End Sub
```

How It Works

The process of opening and sending notes to the MIDI device is straightforward and uses only three functions: midiOutOpen, midiOutShortMsg, and midiOutClose. Tables 7-5-2 and 7-5-3 overview the MIDI low-level functions and their parameters.

Table 7-5-2 Low-level MIDI functions

FUNCTION	DESCRIPTION
midiOutOpen	Opens a MIDI output device
midiOutShortMsg	Outputs a 1-3 byte MIDI message
midiOutClose	Closes the MIDI device

Table 7-5-3 Low-level MIDI functions and their parameters

FUNCTION	PARAMETER	DESCRIPTION
midiOutOpen	hMidiOut as long	Contains the handle to the MIDI device
	ByVal DeviceId as integer	The ID number of the MIDI device
		MIDI_MAPPER is used to access the Windows
		MIDI mapper
	ByVal dwCallBack as long	Usually set to 0

FUNCTION	PARAMETER	DESCRIPTION
	ByVal dwInstance as long	Usually set to 0
	ByVal dwFlags as long	Usually set to 0
midiOutShortMsg	ByVal hMidiOut as integer	Pointer to the MIDI device from midiOutOpen
	ByVal MidiMessage as long	The MIDI message to send
midiOutClose	ByVal hMidiOut as integer	Pointer to the MIDI device from midiOutOpen

Each of the functions is fairly easy to use. But building the parameters for the midiOutShortMsg function warrants a closer look.

Most MIDI data contains commands that range from 1 to 3 bytes in length and are handled by the midiOutShortMsg function. There is also a midiOutLongMsg function that can send messages longer than 3 bytes, but to send single notes to the system, midiOutShortMsg will suffice. The messages to turn on the note and to indicate which note is to be played and the velocity (volume) of the note must be incorporated into the 3 bytes of data. The following is the code that accomplishes this:

```
Message = &H7F0000 + (Note * 256) + &H90
```

The hexadecimal format of the message is as follows:

```
ZZYYXX
```

XX is the hex 90 value, YY is the value of the note, and ZZ is the volume of the note. The first set of data (XX), &H90 is hex 90, which indicates to turn the next note on. To set the YY positions, multiply the note value by 256 to set the third and fourth positions. Finally, set the volume of the note to the highest value of 127 (hex 7F). Note that there are four trailing zeros on the value (&H7F0000) so that the ZZ positions are set.

The final result of this command is to tell the system to turn on the note value with the specified volume. The program allows you to flip through the various notes. 127 indicates the highest pitch note; indicates the lowest pitch note.

Using these techniques, you can play a series of MIDI notes along with or in response to specific program actions. A series of MIDI notes can be used as a specific signature for actions in applications such as exit or mouse clicks. This way you do not have to distribute Wave or MIDI files with your application.

Comments

The multimedia extensions provide a wide range of functions that allow for complex manipulation of MIDI devices and data.

8

PUTTING IT ALL TOGETHER

8

PUTTING IT ALL TOGETHER

How do I...

In this chapter, the techniques developed in the last seven chapters will be combined into projects that demonstrate how to develop interactive multimedia projects. These How-Tos will explore various popular methods of implementing multimedia.

Multimedia can benefit the developer in a wide range of topics and methods, including educational use, business presentations, and information delivery. Topics that will be covered include implementing a hypertext system, building a math game, and developing a business presentation.

8.1 Create an About box that plays like interactive movie credits

One popular feature found in today's multimedia software is an About box that scrolls through the producers and developers of the software like movie credits. Also, many developers like to place Easter eggs in their programs for their users to find. This How-To will pull together techniques from Chapters 2 and 3 to implement a full-featured About box.

8.2 Add a pop-up splash screen to my programs

Often a program will take several moments to load. One common indicator to the user that program elements are loading is a splash screen that indicates load status. In this How-To, a splash screen will be developed for the image flip book program developed in How-To 5.3.

8.3 Create a business presentation

Multimedia has become an important communications tools for many businesses today. The techniques developed throughout this book provide a wide variety of methods for developing multimedia presentations. This How-To will utilize many of the techniques developed earlier in the book to build a demo presentation.

8.4 Create a process control simulation

Computers have always been used to simulate different types of processes. With the use of multimedia, graphics, sound, and animation/video can be added to enhance these simulations. This How-To will develop a simple solar system simulation. Three planets will revolve around a glowing sun. The speed of the planets can be controlled, and there is an option to spin the planets off of their rotation.

8.5 Create a computer-based training authoring and delivery system

Interactive multimedia can be used as an effective training tool. Computer-based training is quickly becoming a popular and effective method for teaching employees as well as students. This How-To implements a multiple-choice authoring and delivery system. The implementation combines all of the necessary interactive elements to design and take tests. Also, various multimedia elements are added to enhance the test-taking process.

8.6 Create a hypertext system

Text is an integral part of delivering information to the user. Hypertext has become a common feature in many different types of programs today. The Microsoft Windows Help environment is an excellent example of the use of hypertext. This How-To builds a hypertext system based on a simple text file format.

8.7   Build a complete animated scene with WinG

WinG was introduced in Chapter 6 as an effective tool for performing high-speed graphic manipulation. Several of the How-Tos in that chapter demonstrate animation and sprite techniques. For this project, a complete animated scene will be developed using the techniques developed in Chapter 6.

8.8   Create a multimedia game

Games are some of the most popular uses for multimedia. To demonstrate the interactive use of Visual Basic 4.0 with multimedia elements, an example math tutor program will be developed. Four different types of exercises will be implemented to demonstrate different techniques for interactive multimedia exercises.

8.1   How do I...
Create an About box that plays like interactive movie credits?

COMPLEXITY: INTERMEDIATE

Problem

I would like to develop for my programs an About box that will provide detailed information on the product developers. This information would be given in movie-like credits, along with the ever-popular Easter egg for the user to find.

Technique

In How-To 2.4, a method for scrolling text in a picture box was developed. In this How-To, this technique will be implemented in a class module. Also, the MCI control and some simple checking will be used to implement a surprise Easter egg for the user.

Steps

Open and run 8-1.VBP. Select the About menu item under the Help menu. The About box appears as shown in Figure 8-1-1.

Click on the Credits button to see the scrolling credits for the About box. To see the Easter egg, first click on the image, then click the address labels in succession from top to bottom; the Thank You animation will then run.

1. Create a new project named 8-1.VBP. Add the objects and properties listed in Table 8-1-1 to the form and save the form as 8-1.FRM.

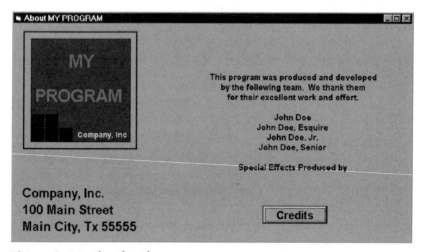

Figure 8-1-1 The About box at runtime

Table 8-1-1 Form 8-1's object and properties

OBJECT	PROPERTY	SETTING
Form	Name	Form1
	Caption	"How-To 8.1"

2. Add the menu items in Table 8-1-2 to the form.

Table 8-1-2 Form 8-1 menu setup

OBJECT	PROPERTY	SETTING
File	Caption	"File"
Edit	Caption	"Edit"
Help	Caption	"Help"
About	Caption	"About"

3. Create a new form named ABOUT.FRM. Add the objects and properties listed in Table 8-1-3 to the form.

Table 8-1-3 The About form's objects and properties

OBJECT	PROPERTY	SETTING
Form	Name	Form2
	Auto3D	-1 'True
	BackColor	&H00C0C0C0&
	Caption	"About MY PROGRAM"
	ScaleMode	3 'Pixel
CommandButton	Name	Credits
	Caption	"Credits"
	Font	
	name	"Arial"
	size	12
Timer	Name	Timer1
	Enabled	0 'False
	Interval	400
PictureBox	Name	ScrollPict
	BackColor	&H00C0C0C0&
	BorderStyle	0 'None
	Font	
	name	"Arial"
	ScaleMode	3 'Pixel
PictureBox	Name	MyIconPict
	AutoSize	-1 'True
	BorderStyle	0 'None
	Picture	(Aboutico.bmp)
MMControl	Name	MMControl2
	Visible	0 'False
MMControl	Name	MMControl1
	Visible	0 'False
Label	Name	CityLabel

continued on next page

continued from previous page

OBJECT	PROPERTY	SETTING
	AutoSize	-1 'True
	BackColor	&H00C0C0C0&
	Caption	"Main City, Tx 55555"
	Font	
	name	"Arial"
	size	13.8
	Index	2
Label	Name	StreetLabel
	AutoSize	-1 'True
	BackColor	&H00C0C0C0&
	Caption	"100 Main Street"
	Font	
	name	"Arial"
	size	13.8
	Index	1
Label	Name	CompanyLabel
	AutoSize	-1 'True
	BackColor	&H00C0C0C0&
	Caption	"Company, Inc."
	Font	
	name	"Arial"
	size	13.8
	Index	0

4. Add the following code to 8-1.FRM.

```
Private Sub About_Click()
'   Show the About Box form
Form2.Show
End Sub
```

5. Add the following code to the general declarations section of ABOUT.FRM. The Scroll class is globally declared, as are variables for performing the scroll and Easter egg.

```
'   Globally declare the Scroll Class
Dim Scroll As Class1
```

```
'   ScrollText will hold the
Dim ScrollText() As String

'   Snum will hold the value of the line
'   of text that is scrolling
Dim Snum As Integer

'   The easter egg variables will be set if the
'   appropriate combination of clicks are done
'   to bring up the Easter Egg Animation
Dim easter1, easter2, easter3 As Integer

'   The Hsav and Wsav variables will hold the Width
'   and Height values of the icon picture.  Thus when
'   the Easter egg is shown, the Icon picture can be
'   resized.
Dim Hsav As Integer
Dim Wsav As Integer
```

6. SetText handles filling the ScrollText array with the text to be scrolled.

```
Private Sub SetText()
'   Setup the text to be scrolled
    ScrollText(1) = "This program was produced and developed"
    ScrollText(2) = "by the following team.  We thank them"
    ScrollText(3) = "for their excellent work and effort."
    ScrollText(4) = ""
    ScrollText(5) = "John Doe"
    ScrollText(6) = "John Doe, Esquire"
    ScrollText(7) = "John Doe, Jr."
    ScrollText(8) = "John Doe, Senior"
    ScrollText(9) = ""
    ScrollText(10) = "Special Effects Produced by"
    ScrollText(11) = "John Doe, Inc."
    ScrollText(12) = ""
    ScrollText(13) = "Original Script Developed by"
    ScrollText(14) = "Sir John Doe."
    ScrollText(15) = ""
    ScrollText(16) = ""
    ScrollText(17) = "If you have ideas for a Company, Inc."
    ScrollText(18) = "production, please feel free to"
    ScrollText(19) = "contact our Research Developer,"
    ScrollText(20) = "John Doe the Third."
    ScrollText(21) = ""
    ScrollText(22) = "Thank You for Using MY PROGRAM!!"
End Sub
```

7. When the CityLabel is selected, a check is done to see if the picture and other two address labels have been selected. If so, then the Easter egg animation is shown.

```
Private Sub CityLabel_Click(Index As Integer)

'   The last text label has to be selected for the
'   Easter Egg to be shown.  The check is done to see
'   if all of the correct selections have been made to
```

continued on next page

continued from previous page

```
'   show the Easter Egg.
      If easter1 = 1 And easter2 = 1 And easter3 = 1 Then
            '   Setup the playing of the animation
            MMControl1.FileName = App.Path + "\letthank.avi"
            MMControl1.Command = "close"
            MMControl1.Command = "open"

            '   Setup the picture to show the animation
            MyIconPict.Width = MyIconPict.Width * 1.2
            MyIconPict.Height = MyIconPict.Height * 1.2
            MMControl1.hWndDisplay = MyIconPict.hWnd
            MMControl1.Command = "play"

            '   Reset the Easter variables
            easter1 = 0
            easter2 = 0
            easter3 = 0
      End If
End Sub
```

8. When the Credits button is selected and the scrolling has not started, the timer is enabled to start the scrolling process.

```
Private Sub Credits_Click()

      '   if the timer is not enabled, then the
      '   animation is started
      If timer1.Enabled = False Then
            '   Reset the scroll count and start
            '   the timer
            Snum = 0
            timer1.Enabled = True
      Else


      End If
End Sub
```

9. The appropriate Easter egg variable is set when the CompanyLabel is selected.

```
Private Sub CompanyLabel_Click(Index As Integer)
      '   Set the appropriate Easter Variable
      easter2 = 1
End Sub
```

10. When the form is loaded, the width and height of the picture are stored. This is done so that when the Easter egg is finished playing, the picture is reset. Also, the Scroll class is set up and the text to be scrolled is set up.

```
Private Sub Form_Load()
      '   Store the width and height of the
      '   icon picture
      Wsav = MyIconPict.Width
      Hsav = MyIconPict.Height
```

```
'  Set the height of the picture that will
'   scroll the text to 0
scrollpict.Height = 0

'  Dimension the ScrollText variable
ReDim ScrollText(22) As String

'  Declare the new class
Set Scroll = New Class1

'  Set the scrolling picture
Set Scroll.Pict = scrollpict

'  Set the timer for the scroll
Set Scroll.Time = timer1

'  Setup the scroll text
SetText

'  Setup the playing of the background music
MMControl2.FileName = "c:\windows\media\passport.mid"
MMControl2.Command = "close"
MMControl2.DeviceType = "sequencer"
MMControl2.Command = "open"
MMControl2.Command = "play"
End Sub
```

11. When the picture is selected, the width and height are reset in case the animation is being shown. Also, the appropriate Easter egg variable is set.

```
Private Sub MyIconPict_Click()
'  When the Picture is selected,
'  the width and height will be reset
'  Thus if the Easter Egg was shown,
'  the original picture will be setup
MyIconPict.Width = Wsav
MyIconPict.Height = Hsav
MyIconPict.Refresh

'  Set the appropriate Easter Flag
easter1 = 1
End Sub
```

12. When StreetLabel is selected, the appropriate Easter egg variable is set.

```
Private Sub StreetLabel_Click(Index As Integer)
'  Set the appropriate Easter Flag
easter3 = 1
End Sub
```

13. The timer handles scrolling the text. When all of the text is displayed, the Scroll class ExitClear function is called to clear the text out.

```
Private Sub Timer1_Timer()
```

continued on next page

continued from previous page

```
'   Scroll the text until all of the text has
'   been shown
If Snum < 22 Then
    '   Increment the scroll line number
    Snum = Snum + 1
    '   Set the scroll number in the text
    Scroll.Lns = Snum
    '   Scroll the text
    Scroll.TextScroll ScrollText
Else
    '   When all of the lines have been shown, the
    '   exitclear function is called to continue scrolling
    '   the text until it has disappeared
    Scroll.exitclear
End If

End Sub
```

14. Create a new class module called SCROLL.CLS. Add the following to the general declarations section of the form. The global member variables for the class are declared.

```
'   This variable holds the line number
'   to be newly displayed
Private m_Lines

'   This will hold the picture for the
'   text to be displayed on
Private m_Pict As Object

'   m_Timer is the timer that controls
'   the scrolling
Private m_Timer As Object

'   m_StartTop holds the top starting
'   position of the m_Pict object
Private m_StartTop
```

15. The Clear function handles scrolling the text off the picture. When the text is cleared, the timer is disabled and the picture is reset.

```
Private Sub Clear()

        '   Move the picture up one the height of line of text
        m_Pict.Top = m_Pict.Top - m_Pict.TextHeight("aWy")

        '   Check to see if the Top of the picture has
        '   moved up far enough to not be visible.
        '   When this is done, the timer is stopped
        '   the picture is reset and moved to its
        '   original position
        If m_Pict.Top + m_Pict.Height < 0 Then
            m_Timer.Enabled = False
            m_Pict.Height = 0
            m_Pict.Top = m_StartTop
```

```
                m_Pict.CurrentX = 0
                m_Pict.CurrentY = 0
            End If
End Sub
```

16. The Scroll function handles scrolling the text. The m_Lines variable indicates the next line of text in the array to be printed.

```
Private Sub Scroll(a() As String)

    '  Move the picture up
    m_Pict.Top = m_Pict.Top - m_Pict.TextHeight(a(m_Lines))

    '  Increase the height for the new line of text
    m_Pict.Height = m_Pict.Height + m_Pict.TextHeight(a(m_Lines))

    '  Center the text by setting the currentx
    m_Pict.CurrentX = (m_Pict.ScaleWidth - m_Pict.TextWidth(a(m_Lines))) / 2

    '  Print the text
    m_Pict.Print a(m_Lines)

End Sub
```

17. ExitClear calls the Clear function to clear the text off the picture.

```
Public Sub ExitClear()
    '  Call the clear function
    Clear
End Sub
```

18. TextScroll calls the Scroll function to handle scrolling the text.

```
Public Sub TextScroll(s() As String)
    '  Call the scroll function and pass the string
    Scroll s()
End Sub
```

19. The following property statements set the Picture box for the scrolling, the timer control, and the Lns property.

```
Public Property Set Pict(aControl As Object)
    '  Set the Picture property and store
    '  the top value
    Set m_Pict = aControl
    m_StartTop = m_Pict.Top
End Property

Public Property Set Time(aControl As Object)
    '  Set the timer property
    Set m_Timer = aControl
End Property

Public Property Let Lns(n As Integer)
    '  Set the lines property
```

continued on next page

continued from previous page

```
    m_Lines = n
End Property
```

How It Works

The Scroll class involves taking the techniques developed in How-To 2.4 and implementing them into a new class. The class is driven by the timer. With each tick of the timer, the next line of text is displayed, with the other lines scrolled up. When all of the text has been displayed, the text can then be cleared using the ExitClear function of the class. This will scroll the text until the last line has scrolled off the picture. Then the class disables the timer and resets the picture.

The Easter egg is easily implemented by the user, who enters in a specific set of actions to enable the Easter egg. In this case, the Easter egg is the playing of an animation with the MCI control and the set of actions is clicking the picture and address label objects. Note that it is important for the CityLabel to be clicked last, otherwise the sequence of the clicks is not important.

Comments

Many different types of methods could be used to enhance the About box. For example, the ScreenBuild class from How-To 4.7 could be used to do a fade in of the picture.

8.2 How do I...
Add a pop-up splash screen to my programs?

COMPLEXITY: INTERMEDIATE

Problem

Often a program will take a while to load, or at certain points will take several minutes for execution. I would like to be able to add a splash screen to my application that informs the user of the load status and at the same time blocks the user from performing other program actions.

Technique

A new Windows API function, SetWindowWord, will be introduced to make the splash screen a child of the primary form (window). With the splash screen as a child, it will be shown until unloaded regardless of action taken on the parent form. How-To 5.3 will be used as the basis for demonstrating the splash screen.

Steps

Open and run 8-2.VBP. The running program appears as shown in Figure 8-2-1.

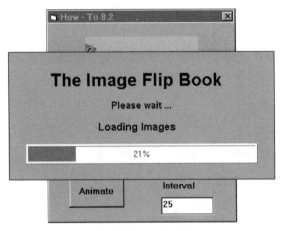

Figure 8-2-1 The form as it loads

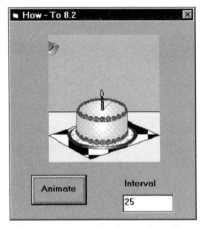

Figure 8-2-2 The form after all images are loaded

As each image is loaded in the flip book, the percentage indicator on the splash screen is increased. Once all of the images are loaded, the primary form is shown (see Figure 8-2-2).

1. Create a new project called 8-2.VBP. Insert a new form and save it as POPUP.FRM. Add the objects and properties listed in Table 8-2-1 to the form.

Table 8-2-1 Project form's objects and properties

OBJECT	PROPERTY	SETTING
Form	Name	PopUp
	Auto3D	-1 'True
	BorderStyle	1 'Fixed Single
	ControlBox	0 'False
	MaxButton	0 'False
	MinButton	0 'False
SSPanel	Name	SSPanel1
	Caption	"SSPanel1"
	Borderwidth	2
	Bevelinner	1
	Floodtype	1
	Floodcolor	65280

continued on next page

CHAPTER 8

continued from previous page

OBJECT	PROPERTY	SETTING
Label	Name	Wait
	AutoSize	-1 'True
	BackStyle	0 'Transparent
	Caption	"Please wait ..."
	Font	
	name	"Arial"
	size	9
	ForeColor	&H00FF0000&
Label	Name	Images
	Alignment	2 'Center
	AutoSize	-1 'True
	BackStyle	0 'Transparent
	Caption	"Loading Images"
	Font	
	name	"Arial"
	size	10.2
Label	Name	Title
	Alignment	2 'Center
	AutoSize	-1 'True
	BackStyle	0 'Transparent
	Caption	"The Image Flip Book"
	Font	
	name	"Arial"
	size	16.2
	ForeColor	&H00800000&

2. Add the objects and properties listed in Table 8-2-2 to Form1 and save the form as 8-2.FRM.

Table 8-2-2 Project form's objects and properties

OBJECT	PROPERTY	SETTING
Form	Name	Form1
	Auto3D	-1 'True
	BackColor	&H00C0C0C0&

OBJECT	PROPERTY	SETTING
	BorderStyle	3 'Fixed Double
	Caption	"How To 8.2"
	ScaleMode	3 'Pixel
TextBox	Name	Text1
	Text	"25"
CommandButton	Name	Animate
	Caption	"Animate"
Timer Timer1	Enabled	0 'False
	Interval	25
Label Label1	AutoSize	-1 'True
	BackStyle	0 'Transparent
	Caption	"Interval"
Image	Name	flip
	Index	0

3. Add the following code to the general declarations section of the form. The SetWindowWord function is declared, along with appropriate constants for the function.

```
'   The SetWindowWord function will be used to designate
'   the splash screen
Private Declare Function SetWindowWord Lib "User" (ByVal hWnd As Integer, ↵
ByVal nIndex As Integer, ByVal wNewWord As Integer) As Integer

'   Constant for the SetWindowWord function
Const GWW_HWNDPARENT = (-8)

'   n will be used to count through the image
'   controls
Dim n As Integer
```

4. Add the following code to the general declarations section of the form. The Pause function pauses the execution of the program for the specified number of seconds.

```
Sub Pause(Seconds As Single)

'   The following code gets the current time and
```

continued on next page

continued from previous page

```
'   loops until the timer has moved forward the
'   specified number of seconds.
    StartTime = Timer
    Do While Timer < StartTime + Seconds
        DoEvents
    Loop

End Sub
```

5. When the Animate button is selected, the timer is started and the animation is set up.

```
Private Sub Animate_Click()

'   Reset n to -1, note it will be
'   incremented immediately
n = -1

'   Set the timer interval
timer1.Interval = Val(text1.Text)

'   Enable the timer
timer1.Enabled = True

'   Make sure the last image is not visible
'   from the last animation.
flip(23).Visible = False

End Sub
```

6. When the form is loaded, Form1 and the Popup form are centered on the screen. Also, the mouse pointer is changed to that of the hourglass for the load. The Popup form is set to be a child of Form1 using the SetWindowWord function. Form1 is set up for the loading of the images. While the images are loaded, the SSPanel is updated to show the appropriate percentages.

```
Private Sub Form_Load()

'   Center the form and splash screen
Form1.Top = (Screen.Height - Form1.Height) / 2
Form1.Left = (Screen.Width - Form1.Width) / 2

Popup.Top = (Screen.Height - Popup.Height) / 2
Popup.Left = (Screen.Width - Popup.Width) / 2

'   Set the hourglass mouse pointer while the
'   images are loading
Popup.MousePointer = 11
Form1.MousePointer = 11

'   Enable the form and show it
Form1.Enabled = False
Form1.Show
```

```
'  Set the FloodPercent and show the
'  splash form
Popup.SSPanel1.FloodPercent = 0
Popup.Show

'  Pause for 2 seconds
Pause 2

'  Make the splash form the child
'  of form1
RtnCode = SetWindowWord(Popup.hWnd, GWW_HWNDPARENT, Form1.hWnd)

'  Load the images
For n = 1 To 23
    Load flip(n)
    flip(n - 1).Picture = LoadPicture(App.Path + "\" + Right$(Str$(n), ↵
             Len(Str$(n)) - 1) + ".bmp")

    Popup.SSPanel1.FloodPercent = (100 * (n / 24))
    Pause 0.5
Next n

'  Load the final image
n = 24
flip(n - 1).Picture = LoadPicture(App.Path + "\" + Right$(Str$(n), ↵
Len(Str$(n)) - 1) + ".bmp")

Popup.SSPanel1.FloodPercent = (100 * (n / 24))
Pause 2

'  Enable form1, set the focus and
'  reset the mousepointer
Form1.Enabled = True
Form1.SetFocus
Form1.MousePointer = 0

'  Unload the splash  screen
Unload Popup

End Sub
```

7. The timer handles flipping through the images and producing the animation.

```
Private Sub Timer1_Timer()

'  Increment n
n = n + 1

'  Check to see if we have reached the next to
'  last picture
If n = 22 Then timer1.Enabled = False

'  For each timer iteration, we will make
'  the currently displayed image invisible
'  and make the image to be displayed visible
```

continued on next page

continued from previous page

```
flip(n).Visible = False
flip(n + 1).Visible = True

End Sub
```

How It Works

The key to building the splash screen is using the Windows SetWindowWord function. The start-up form, Form1, must be set as the parent of the splash screen form, Popup. When Form1 is set as the parent window for the Popup form, it allows the Popup form to stay on top of Form1 despite actions taking place on Form1. When the load is finished, the Popup form simply needs to be unloaded to end its use.

The basis for building the splash screen is How-To 5.3. You may have noted when reviewing this How-To that a short pause takes place when loading the 24 images of the flip book animation. This is an ideal place for a splash screen to be used to give the load status of the images. But to make this demo clearer (and slower), the Pause function is used to count 2 seconds between the load of each image. For additional information on how the image flip book works, see How-To 5.3.

Comments

This general technique can be used to give information about any process to the user. In this case, the percentage of the load is used as an indicator of the process status. The number of images loaded could be given instead of the percentage.

8.3 How do I...
Create a business presentation?

COMPLEXITY: INTERMEDIATE

Problem

Multimedia is an important tool for businesses. The business presentation has become a popular vehicle for providing interactive information about a business and its products and services. I would like to be able to develop a business presentation based on the techniques developed in this book.

Technique

Several techniques previously developed will be called on to build the presentation. The techniques from Chapter 2 will be used to provide eye-catching text for the presentation. The presentation will use the font manipulation techniques from How-To 2.7. Also, several of the methods from Chapter 5 will be used to display video and animation clips as well as perform simple animations using the line control. Note that this presentation makes use of a MDIForm as a backdrop to the presentation.

Figure 8-3-1 The start of the presentation

Steps

Open and run 8-3.VPB. The start of the presentation appears as shown in Figure 8-3-1. The second and third screens show text that transitions from right to left over the background pictures. Figure 8-3-2 shows the second bullet screen. Figure 8-3-3 shows the interactive demo screen of the presentation. To play the various media clips, select the appropriate button. The clips can be replayed, fast forwarded, etc., by using the MCI control buttons. The final screen is shown in Figure 8-3-4. To end the program, click on the form when indicated.

1. Create a new project named 8-3.VBP. Add the object and properties listed in Table 8-3-1 and save the form as 8-3.FRM. Note this is a MDIForm.

Table 8-3-1 The MDIform's object and properties

OBJECT	PROPERTY	SETTING
MDIForm	Name	MDIForm1
	BackColor	&H00000000&
	Caption	"How-To 8.3"
	WindowState	2 'Maximized

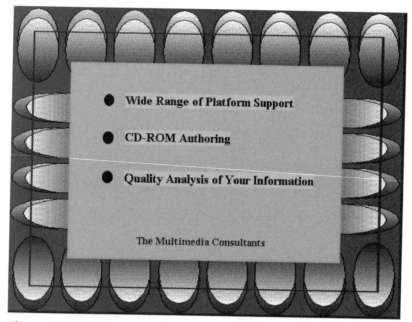

Figure 8-3-2 Presentation information screen

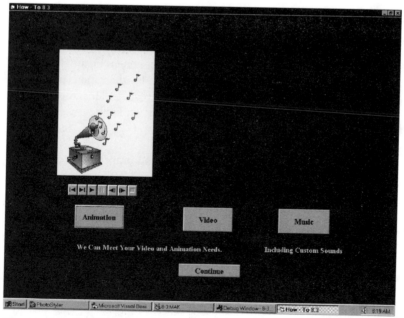

Figure 8-3-3 Presentation demo screen

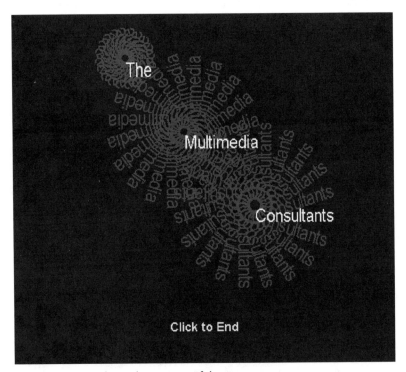

Figure 8-3-4 The ending screen of the presentation

2. Insert a new form named INTRO.FRM. Add the objects and properties listed in Table 8-3-2.

Table 8-3-2 The intro form's objects and properties

OBJECT	PROPERTY	SETTING
Form	Name	Form1
	BackColor	&H00C00000&
	BorderStyle	1 'Fixed Single
	Caption	"Form1"
	MDIChild	-1 'True
	WindowState	2 'Maximized
Timer	Name	Timer3
	Enabled	0 'False
	Interval	2500

continued on next page

continued from previous page

OBJECT	PROPERTY	SETTING
Timer	Name	Timer2
	Enabled	0 'False
	Interval	20
Timer	Name	Timer1
	Interval	1
Label	Name	Consultants
	AutoSize	-1 'True
	BackColor	&H00C00000&
	Caption	"Consultants"
	Font	
	name	"Times New Roman"
	size	48
	ForeColor	&H0000FF00&
	Visible	0 'False
Label	Name	Multimedia
	AutoSize	-1 'True
	BackColor	&H00C00000&
	Caption	"Multimedia"
	Font	
	name	"Times New Roman"
	size	48
	ForeColor	&H0000FF00&
	Visible	0 'False
Label	Name	The
	AutoSize	-1 'True
	BackColor	&H00C00000&
	Caption	"The"
	Font	
	name	"Times New Roman"
	size	48
	ForeColor	&H0000FF00&
	Visible	0 'False

OBJECT	PROPERTY	SETTING
Line	Name	Line1
	BorderColor	&H00000000&
	BorderWidth	10
	Index	3
Line	Name	Line1
	BorderColor	&H00000000&
	BorderWidth	10
	Index	2
Line	Name	Line1
	BorderColor	&H00000000&
	BorderWidth	10
	Index	1
VB.Line	Name	Line1
	BorderColor	&H00000000&
	BorderWidth	10
	Index	0

3. Insert a new form named SCRN2.FRM. Add the objects and properties listed in Table 8-3-3.

Table 8-3-3 Scrn2 objects and properties

OBJECT	PROPERTY	SETTING
Form	Name	Form2
	BackColor	&H00000000&
	BorderStyle	1 'Fixed Single
	Caption	"Form2"
	MDIChild	-1 'True
	WindowState	2 'Maximized
Timer	Name	Timer2
	Enabled	0 'False
	Interval	2500

continued on next page

continued from previous page

OBJECT	PROPERTY	SETTING
Timer	Name	Timer1
	Interval	1
PictureBox	Name	Background
	AutoSize	-1 'True
	BorderStyle	0 'None
	Picture	(Border1.bmp)
	Visible	0 'False
Shape	Name	Shape2
	BackColor	&H000000FF&
	BackStyle	1 'Opaque
	BorderStyle	0 'Transparent
	Shape	2 'Oval
Shape	Name	Shape1
	BackColor	&H000000FF&
	BackStyle	1 'Opaque
	BorderStyle	0 'Transparent
	Shape	2 'Oval
Label	Name	Label4
	AutoSize	-1 'True
	BackColor	&H0000FFFF&
	BackStyle	0 'Transparent
	Caption	"The Multimedia Consultants"
	Font	
	name	"Times New Roman"
	size	10.2
	ForeColor	&H0000FFFF&
Shape	Name	Shape3
	BackColor	&H000000FF&
	BackStyle	1 'Opaque
	BorderStyle	0 'Transparent
	Shape	2 'Oval

OBJECT	PROPERTY	SETTING
Label	Name	Slide3
	AutoSize	-1 'True
	BackColor	&H00C0C0FF&
	Caption	"Superior Multimedia Knowledge"
	Font	
	name	"Times New Roman"
	size	12
Label	Name	Slide2
	AutoSize	-1 'True
	BackColor	&H00C0C0FF&
	Caption	"Over 10 Years Industry Experience"
	Font	
	name	"Times New Roman"
	size	12
Label	Name	Slide1
	AutoSize	-1 'True
	BackColor	&H00C0C0FF&
	Caption	"Consulting Services You Can Use"
	Font	
	name	"Times New Roman"
	size	12

4. Insert a new form named SCRN.FRM. Add the objects and properties listed in Table 8-3-4.

Table 8-3-4 Scrn3 objects and properties

OBJECT	PROPERTY	SETTING
Form	Name	Form3
	BackColor	&H00000000&
	BorderStyle	1 'Fixed Single
	Caption	"Form3"
	MDIChild	-1 'True
	Visible	0 'False
	WindowState	2 'Maximized

continued on next page

continued from previous page

OBJECT	PROPERTY	SETTING
Timer	Name	Timer2
	Enabled	0 'False
	Interval	2500
Timer	Name	Timer1
	Interval	1
PictureBox	Name	Background
	AutoSize	-1 'True
	BorderStyle	0 'None
	Picture	(Border2.bmp)
	Visible	0 'False
Shape	Name	Shape2
	BackColor	&H00FF0000&
	BackStyle	1 'Opaque
	BorderStyle	0 'Transparent
	Shape	2 'Oval
Shape	Name	Shape1
	BackColor	&H00FF0000&
	BackStyle	1 'Opaque
	BorderStyle	0 'Transparent
	Shape	2 'Oval
Label	Name	Label4
	AutoSize	-1 'True
	BackColor	&H0000FFFF&
	BackStyle	0 'Transparent
	Caption	"The Multimedia Consultants"
	Font	
	name	"Times New Roman"
	size	10.2
	ForeColor	&H00FF0000&
Shape	Name	Shape3
	BackColor	&H00FF0000&

OBJECT	PROPERTY	SETTING
	BackStyle	1 'Opaque
	BorderStyle	0 'Transparent
	Shape	2 'Oval
Label	Name	Slide3
	AutoSize	-1 'True
	BackColor	&H00E0E0E0&
	Caption	"Quality Analysis of Your Information"
	Font	
	name	"Times New Roman"
	size	12
Label	Name	Slide2
	AutoSize	-1 'True
	BackColor	&H00E0E0E0&
	Caption	"CD-ROM Authoring"
	Font	
	name	"Times New Roman"
	size	12
Label	Name	Slide1
	AutoSize	-1 'True
	BackColor	&H00E0E0E0&
	Caption	"Wide Range of Platform Support"
	Font	
	name	"Times New Roman"
	size	12

5. Insert a new form named DEMO.FRM. Add the objects and properties listed in Table 8-3-5.

Table 8-3-5 The Demo form's objects and properties

OBJECT	PROPERTY	SETTING
Form	Name	Form4
	BackColor	&H00000000&
	BorderStyle	0 'None
	Caption	"Form4"

continued on next page

continued from previous page

OBJECT	PROPERTY	SETTING
	MDIChild	-1 'True
CommandButton	Name	Continue
	Caption	"Continue"
	Font	
	name	"Times New Roman"
	size	12
MMControl	Name	MMControl3
	EjectVisible	0 'False
	PrevVisible	0 'False
	Visible	0 'False
CommandButton	Name	Music
	Caption	"Music"
	Font	
	name	"Times New Roman"
	size	12
CommandButton	Name	Video
	Caption	"Video"
	Font	
	name	"Times New Roman"
	size	12
CommandButton	Name	animation
	Caption	"Animation"
	Font	
	name	"Times New Roman"
	size	12
PictureBox	Name	Dog
	BackColor	&H00FFFFFF&
	BorderStyle	0 'None
	Visible	0 'False

OBJECT	PROPERTY	SETTING
PictureBox	Name	Victrola
	BackColor	&H00FFFFFF&
	BorderStyle	0 'None
	Visible	0 'False
MMControl	Name	MMControl2
	EjectVisible	0 'False
	RecordVisible	0 'False
	Visible	0 'False
MMControl	Name	MMControl1
	EjectVisible	0 'False
	RecordVisible	0 'False
	Visible	0 'False
Label	Name	Label2
	AutoSize	-1 'True
	BackColor	&H00000000&
	Caption	"Including Custom Sounds"
	Font	
	name	"Times New Roman"
	size	10.8
	ForeColor	&H0000FFFF&
Label	Name	Label1
	AutoSize	-1 'True
	BackColor	&H00000000&
	Caption	"We Can Meet Your Video and Animation Needs."
	Font	
	name	"Times New Roman"
	size	10.8
	ForeColor	&H0000FFFF&

6. Insert a new form named END.FRM. Add the objects and properties listed in Table 8-3-6.

Table 8-3-6 The End form's objects and properties

OBJECT	PROPERTY	SETTING
Form	Name	Form5
	BackColor	&H00000000&
	BorderStyle	1 'Fixed Single
	Caption	"Introduction"
	Font	
	name	"Arial"
	size	7.8
	MDIChild	-1 'True
	WindowState	2 'Maximized
Timer	Name	Timer2
	Enabled	0 'False
	Interval	3500
PictureBox	Name	AniPict
	BorderStyle	0 'None
	Visible	0 'False
MMControl	Name	MMControl1
	EjectVisible	0 'False
	RecordVisible	0 'False
	Visible	0 'False
Timer	Name	Timer1
	Enabled	0 'False
	Interval	10
PictureBox	Name	DispPict
	BackColor	&H00000000&
	BorderStyle	0 'None
	Font	
	name	"MS Sans Serif"
	size	7.8
	ScaleMode	3 'Pixel

OBJECT	PROPERTY	SETTING
Label	Name	Label1
	AutoSize	-1 'True
	BackStyle	0 'Transparent
	Caption	"Click to End"
	Font	
	name	"Arial"
	size	10.2
	ForeColor	&H0000FFFF&
	Visible	0 'False

7. Add the following code to the MCIForm_Load procedure in 8-3.FRM. The first form of the presentation is loaded.

```
Private Sub MDIForm_Load()
'  Load the first form
Form1.Show
```

8. Add the following code to the general declarations section of INTRO.FRM. The global variables for storing the starting label positions on the form are declared, as well as the First variable for executing the code in the Form_Paint function once.

```
'  First will be used to execute the code
'  in the Form_Paint event once
Private First As Integer

'  The following three variables will be used
'  to store the original Heights of each label
Private TheOriginal As Integer
Private multimediaoriginal As Integer
Private consultantsoriginal As Integer
```

9. The following code will only be executed once. At start up, the form is centered and the three labels are given a 0 height. Their original heights are stored for later use.

```
Private Sub Form_Paint()

'  The first time the form is painted, the
'  following code executed
If First = 0 Then

    '  Set the First Variable
    First = 1

    '  Center and place each label
    The.Move Form1.Width / 2 - The.Width / 2, Form1.Height / 2 - The.Height ↵
```

continued on next page

continued from previous page

```
              / 2 - 1800

    Multimedia.Move Form1.Width / 2 - Multimedia.Width / 2, Form1.Height / 2 ↵
    - Multimedia.Height / 2

    Consultants.Move Form1.Width / 2 - Consultants.Width / 2, Form1.Height / 2 ↵
    - Consultants.Height / 2 + 1800

    '   Store the heights of each of the labels
    TheOriginal = The.Height
    multimediaoriginal = Multimedia.Height
    consultantsoriginal = Consultants.Height

    '   Set the heights to 0
    The.Height = 0
    Multimedia.Height = 0
    Consultants.Height = 0

    '   Ensure the labels are not visible
    The.Visible = True
    Multimedia.Visible = True
    Consultants.Visible = True

End If

End Sub
```

10. In the first timer, the line controls are lengthened in the appropriate directions so that a box is drawn around the outer edge of the form.

```
Private Sub Timer1_Timer()

'   Increase the length of each line in the appropriate
'   direction with each timer movement
Line1(0).X2 = Line1(0).X2 + 395
Line1(1).X2 = Line1(1).X2 - 395
Line1(2).Y2 = Line1(2).Y2 - 330
Line1(3).Y2 = Line1(3).Y2 + 345

'   Check to see if the lines have crossed
'   the entire form
If Line1(1).X2 < 0 Then Timer1.Enabled = False: Timer2.Enabled = True
End Sub
```

11. The second timer handles showing the labels. The height of each label is increased until the original height is reached. When all three labels are visible, Timer3 is started. Timer3 allows the form to be visible for a short period of time before the next form is loaded.

```
Private Sub Timer2_Timer()

'   Each label is incrementally exposed in order
'   from the The label to the Consultants label
If The.Height < TheOriginal Then
```

```
    The.Height = The.Height + 150
Else
    If Multimedia.Height < multimediaoriginal Then
        Multimedia.Height = Multimedia.Height + 150
    Else
        If Consultants.Height < consultantsoriginal Then
            Consultants.Height = Consultants.Height + 150
        Else
            Timer2.Enabled = False
            Form1.BackColor = QBColor(5)
            Timer3.Enabled = True
        End If
    End If
End If

End Sub
```

12. After the screen is visible for viewing, the next form is loaded.

```
Private Sub Timer3_Timer()
'  Make the form non-visible
Form1.Visible = False

'  Show the next form
Form2.Show

'  Unload the form
Unload Form1
End Sub
```

13. Add the following code to the general declarations section of SCRN2.FRM. First is used to execute the code in the Form_Paint procedure only once. Inc is used as the moving increment of the label controls. LeftOrg stores the original left position of the label controls.

```
'  First will be used to execute the code
'  in the Form_Paint event only once
Private First As Integer

'  Inc will hold the value to move the labels
'  with each timer event
Private Inc As Integer

'  LeftOrg will hold the original left
'  value of the three labels
Private LeftOrg As Integer
```

14. The code in the Form_Paint procedure is executed only once. The form is centered and the label controls are moved to the right of the form. Note that the left origin of the label controls is stored and the increment for the movement of the label controls is calculated.

```
Private Sub Form_Paint()
```

continued on next page

continued from previous page

```
'   The following code is only executed once
'   when the form is loaded
If First = 0 Then

    '   Center the background picture on the form
    background.Move Form2.Width / 2 - background.Width / 2, Form2.Height / 2 ↵
    - background.Height / 2

    '   Store the left origin of the sliding
    '   labels
    LeftOrg = Slide1.Left

    '   Inc will hold the incremental move to the left
    '   for each timer event.
    Inc = (background.Width - Slide1.Left) / 50

    '   Move the labels off to the right of the form
    Slide1.Left = background.Width
    Slide2.Left = background.Width
    Slide3.Left = background.Width

    '   set First
    First = 1

    '   Show the background image
    background.Visible = True
End If

End Sub
```

15. Timer1 handles sliding the label controls to their start up positions. Note that Timer2 is started to allow a delay for the user to read the text.

```
Private Sub Timer1_Timer()

'   Each label is slid to the left
'   in succession.
If Slide1.Left > LeftOrg Then
    Slide1.Left = Slide1.Left - Inc
Else
    If Slide2.Left > LeftOrg Then
        Slide2.Left = Slide2.Left - Inc
    Else
        If Slide3.Left > LeftOrg Then
            Slide3.Left = Slide3.Left - Inc
        Else
        Timer1.Enabled = False
        '   Timer2 is used to keep the form visible
        '   at the end of the label slides
        Timer2.Enabled = True
        End If
    End If

End If
```

```
End Sub
```

16. Once the user has a brief period to view the form, the next form is loaded.

```
Private Sub Timer2_Timer()

'   Make the form invisible
Form2.Visible = False

'   Unload the form
Unload Form2

'   Show the next form
Form3.Show

End Sub
```

17. Add the following code to SCRN3.FRM. The logic in this form follows the same basic techniques as that of the last form. Refer to the documentation for SCRN2.FRM for the techniques used.

```
'   This form is essentially the same
'   as form2
Private First As Integer
Private Inc As Integer
Private LeftOrg As Integer

Private Sub Form_Paint()

If First = 0 Then
    background.Move Form3.Width / 2 - background.Width / 2, Form3.Height / 2 ↵
    - background.Height / 2

        LeftOrg = Slide1.Left
    Inc = (background.Width - Slide1.Left) / 50
    Slide1.Left = background.Width
    Slide2.Left = background.Width
    Slide3.Left = background.Width
    First = 1
    background.Visible = True
End If

End Sub

Private Sub Timer1_Timer()

If Slide1.Left > LeftOrg Then
    Slide1.Left = Slide1.Left - Inc
Else
    If Slide2.Left > LeftOrg Then
        Slide2.Left = Slide2.Left - Inc
    Else
        If Slide3.Left > LeftOrg Then
            Slide3.Left = Slide3.Left - Inc
        Else
```

continued on next page

continued from previous page

```
            Timer1.Enabled = False
            Timer2.Enabled = True
            End If
      End If

End If

End Sub

Private Sub Timer2_Timer()

Form3.Visible = False
Unload Form3
Form4.Show

End Sub
```

18. Add the following code to DEMO.FRM. When the Animation button is clicked, the Victrola animation is played. Note that the Dog picture is made invisible and the multimedia control is also made invisible.

```
Private Sub Animation_Click()

'  When the animation is to be shown,
'  the Dog picture and the second Multimedia
'  control are to be invisible
Dog.Visible = False
MMControl2.Visible = False

'  Ensure the Victrola picture is visible
'  As well as the MCI control
Victrola.Visible = True
MMControl1.Visible = True

'  Play the animation
MMControl1.Command = "open"
MMControl1.Command = "play"

End Sub
```

19. When the Video button is clicked, the Dog video is played. Note that the picture for the Victrola is made invisible, as well as its multimedia control.

```
Private Sub Video_Click()

'  Ensure that the Victrola picture and
'  first Multimedia control are not visible
Victrola.Visible = False
MMControl1.Visible = False

'  Ensure that the Dog picture and first
'  multimedia control are visible
Dog.Visible = True
MMControl2.Visible = True
```

```
'  Play the video
MMControl2.Command = "open"
MMControl2.Command = "play"

End Sub
```

20. When the Music button is selected, the music clip is played and the MCI control is made visible.

```
Private Sub Music_Click()

'  Play the Music Clip
MMControl3.Visible = True
MMControl3.Command = "open"
MMControl3.Command = "play"

End Sub
```

21. When the Continue button is selected, the multimedia controls are closed and the next form is loaded.

```
Private Sub Continue_Click()

'  Ensure all controls are closed
MMControl1.Command = "close"
MMControl2.Command = "close"
MMControl3.Command = "close"

'  Ensure this form is not
'  visible
Form4.Visible = False

'  Unload this form and show the next
Unload Form4
Form5.Show
End Sub
```

22. When the form is loaded, the form is centered on the screen. Also, the multimedia controls are set up to play the appropriate clips.

```
Private Sub Form_Load()

'  Center this form
Form4.Move Screen.Width / 2 - Form4.Width / 2, Screen.Height / 2 - ↵
Form4.Height / 2

'  Set up the files for the multimedia controls
MMControl1.FileName = App.Path + "\victrola.avi"
MMControl2.FileName = App.Path + "\dog.avi"
MMControl3.FileName = "C:\windows\media\passport.mid"

'  Set the Device Types
MMControl1.DeviceType = "AVIVideo"
MMControl2.DeviceType = "AVIVideo"
MMControl3.DeviceType = "Sequencer"
```

continued on next page

continued from previous page

```
'   Set the display pictures
MMControl1.hWndDisplay = Victrola.hWnd
MMControl2.hWndDisplay = Dog.hWnd

End Sub
```

23. Add the following code to the general declarations section of END.FRM. First will be used to execute the code in the Form_Paint procedure once.

```
'   First will be used to display the
'   code in the Form_Paint procedure once
Dim First As Integer
```

24. When the user clicks on the DispPict control, the program will end if the ending text animation is finished.

```
Private Sub DispPict_Click()

'   If the user clicks on the picture
'   and all of the events are finished
'   then the presentation is done
If Event = "IntroTextDone" Then
    End
End If

End Sub
```

25. When the user clicks on the form, the program will end if the ending text animation is finished.

```
Private Sub Form_Click()

'   If the user clicks on the picture
'   and all of the events are finished
'   then the presentation is done
If Event = "IntroTextDone" Then
    End
End If

End Sub
```

26. When the form is loaded, the MCI control is set up to display the Thank You animation.

```
Private Sub Form_Load()

'   Set the file name, device type and
'   picture for the playing of the
'   animation
MMControl1.FileName = App.Path + "\letthank.avi"
MMControl1.DeviceType = AVIVideo
MMControl1.hWndDisplay = AniPict.hWnd

End Sub
```

27. When the form is painted for the first time, the animation picture is centered and the animation is played.

```
Private Sub Form_Paint()

'  Only execute this code once
If First = 0 Then

'  Center the picture on the form
AniPict.Move Form5.Width / 2 - AniPict.Width / 2, Form5.Height / 2 ↵
- AniPict.Height / 2

'  Make the picture visible
AniPict.Visible = True

'  Play the animation
MMControl1.Command = "open"
MMControl1.Command = "play"

'  set the first variable
First = 1

End If
End Sub
```

28. When the animation is done playing, Timer2 is enabled.

```
Private Sub MMControl1_Done(NotifyCode As Integer)

'  When the animation is finished, start the second timer
Timer2.Enabled = True

End Sub
```

29. Timer1 handles displaying the ending text animation. It uses the code in FINAL.BAS. Event is a global variable that stores the status of the text animation. The IntroFirstTimer function handles displaying the first set of text, IntroSecondTimer the second set of text, and IntroThirdTimer the third set of text. Finally, when the Event variable is set to IntroTextDone, the timer is disabled and the Click to Continue label is shown.

```
Private Sub Timer1_Timer()

'  Depending on which step we are in in displaying
'  the text, the appropriate function is called
If Event = "INTROTEXT1" Then IntroFirstTimer
If Event = "INTROTEXT2" Then IntroSecondTimer
If Event = "INTROTEXT3" Then IntroTHirdTimer
If Event = "IntroTextDone" Then Timer1.Enabled = False: Label1.Visible = True

End Sub
```

30. Timer2 handles starting the display of text animation. It sets up the picture box to show the text animation and then starts Timer1.

```
Private Sub Timer2_Timer()

'  Make the picture visible
AniPict.Visible = False

'  Center the picture to display
'  the text
DispPict.Move Form5.Width / 2 - DispPict.Width / 2, Form5.Height / 2 ↵
- DispPict.Height / 2

'  setup the display of the text
'  by calling the ShowText function
ShowText Timer1, DispPict

'  Start the second timer.
Timer2.Enabled = False
End Sub
```

31. Add the following to the general declarations section of the FINAL.BAS module. Event stores the messages sent between the text animation functions and the timer.

```
Public Event As String

'  The following type declaration describes the
'  Windows API LOGFONT structure.  THE LOGFONT
'  structure is used by several of the WIN API
'  text functions.
```

32. The font procedures used in this module are the same as those developed in How-To 2.7. Refer to that section for additional discussion of how these techniques work.

```
Type LOGFONT
    lfHeight As Integer
    lfWidth As Integer
    lfEscapement As Integer
    lfOrientation As Integer
    lfWeight As Integer
    lfItalic As String * 1
    lfUnderline As String * 1
    lfStrikeOut As String * 1
    lfCharSet As String * 1
    lfOutPrecision As String * 1
    lfClipPrecision As String * 1
    lfQuality As String * 1
    lfPitchAndFamily As String * 1
    lfFaceName As String * 24
End Type

'  Declare the Windows API DeleteObject function
```

```
Private Declare Function DeleteObject Lib "GDI" (ByVal hObject As Integer) ↵
As Integer

'  Declare the Windows API CreateFontIndirect function
Private Declare Function CreateFontIndirect Lib "GDI" (lpLogFont As LOGFONT) ↵
As Integer

'  Declare the Windows API SelectObject function
Private Declare Function SelectObject Lib "GDI" (ByVal hDC As Integer, ↵
ByVal hObject As Integer) As Integer

'  Declare the Windows API TextOut function
Private Declare Function TextOut Lib "GDI" (ByVal hDC As Integer, ByVal x As ↵
Integer, ByVal y As Integer, ByVal lpString As String, ByVal nCount As ↵
Integer) As Integer

Private Timer As Control
Private IntroPic As Control


'  CFONT will be our font structure for the text
Private CFONT As LOGFONT

'  ESCAPE will hold the current ESCAPEMENT of the
'  displayed font
Private escape As Integer

'  ChangeX and ChangeY will hold the increment to move
'  the text to the upperleft corner.
Private ChangeX As Integer
Private ChangeY As Integer

Private n As Integer

Private Text As String
```

33. FontOut handles creating the specified font on the specified device.

```
Private Sub FontOut(Text$, Pict, xx, yy, FontStruct As LOGFONT)

'  Create the new font
NewFont% = CreateFontIndirect(FontStruct)

'  Select the new font into the picture
'  device context
OldFont% = SelectObject(Pict.hDC, NewFont%)

'  Display the text
Throw% = TextOut(Pict.hDC, xx, yy, Text$, Len(Text$))

'  Select the font back for the original device context
Throw% = SelectObject(Pict.hDC, OldFont%)

'  Delete the newly created font
Throw% = DeleteObject(NewFont%)
```

continued on next page

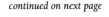

continued from previous page

```
End Sub
```

34. ShowText handles setting up the creation and animation of the text.

```
Public Sub ShowText(t As Object, Pict As Control)

Event = "INTROTEXT1"

Set Timer = t
Set IntroPic = Pict

'   Set the scalemode to 3 (pixels) for the picture
IntroPic.ScaleMode = 3

'   Set up the initial font structure.  We will
'   use a height of 30 and a width of 10.  The
'   weight will be medium (non-bold), and will
'   use Arial.
CFONT.lfHeight = 30
CFONT.lfWidth = 10
CFONT.lfEscapement = 0
CFONT.lfWeight = 400
CFONT.lfItalic = Chr$(0)
CFONT.lfUnderline = Chr$(0)
CFONT.lfStrikeOut = Chr$(0)
CFONT.lfOutPrecision = Chr$(0)
CFONT.lfClipPrecision = Chr$(0)
CFONT.lfQuality = Chr$(0)
CFONT.lfPitchAndFamily = Chr$(0)
CFONT.lfCharSet = Chr$(0)
CFONT.lfFaceName = "Arial" + Chr$(0)

'   Locate the currentx and currenty for the first text display
IntroPic.CurrentX = (IntroPic.ScaleWidth - IntroPic.TextWidth("Introducing...↵
")) / 2 + 90

IntroPic.CurrentY = (IntroPic.ScaleHeight - ↵
IntroPic.TextHeight("Introducing...")) / 2 + 90

'   Caculate the changes for 20 moves of "Introducing..." to the upper corner.
ChangeX = IntroPic.CurrentX / 20
ChangeY = IntroPic.CurrentY / 20

'   Start timer1
Timer.Enabled = True

IntroPic.ForeColor = RGB(255, 0, 0)

Text$ = "Consultants"
End Sub
```

35. IntroFirstTimer handles printing the rotated Consultants text. The technique used to rotate the text was developed in How-To 2.7.

```
Public Sub IntroFirstTimer()

'  Set the new escapement
CFONT.lfEscapement = CFONT.lfEscapement + 180

'  Calculate the center of the text
x = (IntroPic.ScaleWidth - IntroPic.TextWidth(Text$)) / 2 + 100
y = (IntroPic.ScaleHeight - IntroPic.TextHeight(Text$)) / 2 + 100

'  For the last print when the font color is white, we will
'  clear the picture and print the text in black
If CFONT.lfEscapement = 3600 Then

    IntroPic.ForeColor = RGB(255, 255, 255)

    Event = "INTROTEXT2"
    CFONT.lfEscapement = 0
End If

'  Call the FontOut procedure to display the text
FontOut Text$, IntroPic, x, y, CFONT

IntroPic.ForeColor = RGB(255, 0, 0)

If CFONT.lfEscapement = 0 Then
    Text$ = "Multimedia"
End If

End Sub
```

36. IntroSecondTimer handles printing the rotated Multimedia text.

```
Public Sub IntroSecondTimer()

'  Set the new escapement
CFONT.lfEscapement = CFONT.lfEscapement + 180

'  Calculate the center of the text
x = (IntroPic.ScaleWidth - IntroPic.TextWidth(Text$)) / 2
y = (IntroPic.ScaleHeight - IntroPic.TextHeight(Text$)) / 2

'  For the last print when the font color is white, we will
'  clear the picture and print the text in black
If CFONT.lfEscapement = 3600 Then

    IntroPic.ForeColor = RGB(255, 255, 255)
    Event = "INTROTEXT3"
    CFONT.lfEscapement = 0

End If

'  Call the FontOut procedure to display the text
FontOut Text$, IntroPic, x, y, CFONT
IntroPic.ForeColor = RGB(255, 0, 0)
```

continued on next page

continued from previous page

```
If CFONT.lfEscapement = 0 Then
    Text$ = "The"
End If

End Sub
```

37. IntroThirdTimer handles printing the rotated The text.

```
Public Sub IntroThirdTimer()

'  Set the new escapement
CFONT.lfEscapement = CFONT.lfEscapement + 180

'  Calculate the center of the text
x = (IntroPic.ScaleWidth - IntroPic.TextWidth(Text$)) / 2 - 100
y = (IntroPic.ScaleHeight - IntroPic.TextHeight(Text$)) / 2 - 100

'  For the last print when the font color is white, we will
'  clear the picture and print the text in black
If CFONT.lfEscapement = 3600 Then

    IntroPic.ForeColor = RGB(255, 255, 255)

    Event = "IntroTextDone"

End If

'  Call the FontOut procedure to display the text
FontOut Text$, IntroPic, x, y, CFONT
IntroPic.ForeColor = RGB(255, 0, 0)

End Sub
```

How It Works

The presentation developed is for a fictional company, The Multimedia Consultants. For the backdrop of the presentation, a maximized MDIForm is used. Each successive form is a MDIChild of the MDIForm. Each MDIChild acts as a separate screen of the presentation.

The first screen consists of the introduction. A box is built around the screen using the techniques developed in How-To 5.2. The timer control and the line control provide for an effective animated box. The title labels are transitioned in by successively increasing their heights until they are visible.

The next two screens build a familiar presentation look of bulleted text being transitioned from the right to stop at the appropriate bullet. This is performed for each label. Following these two screens is an interactive demo that presents sample clips of the fictional company. The MCI control is used to open and play the clips. The MCI control is kept visible so that the user can replay the clips.

The final form begins with an animation clip. The technique developed in How-To 3.12 to know when the clip has finished playing is used to transition into the final animated text display. The Windows API techniques for displaying rotated text from How-To 2.7 are used. The name of the company is displayed in rotated text. The primary routines to handle the text rotation are in the FINAL.BAS module. The global Event variable in the basic module is used as a message carrier between the timer control on the form and the routines in the module. The timer then checks the status of the variable to call the appropriate routine to display the text. This module can be used in any application by simply changing the text to be displayed.

Comments

The screen-by-screen approach of combining MDIForms with MDIChild forms can provide effective screen-by-screen presentations. For greater precision and control over the playing of the animations, video, and music, consider using the MCI command string interface instead of the MCI control.

8.4 How do I...
Create a process control simulation?

COMPLEXITY: ADVANCED

Problem

I would like to be able to simulate processes graphically and to control the input variables to control the process in real time. How can I do this using Visual Basic 4.0?

Technique

The familiar rotation of planets around a sun will be used to demonstrate a control process. The TransCopy class from How-To 4.8 will be used to move the planets around the sun transparently. Also, a derivative of using the image controls for hot spots will be used to define the path of the planets. The speed of the rotation will also be controlled. Note: This How-To is best run in 1024x768 video mode.

Steps

Open and run 8-4.VBP. The running program appears as shown in Figure 8-4-1.

To control the speed of the rotating planets use the spinner controls to change the timer. To spin off a planet, select the appropriate check box and watch the planet spin off out of orbit.

1. Create a new project called 8-4.VBP. Add the objects and properties listed in Table 8-4-1 to Form1 and save the form as 8-4.FRM.

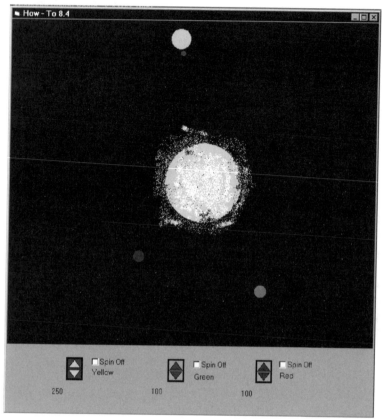

Figure 8-4-1 The form at runtime

Table 8-4-1 The form's objects and properties

OBJECT	PROPERTY	SETTING
Form	Name	Form1
	Auto3D	-1 'True
	Caption	"How-To 8.4"
PictureBox	Name	Background
	AutoSize	-1 'True
	BackColor	&H00FF0000&
	BorderStyle	0 'None
	Picture	(Solar.bmp)
	ScaleMode	3 'Pixel

OBJECT	PROPERTY	SETTING
Image	Name	Image4
Image	Name	Image3
	Index	0 - 47
Image	Name	Image2
	Index	0 - 43
Image	Name	Image1
	Index	0 - 43
PictureBox	Name	YellowMask
	AutoRedraw	-1 'True
	AutoSize	-1 'True
	BorderStyle	0 'None
	Index	0 - 9
	Picture	(y1mask.bmp - y10mask.bmp)
	ScaleMode	3 'Pixel
PictureBox	Name	YellowFull
	AutoRedraw	-1 'True
	AutoSize	-1 'True
	BorderStyle	0 'None
	Index	0 - 9
	Picture	(Yell1.bmp - Yell10.bmp)
	ScaleMode	3 'Pixel
CheckBox	Name	YOff
	Caption	"Spin Off"
CheckBox	Name	GOff
	Caption	"Spin Off"
CheckBox	Name	ROff
	Caption	"Spin Off"
Timer	Name	Timer4
	Interval	500

continued on next page

continued from previous page

OBJECT	PROPERTY	SETTING
PictureBox	Name	Sun4
	AutoRedraw	-1 'True
	AutoSize	-1 'True
	BorderStyle	0 'None
	Picture	(sun4.bmp)
	ScaleMode	3 'Pixel
PictureBox	Name	Sun3
	AutoRedraw	-1 'True
	AutoSize	-1 'True
	BorderStyle	0 'None
	Picture	(sun3.bmp)
	ScaleMode	3 'Pixel
PictureBox	Name	Sun2
	AutoRedraw	-1 'True
	AutoSize	-1 'True
	BorderStyle	0 'None
	Picture	(sun2.bmp)
	ScaleMode	3 'Pixel
PictureBox	Name	Sun1
	AutoRedraw	-1 'True
	AutoSize	-1 'True
	BorderStyle	0 'None
	Picture	(sun1.bmp)
	ScaleMode	3 'Pixel
Timer	Name	Timer3
	Enabled	0 'False
	Interval	100
Timer	Name	Timer2
	Enabled	0 'False
	Interval	100

OBJECT	PROPERTY	SETTING
PictureBox	Name	TempBackground
	AutoRedraw	-1 'True
	AutoSize	-1 'True
	BorderStyle	0 'None
	Picture	(Solar.bmp)
	ScaleMode	3 'Pixel
Timer	Name	Timer1
	Enabled	0 'False
	Interval	250
PictureBox	Name	GreenMask
	AutoRedraw	-1 'True
	AutoSize	-1 'True
	BorderStyle	0 'None
	Picture	(grnmask.bmp)
	ScaleMode	3 'Pixel
PictureBox	Name	Redmask
	AutoRedraw	-1 'True
	AutoSize	-1 'True
	BorderStyle	0 'None
	Picture	(redmask.bmp)
	ScaleMode	3 'Pixel
PictureBox	Name	RedFull
	AutoRedraw	-1 'True
	AutoSize	-1 'True
	BorderStyle	0 'None
	Picture	(red.bmp)
	ScaleMode	3 'Pixel
PictureBox	Name	GreenFull
	AutoRedraw	-1 'True
	AutoSize	-1 'True
	BorderStyle	0 'None

continued on next page

continued from previous page

OBJECT	PROPERTY	SETTING
	Picture	(green.bmp)
	ScaleMode	3 'Pixel
Label	Name	Label6
	AutoSize	-1 'True
	Caption	"Yellow"
Label	Name	Label5
	AutoSize	-1 'True
	Caption	"Green"
Label	Name	Label4
	AutoSize	-1 'True
	Caption	"Red"
Label	Name	Rint
SpinButton	Name	SpinButton3
	Forecolor	255
	Backcolor	12632256
	Borderthickness	3
	Delay	75
SpinButton	Name	SpinButton2
	Forecolor	8421376
	Backcolor	-2147483633
	Borderthickness	3
	Delay	75
Label	Name	Gint
Label	Name	Yint
SpinButton	Name	SpinButton1
	Forecolor	65535
	Backcolor	8421376

OBJECT	PROPERTY	SETTING
	Bordercolor	0
	Borderthickness	3
	Delay	75

Note: The TransCopy class from How-To 4.8 is used in this How-To. For documentation and description of the class, refer to How-To 4.8.

2. Add the following code to the general declarations section of the form. The BitBlt function is used to transfer the Sun images to the display. The variables for tracking the movement of the planets are also declared, and the global declarations of the TransCopy class are made.

```
'  BitBlt will be used to make the transparent effect.
Private Declare Function BitBlt Lib "GDI" (ByVal hDestDC As Integer, ByVal x ↵
As Integer, ByVal y As Integer, ByVal nWidth As Integer, ByVal nHeight As ↵
Integer, ByVal hSrcDC As Integer, ByVal XSrc As Integer, ByVal YSrc As ↵
Integer, ByVal dwRop As Long) As Integer

'  Constants for BitBlt and StrechBlt
Const SRCCOPY = &HCC0020

'  Moon will count through the moons
'  for the Yellow Planet
Dim Moon As Integer

'  These variables will count through the image
'  controls for the three planets
Dim n1 As Integer
Dim n2 As Integer
Dim n3 As Integer

'  These variables will hold the last position
'  of each planet so that the section can be covered
'  up
Dim x1last As Integer
Dim y1last As Integer
Dim x2last As Integer
Dim y2last As Integer
Dim x3last As Integer
Dim y3last As Integer

'  Globally declare out three TransCopy
'  classes
Dim trans1 As TransCopy
Dim trans2 As TransCopy
Dim trans3 As TransCopy
```

3. In the Form_Load procedure, the TransCopy class properties are set. Also the initial settings for the timer interval displays are set up.

```
Private Sub Form_Load()
' Seed the random number generator
Randomize

'  Set the display of the timer values
Yint.Caption = Timer1.Interval
Gint.Caption = Timer2.Interval
Rint.Caption = Timer3.Interval

'  Move the background to the top of the form
background.Move background.Left, 0

'  Create the new classes
Set trans1 = New TransCopy
Set trans2 = New TransCopy
Set trans3 = New TransCopy

'  Send in the three pictures for the class
Set trans1.BackGroundPict = background
Set trans1.MaskPict = YellowMask(0)
Set trans1.PrimaryPict = YellowFull(0)

'  Send in the three pictures for the class
Set trans2.BackGroundPict = background
Set trans2.MaskPict = GreenMask
Set trans2.PrimaryPict = GreenFull

'  Send in the three pictures for the class
Set trans3.BackGroundPict = background
Set trans3.MaskPict = redmask
Set trans3.PrimaryPict = RedFull
End Sub
```

4. In the Form_Paint procedure, the timers are enabled and the initial Sun graphic is transferred to the displayed picture.

```
Private Sub Form_Paint()

'  Copy the sun onto the displayed picture
throw% = BitBlt(background.hDC, Image4.Left, Image4.Top, Sun4.ScaleWidth, ↵
Sun4.ScaleHeight, Sun1.hDC, 0, 0, SRCCOPY)

'  Enable the timers
Timer1.Enabled = True
Timer2.Enabled = True
Timer3.Enabled = True
Timer4.Enabled = True
End Sub
```

5. Each of the Spin button events handles incrementing or decrementing the timer interval by a value of 10. This controls the speed of a planet's rotation.

```
Private Sub SpinButton1_SpinDown()

'  If the timer interval is not 0 then
```

```
'   decrement the value by 10
If Timer1.Interval <> 0 Then
    Timer1.Interval = Timer1.Interval - 10
    Yint.Caption = Timer1.Interval
End If

End Sub

Private Sub SpinButton1_SpinUp()

'   Increase the timer value
Timer1.Interval = Timer1.Interval + 10
Yint.Caption = Timer1.Interval
End Sub

Private Sub SpinButton2_SpinDown()

'   If the timer interval is not 0 then
'   decrement the value by 10
If Timer2.Interval <> 0 Then
    Timer2.Interval = Timer2.Interval - 10
    Gint.Caption = Timer2.Interval
End If

End Sub

Private Sub SpinButton2_SpinUp()

'   Increase the timer value
Timer2.Interval = Timer2.Interval + 10
Gint.Caption = Timer2.Interval

End Sub

Private Sub SpinButton3_SpinDown()

'   If the timer interval is not 0 then
'   decrement the value by 10
If Timer3.Interval <> 0 Then
    Timer3.Interval = Timer3.Interval - 10
    Rint.Caption = Timer3.Interval
End If

End Sub

Private Sub SpinButton3_SpinUp()

'   Increase the timer value
Timer3.Interval = Timer3.Interval + 10
Rint.Caption = Timer3.Interval

End Sub
```

6. The first timer handles the yellow planet's rotation. Because the yellow planet has a revolving moon, the image that is copied to the main display changes depending on the next rotation of the moon. The Moon variable counts through yellow planet images. Note that the original position of the planet is covered with an original copy of the background from the back-up copy of the background image. Also, a check is done to see if the planet should be spun off. If it is to be spun off, then the left and top positions of the image control are moved.

```
Private Sub Timer1_Timer()

'  Increase the moon counter
Moon = Moon + 1

'  if the final moon has been reached,
'  move back to the original
If Moon = 10 Then Moon = 0

'  Set the class properties
Set trans1.MaskPict = YellowMask(Moon)
Set trans1.PrimaryPict = YellowFull(Moon)

'  Increase the Image Index Counter
n1 = n1 + 1

'  If the final Image array has been reached
'  then reset to the first index
If n1 = 42 Then n1 = 0

'  Set the left and top values for
'  the transfer
x = Image1(n1).Left
y = Image1(n1).Top

'  If the spin off check box is selected
'  then begin spinning the moon off
If YOff.Value = 1 Then
    Image1(n1).Left = Image1(n1).Left - 10
    Image1(n1).Top = Image1(n1).Top - 10
End If

'  Copy from the backup copy of the background to the display
'  to the last position of the planet
throw% = BitBlt(background.hDC, x1last, y1last, YellowMask(Moon).ScaleWidth, ↵
YellowMask(Moon).ScaleHeight, TempBackground.hDC, x1last, y1last, SRCCOPY)

'  Build the transparent planet
trans1.showtrans x, y

'  Store the current position of the planet
x1last = x
y1last = y

End Sub
```

7. The second timer handles the rotation of the green planet. The same techniques as used with Timer1 are used here. Note that there is no moon for this planet.

```
Private Sub Timer2_Timer()

'  Increase the Image Index Counter
n2 = n2 + 1

'  If the final Image array has been reached
'  then reset to the first index
If n2 = 54 Then n2 = 0

'  Set the left and top values for
'  the transfer
x = Image2(n2).Left
y = Image2(n2).Top

'  If the spin off check box is selected
'  then begin spinning the moon off
If GOff.Value = 1 Then
    Image2(n2).Left = Image2(n2).Left - 20
    Image2(n2).Top = Image2(n2).Top - 20
End If

'  Copy from the backup copy of the background to the display
'  to the last position of the planet
throw% = BitBlt(background.hDC, x2last, y2last, GreenMask.ScaleWidth,
GreenMask.ScaleHeight, TempBackground.hDC, x2last, y2last, SRCCOPY)

'  Build the transparent planet
trans2.showtrans x, y

'  Store the current position of the planet
x2last = x
y2last = y

End Sub
```

8. The third timer handles the rotation of the red planet. The same techniques as used with Timer2 are used here. Note that there is no moon for this planet.

```
Private Sub Timer3_Timer()

'  Increase the Image Index Counter
n3 = n3 + 1

'  If the final Image array has been reached
'  then reset to the first index
If n3 = 55 Then n3 = 0

'  Set the left and top values for
'  the transfer
x = Image3(n3).Left
y = Image3(n3).Top
```

continued on next page

continued from previous page

```
'  If the spin off check box is selected
'  then begin spinning the moon off
If ROff.Value = 1 Then
     Image3(n3).Left = Image3(n3).Left + 20
     Image3(n3).Top = Image3(n3).Top + 20
End If


'  Copy from the backup copy of the background to the display
'  to the last position of the planet
throw% = BitBlt(background.hDC, x3last, y3last, redmask.ScaleWidth,
redmask.ScaleHeight, TempBackground.hDC, x3last, y3last, SRCCOPY)


'  Build the transparent planet
trans3.showtrans x, y


'  Store the current position of the planet
x3last = x
y3last = y


End Sub
```

9. This timer handles displaying the different suns. A random number is generated with each timer tick to choose which version of the sun will be displayed.

```
Private Sub Timer4_Timer()


'  Randomly get the number of the sun
'  to display
num = Int((4 - 1 + 1) * Rnd + 1)


'  Copy the appropriate sun to the displayed
'  image
If num = 1 Then throw% = BitBlt(background.hDC, Image4.Left, Image4.Top, ↵
Sun4.ScaleWidth, Sun4.ScaleHeight, Sun1.hDC, 0, 0, SRCCOPY)


If num = 2 Then throw% = BitBlt(background.hDC, Image4.Left, Image4.Top, ↵
Sun4.ScaleWidth, Sun4.ScaleHeight, Sun2.hDC, 0, 0, SRCCOPY)


If num = 3 Then throw% = BitBlt(background.hDC, Image4.Left, Image4.Top, ↵
Sun4.ScaleWidth, Sun4.ScaleHeight, Sun3.hDC, 0, 0, SRCCOPY)


If num = 4 Then throw% = BitBlt(background.hDC, Image4.Left, Image4.Top, ↵
Sun4.ScaleWidth, Sun4.ScaleHeight, Sun4.hDC, 0, 0, SRCCOPY)


End Sub
```

How It Works

The planet paths are defined by image controls. Look at the form and notice how the image controls are placed along the planet black line paths. It is important to make sure that the image controls are the same size as the planet for that path. The easiest way to do this is to load one of the planet images into the control and then delete the picture. In this way, the first image in the control array is properly sized and the subsequent members of the control array are properly sized.

For the transparent display of the planets, the techniques developed in How-To 4.8 are used. A black and white mask of each planet is developed and the TransCopy class is used to display a transparent copy of the planets. Each image control array is looped through, with the origin point of each image control used as the placement position to which to transfer the image of the planet. It is important to cover up the last position of the planet with the original background. Each timer accomplishes this by copying from the back-up copy of the background image the necessary portion of the background.

A moon revolves around the yellow planet while the planet is in motion. With each tick of the timer, the next image in the moon image sequence is used so that it appears to be rotating around the planet.

The interaction with simulation is controlled in two ways. First, the speed of the rotation of the planets around the sun can be changed with the Spin buttons. The spinning of the planets can be stopped by scrolling the timer speed to 0. Second, the planets can be spun off course by selecting the Spin Off check boxes. When this happens, the planet path origins are moved with each tick of the timer. Over time (depending on the rotation speed), the planets will spin off course and off the form.

Comments

Many different types of interaction could be added to this simulation. A collision between the sun and the planets and collisions between the planets could be detected and appropriate action can be taken. You could store the origin points of the image controls by writing a simple function to write their origin points out to a file and then read them in at runtime. An example of this can be found in How-To 4.4. By doing this, your final program would not have the additional overhead of the image controls being loaded at runtime. (In this example, the primary resources of the application are tied up in the storage and manipulation of the graphics.) Finally, the interaction of outside objects such as comets and asteroids could easily be added to affect the simulation.

8.5 How do I...
Create a computer-based training authoring and delivery system?

COMPLEXITY: ADVANCED

Problem

Computer-based training is an important part of the computer industry that has become enhanced through the use of multimedia. How can I use the techniques developed in this book to build a multiple-choice authoring and delivery system?

Technique

There will be two major parts to this How-To. The first is authoring the multiple-choice tests and the second is taking the multiple-choice test. The basic layout of the test design and the test-taking modules fall well within the purview of standard Visual Basic 4.0 features. Added to this familiar use of Visual Basic 4.0 will be the use of sound, animation, and picture images.

Steps

Open and run 8-5.VBP. The running program appears as shown in Figure 8-5-1.

You can select to take a test, create a new test, or edit an existing test. If you choose to create or edit a test, you must enter a password. The password is "TEST". Once the password is entered, click the Done button. In each option, you will need to select an existing file or, in the case of creating a new file, enter a test file name.

The design mode appears as is shown in Figure 8-5-2.

You can enter up to 50 questions for each single test. You do not have to enter questions in sequence (e.g. 1, 2,…). Simply enter in the question number or browse using the command buttons and enter in the question text, answer(s), and explanation. There are two types of answers, text and picture. If it is a picture answer, then enter in the bitmap file name. The bitmap files should be located in the same directory as the running program. To indicate the correct response to a question, select the appropriate option button answer. To save a question, click the Save Question button. To finish the design stage, click the Done button.

The test-taking module appears as shown in Figure 8-5-3.

When the test-taking mode starts up, an animation stating "Good Luck" is played. Then the first question is shown. The user can select any one of the answers. An answer can only be selected once. If the answer is correct, then the DING.WAV

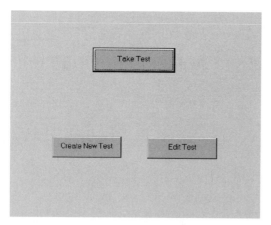

Figure 8-5-1 The set-up phase of the program

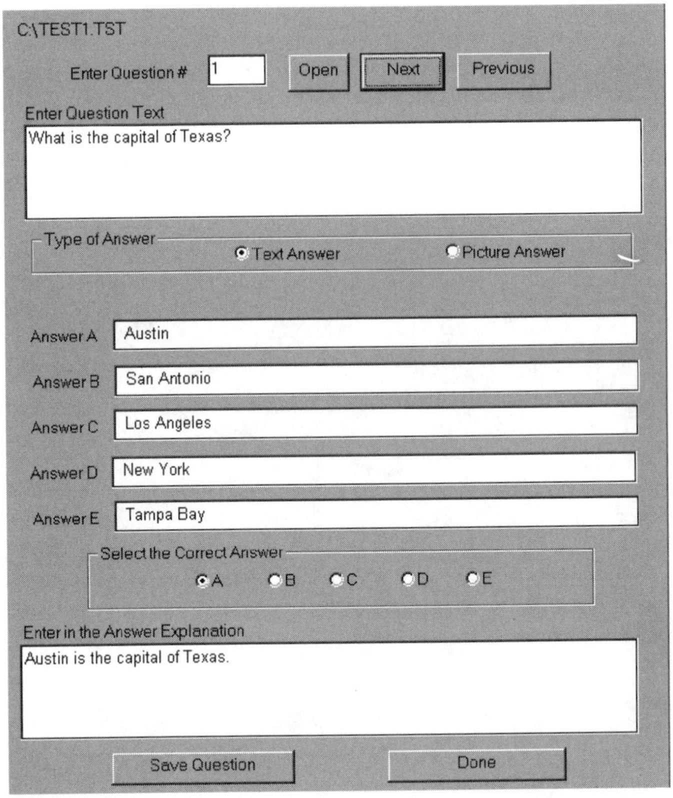

Figure 8-5-2 The test design mode

file is played. If the answer is incorrect, then the CHORD.WAV file is played and the answer explanation is given. For the picture answers, the selection is made by clicking on the appropriate picture to answer the question.

1. Create a new project called 8-5.VBP. Add the object and properties listed in Table 8-5-1 to Form1 and save the form as 8-5.FRM.

Table 8-5-1 The MDIform's object and properties

OBJECT	PROPERTY	SETTING
MDIForm	Name	MDIForm1
	BackColor	&H8000000C&
	Caption	"How-To 8.5"
	WindowState	2 'Maximized

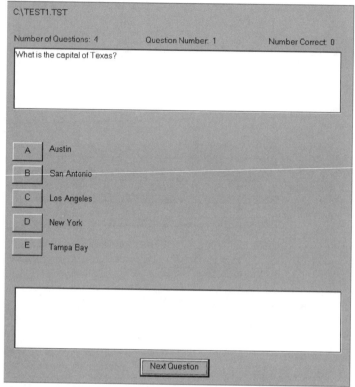

Figure 8-5-3 The test-taking phase of the program

2. Add a new form to the project and save it as OPEN.FRM. Add the objects and properties from Table 8-5-2 to the form.

Table 8-5-2 The Open form's objects and properties

OBJECT	PROPERTY	SETTING
Form	Name	Form2
	BorderStyle	0 'None
	Caption	"Form2"
	MDIChild	-1 'True
CommandButton	Name	Done
	Caption	"Done"
	Visible	0 'False

OBJECT	PROPERTY	SETTING
TextBox	Name	PassText
	Visible	0 'False
CommandButton	Name	Edit
	Caption	"Edit Test"
CommandButton	Name	Create
	Caption	"Create New Test"
CommandButton	Name	TakeTest
	Caption	"Take Test"
CommonDialog	Name	CommonDialog1
	filename	"*.tst"
Label	Name	Label1
	AutoSize	-1 'True
	Caption	"Enter Password"
	Visible	0 'False

3. Add a new form to the project and save it as DESIGN.FRM. Add the objects and properties from Table 8-5-3 to the form.

Table 8-5-3 The Design form's objects and properties

OBJECT	PROPERTY	SETTING
Form	Name	Form1
	Auto3D	-1 'True
	BackColor	&H00E0E0E0&
	BorderStyle	0 'None
	Caption	"Form1"
	MDIChild	-1 'True
CommandButton	Name	Done
	Caption	"Done"
CommandButton	Name	Previous

continued on next page

continued from previous page

OBJECT	PROPERTY	SETTING
	Caption	"Previous"
CommandButton	Name	Next
	Caption	"Next"
Frame	Name	Frame2
	Caption	"Select the Correct Answer"
OptionButton	Name	OptA
	Caption	"A"
	Value	-1 'True
OptionButton	Name	OptB
	Caption	"B"
OptionButton	Name	OptC
	Caption	"C"
OptionButton	Name	OptD
	Caption	"D"
OptionButton	Name	OptE
	Caption	"E"
Frame	Name	Frame1
	Caption	"Type of Answer"
OptionButton	Name	PictOption
	Caption	"Picture Answer"
OptionButton	Name	TextOption
	Caption	"Text Answer"
	Value	-1 'True
CommandButton	Name	Open
	Caption	"Open"

OBJECT	PROPERTY	SETTING
CommandButton	Name	Save
	Caption	"Save Question"
TextBox	Name	ExpTExt
	Font	
	name	"Arial"
	MultiLine	-1 'True
TextBox	Name	AnswerE
	Font	
	name	"Arial"
TextBox	Name	AnswerD
	Font	
	name	"Arial"
TextBox	Name	AnswerC
	Font	
	name	"Arial"
TextBox	Name	AnswerB
	Font	
	name	"Arial"
TextBox	Name	AnswerA
	Font	
	name	"Arial"
TextBox	Name	QuestNum
TextBox	Name	QuestText
	Font	
	name	"Arial"
	MultiLine	-1 'True
Label	Name	File
	AutoSize	-1 'True
	Caption	"Label11"

continued on next page

CHAPTER 8

continued from previous page

OBJECT	PROPERTY	SETTING
Label	Name	Label10
	AutoSize	-1 'True
	Caption	"Enter in the Answer Explanation"
Label	Name	Label9
	AutoSize	-1 'True
	Caption	"Answer E"
Label	Name	Label8
	AutoSize	-1 'True
	Caption	"Answer D"
Label	Name	Label7
	AutoSize	-1 'True
	Caption	"Answer C"
Label	Name	Label6
	AutoSize	-1 'True
	Caption	"Answer B"
Label	Name	Label5
	AutoSize	-1 'True
	Caption	"Enter the Filename of the Picture file (BMP format only)."
	Visible	0 'False
Label	Name	Label4
	AutoSize	-1 'True
	Caption	"Answer A"
Label	Name	Label3
	AutoSize	-1 'True
	Caption	"Enter Question Text"
Label	Name	Label1
	AutoSize	-1 'True
	Caption	"Enter Question #"

4. Add a new form to the project and save it as TEST.FRM. Add the objects and properties from Table 8-5-4 to the form.

Table 8-5-4 The Test form's objects and properties

OBJECT	PROPERTY	SETTING
Form	Name	Form3
	Auto3D	-1 'True
	BackColor	&H00C0C0C0&
	BorderStyle	0 'None
	Caption	"Form3"
	MDIChild	-1 'True
Timer	Name	Timer3
	Enabled	0 'False
	Interval	2350
MMControl	Name	MMControl2
Timer	Name	Timer2
	Enabled	0 'False
	Interval	2300
MMControl	Name	MMControl1
PictureBox	Name	AnimPict
	BorderStyle	0 'None
PictureBox	Name	Picture15
	AutoSize	-1 'True
	BorderStyle	0 'None
PictureBox	Name	Picture14
	AutoSize	-1 'True
	BorderStyle	0 'None
PictureBox	Name	Picture13

continued on next page

continued from previous page

OBJECT	PROPERTY	SETTING
	AutoSize	-1 'True
	BorderStyle	0 'None
PictureBox	Name	Picture12
	AutoSize	-1 'True
	BorderStyle	0 'None
PictureBox	Name	Picture11
	AutoSize	-1 'True
	BorderStyle	0 'None
PictureBox	Name	Picture10
	AutoSize	-1 'True
	BorderStyle	0 'None
PictureBox	Name	Picture9
	AutoSize	-1 'True
	BorderStyle	0 'None
PictureBox	Name	Picture8
	AutoSize	-1 'True
	BorderStyle	0 'None
PictureBox	Name	Picture7
	AutoSize	-1 'True
	BorderStyle	0 'None
PictureBox	Name	Picture6
	AutoSize	-1 'True
	BorderStyle	0 'None
PictureBox	Name	Picture5
	AutoSize	-1 'True
	BorderStyle	0 'None
PictureBox	Name	Picture4

OBJECT	PROPERTY	SETTING
	AutoSize	-1 'True
	BorderStyle	0 'None
Timer	Name	Timer1
	Enabled	0 'False
	Interval	50
PictureBox	Name	Picture3
	AutoSize	-1 'True
	BorderStyle	0 'None
PictureBox	Name	Picture2
	AutoSize	-1 'True
	BorderStyle	0 'None
PictureBox	Name	Picture1
	AutoSize	-1 'True
	BorderStyle	0 'None
CommandButton	Name	NextQuest
	Caption	"Next Question"
TextBox	Name	questText
	Enabled	0 'False
	MultiLine	-1 'True
CommandButton	Name	QSelect
	Caption	"E"
	Index	4
	Visible	0 'False
CommandButton	Name	QSelect
	Caption	"B"
	Index	1
	Visible	0 'False

continued on next page

continued from previous page

OBJECT	PROPERTY	SETTING
CommandButton	Name	QSelect
	Caption	"D"
	Index	3
	Visible	0 'False
CommandButton	Name	QSelect
	Caption	"C"
	Index	2
	Visible	0 'False
CommandButton	Name	QSelect
	Caption	"A"
	Index	0
	Visible	0 'False
TextBox	Name	ExpText
	Enabled	0 'False
	MultiLine	-1 'True
PictureBox	Name	PictAnsw4
	AutoSize	-1 'True
	BackColor	&H00000000&
	Visible	0 'False
PictureBox	Name	PictAnsw3
	AutoSize	-1 'True
	BackColor	&H00000000&
	Visible	0 'False
PictureBox	Name	PictAnsw1
	AutoSize	-1 'True
	BackColor	&H00000000&
	Visible	0 'False
PictureBox	Name	PictAnsw0
	AutoSize	-1 'True

OBJECT	PROPERTY	SETTING
	BackColor	&H00000000&
	Visible	0 'False
PictureBox	Name	PictAnsw2
	AutoSize	-1 'True
	BackColor	&H00000000&
	Visible	0 'False
Label	Name	File
	Caption	"Label1"
	Visible	0 'False
Label	Name	TotalQuestions
	AutoSize	-1 'True
	Caption	"Number of Questions: 50"
	Visible	0 'False
Label	Name	NCorrect
	AutoSize	-1 'True
	Caption	"Number Correct: 50"
	Visible	0 'False
Label	Name	QNumber
	AutoSize	-1 'True
	Caption	"Question Number: 50"
	Visible	0 'False
Label	Name	B
	Font	
	name	"Arial"
	Visible	0 'False
Label	Name	C
	Font	
	name	"Arial"
	Visible	0 'False

continued on next page

continued from previous page

OBJECT	PROPERTY	SETTING
Label	Name	D
	Font	
	name	"Arial"
	Visible	0 'False
Label	Name	E
	Font	
	name	"Arial"
	Visible	0 'False
Label	Name	A
	BackColor	&H00FFFFFF&
	Font	
	name	"Arial"
	ForeColor	&H00000000&
	Visible	0 'False

5. Add the following code to the MDIForm_Load procedure. The main form for starting the test procedure is loaded.

```
Private Sub MDIForm_Load()
'   Load Form2
Form2.Show
End Sub
```

6. Add the following code to the general declarations section of OPEN.FRM. The QuestRecord data type defines each multiple-choice question. The KeyArray is used to enter and check the password.

```
'  Declare the question record data type
Dim QuestRec As QuestRecord

'  KeyArray will be used to check the
'  text password
Dim keyarray() As String

'  Cnt will be used to count the password
'  keys entered
Dim Cnt As Integer
```

7. Add the following code to the general declarations section of the form. Password sets up for the entering of the password.

```
Private Sub Password()

'  Clear out the Password text
PassText.Text = ""

'  Dimension and clear the keyarray
ReDim keyarray(4) As String

'  Reset Cnt
Cnt = 1

'  Make the label, text box, and Done
'  command button
PassText.Visible = True
Label1.Visible = True
Done.Visible = True

End Sub
```

8. When the Create button is selected, the Password function is called to set up entering the password.

```
Private Sub Create_Click()

'  NewEdit will indicate that a new
'  test is to be created
NEWEDIT = 1

'  Call the password function to allow
'  for the password to be entered
password

End Sub
```

9. When the Edit button is selected, the Password function is called to set up entering the password.

```
Private Sub Edit_Click()

'  NewEdit will indicate that a
'  test is to be edited
NEWEDIT = 2

'  Call the password function to allow
'  for the password to be entered
password

End Sub
```

10. When the user selects the Done button, the text entered is checked to see if it meets the password. If so, then the file dialog box is shown so the user can select

a file. The appropriate checks are made to ensure the file exists if it is to be opened, and does not exist if it is to be created.

```
Private Sub Done_Click()

'  Set flag
Flag = 0

'  check to see if the TEST password
'  has been finished
If keyarray(1) <> "T" Then Flag = 1
If keyarray(2) <> "E" Then Flag = 1
If keyarray(3) <> "S" Then Flag = 1
If keyarray(4) <> "T" Then Flag = 1

'  If the flag is still 0 then the
'  flag is still 0
If Flag = 0 Then

Top:

    '  Depending on the command button selected, the
    '  appropriate dialogue box is shown
    If NEWEDIT = 1 Then CommonDialog1.ShowSave
    If NEWEDIT = 2 Then CommonDialog1.ShowOpen

    '  If the filename was not entered, or the filename
    '  is a wildcard, then the sub is exited
    If CommonDialog1.filename = "" Or Left(CommonDialog1.filename, 1) = "*" ↵
    Then Exit Sub

    If NEWEDIT = 2 Then

        '  Check will equal the directory of the filename
        check = Dir(CommonDialog1.filename)

        '  If check is empty then the file was not found, the filename
        '  of the dialogue box filename is cleared and the top of the
        '  sub is jumped to to start over the file name selection process
        If check = "" Then MsgBox "Test File Not Found.": ↵
        CommonDialog1.filename = "": GoTo Top

        '  Set the filename to the selected file
        filename = CommonDialog1.filename

    Else

        '  Check will equal the directory of the filename
        check = Dir(CommonDialog1.filename)

        '  If the file exits, then a new test can not be
        '  created.  Start the file selection process over
        If check <> "" Then MsgBox "This file exists, select 'Edit Test'.": ↵
        CommonDialog1.filename = "": GoTo Top
```

```
     '  Set the filename
     filename = CommonDialog1.filename

     '  check to see if an extension is on the filename
     '  if not add the .tst extension.
     If InStr(1, filename, ".") = 0 Then filename = filename + ".tst"

     '  Load the design form
     Load Form1

     '   Unload this form
     Unload Form2

   End If

   '  Load the design form
   Load Form1

   '   Unload this form
   Unload Form2

Else

     '  Clear password text box
     '  if an incorrect password
     '  is entered
     PassText.Text = ""

End If

'  reset count
Cnt = 1

End Sub
```

11. When the form is resized, the form is centered.

```
Private Sub form_Resize()

'  Center the form
centerform Form2

End Sub
```

12. When the Take Test button is selected, the file dialog box is shown so the user can select the test to be taken. The appropriate checks are made to ensure the file exists and is a test file.

```
Private Sub TakeTest_Click()

Top:

'  Show the open dialog
```

continued on next page

continued from previous page

```
CommonDialog1.ShowOpen

'  If no file was selected or a wild card in
'  the filename then exit the sub
If CommonDialog1.filename = "" Or Left(CommonDialog1.filename, 1) = "*" ↵
Then Exit Sub

'  Check will equal the directory listing
check = Dir(CommonDialog1.filename)

'  if check is blank then the file does not
'  exist.
If check = "" Then MsgBox "Test File Not Found.": CommonDialog1.filename = ""↵
: GoTo Top

'  Set the filename
filename = CommonDialog1.filename

'  Reset the Total value
Total = 0

'  Flag will be used to indicate when
'  a valid question is found
Flag = 0

'  Open the file
Open filename For Random As #1 Len = Len(QuestRec)

'  Go through the 50 question records
For n = 1 To 50
     '   Read in the record
     Get #1, Val(n), QuestRec

     '  Check to see if the Qtype is not 3, if so
     '  then we know that that record is a valid question
     '  and we increment total
     If QuestRec.QType <> 3 Then Total = Total + 1

     '  We will set flag to 1 when a valid question is found
     If QuestRec.QType = 3 Or QuestRec.QType = 2 Or QuestRec.QType = 1 Then ↵
     Flag = 1
Next n

'  Close the file
Close #1

'  If flag is still 0 then this is not a valid test file.
If Flag = 0 Then MsgBox "This is not a valid test file.": ↵
CommonDialog1.filename  = "": GoTo Top

'  Unload this form and load
'  the test form
Unload Form2
Load Form3
```

```
End Sub
```

13. When the user enters the password text, the first four characters are stored to be checked.

```
Private Sub PassText_KeyPress(KeyAscii As Integer)

'   For the first four characters entered, they
'   are stored for checking
If Cnt < 5 Then keyarray(Cnt) = Chr$(KeyAscii): Cnt = Cnt + 1

'   In order for the key not to be shown, the KeyAscii
'   value is set to 0
KeyAscii = 0

End Sub
```

14. Add the following code to the general declarations section of DESIGN.FRM. The standard data structure for the multiple-choice data record is declared.

```
'   Globally declare the question
'   data type
Dim QuestRec As QuestRecord
```

15. When the Next button is selected, the next record in the file is opened.

```
Private Sub Next_Click()

'   Set the question number text
'   to the current reccord + 1
QuestNum.Text = Val(QuestNum.Text) + 1

'   Open the question
Open_Click

End Sub
```

16. When the Previous button is selected, the previous record in the file is opened.

```
Private Sub Previous_Click()

'   Set the question number text
'   to the current reccord - 1
QuestNum.Text = Val(QuestNum.Text) - 1

'   Open the question
Open_Click

End Sub
```

17. When the Done button is selected, the form is unloaded and the Open form is loaded.

```
Private Sub Done_Click()
```

continued on next page

623

continued from previous page

```
'  Unload this form
Unload Form1

'  Load Form2
Load Form2

End Sub
```

18. When the form is loaded, a check is done to see if this is a new test being created. If this is a new test, then the test should be initialized.

```
Private Sub Form_Load()

'  Set the file label caption to the filename
file.Caption = filename

'  Autosize the label
file.AutoSize = True

'  Open the filename as random with
'  the length of the question records
Open filename For Random As #1 Len = Len(QuestRec)

'  If this is a new question file then
'  it needs to be initialized
If NEWEDIT = 1 Then
    QuestRec.QText = ""

    '  Note Qtype is set to 3 to indicate
    '  that this is a newly initialized question
    QuestRec.QType = 3
    QuestRec.AnswerA = ""
    QuestRec.AnswerB = ""
    QuestRec.AnswerC = ""
    QuestRec.AnswerD = ""
    QuestRec.AnswerE = ""
    QuestRec.CorrectAnsw = ""
    QuestRec.Explanation = ""

    '  Write the 50 questions out
    For n = 1 To 50
        Put #1, n, QuestRec
    Next n
End If

End Sub
```

19. When the form is resized, the form is automatically centered. This includes the start up of the form.

```
Private Sub form_Resize()

'  Center the form
centerform Form1
```

```
End Sub
```

20. When the form is unloaded, the test file is closed.

```
Private Sub form_Unload(Cancel As Integer)

'  Close the file
Close #1

End Sub
```

21. When the Open button is selected, the record entered in the QuestNum text box is opened and the data is read in and displayed.

```
Private Sub Open_Click()

'  Don't let a record greater than 50 and less
'  than 1 be opened
If Val(QuestNum) > 50 Then QuestNum.Text = 50: Exit Sub
If Val(QuestNum) < 1 Then QuestNum.Text = 1:  Exit Sub

'  Get the record
Get #1, Val(QuestNum), QuestRec

'  Display the Question Text
QuestText.Text = QuestRec.QText

'  Set the Text or Picture answer option
If QuestRec.QType = 1 Then TextOption.Value = True
If QuestRec.QType = 2 Then PictOption.Value = True

'  Show the answers
AnswerA.Text = QuestRec.AnswerA
AnswerB.Text = QuestRec.AnswerB
AnswerC.Text = QuestRec.AnswerC
AnswerD.Text = QuestRec.AnswerD
AnswerE.Text = QuestRec.AnswerE

'  Set the option button for the Correct answer
If QuestRec.CorrectAnsw = "A" Then OptA.Value = True
If QuestRec.CorrectAnsw = "B" Then OptB.Value = True
If QuestRec.CorrectAnsw = "C" Then OptC.Value = True
If QuestRec.CorrectAnsw = "D" Then OptD.Value = True
If QuestRec.CorrectAnsw = "E" Then OptE.Value = True

'   Show the explanation text
ExpTExt.Text = QuestRec.Explanation

End Sub
```

22. When the Picture answer button is selected, the instructions for entering in the picture answers are shown.

```
Private Sub PictOption_Click()
```

continued on next page

continued from previous page

```
'   If it is a picture answer then the
'   instructions in label5 are shown
If PictOption.Value = True Then
    Label5.Visible = True
Else
    Label5.Visible = False
End If

End Sub
```

23. When the Save Question button is selected, the QuestRec data type is filled out and written to file.

```
Private Sub Save_Click()

'   Do not save the record if the value is greater than 50
'   or less than 1
If Val(QuestNum) > 50 Or Val(QuestNum) < 1 Then MsgBox "Enter a Valid Question
Number": Exit Sub

'   Do not allow the question to be saved if there is no
'   question text
If QuestText.Text = "" Then MsgBox "Enter Text for your Question"

'   There must be at least one answer and it must start in A
If AnswerA.Text = "" Then MsgBox "You must have at least one answer in A"

'   Set the text
QuestRec.QText = QuestText.Text

'   Set the option value
If TextOption.Value = True Then QuestRec.QType = 1
If PictOption.Value = True Then QuestRec.QType = 2

'   Set the answers
QuestRec.AnswerA = AnswerA.Text
QuestRec.AnswerB = AnswerB.Text
QuestRec.AnswerC = AnswerC.Text
QuestRec.AnswerD = AnswerD.Text
QuestRec.AnswerE = AnswerE.Text

'   Store the correct answer
If OptA.Value = True Then QuestRec.CorrectAnsw = "A"
If OptB.Value = True Then QuestRec.CorrectAnsw = "B"
If OptC.Value = True Then QuestRec.CorrectAnsw = "C"
If OptD.Value = True Then QuestRec.CorrectAnsw = "D"
If OptE.Value = True Then QuestRec.CorrectAnsw = "E"

'   Store the explanation text
QuestRec.Explanation = ExpTExt.Text

'   Write the record
Put #1, Val(QuestNum), QuestRec

End Sub
```

24. When the Text option button is selected, the directions for the picture box answers are made invisible.

```
Private Sub TextOption_Click()

'  If the answer is a picture then show the
'  picture instructions
If PictOption.Value = True Then
    Label5.Visible = True
Else
    Label5.Visible = False
End If

End Sub
```

25. Add the following code to the general declarations section of TEST.FRM. The sndPlaySound function is declared for playing Wave files, the CrossHatch classes are declared for fading in the picture box answers, and various variables are globally declared for taking the test.

```
'  Declare the sndPlaySound function, which will be used to
'  play feedback sounds to the user
Private Declare Function sndPlaySound Lib "MMSYSTEM" (ByVal lpszSoundName ↵
As String, ByVal uFlags As Integer) As Integer

'  Declare our five crosshatch classes
Dim CrossHatch1 As CrossHatch
Dim CrossHatch2 As CrossHatch
Dim CrossHatch3 As CrossHatch
Dim CrossHatch4 As CrossHatch
Dim CrossHatch5 As CrossHatch

'  Click will be used to indicate when an answer
'  has been selected
Dim click

'  RecNumber will hold the current record
'  in the file
Dim RecNumber As Integer

'  Question Number will hold the number of the
'  questions currently being worked on
Dim QuestionNumber As Integer

'  QuestRec will be the record to hold the
'  multiple choice question
Dim QuestRec As QuestRecord

'  NumCorrect will count each correct answer
Dim NumCorrect As Integer
```

627

26. Add the following code to the general declarations section of the form. Correct is called to play the DING.WAV and update the appropriate variables to track the user's score.

```
Public Sub Correct()

'  Play the ding sound when a correct answer
'  has been given
throw% = sndPlaySound("c:\windows\media\ding.wav", &H0)

'  Show that the answer was correct and
'  Increment the number correct value
ExpTExt.Text = "Correct!"
NumCorrect = NumCorrect + 1

'  Update the display of the number correct
NCorrect.Caption = "Number Correct: " + Str$(NumCorrect)
NCorrect.AutoSize = True

End Sub
```

27. Add the following code to the general declarations section of the form. Incorrect is called to play the CHORD.WAV and update the appropriate variables to track the user's score.

```
Public Sub Incorrect()

'  Play the chord wave to indicate
'  an incorrect answer
throw% = sndPlaySound("c:\windows\media\chord.wav", &H0)

'  Show the explanation
ExpTExt.Text = QuestRec.Explanation

End Sub
```

28. Add the following code to the general declarations section of the form. The Done routine handles ending the test. If the user answers all the questions correctly, then a Congratulations animation is shown.

```
Public Sub Done()

'  Show the number correctly answered and
'  the percentage
MsgBox "You answered" + Str$(NumCorrect) + " out of" + Str$(Total) + " questions
correctly.  This is a score of" + Str$((NumCorrect / Total) * 100) + "%."

'  Check to see if the user answered 100% correct
If (NumCorrect / Total) * 100 = 100 Then

    '  Turn off the Ncorrect label
    NCorrect.Visible = False

    '  Turn off the question number label
```

```
        QNumber.Visible = False

        '  Turn off the total # Questions label
        totalquestions.Visible = False

        '  Turn off the file name label
        file.Visible = False

        '  Clear the two text boxes
        QuestText.Text = ""
        ExpTExt.Text = ""

        '  Make sure the answer commands are
        '  not displayed
        For n = 0 To 4
            QSelect(n).Visible = False
        Next n

        '  Ensure all of the picture answers are not
        '  visible
        PictAnsw0.Visible = False
        PictAnsw1.Visible = False
        PictAnsw2.Visible = False
        PictAnsw3.Visible = False
        PictAnsw4.Visible = False

        '  Ensure the label answers are not visible
        a.Visible = False
        B.Visible = False
        C.Visible = False
        D.Visible = False
        E.Visible = False

        '  Play the animation
        MMControl2.Command = "close"
        MMControl2.DeviceType = "AVIVideo"
        MMControl2.Filename = App.Path + "\raccong.avi"
        AnimPict.Visible = True
        MMControl2.hWndDisplay = AnimPict.hWnd
        MMControl2.Command = "open"
        MMControl2.Command = "play"

Else

        '  Unload this form
        Unload Form3

        '  Load the form
        Load Form2

End If

End Sub
```

29. Add the following code to the general declarations section of the form. The LoadQuestion routine handles reading in and loading the next question. It also handles fading in the bitmap images if the answers are pictures.

```
Public Sub LoadQuestion()

'   Ensure that the last record is not passed
If QuestionNumber > 50 Then Done: Exit Sub

'   Make sure the answer labels are not visible
For n = 0 To 4
    QSelect(n).Visible = False
Next n

'   Ensure the picture answer images are not visible
PictAnsw0.Visible = False
PictAnsw1.Visible = False
PictAnsw2.Visible = False
PictAnsw3.Visible = False
PictAnsw4.Visible = False

'   Ensure the answers are not visible
a.Visible = False
B.Visible = False
C.Visible = False
D.Visible = False
E.Visible = False

'   Decrement RecNumber noting that it
'   is immediately incremented in the do
'   loop
RecNumber = RecNumber - 1

'   Search to find the next valid question
Do
    '   Increment the record number
    RecNumber = RecNumber + 1

    '   Make sure the last record is not passed
    '   If it has been reached then the test is
    '   done
    If RecNumber > 50 Then Done: Exit Sub

    '   Get the record
    Get #1, Val(RecNumber), QuestRec

Loop Until QuestRec.QType <> 3

' Increment the question number
QuestionNumber = QuestionNumber + 1

'   Display the new question number
QNumber.Caption = "Question Number: " + Str$(QuestionNumber)

'   Autosize the label
```

```
QNumber.AutoSize = True

'   Display the question text
QuestText.Text = QuestRec.QText

'  Check to see if it is a text answer
'  or a picture answer
If QuestRec.QType = 1 Then

        '  There is no answer if the answer field is a string of 128 spaces
        '  if there is an answer, it is displayed
        If QuestRec.AnswerA <> String(128, " ") Then a.Caption = QuestRec.AnswerA ↵
        : a.Visible = True: QSelect(0).Visible = True

        If QuestRec.AnswerB <> String(128, " ") Then B.Caption = QuestRec.AnswerB↵
        : B.Visible = True: QSelect(1).Visible = True

        If QuestRec.AnswerC <> String(128, " ") Then C.Caption = QuestRec.AnswerC↵
        : C.Visible = True: QSelect(2).Visible = True

        If QuestRec.AnswerD <> String(128, " ") Then D.Caption = QuestRec.AnswerD↵
        : D.Visible = True: QSelect(3).Visible = True

        If QuestRec.AnswerE <> String(128, " ") Then E.Caption = QuestRec.AnswerE↵
        : E.Visible = True: QSelect(4).Visible = True

Else

        '  Check to see if there is a bitmap file name in answer a
        If QuestRec.AnswerA <> String(128, " ") Then

            '  Load the picture into picture1
            picture1.Picture = LoadPicture(App.Path + "\" + RTrim(QuestRec.AnswerA))

            '  Make the first picture answer visible
            PictAnsw0.Visible = True

            '  Set the width and height of the picture
            PictAnsw0.Width = picture1.Width
            PictAnsw0.Height = picture1.Height

            '  Set the class pict1 property
            Set CrossHatch1.Pict1 = PictAnsw0

            '  Setup the fade
            CrossHatch1.setup

            '  Begin the fadein process
            CrossHatch1.fadein
        End If


        '  The following if statements check to see
        '  if there is an answer in each field and follows
        '  the same logic as the last section
```

continued on next page

continued from previous page

```
    If QuestRec.AnswerB <> String(128, " ") Then

        picture4.Picture = LoadPicture(App.Path + "\" + ↵
        RTrim(QuestRec.AnswerB)): PictAnsw1.Visible = True

        PictAnsw1.Width = picture4.Width
        PictAnsw1.Height = picture4.Height
        Set CrossHatch2.Pict1 = PictAnsw1
        CrossHatch2.setup
        CrossHatch2.fadein
    End If

    If QuestRec.AnswerC <> String(128, " ") Then
        picture7.Picture = LoadPicture(App.Path + "\" + ↵
        RTrim(QuestRec.AnswerC)): PictAnsw2.Visible = True

        PictAnsw2.Width = picture7.Width
        PictAnsw2.Height = picture7.Height
        Set CrossHatch3.Pict1 = PictAnsw2
        CrossHatch3.setup
        CrossHatch3.fadein
    End If

    If QuestRec.AnswerD <> String(128, " ") Then
        picture10.Picture = LoadPicture(App.Path + "\" + ↵
        RTrim(QuestRec.AnswerD)): PictAnsw3.Visible = True

        PictAnsw3.Width = picture10.Width
        PictAnsw3.Height = picture10.Height
        Set CrossHatch4.Pict1 = PictAnsw3
        CrossHatch4.setup
        CrossHatch4.fadein
    End If

    If QuestRec.AnswerE <> String(128, " ") Then
        picture13.Picture = LoadPicture(App.Path + "\" + ↵
        RTrim(QuestRec.AnswerE)): PictAnsw4.Visible = True

        PictAnsw4.Width = picture13.Width
        PictAnsw4.Height = picture13.Height
        Set CrossHatch5.Pict1 = PictAnsw4
        CrossHatch5.setup
        CrossHatch5.fadein
    End If

End If

End Sub
```

30. When form is loaded, the Good Luck animation is shown.

```
Private Sub form_Load()

'   Play the Good Luck animation
MMControl1.Command = "close"
```

```
MMControl1.DeviceType = "AVIVideo"
MMControl1.Filename = App.Path + "\racgood.avi"
MMControl1.hWndDisplay = AnimPict.hWnd
MMControl1.Command = "open"
MMControl1.Command = "play"

End Sub
```

31. Any time the form is resized, the form is centered on the screen.

```
Private Sub form_Resize()

'  Center the form
centerform Form3

End Sub
```

32. When the form is unloaded, the test file is closed.

```
Private Sub form_Unload(Cancel As Integer)

'  Close the file
Close #1

End Sub
```

33. When the animation is finished playing, the timer is enabled. This allows the user to see the end of the animation for a short period of time.

```
Private Sub MMControl1_Done(NotifyCode As Integer)

'  Enable the timer so that the animation
'  can be visible for a short period
Timer2.Enabled = True

End Sub
```

34. When the animation is finished playing, the timer is enabled. This allows the user to see the end of the animation for a short period of time.

```
Private Sub MMControl2_Done(NotifyCode As Integer)

'  Enable the timer so that the animation
'  can be visible for a short period
timer3.Enabled = True

End Sub
```

35. When the Next Question button is selected, a check is done to ensure that the user entered an answer. If so, then the LoadQuestion routine is called.

```
Private Sub NextQuest_Click()

'  If click is equal to 1 then an answer
'  has been given so the next question can
```

continued on next page

continued from previous page

```
'   be loaded
If click = 1 Then
    '   Reset click
    click = 0
    '   Clear out the Explanation text
    ExpTExt.Text = ""
    '   Increase the record number
    RecNumber = RecNumber + 1
    '   Load the next question
    LoadQuestion
Else
    '   Notify the user an answer must be selected
    MsgBox "You must select an answer."
End If

End Sub
```

36. Add the following code to the general declarations section of the form. If the answer is a picture, then when one of the pictures is clicked on, a check is done to see if the correct answer has been given.

```
Private Sub PictAnsw(index As Integer)

'   Check to make sure no answer has been given
If click <> 1 Then

'   Set click to indicate an answer has been given
click = 1

'   Check for a correct answer and if so then
'   call the correct function
If (index = 0) And (QuestRec.CorrectAnsw = "A") Then correct: Exit Sub
If (index = 1) And (QuestRec.CorrectAnsw = "B") Then correct: Exit Sub
If (index = 2) And (QuestRec.CorrectAnsw = "C") Then correct: Exit Sub
If (index = 3) And (QuestRec.CorrectAnsw = "D") Then correct: Exit Sub
If (index = 4) And (QuestRec.CorrectAnsw = "E") Then correct: Exit Sub

'   If no correct answer was given then call the
'   incorrect function
incorrect

End If

End Sub
```

37. When one of the picture answers is selected, the PictAnsw function is called.

```
Private Sub PictAnsw0_Click()

'   Call the PictAnsw function indicating the
'   first image was selected
PictAnsw 0

End Sub
```

```
Private Sub PictAnsw1_Click()

'  Call the PictAnsw function indicating the
'  second image was selected
PictAnsw 1

End Sub

Private Sub PictAnsw2_Click()

'  Call the PictAnsw function indicating the
'  third image was selected
PictAnsw 2

End Sub

Private Sub PictAnsw3_Click()

'  Call the PictAnsw function indicating the
'  fourth image was selected
PictAnsw 3

End Sub

Private Sub PictAnsw4_Click()

'  Call the PictAnsw function indicating the
'  fifth image was selected
PictAnsw 4

End Sub
```

38. When one of the answer buttons is selected, a check is done to see if it is a correct answer and to take appropriate action.

```
Private Sub QSelect_Click(index As Integer)

'  If no answer has been given then check the
'  answer given
If click <> 1 Then

'  Set the click variable so no answer will be checked
'  again
click = 1

'  Check for a correct answer and if so then
'  call the correct function
If (index = 0) And (QuestRec.CorrectAnsw = "A") Then correct: Exit Sub
If (index = 1) And (QuestRec.CorrectAnsw = "B") Then correct: Exit Sub
If (index = 2) And (QuestRec.CorrectAnsw = "C") Then correct: Exit Sub
If (index = 3) And (QuestRec.CorrectAnsw = "D") Then correct: Exit Sub
If (index = 4) And (QuestRec.CorrectAnsw = "E") Then correct: Exit Sub

'  If no correct answer was given then call the
'  incorrect function
```

continued on next page

continued from previous page

```
incorrect

End If

End Sub
```

39. No text is allowed to be entered in the QuestText text box.

```
Private Sub QuestText_KeyPress(KeyAscii As Integer)

'  Do not allow any keys to be entered
KeyAscii = 0

End Sub
```

40. Timer1 is used to handle the cross hatch fade in of the picture answers.

```
Private Sub timer1_Timer()

'  The intick function will be called for each
'  answer that contains an image
If QuestRec.AnswerA <> String(128, " ") Then
    CrossHatch1.intick
End If

If QuestRec.AnswerB <> String(128, " ") Then
    CrossHatch2.intick
End If

If QuestRec.AnswerC <> String(128, " ") Then
    CrossHatch3.intick
End If

If QuestRec.AnswerD <> String(128, " ") Then
    CrossHatch4.intick
End If

If QuestRec.AnswerE <> String(128, " ") Then
    CrossHatch5.intick
End If

End Sub
```

41. Timer2 is called once the introductory animation is finished. It handles opening the test file and setting up the question-taking process. Also, the CrossHatch classes for the fade in of the picture answers are set up.

```
Private Sub Timer2_Timer()

'  Disable the timer
Timer2.Enabled = False

'  Make the animation picture visible
AnimPict.Visible = False
```

```
'  Set the file label
file.Caption = Filename
file.AutoSize = True

'  Set up the counting variables
QuestionNumber = 0
NumCorrect = 0
RecNumber = 1

'  Setup the number correct label
NCorrect.Caption = "Number Correct: " + Str$(NumCorrect)
NCorrect.AutoSize = True

'  Open the file name
Open Filename For Random As #1 Len = Len(QuestRec)

'  Setup the Totalquestions label
totalquestions.Caption = "Number of Questions: " + Str$(Total)
totalquestions.AutoSize = True

'  Load the first question
LoadQuestion

'  Declare the new classes
Set CrossHatch1 = New CrossHatch
Set CrossHatch2 = New CrossHatch
Set CrossHatch3 = New CrossHatch
Set CrossHatch4 = New CrossHatch
Set CrossHatch5 = New CrossHatch

'  Set the crosshatch properties
Set CrossHatch1.Pict1 = picture1
Set CrossHatch1.pict2 = picture1
Set CrossHatch1.pict3 = picture2
Set CrossHatch1.pict4 = picture3

Set CrossHatch2.pict2 = picture4
Set CrossHatch2.pict3 = picture5
Set CrossHatch2.pict4 = picture6

Set CrossHatch3.pict2 = picture7
Set CrossHatch3.pict3 = picture8
Set CrossHatch3.pict4 = picture9

Set CrossHatch4.pict2 = picture10
Set CrossHatch4.pict3 = picture11
Set CrossHatch4.pict4 = picture12

Set CrossHatch5.pict2 = picture13
Set CrossHatch5.pict3 = picture14
Set CrossHatch5.pict4 = picture15

'  Indicate no blow up of the pattern will be
'  shown
Let CrossHatch1.blowup = 0
```

continued on next page

continued from previous page

```
Let CrossHatch2.blowup = 0
Let CrossHatch3.blowup = 0
Let CrossHatch4.blowup = 0
Let CrossHatch5.blowup = 0

'  Pass the timer to the class
Set CrossHatch1.timer = timer1
Set CrossHatch2.timer = timer1
Set CrossHatch3.timer = timer1
Set CrossHatch4.timer = timer1
Set CrossHatch5.timer = timer1


'  Call the setup bitmap function
CrossHatch1.buildbitmap
CrossHatch2.buildbitmap
CrossHatch3.buildbitmap
CrossHatch4.buildbitmap
CrossHatch5.buildbitmap

'  Build the cross hatch screens
CrossHatch1.BuildScrns 1
CrossHatch2.BuildScrns 1
CrossHatch3.BuildScrns 1
CrossHatch4.BuildScrns 1
CrossHatch5.BuildScrns 1

'  Make all of the labels visible
file.Visible = True
totalquestions.Visible = True
QNumber.Visible = True
NCorrect.Visible = True

End Sub
```

42. If the final Congratulations animation is run, then Timer3 is enabled when the animation is finished to allow the user a short period to view it. When the timer starts, the form is unloaded and the open form is loaded.

```
Private Sub timer3_Timer()

'  Unload this form
Unload Form3

'  Load form2
Load Form2

End Sub
```

43. Create a new module called MODULE.BAS. Add the following code to the general declarations section of the form. Global variables for the project are declared here, as is the multiple-choice data type.

```
'  When a test is to be taken, Total will
```

```
'   contain the total number of questions in the
'   test.  This is calculated in Form2 and used by
'   Form3
Public Total As Integer

'   Filename will hold the location and name
'   of the file to be worked on
Public Filename As String

'   NewEdit will indicate whether the test is to
'   be created or edited
Public NEWEDIT As Integer

'   The QuestRecord data type is the
'   format for each question
Public Type QuestRecord
     '   The question text
     QText As String * 1024

     '   Qtype indicates whether it is a text
     '   or picture question
     QType As Integer

     '   Each variable holds the answer
     '   appropriate answer
     AnswerA As String * 128
     AnswerB As String * 128
     AnswerC As String * 128
     AnswerD As String * 128
     AnswerE As String * 128

     '   Correct answer holds the correct answer
     '   to the queston
     CorrectAnsw As String * 1

     '   Explanation holds the explanation of the correct
     '   answer
     Explanation As String * 1024
End Type
```

44. The CenterForm function handles centering the specified form on the screen.

```
Public Sub CenterForm(form As Object)

     '   As long as the form is not minimized, then
     '   the form is centered on the screen.
     If form.WindowState = 0 Then
         form.Move (Screen.Width - form.Width) / 2, (Screen.Height - ↵
         form.Height) / 2
     End If

End Sub
```

How It Works

The central focus of this How-To is the multiple-choice test. The QuestRecord data type defines each record of the test file. This makes reading and writing from the test files simple by using the Visual Basic 4.0 random file support with the Get and Put functions. With these functions, the entire record can be read to and written from the data record easily.

Each basic question consists of the question statement, the answers, and the explanation. There can be two different types of answers, text and picture. If it is a picture answer, then the name of the BMP format file is stored in design mode. In the test-taking mode, the bitmap files are loaded into the picture boxes and then the CrossHatch class is used to fade in the graphics.

In the test mode, an animation is added at the beginning of the test mode to tell the user "Good Luck." At the end, if the user has answered all of the questions correctly, an animation tells the user "Congratulations." Feedback is given to the user after answering each question with the use of the sndPlaySound function. When a correct answer is given, appropriate feedback is given with DING.WAV. When an answer is incorrect, the CHORD.WAV file is played. At that point, an explanation of the correct answer is given. You may wish to show the explanation even when the question is correct, in case the user had a lucky guess and would like to know the explanation.

You do not have to enter the questions in numerical record sequence. When a new test is created, all the records are initialized. To check whether or not a record is a valid question, check the question type. This field is initialized to 3 when the file is created. When the test is taken, each record out of the 50 is checked to see if it is a valid question. The value of the question type field is either 1 for a text answer or 2 for a picture answer.

Comments

Additional multimedia elements as answers could easily be added to this straightforward authoring and delivery system. Video, sound, and animation answers could easily be implemented.

8.6 How do I...
Create a hypertext system?

COMPLEXITY: ADVANCED

Problem

Hypertext is an important tool for delivering text information to users. I would like to be able to develop my text information into a hypertext format that includes pop-up text, hyperlinks, and graphics.

Technique

The central idea behind hypertext is the ability to embed character sequences in a document that indicate when text should be processed as a hyperlink, pop up, and the like. A document structure must be developed to indicate where hyperjumps "jump" or link to. A simple document structure will be developed, along with a Visual Basic 4.0 class to read and process the document.

Steps

Open and run 8-6.VBP. The running program appears as shown in Figure 8-6-1. The running program is a hypertext browser, which allows you to navigate the document easily and fully. The text in underlined pink represents pop-up definitions. Click on any one of these and a pop-up window with text will be shown. When a graphic is available for viewing, the text will be shown in small blue print (Graphic). To see more text for this section, click on the More button. If there is additional text, it will be shown. In this case, you will see in the next section the Comments text in red. This indicates a hyperjump to a new section of the text. Click on the Comments keyword and the comments section of the document will be shown. Once you have

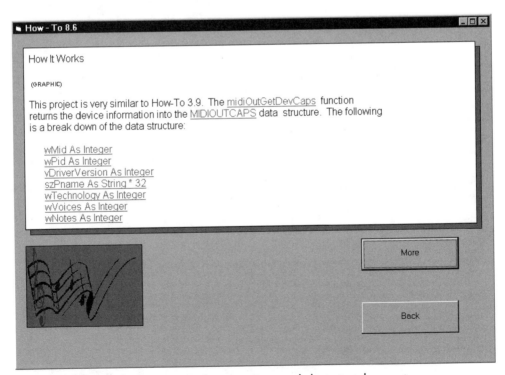

Figure 8-6-1 The form at runtime depicting an example hypertext document

made this jump, you can go back to the original section by clicking on the Back button.

1. Create a new project called 8-6.VBP. Add the objects and properties listed in Table 8-6-1 to Form1 and save the form as 8-6.FRM.

Table 8-6-1 The project's objects and properties

OBJECT	PROPERTY	SETTING
Form	Name	Form1
	Auto3D	-1 'True
	Caption	"How-To 8.6"
PictureBox	Name	PopDisp
	Font	
	name	"Arial"
	size	10.2
	ForeColor	&H00000000&
	Visible	0 'False
PictureBox	Name	PopShadow
	BackColor	&H00808080&
	Font	
	name	"Arial"
	size	10.2
	ForeColor	&H00000000&
	Visible	0 'False
CommandButton	Name	More
	Caption	"More"
CommandButton	Name	Back
	Caption	"Back"
PictureBox	Name	PictDisp
	BackColor	&H00FFFFFF&
	ForeColor	&H000000FF&
	Visible	0 'False

OBJECT	PROPERTY	SETTING
PictureBox	Name	TextDisp
	Font	
	name	"Arial"
	size	9.6
PictureBox	Name	TextShadow
	BackColor	&H00808080&
	Font	
	name	"Arial"
	size	9.6

2. Add the following code to the general declarations section of the form. The First variable is used to execute the code in Form_Paint once. The Hyper class is declared globally.

```
'  First will be used to execute the code in the
'  Form_Paint event only once
Dim First As Integer

'  Globally declare our Hyper Class
Dim Hyper As Hyper
```

3. When the Back button is selected, the Back function of the class is called. This jumps back to the previous link (section) that the current link was jumped to from.

```
Private Sub Back_Click()

'  Go to the previous link
Hyper.Back

End Sub
```

4. When the More button is selected, a refresh of the hypertext needs to be performed if the pop-up picture is visible. Then the DisplayLink function is called to update the hypertext.

```
Private Sub More_Click()

'  If the Pop Up Picture is visible
'  and the More button is selected,
'  then the main text needs to be
'  refreshed
If PopDisp.Visible = True Then
    Hyper.Refresh
End If

'  Call the Display Link function, which
```

continued on next page

continued from previous page

```
'  will move to the next screen if there
'  is additional text
Hyper.DisplayLink

End Sub
```

5. When the form is loaded, various picture boxes are set to the appropriate widths and heights. Also, the class is created and the indexes for the hypertext file are set up. This only has to be done once for each hypertext file.

```
Private Sub Form_Load()

'  Make the pop up picture the same width and
'  height as the display text.
PopDisp.Width = TextDisp.Width
PopDisp.Height = TextDisp.Height

'  Make the pop up shadow picture the same width and
'  height as the display text.
PopShadow.Width = PopDisp.Width
PopShadow.Height = PopDisp.Height

'  Set the height of the Text Display
'  function
TextDisp.Height = TextDisp.TextHeight("HelloWorld") * 16

'  Set the Text Shadow to the same
'  dimensions as the Text Display
TextShadow.Height = TextDisp.Height
TextShadow.Width = TextDisp.Width

'  Offset the Text Shadow
TextShadow.Move TextDisp.Left + 100, TextDisp.Top + 100

'  Create the new Hyper Class
Set Hyper = New Hyper

'  Build the indexes for the text.
'  Note, this only needs to be done
'  once
Hyper.buildindex App.Path + "\hyper.txt", App.Path + "\hyper.idx"

'  Set the number of lines in the hypertext
Let Hyper.LineCount = 14

'  Set the main text display
Set Hyper.TextDisp = TextDisp

'  Set the pop up display
Set Hyper.PopPict = PopDisp

'  Set the pop up shadow
Set Hyper.PopShadow = PopShadow

'  Set the display picture for the graphics
```

```
Set Hyper.DispPict = PictDisp

'  Set the number of characters per line
Let Hyper.CharsPerLine = 80

'  Set the text file and index file
Let Hyper.filename = App.Path + "\hyper.txt"
Let Hyper.fileindex = App.Path + "\hyper.idx"

End Sub
```

6. The first time the form is painted, the Setup function of the Hyper class is called to set up the display of the hypertext and show the first screen.

```
Private Sub Form_Paint()

'  On the first Form_Paint event,
'  setup the hypertext class
If First = 0 Then
    '  Setup the hypertext
    Hyper.setup
    First = 1
End If

End Sub
```

7. When the TextDisp picture is clicked, a refresh is done on the hypertext if the pop-up picture is displayed. Then the TextClick function of the class is called to check for a click on a hypertext keyword.

```
Private Sub TextDisp_MouseDown(Button As Integer, Shift As Integer, x As Single, y
As Single)

'  If the main text display is selected and the
'  pop up picture is visible, then it needs to
'  be refreshed
If PopDisp.Visible = True Then
    Hyper.Refresh
End If

'  Call the textclick function with the x and
'  y coords. of the text click
Hyper.TextClick x, y

End Sub
```

8. Insert a new class into the project and save it as HYPER.CLS. Add the following code to the general declarations section of the form. The global members and objects of the class are declared.

```
'  Declare the member objects.  These include the
'  Text display, the popup pictures, and the graphic
'  display picture
Private m_TextDisp As Object
```

continued on next page

continued from previous page

```
Private m_PopPict As Object
Private m_PopShadow As Object
Private m_DispPict As Object

'   These are the hypertext file and
'   the index file
Private m_filename As String
Private m_fileindex As String

'   m_CharsPerLine holds the number
'   of characters to be displayed on
'   each line
Private m_CharsPerLine As Integer

'   m_Index will store the index into the
'   m_LinkIndex array
Private m_Index As Integer

'   m_IndexLast will store the index into the
'   m_LinkIndex array for the last link shown
Private m_IndexLast As Integer

'   m_GlobalCount holds the current byte position in
'   the hypertext file for the current link.
'   m_GlobalCountLast holds the bytecount for the last
'   screen shown
Private m_GlobalCount As Integer
Private m_GlobalCountLast As Integer

'   m_LineCount holds the number of lines to be shown
'   on any one screen
Private m_Linecount As Integer

'   m_BackGlobalLast holds the bytecount for
'   the previous link jumped from
Private m_BackGlobalLast As Integer

'   This array stores the starting point for
'   each link in the array
Dim m_LinkIndex() As Integer

'   This array stores the starting bytes for
'   each jump with in a link
Dim m_JumpIndex() As String
```

9. The following sets up the properties of the classes. These include the file name for the hypertext, the picture to display the text on, the pop-up picture, and shadow picture.

```
'   The following are the property settings
'   for most of the member variables
Public Property Let LineCount(n As Integer)
    Let m_Linecount = n
End Property
```

```
Public Property Let CharsPerLine(n As Integer)
    Let m_CharsPerLine = n
End Property

Public Property Let filename(file As String)
    Let m_filename = file
End Property

Public Property Let fileindex(file As String)
    Let m_fileindex = file
End Property

Public Property Set TextDisp(acontrol As Control)
    Set m_TextDisp = acontrol
End Property

Public Property Set PopShadow(acontrol As Control)
    Set m_PopShadow = acontrol
End Property

Public Property Set PopPict(acontrol As Control)
    Set m_PopPict = acontrol
End Property

Public Property Set DispPict(acontrol As Control)
    Set m_DispPict = acontrol
End Property
```

10. The Setup function handles reading in the indexes for the links in the hypertext file.

```
Public Sub Setup()

'   Dimension the Link array.  Note that there can only be
'   250 links within one hypertext file
ReDim m_LinkIndex(250, 2) As Integer

'   Open the index file for input
Open m_fileindex For Input As #1

'   Read until the end of the file
Do Until EOF(1)

    '   Read in one line
    Line Input #1, LN$

    '   Find the colon in the line
    p = InStr(1, LN$, ":")

    '   Increment our n counter
    n = n + 1

    '   Check for a link index
    If Left$(LN$, 1) = "L" Then
```

continued on next page

continued from previous page

```
            '  Increment our array counter
            cnt = cnt + 1

            '  Get the bytecount and store it
            m_LinkIndex(cnt, 1) = Val(Mid$(LN$, p + 1, Len(LN$)))

            '  store the line number in the index
            '  where the link is found
            m_LinkIndex(cnt, 2) = n
        End If

Loop

'  Close the file
Close #1

'  Set the index to the first element
'  in the m_LinkIndex array
m_Index = 1

'  Display the first link
displayLink

End Sub
```

11. The DisplayLink function is the workhorse behind displaying each link (or section) of the document. It handles displaying the static text as well as the various types of hypertext keywords. It also tracks where in the link it is currently positioned. Thus, when the More button is selected, the next section of the link is automatically displayed. This includes wrapping from the bottom of the link back to the top.

```
Public Sub DisplayLink()

'  redimension and clear the jump array
ReDim m_JumpIndex(50, 5) As String

'  Open the hypertext file
Open m_filename For Binary Access Read Lock Read As #1

'  The read variables are used to read various lengths
'  of data from the file.
read1$ = " ": Read2$ = "   ": Read3$ = "       "

'  Check to see if we are not on the
'  first screen
If m_GlobalCount <> 0 Then

    '  Store the current position in the file
    m_GlobalCountLast = m_GlobalCount

    '  Set the bytecount to the current count
    bytecount = m_GlobalCount
```

```
    '  Reset the global count
    m_GlobalCount = 0

    '  if the pop up picture is not visible
    '  then clear the screen
    If m_PopPict.Visible = False Then
        m_TextDisp.Cls
    Else
        '  Make sure the pop up pictures are not
        '  visible
        m_PopShadow.Visible = False
        m_PopPict.Visible = False
    End If
Else

    '  On the first screen of the link, set the
    '  bytecount
    bytecount = m_LinkIndex(m_Index, 1)
    bytecount = bytecount + Len("~~L" + Right$(Str$(m_Index), ↵
    Len(Str$(m_Index)) - 1)) + 1


    '  If the pop up pictures are not visible
    '  then clear the text screen or else
    '  turn off the pictures
    If m_PopPict.Visible = False Then
            m_TextDisp.Cls
    Else
        m_PopShadow.Visible = False
        m_PopPict.Visible = False
    End If

    '  Reset m_GlobalCountLast variable
    '  since we are on the first screen
    m_GlobalCountLast = 0
End If

'  Set the starting position for the start of the text
m_TextDisp.CurrentX = 100
m_TextDisp.CurrentY = 100

Rem ****************************Start Printing********************************

Do Until flag = 1

    '  n will be used to count the number of
    '  characters printed on each line
    n = n + 1

    '  If we have reached the maximum number of characters
    '  per line then we need to check for the next space
    '  so that the current word will not be broken up
    If n = m_CharsPerLine Then
        checkspace = 1
    End If
```

continued on next page

649

continued from previous page

```
'  Read the next character
Get #1, bytecount, read1$

'  If a space character was read and the checkspace
'  flag is set
If read1$ = " " And checkspace = 1 Then

    '  Print a new line
    m_TextDisp.Print

    '  Set the x
    m_TextDisp.CurrentX = 100

    '  Increment the line counter
    NewLine = NewLine + 1

    '  Check to see if the maximum number of lines
    '  to be printed have been printed
    If NewLine > m_Linecount Then

        '  Store the current bytecount
        m_GlobalCount = bytecount

        '   Set the flag so the do loop ends
        flag = 1
    End If

    '  Reset the checkspace and n
    '  variables
    checkspace = 0
    n = 0
End If

'  Check for a special character in the text
If read1$ = "\" Then

    '  Read in the next several characters
    Get #1, bytecount + 1, Read3$

    '  BFlag will be reset
    BFlag = 0

    '  Check for a paragraph return in the text
    If Left$(Read3$, 2) = "\T" Or Left$(Read3$, 2) = "\B" Then

        '  Set BFlag if this is a single line feed
        If Left$(Read3$, 2) = "\B" Then BFlag = 1

        '  Reset the character counter
        n = 0
        '  Reset the checkspace flag
        checkspace = 0

        '  If this is the first screen in, increment the newline
```

```
'  counter.   Note if this is a single line feed then
'  NewLine is only incremented once
If m_GlobalCountLast = 0 And BFlag = 0 Then NewLine = NewLine + 2
If m_GlobalCountLast = 0 And BFlag = 1 Then NewLine = NewLine + 1


'  If NewLine is not the first line
'  of the screen then do two prints
'  and set the currentx
If NewLine > 0 Then
    m_TextDisp.Print
    '  If only one line feed then only print
    '  once.
    If BFlag = 0 Then m_TextDisp.Print
    m_TextDisp.CurrentX = 100
End If


'  If this is not the first screen then increment
'  NewLine now.  Only increment once if this is
'  a single line feed
If m_GlobalCountLast <> 0 And BFlag = 0 Then NewLine = NewLine + 2
If m_GlobalCountLast <> 0 And BFlag = 1 Then NewLine = NewLine + 1


'  Check to see if Newline is greater than the max
'  lines on the screen
If NewLine > m_Linecount Then
      '  Store the ByteCount
      m_GlobalCount = bytecount

      '  Set flag to end the loop
      flag = 1

End If

'  Increment ByteCount past the special characters
bytecount = bytecount + 2
End If

'  Check to see if a graphic has been shown
If Left$(Read3$, 2) = "\G" Then

    '  Increment ByteCount past the special characters
    bytecount = bytecount + 4

    '  Clear the file variable that will hold the
    '  graphic filename
    file = ""

    '  Read in the next character
    Get #1, bytecount, read1$

    '  If the next character is a back slash
    '  then we need to move one further for the
    '  start of the filename
    If read1$ <> "\" Then bytecount = bytecount + 1
```

continued on next page

continued from previous page

```
                    '  Increment ByteCount to read the next character
                    bytecount = bytecount + 1

                    '  Read in the next character
                    Get #1, bytecount, read1$

                    '  Read the filename until the next back
                    '  slash
                    Do Until read1$ = "\"
                        '  Store the next character
                        file = file + read1$

                        '  Increment Bytecount
                        bytecount = bytecount + 1

                        '  Read the next character
                        Get #1, bytecount, read1$
                    Loop

                    '  Decrement the bytecount since the
                    bytecount = bytecount - 1

                    '  increment the jump counter into the JumpIndex array
                    Jump = Jump + 1

                    '  Store the filename in the JumpIndex array
                    m_JumpIndex(Jump, 1) = file

                    '  Display the graphic
                    dispgraphictext Jump

                    '  Start a new line
                    m_TextDisp.Print
                    m_TextDisp.CurrentX = 100
                    bytecount = bytecount + 1

                    '  Set the character count to the
                    '  beginning of the line
                    n = 0

                    '  Clear the checkspace character
                    checkspace = 0

                    '  Increase the NewLine counter
                    NewLine = NewLine + 1
                End If

            '  Check for a popup display or a LinkJump
            If Left$(Read3$, 1) = "P" Or Left$(Read3$, 1) = "L" Then

                '  Check for the slash following the
                '  \P or \L
                p = InStr(1, Read3$, "\")
                If p <> 0 Then
```

```
'  Increment the Jump character
Jump = Jump + 1


'  Store the Index Name (i.e. P1 or L2)
m_JumpIndex(Jump, 1) = Left$(Read3$, p - 1)


'  Get the number of the pop up or link
num$ = Right$(m_JumpIndex(Jump, 1), Len(m_JumpIndex(Jump, 1)) ↵
- 1)


'  Check to see if the index is a single digit  and
'  increment the bytecount appropriately
If Len(num$) = 1 Then bytecount = bytecount + 4 Else ↵
bytecount = bytecount + 5


'  If this is a pop up or link, then change the color
'  appropriately and underline property
If Left$(Read3$, 1) = "P" Then
    m_TextDisp.ForeColor = RGB(255, 0, 255)
    m_TextDisp.FontUnderline = True
Else
    m_TextDisp.ForeColor = RGB(255, 0, 0)
End If


'  Read the next character
Get #1, bytecount, read1$


'  Increment the ByteCount
bytecount = bytecount + 1


'  Store the currentx and y of the picture box
'  this will be the origin of the text hot spot
'  for checking for a click
m_JumpIndex(Jump, 2) = m_TextDisp.CurrentX
m_JumpIndex(Jump, 3) = m_TextDisp.CurrentY


'  Clear out the Text variable
Text$ = ""


'  Read until the back slash is found
Do Until read1$ = "\"
    '  Add up the Text Variable
    Text$ = Text$ + read1$

    '  Make sure that this is not the first character
    '  on the line.  If not then increment the counter
    If n <> 1 Then n = n + 1

    '  Check to see if the end of the line
    '  has been reached
    If n = m_CharsPerLine Then
        '  Reset n
        n = 0

        '  Increment the line couunter
```

continued on next page

continued from previous page

```
                        NewLine = NewLine + 1

                        '  Check to see if the end of the
                        '  display has been reached
                        If NewLine > m_Linecount Then
                            m_GlobalCount = bytecount
                            flag = 1
                        End If
                    End If

                    '  Print the character
                    m_TextDisp.Print read1$;

                    '  Read the next character
                    Get #1, bytecount, read1$

                    '  Increment the bytecount
                    bytecount = bytecount + 1
                Loop

                '  Set the next line up
                If n = 0 Then
                    checkspace = 0
                    m_TextDisp.Print
                    m_TextDisp.CurrentX = 100
                End If

                '  Store the ending point of the hyper hot spot
                m_JumpIndex(Jump, 4) = m_TextDisp.TextWidth(Text$)
                m_JumpIndex(Jump, 5) = m_TextDisp.TextHeight(Text$)

                '  Reset the text color and underline properties
                m_TextDisp.ForeColor = RGB(0, 0, 0)
                m_TextDisp.FontUnderline = False
            End If
        End If

Else

Rem *****************************Normal Text Print*****************************

    '  Check to see if the four star ending to the
    '  link has been found.  If so, end the pringin
    If read1$ = "*" Then
        Get #1, bytecount + 1, Read2$
        If Read2$ = "**" Then flag = 1: read1$ = " "
    Else

        '  Check for the new line or end of line characters
        If read1$ <> Chr$(10) And read1$ <> Chr$(13) Then

            '  Make sure this is not a newline or that
            '  so that a space will not be printed
            If n <> 0 Or read1$ <> " " Then
                m_TextDisp.Print read1$;
```

```
              End If

       Else

              '  If this is not a new line and this is
              '  not the first position on the line then
              '  print a space for the return entered in
              '  the text
              If checkspace <> 1 Then
                  If n > 2 Then
                      m_TextDisp.Print " ";
                  End If
              Else
                  ' Start a new line
                  checkspace = 0
                  n = 0
                  m_TextDisp.Print
                  m_TextDisp.CurrentX = 100
                  NewLine = NewLine + 1

                  '  Check to see if the end of the screen
                  '  has been reached
                  If NewLine > m_Linecount Then
                      m_GlobalCount = bytecount
                      flag = 1
                  End If
              End If

       End If
     End If

End If

'  Increment bytecount
bytecount = bytecount + 1
Loop

'  Close the file
Close #1
End Sub
```

12. The TextClick function processes the mouse click to see if one of the hypertext keywords has been selected. If so, then the appropriate function is called to process the type of action to be taken (i.e., display a graphic, jump to a new section, or pop up text).

```
Public Sub TextClick(x, y)

'  Loop through the jump index
For n = 1 To 50

     '  Check to see if the jump is blank.  If
     '  so the end of the jumps have been found
     If m_JumpIndex(n, 1) = "" Then Exit Sub
```

continued on next page

continued from previous page

```
     '  Get the starting positions of the
     '  hypertext
     xx = Val(m_JumpIndex(n, 2))
     yy = Val(m_JumpIndex(n, 3))

     '  Get the width and height of the
     '  hyper text
     twidth = Val(m_JumpIndex(n, 4))
     theight = Val(m_JumpIndex(n, 5))

     '  Check to see if the click fell within the
     '  bounds of the text
     If ((x > xx) And (x < xx + twidth)) And ((y > yy) And (y < yy + ↵
     theight)) Then
          '  store n
          Sav = n
          '  Set n to end the loop
          n = 101
     End If
Next n

'  Reset n
n = Sav

'  Call the Display Graphic function to display the Graphic in
'  the jump
If InStr(1, m_JumpIndex(n, 1), ".") Then DisplayGraphic n

'  Call the DisplayPop function if a pop up definition is to be displayed.
If Left$(m_JumpIndex(n, 1), 1) = "P" Then DisplayPop n, x, y

'  Call the Linkjump function if a new link is to
'  be called
If Left$(m_JumpIndex(n, 1), 1) = "L" Then linkjump n

End Sub
```

13. When the Back button is selected, the appropriate variables are reset so that the last link is redisplayed.

```
Public Sub Back()

'  If this is not the first link
'  Then go back to the last link
If m_Index <> 1 Then

     '  Make sure the graphic display is not visible
     m_DispPict.Visible = False

     '  Clear the Text Display
     m_TextDisp.Cls

     '  Sav the Index in to the link array
     Sav = m_Index
```

```
        ' Set the Index to the last link
        m_Index = m_IndexLast

        ' Sav the current link in the m_IndexLast
        m_IndexLast = Sav

        ' set the GlobalCount variable to the
        ' bytecount of the last link
        m_GlobalCount = m_BackGlobalLast

        ' Display the new link
        displayLink
    End If

End Sub
```

14. The Refresh function resets the m_GlobalCount variable to the position in the hypertext file so that present section of the link is redisplayed.

```
Public Sub Refresh()
    ' When a refresh is done, the beginning
    ' bytecount of the screen
    m_GlobalCount = m_GlobalCountLast
    displayLink
End Sub
```

15. The DisplayGraphic function is called when the Graphic keyword is selected. It handles showing the specified graphic.

```
Private Sub DisplayGraphic(Index)

    ' Load the graphic into the picture
    m_DispPict.Picture = LoadPicture(App.Path + "\" + m_JumpIndex(Index, 1))

    ' Autosize the picture
    m_DispPict.AutoSize = True

    ' Move the picture to the lower left of the Text Display
    m_DispPict.Move m_TextDisp.Left, m_TextDisp.Top + m_TextDisp.Height + 300

    ' Make the picture visible
    m_DispPict.Visible = True
End Sub
```

16. DisplayPop handles reading the pop-up text from the hypertext file and displaying it. Note that to size the pop-up windows appropriately, the text is read into an array and then the pop-up window is sized according to the number of lines to be displayed.

```
Private Sub DisplayPop(Index, x, y)

' S will be used to store each line of
' the text to be displayed
```

continued on next page

continued from previous page

```
ReDim s(30) As String

'  Get the starting position in the file of the
'  pop up text
bytecount = GetPopByteCount(Index)

'  Setup our read variables
read1$ = " ": Read2$ = " ": Read3$ = "  "

'  Set line count to 1
Lcount = 1

'   Open the hyper text file for reading
Open m_filename For Binary Access Read Lock Read As #1

'  Loop until flag is set to 1
Do Until flag = 1

    '  Read the first character
    Get #1, bytecount, read1$

    '  If we are checking for a space to end the line
    '  on then a new line is started
    If read1$ = " " And checkspace = 1 Then
        n = 0
        checkspace = 0
        Lcount = Lcount + 1
    End If

    '  Check for the end of the popup text
    If read1$ = "#" Then
        '   Read the next character
        Get #1, bytecount + 1, Read2$
            '  If it is a # then set flag to 1 and
            '  clear out the read1$ variable
            If Read2$ = "#" Then
                flag = 1
                read1$ = ""
            End If
    End If

    '  Check for a paragraph return
    If read1$ = "\" Then
        '   Read the next character
        Get #1, bytecount + 1, Read3$
            '  Check for the \T character
            If Left$(Read3$, 2) = "\T" Then
                '   Reset the character counter
                n = 0
                '   reset checkspace
                checkspace = 0
                '   Increment the line count by two
                Lcount = Lcount + 2
                '   Increment bytecound by two
                bytecount = bytecount + 2
```

```
                        read1$ = " "
                    End If
            End If

            '   Increment the characters on the line counter
            n = n + 1

            '   Check to see if the max number of characters
            '   on the line has been reached.
            If n = m_CharsPerLine Then
                checkspace = 1
            End If

            '   Check to make sure a line feed or carriage return
            '   is not the character
            If read1$ <> Chr$(10) And read1$ <> Chr$(13) Then
                '   Store the character in the array
                s(Lcount) = s(Lcount) + read1$
            End If

            '   Increment bytecount
            bytecount = bytecount + 1
Loop

'   Since Lcount contains the number of lines in the text
'   the picture box can be sized to the size of the lines
m_PopPict.Height = (Lcount + 2) * m_PopPict.TextHeight("HelloWorld")

'   Move the picture to right below the hypertext
m_PopPict.Move m_TextDisp.Left + 105, m_TextDisp.Top + y + 125

'   Move the drop shadow slightly to the left and right of
'   the pop up picture
m_PopShadow.Height = (Lcount + 2) * m_PopPict.TextHeight("HelloWorld")
m_PopShadow.Move m_TextDisp.Left + 165, m_TextDisp.Top + y + 195

'   Clear the popup picture and the drop shadow
'   picture and make them visible
m_PopPict.Cls: m_PopPict.Visible = True
m_PopShadow.Cls: m_PopShadow.Visible = True

'   Move down the picture the height of one line of text
m_PopPict.CurrentY = 0 + m_PopPict.TextHeight("HelloWorld")

'   Loop through the s array to display
'   the text
For n = 1 To Lcount
    m_PopPict.CurrentX = 100
    m_PopPict.Print s(n)
Next n

'   Close the file
Close #1

End Sub
```

CHAPTER 8

17. LinkJump handles the jump to a new link. This function is called when the red
keywords are selected.

```
Public Sub LinkJump(Index)

'  Make the graphic display picture invisible
m_DispPict.Visible = False

'  Store the current index in
'  the m_IndexLast variable
m_IndexLast = m_Index

'  Get the index for the new link
m_Index = Val(Right$(m_JumpIndex(Index, 1), Len(m_JumpIndex(Index, 1)) - 1))

'  Clear the text display
m_TextDisp.Cls

'  Store the Global count for the starting point of the
'  present link screen in the m_BackGlobalLast variable
m_BackGlobalLast = m_GlobalCountLast

'  Reset the Global count variables
m_GlobalCount = 0
m_GlobalCountLast = 0

'  Display the new link
displayLink

End Sub
```

18. The DispGraphicText function handles displaying the Graphic keyword in the
hypertext.

```
Public Sub DispGraphicText(Jump)

'  Set the color of the text to blue
m_TextDisp.ForeColor = QBColor(1)

'  Save the current font size
Sav = m_TextDisp.FontSize

'  Store the CurrentX and CurrentY of the display
x = m_TextDisp.CurrentX
y = m_TextDisp.CurrentY

'  Store the Currentx and CurrentY in the JumpIndex array
m_JumpIndex(Jump, 2) = x
m_JumpIndex(Jump, 3) = y

'  Move partly down the height of the
'  text
m_TextDisp.CurrentY = m_TextDisp.CurrentY + m_TextDisp.TextHeight("Wja") / 2
```

660

```
'  Print the hot spot text
m_TextDisp.Print " (GRAPHIC)";

'  Store the width and height of the text
m_JumpIndex(Jump, 4) = m_TextDisp.TextWidth(" (GRAPHIC)")
m_JumpIndex(Jump, 5) = m_TextDisp.TextHeight(" (GRAPHIC)")

'  Reset the CurrentX and CurrentY
m_TextDisp.CurrentX = x
m_TextDisp.CurrentY = y

'  Reset the font size
m_TextDisp.FontSize = Sav

'  Reset the font color
m_TextDisp.ForeColor = RGB(0, 0, 0)

End Sub
```

19. GetPopByteCount handles finding the starting byte position for the specified pop-up picture text. It then returns the value to the Calling function.

```
Private Function GetPopByteCount(Index) As Integer

'  Get the number of the Pop Up Text
PopNum = Val(Right$(m_JumpIndex(Index, 1), Len(m_JumpIndex(Index, 1)) - 1))

'  Get the LineNumber of where the index starts in the index file
LineNum = m_LinkIndex(m_Index, 2)

'  Open the index file
Open m_fileindex For Input As #2

'  Seek to the starting of the link
For B = 1 To LineNum
    Line Input #2, LN$
Next B

'  Loop until flag is set to 1
Do Until flag = 1
    '  Get the next line
    Line Input #2, LN$

    '  Check to see if the Pop Up index has been found
    If m_JumpIndex(Index, 1) = Mid$(LN$, 1, Len(m_JumpIndex(Index, 1))) Then
        flag = 1
    End If
Loop

'  Find the : in the Pop Up index
p = InStr(1, LN$, ":")

'  Get the bytecount stored in the index
```

continued on next page

continued from previous page

```
bytecount = Val(Mid$(LN$, p + 1, Len(LN$)))

' Seek past the beginning of the Pop Up setup information
bytecount = bytecount + Len("##") + Len(m_JumpIndex(Index, 1))

' Set the value of the function to the bytecount
GetPopByteCount = bytecount

' Close the file
Close #2

End Function
```

20. BuildIndex builds the index file for the hypertext file. This function only needs to be called once for a hypertext file. But if you change the hypertext file in any way, it needs to be called again.

```
Public Sub BuildIndex(TextFile, IndexFile)

' Open the text file and the Index file
Open TextFile For Binary Access Read Lock Read As #1
Open IndexFile For Output As #2

' Set the read variables
read1$ = " ": Read2$ = "   "

' Read until the end of the file
Do While Not EOF(1)

' Increment the cnt variable, which is used
' to count the bytes
cnt = cnt + 1

' Read the next character
Get #1, cnt, read1$

' Check for the possible starting of a link
If read1$ = "~" Then

    ' Read the next two characters
    Get #1, cnt + 1, Read2$

    ' Check if the link is found
    If Read2$ = "~L" Then

        ' Increment the linknum counter
        linknum = linknum + 1

        ' Make the linknumber into a string
        lnum$ = Str$(linknum)
        lnum$ = Right$(lnum$, Len(lnum$) - 1)

        ' Make a string out of the cnt variable
```

```
        C$ = Str$(cnt)
        C$ = Right$(C$, Len(C$) - 1)

        '  Print into the index file the index to
        '  the link
        Print #2, "L" + lnum$ + ":" + C$

        '  Reset PCount, which counts the pop up links
        PCount = 0
    End If
End If

'  Check for the start of a Pop Up Pict section
If read1$ = "#" Then

    '  Read the next character
    Get #1, cnt + 1, Read2$

    '  Check for the #P start of the Pop Up section
    If Read2$ = "#P" Then

        '  Increment the PCount variable
        PCount = PCount + 1

        '  Make a string out of the Pcount variable
        Pnum$ = Str$(PCount)
        Pnum$ = Right$(Pnum$, Len(Pnum$) - 1)

        '  Make a string out of the cnt variable
        C$ = Str$(cnt)
        C$ = Right$(C$, Len(C$) - 1)

        '   Write the Pop Up index
        Print #2, "P" + Pnum$ + ":" + C$
    End If
End If

Loop

'  Close the two files
Close #1
Close #2

End Sub
```

How It Works

The key to developing a hypertext system is to develop a method for structuring the document into sections, and within those sections defining the keywords from which an action will be taken. Table 8-6-2 identifies the methods used in this How-To.

Table 8-6-2 The hypertext document's embedded characters and commands

COMMAND	ACTION
~~L#	Indicates the start of a link where # is the section number
\\T	Indicates that a double return should be performed
\\G#\ (Graphic File) \	Specifies that the Graphic keyword should be displayed, as should the file name of the graphic (Note that this embedded command must be either on its own line or at the end of a line. The program will automatically make a line break at the end of the command.)
\\B	Indicates that a single return should be performed
\P#\ (Key Words) \P	The \P#P indicates the start of pop up keywords where pound is the pop up number. The keywords are ended with the \P
\L#\ (Key Words) \L	Indicates a jump to another link where # indicates the link to jump to
****	Specifies the end of the main body of text for the link
##P(##)	Specifies the start of the pop-up text, where (##) indicates the number of the pop up. This number corresponds with \P#\
##	Indicates the end of the link and the end of the pop-up definitions

Note that the \\T embedded command can also be used in the pop-up definitions. None of the other embedded commands are implemented in displaying the pop-up text (but could be quite easily).

Review the HYPER.TXT file that comes with this project to see the document set up for the example given. As you will notice, the length of text on each line is not important. One of the properties of the class is the m_CharsPerLine variable. This variable is set with the CharsPerLine property of the class to indicate the number of characters to be printed on each line. In the DisplayLink function, each character is printed up to the number of characters per line and a check is done to ensure that a word is not broken in half. So each line may contain more than the specified number of characters; this should be considered when setting this variable to ensure your line breaks come out as desired.

The two workhorse functions of the hypertext class are the DisplayLink and DisplayPop functions. The DisplayLink function makes the following determinations.

1. It checks to see if an embedded character has been found in the text. If so, the character is then processed. The m_JumpIndex array holds (in order) the different embedded commands in a section. For a graphic, the name of the bitmap file is stored. For a pop-up command, the number of the pop up is stored. For a link jump, the link to jump to is stored. In each case, the bounding box of the hypertext is stored so that a text click can be checked. See How-To 2.2 for additional information on checking text clicks to see if they fall in the bounds of the keywords.

2. It counts each character on the line. When the maximum number of characters to be printed is reached, a check is done to ensure that a word is not broken and continued on the next line.

3. The primary method used to track the position in the hypertext is the use of the current byte position. Because there is a maximum number of lines that can be printed on the text display, the text may have to be scrolled. The m_ByteCount and m_ByteCountLast variables store the current position and the last position in the file. By using these variables, each time the DisplayLink function is called, the next section of the link is displayed. When the Refresh button is selected, the current position (m_ByteCount) is reset to the previous position (m_ByteCountLast) so that the same text will be redisplayed.

When a new link is jumped to, the byte position in the current link is stored in the m_BackByteCount variable. Thus, when the Back function is selected, the byte count is reset to the last position in the last link. Also, the index into the m_LinkIndex array is reset to the last link index (stored in m_IndexLast).

In the DisplayPop function, a problem is encountered in knowing how large to size the pop-up picture. The size of the picture depends on the size of the pop-up text and the number of characters that can be printed on each line. Instead of printing the text directly to the displayed picture box, text is stored in an array. With each new line to be printed, the next index in the array is set. The total number of indexes in the array is the number of lines the picture box needs to be set to. Then the text in the array can be easily printed to the pop-up picture.

The index file is built to make finding the byte starting positions of the links and pop-up definitions easily. Each line in the index contains the type of index and the starting byte position in the file. The following is an example index file:

```
L1:1
P1:1080
P2:1106
L2:1452
P1:1751
```

L1:1 indicates that link 1 starts at byte position 1. P1:1751 indicates that the first pop up in the second link starts at byte 1751. The m_IndexArray member variable of the class is filled with the starting byte positions of each link. Thus, when the link is to be displayed, it is easy to find its starting byte position. Likewise, it is easy to find the starting byte position of each pop up within the link.

To build the index file, the BuildIndex function can be called. In this example, it is called each time the project is loaded. The BuildIndex function simply reads through the file and searches for the embedded pop-up and link jump lines. It then stores the starting byte positions for each.

As you can see, the implementation of Form1 is quite simple. And the hypertext class can be easily integrated into existing applications. The hypertext file can be built in any DOS or Windows word processor. But it is important to save the file out as text formatted.

Comments

It would be quite easy to integrate additional multimedia elements into the hypertext capabilities. Additional embedded commands could be added to play video, animation, and sound files along with displaying the graphic images.

8.7 How do I...
Build a complete animated scene with WinG?

COMPLEXITY: INTERMEDIATE

Problem

In Chapter 6, WinG was used to build high-speed sprites and animations. I would like to be able to use WinG to develop an animated scene complete with independent moving objects and sounds. How do I solve the complex timing and tracking necessary to develop a full-featured animated scene using WinG?

Technique

The Sprite class and images found in How-To 6.10 will be used to develop an animated scene. The scene will be complete with background music, action sounds, three individual fish, a school of fish, and a sinking anchor. The timing and tracking necessary to give the fish realistic swimming movement will also be developed.

Steps

Open and run 8-7.VBP. The running program appears as shown in Figure 8-7-1.

1. Create a new project called 8-7.VBP. Add the objects and properties listed in Table 8-7-1 to Form1 and save the form as 8-7.FRM.

Figure 8-7-1 The form as it appears at runtime

Table 8-7-1 Project form's objects and properties

OBJECT	PROPERTY	SETTING
Form	Name	Form1
	Auto3D	-1 'True
	aption	"How-To 8.7"
	ScaleMode	3 'Pixel
PictureBox	Name	Picture6
	AutoRedraw	-1 'True
	AutoSize	-1 'True
	ScaleMode	3 'Pixel
PictureBox	Name	Picture5
	AutoRedraw	-1 'True
	AutoSize	-1 'True
	ScaleMode	3 'Pixel

OBJECT	PROPERTY	SETTING
PictureBox	Name	Picture4
	AutoRedraw	-1 'True
	AutoSize	-1 'True
	ScaleMode	3 'Pixel
PictureBox	Name	Picture3
	AutoRedraw	-1 'True
	AutoSize	-1 'True
	ScaleMode	3 'Pixel
PictureBox	Name	Picture2
	AutoRedraw	-1 'True
	AutoSize	-1 'True
	ScaleMode	3 'Pixel
Timer	Name	Timer1
	Enabled	0 'False
	Interval	1
PictureBox	Name	Picture1
	BorderStyle	0 'None
	ScaleMode	3 'Pixel
MMControl	Name	MMControl1
	Visible	0 'False
	borderstyle	1

2. Add the following code to the general declarations section of the form. The appropriate WinG functions and global variables for tracking the scene objects are declared.

```
'  WinG Functions
Private Declare Function WinGBitBlt Lib "wing.dll" (ByVal hdcDest As Integer, ↵
ByVal nXOriginDest As Integer, ByVal nYOriginDest As Integer, ByVal ↵
nWidthDest As Integer, ByVal nHeightDest As Integer, ByVal hdcSrc As Integer, ↵
ByVal nXOriginSrc As Integer, ByVal nYOriginSrc As Integer) As Boolean

Private Declare Function WinGCreateDC Lib "wing.dll" () As Integer

'  Delete Device Context
Private Declare Function DeleteDC Lib "GDI" (ByVal hDC As Integer) As Integer
```

```
'   Used to play the Ding.Wav sound
'   when the chest shuts
Private Declare Function sndPlaySound Lib "mmSYstem" (ByVal lpszSoundName As ↵
String, ByVal uFlags As Integer) As Integer

'   Play the sounds and let system
'   continue
Const SND_ASYNC = &H1                        '   play asynchronously

'   The primary WinG surface
'   for building the animation
Dim WinGSurface As Long

'   These are the tracking X and Y
'   variables for the sprites
Dim GreenX As Integer
Dim GreenY As Integer
Dim SchoolX As Integer
Dim SchoolY As Integer
Dim RedX As Integer
Dim RedY As Integer
Dim AnchorY As Integer
Dim AnchorX As Integer
Dim SlimY As Integer
Dim SlimX As Integer

'   These are the step variables for
'   the sprites
Dim SchoolXStep As Integer
Dim SchoolYStep As Integer
Dim SlimStep As Integer
Dim GreenXStep As Integer
Dim GreenYStep As Integer
Dim RedXStep As Integer

'   First will be used to execute the code in
'   the form paint event  once
Dim First As Integer

'   These are the direction tracking
'   variables for the sprites
Dim GreenDirect As String
Dim RedDirect As String
Dim SchoolDirect As String
Dim SlimDirection As String

'   Declare the working and backup
'   backgrounds
Dim Back As WinG
Dim Back2 As WinG

'   Globally declare the sprites
Dim SchoolRight As WinGSprite
Dim SchoolLeft As WinGSprite
Dim GreenRIght As WinGSprite
```

continued on next page

continued from previous page

```
Dim GreenLeft As WinGSprite
Dim RedFish As WinGSprite
Dim SlimFish As WinGSprite
Dim Anchor As WinGSprite

'  Declare the Chest Bitmaps
Dim Chest(9) As WinG

'  The WinG device contexts
Dim wingDC1 As Integer
Dim wingDC2 As Integer
Dim wingDC3 As Integer

'  N will be used to count times
'  for the chest animations
Dim N As Integer

'  BoxCount is used to count
'  through the chest bitmaps
Dim BoxCount As Integer
```

3. Add the following code to the general declarations section of the form. The SlimMove function handles moving and tracking the brightly colored slim fish. Note that the X direction movement (SlimStep) is randomly generated. The X movement is not a uniform number and provides a more realistic "swaying" movement when the fish swim.

```
Private Sub SlimMove()

'  Check to see if the fish
'  has hit the right side of the
'  background.  If so, change the
'  direction and reset the x
'  coordinate
If SlimDirection = "UL" Then SlimDirection = "UR": SlimX = -150

'  Increase the X position
SlimX = SlimX + SlimStep

'  Move the fish
SlimFish.MoveImage SlimX, SlimY + 200

'  Check for a collision
SlimFish.collide SlimX, SlimY, SlimDirection, Picture3.ScaleWidth,
Picture3.ScaleHeight

'  Get a new step size
SlimStep = Int((9 - (-2) + 1) * Rnd + (-2))

End Sub
```

4. Add the following code to the general declarations section of the form. The AnimateChest function handles displaying the next appropriate chest frame.

```
Private Sub AnimateChest()

'   Copy the chest
Chest(BoxCount).transbits2 65, 280

End Sub
```

5. The SchoolMove function handles moving the school of fish. If you have ever watched a school of fish swim, the fish appear to change direction quickly and randomly while swimming. To make this happen, a counter value is passed into the function. When the value equals 39, a new direction for the school is randomly selected. Of course, a check is always done to see if the school has collided with one of the boundaries and its direction is updated appropriately.

```
Private Sub SchoolMove(N)

'   Every 39 moves a new random direction
'   will be picked for the school of fish
'   This will give them a more random movement
If N Mod 39 = 0 Then
    v = Int((4 - 1 + 1) * Rnd + 1)
    If v = 1 Then SchoolDirect = "UR"
    If v = 2 Then SchoolDirect = "DR"
    If v = 3 Then SchoolDirect = "DL"
    If v = 4 Then SchoolDirect = "UL"
End If

'   Depending on the GreenDirect, we will increment or
'   decrement GreenX and GreenY appropriately.  Then the image
'   is moved and we check for a collision with the
'   collide function.
Select Case SchoolDirect

    Case "UL"
        SchoolX = SchoolX - SchoolXStep
        SchoolY = SchoolY - SchoolYStep
        SchoolLeft.MoveImage SchoolX, SchoolY
        SchoolLeft.collide SchoolX, SchoolY, SchoolDirect, ↵
            Picture6.ScaleWidth, Picture6.ScaleHeight

    Case "UR"
        SchoolX = SchoolX + SchoolXStep
        SchoolY = SchoolY - SchoolYStep
        SchoolRight.MoveImage SchoolX, SchoolY
        SchoolRight.collide SchoolX, SchoolY, SchoolDirect, ↵
            Picture6.ScaleWidth, Picture6.ScaleHeight

    Case "DL"
        SchoolX = SchoolX - SchoolXStep
        SchoolY = SchoolY + SchoolYStep
        SchoolLeft.MoveImage SchoolX, SchoolY
        SchoolLeft.collide SchoolX, SchoolY, SchoolDirect, ↵
            Picture6.ScaleWidth, Picture6.ScaleHeight
```

continued on next page

continued from previous page

```
    Case "DR"
        SchoolX = SchoolX + SchoolXStep
        SchoolY = SchoolY + SchoolYStep
        SchoolRight.MoveImage SchoolX, SchoolY
        SchoolRight.collide SchoolX, SchoolY, SchoolDirect, ↵
            Picture6.ScaleWidth, Picture6.ScaleHeight

    End Select


'   Randomly generate the next step size
SchoolXStep = Int((10 - 0 + 1) * Rnd + 0)
SchoolYStep = Int((6 - 0 + 1) * Rnd + 0)

End Sub
```

6. Add the following code to the general declarations section of the form. The GreenMove function handles moving and tracking the green fish. Note that the X and Y direction movements (GreenXStep and GreenYStep) are randomly generated. Their values are not uniform numbers and provide a more realistic "swaying" movement when the fish swim.

```
Private Sub GreenMove()

'   Depending on the GreenDirect, we will increment or
'   decrement GreenX and GreenY appropriately.  Then the image
'   is moved and we check for a collision with the
'   collide function.
Select Case GreenDirect

Case "UL"
    GreenX = GreenX - GreenXStep
    GreenY = GreenY - GreenYStep
    GreenLeft.MoveImage GreenX, GreenY
    GreenLeft.collide GreenX, GreenY, GreenDirect, ↵
        Picture2.ScaleWidth, Picture2.ScaleHeight

Case "UR"
    GreenX = GreenX + GreenXStep
    GreenY = GreenY - GreenYStep
    GreenRIght.MoveImage GreenX, GreenY
    GreenRIght.collide GreenX, GreenY, GreenDirect, ↵
        Picture2.ScaleWidth, Picture2.ScaleHeight

Case "DL"
    GreenX = GreenX - GreenXStep
    GreenY = GreenY + GreenYStep
    GreenLeft.MoveImage GreenX, GreenY
    GreenLeft.collide GreenX, GreenY, GreenDirect, ↵
        Picture2.ScaleWidth, Picture2.ScaleHeight

Case "DR"
    GreenX = GreenX + GreenXStep
    GreenY = GreenY + GreenYStep
```

```
        GreenRIght.MoveImage GreenX, GreenY
        GreenRIght.collide GreenX, GreenY, GreenDirect, ↵
            Picture2.ScaleWidth, Picture2.ScaleHeight

    End Select

'  Randomly generate the next step size
GreenXStep = Int((42 - 0 + 1) * Rnd + 0)
GreenYStep = Int((29 - 0 + 1) * Rnd + 0)

End Sub
```

7. Add the following code to the general declarations section of the form. The anchor is moved to the bottom of the sea and stops on the rock shelf. To give the anchor a more realistic descent, a swaying motion in the fall is developed by changing the X origin value of where the next anchor should be drawn. Thus, the anchor sways from left to right in its descent.

```
Private Sub AnchorMove()

'  The anchor will move to the
'  bottom of the background then stop
If AnchorY < 250 Then
    AnchorY = AnchorY + 7
    Anchor.MoveImage 500 + AnchorX, AnchorY
    AnchorX = Int((2 - (-2) + 1) * Rnd + (-2))
Else
    Anchor.MoveImage 500 + AnchorX, AnchorY
End If

End Sub
```

8. Add the following code to the general declarations section of the form. The CreateGreen function creates and sets up the fish object. Note that the green fish consists of a left- and right-pointing sprite.

```
Private Sub CreateGreen()

'  Our GreenDirect is Down and Right
'  To begin with
GreenDirect = "DR"

'  Start out at the origin
GreenY = 0
GreenX = 0

'  Set the X and Y step
GreenXStep = 10
GreenYStep = 5

'  Setup the sprites
Set GreenRIght = New WinGSprite
Let GreenRIght.filename = App.Path + "\fish1.bmp"
Set GreenRIght.dispback = picture1
```

continued on next page

CHAPTER 8

continued from previous page

```
Set GreenLeft = New WinGSprite
Let GreenLeft.filename = App.Path + "\fish2.bmp"
Set GreenLeft.dispback = picture1

'  Create
GreenRIght.create
GreenLeft.create

'  Set the surface to copy to
GreenRIght.surface = WinGSurface

'  Set the surface to copy to
GreenLeft.surface = WinGSurface

'  Set the boundaries for the fish movements
Let GreenRIght.Leftbound = 0
Let GreenRIght.TopBound = 0
Let GreenRIght.RightBound = picture1.ScaleWidth
Let GreenRIght.Bottombound = picture1.ScaleHeight

Let GreenLeft.Leftbound = 0
Let GreenLeft.TopBound = 0
Let GreenLeft.RightBound = picture1.ScaleWidth
Let GreenLeft.Bottombound = picture1.ScaleHeight

End Sub
```

9. Add the following code to the general declarations section of the form. The CreateSchool function creates and sets up the fish school object. Note that the school consists of left- and right-pointing sets of sprites.

```
Private Sub CreateSchool()

'  Set the starting direction
SchoolDirect = "DR"

'  Set the starting positions
SchoolX = 20
SchoolY = 10

'  Setup the sprite
Set SchoolRight = New WinGSprite
Set SchoolLeft = New WinGSprite
SchoolRight.filename = App.Path + "\school1.bmp"
SchoolLeft.filename = App.Path + "\school2.bmp"
Set SchoolRight.dispback = picture1
Set SchoolLeft.dispback = picture1

'  Create
SchoolRight.create
SchoolLeft.create

'  Set the surface to copy to
SchoolRight.surface = WinGSurface
```

674

```
SchoolLeft.surface = WinGSurface

'  Set the boundaries
Let SchoolRight.Leftbound = 0
Let SchoolRight.TopBound = 0
Let SchoolRight.RightBound = picture1.ScaleWidth
Let SchoolRight.Bottombound = picture1.ScaleHeight

Let SchoolLeft.Leftbound = 0
Let SchoolLeft.TopBound = 0
Let SchoolLeft.RightBound = picture1.ScaleWidth
Let SchoolLeft.Bottombound = picture1.ScaleHeight

End Sub
```

10. Add the following code to the general declarations section of the form. The CreateRed function creates and sets up the red fish object, which consists of one right-pointing fish sprite.

```
Private Sub CreateRed()

'  Set the starting direction
RedDirect = "UR"

'  Set the starting origin
RedX = -150
RedY = 50

'  Setup the sprite
Set RedFish = New WinGSprite
RedFish.filename = App.Path + "\Fish3.bmp"
Set RedFish.dispback = picture1

'  Create
RedFish.create

'  Set the surface to copy to
RedFish.surface = WinGSurface

'  Set the boundaries
Let RedFish.Leftbound = 0
Let RedFish.TopBound = 0
Let RedFish.RightBound = picture1.ScaleWidth + Picture3.ScaleWidth * 2
Let RedFish.Bottombound = picture1.ScaleHeight

End Sub
```

11. Add the following code to the general declarations section of the form. The CreateSlim function creates and sets up the slim fish object, which consists of one right-pointing fish sprite.

```
Private Sub CreateSlim()

'  Set the starting direction
```

continued on next page

continued from previous page

```
SlimDirection = "UR"

'   Set the starting Y position
SlimY = 47

'   Setup the sprites
Set SlimFish = New WinGSprite
SlimFish.filename = App.Path + "\Fish4.bmp"
Set SlimFish.dispback = picture1
SlimFish.create
SlimFish.surface = WinGSurface

'   Set the boundaries
Let SlimFish.Leftbound = 0
Let SlimFish.TopBound = 0
Let SlimFish.RightBound = picture1.ScaleWidth + Picture3.ScaleWidth * 2
Let SlimFish.Bottombound = picture1.ScaleHeight

End Sub
```

12. Add the following code to the general declarations section of the form. The CreateAnchor function handles creating and setting up the anchor object.

```
Private Sub CreateAnchor()

'   Set the starting Y
AnchorY = -100

'   Setup the sprite
Set Anchor = New WinGSprite
Anchor.filename = App.Path + "\anchor2.bmp"
Set Anchor.dispback = picture1

'   Create
Anchor.create

'   Set the surface to copy to
Anchor.surface = WinGSurface

End Sub
```

13. Add the following code to the general declarations section of the form. The RedMove function handles moving the red fish. Note that the X directional movement (RedXStep) value is randomly generated to give the fish a more realistic "swaying" swimming motion.

```
Public Sub RedMove()

'   Check to see if the Red fish has changed GreenDirect
'   If so reset to the left of the picture and set
'   the GreenDirect back
If RedDirect = "UL" Then RedDirect = "UR": RedX = -150

'   Increase the Red fish position
```

```
RedX = RedX + RedXStep

'   Move the Red Fish and check for a collision
RedFish.MoveImage RedX, RedY
RedFish.collide RedX, RedY, RedDirect, Picture3.ScaleWidth, Picture3.ScaleHeight

'   Randomly set the Xstep
RedXStep = Int((12 - 0 + 1) * Rnd + 0)

End Sub
```

14. Add the following code to the general declarations section of the form. The CreateBackground function handles creating and setting up the working background and the back up copy of the background.

```
Private Sub CreateBackground()

'   Create the background instances
Set Back = New WinG
Set Back2 = New WinG

'   Create the WinG Device Contexts
wingDC1 = WinGCreateDC()
wingDC2 = WinGCreateDC()
wingDC3 = WinGCreateDC()

'   Setup the backgrounds
Let Back.filename = App.Path + "\sea.bmp"
Let Back.wdc = wingDC1
Set Back.picture = picture1

Let Back2.filename = App.Path + "\sea.bmp"
Let Back2.wdc = wingDC3
Set Back2.picture = picture1

'   Make the background WinG bitmaps
Back.MakeWinGBit
Back2.MakeWinGBit

'   Set the palette for the animation
Back.setpal

'   Get the surface to copy to
WinGSurface = Back.surface

End Sub
```

15. Add the following code to the general declarations section of the form. The CreateChest function creates and sets up the nine WinG bitmaps for the different chest frames.

```
Private Sub CreateChest()

'   Create the chest WinG bitmaps
```

continued on next page

continued from previous page

```
For A = 1 To 9

    ' Create the WinG instance
    Set Chest(A) = New WinG

    ' Get the string representation of A
    num$ = Str$(A)
    num$ = Right$(num$, Len(num$) - 1)

    ' Set the chest file name, WinG device context
    ' and picture
    Let Chest(A).filename = App.Path + "\c00" + num$ + ".bmp"
    Let Chest(A).wdc = wingDC2
    Set Chest(A).picture = picture1

    ' Make the WinG bitmap
    Chest(A).MakeWinGBit

    ' Set the surface to copy to
    Chest(A).surface = WinGSurface

Next A

End Sub
```

16. When the form is loaded, the random number generator is seeded with the Randomize function and the two global counting variables are initialized. Also, the various sprites and animations are created by calling their Create functions. Note that it is important to call the CreateBackground function first. The working background is the surface for all of the sprites to be copied to. Finally, the background MIDI music is played.

```
Private Sub Form_Load()

' Seed the random number generator
Randomize

' Initialize BoxCount and N to 1
BoxCount = 1
N = 1

' Create the sprites
CreateBackground
CreateGreen
CreateSchool
CreateRed
CreateSlim
CreateAnchor
CreateChest

' Start the play of the music
MMControl1.DeviceType = "Sequencer"
MMControl1.filename = "c:\windows\media\canyon.mid"
MMControl1.Command = "close"
```

```
MMControl1.Command = "open"
MMControl1.Command = "play"

End Sub
```

17. When the form is painted the first time, the background images are set up and the background is displayed using WinGBitBlt.

```
Private Sub Form_Paint()

'   The first time the form is painted
'   execute the following actions
If First = 0 Then
    '   Copy the bitmap bits into
    '   the background WinG bitmap
    Back.transbits
    Back2.transbits

    '   Display the background
    Call WinGBitBlt(picture1.hDC, 0, 0, picture1.ScaleWidth, ↵
        picture1.ScaleHeight, wingDC1, 0, 0)

    First = 1
    Timer1.Enabled = True
End If
End Sub
```

18. When the form is unloaded, it is important to delete the WinG device contexts and to set all of the Sprite classes to nothing.

```
Private Sub Form_Unload(Cancel As Integer)

'   Delete the WinG instances
throw = DeleteDC(wingDC1)
throw = DeleteDC(wingDC2)
throw = DeleteDC(wingDC3)

'   Terminate the Chest bitmaps
For A = 1 To 9
    Set Chest(A) = Nothing
Next A

'   Terminate the backgrounds
Set Back = Nothing
Set Back2 = Nothing

Set SchoolRight = Nothing
Set SchoolLeft = Nothing

'   Terminate the Fish instances
Set GreenRIght = Nothing
Set GreenLeft = Nothing
Set RedFish = Nothing
Set SlimFish = Nothing
Set Anchor = Nothing
```

continued on next page

continued from previous page

```
'   Close the multimedia device
MMControl1.Command = "close"
End Sub
```

19. The timer is the controller for all the movements in the animated scene. Note that the chest only moves on every fourth tick of the timer. The ding Wave is played right before the chest is to be closed. The primary difference between this implementation and that in Chapter 6 is that instead of copying the background individually over each object's last position, the whole background is repainted on the working device context. With the number of objects in this scene, it is as efficient to repaint the entire background once as it is to call WinGBitBlt several times. With each tick of the timer, the appropriate Move function for each object is called.

```
Private Sub Timer1_Timer()

'   When N reaches 40 set N to 1
If N = 40 Then N = 1

'   When BoxCount reaches 10 then set to 1
If BoxCount = 10 Then BoxCount = 1

'   When the box is about to shut,
'   play the ding wave
If N = 28 Then throw = sndPlaySound("c:\windows\media\ding.wav", SND_ASYNC)

'   Copy the original background over the current
'   fish and chest positions
Call WinGBitBlt(wingDC1, 0, 0, picture1.ScaleWidth, picture1.ScaleHeight, wingDC3,
0, 0)

'   Update the Sprites
SlimMove
AnchorMove
AnimateChest
GreenMove
SchoolMove N
RedMove

'   Copy the three objects to the screen
Call WinGBitBlt(picture1.hDC, 0, 0, picture1.ScaleWidth, ↵
picture1.ScaleHeight, wingDC1, 0, 0)

'   Check to see if four ticks on the clock
'   have counted off.  If so, then increment
'   BoxCount
If N Mod 4 = 0 Then BoxCount = BoxCount + 1

'   Increment N
N = N + 1

End Sub
```

20. Add the WinG class from How-To 6.7 to the project. For complete documentation on how the code in this class works, see How-To 6.7. Important highlights are commented on in the following code.

```
Private Declare Function TransparentDIBits Lib "winghelp.dll" (dstInfo As ↵
Any, dstBuffer As Any, ByVal destx As Integer, ByVal desty As Integer, ↵
srcBuffer As Any, srcInfo As Any, ByVal srcx As Integer, ByVal srcy As ↵
Integer, ByVal iUsage As Integer, ByVal TransparentColor As Byte) As Boolean

Private Declare Function WinGCreateDC Lib "wing.dll" () As Integer

Private Declare Function WinGRecommendDIBFormat Lib "wing.dll" (pBitmapInfo ↵
As Any) As Boolean

Private Declare Function WinGCreateBitmap Lib "wing.dll" (ByVal wingDC As ↵
Integer, pBitmapInfo As Any, ppBits As Any) As Integer

Private Declare Function WinGGetDIBPointer Lib "wing.dll" (ByVal WinGBitmap ↵
As Integer, pBitmapInfo As Any) As Long

Private Declare Function WinGGetDIBColorTable Lib "wing.dll" (ByVal wingDC As ↵
Integer, ByVal StartIndex As Integer, ByVal NumberOfEntries As Integer, ↵
pRgbQuadColors As Any) As Integer

Private Declare Function WinGSetDIBColorTable Lib "wing.dll" (ByVal wingDC As ↵
Integer, ByVal StartIndex As Integer, ByVal NumberOfEntries As Integer, ↵
pRgbQuadColors As Any) As Integer

Private Declare Function WinGCreateHalftonePalette Lib "wing.dll" () As Integer

Private Declare Function WinGCreateHalftoneBrush Lib "wing.dll" (ByVal Context As
Integer, ByVal crColor As Long, ByVal DitherType As Integer) As Integer

Private Declare Function WinGBitBlt Lib "wing.dll" (ByVal hdcDest As Integer, ↵
ByVal nXOriginDest As Integer, ByVal nYOriginDest As Integer, ByVal ↵
nWidthDest As Integer, ByVal nHeightDest As Integer, ByVal hdcSrc As Integer, ↵
ByVal nXOriginSrc As Integer, ByVal nYOriginSrc As Integer) As Boolean

Private Declare Function WinGStretchBlt Lib "wing.dll" (ByVal hdcDest As ↵
Integer, ByVal nXOriginDest As Integer, ByVal nYOriginDest As Integer, ByVal ↵
nWidthDest As Integer, ByVal nHeightDest As Integer, ByVal hdcSrc As Integer, ↵
ByVal nXOriginSrc As Integer, ByVal nYOriginSrc As Integer, ByVal nWidthSrc ↵
As Integer, ByVal nHeightSrc As Integer) As Boolean

Private Declare Function DeleteObject Lib "GDI" (ByVal hObject As Integer) ↵
As Integer

Private Declare Function CreatePalette Lib "GDI" (lpLogPalette As LOGPALETTE) ↵
As Integer

Private Declare Function SelectPalette Lib "User" (ByVal hDC As Integer, ↵
ByVal hPalette As Integer, ByVal bForceBackground As Integer) As Integer
```

continued on next page

continued from previous page

```
Private Declare Function RealizePalette Lib "User" (ByVal hDC As Integer) ↵
As Integer

Private Declare Function SelectObject Lib "GDI" (ByVal hDC As Integer, ↵
ByVal hObject As Integer) As Integer

Private Declare Function lopen Lib "Kernel" Alias "_lopen" (ByVal lpPathName ↵
As String, ByVal iReadWrite As Integer) As Integer

Private Declare Function lread Lib "Kernel" Alias "_lread" (ByVal hfile ↵
As Integer, lpBuffer As Any, ByVal wBytes As Integer) As Integer

Private Declare Function lclose Lib "Kernel" Alias "_lclose" (ByVal hfile ↵
As Integer) As Integer

Private Declare Function hread Lib "Kernel" Alias "_hread" (ByVal hfile ↵
As Integer, buffer As Any, ByVal n As Long) As Long

Private Declare Function hwrite Lib "Kernel" Alias "_hwrite" (ByVal hfile ↵
As Integer, buffer As Any, ByVal n As Long) As Long

Private Declare Function lstrcpy Lib "Kernel" (dest As Any, src As Any) As Long

Const OPEN_READ = 0

Const SRCCOPY = &HCC0020
Const WHITENESS = &HFF0062
Const BLACKNESS = &H42&

Private Type RGBQUAD
    rgbBlue      As String * 1
    rgbGreen     As String * 1
    rgbRed       As String * 1
    rgbReserved  As String * 1
End Type

Private Type PALETTEENTRY
    peRed    As String * 1
    peGreen  As String * 1
    peBlue   As String * 1
    peFlags  As String * 1
End Type

Private Type LOGPALETTE
    version            As Integer
    nEntries           As Integer
    palpalentry(256)   As PALETTEENTRY
End Type

Const PC_RESERVED = &H1    '  palette index used for animation
Const PC_NOCOLLAPSE = &H4 '  do not match color to system palette
Const DIB_RGB_COLORS = 0   '  color table in RGBTriples

Private Type BITMAPFILEHEADER
    bfType       As Integer
```

```
    bfSize        As Long
    bfReserved1   As Integer
    bfReserved2   As Integer
    bfOffBits     As Long
End Type


Private Type BITMAPINFOHEADER
    biSize          As Long
    biWidth         As Long
    biHeight        As Long
    biPlanes        As Integer
    biBitCount      As Integer
    biCompression   As Long
    biSizeImage     As Long
    biXPelsPerMeter As Long
    biYPelsPerMeter As Long
    biClrUsed       As Long
    biClrImportant  As Long
End Type


Private Type BITMAPINFO
    bmiHeader       As BITMAPINFOHEADER
    bmiColors(256) As RGBQUAD
End Type



Private hbitmap      As Integer
Private m_pict       As Object
Private m_WinGDc     As Integer
Private WGBminfo     As BITMAPINFO
Private bminfo       As BITMAPINFO
Private psurface     As Long
Private pal          As Integer
Private bitdata()    As Byte
Private m_filename   As String
Private m_psurface   As Long



Private Sub ReadBitmap()

Dim LogicalPal As LOGPALETTE
Dim FileHeader As BITMAPFILEHEADER

FileP = lopen(m_filename, OPEN_READ)

throw = lread(FileP, FileHeader, Len(FileHeader)) = Len(FileHeader)
throw = lread(FileP, bminfo.bmiHeader.biSize, Len(bminfo.bmiHeader))
throw = lread(FileP, bminfo.bmiColors(0), Len(bminfo.bmiColors(0)) * 256)

For n = 0 To 255
    LogicalPal.palpalentry(n).peRed = bminfo.bmiColors(n).rgbRed
    LogicalPal.palpalentry(n).peGreen = bminfo.bmiColors(n).rgbGreen
    LogicalPal.palpalentry(n).peBlue = bminfo.bmiColors(n).rgbBlue
    If (n > 9) And (n < 246) Then
            LogicalPal.palpalentry(n).peFlags = Chr$(PC_RESERVED)
```

continued on next page

CHAPTER 8

continued from previous page

```
        Else
            LogicalPal.palpalentry(n).peFlags = Chr$(0)
    End If
Next n

LogicalPal.version = &H300
LogicalPal.nEntries = 256
pal = CreatePalette(LogicalPal)

ReDim bitdata(bminfo.bmiHeader.biSizeImage)
throw = hread(FileP, bitdata(0), bminfo.bmiHeader.biSizeImage)

Call lclose(FileP)

End Sub


Public Sub MakeWinGBit()

ReadBitmap

WGBminfo.bmiHeader.biSize = 40
WGBminfo.bmiHeader.biWidth = m_pict.ScaleWidth
WGBminfo.bmiHeader.biHeight = m_pict.ScaleHeight
WGBminfo.bmiHeader.biPlanes = 1
WGBminfo.bmiHeader.biBitCount = 8
WGBminfo.bmiHeader.biCompression = 0
WGBminfo.bmiHeader.biSizeImage = 0
WGBminfo.bmiHeader.biXPelsPerMeter = 0
WGBminfo.bmiHeader.biYPelsPerMeter = 0
WGBminfo.bmiHeader.biClrUsed = 256
WGBminfo.bmiHeader.biClrImportant = 0

hbitmap = WinGCreateBitmap(m_WinGDc, WGBminfo, psurface)
throw = SelectObject(m_WinGDc, hbitmap)

Call WinGSetDIBColorTable(m_WinGDc, 0, 256, bminfo.bmiColors(0))

End Sub

Public Sub setpal()
holdPal = SelectPalette(m_pict.hDC, pal, False)

throw = DeleteObject(holdPal)

Call RealizePalette(m_pict.hDC)

End Sub
```

21. The Transbits function copies this WinG bitmap's contents on to its own surface.

```
Public Sub Transbits()
BytesAsLong& = lstrcpy(bitdata(0), bitdata(0))
InfoAsLong& = lstrcpy(bminfo, bminfo)

Call TransparentDIBits(WGBminfo, ByVal psurface, 0, 0, ByVal BytesAsLong&, ↵
```

```
ByVal InfoAsLong&, 0, 0, 0, 1)

End Sub
```

22. Transbits2 copies this WinG bitmap's bits onto the m_psurface bitmap at the specified X and Y positions.

```
Public Sub Transbits2(X, Y)

BytesAsLong& = lstrcpy(bitdata(0), bitdata(0))
InfoAsLong& = lstrcpy(bminfo, bminfo)

Call TransparentDIBits(WGBminfo, ByVal m_psurface, x, y, ByVal BytesAsLong&, ↵
ByVal InfoAsLong&, 0, 0, 0, 0)

End Sub


Public Property Set picture(acontrol As Control)
Set m_pict = acontrol
End Property

Public Property Let wdc(n As Integer)
Let m_WinGDc = n
End Property

Public Property Let filename(s As String)
Let m_filename = s
End Property

Public Property Let surface(n As Long)
    m_psurface = n
End Property

Public Property Get surface() As Long
    surface = psurface
End Property

Private Sub Class_Terminate()
throw = DeleteObject(hbitmap)
End Sub
```

23. Add the Sprite class from How-To 6.9 to the project. For complete documentation on how the code in this class works, see How-To 6.9. Important hightlights are commented on in the following code.

```
'   Standard WinG functions
Private Declare Function DeleteDC Lib "GDI" (ByVal hDC As Integer) As Integer
Private Declare Function WinGCreateDC Lib "wing.dll" () As Integer

'   Globally declare the WinG bitmap
'   for the sprite
Dim WinGBitmap As WinG

Dim m_dispback As Object
```

continued on next page

CHAPTER 8

continued from previous page

```
'  Declare the boundaries for detecting collisions
Dim m_rightbound As Integer
Dim m_bottombound As Integer
Dim m_topbound As Integer
Dim m_leftbound As Integer

'  The surface to copy the bitmap onto
Dim m_psurface As Long

'  The filename to open
Dim m_filename As String

'  The device WinG context for the sprite
Dim WInGDC As Integer

'  Set the right boundary
Public Property Let RightBound(N As Integer)
    Let m_rightbound = N
End Property

'  Set the bottom boundary
Public Property Let Bottombound(N As Integer)
    Let m_bottombound = N
End Property

'  Set the Top boundary
Public Property Let TopBound(N As Integer)
    Let m_topbound = N
End Property

'  Set the left boundary
Public Property Let Leftbound(N As Integer)
    Let m_leftbound = N
End Property

'  This is the background to be displayed
Public Property Set dispback(acontrol As Object)
    Set m_dispback = acontrol
End Property

'  The file to be opened
Public Property Let filename(s As String)
    Let m_filename = s
End Property

Public Sub collide(X, Y, direction, width, height)

'  We check to see if the sprite has reached the right
'  side of the form.  If so, we change direction
'  appropriately
If X + width > m_rightbound Then
    If direction = "UR" Then direction = "UL"
    If direction = "DR" Then direction = "DL"
End If
```

686

```
'  We check to see if the sprite has reached the left
'  side of the form.  If so, we change direction
'  appropriately
If X < m_leftbound Then
    If direction = "UL" Then direction = "UR"
    If direction = "DL" Then direction = "DR"
End If


'  We check to see if the sprite has reached the
'  bottom side of the form.  If so, we change direction
'  appropriately
If Y + height > m_bottombound Then
    If direction = "DL" Then direction = "UL"
    If direction = "DR" Then direction = "UR"
End If


'  We check to see if the sprite has reached the top
'  side of the form.  If so, we change direction
'  appropriately
If Y < m_topbound Then
    If direction = "UL" Then direction = "DL"
    If direction = "UR" Then direction = "DR"
End If

End Sub
```

24. MoveImage copies this WinG sprite's bitmap bits on to the working WinG surface specified by m_psurface.

```
Public Sub MoveImage(X, Y)

'  Set the surface to copy the bits to
WinGBitmap.surface = m_psurface

'  Copy the bits
WinGBitmap.transbits2 X, Y

End Sub
```

25. Sets the surface for the sprite's bitmap bits to be copied on to.

```
'  Set the surface for bits to be
'  copied to
Public Property Let surface(N As Long)
    m_psurface = N
End Property

'  Create the WinG bitmap for the sprite
Public Sub create()
    Let WinGBitmap.filename = m_filename
    Set WinGBitmap.picture = m_dispback
    WinGBitmap.MakeWinGBit

    '  Delete the device context because
```

continued on next page

continued from previous page

```
   '  it will not be used any more
      throw = DeleteDC(WInGDC)
End Sub


   '  When the class is intialized, the
   '  new WinG device context is set
   '  and the WinGBitmap created
Private Sub Class_Initialize()
      WInGDC = WinGCreateDC()
      Set WinGBitmap = New WinG
      Let WinGBitmap.wdc = WInGDC
End Sub


   '  Be sure to terminate the
   '  WinG bitmap and delete the
   '  device context.
Private Sub Class_Terminate()
      Set WinGBitmap = Nothing
End Sub
```

How It Works

For the basics on how the Sprite and WinG class work and the overall animation and sprite techniques used, see Chapter 6, How-Tos 6.7 through 6.10. The primary additions made here include developing a technique for giving the fish more realistic movement and the addition of the fish school and the anchor.

The fish school requires an additional movement element to make its swimming motions more realistic. If you have ever watched a school of fish swim, you have probably noticed that the fish change directions suddenly and for no apparent reason. Thus, the direction of the school needs to be changed randomly every so often. The SchoolMove function accomplishes this by randomly changing the fish direction on every 39th tick of the timer. The new direction is randomly generated and set. Also, checks are done to see if the school of fish has crossed any of the boundaries; if so, the direction is updated appropriately.

Another feature of fish swimming is that their movement is not usually smooth and uniform. They tend to speed up and slow down and generally to move in a swaying motion. In the sprites developed in Chapter 6, the fish all moved evenly with every timer tick. To help give the fish more realistic movement, the amount of movement for each timer tick is randomly generated to fall in a specified range. The following is the sample code for the X and Y movement of the green fish:

```
GreenXStep = Int((42 - 0 + 1) * Rnd + 0)
GreenYStep = Int((29 - 0 + 1) * Rnd + 0)
```

The Xstep falls between a value of 0 and 49. The Ystep falls between 29 and 0. When the program is run, you will notice that the green fish swims in a general direction, but does not move in straight or even movements. The other two fish move in only one direction; the speed of the movement is also randomly generated.

The anchor is an example of a sprite that has limited action. It moves until it reaches the bottom and rests on the rocks. The swaying motion of the anchor falling is developed by also randomly generating its X position. The anchor could fall straight down, or the speed of the fall could be randomly generated, or, the anchor could fall in a certain direction, such as from left to right.

The basic framework developed in this How-To enables you to add sprites or animations easily. Any new objects developed need a Create function similiar to the ones found, a set of variables for tracking the object, and a Move function. The Create function should be called from the Form_Load procedure and the Move function should be called from the timer. Note that a new sprite or other object must use the surface of the primary working background for drawing its bits on to. The global variable used in this How-To for the working surface is WinGSurface. The following code is an example of how the school sprite's drawing surfaces are set.

```
SchoolRight.surface = WinGSurface
SchoolLeft.surface = WinGSurface
```

Comments

This How-To demostrates how the power and speed of WinG can be used to develop highly active animated scenes. The examples provided here are only a few of the many different types of animations that could be developed. More sprites could be added to the project, as could other animated objects like the chest. One feature not implemented in the WinG sprites but implemented in the sprites from Chapter 5 and the next How-To is a collision-detecting method that checks for collisions between two sprites. This would allow you to move the fish sprites appropriately when they collide.

8.8 How do I...
Create a multimedia game?

Problem

Some of the best examples of uses of multimedia are in educational games. How would I go about using the techniques developed in this book to develop a multimedia game?

Technique

The many different techniques developed in the book could be used in a wide variety of methods to implement a multimedia game. The example developed in this section will be that of a math tutor. A wide range of techniques developed throughout the book will be drawn on to implement four different types of demonstration exercises.

Steps

Open and run 8-8.VBP. The running program appears as shown in Figure 8-8-1. Figure 8-8-1 shows the start up of the program. Figure 8-8-2 shows the second game in the Math Tutor. The first game is not shown because it follows the same basic concept as developed in How-To 3.12. To play the game in Figure 8-8-2, click on the boxes of the picture. With each click, an equation is built at the bottom of the screen. The equation must then be solved and the answer must be entered. If the answer is correct, the Congratulations animation is shown.

Figure 8-8-3 depicts the third game. The primary concept behind this game is learning how to use the calculator. An equation to be solved is given at the bottom of the screen. The hot spot concept developed in How-To 4.3 is used to create hot spots on the calculator buttons. When the hot spots are clicked on, the name of the key is spoken. When the equation has been entered into the calculator, click the Check button to compare the answer with the correct answer.

The final exercise (Figure 8-8-4) implements the use of sprites from Chapter 5. With each new round of the exercise, an equation is stated. Then the boxes at the bottom of the screen are filled with numbers, one of which is the correct answer. The goal is to move the fish to the box with the correct answer.

1. Create a new project called 8-8.VBP. Add the object and properties listed in Table 8-8-1 to MDIForm1 and save the form as 8-8.FRM.

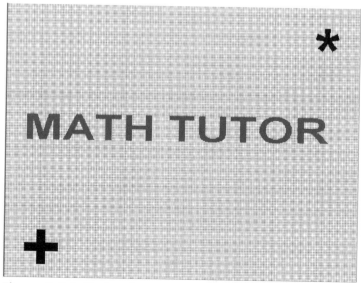

Figure 8-8-1 The introductory screen of the Math Tutor

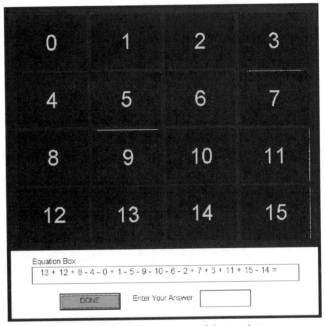

Figure 8-8-2 The second exercise of the Math Tutor

Table 8-8-1 The MDIForm's object and properties

OBJECT	PROPERTY	SETTING
MDIForm	Name	MDIForm1
	Auto3D	-1 'True
	BackColor	&H8000000C&
	Caption	"How-To 8.8"
	WindowState	2 'Maximized

2. Create a new form called INTRO.FRM. Add the objects and properties listed in Table 8-8-2 to the form.

Table 8-8-2 The Intro form's objects and properties

OBJECT	PROPERTY	SETTING
Form	Name	Form1
	BorderStyle	0 'None
	Caption	"Introduction"

continued on next page

continued from previous page

OBJECT	PROPERTY	SETTING
	Font	
	name	"Arial"
	MDIChild	-1 'True
	Visible	0 'False
Timer	Name	Timer1
	Enabled	0 'False
	Interval	10
PictureBox	Name	DispPict
	BackColor	&H00C0C0FF&
	BorderStyle	0 'None
	ScaleMode	3 'Pixel
Label	Name	Label2
	AutoSize	-1 'True
	BackStyle	0 'Transparent
	Caption	"*"
	Font	
	name	"Arial"
	size	72
Label	Name	Label1
	AutoSize	-1 'True
	BackStyle	0 'Transparent
	Caption	"+"
	Font	
	name	"Arial"
	size	72
MMControl	Name	MMControl1
	Visible	0 'False
	BorderStyle	1

3. Create a new form called ABOUT.FRM. Add the objects and properties listed in Table 8-8-3 to the form.

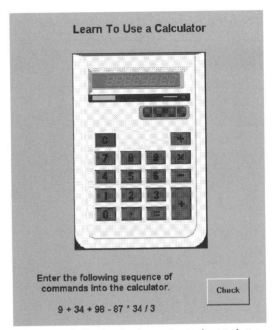

Figure 8-8-3 The third exercise in the Math Tutor

Figure 8-8-4 The final exercise in the Math Tutor

Table 8-8-3 The About form's objects and properties

OBJECT	PROPERTY	SETTING
Form	Name	Form2
	Auto3D	-1 'True
	BackColor	&H00C0C0C0&
	BorderStyle	0 'None
	Caption	"MATH TUTOR Instructions"
	MDIChild	-1 'True
	ScaleMode	3 'Pixel
	Visible	0 'False
CommandButton	Name	Continue
	Caption	"Continue"
	Font	
	name	"Arial"
	size	12
Timer	Name	Timer1
	Enabled	0 'False
	Interval	400
PictureBox	Name	ScrollPict
	BackColor	&H00C0C0C0&
	BorderStyle	0 'None
	Font	
	name	"Arial"
	size	12
	ScaleMode	3 'Pixel
MMControl	Name	MMControl1
	Visible	0 'False
	BorderStyle	1

4. Create a new form called EXER1.FRM. Add the objects and properties listed in Table 8-8-4 to the form.

Table 8-8-4 The Exer1 form's objects and properties

OBJECT	PROPERTY	SETTING
Form	Name	exer1
	BackColor	&H00404000&
	BorderStyle	0 'None
	Caption	"Exercise One"
	Font	
	name	"Arial"
	size	12
	ForeColor	&H0000FFFF&
	MDIChild	-1 'True
	Visible	0 'False
PictureBox	Name	BackDrop
	BackColor	&H00C0C0C0&
	BorderStyle	0 'None
	Font	
	name	"MS Sans Serif"
	Visible	0 'False
Label	Name	Number
	AutoSize	-1 'True
	Caption	"95874"
	DragMode	1 'Automatic
	Font	
	name	"Arial"
	size	10.2
	ForeColor	&H00800000&
	Index	8
Label	Name	Number
	AutoSize	-1 'True
	Caption	"58965"
	DragMode	1 'Automatic
	Font	
	name	"Arial"
	size	10.2

continued on next page

continued from previous page

OBJECT	PROPERTY	SETTING
	ForeColor	&H000000C0&
	Index	7
Label	Name	Number
	AutoSize	-1 'True
	Caption	"19875"
	DragMode	1 'Automatic
	Font	
	name	"Arial"
	size	10.2
	ForeColor	&H00808080&
	Index	6
Label	Name	Number
	AutoSize	-1 'True
	Caption	"1258.21"
	DragMode	1 'Automatic
	Font	
	name	"Arial"
	size	10.2
	ForeColor	&H00800000&
	Index	5
Label	Name	Number
	AutoSize	-1 'True
	Caption	"588.999"
	DragMode	1 'Automatic
	Font	
	name	"Arial"
	size	10.2
	ForeColor	&H00C000C0&
	Index	4
Label	Name	Number
	AutoSize	-1 'True
	Caption	"588.99"
	DragMode	1 'Automatic

OBJECT	PROPERTY	SETTING
	Font	
	name	"Arial"
	size	10.2
	ForeColor	&H00004000&
	Index	3
Label	Name	Number
	AutoSize	-1 'True
	Caption	"176.5"
	DragMode	1 'Automatic
	Font	
	name	"Arial"
	size	10.2
	ForeColor	&H00FF0000&
	Index	2
Label	Name	Number
	AutoSize	-1 'True
	BackColor	&H00FFFFFF&
	Caption	"95"
	DragMode	1 'Automatic
	Font	
	name	"Arial"
	size	10.2
	ForeColor	&H000000FF&
	Index	1
Label	Name	Number
	AutoSize	-1 'True
	Caption	"27"
	DragMode	1 'Automatic
	Font	
	name	"Arial"
	size	10.2
	Index	0
CommandButton	Name	Done

continued on next page

continued from previous page

OBJECT	PROPERTY	SETTING
	Caption	"CONTINUE"
	Font	
	name	"Arial"
	size	7.8
MMControl	Name	MMControl1
	AutoEnable	0 'False
	BorderStyle	1
Label	Name	Click
	Alignment	2 'Center
	AutoSize	-1 'True
	BackColor	&H00E0E0E0&
	Caption	"Click the Done Button When Finished."
	Font	
	name	"MS Sans Serif"
	size	12
	ForeColor	&H000000FF&
	Visible	0 'False

5. Create a new form called EXER2.FRM. Add the objects and properties listed in Table 8-8-5 to the form.

Table 8-8-5 The Exer2 form's objects and properties

OBJECT	PROPERTY	SETTING
Form	Name	Exer2
	BorderStyle	0 'None
	Caption	"Exercise Two"
	Font	
	name	"Arial"
	size	12
	MDIChild	-1 'True
Timer	Name	Timer2
	Enabled	0 'False
	Interval	1000

OBJECT	PROPERTY	SETTING
PictureBox	Name	AnimPict
	BackColor	&H00000000&
	Enabled	0 'False
	Visible	0 'False
MMControl	Name	MMControl1
	DeviceType	"AVIVideo"
	FileName	"festcong.avi"
PictureBox	Name	CoverPict
	BackColor	&H00000000&
	Font	
	name	"Arial"
	size	25.8
	ForeColor	&H0000FFFF&
	Visible	0 'False
Timer	Name	Timer1
	Enabled	0 'False
	Interval	1
TextBox	Name	Answer
	Font	
	name	"Arial"
	size	10.2
	Visible	0 'False
TextBox	Name	Equation
	Font	
	name	"Arial"
	size	10.2
	Visible	0 'False
CommandButton	Name	Continue
	Caption	"Continue"

continued on next page

continued from previous page

OBJECT	PROPERTY	SETTING
Label	Name	Label2
	AutoSize	-1 'True
	Caption	"Equation Box"
	Font	
	name	"Arial"
	size	9
	Visible	0 'False
Label	Name	Label1
	AutoSize	-1 'True
	Caption	"Enter Your Answer"
	Font	
	name	"Arial"
	size	9
	Visible	0 'False
Image	Name	BoxNum
	Index	0 - 15

6. Create a new form called EXER3.FRM. Add the objects and properties listed in Table 8-8-6 to the form.

Table 8-8-6 The Exer3 form's objects and properties

OBJECT	PROPERTY	SETTING
Form	Name	Exer3
	Auto3D	-1 'True
	BackColor	&H00404040&
	BorderStyle	0 'None
	Caption	"Exercise Three"
	MDIChild	-1 'True
CommandButton	Name	Command2
	Caption	"Continue"
CommandButton	Name	Command1
	Caption	"Check"

OBJECT	PROPERTY	SETTING
	Visible	0 'False
Timer	Name	Timer1
	Enabled	0 'False
	Interval	10
PictureBox	Name	Picture3
PictureBox	Name	Picture2
	AutoSize	-1 'True
	Picture	(Calc.bmp)
PictureBox	Name	Picture1
	AutoSize	-1 'True
	BackColor	&H00404040&
	Visible	0 'False
Label	Name	FeedBack
	Alignment	1 'Right Justify
	Font	
	name	"Arial"
	size	10.8
	Visible	0 'False
Image	Name	Image2
	Index	0 - 15
Label	Name	Instruct
	Alignment	2 'Center
	Font	
	name	"Arial"
	size	10.2
	Visible	0 'False
Label	Name	ClickLabel
	AutoSize	-1 'True

continued on next page

continued from previous page

OBJECT	PROPERTY	SETTING
	BackColor	&H008080FF&
	Caption	" Learn To Use a Calculator "
	Font	
	name	"Arial"
	size	12
	Visible	0 'False

7. Create a new form called EXER4.FRM. Add the objects and properties listed in Table 8-8-7 to the form.

Table 8-8-7 The Exer4 form's objects and properties

OBJECT	PROPERTY	SETTING
Form	Name	Exer4
	BackColor	&H00C0C0C0&
	BorderStyle	0 'None
	Caption	" "
	Font	
	name	"Arial"
	size	12
	KeyPreview	-1 'True
	MDIChild	-1 'True
	Visible	0 'False
CommandButton	Name	Command1
	Caption	"Begin"
	Font	
	name	"Arial"
PictureBox	Name	Mask4
	AutoSize	-1 'True
	BorderStyle	0 'None
	Picture	(f3mask.bmp)
PictureBox	Name	TempPict4
	AutoSize	-1 'True
	BackColor	&H00FFFFFF&

OBJECT	PROPERTY	SETTING
	BorderStyle	0 'None
	Picture	(f3right.bmp)
PictureBox	Name	Transf3
	AutoSize	-1 'True
	BorderStyle	0 'None
PictureBox	Name	Transf2
	AutoSize	-1 'True
	BorderStyle	0 'None
Timer	Name	Timer1
	Enabled	0 'False
	Interval	500
PictureBox	Name	TempPict3
	AutoSize	-1 'True
	BackColor	&H00FFFFFF&
	BorderStyle	0 'None
	Picture	(f2right.bmp)
PictureBox	Name	Mask3
	AutoSize	-1 'True
	BorderStyle	0 'None
	Picture	(f2mask.bmp)
PictureBox	Name	Mask2
	AutoSize	-1 'True
	BorderStyle	0 'None
	Picture	(f1lmask.bmp)
PictureBox	Name	TempPict2
	AutoSize	-1 'True
	BackColor	&H00FFFFFF&
	BorderStyle	0 'None
	Picture	(f1left.bmp)

continued on next page

continued from previous page

OBJECT	PROPERTY	SETTING
PictureBox	Name	Picture2
	AutoSize	-1 'True
	BorderStyle	0 'None
PictureBox	Name	Transf1
	AutoSize	-1 'True
	BorderStyle	0 'None
PictureBox	Name	Mask1
	AutoSize	-1 'True
	BorderStyle	0 'None
	Picture	(f1rmask.bmp)
PictureBox	Name	TempPict
	AutoSize	-1 'True
	BackColor	&H00FFFFFF&
	BorderStyle	0 'None
	Picture	(f1right.bmp)
PictureBox	Name	Picture1
	AutoSize	-1 'True
	BackColor	&H00C0C0C0&
	BorderStyle	0 'None
	Picture	(sea.bmp)
	Visible	0 'False
PictureBox	Name	CheckNum
	BackColor	&H000000FF&
	BorderStyle	0 'None
	ForeColor	&H00000000&
	Index	2
	ScaleMode	3 'Pixel
PictureBox	Name	CheckNum
	BackColor	&H000000FF&
	BorderStyle	0 'None

OBJECT	PROPERTY	SETTING
	ForeColor	&H00000000&
	Index	3
	ScaleMode	3 'Pixel
PictureBox	Name	CheckNum
	BackColor	&H000000FF&
	BorderStyle	0 'None
	ForeColor	&H00000000&
	Index	4
	ScaleMode	3 'Pixel
PictureBox	Name	CheckNum
	BackColor	&H000000FF&
	BorderStyle	0 'None
	ForeColor	&H00000000&
	Index	0
	ScaleMode	3 'Pixel
PictureBox	Name	CheckNum
	BackColor	&H000000FF&
	BorderStyle	0 'None
	ForeColor	&H00000000&
	Index	1
	ScaleMode	3 'Pixel

8. Create a new form called FINAL.FRM. Add the objects and properties listed in Table 8-8-8 to the form.

Table 8-8-8 The Final form's objects and properties

OBJECT	PROPERTY	SETTING
Form	Name	Final
	Auto3D	-1 'True
	BackColor	&H00C0C0C0&
	BorderStyle	0 'None
	MDIChild	-1 'True

continued on next page

CHAPTER 8

continued from previous page

OBJECT	PROPERTY	SETTING
CommandButton	Name	End
	Caption	"Click to End"
	Font	
	name	"Arial"
	size	10.8
MMControl	Name	MMControl1
Label	Name	Label4
	AutoSize	-1 'True
	Caption	"Thank You and Play Again!"
	Font	
	name	"Arial"
	size	10.8
Label	Name	Correct
	AutoSize	-1 'True
	Caption	"You answered 20 Correctly."
	Font	
	name	"Arial"
	size	13.8
Label	Name	Label2
	AutoSize	-1 'True
	Caption	"There are a total of 20 Questions."
	Font	
	name	"Arial"
	size	13.8
Label	Name	Label1
	AutoSize	-1 'True
	BackColor	&H00C0C0C0&
	Caption	"Your Score"
	Font	
	name	"Arial"
	size	36
	ForeColor	&H000000FF&

9. Add the following code to the general declarations section of MDIForm. The first form of the project is loaded.

```
Private Sub MDIForm_Load()
'  Load the first form
Load Form1

End Sub
```

10. Add the following code to the general declarations section of INTRO.FRM. First is used to execute the code in the Form_Paint procedure once.

```
'  First will be used to execute the code in the
'  Form_Paint procedure only once
Dim First As Integer
```

11. When the form is loaded, the form is sized and the animated text is set up.

```
Private Sub Form_Load()

'  Move the picture to the top left of the form
DispPict.Move 0, 0

'  Set the form to be the same size as the picture.
Form1.width = DispPict.width
Form1.height = DispPict.height

'  Start the text display
ShowIntro timer1, DispPict

End Sub
```

12. The code in the Form_Paint procedure is executed only once. The form does not start out visible so any resizing is not visible.

```
Private Sub Form_Paint()

'  On the first load make the form visible
If First = 0 Then
    Form1.Visible = True
    First = 1
End If

End Sub
```

13. When the form is resized, it will be centered.

```
Private Sub form_Resize()

'  center the form
centerform Form1

End Sub
```

14. The primary work of the introductory form is done in the INTROTXT.BAS module. Depending on the status of any one part of the animated text, the appropriate function is called from the timer.

```
Private Sub Timer1_Timer()

'   Until the first text display is done, call
'   the IntroFirstTimer
If Event = "INTROTEXT1" Then IntroFirstTimer

'   Until the Second text display is done, call
'   the IntroSecondTimer
If Event = "INTROTEXT2" Then IntroSecondTimer

'   Until the third text display is done, call
'   the IntroThirdTimer
If Event = "INTROTEXT3" Then IntroTHirdTimer

'   When the text display is done, this form is unloaded
'   and the next form loaded
If Event = "IntroTextDone" Then
    Unload Form1
    Load Form2
End If

End Sub
```

Note: The Scroll class developed in How-To 8.1 is used in this exercise.

15. Add the following code to the general declarations section of ABOUT.FRM. The global Scroll class is declared, along with variables for performing the scrolling of the text.

```
'   First will be used to execute the code in the
'   Form_Paint procedure only once
Dim First As Integer

'   Globally declare the scroll class
Dim Scroll As Class1

'   ScrollText will hold the text to be
'   displayed
Dim ScrollText() As String

'   Snum will count through the text
Dim Snum As Integer
```

16. Add the following code to the general declarations section of the form. SetText handles setting the text for the ScrollText array.

```
Private Sub SetText()

'   Set the text to be displayed
ScrollText(1) = "The MATH TUTOR program takes you through a series of exercises"
```

```
ScrollText(2) = "to help develop your basic math skills.  Before each exercise,"
ScrollText(3) = "instructions will be given to you regarding the task to be ↵
solved."

ScrollText(4) = ""
ScrollText(5) = "The number of correct answers given will be tallied at the ↵
end of"

ScrollText(6) = "the program and reported to you."
ScrollText(7) = ""
ScrollText(8) = "When you receive a wrong answer, the correct answer will be
given."
ScrollText(10) = ""
ScrollText(11) = "Good Luck, and we hope you enjoy MATH TUTOR!"
ScrollText(12) = ""
ScrollText(13) = ""

End Sub
```

17. When the Continue button is selected, the MCI device is closed and the first exercise is loaded.

```
Private Sub Continue_Click()

'  Close the multimedia control
mmcontrol1.Command = "Close"

'  Unload this form
Form2.Hide

'  Load the first exercise
exer1.Show

End Sub
```

18. When the form is loaded, the Scroll class is declared and set up. Also, the MIDI file starts playing.

```
Private Sub Form_Load()

'  Make sure the picture height is 0
ScrollPict.height = 0

'  Dimension the scroll text array
ReDim ScrollText(13) As String

'  Create the new class
Set Scroll = New Class1

'  Set the scrolling picture
Set Scroll.Pict = ScrollPict

'  Set the scrolling timer
Set Scroll.Time = timer1
```

continued on next page

continued from previous page

```
'  Setup the text
SetText

'  Play the passport MIDI file
mmcontrol1.filename = "c:\windows\media\passport.mid"
mmcontrol1.Command = "close"
mmcontrol1.DeviceType = "sequencer"
mmcontrol1.Command = "open"
mmcontrol1.Command = "play"

' Set Snum
Snum = 0

'  Enable the timer
timer1.Enabled = True

'  Make this form visible
Form2.Visible = True

End Sub
```

19. The first time the form is painted, the form is centered and made visible.

```
Private Sub form_Paint()

'  Execute this code at startup
If First = 0 Then
    Form2.Visible = True
    First = 1
    '  Center the form
    CenterForm Form2
End If

End Sub
```

20. With each timer tick, the text is scrolled. See How-To 8.1 for additional information on how the Scroll class works.

```
Private Sub Timer1_Timer()

    '  Scroll the text until the last
    '  line is reached
    If Snum < 12 Then
        Snum = Snum + 1
        Scroll.Lns = Snum
        Scroll.TextScroll ScrollText
    End If

End Sub
```

Note: This exercise is very similar to How-To 3.12. Additions allow the exercise to be run five times with different sets of numbers, but the logic is the same.

21. Add the following code to the general declarations section of EXER1.FRM. Appropriate variables are declared to perform the exercises.

```
'   First will be used to execute the
'   the code in the Form_Paint event
'   only once
Dim First As Integer

'   Paint will be used to execute the
'   the code in the Form_Paint event
'   only once
Dim Paint As Integer

'   Round will be used to run this
'   exercise once
Dim Round As Integer

'   Pos stores the positions of the
'   number labels
Dim pos(9, 2)
```

22. ShowInstruct handles displaying the instructions for the exercise.

```
Private Sub ShowInstruct()

'   Display the Instructions
OutText exer1, "", 1
OutText exer1, "The goal on this first exercise is to align the numbers", 1
OutText exer1, "in sequence from left to right.  The numbers should be", 1
OutText exer1, "in order from smallest to largest in value.", 1
OutText exer1, "", 1
OutText exer1, "Click the DONE button when you are finished aligning the", 1
OutText exer1, "numbers.  You have until the finish of the music to align", 1
OutText exer1, "the numbers.  The exercise will be run five times for a ", 1
OutText exer1, "total of five points.", 1
OutText exer1, "", 1
OutText exer1, "", 1
OutText exer1, "Good Luck!!!", 2

End Sub
```

23. The StorePos function stores the starting positions of the labels so that when the numbers are aligned, they can be rescrambled.

```
Private Sub StorePos()

'   Store the starting positions of the labels
For N = 0 To 8
    pos(N, 1) = Number(N).Left
    pos(N, 2) = Number(N).Top
Next N

End Sub
```

24. RestorePos handles rescrambling the numbers to their original positions.

```
Private Sub RestorePos()

'  Restore the starting positions of the labels
For N = 0 To 8
    Number(N).Left = pos(N, 1)
    Number(N).Top = pos(N, 2)
Next N

End Sub
```

25. The CheckAlign function checks to see if the numbers are aligned. Depending on a correct or incorrect answer, appropriate feedback is given. The next set of numbers is then loaded and the process starts over.

```
Private Sub CheckAlign()

'  Check to see if the numbers are in order.  We
'  will do this by checking to see if the left
'  values are incrementally larger
For N = 0 To 7

    '  If any one of the labels is further to the
    '  left than its predeccesor, then tell the
    '  user that there is an error
    If Number(N).Left > Number(N + 1).Left Then

        '  Notify the user that the answer was incorrect
        MsgBox "Sorry, Try Again Next Time!"

        '  Move the first label to the left
        Number(0).Left = 200

        For NN = 1 To 8
            '  Put the labels in order.
            Number(NN).Left = Number(NN - 1).Left + Number(NN - 1).width + 90
            Number(NN).Top = Number(NN - 1).Top
        Next NN

        '  Let the user see the correct answer
        MsgBox "Take a Quick Look at How this Puzzle is Solved."

        '  Go to the next round
        GoTo NextRound

    End If

Next N

'  Contgratulate the user
MsgBox "Congratulations, You Have Just Increased Your Score!"

'  Increase the number correct
NumAnswCorrect = NumAnswCorrect + 1

NextRound:
```

```
'   Restore the label positions
RestorePos

'   Each round has a different set of numbers to be ordered
Round = Round + 1

If Round = 2 Then
    Number(0) = ".1"
    Number(1) = ".11"
    Number(2) = ".111"
    Number(3) = ".1111"
    Number(4) = ".25"
    Number(5) = ".27"
    Number(6) = "1.8"
    Number(7) = "1.9"
    Number(8) = "1.99"
End If

If Round = 3 Then
    Number(0) = "24"
    Number(1) = "42"
    Number(2) = "422"
    Number(3) = "4222"
    Number(4) = "5987"
    Number(5) = "6300"
    Number(6) = "6303"
    Number(7) = "6330"
    Number(8) = "6333"
End If

If Round = 4 Then
    Number(0) = "6"
    Number(1) = "12"
    Number(2) = "18"
    Number(3) = "24"
    Number(4) = "30"
    Number(5) = "35"
    Number(6) = "53"
    Number(7) = "68"
    Number(8) = "86"
End If

If Round = 5 Then
    Number(0) = "6.01"
    Number(1) = "6.011"
    Number(2) = "66.01"
    Number(3) = "66.06"
    Number(4) = "568"
    Number(5) = "569"
    Number(6) = "875.3456"
    Number(7) = "875.3457"
    Number(8) = "987"
End If
```

continued on next page

continued from previous page

```
'   Reset First
First = 1

done.Caption = "CONTINUE"

If Round = 6 Then
    Unload exer1
    Exer2.Show
End If

End Sub
```

26. When the Done button is selected, the program is in either the continue or done mode. If it is in the continue mode, then the exercise is started or continued. If it is in the done mode, then the user has finished one round of the exercise and the answer is checked.

```
Private Sub Done_Click()

'   First will be 1 after the instructions have been shown
If First = 1 Then

    '   Make the picture visible
    BackDrop.Visible = True

    '   Make the Click label visible
    Click.Visible = True

    '   Set the filename to the canyon MIDI file
    '   found in the Windows directory
    mmcontrol1.filename = "c:\windows\media\canyon.mid"

    '   Set the device type to the sequencer for MIDI
    mmcontrol1.DeviceType = "sequencer"

    '   Open the device
    mmcontrol1.Command = "open"

    '   Start from the beginning of the piece
    mmcontrol1.From = 0

    '   Play only for a quarter of the length of
    '   the selection
    mmcontrol1.To = mmcontrol1.Length / 4

    '   Turn on the notify feature
    mmcontrol1.Notify = True

    '   Play the selection
    mmcontrol1.Command = "play"

    '   Set First to Two
    First = 2
```

```
    '   Clear the form
    exer1.Cls

    '   Set the caption to Done
    done.Caption = "DONE"
Else

    '   Close the Device
    mmcontrol1.Command = "Close"

    '   Check the alignment of the numbers
    CheckAlign

End If

End Sub
```

27. When the form is loaded, the first set of numbers is loaded and the original positions of the labels are stored.

```
Private Sub Form_Load()

'   Set the first round and
'   setup the first set of numbers
Round = 1
Number(0) = "27"
Number(1) = "95"
Number(2) = "176.5"
Number(3) = "588.99"
Number(4) = "588.999"
Number(5) = "1258.21"
Number(6) = "19875"
Number(7) = "58965"
Number(8) = "95874"

'   Store the positions
StorePos

End Sub
```

28. When the form is painted the first time, the instructions are shown and the form is centered.

```
Private Sub Form_Paint()

'   This code will only be executed
'   the first time the form is loaded
If Paint = 0 Then
    ShowInstruct
    Paint = 1
    First = 1

    '   Center the form
    CenterForm exer1
```

continued on next page

continued from previous page

```
        exer1.Visible = True
End If

End Sub
```

29. When the form is unloaded, the multimedia device is closed.

```
Private Sub Form_Unload(Cancel As Integer)

'  Close the sequencer
mmcontrol1.Command = "close"

End Sub
```

30. When the music is done playing, the user's time is up and the answer is checked.

```
Private Sub MMcontrol1_Done(NotifyCode As Integer)

'  If it was a normal ending of the playing
'  of our MIDI file then we will check the
'  alignment of numbers.
If NotifyCode = 1 Then CheckAlign

End Sub
```

31. When the labels are dragged and dropped on the backdrop picture, they are moved to the new locations.

```
Private Sub BackDrop_DragDrop(source As Control, x As Single, y As Single)

If First = 2 Then

'   We are dragging and dropping the labels on
'   the picture control.  When the drop has taken place,
'   we will move the label to the new position.  Note that
'   source contains the control that is being dragged and
'   dropped
    source.Left = x - (source.width / 2)
    source.Top = y - (source.height / 2)
End If

End Sub
```

32. Add the following code to the general declarations section of EXER2.FRM. Appropriate global variables are declared to perform the exercise.

```
'  First will be used to
'  indicate the status of the program in
'  checking to see if all of the boxes have
'  been uncovered
Dim First As Integer

'  Cnt will be used to count the number
'  of boxes uncovered
```

```
Public Cnt As Integer

'   Sum will hold running
'   total of the equation
Public Sum As Integer

'   Last indicates what the
'   last math operation was
Public Last As Integer

'   Is used as a counter in the timer
Dim N As Integer

'   GlobalIndex indicates what the last picture
'   uncovered was
Dim globalindex As Integer

'   Round will be used to run
'   the exercise 5 times
Dim Round As Integer
```

33. ShowInstruct handles showing the instructions for the exercise.

```
Private Sub ShowInstruct()

'   Display the instruction text
OutText Exer2, "", 2
OutText Exer2, "", 2
OutText Exer2, "", 2
OutText Exer2, "The goal on this second exercise is to build a math equation", 1
OutText Exer2, "that you must solve.  Each of the boxes that will appear on", 1
OutText Exer2, "the puzzle need to be selected.  When this happens, the ↵
number", 1

OutText Exer2, "of the box will be placed in the equation box below, with ↵
either", 1

OutText Exer2, "a plus or minus sign.  You must click on all of the boxes to", 1
OutText Exer2, "place all of the numbers in the equation.  Then, carefully", 1
OutText Exer2, "figure out the total of the equation and enter it in the", 1
OutText Exer2, "next text box.  If you get it right, see what happens!", 1
OutText Exer2, "", 1
OutText Exer2, "You will work through the exercise five times for a total of", 1
OutText Exer2, "five points.", 1
OutText Exer2, "", 1
OutText Exer2, "Good Luck!!!", 1

End Sub
```

34. When one of the BoxNum image controls is selected that has not been previously selected, it is covered with a picture. The timer is enabled to perform the covering. Also, the equation is updated and the running total is kept.

```
Private Sub BoxNum_Click(Index As Integer)
```

continued on next page

CHAPTER 8

continued from previous page

```
'  If the timer is running then do not
'  perform these checks
If timer1.Enabled = True Then Exit Sub

'  Check to see if the box is enabled
If BoxNum(Index).Enabled = True Then
    '  Make the box disabled
    BoxNum(Index).Enabled = False
    '  Enable the timer
    timer1.Enabled = True
    '  Move the coverpicture image to cover
    '  the box on the screen
    CoverPict(Index).Move BoxNum(Index).Left, BoxNum(Index).Top

    '  Set the height to 0
    CoverPict(Index).height = 0

    '  Set the width to that of the image width
    CoverPict(Index).width = BoxNum(Index).width

    '  Make the cover picture visible
    CoverPict(Index).Visible = True

    '  Store the index in the GlobalIndex
    globalindex = Index
End If

'  Increase out counter
Cnt = Cnt + 1

'  Clear the Sym variable
sym = ""

'  As long as this is not the first number entered
If Cnt > 1 Then

    '  Last indicates what the last operation
    '  was and the current number selected by the
    '  user is then added or subtracted to the total
    '  sum
    If Last = 1 Then Sum = Sum - Index
    If Last = 2 Then Sum = Sum + Index

Else

'  If this is the first number entered then
'  sum is equal to the number selected
Sum = Index

End If

'  Generate a random number that will indicate
'  the math operation to take place
rand = Int((2 - 1 + 1) * Rnd + 1)
```

```
'   As long as the last number was not selected,
'   then set the Last variable, which indicates the
'   math operation to be performed next.
If Cnt <> 16 Then

        '   A 1 value indicates subtraction, 2 indicates
        '   addition
        If rand = 1 Then sym = "-": Last = 1
        If rand = 2 Then sym = "+": Last = 2

Else

        '   If this is the last number then the
        '   next symbol is the = sign
        sym = "= "

End If

'   Add the index value to the equation and the
'   symbol
Equation.Text = Equation.Text + Str$(Index) + " " + sym

End Sub
```

35. When the Continue button is selected, the program is in either the continue or done mode. In continue mode, the instructions are cleared and the main exercise set up. In done mode, the answer entered by the user is checked to see if the correct total was entered.

```
Private Sub Continue_Click()

'   If the command box is used to continue to
'   pass the instructions then the following
'   is executed
If First = 1 Then

        '   Make the various parts of the game
        '   visible
        Equation.Visible = True
        Label1.Visible = True
        Answer.Visible = True
        Label2.Visible = True

        '   Set First to 2 so that this
        '   code is not executed again
        First = 2

        '   Change the caption
        Continue.Caption = "DONE"

        '   Load the picture
        Exer2.Picture = LoadPicture(App.Path + "\pyramid1.bmp")

Else
```

continued on next page

719

continued from previous page

```
'  We check to see if the full equation
'  has been built
If InStr(1, Equation.Text, "=") = 0 Then
     '  Indicate to the user that not all
     '  of the boxes have been pushed
     MsgBox "You still have more boxes to push"

Else

     '  Round calculates the number of times
     '  this game has been run.
     Round = Round + 1

     '  Check to see if the text in the
     '  text box equals the sum value
     If Val(Answer.Text) = Sum Then

         Exer2.Picture = LoadPicture("")

         '  Setup for the showing of the animation
         ClearCover

         '  Display the animation picture
         AnimPict.Enabled = True
         AnimPict.Visible = True

         '  Play the animation
         mmcontrol1.Command = "close"
         mmcontrol1.hWndDisplay = AnimPict.hWnd
         mmcontrol1.DeviceType = "AVIVideo"
         mmcontrol1.filename = App.Path + "\festcong.avi"
         mmcontrol1.Command = "open"
         mmcontrol1.Notify = True
         mmcontrol1.Command = "play"

         '  Increase the number of answers correct
         NumAnswCorrect = NumAnswCorrect + 1

     Else


         '  Indicate an incorrect answer
         MsgBox "Sorry, Try Again!  The correct answer was" + Str$(Sum) + ↵
         "  Watch your math closely!"

         '  Clear the cover pictures
         ClearCover

     End If

  End If

End If
```

```
' Check to see if this is the last round
If Round = 5 Then
    ' Unload this form
    Unload Exer2

    ' Show the next form
    Exer3.Show
End If

End Sub
```

36. When one of the CoverPict pictures is selected, the ding Wave is played to indicate that no action can be taken.

```
Private Sub CoverPict_Click(Index As Integer)

    ' If a cover picture is clicked on then indicate
    ' to the user with a ding that this picture has
    ' already been selected
    throw% = sndPlaySound("c:\windows\media\ding.wav", 0)

End Sub
```

37. When the form is loaded, the CoverPict control array is dimensioned out to enough pictures to cover the boxes on the background.

```
Private Sub Form_Load()

' Load the Coverpictures to
' display the numbers
For NN = 0 To 15
    Load CoverPict(NN)
Next NN

' Seed the random number generator
Randomize

End Sub
```

38. The first time the form is painted, the instructions for performing the exercise are shown.

```
Private Sub form_Paint()

' If this is the first time
' for the form to be painted then
' show the instructions
If First = 0 Then ShowInstruct: First = 1

End Sub
```

39. When the form is resized, the form is centered.

```
Private Sub form_Resize()
```

continued on next page

continued from previous page

```
'   Center the form
CenterForm Exer2

End Sub
```

40. When the Congratulatory animation is done playing, the timer is started to allow the animation to be visible for a short period of time.

```
Private Sub MMcontrol1_Done(NotifyCode As Integer)

'   Enable the timer
timer2.Enabled = True

End Sub
```

41. Timer1 handles showing the CoverPict pictures of the boxes on the background. It then prints the number on the picture.

```
Private Sub Timer1_Timer()

'   Inc will be the amount to uncover the picture
'   with each timer tick
Inc = BoxNum(globalindex).height / 2

'   Increment N
N = N + 1

'   Uncover the height by the increment
CoverPict(globalindex).height = CoverPict(globalindex).height + Inc

'   End the timer when the picture
'   is uncovered
If N = 2 Then

    timer1.Enabled = False

    '   Reset N
    N = 0

    '   Set the scalemode of the
    '   picture
    CoverPict(globalindex).ScaleMode = 3

    '   Globalindex has the number that was
    '   uncovered
    num$ = Str$(globalindex)
    num$ = Right$(num$, Len(num$) - 1)

    '   Calculate the center to print the text
    '   on the coverpict
    x = CoverPict(globalindex).ScaleWidth / 2 - ↵
    CoverPict(globalindex).TextWidth(num$) / 2

    y = CoverPict(globalindex).ScaleHeight / 2 - ↵
    CoverPict(globalindex).TextHeight(Str$(globalindex)) / 2
```

```
    ' Set the CurrentX and CurrentY
    CoverPict(globalindex).CurrentX = x
    CoverPict(globalindex).CurrentY = y

    ' Print the number
    CoverPict(globalindex).Print num$

End If

End Sub
```

42. ClearCover handles moving the CoverPict pictures out of view and resetting the exercise to be run again.

```
Private Sub ClearCover()

' Reset the counting
' of the numbers uncovered
Cnt = 0

' Make the cover pictures invisible and
' move them off the main picture
For NN = 0 To 15
    BoxNum(NN).Enabled = True
    CoverPict(NN).Visible = False
    CoverPict(NN).Move 0, 0
Next NN

' Close the device
mmcontrol1.Command = "close"

' Clear the text boxes
Equation.Text = ""
Answer.Text = ""

End Sub
```

43. Timer2 is called to show the animation for a short period after it is done running. The background image is then loaded.

```
Private Sub Timer2_Timer()

' Make the Animation picture invisible
AnimPict.Visible = False

' Load the picture
Exer2.Picture = LoadPicture(App.Path + "\pyramid1.bmp")

' Enable the timer
timer2.Enabled = False

End Sub
```

Note: The Wipe class developed in How-To 4.6 and the WaveTools class from How-To 7.2 are used in this exercise.

44. Add the following code to the general declarations section of EXER3.FRM. The Wipe class and WaveTools class are declared globally, along with the necessary variables needed to perform this exercise.

```
'   Round will be used to count out
'   five rounds of the exercise
Dim Round As Integer

'   Declare the Wave tools
'   class
Dim Wave As WaveTools

'   Declare the WipeClass
Dim wipeclass As wipeclass

'   Nums will hold the last number selected
Dim Nums As String

'   LastKey indicates the last math
'   function key selected (+,-,*,/)
Dim LastKey As Integer

'   Sum will hold the continuous sum of the
'   equation
Dim Sum As Double

'   Answ holds the answer to the equation
Dim Answ As Double

'   EqFlag indicates that the equal sign was
'   selected
Dim EqFlag As Integer
```

45. The PlayWave function handles playing the Wave file (specified by index) for the button clicked on. It uses the WaveTools class to control playing the Wave files.

```
Public Sub PlayWave(Index)

'   Make sure the wave file is closed
Wave.closewave
'   Depending on the button pushed, play
'   the appropriate wave
If Index = 0 Then filename = App.Path + "\zero.wav"
If Index = 1 Then filename = App.Path + "\one.wav"
If Index = 2 Then filename = App.Path + "\two.wav"
If Index = 3 Then filename = App.Path + "\three.wav"
If Index = 4 Then filename = App.Path + "\four.wav"
If Index = 5 Then filename = App.Path + "\five.wav"
If Index = 6 Then filename = App.Path + "\six.wav"
If Index = 7 Then filename = App.Path + "\seven.wav"
```

```
If Index = 8 Then filename = App.Path + "\eight.wav"
If Index = 9 Then filename = App.Path + "\nine.wav"
If Index = 10 Then filename = App.Path + "\period.wav"
If Index = 11 Then filename = App.Path + "\equal.wav"
If Index = 12 Then filename = App.Path + "\plus.wav"
If Index = 13 Then filename = App.Path + "\minus.wav"
If Index = 14 Then filename = App.Path + "\times.wav"
If Index = 15 Then filename = App.Path + "\divide.wav"
If Index = 16 Then filename = App.Path + "\clear.wav"

' Set the filename
Wave.filename = filename

' Read the wave file
Wave.readwave filename

' Play the wave file
Wave.playwave

End Sub
```

46. When the Check button is selected, the answer is checked and appropriate feedback is given. Then the next question is loaded.

```
Private Sub Check_Click()

' Check to see if the answer was correct
' or incorrect
If Sum = Answ Then
    MsgBox "Way to Go!!!"
    NumAnswCorrect = NumAnswCorrect + 1

Else
    MsgBox "The correct answer is" + Str$(Answ) + "."
End If

' Go to the next round
Round = Round + 1

' Setup the display of the equation
a$ = "Enter in the following sequence of commands into the calculator." + ↵
Chr$(13) + Chr$(13)

' Depending on the round, put forth the appropriate equation
' Answ holds the answer to the equation.
If Round = 2 Then a$ = a$ + "99.34 + 8.77 * .8 - 7.5 * 100 / 2": Answ = 3949.4
If Round = 3 Then a$ = a$ + "100 / .1 + 67 * 2.8 - 98": Answ = 2889.6
If Round = 4 Then a$ = a$ + "10 + 2 / 2 * 4 - 5 + 6 / 1 * 8 - 9": Answ = 191
If Round = 5 Then a$ = a$ + ".1 + .1 * 10.00 - 5 * 2 / 2": Answ = -3

' Show the instructons
Instruct.Caption = a$

' Check to see if this is the last round
If Round = 5 Then
```

continued on next page

continued from previous page

```
        Unload Exer3
        Load Exer4
    End If

End Sub
```

47. When the Continue button is selected, the instructions are cleared and the exercise is set up.

```
Private Sub Continue_Click()

'   Make this command invisible
Continue.Visible = False

'   Clear the form
Exer3.Cls

'   Make the various objects visible
Picture1.Visible = True
Check.Visible = True
Instruct.Visible = True
ClickLabel.Visible = True
Feedback.Visible = True

'   Perform the wipe of the image
wipeclass.setup 5, 40, 50

End Sub
```

48. The first time the form is painted, the instructions are shown.

```
Private Sub Form_Paint()

'   Show the instructions when the form is loaded
If First = 0 Then ShowInstruct: First = 1

End Sub
```

49. When the form is resized, it is centered.

```
Private Sub Form_Resize()

'   Center the form
CenterForm Exer3

End Sub
```

50. The timer handles performing the Snake wipe of the calculator.

```
Private Sub Timer1_Timer()

'   Run the Wipe method for
'   the wipe specified in Button
wipeclass.Wipe 5

'   Check to see if the wipe has
```

```
'  been finished.
If wipeclass.done = 1 Then timer1.Enabled = False: Feedback.Visible = True⏎
: Unload Exer2

End Sub
```

51. Add the following code to the general declarations section of the form. The ShowInstruct function handles displaying the instructions for the exercise.

```
Private Sub ShowInstruct()

'  Display the instruction text
OutText Exer3, "", 2
OutText Exer3, "", 2
OutText Exer3, "", 2
OutText Exer3, "In this exercise you will learn to use a simple calculator.", 1
OutText Exer3, "An equation will be given below the calculator for you to", 1
OutText Exer3, "solve.  Enter the equation into the calculator, and when you", 1
OutText Exer3, "are done, click on the equal sign and click the check ⏎
button.", 1

OutText Exer3, "", 1
OutText Exer3, "You will work through the exercise five times for a total of", 1
OutText Exer3, "five points.", 1
OutText Exer3, "", 1
OutText Exer3, "Good Luck!!!", 1

End Sub
```

52. Add the following code to the general declarations section of the form. CalcSum handles performing the operation specified on the calculator.

```
Private Sub CalcSum()

'  Depending on the last key, perform the appropriate
'  operation
If LastKey = 1 Then Sum = Sum + Val(Nums$)
If LastKey = 2 Then Sum = Sum - Val(Nums$)
If LastKey = 3 Then Sum = Sum * Val(Nums$)

'  Since a number can not be divided by zero, the
'  following check is performed
On Error GoTo ErrDivide

'  Divide the two values
If LastKey = 4 Then Sum = Sum / Val(Nums$)

'  Show the new sum in the feedback label
Feedback.Caption = Sum
Exit Sub

'  Notify the user of a divide by 0
ErrDivide:

MsgBox "You can not divide a number by 0."
```

continued on next page

continued from previous page

```
Feedback.Caption = Sum
End Sub
```

53. When the form is loaded, the two classes are declared and set up. The first equation is set up and the instructions are shown.

```
Private Sub Form_Load()

Set Wave = New WaveTools

'  Declare the new WipeClass object
Set wipeclass = New wipeclass

'  Initialize WipeClass with the appropriate timer
'  and three picture controls.
Set wipeclass.Timer = timer1
Set wipeclass.Pict1 = Picture1
Set wipeclass.Pict2 = Picture2
Set wipeclass.Pict3 = picture3

'  Setup the pictures for the wipe
wipeclass.pictset

'  Set round
Round = 1

'  Show the first equation
a$ = "Enter the following sequence of commands into the calculator." ↵
+ Chr$(13) + Chr$(13)

a$ = a$ + "9 + 34 + 98 - 87 * 34 / 3": Answ = 612

'  Show the instructions
Instruct.Caption = a$

'  Set lastkey to +
LastKey = 1

End Sub
```

54. When one of the hot spot images is selected, it is processed depending on the key selected. The appropriate actions are taken to perform all of the functions of the calculator. The CalcSum function is used to perform the actual math and track the total.

```
Private Sub Image2_Click(Index As Integer)

'  If the equal key was pressed
If EqFlag = 1 Then
    '  Reset the equal flag
    EqFlag = 0
    '  If the new index is a number then
    '  clear out the total
```

```
      If Index < 10 Then Sum = 0

End If

'  Play the appropriate wave file for the
'  index entered
playwave (Index)

'  Depending on the selection the appropriate
'  actions will be taken
Select Case Index

'  Check for a number
Case 0 To 9
    '  Show the number
    Nums$ = Nums$ + Right$(Str$(Index), Len(Str$(Index)) - 1)
    Feedback.Caption = Nums$

Case 10
    '  Show the point
    Nums$ = Nums$ + "."
    Feedback.Caption = num$

Case 11
    '  Calculate the sum
    calcsum
    '  Set lastkey to +
    LastKey = 1
    Nums$ = ""
    EqFlag = 1

Case 12
    '  As long as there have been
    '  numbers entered then calculate
    '  the sum and clear the nums$ variable
    If Nums$ <> "" Then
        calcsum
        Nums$ = ""
    End If

    '  Set LastKey to +
    LastKey = 1

Case 13
    '  As long as there have been
    '  numbers entered then calculate
    '  the sum and clear the nums$ variable
    If Nums$ <> "" Then
        calcsum
        Nums$ = ""
    End If

    '  set LastKey to minus
    LastKey = 2
```

continued on next page

continued from previous page

```
Case 14
    '   As long as there have been
    '   numbers entered then calculate
    '   the sum and clear the nums$ variable
    If Nums$ <> "" Then
        calcsum
        Nums$ = ""
    End If

    '   Set lastkey to multiplication
    LastKey = 3

Case 15
    '   As long as there have been
    '   numbers entered then calculate
    '   the sum and clear the nums$ variable
    If Nums$ <> "" Then
        calcsum
        Nums$ = ""
    End If

    '   Set LastKey to divide
    LastKey = 4

Case 16
    '   Clear out all variables
    Sum = 0
    Nums$ = ""
    LastKey = 1
    Feedback.Caption = ""

End Select

End Sub
```

Note: The WaveTools class from How-To 7.2 is used. The Sprite class used for this exercise is very similar to the classes developed in Chapter 5. The primary differences are discussed in the How It Works section at the end of this How-To.

55. Add the following code to the general declarations section of EXER4.FRM. The global declarations of the Wipe and Sprite class are made and variables needed to perform the exercises are declared.

```
'   DispPict is value of the correct
'   picture answer
Dim DispPict

'   Declare the wavetools class
Dim Wave As WaveTools

'   Declare the four sprites
Dim sprite1 As Sprite
Dim sprite2 As Sprite
```

```
Dim sprite3 As Sprite
Dim sprite4 As Sprite

'  Round will count the number of
'  times the exercise is run
Dim Round As Integer

'  Direction indicates the left or
'  right direction of the user
'  controlled sprite
Dim direction As Integer

'  x and y will be used to hold the current location
'  of the sprite
Dim x As Integer
Dim y As Integer

'  xx and yy will track the second sprite
Dim xx As Integer
Dim yy As Integer

'  xxx and yyy will track the third sprite
Dim xxx As Integer
Dim yyy As Integer

'  Mstep will be used to calculate the amount of
'  movement for each sprite movement
Dim Mstep As Integer
Dim mstep2 As Integer

'  First is used to execute
'  the code in Form_Paint once
Dim First As Integer

'  The sprite is moved around using the arrow keys
'  These are the constant values for each key
Const KEY_LEFT = &H25
Const KEY_UP = &H26
Const KEY_RIGHT = &H27
Const Key_Down = &H28
```

56. Add the following code to the general declarations section of the form. The ShowInstruct function shows the instructions for the exercise.

```
Private Sub ShowInstruct()

'  Display the instruction text
OutText Exer4, "", 2
OutText Exer4, "", 2
OutText Exer4, "", 2
OutText Exer4, "In this last exercise you will solve basic math problems.", 2
OutText Exer4, "The program will speak to you a simple math equation.", 2
OutText Exer4, "You then need to swim your fish to the red box on the sea", 2
OutText Exer4, "floor that contains the correct answer.", 2
OutText Exer4, "", 2
```

continued on next page

continued from previous page

```
OutText Exer4, "You will work through the exercise five times ", 2
OutText Exer4, "for a total of five points.", 2
OutText Exer4, "", 2
OutText Exer4, "Good Luck!!!", 2

End Sub
```

57. Add the following code to the general declarations section of the form. The BuildEquation function handles building the equation, including playing the Wave file for each number and the operand, and calculating the answer. It then places the correct answer in one of the picture boxes and fills the others with incorrect answers.

```
Private Sub BuildEquation()

'   Clear the picture
Picture1.Cls

'   Show the fish
Form_KeyDown KEY_RIGHT, 0

'   Increment the round
Round = Round + 1

'   Get the first number
Firstnum = Int((9 - 0 + 1) * Rnd + 0)

'   Get the operator
operator = Int((4 - 1 + 1) * Rnd + 1)

'   Get the second number
secondnum = Int((9 - 0 + 1) * Rnd + 0)

'   Ensure that a divide by 0 can not take place
If operator = 4 And secondnum = 0 Then secondnum = 1

'   Perform the operation depending on the
'   operator
If operator = 1 Then Answ = Firstnum + secondnum
If operator = 2 Then Answ = Firstnum - secondnum
If operator = 3 Then Answ = Firstnum * secondnum
If operator = 4 Then Answ = Firstnum / secondnum

'   Make sure the wave device is closed
Wave.closewave

'   Depending on the first number,
'   play the appropriate file
Select Case Firstnum

Case 0
    filename = App.Path + "\zero.wav"

Case 1
```

```
        filename = App.Path + "\One.wav"

Case 2
        filename = App.Path + "\Two.wav"

Case 3
        filename = App.Path + "\three.wav"

Case 4
        filename = App.Path + "\four.wav"

Case 5
        filename = App.Path + "\five.wav"

Case 6
        filename = App.Path + "\six.wav"

Case 7
        filename = App.Path + "\Seven.wav"

Case 8
        filename = App.Path + "\eight.wav"

Case 9
        filename = App.Path + "\nine.wav"

End Select

'   Set the filename
Wave.filename = filename

'   Read the wave file
Wave.readwave filename

'   Play the wave file
Wave.playwave

'   Close the wave file
Wave.closewave

'   Set the operator file
Select Case operator

Case 1
        filename = App.Path + "\plus.wav"

Case 2
        filename = App.Path + "\Minus.wav"

Case 3
        filename = App.Path + "\Times.wav"

Case 4
        filename = App.Path + "\Divide.wav"
```

continued on next page

continued from previous page

```
End Select

Wave.filename = filename

'   Read the wave file
Wave.readwave filename
Wave.playwave
Wave.closewave

'   Set the file for the second
'   number
Select Case secondnum

Case 0
    filename = App.Path + "\zero.wav"

Case 1
    filename = App.Path + "\One.wav"

Case 2
    filename = App.Path + "\Two.wav"

Case 3
    filename = App.Path + "\three.wav"

Case 4
    filename = App.Path + "\four.wav"

Case 5
    filename = App.Path + "\five.wav"

Case 6
    filename = App.Path + "\six.wav"

Case 7
    filename = App.Path + "\Seven.wav"

Case 8
    filename = App.Path + "\eight.wav"

Case 9
    filename = App.Path + "\nine.wav"

End Select

Wave.filename = filename

'   Read the wave file
Wave.readwave filename
Wave.playwave

'   Choose which picture will show the
'   correct answer
DispPict = Int((4 - 0 + 1) * Rnd + 0)
```

```
' Clear the picture
CheckNum(DispPict).Cls

' Set up the correct number to be displayed
If Len(Str$(Answ)) > 3 Then d$ = Left$(Str$(Answ), 4): Else d$ = Str$(Answ)
If Left$(d$, 1) <> "-" Then d$ = Right$(d$, Len(d$) - 1)

' Center and print the number
CheckNum(DispPict).CurrentX = CheckNum(DispPict).ScaleWidth / 2 - ↵
CheckNum(DispPict).TextWidth(d$) / 2

CheckNum(DispPict).CurrentY = CheckNum(DispPict).ScaleHeight / 2 - ↵
CheckNum(DispPict).TextHeight(d$) / 2

CheckNum(DispPict).Print d$

' Display numbers in the other pictures
For NN = 0 To 4

    ' Make sure that we don't overwrite
    ' the picture with the correct answer
    If NN <> DispPict Then

        ' Generate the random number
        num = Int((81 - (-81) + 1) * Rnd + (-81))

        ' Make sure the answer does not equal
        ' the correct answer.  If it does, then divide
        ' it by 2
        If num = Answ Then num = num / 2

        ' Generate another random number between
        ' 1 and 5
        Temp = Int((5 - 1 + 1) * Rnd + 1)

        ' When Temp = 4 then we will
        ' make a number that is a fraction
        If Temp = 4 Then
            ' Generate another number between
            ' 1 and 10
            Temp = Int((10 - 1 + 1) * Rnd + 1)
            ' Divide the number by 3
            num = Temp / 3
        End If

        ' d$ will equal the string of the number
        If Len(Str$(num)) > 3 Then d$ = Left$(Str$(num), 4): Else d$ = Str$(num)
        If Left$(d$, 1) <> "-" Then d$ = Right$(d$, Len(d$) - 1)

        ' Center the number and print it
        CheckNum(NN).Cls
        CheckNum(NN).CurrentX = CheckNum(NN).ScaleWidth / 2 - ↵
        CheckNum(NN).TextWidth(d$) / 2

        CheckNum(NN).CurrentY = CheckNum(NN).ScaleHeight / 2 - ↵
```

continued on next page

continued from previous page

```
            CheckNum(NN).TextHeight(d$) / 2

            CheckNum(NN).Print d$

    End If

    Next NN

    End Sub
```

58. When the Begin button is clicked, the form is cleared and the exercise is set up.

```
Private Sub Begin_Click()

'   Set First
First = 0

'   Display the picture
Picture1.Visible = True

'   Start the Timer
timer1.Enabled = True

Exer4.Cls

'   Call the Form_Paint procedure to
'   start the animation
'   When the form is first painted,
'   the sprites need to be setup
sprite1.setup
sprite2.setup
sprite3.setup
sprite4.setup

'   Show the fish
Form_KeyDown Key_Down, 0

Exer4.height = Picture1.height

'   Make the command button invisible
Begin.Visible = False

'   Build the first equation
BuildEquation

End Sub
```

59. As with the sprite exercises in Chapter 5, the primary sprite is controlled by the user with the arrow keys. For a detailed description of how this process works, see How-Tos 5.4, 5.5, and 5.6. Additional logic is added to check for a collision with the answer boxes and to see if the correct answer is selected.

```
Private Sub Form_KeyDown(KeyCode As Integer, Shift As Integer)
```

```
'  Depending on the key selected, we increment or
'  decrement x or y and call MoveImage function of
'  the sprite.
If KeyCode = KEY_RIGHT Then x = x + Mstep: direction = 1
If KeyCode = KEY_LEFT Then x = x - Mstep: direction = 0
If KeyCode = Key_Down Then y = y + Mstep
If KeyCode = KEY_UP Then y = y - Mstep


'  W will be with width of Mask1
'  and H the height
W = Mask1.ScaleWidth
H = Mask1.ScaleHeight


'  WW will be with width of Mask2
'  and HH the height
WW = Mask4.ScaleWidth
HH = Mask4.ScaleHeight


'  Check for a collision with the two fish sprites
sprite3.collide xx, yy, x, y, W, H, Mstep, Coll1
sprite4.collide xxx, yyy, x, y, W, H, mstep2, Coll2


'  Move the fish depending on the direction
If direction = 1 Then
     sprite1.MoveImage x, y, Mstep
Else
     sprite2.MoveImage x, y, Mstep
End If


'  If there was a collision then update the
'  sprite that was collided with.  This will make
'  sure that the collided image was not overwritten
If Coll1 = "True" Then sprite3.update xx, yy, Mstep
If Coll2 = "True" Then sprite4.update xxx, yyy, mstep2


'  A check is done to see if the fish has collided
'  with any of the picture boxes
For NN = 0 To 4


'  Get the values of the position and dimension of each
'  picture box.  Note that the width and height are divided
'  in half to ensure that the actual fish part of the mask
'  has collided with the picture box.
L = CheckNum(NN).Left + CheckNum(NN).ScaleWidth / 2
R = CheckNum(NN).Top + CheckNum(NN).ScaleHeight / 2
W = CheckNum(NN).ScaleWidth / 30
H = CheckNum(NN).ScaleHeight / 30


'  Depending on which direction a check is done
'  to see if a collision has taken place
If direction = 1 Then
     sprite1.collide x, y, L, R, W, H, 0, Coll
Else
     sprite2.collide x, y, L, R, W, H, 0, Coll
End If
```

continued on next page

continued from previous page

```
'  Check to see if a collision has happened with
'  the correct picture
If (Coll = "True") And (NN = DispPict) Then

    '  Reset the location of the user controlled fish
    x = 0
    y = 0

    '  Increase the number answered correct
    NumAnswCorrect = NumAnswCorrect + 1

    '  Notify the user of a correct answer
    MsgBox "Congratulations, that is a correct score!"

    '  Check to see if the last round has been reached
    If Round = 5 Then
        Unload Exer4
        Load Final
    Else
        '  Build the next equation and start over
        BuildEquation
    End If

    Exit Sub

End If

'  Check to see if an incorrect picture answer
'  was selected
If (Coll = "True") And (NN <> DispPict) Then

    '  Reset the x and y coordinates of the
    '  user controlled fish
    x = 0
    y = 0

    '  Notify the user of an incorrect response
    MsgBox "Sorry, try again!"

    If Round = 5 Then
        Unload Exer4
        Load Final
    Else
        '  Build the next equation
        BuildEquation
    End If

    Exit Sub

End If

Next NN

End Sub
```

60. When the form is loaded, the various sprites are set up and the initial variables for the sprite movements are set.

```
Private Sub Form_Load()

'   Set Round
Round = 0

'   Seed the random number generator
Randomize

'   Start out the direction to be pointing right
direction = 1

'   Create the new wave class
Set Wave = New WaveTools

'   Create a new instance of the class
Set sprite1 = New Sprite
Set sprite2 = New Sprite
Set sprite3 = New Sprite
Set sprite4 = New Sprite

'   Pass in the appropriate images
'   to initialize the class
Set sprite1.mask1pict = Mask1
Set sprite1.background = Picture1
Set sprite1.dispback = Picture2
Set sprite1.transf1pict = Transf1
Set sprite1.primarypict = temppict

Set sprite2.mask1pict = Mask2
Set sprite2.background = Picture1
Set sprite2.dispback = Picture2
Set sprite2.transf1pict = Transf1
Set sprite2.primarypict = TempPict2

Set sprite3.mask1pict = Mask3
Set sprite3.background = Picture1
Set sprite3.dispback = Picture2
Set sprite3.transf1pict = Transf2
Set sprite3.primarypict = TempPict3

Set sprite4.mask1pict = Mask4
Set sprite4.background = Picture1
Set sprite4.dispback = Picture2
Set sprite4.transf1pict = Transf3
Set sprite4.primarypict = TempPict4


'   Move the picture to the upper
'   left corner and size the form
'   to the picture
Picture1.Move 0, 0
```

continued on next page

continued from previous page

```
Exer4.width = Picture1.width + 6
Exer4.height = Picture1.height + 1100

'   Mstep holds the amount of each movement
Mstep = 15
mstep2 = 14

'   Start x amd y as 0
y = 0
x = 0

'   Set the starting positions for the two self moving fish
xx = xx + Mstep * 5
yy = 100

xxx = xxx + mstep2
yyy = 300

End Sub
```

61. When the form is painted the first time, the form is centered and the instructions are shown.

```
Private Sub Form_Paint()

'   Make sure this code is only
'   executed once.
If First = 0 Then

    '   Center the form
    CenterForm Exer4

    '   Set First
    First = 1

    '   Show the instructions
    ShowInstruct

End If

End Sub
```

62. When the form is unloaded, the Wave device is closed.

```
Private Sub Form_Unload(Cancel As Integer)

'   Make sure the wave device is closed
Wave.closewave

End Sub
```

63. The timer handles moving the two independent fish. Each time the fish are moved, collision with the user sprite is checked. Also, a check is done to see if

the sprites have collided with the right side of the background picture. If they
have, then they are reset to swim from the left again.

```
Private Sub Timer1_Timer()

    '  Increment the movements of the two fish
    xx = xx + Mstep
    xxx = xxx + mstep2

    '  Move the first sprite
    sprite3.MoveImage xx, yy, Mstep

    '  Get the width and height of the fish
    W = Mask1.ScaleWidth
    H = Mask1.ScaleHeight

    '  Check for a collision with the user controlled sprite
    '  Depending on direction
    If direction = 1 Then
        sprite3.collide xx, yy, x, y, W, H, Mstep, Coll
        '  If there was a collision then first update the user controlled
        '  sprite then update sprite3.  This will ensure that sprite3  appears
        '  to always be on top
        If Coll = "True" Then sprite1.update x, y, Mstep: sprite3.update xx, ↵
        yy, Mstep
    Else
        sprite3.collide xx, yy, x, y, W, H, Mstep, Coll
        '  If there was a collision then first update the user controlled
        '  sprite then update sprite3.  This will ensure that sprite3  appears
        '  to always be on top
        If Coll = "True" Then sprite2.update x, y, Mstep: sprite3.update xx, ↵
        yy, Mstep
    End If


    '  Set W to the width of the mask plus the width of the picture
    W = Picture1.ScaleWidth + Mask3.ScaleWidth * 2

    '  Set H to the height of the picture
    H = Picture1.ScaleHeight

    '  HH is the height of the mask
    HH = Mask3.ScaleHeight

    '  We are checking for a collision with an imaginary
    '  box on the right of the picture.  This is essentially
    '  a box on the right edge of the picture.  If our
    '  sprite has collided with this box then the sprite needs to move back
    '  to the left to give an appearance of wrapping around
    sprite3.collide xx, yy, W, yy, Mstep * 4, HH / 2, Mstep, Coll

    '  If a collision took place then move the
    '  fish back to the left side of the form
    If Coll = "True" Then xx = -50
```

continued on next page

continued from previous page

```
'  Move the second fish
sprite4.MoveImage xxx, yyy, mstep2

'  Get the width and height of the fish
W = Mask1.ScaleWidth
H = Mask1.ScaleHeight

'  Check for a collision with the user controlled sprite
'  Depending on direction
If direction = 1 Then
    sprite4.collide xxx, yyy, x, y, W, H, mstep2, Coll
    '  If there was a collision then first update the user controlled
    '  sprite then update sprite4.  This will ensure that sprite4 appears
    '  to always be on top
    If Coll = "True" Then sprite1.update x, y, Mstep: sprite4.update xxx, ↵
    yyy, mstep2
Else
    sprite4.collide xxx, yyy, x, y, W, H, mstep2, Coll
    '  If there was a collision then first update the user controlled
    '  sprite then update sprite4.  This will ensure that sprite4 appears
    '  to always be on top
    If Coll = "True" Then sprite2.update x, y, Mstep: sprite4.update xxx, ↵
    yyy, mstep2
End If

'  Check to see if the sprite has collided with
'  the right side of the picture  See above for
'  additional details
W = Picture1.ScaleWidth + Mask4.ScaleWidth * 2
H = Picture1.ScaleHeight
HH = Mask4.ScaleHeight

sprite4.collide xxx, yyy, W, yyy, Mstep * 4, HH, Mstep, Coll

If Coll = "True" Then xxx = -50

End Sub
```

64. Add the following code to FINAL.FRM. When the End button is selected, the program is finished.

```
Private Sub End_Click()
    mmcontrol1.Command = "close"
    End
End Sub
```

65. When the form is loaded, the MIDI music is played and the total number of answers correct is displayed.

```
Private Sub form_Load()

Correct.Caption = "You answered" + Str$(NumAnswCorrect) + "correctly."

mmcontrol1.filename = "C:\windows\media\passport.mid"
mmcontrol1.DeviceType = "Sequencer"
```

```
mmcontrol1.Command = "open"
mmcontrol1.Command = "play"
```

```
End Sub
```

66. When the form is resized, it is centered on the screen.

```
Private Sub form_Resize()
```

```
CenterForm Final
```

```
End Sub
```

67. Create a new module and save it as GLOBAL.BAS. Add the following code to the general declarations section of the module. The sndPlaySound is declared for playing various sounds in the program and several global project variables are declared.

```
'  Globally declare the sndPlaySound API function
Public Declare Function sndPlaySound Lib "MMSystem" (ByVal lpszSoundName As ↵
String, ByVal uFlags As Integer) As Integer

'  Event will be used in the Intro form and
'  introtxt.bas
Public Event As String

'  NumAnswCorrect will be used to tally the
'  number of correct answers given
Public NumAnswCorrect As Integer
```

68. Add the following code to the module. The OutText function prints the specified text on the form. The text can be centered or left-justified.

```
'  OutText will be used to display the text
'  on the specified object
Public Sub OutText(Obj As Object, Txt As String, Centered)

'  Check to see whether or not the text should be centered
'  on the object
If Centered = 2 Then
    '  Find the center
    Obj.CurrentX = (Obj.ScaleWidth - Obj.TextWidth(Txt)) / 2
Else
    '  Print slightly to the right of the
    '  left of the object
    Obj.CurrentX = 250
End If

'  Print the text
Obj.Print Txt

End Sub
```

69. CenterForm handles centering the specified form on the screen.

```
Public Sub CenterForm(form As Object)

    '   Center the form as long as it
    '   is not minimized
    If form.WindowState = 0 Then
        form.Move (Screen.width - form.width) / 2, (Screen.height - ↵
                form.height) / 2
    End If

End Sub
```

70. Create a new module and save it as INTROTXT.BAS. Add the following code to the general declarations section of the module. See How-To 2.7 for additional information on the declarations made. In general, this module is similar to the FINAL.BAS module in How-To 8.3 and How-To 2.7.

```
'   The following type of declaration describes the
'   Windows API LOGFONT structure.  THE LOGFONT
'   structure is used by several of the WIN API
'   text functions.
Type LOGFONT
    lfHeight As Integer
    lfWidth As Integer
    lfEscapement As Integer
    lfOrientation As Integer
    lfWeight As Integer
    lfItalic As String * 1
    lfUnderline As String * 1
    lfStrikeOut As String * 1
    lfCharSet As String * 1
    lfOutPrecision As String * 1
    lfClipPrecision As String * 1
    lfQuality As String * 1
    lfPitchAndFamily As String * 1
    lfFaceName As String * 24
End Type

'   Declare the Windows API DeleteObject function
Private Declare Function DeleteObject Lib "GDI" (ByVal hObject As Integer) ↵
As Integer

'   Declare the Windows API CreateFontIndirect function
Private Declare Function CreateFontIndirect Lib "GDI" (lpLogFont As LOGFONT) ↵
As Integer

'   Declare the Windows API SelectObject function
Private Declare Function SelectObject Lib "GDI" (ByVal hDC As Integer, ByVal ↵
hObject As Integer) As Integer

'   Declare the Windows API TextOut function
Private Declare Function TextOut Lib "GDI" (ByVal hDC As Integer, ByVal x As ↵
Integer, ByVal y As Integer, ByVal lpString As String, ByVal nCount As ↵
Integer) As Integer
```

```
'   These are the two controls that will be used to
'   display the text
Private Timer As Control
Private IntroPic As Control

'   CFONT will be our font structure for the text
Private CFONT As LOGFONT

'   ESCAPE will hold the current ESCAPEMENT of the
'   displayed font
Private escape As Integer

'   ChangeX and ChangeY will hold the increment to move
'   the text to the upperleft corner.
Private ChangeX As Integer
Private ChangeY As Integer

'   N will be used as a counter in the IntroThird
'   Function
Private N As Integer

Private Sub FontOut(Text$, Pict, xx, yy, FontStruct As LOGFONT)

'   Create the new font
NewFont% = CreateFontIndirect(FontStruct)

'   Select the new font into the picture
'   device context
OldFont% = SelectObject(Pict.hDC, NewFont%)

'   Display the text
throw% = TextOut(Pict.hDC, xx, yy, Text$, Len(Text$))

'   Select the font back for the original device context
throw% = SelectObject(Pict.hDC, OldFont%)

'   Delete the newly created font
throw% = DeleteObject(NewFont%)

End Sub

Public Sub ShowIntro(T As Control, Pict As Control)

'   Set the first event
Event = "INTROTEXT1"

'   set the Timer and IntroPic controls for the
'   display of the text
Set Timer = T
Set IntroPic = Pict

'   Set the scalemode to 3 (pixels) for the picture
IntroPic.ScaleMode = 3

'   Set up the initial font structure.  We will
```

continued on next page

continued from previous page

```
'   use a height of 30 and a width of 10.   The
'   weight will be medium (non-bold), and will
'   use Arial.
CFONT.lfHeight = 30
CFONT.lfWidth = 10
CFONT.lfEscapement = 0
CFONT.lfWeight = 400
CFONT.lfItalic = Chr$(0)
CFONT.lfUnderline = Chr$(0)
CFONT.lfStrikeOut = Chr$(0)
CFONT.lfOutPrecision = Chr$(0)
CFONT.lfClipPrecision = Chr$(0)
CFONT.lfQuality = Chr$(0)
CFONT.lfPitchAndFamily = Chr$(0)
CFONT.lfCharSet = Chr$(0)
CFONT.lfFaceName = "Arial" + Chr$(0)


'   Locate the currentx and currenty for the first text display
IntroPic.CurrentX = (IntroPic.ScaleWidth - IntroPic.TextWidth(↵
"Introducing...")) / 2 + 90

IntroPic.CurrentY = (IntroPic.ScaleHeight -
IntroPic.TextHeight("Introducing...")) / 2 + 90

'   Calculate the changes for 20 moves of "Introducing..." to the upper corner.
ChangeX = IntroPic.CurrentX / 20
ChangeY = IntroPic.CurrentY / 20

'   Start timer1
Timer.Enabled = True

'   Set the ForeColor for the text to be printed
IntroPic.ForeColor = RGB(255, 0, 0)

End Sub

Private Sub PLast()

'   Create a new font with a larger width and height
CFONT.lfWidth = CFONT.lfWidth + 10
CFONT.lfHeight = CFONT.lfHeight + 2

'   Set the color for the font
IntroPic.ForeColor = RGB(255, 80, 255)
'   Call the FontOut procedure to display the text
FontOut "Introducing...", IntroPic, x, y, CFONT

End Sub

Public Sub IntroFirstTimer()

'   Set the new escapement
CFONT.lfEscapement = CFONT.lfEscapement + 180
```

```
'  Calculate the center of the text
x = (IntroPic.ScaleWidth - IntroPic.TextWidth("Introducing...")) / 2 + 90
y = (IntroPic.ScaleHeight - IntroPic.TextHeight("Introducing...")) / 2 + 90

'  For the last print when the font color is white, we will
'  clear the picture and print the text in black
If CFONT.lfEscapement = 3600 Then

    '   Set the forecolor back to black
    IntroPic.ForeColor = RGB(0, 0, 0)

    '  Set the next event
    Event = "INTROTEXT2"

End If

'  Call the FontOut procedure to display the text
FontOut "Introducing...", IntroPic, x, y, CFONT

End Sub

Public Sub IntroSecondTimer()

'  Move up and to the left by the
'  increment stored in ChangeX and ChangeY
x = IntroPic.CurrentX - ChangeX
y = IntroPic.CurrentY - ChangeY

'  Set the new x and y.  Note, we are storing
'  the x and y values here.
IntroPic.CurrentX = x
IntroPic.CurrentY = y

'  Call the FontOut procedure to display the text
FontOut "Introducing...", IntroPic, x, y, CFONT

'  If x is greater than 0 but less than the amount
'  of the incremental move (by 1), then we need to stop
'  moving or else the text will not be visible.
If (x > 0) And (x < (ChangeX * 3)) Then

    '  Set the next event
    Event = "INTROTEXT3"

    '  Set the timer interval to pause the display
    Timer.interval = 5000

    '  Call the Plast routine to print the final larger
    '  "Introducing..." text
    PLast

End If

End Sub
```

continued on next page

continued from previous page

```
Public Sub IntroThirdTimer()

'   Execute this code the second time this
'   function is called
N = N + 1

If N = 2 Then

'   Calculate the center of the text
x = (IntroPic.ScaleWidth - IntroPic.TextWidth("MATH TUTOR")) / 2 - 235
y = (IntroPic.ScaleHeight - IntroPic.TextHeight("MATH TUTOR")) / 2 - 50

'   Refresh the picture
IntroPic.Refresh

'   Set up the initial font structure.  We will
'   use a height of 30 and a width of 10.  The
'   weight will be medium (non-bold), and will
'   use Arial.
CFONT.lfHeight = 70
CFONT.lfWidth = 40
CFONT.lfEscapement = 0
CFONT.lfWeight = 700
CFONT.lfItalic = Chr$(0)
CFONT.lfUnderline = Chr$(0)
CFONT.lfStrikeOut = Chr$(0)
CFONT.lfOutPrecision = Chr$(0)
CFONT.lfClipPrecision = Chr$(0)
CFONT.lfQuality = Chr$(0)
CFONT.lfPitchAndFamily = Chr$(0)
CFONT.lfCharSet = Chr$(0)
CFONT.lfFaceName = "Arial" + Chr$(0)

'   Display the MATH TUTOR text
FontOut "MATH TUTOR", IntroPic, x, y, CFONT

End If

'   The third time this routine is called then the
'   text display is finished
If N = 3 Then
    Event = "IntroTextDone"
End If

End Sub
```

71. Create a new class and save it as SPRITE2.CLS. This Sprite class is very similar to that found in How-Tos 5.4, 5.5, and 5.6. The differences are discussed in the How It Works section at the end of this How-To.

```
'   BitBlt will be our primary function to handle
'   the sprite animation
Private Declare Function BitBlt Lib "GDI" (ByVal hDestDC As Integer, ByVal x ↵
```

```
As Integer, ByVal y As Integer, ByVal nWidth As Integer, ByVal nHeight As ↵
Integer, ByVal hSrcDC As Integer, ByVal XSrc As Integer, ByVal YSrc As ↵
Integer, ByVal dwRop As Long) As Integer

'  We will use the transparent bitmap techniques
'  developed in chapter4
Const SRCAND = &H8800C6
Const SRCINVERT = &H660046
Const SRCCOPY = &HCC0020


'  Mstep will be used to calculate the amount of
'  movement for each sprite movement
Dim Mstep As Integer

'  These are the global members of the class
Dim m_mask1pict As Object
Dim m_background As Object
Dim m_dispback As Object
Dim m_transf1pict As Object
Dim m_primarypict As Object


'  This is the first mask
Public Property Set mask1pict(acontrol As Object)
    Set m_mask1pict = acontrol
End Property


'  This is the displayed background
Public Property Set background(acontrol As Object)
    Set m_background = acontrol
End Property


'   This is the background to be displayed
Public Property Set dispback(acontrol As Object)
    Set m_dispback = acontrol
End Property


'  This will be the working picture for building
'  the movement of the sprite.
Public Property Set transf1pict(acontrol As Object)
    Set m_transf1pict = acontrol
End Property


'  This will hold the mask which converts the
'  background around the sprite to black
Public Property Set primarypict(acontrol As Object)
    Set m_primarypict = acontrol
End Property


Public Sub collide(x, y, x1, y1, width, height, Mstep, Coll)

'  Remember that the actual displayed
'  width includes a border around the
'  masks that is the size of the Mstep
'  variables
width = width + Mstep
```

continued on next page

CHAPTER 8

continued from previous page

```
height = height + Mstep

'  Set Coll to False to begin with
Coll = "False"

'  Set m_x1 and M_y1
M_x1 = x
M_y1 = y

'  Get the points for the upper right
'  corner of the sprite
M_x2 = x + m_mask1pict.ScaleWidth + Mstep * 2
M_y2 = y

'  Get the points for the lower right
'  corner of the sprite
m_x3 = x
m_y3 = y + m_mask1pict.ScaleHeight + Mstep * 2

'  Get the bottom right corner of the sprite
m_x4 = x + m_mask1pict.ScaleWidth + Mstep * 2
m_y4 = y + m_mask1pict.ScaleHeight + Mstep * 2

'  Get the upper right corner point of
'  the passed in box
X2 = x1 + width
Y2 = y1

'  Get the lower left point of the
'  passed in box
x3 = x1
y3 = y1 + height

'  Get the lower right corner of
'  the point
x4 = x1 + width
y4 = y1 + height

'  Get the Mid point of the top
'  box line
Topx = (x1 + X2) / 2
TopY = y1

'  Get the mid point of the right
'  box line
Rightx = X2
RightY = (Y2 + y4) / 2

'  Get the mid point of the left
'  box line
Leftx = x1
LeftY = (y1 + y3) / 2

'  Get the mid point of the bottom
'  box line
```

```
Bottomx = (x3 + x4) / 2
BottomY = y3

'  The following four statements check to see if the points of
'  passed in box fall within the sprite boundaries
If (x1 >= M_x1) And (x1 <= m_x4) And (y1 <= m_y4) And (y1 >= M_y1) Then Coll ↵
= "True":  Exit Sub

If (X2 >= M_x1) And (X2 <= m_x4) And (Y2 <= m_y4) And (Y2 >= M_y1) Then Coll ↵
= "True": Exit Sub

If (x3 >= M_x1) And (x3 <= m_x4) And (y3 <= m_y4) And (y3 >= M_y1) Then Coll ↵
= "True": Exit Sub

If (x4 >= M_x1) And (x4 <= m_x4) And (y4 <= m_y4) And (y4 >= M_y1) Then Coll ↵
= "True": Exit Sub

'  Also it is important to check and see if the edges of the passed in box
'  have crossed into the sprite.
If (Topx >= M_x1) And (Topx <= M_x2) And (TopY <= m_y3) And (TopY >= M_y1) ↵
Then Coll = "True": Exit Sub

If (Rightx >= M_x1) And (Rightx <= M_x2) And (RightY <= m_y3) And (RightY >= ↵
 M_y1) Then Coll = "True": Exit Sub

If (Bottomx >= M_x1) And (Bottomx <= M_x2) And (BottomY <= m_y3) And (BottomY ↵
>= M_y1) Then Coll = "True": Exit Sub

If (Leftx >= M_x1) And (Leftx <= M_x2) And (LeftY <= m_y3) And (LeftY >= ↵
M_y1) Then Coll = "True": Exit Sub

End Sub

Public Sub MoveImage(x, y, Mstep)

'  First copy the background from the backup
'  of the background.  The copy is made from where
'  the sprite is to be placed minus the move of
'  the sprite.
throw% = BitBlt(m_transf1pict.hDC, 0, 0, m_transf1pict.ScaleWidth + (Mstep * ↵
2), m_transf1pict.ScaleHeight + (Mstep * 2), m_dispback.hDC, x - Mstep, y - ↵
Mstep, SRCCOPY)

'  Build the sprite on the new section of the background  Using
'  the transparent techniques developed in How-To 4.8
throw% = BitBlt(m_transf1pict.hDC, Mstep, Mstep, m_mask1pict.ScaleWidth, ↵
m_mask1pict.ScaleHeight, m_mask1pict.hDC, 0, 0, SRCAND)

throw% = BitBlt(m_transf1pict.hDC, Mstep, Mstep, m_primarypict.ScaleWidth, ↵
m_primarypict.ScaleHeight, m_primarypict.hDC, 0, 0, SRCINVERT)

'  Copy the new image to the displayed background.  Note that
'  the image is placed where the previous sprite was
'  located.  This will cover the old sprite with background.
throw% = BitBlt(m_background.hDC, x - Mstep, y - Mstep, ↵
```

continued on next page

continued from previous page

```
    m_transf1pict.ScaleWidth, m_transf1pict.ScaleHeight, m_transf1pict.hDC, ↵
    0, 0, SRCCOPY)

End Sub

Public Sub setup()

'   Make sure that our picture that will hold
'   the background is the same size as the
'   background.
m_dispback.width = m_background.width
m_dispback.height = m_background.height

m_mask1pict.width = m_mask1pict.width
m_mask1pict.height = m_mask1pict.height

m_primarypict.width = m_mask1pict.width
m_primarypict.height = m_mask1pict.height

'   The picture used for building the movements
'   of the sprite needs to be large enough to hold
'   the additional background to cover the previous
'   location of the sprite.
m_transf1pict.width = m_mask1pict.width * 1.3
m_transf1pict.height = m_mask1pict.height * 1.5

'   The following statements ensure that
'   all of the images are operating with
'   a pixel scalemode
m_primarypict.ScaleMode = 3
m_mask1pict.ScaleMode = 3
m_transf1pict.ScaleMode = 3
m_dispback.ScaleMode = 3
m_background.ScaleMode = 3

'   All but the displayed background needs
'   to be set to autoredraw so the bit manipulations
'   can be done while the images are not visible.
m_primarypict.AutoRedraw = True
m_mask1pict.AutoRedraw = True
m_transf1pict.AutoRedraw = True
m_dispback.AutoRedraw = True

'   Transfer background to the dispback
'   picture which will hold a copy of it
throw% = BitBlt(m_dispback.hDC, 0, 0, m_background.ScaleWidth, ↵
m_background.ScaleHeight, m_background.hDC, 0, 0, SRCCOPY)

End Sub

Public Sub update(x, y, Mstep)
'   Note that x and y were not updated
'   and should be in the same position as the
'   last sprite move
```

```
'   First copy the background from the displayed
'   background to the transf1 picture.  This will
'   ensure that any new sprites around this sprite will
'   be transferred in.
throw% = BitBlt(m_transf1pict.hDC, 0, 0, m_transf1pict.ScaleWidth + (Mstep * ↵
2), m_transf1pict.ScaleHeight + (Mstep * 2), m_background.hDC, x - Mstep, y - ↵
Mstep, SRCCOPY)

'   Build the sprite on the new section of the background using
'   the transparent techniques developed in How-To 4.8
throw% = BitBlt(m_transf1pict.hDC, Mstep, Mstep, m_mask1pict.ScaleWidth, ↵
m_mask1pict.ScaleHeight, m_mask1pict.hDC, 0, 0, SRCAND)

throw% = BitBlt(m_transf1pict.hDC, Mstep, Mstep, m_primarypict.ScaleWidth, ↵
m_primarypict.ScaleHeight, m_primarypict.hDC, 0, 0, SRCINVERT)

'   Copy the new image to the displayed background.  Note that
'   the image is placed where the previous sprite was
'   located.  This will cover the old sprite with background.
throw% = BitBlt(m_background.hDC, x - Mstep, y - Mstep,
m_transf1pict.ScaleWidth, m_transf1pict.ScaleHeight, m_transf1pict.hDC, 0, 0, ↵
SRCCOPY)

End Sub
```

How It Works

The game is divided into seven sections. Table 8-8-9 is a breakdown of each section. Several specific programming points of the various sections will be singled out for a closer look.

Table 8-8-9 The Math Tutor sections explanation

SECTION	DESCRIPTION
Introduction	This section pulls on the techniques developed in How-To 2.7 and the code in the Introtxt module. A similar implementation of animated text can be found in How-To 8.3.
About	This section utilizes the Scroll class developed in How-To 8.1.
Exercise 1	How-To 3.12 is used for this exercise. The Done event of the MCI control is used to determine when a multimedia file has finished playing.
Exercise 2	This exercise implements an interactive game where math equations are built in real time. The hot spot methods from How-To 4.3 are used to implement the interactive clicking on the picture.

continued on next page

continued from previous page

SECTION	DESCRIPTION
Exercise 3	In this exercise, the calculator from How-To 4.3 is redefined to build a simple calculator. When the buttons of the calculators are selected, the appropriate Wave file is played. The WaveTools class developed in Chapter 7 is used to play the Wave files.
Exercise 4	The sprite tools developed in Chapter 5 are slightly modified to build this exercise. Three sprites are being controlled; two by the timer control and one by the user. Various collisions and manipulations are performed to make this exercise successful.
Final	This simple form shows the user's final score.

As Table 8-8-9 reveals, most of this example pulls from other How-Tos in this book. A few specific programming points need to be elaborated on.

In Exercise 3, the WaveTools class is used for playing the Wave files. It is important to note that the flexibility of the low-level Wave methods the class uses helps enhance this exercise. The speedy response of the Wave file after the button is clicked is a plus over the interpretation that the MCI command string interface forces on the system.

Also in Exercise 3, the logic for a basic calculator is implemented. The basic functions work the same as those in the calculator that comes with Windows. A running total of the operations is kept, as opposed to calculators that store the equation and then solve the equation based on the standard order of operations. Each time a math operation button is selected, the previous math operation is performed. For example, if the running total is 80 and the last operator entered is +, when the new number is entered (say 20) and the multiplication button is selected, then the 80 + 20 operation is made for a total of 100. This process continues with each operation button selected.

The Sprite class implemented in Exercise 4 is similar to the Sprite classes developed in Chapter 5. There are three primary differences:

1. Instead of the transparent graphic implementation of the two masks from How-To 4.9, the simpler method of How-To 4.8 is used. By doing this, one step is reduced in setting up the sprites and less overhead resources are used in the program.

2. The Collide routine has been updated to make it easier to draw an imaginary box with the coordinates passed in. The origin coordinates and the width and height of the object to check for a collision with are passed into the function. This makes it easy to draw imaginary boxes for the sprite to run into, as when

checking to see if the sprite has collided with the right side of the background picture. The coordinates of the right side of the background picture are passed into the Collide function.

3. An Update function has been added that redraws the transparent bitmap in its present position directly on the displayed background. The Move function could be used, but, it would first copy an original copy of the background to the sprite's last position. This is not needed when the sprite has not moved. The Update function is useful for making sure all sprites are visible when they have collided.

Each of the Sprite classes is useful depending on the type of sprites you will be implementing, and the same basic techniques for setting up and moving the sprites can be found in all of the classes.

Comments

This example program demonstrates only a few ways in which math tutorials could be implemented. The developer's imagination is the limit as to what can be accomplished given the tools and techniques developed in this book.

The Annotated MCI Command String Reference

The MCI command string interface provides an easy English-like interface for controlling multimedia devices. These devices include MIDI sequencers, wave audio, digital video (AVI), and compact disc (CD). The following breaks down the MCI functions and commands.

MCI Functions

Name
mciExecute

Declaration

```
Declare Function mciExecute Lib "mmsystem" (ByVal lpstrCommand As String) As Integer
```

Description

mciExecute is very similar to mciSendString. The primary difference is the return value from the function. If the command is carried out correctly, then the return value is true; otherwise it is false.

Name

mciSendString

Declaration

```
Declare Function mciSendString Lib "mmsystem" (ByVal lpstrCommand As String, ByVal
lpstrReturnString As String, ByVal uReturnLength As Integer, ByVal hWndCallback As
Integer) As Long
```

Description

mciSendString provides for full access to the MCI command string interface. As with mciExecute, you can provide commands to the system. But it provides a method for returning either the requested information or the status of the last message. This is done with the lpstrReturnString parameter of the function. Depending on the command sent to the system, this parameter is set appropriately. For example, if the <Status Track Length 1> command is sent to the system, the lpstrReturnString parameter contains the length of the first track of the device. The return value from the function can be interpreted by the mciGetErrorString function. The third parameter specifies the length of the lpstrBuffer buffer (string).

Name

mciGetErrorString

Declaration

```
Declare Function mciGetErrorString Lib "mmsystem" (ByVal wError As Long, ByVal
lpstrBuffer As String, ByVal uLength As Integer) As Integer
```

Description

The first parameter of the function is the value returned from the mciSendString function. The interpretation of the error is returned in the lpstrBuffer parameter. The third parameter specifies the length of the lpstrBuffer buffer (string).

MCI Devices

A number of devices can be accessed by the MCI command string interface. The following is a table of the most common ones.

TYPE OF DEVICES	DESCRIPTION
WaveAudio	Plays wave (.WAV) audio
Sequencer	MIDI device that plays MIDI (.MID) files
DigitalVideo	Plays Video for Windows (.AVI)
CDAudio	Plays compact discs
Animation	Plays animation files
Video Disc	Controls the play of a video disc
VCR	Controls the play of a VCR

System Commands

break

Command
break <argument>

Description
Sets a break key for an MCI device.

<argument>
Specifies a key to abort a Wait command. One of the following items modifies break.

on <virtual key>
Specifies the Windows virtual key that breaks the Windows playing of the device and returns control to the application.

off
Disables the current break key.

sound

Command
sound

Description
Plays sounds from the [sounds] section of the WIN.INI file.

sysinfo

Command
sysinfo <argument>

Description

Returns information about MCI devices.

<argument>

Specifies that the following information will be returned.

quantity

Returns the number of MCI devices listed in the SYSTEM.INI file of the type specified in the device name field. The device name must be a standard MCI device type. Any digits after the name are ignored. The special device name returns the total number of MCI devices in the system.

quantity open

Returns the number of open MCI devices of the type specified in the device name field. The device name must be a standard MCI device type. Any digits after the name are ignored. The name returns the total number of MCI devices in the system that are open.

Required Commands

capability

Command

capability <argument>

Description

Obtains the capabilities of a device.

<argument>

Requests information about a particular capability of a device.

can eject

Returns true if the device can eject the media.

can play

Returns true if the device can play.

can record

Returns true if the device supports recording.

can save

Returns true if the device can save data.

compound device

Returns true if the device requires an element (file) name.

device type

Returns the device type of the device.

has audio
Returns true if the device supports audio playback.

has video
Returns true if the device supports video.

uses files
Returns true if the element of a compound device is a path and file name.

close

Command
close

Description
Closes the device. For a compound device, the file is closed. For a simple device, the device is closed.

info

Command
info <argument>

Description
Obtains textual information from a device.

<argument>
Requests the specified information.

product
Returns a null-terminated string with the product name.

open

Command
open <argument>

Description
Initializes the device.

<argument>
Opens the device as specified.

alias   <device alias>
Specifies an alternate name for the given device. If specified, it must be used for later references to the device.

shareable
Initializes the device or element as shareable. Later attempts to open the device will fail unless the device is set as shareable.

type   <device type>
Specifies the device type of a device element.

status

Command
status <argument>

Description
Obtains status information from the device.

<argument>
Checks the specified status.

mode
Returns the mode of the device. These include not ready, paused, playing, and stopped.

ready
Returns true if the device is ready.

Animation

capability

Command
capability <argument>

Description
Requests information about the capabilities of the graphics driver.

<argument>
Specifies the capability to be checked.

can eject
Returns true if the device can eject the media.

can play
Returns true if the device can play.

can record
Returns false, because animation devices cannot record.

can reverse
Returns true if the animation device can play the animation in reverse.

can save
Returns false, because animation devices cannot save.

can stretch
Returns true if the device can stretch frames to fill a given display rectangle.

compound device
Returns true if the device requires a file name.

device type
Returns animation.

fast play rate
Returns the fast play rate in frames per second.

has audio
Returns true if the device supports audio playback.

has video
Returns true if the animation devices are video output.

normal play rate
Returns normal play rate in frames per second.

slow play rate
Returns the slow play rate in frames per second.

uses files
Returns true if the element of a compound device is a path and file name.

uses palettes
Returns true if the device uses palettes.

windows
Returns the number of windows the device can support.

close

Command
close

Description
Closes a device element (file) and any associated resources.

info

Command
info <argument>

Description

Returns information on the specified item.

<argument>

Specifies the item to retrieve information on.

file

Returns the name of the file used by the animation device or movie player in a null-terminated string.

product

Returns the product name and model of the current device in a null-terminated string.

window text

Returns the caption of the window used by the device.

open

Command

open <arguments>

Description

Initializes and opens the animation device.

<arguments>

Specifies the way in which the device should be opened.

alias <device alias>

Specifies an alternate name for the animation. If specified, it must also be used in subsequent references to the animation.

nostatic

Indicates that the device should reduce the number of colors in the system palette to maximize the number of colors the animation can control.

parent <hwnd>

Specifies the window handle of the parent window.

shareable

Initializes the device or element as shareable. Later attempts to open the device will fail unless the device is set as shareable.

style <child, overlapped, or pop up>

child	Opens a window with a child window style.
overlapped	Opens a window with an overlapped window style.
pop up	Opens a window with a pop-up window style.

type <device type>

Specifies the device type of the device element.

pause

Command

pause

Description

Pauses the display of the animation and keeps the current position.

play

Command

play items

Description

Begins the play of the animation device.

fast

Plays the animation sequence at fast speed.

from <position>

Specifies the frame at which to start playing. If this is not included in the command, then play starts at the current position.

to <position>

Specifies the frame at which to stop playing. If this is not included in the command, then play stops at the end of the clip.

reverse

Indicates that the play direction is backwards.

scan

Plays the animation sequence as fast as possible without disabling video.

slow

Plays the animation sequence at a slow rate.

speed fps

Plays the animation sequence at the specified speed in frames per second.

put

Command

put <arguments>

Description

Defines the area of the source image and destination window used for display.

<arguments>

Specifies the display options for the animation.

destination
Sets the whole window as the destination window.

destination <at rectangle>
Specifies a rectangle for the area of the window used to display the image. The rectangle coordinates are relative to the window origin and are specified as X1, Y1, X2, and Y2, with X1 and Y1 as the top-left origin. X2 and Y2 are the width and height.

source
Selects the whole image for display in the destination window.

source <at rectangle>
Specifies a rectangle for the image area used for display. The rectangle coordinates are relative to the image origin and are specified as X1, Y1, X2, and Y2, with X1 and Y1 as the top-left origin. X2 and Y2 are the width and height.

set

Command
set <arguments>

Description
Sets the various options for the play of the animation.

<arguments>
Specifies the options to be set.

audio all off
Disables audio output.

audio all on
Enables audio output.

audio left off
Disables output to the left audio channel.

audio left on
Enables output to the left audio channel.

audio right off
Disables output to the right audio channel.

audio right on
Enables output to the right audio channel.

time format frames
Sets the time format to frames. When the device is first opened, frames is the default.

time format milliseconds
Sets the time format to milliseconds.

video off
Disables video output.

video on
Enables video output.

status

Command
status <argument>

Description
Obtains status information for the device.

<argument>
Specifies the item to be checked.

current track
Returns the current track.

forward
Returns true if the play direction is forward or not playing.

length
Returns the total length of the animation in the present time format (milliseconds or frames).

length track <track number>
Returns the length of the specified track in the present time format.

media present
Returns true if the media is inserted in the device; otherwise returns false.

mode
Returns not ready, paused, playing, seeking, or stopped.

number of tracks
Returns the number of tracks for the animation.

palette handle
Returns the handle of the palette used for the animation in the LowOrder word of the return value.

position
Returns the current position in the animation.

position track <number>
Returns the starting position of the specified track.

ready
Returns true if the device is ready.

speed
Returns the current speed.

start position
Returns the starting position of the animation.

time format
Returns the present time format.

window handle
Returns the handle of the window used for the animation in the LowOrder word of the return value.

step

Command
step <arguments>

Description
Steps the play one or more frames forward or backward.

<arguments>
Specifies the type of step to be performed.

by <frames>
Indicates the number of frames to step.

reverse
Indicates the steps should be done in reverse.

stop

Command
stop

Description
Stops the play of the device.

update

Command
update <arguments>

Description
Updates the display of the current frame.

<arguments>
Specifies how the update is to be performed.

at rectangle
Specifies the clipping rectangle for the animation. X1, Y1, X2, and Y2 are the coordinates, with X1 and Y1 as the origin. X2 and Y2 are the width and height.

hdc <hdc>
Specifies the handle of the display context to paint.

where

Command
where

Description
Obtains the rectangle specifying the source or destination area.

destination
Requests the destination offset and extent.

source
Requests the source offset and extent.

window

Command
window

Description
Specifies the windows that the animation should be played in.

handle <hWnd>
Specifies the window handle that the animation should be played in.

handle default
Specifies that the animation device should handle displaying the animation in its own window.

state hide
Hides the playing window

state iconic
Indicates that the animation window should be iconisized.

state maximize
Maximizes the display window.

state minimized
Indicates that the animation window should be minimized.

state no action
Displays the window in its static state.

state no activate
Restores the window to its last dimensions.

state normal
Restores the window to its initialization state.

state show
Shows the display window.

text <title text>
Indicates the text for the title bar of the animation window.

CD Audio

capability

Command
capability <arguments>

Description
Requests information about the capabilities of the CD audio device.

<arguments>
Specifies the capability to be checked.

can eject
Returns true if the CD audio device can eject the disk.

can play
Returns true if the CD audio device can play the disk.

can record
Returns false, because CD audio devices cannot record.

can save
Returns false, because CD audio devices cannot save data.

compound device
Returns false, because CD audio devices are simple devices.

device type
Returns cdaudio.

has audio
Returns true, because CD audio devices can store and play sound.

has video
Returns false, because CD audio devices do not support video play.

uses files

Returns false, because simple devices do not use files.

close

Command

close

Description

Closes the device.

info

Command

info <arguments>

Description

Requests information on the specified item.

<arguments>

Specifies the item to retrieve information on.

product

Returns the product name and model of the current audio device.

open

Command

open <arguments>

Description

Opens the CD audio device for play.

<arguments>

Specifies how the device should be opened.

alias <device alias>

Specifies an alternate name for the CD device. This name must be used in subsequent calls.

shareable

Initializes the device or element as shareable. Later attempts to open the device will fail unless the device is set as shareable.

pause

Command

pause

Description

Pauses playing.

play

Command

play <arguments>

Description

Starts playing audio. The following optional items modify play.

<arguments>

Specifies the starting and ending position of the play.

from <position>

Specifies the starting position to begin play. If this is not specified, then the current position is used.

to <position>

Specifies the ending position to end play. If this is not specified, then the stop is the end of the disk.

resume

Command

resume

Description

Resumes playing of a paused device.

seek

Command

seek <arguments>

Description

Seeks to the specified position.

<arguments>

Specifies the position to seek to.

to <position>

Specifies the position to seek to.

to <start>

Specifies the starting position of the disc.

to end

Specifies seek to the end of the audio data on the disc.

status

Command

status <arguments>

Description

Obtains the specified information about the device.

<arguments>

Specifies the item to be checked.

current track

Returns the current track.

length

Returns the total length of the disc.

length track <track number>

Returns the length of the track specified.

media present

Returns true if the disc is inserted in the drive.

mode

Returns not ready, open, paused, playing, seeking, or stopped for the current mode of the device.

number of tracks

Returns the number of tracks on the disc.

position

Returns the current position.

position track <track no>

Returns the starting position of the track specified.

ready

Returns True if the device is ready.

start position

Returns the starting position of the disc.

time format
Returns the present time format.

stop

Command
stop

Description
Stops playing.

MIDI Sequencer

capability

Command
capability <arguments>

Description
Requests information about the capabilities of the MIDI sequencer.

<arguments>
Specifies the item to be checked.

can eject
Returns false, because MIDI devices cannot eject.

can play
Returns true.

can record
Returns true if the sequencer can record.

can save
Returns true if the sequencer can save.

compound device
Returns true, because sequencers are compound devices (support files).

device type
Returns sequencer.

has audio
Returns true, because MIDI devices support playback.

has video
Returns false, because MIDI devices do not support video.

uses files

Returns true, because MIDI devices use files to play data.

close

Command

close

Description

Closes the MIDI device and any files associated with it.

info

Command

info <arguments>

Description

Retrieves the specified information.

<arguments>

Specifies the item to retrieve information on.

product

Returns the product name of the sequencer.

open

Command

open <arguments>

Description

Opens the device.

<arguments>

Specifies how the device should be opened.

alias   <device alias>

Specifies an alternate name for the MIDI device. This name must be used in subsequent calls.

shareable

Initializes the device or element as shareable. Later attempts to open the device will fail unless the device is set as shareable.

type   <device type>

Specifies the device type of the device element.

pause

Command
pause

Description
Pauses playing.

play

Command
play <arguments>

Description
Starts playing the sequencer.

<arguments>
Specifies the starting and ending points of the play.

from   <position>
Specifies the position to start playing from. If this is not part of the command, the starting point is the current position.

to   <position>
Specifies the position to stop playing. If this is not part of the command, then playing stops at the end of the data.

record

Command
record <arguments>

Description
Starts the MIDI recording.

<arguments>
Specifies the position and mode of the recording.

insert
Specifies that new data is added to the device element (file).

from   <position>
Specifies the position to start recording.

to   <position>
Specifies the position to stop recording.

overwrite
Specifies that new data will replace data in the device element.

resume

Command

resume

Description

Resumes playing or recording from the current position.

set

Command

set <arguments>

Description

Sets various items to control the playing of the MIDI data.

<arguments>

Specifies the items to be set.

audio all off

Turns off audio.

audio all on

Turns on audio.

audio left off

Disables left channel output.

audio left on

Enables left channel output.

audio right off

Disables right channel output.

audio right on

Enables right channel output.

port   <port number>

Indicates the MIDI port that should receive the MIDI data (messages).

port mapper

Sets the MIDI mapper as the port for the MIDI data (messages).

port none

Closes the MIDI port and stops sending MIDI messages.

time format milliseconds

Sets the time format to milliseconds.

save

Command

save <arguments>

Description

Saves the MIDI data to the specified item.

<arguments>

Specifies the file name.

filename

Specifies the destination path and file.

seek

Command

seek <arguments>

Description

Moves to the specified position in the MIDI data.

<arguments>

Specifies the position to seek to.

to <position>

Specifies the final position for the seek.

to start

Specifies to seek to the start of the sequence.

to end

Specifies to seek to the end of the sequence.

status

Command

seek <arguments>

Description

Obtains the specified information about the device.

<arguments>

Specifies the item to be checked.

current track

Returns the current track number.

division type

Returns one of the following file division types: PPQN, SMPTE 24 frame, SMPTE 25 frame, SMPTE 30 drop frame, or SMPTE 30 frame. Use this information to determine the format of the MIDI file and the meaning of tempo and position.

length

Returns the length of a sequence in the current time format.

length track <track number>

Returns the length of the track in the current time format.

media present

Returns true.

mode

Returns not ready, paused, playing, seeking, or stopped.

number of tracks

Returns the number of tracks.

offset

Returns the offset of a SMPTE-based file. The offset is the start time of a SMPTE-based sequence. The time is returned as hh:mm:ss:ff.

port

Returns the MIDI port number assigned to the sequence.

position

Returns the current position in the current time format.

position track <track number>

Returns the position of the specified track.

ready

Returns true if the device is ready.

start position
Returns the starting position of the media or device element.

tempo
Returns the current tempo of a sequence in the current time format.

time format
Returns the time format.

stop

Command
stop

Description
Stops play of the MIDI device.

Waveform Audio

capability

Commands
capability <arguments>

Description
Requests capability information about the specified item.

<arguments>
Specifies the capability to be checked.

can eject
Returns false, because wave audio devices have no media that can be ejected.

can play
Returns true if the device can play.

can record
Returns true if the device can record.

can save
Returns true if the Wave device can save data.

compound device
Returns true, because Wave devices are compound devices.

device type
Returns waveaudio.

has audio
Returns true.

has video
Returns false, because Wave devices do not support video.

inputs
Returns the total number of input devices.

outputs
Returns the total number of output devices.

uses files
Returns true, because Wave devices use files for operation.

close

Command
close

Description
Closes the audio device and any files associated with it.

cue

Command
cue <arguments>

Description
Prepares for playing or recording. The command does not have to be used but can help to increase the reaction time to a play or record request.

<arguments>
Specifies the type of request to be cued for.

input
Prepares for recording.

output
Prepares for playing (default).

delete

Command
delete <arguments>

Description
Deletes a section of the Wave data.

<arguments>

Specifies the beginning and end of the section to be deleted.

from <position>

Specifies the position to start deleting data. If not specified, the current position is used.

to <position>

Specifies the position to stop deleting data. If not specified, the end of the file is used.

info

Command

info <arguments>

Description

Retrieves the information on the specified item.

<arguments>

Specifies the item to retrieve the information about.

input

Returns the description of the current wave form audio input device. The default driver returns wave audio input and output device.

file

Returns the current file name.

output

Returns the description of the current wave form audio output device. The standard driver returns wave audio input and output device.

product

Returns the description of the current wave form audio output device. The default driver returns wave audio input and output device.

open

Command

open <arguments>

Description

Opens the device for play.

<arguments>

Specifies the way in which the device will be opened.

alias <device alias>
Specifies an alternate name for the wave device. This name must be used in subsequent calls.

buffer <buffer size>
Sets the size of the wave audio device buffer in seconds. The default is 4.

shareable
Initializes the device or element as shareable. Later attempts to open the device will fail unless the device is set as shareable.

type <device type>
Specifies the device type of a device element.

pause

Command
pause

Description
Pauses playing or recording.

play

Command
play <arguments>

Description
Starts the play of the audio data.

<arguments>
Specifies the starting and ending position of the play.

from <position>
Specifies the position to start playing. If not set in the command, the current position in the Wave data is used.

to <position>
Specifies the position to stop playing. If not set in the command, the end of the Wave data is used.

record

Command
record <arguments>

Description
Begins the recording of the Wave data.

\<arguments>
Specifies the type and position of the recording.

insert
Specifies that new data is added to the device element.

from   \<position>
Specifies the position to start recording. If not part of the command, the current position is used.

to   \<position>
Specifies the position to stop recording. If not part of the command, then recording continues until a pause or stop is issued to the system.

resume

Command
resume

Description
Resumes playing or recording of the device.

save

Command
save \<arguments>

Description
Saves the data to the file.

\<arguments>
Specifies the file name for the data to be written to.

filename
Specifies the path and file name used to save data.

seek

Command
seek \<arguments>

Description
Moves to the specified location in the Wave data.

\<arguments>
Specifies the position to seek to.

to <position>
Specifies the position to seek to.

to <start>
Specifies to seek to the start of the beginning of the file.

to <end>
Specifies to seek to the end of the file.

status

Command
status <arguments>

Description
Obtains information about the specified items.

<arguments>
Specifies the item for the status to be checked.

alignment
Returns the block alignment of data in bytes.

bitspersample
Returns the bits per sample.

bytespersec
Returns the average number of bytes per second played or recorded.

channels
Returns the number of channels. 1 is mono and 2 is stereo.

current track
Returns the index for the current track (1 for the default device).

format tag
Returns the format for playing and recording.

input
Returns the input set.

length
Returns the total length of the Wave file.

length track <track number>
Returns the length of the specified track.

level
Returns the current audio sample value.

media present
Returns true.

mode
Returns not ready, paused, playing, stopped, recording, or seeking.

number of tracks
Returns the number of tracks (1 for the default device).

position
Returns the current position.

ready
Returns true if the device is ready.

samplespersec
Returns the number of samples per second played or recorded.

time format
Returns the current time format.

stop

Command
stop

Description
Stops playing or recording.

Digital Video

capability

Command
capability <argument>

Description
Requests information about the capabilities of the graphics driver.

<argument>
Specifies the capability to check.

can eject
Returns false, because digital video has no media to eject.

can freeze
Returns false, because digital video cannot be frozen.

can lock
Returns true if digital video can lock.

can play
Returns true if the device can play.

can record
Returns false, because digital video devices cannot record.

can save
Returns false.

can stretch
Returns true if the device can stretch frames to fill the display.

compound device
Returns true, because digital video uses files.

device type
Returns digitalvideo.

has audio
Returns true if the device supports audio playback.

has video
Returns true.

uses files
Returns true.

uses palettes
Returns true, because digital video uses palettes.

close

Command
close

Description
Closes a device element (file) and any associated resources.

info

Command
info <argument>

Description
Returns information on the specified item.

<argument>
Specifies the item to retrieve information on.

file
Returns the name of the file used by the device.

product
Returns Video for Windows.

window text
Returns the text in the window of the digital video device.

open

Command
open <arguments>

Description
Initializes and opens the animation device.

<arguments>
Specifies the way in which the device should be opened.

alias   <device alias>
Specifies an alternate name for the digital video device. This name must be used in subsequent calls.

parent   <hwnd>
Specifies the window handle of the parent window.

shareable
Initializes the device or element as shareable. Later attempts to open the device will fail unless the device is set as shareable.

style <child, overlapped, or pop up>
child	Opens a window with a child window style.
overlapped	Opens a window with an overlapped window style.
pop up	Opens a window with a pop-up window style.

type   <device type>
Specifies the device type of the device element.

pause

Command
pause

Description
Pauses the display of the animation and keeps the current position.

play

Command

play items

Description

Begins the play of the animation device.

from <position>

Specifies the frame at which to start playing. If this is not a part of the command, the current position is used.

to <position>

Specifies the frame at which to stop playing. If this is not specified, then the play continues to the end of the data.

fullscreen

Tells the system to display the full video screen.

put

Command

put <arguments>

Description

Defines the area of the source image and destination window used for display.

<arguments>

Specifies the display options for the animation.

destination

Sets the whole window as the destination window.

destination at rectangle

Specifies a rectangle for the area of the window used to display the image. The rectangle coordinates are relative to the window origin and are specified as X1, Y1, X2, and Y2. The coordinates X1 and Y1 specify the top-left corner. The coordinates X2 and Y2 specify the width and height of the rectangle. If the device supports stretching, the video will be stretched to fit the display.

source

Selects the whole image for display in the destination window.

source at rectangle

Specifies a rectangle for the image area used for display. The rectangle coordinates are relative to the image origin and are specified as X1, Y1, X2, and Y2. The coordinates X1 and Y1 specify the top-left origin. The coordinates X2 and Y2 specify the width and height of the rectangle.

status

Command

status <argument>

Description

Obtains status information for the device.

<argument>

Specifies the item to be checked.

audio

Returns on if either speaker is enabled and off if a speaker is disabled.

forward

Returns true if the play direction is forward.

length

Returns the length of the clip.

media present

Returns true if the video file is loaded.

mode

Returns not ready, paused, playing, seeking, or stopped for the current mode.

position

Returns the current position.

ready

Returns true if the device is ready.

seek exactly

Returns on or off to indicate whether or not seek is exactly set.

speed

Returns the current playback speed.

start position

Returns the starting position of the video file.

time format

Returns the current time format.

window handle

Returns the handle of the window for the video display.

window visible

Returns true if the window is not hidden.

window maximized

Returns true if the window is maximized.

window minimized
Returns true if the window is minimized.

step

Command
step <arguments>

Description
Step the play one or more frames forward or reverse.

<arguments>
Specifies the type of step to be performed.

by <frames>
Indicates the number of frames to step.

reverse
Steps the frames in reverse.

stop

Command
stop

Description
Stops the play of the device.

update

Command
update <arguments>

Description
Updates the display of the current frame.

<arguments>
Specifies how the update is to be performed.

at rectangle
Specifies the clipping rectangle relative to the display rectangle. X1 and Y1 are the top-left origin coordinates. X2 and Y2 are the width and height.

hdc <hdc>
Specifies the handle of the display context to paint.

where

Command
where

Description
Obtains the rectangle specifying the source or destination area.

destination
Requests the destination offset and extent.

destination max
Returns the current size of the rectangle.

source
Requests the source offset and extent.

source max
Returns the maximum size of the frame buffer.

window
Returns the current size and position of the display window.

window max
Returns the size of the display.

window

Command
window

Description
Specifies the windows that the animation should be played in.

handle   <hWnd>
Specifies the window handle that the video should be played in.

handle default
Specifies that the video device should handle displaying the animation in its own window.

state hide
Hides the playing window.

state iconic
Indicates that the animation window should be iconisized.

state maximize
Maximizes the display window.

state minimized

Indicates that the animation window should be minimized.

state no action

Displays the window in its static state.

state no activate

Restores the window to its last dimensions.

state normal

Restores the window to its initialization state.

state show

Shows the display window.

text <title text>

Indicates the text for the title bar of the animation window.

B

Guide to the Windows APIs Referenced in the How-Tos

A wide range of Windows API calls are made throughout this book. This appendix gives you a quick reference guide to each API call, including the multimedia APIs and WinG. Detailed information on each function can be found in the Windows SDK Help file provided with Visual Basic 4.0.

AnimatePalette

Declaration
```
Declare Sub AnimatePalette Lib "GDI" (ByVal hPalette As Integer, ByVal wStartIndex
As Integer, ByVal wNumEntries As Integer, lpPaletteColors As PALETTEENTRY)
```

Description
Replaces entries in the specified logical palette. The new entries are automatically updated to the system palette.

BitBlt

Declaration

```
Declare Function BitBlt Lib "GDI" (ByVal hDestDC As Integer, ByVal X As Integer,
ByVal Y As Integer, ByVal nWidth As Integer, ByVal nHeight As Integer, ByVal
hSrcDC As Integer, ByVal XSrc As Integer, ByVal YSrc As Integer, ByVal dwRop As
Long) As Integer
```

Description

Transfers image data between two device contexts.

CreateCompatibleBitmap

Declaration

```
Declare Function CreateCompatibleBitmap Lib "GDI" (ByVal hDC As Integer, ByVal
nWidth As Integer, ByVal nHeight As Integer) As Integer
```

Description

Creates a bitmap that is compatible with the specified device.

CreateCompatibleDC

Declaration

```
Declare Function CreateCompatibleDC Lib "GDI" (ByVal hDC As Integer) As Integer
```

Description

Creates a memory device context that is compatible with the specified device.

CreateDIBitmap

Declaration

```
Declare Function CreateDIBitmap Lib "GDI" (ByVal hDC As Integer, lpInfoHeader As
BITMAPINFOHEADER, ByVal dwUsage As Long, ByVal lpInitBits As String, lpInitInfo As
BITMAPINFO, ByVal wUsage As Integer) As Integer
```

Description

Creates a DIB bitmap from the BITMAPINFOHEADER and BITMAPINFO structures.

CreateFontIndirect

Declaration

```
Declare Function CreateFontIndirect Lib "GDI" (lpLogFont As LOGFONT) As Integer
```

Description

Uses the LOGFONT structure to create the specified font.

CreateHatchBrush

Declaration

```
Declare Function CreateHatchBrush Lib "GDI" (ByVal nIndex As Integer, ByVal
crColor As Long) As Integer
```

Description

Creates a hatch brush specified by the nIndex parameter with the color specified by crColor.

CreatePalette

Declaration

```
Declare Function CreatePalette Lib "GDI" (lpLogPalette As LOGPALETTE) As Integer
```

Description

Creates a palette from the specified logical palette structure.

CreatePatternBrush

Declaration

```
Declare Function CreatePatternBrush Lib "GDI" (ByVal hBitmap As Integer) As Integer
```

Description

Creates a font specified by the bitmap referenced. It only uses the first 8x8 bits of the bitmap.

CreatePen

Declaration

```
Declare Function CreatePen Lib "GDI" (ByVal nPenStyle As Integer, ByVal nWidth As
Integer, ByVal crColor As Long) As Integer
```

Description

Creates the pen with the specified style, width, and color.

CreatePolygonRgn

Declaration

```
Declare Function CreatePolygonRgn Lib "GDI" (lpPoints As POINTAPI, ByVal nCount As
Integer, ByVal nPolyFillMode As Integer) As Integer
```

Description

Creates a polygonal region based on the given coordinates. The polygon is closed off automatically if the first and last points do not match.

CreateSolidBrush

Declaration
```
Declare Function CreateSolidBrush Lib "GDI" (ByVal crColor As Long) As Integer
```

Description
Creates a solid color brush with the specified color.

DeleteDC

Declaration
```
Declare Function DeleteDC Lib "GDI" (ByVal hDC As Integer) As Integer
```

Description
Deletes the specified device context.

DeleteObject

Declaration
```
Declare Function DeleteObject Lib "GDI" (ByVal hObject As Integer) As Integer
```

Description
Deletes the specified object.

GetDC

Declaration
```
Declare Function GetDC Lib "User" (ByVal hWnd As Integer) As Integer
```

Description
Retrieves the device context of an object from the handle to the object.

GlobalAlloc

Declaration
```
Declare Function GlobalAlloc Lib "Kernel" (ByVal wFlags As Integer, ByVal dwBytes As Long) As Integer
```

Description
Allocates blocks of memory using GlobalAlloc.

GlobalFree

Declaration
```
Declare Function GlobalFree Lib "Kernel" (ByVal hMem As Integer) As Integer
```

Description
Frees up allocated memory with GlobalFree.

GlobalHandleToSel

Declaration
```
Private Declare Function GlobalHandleToSel Lib "ToolHelp.DLL" (ByVal hMem As
Integer) As Integer
```

Description
Provides a Windows selector for the specified memory block.

GlobalLock

Declaration
```
Declare Function GlobalLock Lib "Kernel" (ByVal hMem As Integer) As Long
```

Description
Performs operations on memory on a memory block; it must first be locked.

GlobalUnlock

Declaration
```
Declare Function GlobalUnlock Lib "Kernel" (ByVal hMem As Integer) As Integer
```

Description
Unlocks a memory block locked with GlobalLock.

hread

Declaration
```
Private Declare Function hread Lib "Kernel" Alias "_hread" (ByVal hfile As
Integer, buffer As Any, ByVal N As Long) As Long
```

Description
Reads data from the specified file. Supports memory blocks larger than 64K.

lclose

Declaration
```
Private Declare Function lclose Lib "Kernel" Alias "_lclose" (ByVal hfile As
Integer) As Integer
```

Description
Closes the specified file.

lopen

Declaration
```
Private Declare Function lopen Lib "Kernel" Alias "_lopen" (ByVal lpPathName As
String, ByVal iReadWrite As Integer) As Integer
```

Description
Opens an existing file and sets the file pointer to the beginning of the file.

lread

Declaration
```
Private Declare Function lread Lib "Kernel" Alias "_lread" (ByVal hfile As
Integer, lpBuffer As Any, ByVal wBytes As Integer) As Integer
```

Description
Reads data from the specified file.

lstrcpy

Declaration
```
Private Declare Function lstrcpy Lib "Kernel" (dest As Any, src As Any) As Long
```

Description
Copies one string to another and returns a pointer to the new string.

mciGetErrorString

Declaration
```
Declare Function mciGetErrorString Lib "mmsystem" (ByVal wError As Long, ByVal
lpstrBuffer As String, ByVal uLength As Integer) As Integer
```

Description
Interprets the error code returned from mciSendString.

mciSendCommand

Declaration
```
Declare Function mciSendCommand Lib "mmsystem" (ByVal udeviceid As Integer, ByVal
uMessage As Integer, ByVal dwParam1 As Long, ByVal dwParam2 As Long) As Long
```

Description
Sends MCI commands to the system.

mciSendString

Declaration
```
Declare Function mciSendString Lib "mmsystem" (ByVal lpstrCommand As String, ByVal
lpstrReturnString As String, ByVal uReturnLength As Integer, ByVal hWndCallback As
Integer) As Long
```

Description
Sends MCI message strings to the system. Error codes returned from the function are interpreted by mciGetErrorString.

MemoryRead

Declaration
```
Private Declare Function MemoryRead Lib "ToolHelp.DLL" (ByVal wSel As Integer,
ByVal dwOffset As Long, lpvBuf As Any, ByVal dwcb As Long) As Long
```

Description
Reads data from memory. This memory is allocated from GlobalAlloc and should be locked with GlobalLock.

MemoryWrite

Declaration
```
Private Declare Function MemoryWrite Lib "ToolHelp.DLL" (ByVal wSel As Integer,
ByVal dwOffset As Long, lpvBuf As Any, ByVal dwcb As Long) As Long
```

Description
Writes data to memory. This memory is allocated from GlobalAlloc and should be locked with GlobalLock.

MessageBeep

Declaration
```
Declare Sub MessageBeep Lib "User" (ByVal wType As Integer)
```

Description
Plays one of the standard system messages including MB_ICONASTERISK, MB_ICONEXCLAMATION, MB_ICONHAND, MB_ICONQUESTION, and MB_OK.

midiOutClose

Declaration
```
Private Declare Function midiOutClose Lib "mmsystem.dll" (ByVal hMidiOut As
Integer) As Integer
```

Description

Closes the specified MIDI device.

midiOutGetDevCaps

Declaration

```
Declare Function midiOutGetDevCaps Lib "MMSYSTEM" (ByVal udeviceid As Integer,
lpCaps As MIDIOUTCAPS, ByVal uSize As Integer) As Integer
```

Description

Retrieves information on the specified MIDI device.

midiOutGetNumDevs

Declaration

```
Declare Function midiOutGetNumDevs Lib "MMSYSTEM" () As Integer
```

Description

Retrieves the number of installed MIDI devices.

midiOutOpen

Declaration

```
Declare Function midiOutOpen Lib "MMSYSTEM" (lphMidiOut As Integer, ByVal udevi-
ceid As Integer, ByVal dwCallback As Long, ByVal dwInstance As Long, ByVal dwFlags
As Long) As Integer
```

Description

Opens the specified MIDI device for input.

midiOutShortMsg

Declaration

```
Private Declare Function midiOutShortMsg Lib "mmsystem.dll" (ByVal hMidiOut As
Integer, ByVal MidiMessage As Long) As Integer
```

Description

Sends a short MIDI message to the system.

mmioAscend

Declaration

```
Declare Function mmioAscend Lib "mmsystem" (ByVal hmmio As Integer, lpck As MMCK-
INFO, ByVal uFlags As Integer) As Integer
```

Description

Ascends into the parent chunk of the present chunk and reads in the chunk header.

mmioClose

Declaration
```
Declare Function mmioClose Lib "mmsystem" (ByVal hmmio As Integer, ByVal uFlags As
Integer) As Integer
```

Description
Closes the open file.

mmioCreateChunk

Declaration
```
Declare Function mmioCreateChunk Lib "mmsystem" (ByVal hmmio As Integer, lpck As
MMCKINFO, ByVal uFlags As Integer) As Integer
```

Description
Creates a new RIFF chunk in the file.

mmioDescend

Declaration
```
Declare Function mmioDescend Lib "mmsystem" (ByVal hmmio As Integer, lpck As MMCK-
INFO, lpckParent As MMCKINFO, ByVal uFlags As Integer) As Integer
```

Description
Moves down one chunk from the present position.

mmioOpen

Declaration
```
Declare Function mmioOpen Lib "mmsystem" (ByVal szFileName As String, mi As
MMIOINFO, lpmmioinfo As MMIOINFO, ByVal dwOpenFlags As Long) As Integer
```

Description
Opens the specified RIFF file and reads in the header information.

mmioRead

Declaration
```
Declare Function mmioRead Lib "mmsystem" (ByVal hmmio As Integer, ByVal pch As
String, ByVal cch As Long) As Long
```

Description
Reads in the RIFF data.

mmioSeek

Declaration

```
Declare Function mmioSeek Lib "mmsystem" (ByVal hmmio As Integer, ByVal lOffset As
Long, ByVal iOrigin As Integer) As Long
```

Description

Seeks to the specified offset in the RIFF file.

mmioWrite

Declaration

```
Declare Function mmioWrite Lib "mmsystem" (ByVal hmmio As Integer, ByVal pch As
String, ByVal cch As Long) As Long
```

Description

Writes the specified data to the RIFF file.

PatBlt

Declaration

```
Declare Function PatBlt Lib "GDI" (ByVal hDC As Integer, ByVal X As Integer, ByVal
Y As Integer, ByVal nWidth As Integer, ByVal nHeight As Integer, ByVal dwRop As
Long) As Integer
```

Description

Paints the specified device context with the current brush using the specified raster
operation.

PtInRegion

Declaration

```
Declare Function PtInRegion Lib "GDI" (ByVal hRgn As Integer, ByVal X As Integer,
ByVal Y As Integer) As Integer
```

Description

Checks to see if the specified coordinates fall into the given region. Returns nonzero
if the point is in the region.

RealizePalette

Declaration

```
Private Declare Function RealizePalette Lib "User" (ByVal hDC As Integer) As
Integer
```

Description

Maps palette entries from the current logical palette to the system palette.

Rectangle

Declaration

```
Declare Function Rectangle Lib "GDI" (ByVal hDC As Integer, ByVal X1 As Integer,
ByVal Y1 As Integer, ByVal X2 As Integer, ByVal Y2 As Integer) As Integer
```

Description

Creates a rectangle on the specified device context.

ReleaseDC

Declaration

```
Declare Function ReleaseDC Lib "User" (ByVal hWnd As Integer, ByVal hDC As
Integer) As Integer
```

Description

Releases the specified device context back to the system.

SelectObject

Declaration

```
Declare Function SelectObject Lib "GDI" (ByVal hDC As Integer, ByVal hObject As
Integer) As Integer
```

Description

Selects the specified object to the specified device context.

SelectPalette

Declaration

```
Private Declare Function SelectPalette Lib "User" (ByVal hDC As Integer, ByVal
hPalette As Integer, ByVal bForceBackground As Integer) As Integer
```

Description

Selects the specified palette into the specified device context.

SetWindowWord

Declaration

```
Declare Function SetWindowWord Lib "User" (ByVal hWnd As Integer, ByVal nIndex As
Integer, ByVal wNewWord As Integer) As Integer
```

Description

Places a word value at the specified offset into the extra window memory of the given window. Is used in this book to make one window the parent of another.

sndPlaySound

Declaration

```
Declare Function sndPlaySound Lib "MMSYSTEM" (ByVal lpszSoundName As String, ByVal
uFlags As Integer) As Integer
```

Description

Plays system sound, WIN.INI sounds, and Wave files.

StretchBlt

Declaration

```
Declare Function StretchBlt% Lib "GDI" (ByVal hDC%, ByVal X%, ByVal Y%, ByVal
nWidth%, ByVal nHeight%, ByVal hSrcDC%, ByVal XSrc%, ByVal YSrc%, ByVal
nSrcWidth%, ByVal nSrcHeight%, ByVal dwRop&)
```

Description

Stretches the specified bits to fit into the specified rectangle size of the device
context.

StretchDIBits

Declaration

```
Declare Function StretchDIBits# Lib "GDI" (ByVal hDC#, ByVal X#, ByVal Y#, ByVal
dX#, ByVal dY#, ByVal SrcX#, ByVal SrcY#, ByVal wSrcWidth#, ByVal wSrcHeight#,
ByVal lpBits As String, lpBitsInfo As BITMAPINFO, ByVal wUsage#, ByVal dwRop&)
```

Description

Copies the bits of a DIB from a source rectangle to a destination rectangle and
stretches the bits as needed to fit the target rectangle.

TextOut

Declaration

```
Declare Function TextOut Lib "GDI" (ByVal hDC As Integer, ByVal X As Integer,
ByVal Y As Integer, ByVal lpString As String, ByVal nCount As Integer) As Integer
```

Description

Places text using the current font in the device context at the specified coordinates.

TransparentDIBits

Declaration

```
Private Declare Function TransparentDIBits Lib "winghelp.dll" (dstInfo As Any,
dstBuffer As Any, ByVal destx As Integer, ByVal desty As Integer, srcBuffer As
Any, srcInfo As Any, ByVal srcx As Integer, ByVal srcy As Integer, ByVal iUsage
As Integer, ByVal TransparentColor As Byte) As Boolean
```

Description

Copies bits from a WinG bitmap onto the surface of a WinG bitmap. Will do a transparent copy so that the background bits are not visible.

waveOutClose

Declaration

```
Declare Function waveOutClose Lib "MMSYSTEM" (ByVal hWaveOut As Integer) As Integer
```

Description

Closes the wave audio device.

waveOutGetDevCaps

Declaration

```
Declare Function waveOutGetDevCaps Lib "MMSYSTEM" (ByVal udeviceid As Integer, lpCaps As
WAVEOUTCAPS, uSize As Integer) As Integer
```

Description

Retrieves information about the specified wave audio device.

waveOutOpen

Declaration

```
Declare Function waveOutOpen Lib "MMSYSTEM" (lpWaveout As Integer, ByVal UINT As
Integer, lpformat As Integer, ByVal dwCallback As Long, ByVal dwInstance As Long, ByVal
flags As Long) As Integer
```

Description

Opens the wave audio device for output.

waveOutPrepareHeader

Declaration

```
Declare Function waveOutPrepareHeader Lib "MMSYSTEM" (ByVal hWaveOut As Integer, WH As
WAVEHDR, ByVal uSize As Integer) As Integer
```

Description

Prepares the wave audio device header for output.

waveOutSetVolume

Declaration

```
Declare Function waveOutSetVolume Lib "MMSYSTEM" (ByVal udeviceid As Integer, ByVal
dwVolume As Long) As Integer
```

Description

Sets the volume of the wave audio device.

waveOutUnprepareHeader

Declaration

```
Declare Function waveOutUnprepareHeader Lib "MMSYSTEM" (ByVal hWaveOut As Integer, WH As
WAVEHDR, ByVal uSize As Integer) As Integer
```

Description

Resets the header of the wave audio device. This should be called before the device is closed.

WinGBitBlt

Declaration

```
Private Declare Function WinGBitBlt Lib "wing.dll" (ByVal hdcDest As Integer, ByVal
nXOriginDest As Integer, ByVal nYOriginDest As Integer, ByVal nWidthDest As Integer,
ByVal nHeightDest As Integer, ByVal hdcSrc As Integer, ByVal nXOriginSrc As Integer,
ByVal nYOriginSrc As Integer) As Boolean
```

Description

Transfers from a WinG device context either to another device context or to a display device context.

WinGCreateBitmap

Declaration

```
Private Declare Function WinGCreateBitmap Lib "wing.dll" (ByVal WInGDC As Integer,
pBitmapInfo As Any, ppBits As Any) As Integer
```

Description

Creates a WinG bitmap from a BITMAPINFO structure.

WinGCreateDC

Declaration

```
Private Declare Function WinGCreateDC Lib "wing.dll" () As Integer
```

Description

Creates a new WinG device context.

WinGCreateHalftoneBrush

Declaration

```
Private Declare Function WinGCreateHalftoneBrush Lib "wing.dll" (ByVal Context As
Integer, ByVal crColor As Long, ByVal DitherType As Integer) As Integer
```

Description
Creates a halftone brush.

WinGCreateHalftonePalette

Declaration
```
Private Declare Function WinGCreateHalftonePalette Lib "wing.dll" () As Integer
```

Description
Creates a halftone palette for converting true color images.

WinGGetDIBColorTable

Declaration
```
Private Declare Function WinGGetDIBColorTable Lib "wing.dll" (ByVal WInGDC As Integer,
ByVal StartIndex As Integer, ByVal NumberOfEntries As Integer, pRgbQuadColors As Any) As
Integer
```

Description
Gets the color table of the WinG bitmap.

WinGGetDIBPointer

Declaration
```
Private Declare Function WinGGetDIBPointer Lib "wing.dll" (ByVal WinGBitmap As Integer,
pBitmapInfo As Any) As Long
```

Description
Gets a pointer to the WinG DIB surface.

WinGRecommendDIBFormat

Declaration
```
Private Declare Function WinGRecommendDIBFormat Lib "wing.dll" (pBitmapInfo As Any) As
Boolean
```

Description
Recommends an optimal DIB format for the WinG bitmap.

WinGSetDIBColorTable

Declaration
```
Private Declare Function WinGSetDIBColorTable Lib "wing.dll" (ByVal WInGDC As Integer,
ByVal StartIndex As Integer, ByVal NumberOfEntries As Integer, pRgbQuadColors As Any) As
Integer
```

Description

Sets the WinG color table from the bmicolors field of the BITMAPINFO structure.

WinGStretchBlt

Declaration

```
Private Declare Function WinGStretchBlt Lib "wing.dll" (ByVal hdcDest As Integer, ByVal
nXOriginDest As Integer, ByVal nYOriginDest As Integer, ByVal nWidthDest As Integer,
ByVal nHeightDest As Integer, ByVal hdcSrc As Integer, ByVal nXOriginSrc As Integer,
ByVal nYOriginSrc As Integer, ByVal nWidthSrc As Integer, ByVal nHeightSrc As Integer)
As Boolean
```

Description

Transfers from a WinG device context to either another device context or to a display
device context. It will stretch the bits to fit the specified dimensions if necessary.

Reference List of Multimedia Product Vendors

The following is a list of multimedia product vendors. These vendors provide a wide range of products, from custom controls for Visual Basic 4.0 to animation and video digitizing packages.

acuris
931 Hamilton Ave.
Menlo Park, CA 94025
1-415-329-1920
Description: Various clip model libraries

Adobe Systems Inc.
1585 Charleston Rd.
P.O. Box 7900
Mountain View, CA 94039-7900
1-800-833-6687
Description: Multimedia image editing and development utilities
Product Titles: Premiere, Photoshop

Asymetrix
110-110th Ave. N.E.
Ste. 700
Bellevue, WA 98004-5840
1-800-448-6543
Description: Authoring and presentation
software
Product Titles: MediaBlitz, Toolbook,
Multimedia Toolbook, Compel

Autodesk
111 McInnis Pkwy.
San Rafael, CA 94903
1-800-228-3601
Description: 3D and 2D animation software
Product Title: 3D Studio Animator

BENNET-TEC Information Systems
50 Jericho Turnpike
Jericho, NY 11753
1-516-997-5596
Description: Image and hypertext Visual
Basic utilities
Product Titles: VBX Artist, ALLText, AllTExt
HT/Pro edition

Caligari
1955 Landings Dr.
Mountain View, CA 94043
1-415-390-9600
Description: 3D animation software
Product Title: TrueSpace

Creative Labs, Inc.
1901 McCarthy Ave.
Milpitas, CA 95134
1-800-998-5227
Description: Multimedia upgrade kits,
sound boards, and CD-ROM drives

Crystal Graphics
3110 Patrick Henry Drive
Santa Clara, CA 95054
1-408-496-6175
Description: 3D animation software
Product Titles: Crystal TOPAS Professional,
Crystal TOPAS, Crystal Flying Fonts,
Crystal Flying Fonts Pro, Crystal 3D
Designer

Diamond Head Software
707 Richards St.
Penthouse #3
Honolulu, HI 96813
1-800-428-6657
Description: Visual Basic imaging utilities
Product Title: Image Basic

Digital Zone
P.O. Box 5562
Bellevue, WA 98006
1-800-538-3113
Description: Various background and digital
image collections

Firstlight, Inc.
15353 NE 90th St.
Redmond, WA 98052
1-800-368-1488
Description: Multimedia clip libraries
Product Titles: Gatekeeper, Multi-Media
Video Library

Gold Disk
3350 Scott Blvd.
Bldg. 14
Santa Clara, CA 95054
1-408-982-0200
Description: Presentation and animation
software
Product Titles: Astound, Animation Works,
Animation Works Interactive

Gryphon
7220 Trade St.
Ste. 120
San Diego, CA 92121
1-619-536-8815
Description: Morphing software
Product Title: Morph

ImageFX
3021 Brighton-Henrietta TL Road
Rochester, NY 14623
1-716-272-8030
Description: Visual Basic special effects tools
Product Title: FXTools

Image North Technologies
180 King Street South
Ste. 360
Waterloo, Ontario, Canada N2J 1P8
1-800-363-3400
Description: Authoring software
Product Title: Image Q

in:sync
6106 MacArthur Blvd.
Ste. 102
Bethesda, MD 20816
1-301-831-5008
Description: Video capture and editing
Product Title: Audio Visual Recorder

Instant Replay Corp.
2 West
2100 St. George Ave.
St. George, UT 84770
1-800-388-8086
Description: Visual Basic visual effect utilities
Product Title: VisualFX

Intel
2200 Mission College Blvd.
Santa Clara, CA 95052-8119
1-800-538-3373
Description: Video digitizing

Product Titles: Smart Video Recorder, Smart Video Recorder Pro

Lenel Systems
290 Woodcliff Office Park
Fairport, NY 14450
1-716-248-9720
Description: Windows-based multimedia tools that include multimedia dll's, database utilities, and drivers
Product Titles: Multimedia Works, Multimedia Works Developers Kit, Media Organizer, MpcOrganizer, Lenel MCI Multimedia Drivers Kit

Macromedia
600 Townsend St.
San Francisco, CA 94103
1-800-288-4797
Description: Presentation and authoring utilities
Product Titles: Action!, Director

Media Architects
7320 SW Hunziker Rd.
Ste. 305
Portland, OR 97223
1-503-639-2505
Description: Visual Basic imaging utilities.
Product Titles: Media Knife/VBX, ImageKnife VBX

MEDIACOM
P.O. Box 36173
Richmond, VA 23235
1-804-794-0700
Description: Clip libraries
Product Title: AdClips

MIDISOFT
P.O. Box 1000
Bellevue, WA 98009
1-206-391-3610
Description: MIDI and Wave utilities and clip libraries

continued on next page

continued from previous page

Product Titles: Studio for Windows, Music Mentor with Recording Session, MIDI Kit with Recording Session, Music Magic Songbook, Sound Impression, Multimedia Music Library, World of Music Sampler, Sound Explorer

Motion Works USA

524 2nd Street
San Francisco, CA 94107
1-800-800-8476
Description: Visual Basic custom controls for multimedia authoring
Product Title: Mediashop

Paul Mace Software Inc.

400 Williamson Way
Ashland, OR 97520
1-503-488-2322
Description: Multimedia authoring
Product Title: Multimedia Grasp 4.5

Pixar, Inc.

1001 West Cutting Blvd.
Richmond, CA 94804
1-510-236-4000
Description: 3D rendering and animation utilities
Product Title: Pixar Typestry

Q.Media

312 East 5th Ave.
Vancouver, B.C., Canada V5T 1H4
1-604-879-1190
Description: Multimedia authoring
Product Title: Q.Media for Windows

Studio Magic

1690 Dell Avenue
Campbell, CA 95008
1-408-378-3838
Description: Video hardware and software
Product Title: The Personal Video Studio

INDEX

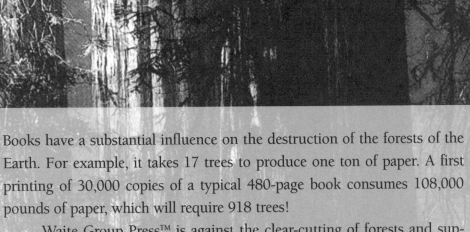

Books have a substantial influence on the destruction of the forests of the Earth. For example, it takes 17 trees to produce one ton of paper. A first printing of 30,000 copies of a typical 480-page book consumes 108,000 pounds of paper, which will require 918 trees!

Waite Group Press™ is against the clear-cutting of forests and supports reforestation of the Pacific Northwest of the United States and Canada, where most of this paper comes from. As a publisher with several hundred thousand books sold each year, we feel an obligation to give back to the planet. We will therefore support organizations which seek to preserve the forests of planet Earth.

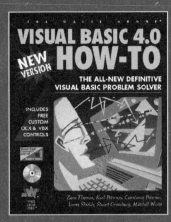

LIMITED WARRANTY

The following warranties shall be effective for 90 days from the date of purchase: (i) The Waite Group, Inc. warrants the enclosed disk to be free of defects in materials and workmanship under normal use; and (ii) The Waite Group, Inc. warrants that the programs, unless modified by the purchaser, will substantially perform the functions described in the documentation provided by The Waite Group, Inc. when operated on the designated hardware and operating system. The Waite Group, Inc. does not warrant that the programs will meet purchaser's requirements or that operation of a program will be uninterrupted or error-free. The program warranty does not cover any program that has been altered or changed in any way by anyone other than The Waite Group, Inc. The Waite Group, Inc. is not responsible for problems caused by changes in the operating characteristics of computer hardware or computer operating systems that are made after the release of the programs, nor for problems in the interaction of the programs with each other or other software.

THESE WARRANTIES ARE EXCLUSIVE AND IN LIEU OF ALL OTHER WARRANTIES OF MERCHANTABILITY OR FITNESS FOR A PARTICULAR PURPOSE OR OF ANY OTHER WARRANTY, WHETHER EXPRESS OR IMPLIED.

EXCLUSIVE REMEDY

The Waite Group, Inc. will replace any defective disk without charge if the defective disk is returned to The Waite Group, Inc. within 90 days from date of purchase.

This is Purchaser's sole and exclusive remedy for any breach of warranty or claim for contract, tort, or damages.

LIMITATION OF LIABILITY

THE WAITE GROUP, INC. AND THE AUTHORS OF THE PROGRAMS SHALL NOT IN ANY CASE BE LIABLE FOR SPECIAL, INCIDENTAL, CONSEQUENTIAL, INDIRECT, OR OTHER SIMILAR DAMAGES ARISING FROM ANY BREACH OF THESE WARRANTIES EVEN IF THE WAITE GROUP, INC. OR ITS AGENT HAS BEEN ADVISED OF THE POSSIBILITY OF SUCH DAMAGES.

THE LIABILITY FOR DAMAGES OF THE WAITE GROUP, INC. AND THE AUTHORS OF THE PROGRAMS UNDER THIS AGREEMENT SHALL IN NO EVENT EXCEED THE PURCHASE PRICE PAID.

COMPLETE AGREEMENT

This Agreement constitutes the complete agreement between The Waite Group, Inc. and the authors of the programs, and you, the purchaser.

Some states do not allow the exclusion or limitation of implied warranties or liability for incidental or consequential damages, so the above exclusions or limitations may not apply to you. This limited warranty gives you specific legal rights; you may have others, which vary from state to state.

SATISFACTION REPORT CARD

Please fill out this card if you wish to know of future updates to
Visual Basic 4.0 Multimedia How-To, or to receive our catalog.

Company Name: _____ Division/Department: _____

Last Name: _____ First Name: _____ Middle Initial: _____

Street Address: _____

City: _____ State: _____ Zip: _____

Daytime Telephone: (   ) _____

Date product was acquired: Month _____ Day _____ Year _____ Your Occupation: _____

Overall, how would you rate *Visual Basic 4.0 Multimedia How-To?*

☐ Excellent   ☐ Very good   ☐ Good
☐ Fair   ☐ Below average ☐ Poor

What did you like MOST about this book? _____

_____

What did you like LEAST about this book? _____

_____
_____

Please describe any problems you encountered using the CD:

_____
_____

How did you use this book (problem solver, tutorial, reference...)?

_____

What is your level of computer expertise?
☐ New   ☐ Dabbler   ☐ Hacker
☐ Power user ☐ Programmer   ☐ Experienced professional

Please describe your computer hardware:
Computer _____ Hard disk _____
5.25" disk drives _____ 3.5" disk drives _____
Video card _____ Monitor _____
Printer _____ Peripherals _____
Sound board _____ CD-ROM_____

What online services do you subscribe to?
☐ CompuServe   ☐ BIX   ☐ America Online
☐ Internet Provider ☐ Delphi   ☐ GEnie

Where did you buy this book?
☐ Bookstore (name): _____
☐ Discount store (name): _____
☐ Computer store (name): _____
☐ Catalog (name): _____
☐ Direct from WGP   ☐ Other _____

What price did you pay for this book? _____

What influenced your purchase of this book?
☐ Recommendation   ☐ Advertisement
☐ Magazine review   ☐ Store display
☐ Mailing   ☐ Book's format
☐ Reputation of Waite Group Press ☐ Other

How many computer books do you buy each year? _____

How many other Waite Group books do you own? _____

What is your favorite Waite Group book? _____

_____

Is there any program or subject you would like to see Waite Group Press cover in a similar approach? _____

_____

Additional comments? _____

_____

Please send to: **Waite Group Press**
                 Attn: *Visual Basic 4.0 Multimedia How-To*
                 200 Tamal Plaza
                 Corte Madera, CA 94925

☐ **Check here for a free Waite Group catalog**

SATISFACTION CARD

BEFORE YOU OPEN THE DISK OR CD-ROM PACKAGE ON THE FACING PAGE, CAREFULLY READ THE LICENSE AGREEMENT.

Opening this package indicates that you agree to abide by the license agreement found in the back of this book. If you do not agree with it, promptly return the unopened disk package (including the related book) to the place you obtained them for a refund.